ALLIES AND RIVALS

ALLIES AND RIVALS

GERMAN-AMERICAN EXCHANGE
AND THE RISE OF THE
MODERN RESEARCH UNIVERSITY

Emily J. Levine

The University of Chicago Press   *Chicago and London*

The University of Chicago Press, Chicago 60637
The University of Chicago Press, Ltd., London
© 2021 by The University of Chicago
Published 2021
Paperback edition 2024
Printed in the United States of America

33 32 31 30 29 28 27 26 25 24   1 2 3 4 5

ISBN-13: 978-0-226-34181-1 (cloth)
ISBN-13: 978-0-226-83332-3 (paper)
ISBN-13: 978-0-226-34195-8 (e-book)
DOI: https://doi.org/10.7208/chicago/9780226341958.001.0001

Library of Congress Cataloging-in-Publication Data

Names: Levine, Emily J., author.
Title: Allies and rivals : German-American exchange and the rise of
the modern research university / Emily J. Levine.
Other titles: German-American exchange and the rise
of the modern research university
Description: Chicago ; London : The University of Chicago Press, 2021.
| Includes bibliographical references and index.
Identifiers: LCCN 2021004007 | ISBN 9780226341811 (cloth) |
ISBN 9780226341958 (ebook)
Subjects: LCSH: Universities and colleges—History—19th century. |
Universities and colleges—United States—History—19th century. |
Universities and colleges—Germany—History—19th century. |
Education, Higher—United States—German influences. | Education,
Higher—United States—History—19th century. | Education, Higher—
Germany—History—19th century. | Germany—Relations—United
States. | United States—Relations—Germany.
Classification: LCC LA181 .L49 2021 | DDC 378.009/034—dc23
LC record available at https://lccn.loc.gov/2021004007

For Matthew

Universities, like families and like nations, live only as they are continually reborn, and rebirth means constant new endeavor of thought and action, and these mean an ever renewed process of change. . . . Tradition looks forward as well as backward. To transmit the powers and achievements of our own day to the future is as important as to transmit the past to the present. Indeed, the more aware we are of the fact that we are builders of a future world, the more likely are we to be intelligent in our attitude to the past and in our estimate of the values we inherit from it.

JOHN DEWEY, 1939

CONTENTS

THE UNIVERSITY'S CENTURY

Autonomy is not a given, but a historical conquest, endlessly having to be undertaken anew.

PIERRE BOURDIEU, 2001

Every nation with a well-developed higher education system claims its research universities as national assets. But the institution and ideals of the modern research university do not belong to any individual country. Like the Elgin Marbles or nuclear physics, the university stands at the junction between the interests of nations and our shared humanity. Throughout the long history of scholarship since antiquity, a tension has persisted between the independence of scholars and higher learning that serves the state. This tension can be seen in Plato's Academy and the career of Socrates, who would rather drink poison than succumb to the demands of the Athenian polis.[1] The research university, which arose from the modern historical milieu and took shape alongside many of modernity's ideologies, including nationalism and cosmopolitanism, became defined by the duality resulting from the productive tension between its values and the world outside its walls.

This complicated reality has led to a series of contradictions. Devoted to the ideals of pure scientific inquiry, the university is also an institution forged of hard compromises. Its scholars enjoy autonomy and at the same time provide services to the wider society. And the modern research university gives the impression of timelessness even as it evolves. As a result, the university is contested and frequently misunderstood. How can we address pressing higher education policy questions of the day if we don't have a clear genealogy of the co-evolution of modernity and the university?[2]

Historical understanding is required to answer such questions as how universities should be supported, who gets to be admitted, and what kind of knowledge they can pursue.[3] We must examine under what terms the university developed to uncover the roots of its prominent place in society and how it differs from other institutions. Only then can we begin to determine whom it serves and what it benefits. Defenders and critics of the university often draw on the words of former University of California president Clark Kerr, who, in his gospel of postwar higher education, observed that "[the university] and the church are the two most persistent institutions society has known."[4] Longevity, however, should not be mistaken for stasis. Universities have survived not because they have remained the same but because they have proved to be remarkably adaptable.

This book integrates the history of the university into the long nineteenth-century story of the emergence of nation-states, the competitive dynamics among cities, and growing global economic and cultural interconnectedness.[5] The long view reveals the mobility of knowledge centers, the fragility of particular institutions of higher learning, and the resilience of core principles. Only by knowing what comes and goes can we make claims about what is worth saving. By excavating the origins of the principles and institutions of higher education we will see that such ideals as meritocracy and academic freedom are the results of tangled and disputed histories—and may deserve rethinking.

Since the university transcends national borders, our exploration of its origins and evolution must do so as well. In the parallel histories of the university and modernity, no two countries are more intertwined than the fast-growing young nations, the United States and Germany. As the émigré historian Fritz Stern wrote, "In the twentieth century these two powers had violent alternations of intimacy and enmity; the American Century began as the German one ended."[6]

In 1904, when the German sociologist Max Weber and his wife Marianne, a sociologist and women's rights activist, visited the United States, academic exchange between the two countries already had a near-century-long history. Max, the future author of *The Protestant Ethic and the Spirit of Capitalism*, was recovering from a bout of mental illness when he received an invitation to present at the Congress of Arts and Science, a scholarly conference held in conjunction with the 1904 World's Fair in St. Louis. Marianne thought that a visit to America would rejuvenate her husband, and so the academic couple seized the opportunity. In the spirit of Alexis de Tocqueville, the French voyager and theorist who traveled to the United States in 1831 and wrote a two-volume history on America's strange habits and customs, the Webers toured Niagara Falls, Boston, Washington, DC, Chicago, and Tuskegee, among other places. They were captivated by America's capitalist spirit, including its skyscrapers and elevators. They were enchanted, in particular, by the vast landscape dotted with "little sects and *colleges*," many of which were "colonies of charming buildings far outside the metropolis . . .—worlds by themselves, full of poetry and the happy intellectual life of the young."[7]

Yet the Webers soon realized that the American colleges' remove from society was illusory. Over the course of their journey the scholars observed a remarkable shift that was occurring in higher education on both sides of the Atlantic: the autonomy that scholars often invoked was under threat. Now scholars were tethered to a university system that was ever more obligated to the state and was managed by an oppressive bureaucracy and business-style leaders. Weber came to believe that America was the source of the model that was bringing on this change, which he thought was corrupting higher education, even in Germany. In a lecture, "Science as a Vocation" (*Wissenschaft als Beruf*), which would later become famous for identifying the perils of the university's modernization, Weber lamented that in America "[a professor] sells me his knowledge and his methods for my father's money, just as the greengrocer sells my mother cabbage."[8] Increasingly outspoken about the shortcomings of the German university, Weber blamed the longtime and influential director of academic affairs in the Prussian Education Ministry Friedrich Althoff for introducing the "American" model into Germany and tainting the pursuit of pure knowledge.[9]

Not surprisingly for a circumspect sociologist, Weber's assessment of America was not all negative. Even the critic of capitalism admitted that the apparent transformation of the American higher education system had the value of spurring domestic competition and vibrant scholarly activity. That a city like Chicago had two universities and the state of Illinois yet another guaranteed in Weber's eyes a genuine academic freedom in America that Germany had nearly lost. Whereas German scholars were subservient to Althoff, whose permission they required to even consider an appointment at another university, American scholars could weigh multiple offers of appointment and, in effect, use the market to their advantage. Nonetheless, each American university had at its helm a leader who aimed to recreate a German-like mini-empire of scholars under his tutelage. In a lecture comparing the two education systems, Weber announced, "The United States have an Althoff at every university. The American university president is such a man."[10] Ambivalent as he was, Weber saw that, as a result of this cross-fertilization, Germany was not only being Americanized, American universities were being Europeanized.

Weber was right to see exchanges across the Atlantic as determinants of the ongoing evolution of higher education in both America and Germany. Drawing on Weber as inspiration, this book treats transatlantic cultural exchange and competition as its topic, methodology, and causal historical mechanism. It uncovers the origins of the research university by pulling apart the strands of the parallel, comparative, and intertwined stories that unfolded on both sides of the Atlantic. Chapters pair individuals and institutions from Germany and America to reveal side-by-side stories about how idealists made compromises to create universities they hoped would bring tangible benefits to their respective communities. Using what Benedict Anderson called the "spectre of comparison," this book also highlights the differences in how these two young nations funded their universities and designed their degrees and programs of study.[11] Our protagonists were not just observers of their counterparts, as Weber understood. An observer can impact her object of study. Americans and Germans traveled back and forth, borrowing ideas they believed held potential at home, and became enmeshed in what I call *competitive emulation*, an energetic dance of cooperation and competition that fueled innovation and, in turn, raised the stakes of that exchange.[12]

Viewing the university from the perspective of German-American exchange, as Weber did, permits us to identify the university's unique features, among them the endless need for external validation and participation in an intellectual community that crosses national borders. Though we often treat the ideals of the university as self-evident, the German-American interchanges show that knowledge institutions were contingent on evolving compromises among academic innovators and their partners. The best of these outcomes rose to become influential models that seemed to transcend their time and place. But knowledge centers, like nation-states, rise and fall. Universities were undoubtedly shaped by nation-states but cannot entirely be explained by them—a contradiction that is essential to understanding their identity. This book's distinctive contribution is to provide a historical account of how the university was enabled by nationalization and globalization while it preserved an internal raison d'être that continues, even today, to diverge from the self-interested politics of nations and the logic of markets.[13]

▲ ▲

Today we take it for granted that science and other forms of advanced research have a natural home within institutions of higher learning. But there is no necessary connection between the two. In the eighteenth century, academies were the primary sites for the production of new knowledge, while universities reinforced received wisdom. The Paris Academy of Sciences, among others, published transactions, distributed prizes and honors, and advised government. Scientists and philosophers in eighteenth-century Germany and America, including Henry Adams and George Bancroft, conducted the bulk of their experiments, writing, and instruction outside the confines of universities. The philosopher Johann Gottfried Herder reflected a general transatlantic belief when he asserted that the most serious and authentic form of higher learning—*Bildung* or self-cultivation—happened in extra-university spaces.[14] It is no surprise, then, that following their medieval pinnacle, eighteenth-century European universities had, despite a handful of exceptions, fallen from their privileged place as centers of knowledge. Ostensibly focused on the professional training of secondary teachers, German universities in the eighteenth century were known for rowdiness and occasional religious subversion. Colleges in the new nation of America, in contrast, were largely finishing schools for young gentlemen. On neither side of the Atlantic did these institutions inspire awe. The rise of the nation-state and its new military, scientific, and social needs, as well as the emergence of scholars with ambitions to impact the wider world, created the conditions of possibility for the formation of a modern university with a renewed purpose.[15]

The nineteenth was the century of both the nation-state and the university, and their parallel rise had consequences for the organization of the university as an institution that united the advancement of knowledge (research) and the dissemination of knowledge (teaching) in one institution.[16] The seed of this hybrid was planted with the founding of the University of Berlin in 1810.[17] The visionary founders of this institution, the philosopher Johann Gottlieb Fichte and the linguist Wilhelm von Humboldt, nurtured, in different ways, aspirations for the university to serve the burgeoning German nation. Incubated in the national sentiment germinating against Napoleon, the University of Berlin unleashed an idea that would have immense power well beyond the German-speaking lands. Universities would provide the requisite academic instruction to train a professional civil service and competitive military, and they would operate as independent institutions that would authenticate and legitimize knowledge. As the sociologist and preeminent Weber scholar Edward Shils later observed, "Universities became part of the symbolic apparatus of progressive civilization, of modernity. . . . The very belief in the need for and the desirability of a university was a part of the image of what a modern society should be and of the proper place of a university within it."[18]

The envy of the British, Russians, and Japanese, as well as the Americans, the ur-modern research university of Berlin created the blueprint for a university as a building block for the nation-state. Universities inspired by Berlin were soon established by aspiring nations across Europe, including the Royal Frederick University in Oslo in 1811, the University of Warsaw in 1816, and the Othonian (later National) University in Athens in 1837. As the historian Richard Evans observed, "The founding of a university was a requirement of any self-respecting state."[19] As the cases of Strasbourg and Basel underscore, universities became arenas for regional battles in nationalization.[20] But they also remained semiautonomous institutions devoted to the ideals of pure inquiry and the open exchange of ideas. Shils noted this paradox: "It was also believed that the majesty of a state and the dignity of a society required the existence of a university within its territory, quite apart from the utility of the knowledge it conveyed for the conduct of the affairs of the state, Church and society."[21] The purpose of the university from the beginning was both utilitarian and symbolic, practical and idealistic.

Satisfied with their "homegrown tradition of research," Americans were initially slow to catch the university fever, but once they did, what the eminent historian of education Laurence Veysey called the "lure" of the university was irreversible.[22] The industrial output and urban development that so impressed the Webers in 1904 was due in no small part to investments the Americans had made in higher education since the Civil War.

But growth in American higher education depended critically on Germany. By the end of the nineteenth century nearly ten thousand Americans had traveled to Germany to study in the universities of Berlin, Göttingen, Leipzig, and other cities, and many came to believe that the German university model had potential for the young American nation.[23] A notable number of these American "returnees" converted their experiences studying abroad into educational reform at home.[24] At least forty-five US university presidents can be traced to the universities of Leipzig and Göttingen alone.[25] When in 1875 one "returnee," Daniel Coit Gilman, became the founding president of the Johns Hopkins University, the first research university in America, that university was called Göttingen at Baltimore."[26] Gilman, for his part, never aimed merely to implement a German formula. Like the American founding fathers Jefferson and Adams, he aspired for America to be a place from which new ideas emanated. When he spoke at the International Congress of Higher Education in Chicago in 1893 Gilman wished aloud for the day "when men of letters, or at least of academic culture, will be sent, as the best representatives of the American people, to the most cultivated courts of Europe."[27]

Germans were divided as to what to make of these American developments. Althoff confided his desire to "found a little German university over there."[28] The Austrian-German philologist Alois Brandl described the German-American relationship in similar expansionist terms: "The American research university is the best conquest that we have made in the world since Goethe."[29] Germans had grown accustomed to writing of America as a land of "unlimited possibility," by which they meant unlimited resources to be extracted; "Americanization" (*Amerikanisierung*) was thus not typically meant as a compliment.[30] As early as 1882, however, the physiologist and permanent secretary of the Prussian Academy of Arts, Emil Du Bois-Reymond, reflected a newfound interest in America when he linked America's industrial progress to its scholarly output: "We must get accustomed to the idea that, much like the center of gravity of a binary star, the economic center of gravity of the civilized world already lies between the old and new continent, in the Atlantic ocean, and that, the scholarly center of gravity will also move more decisively towards the West."[31] Du Bois-Reymond joined a growing cadre of Germans who implored their compatriots to take America more seriously. That the French showed greater interest in the American version of Göttingen than in Göttingen itself was additional evidence of the westward shift.[32]

In spite of the persistent anxieties among Germans, by 1904, when Weber visited America, scholarly traffic was regularly flowing in both directions. The interchanges of knowledge, ideas, and scholars were made increasingly possible by the concurrent urbanization, globalization, and decentralized federalist structures of the two countries.[33] The German American legal scholar Francis Lieber, a leading figure in international law, reflected the cosmopolitanism of the moment when he proposed the revival of the traveling professor of late antiquity: "Why could not the same person teach in New York and Strasbourg?"[34] When the university was permitted greater autonomy and the climate was conducive to robust international exchange, American students flocked to Germany. And when they later in life rose to positions of power, Gilman of Hopkins, as well as Henry P. Tappan, president of the University of Michigan, and Andrew Dickson White of Cornell, eagerly recreated stateside the laboratories and seminars they had experienced in German universities as students. Meanwhile, in Germany, the applied mathematician Felix Klein and the cultural historian Karl Lamprecht, among others, experimented with American innovations, including the private financing of scholarship, the integration of the applied sciences, and coeducation. Rather than an asymmetrical colonial relationship, the Germans and Americans by the early twentieth century enjoyed a two-way diffusion of academic innovations. On both sides of the Atlantic, university leaders borrowed ideas from elsewhere and adapted them to their home contexts to fuel hybrid institutional designs, many of which went on to be the object of further praise and emulation. This process of competitive emulation was as great as any endogenous factor in institutional change.

The transatlantic travelers were no doubt enthralled by the exchange of ideas and the universal pursuit of truth. But they were also motivated by a desire to prove that their nations were at the vanguard of scientific advancement. This rivalrous aspect of competitive emulation was equally potent. Encouraged by his right-hand man, the liberal theologian and education reformer Adolf von Harnack, Althoff came to balance these twin goals—the advancement of science and the aggrandizement of the nation-state—and together devised strategies that would ensure that the new "worldwide enterprise of academic knowledge" (*Weltbetrieb der Wissenschaft*) worked to maintain Germany's "worldwide reputation of German academic research" (*Weltgeltung deutscher Wissenschaft*).[35]

In America and Germany skeptics of international exchange and foreign entanglements rebuffed the efforts of Gilman and Harnack. These nativists called for intellectual self-sufficiency and protectionism—after all, wouldn't guest professors be in a position to steal trade secrets? Despite this resistance, however, international exchange persisted. Gilman knew that he could only achieve his aspirations for Hopkins if its diplomas rose beyond fiat to be "worth [their] face in the currency of the world."[36] Degrees from the new institution had to be accepted by the esteemed Germans as evidence of excellence in training and scholarship. Conversely, the German universities could remain preeminent, Althoff understood, only if their professors were sought by foreigners for training.

In their need for external validation, scholars and universities, then, differed from the nation-states in which they were embedded and from industry, to which they increasingly answered. It is difficult to imagine competitive corporations revealing trade secrets to one another or political rivals sharing military strategies, but precisely such an "open source" value system prevailed in universities avant la lettre.[37] The logic of scientific advancement required that universities keep their gates open. This porosity permitted would-be university builders to enter and emulate the models they found valuable by creating their own similar institutions at home. Remarkably the openness of higher education all but guaranteed that the leading centers of knowledge in one generation would be surpassed in the next.

To be sure, when war broke out, the ideals of pure inquiry and international exchange receded, and the narrower nationalist values that legitimated state power predominated. The university would be pulled toward serving the state and savvy scholars in Germany and America accordingly promoted themselves as scientific experts who could produce knowledge that furthered economic development and military might. Under these constrained circumstances knowledge sharing and open borders remained dormant but did not disappear. Universities continued to rely on peer institutions for the advancement of knowledge and the bestowal of status. Even as universities became more integrated into the world around them, neither the imperatives of nations nor markets took complete hold over

them. Their new currency, based on exchange, trust, and mutual validation, persisted.

▲ ▲

Scholars have tended to approach the history of the university through
either an internalist framework focused on the university "ideal" to the
exclusion of politics, or an institutionalist perspective oriented toward
organizational questions.[38] Those interested in the relationship between
universities and their contexts have largely restricted themselves to the
national or comparative lenses.[39] But just as it is impossible to understand
the dynamism of knowledge centers without the transatlantic framework,
so too does the multifaceted university require an interdisciplinary approach that bridges the historical and sociological. Universities were the
results of both ideals and institutional compromises, and they emerged in
nation-states that were themselves part of an increasingly global world. In
that world universities were neither abstract "vessels which floated on a
stream of desire to acquire the kind of knowledge which they transmitted
and created," as Shils suggested, nor did they sweep over countries in a
spontaneous "wave," as the modern university's medieval predecessors did
in Hastings Rashdall's description. Universities do not behave like abstract
ideas or commodities.[40] They are something different. While scholars have
invoked as explanatory mechanisms such concepts as influence, translation, or export, none of these fully captures the complex process through
which would-be academic entrepreneurs experienced institutions of higher
learning elsewhere, exchanged ideas about how to organize ideas, and then
made calculated decisions about what to recreate at home, inevitably with
different results.[41]

The work of organizational sociologists and sociologists of knowledge,
as well as of historians of modern Europe and America, necessarily provides the two requisite sides of this narrative. In the chapters that follow I draw on various sociological frameworks, including the diffusion
of knowledge, status as a currency in interinstitutional relationships, and
institutional hybridization, to identify the process through which institutions of higher learning emerge and spread.[42] The sociologist Elisabeth
Clemens has argued that sociology's "organizational synthesis is enriched
by incorporating politics." No doubt political and intellectual histories "can
be improved by attending to organizational form."[43] Such "organizational
forms" provide the missing link between the internal history of the university and the external history of modern politics.

When mapping the sociology of knowledge onto an international political context, what becomes clear are the competitive dynamics through which the universities as institutions of higher learning evolved. "The world of letters . . . creates its own geography and its own divisions," the French sociologist Pascale Casanova reminds us, "as against the national boundaries that give rise to political and nationalist feeling."[44] The world of letters developed its own geopolitics in which there were clear winners and losers, but that hierarchy did not necessarily conform to that of nations.[45] Rather, in the university's world, Göttingen or Ann Arbor could be a major player even if it remained politically off the map. By focusing on the multiple levels of identity—local, national, and global—that often facilitated the exchanges of scholars across continents, we can determine the conditions for academic innovation.[46]

As a transatlantic and interdisciplinary history of the university as ideal and institution, the story that follows necessarily takes up diverse perspectives, as it moves back and forth between Germany and America. To present this history otherwise, through a single framework, would come at the cost of fidelity and nuance. The US-German rivalry sheds light on the development of these new nations and their aspirations to become global powers at the turn of the twentieth century. Germany's universities had long been able to claim the mantle of preeminence, but at the beginning of the twentieth century, America's universities, with respect to prestige and research output, seemed poised to take the lead. This occurred in part because of Americans' emulation of what they saw as valuable in the German model. These transatlantic cases, far from exhaustive, provide the connective historical tissue that is essential to make knowledge of past academic innovation useful to the current reform of universities.[47] And this changing of the guard also holds universal meaning for understanding where education innovation originates and the optimal conditions for its diffusion.

▲ ▲

The chapters of this book trace the institutionalization of the modern university ideal, beginning with the founding of the University of Berlin in 1810 and continuing in various permutations on both sides of the Atlantic through the events just after 1933, when political upheaval and mass emigration devastated the German university and created the terms for a new American one rooted in the New Deal. Chapters 1, 2, and 3 examine this institutionalization process as a compromise that I call the academic social contract. That compromise reconciled aspects of the university ideal with broader social needs and political stakeholders.

In my telling, the most significant agents for institutional change were academic innovators, whom the sociologist Randall Collins once described as "the educational entrepreneurs who traveled the country from college to college" and borrowed the best ideas to improve their home institutions.[48] They negotiated compromises and fashioned academic social contracts among willing parties. The university did not emerge in isolation nor was it ever a finished project. Rather, the compromises were constantly renegotiated by these innovators and other social actors amid changing contexts. As the society that the university served evolved, the university coevolved into such forms as the central state university in Berlin, the land grant in California, and the privately funded urban university in Baltimore, and each time the academic social contract was reconstituted.[49]

Given the mutually beneficial contract model, it would be a mistake to judge the university's value system as positive and that of the state as negative. Chapters 4 and 5 underscore this point by tackling the fraught question concerning who gets to belong to these communities of higher learning. Using the perspective of the nineteenth-century German-American encounter, this pair of chapters shows the contradictions that emerged when a group of American reformers adapted the German system, intended for an elite segment of the population, and wedged it into the American democratic tradition.[50]

The modern university ideal never fully reconciled the competing goals of the specialization required for scholarship and the experience of student learning. This conflict led to the founding of new institutions designed solely for one purpose or the other. The stories of these extra-university institutions, a necessary part of any study of academic innovation, are charted in chapters 6, 7, and 8. Chapters 9 and 10 marry the earlier themes of autonomy and power with questions about stratification and exclusion. Hitler's purge of the Jews from universities shows that he was willing to compromise the war effort to serve his aspirations for an ethno-nationalist state, while Americans would absorb scholarly refugees but leave the ethnic and racial hierarchies of their own system intact. Concluding this story where many others begin, this book reflects my contention that the period leading up to and including both world wars shares more similarities with our current world than with the subsequent period that began in 1945, the contractual basis of which is now unraveling.[51] Nonetheless, the balancing acts negotiated by the pre–World War II educational innovators, when they worked, ushered in an indisputable golden age for universities and their societies, from which we continue to reap benefits. The consequences of their compromises are also ours to bear.

CHAPTER ONE

THE HUMBOLDTIAN CONTRACT AND THE FEDERALIST ORIGINS OF THE RESEARCH UNIVERSITY

And he seemed to be much struck when I brought out the apparent paradox that in a democracy with little government things might go badly in detail but well on the whole, while in a monarchy with much and omnipresent government, things might go very pleasingly in detail but poorly on the whole.

CARL SCHURZ ON OTTO VON BISMARCK, 1868

America and Germany hadn't always been at the center of the academic world. In the eighteenth century, Paris was an acknowledged center of scientific thought and progress, and the French thought of themselves as the "scientific pedagogues of Europe."[1] It seemed that only a great metropolitan center like Paris could accumulate commanding levels of cultural capital. In the view of envious Europeans like the German natural scientist Lorenz Oken, "In France most of the scientists live together in Paris . . . in England, the same applies to London . . . we do not have a Paris or London in Germany."[2] Over the course of the nineteenth century, however, the centers of science—and with them, higher learning—shifted from Paris and London to Göttingen and Berlin, and then to Baltimore and Ann Arbor. What did Germany and America have that France and England lacked and might account for the latter's failure to keep pace with the former's development of knowledge centers? Although many possible factors can be identified, what stands out is the federalist political structures of America and Germany. In both countries there was a dynamic relationship between decentralization and central authority. The benefits of center-periphery competition for the advancement of knowledge that Weber identified in 1904 were most fully realized under federalism.[3]

The modern university's origins can be traced, then, to institutions in early nineteenth-century Germany, which at the time was a collection of states but not yet a country, and to others in an American nation on the cusp of industrialization.[4] In the federalist political systems of these kindred countries robust regional centers vied for influence, and leaders debated the proper locus of power.[5] An observer in the southwestern German state of Württemberg in 1860 made clear the salutary cultural effects of the decentralization that German nationalists otherwise lamented: "It may well be true that the fragmentation of Germany into a myriad *Stämme* [tribes] and states has hitherto prevented her from making her political power felt as it should be; it is at least equally true that precisely because of this Germany has become a country second to none with regard to the dissemination of culture and knowledge."[6] In this milieu, emerging academic leaders in both countries faced a parallel challenge—to found universities that they hoped would bring national culture to their disparate states. Crucially, the federalist political context provided the conditions for the unwritten contracts between the nascent university systems and their publics. Germans and Americans would vary the terms of these contracts, but their respective university systems shared characteristics that would be constitutive features of their rise.

HUMBOLDT'S GIFT—THE UNIVERSITY OF BERLIN

Dubbed by Hegel "world spirit on horseback," Napoleon rode into Jena in 1806 during his nineteen-day sweep of Prussia, having soundly defeated the forces of Friedrich Wilhelm III and thus ensuring his ultimate victory. Among other actions intended to solidify his control of the German lands, Napoleon promptly shut twenty-two (or over half) of the German universities because of suspicious political activity. The French takeover was a devastating political loss and a humiliation for the residents, who were forced to accept the presence of French regiments in their fortresses, pay large sums to the invaders, and reduce their army significantly. But the anti-French sentiment motivated a push for national renewal and created the conditions for cultural reform led by the Prussian politicians Karl August von Hardenberg and Karl vom Stein zum Altenstein. The so-called Stein-Hardenberg reforms included freeing serfs, granting limited citizenship to Jews, and creating a modern bureaucracy, most notably institutions devoted to education. While the new state of Westphalia and its esteemed universities, including Halle and Göttingen, were decimated, it was perhaps an indication of its relative unimportance that the royal garrison town of Berlin was allowed a certain leeway in the realm of culture and education.[7] In 1807, allegedly in response to the protestations of faculty from the recently dissolved Halle University, Friedrich Wilhelm III declared, "The state must replace through intellectual powers what it has lost in the way of physical ones."[8] Over the ensuing three years, the University of Berlin would come into existence as an embodiment of a contract between Wilhelm and the faculty: a modern institution sponsored by the state within which consider-able "intellectual powers" coalesced and were preserved.

The University of Berlin did not arise de novo.[9] Even though it had novel features that would prove consequential, the university rested on a founda-tion of scholarly inquiry stretching back to medieval times and distributed among the German states. In the Enlightenment era, reformers, most no-tably at new universities in Halle and Göttingen, had broken with religious orthodoxy, in large part by transforming religious training as preparation for the civil service. At Halle, founded in 1694, innovative professors im-plemented new modes of instruction in historical thinking for teaching theologians how to engage in more active discourse.[10] At the University of Göttingen, founded in 1737, the Hanoverian privy-counselor Gerlach Adolph von Münchhausen encouraged scholarship free from censorship and promoted research in the sciences through interactions between the Göttingen Academy of Sciences (founded in 1751) and the new seminars at the university.[11] These exceptional institutions and the "germ of academic freedom" attracted scholars from the German lands and beyond, including Benjamin Franklin and the English poet Coleridge, and would provide a model for the new Prussian university.[12]

The ground from which the University of Berlin sprouted received ad-ditional fertilization in the form of the philosophical idealism and devo-tion to spiritual freedom expressed by German Romantics like J. G. Fichte, F. W. J. Schelling, G. W. F. Hegel, and Johann Wolfgang von Goethe.[13] In this heady time, Romantics like Fichte and Friedrich Schiller admonished the *Brotstudenten* (literally, the "bread students" or careerists) who were there only for credentials, and instead united around the notion of self-cultivation, or *Bildung*, a uniquely German concept that combined indi-vidual intellectual and moral betterment.[14] Their Romanticism, despite emerging in small private circles outside the old universities like Jena, helped nurture a cultural nationalism under which calls for a new "na-tional" university reached sympathetic ears.[15]

In the winter of 1807–1808, Fichte, who had lectured in Jena in the 1790s and sought refuge from Napoleon's advance in Königsberg and later in Co-penhagen, returned to French-occupied Berlin to deliver his *Addresses to the German Nation*. In fourteen lectures, Fichte, embracing a German philo-sophical tradition in opposition to that of the French, urged the Germans who packed the great hall of the old Academy to overcome their disgrace so the "living force may in all places ignite German minds to decisions and ac-tion. . . . It is only through the common feature of being German that we can avert the downfall of our nation through fusion with foreign countries, and win back a self that rests only on itself and is absolutely incapable of all dependency."[16] To further this goal, he also sent to the Prussian Civil Cabinet a more measured and detailed essay outlining a plan for a new institution of higher learning in Berlin that would be a "school in the art of putting scholarly reason to use."[17] Back in Halle, where only 174 students remained out of the original thirteen hundred, and down-and-out professors now sold their silverware for bread, the Norwegian scholar Henrik Steffens wrote a polemic on "the idea of the university," suggesting that only free thought for the youth would fuel a national revival. The rhetoric of both Fichte and Steffens signaled a significant transformation: universities would become the "guardians of the national spirit and the awakeners of inner freedom." The university in Berlin proposed by Fichte would be their flagship.[18]

In the debate among scholars over just what this institution would look like, one issue was the degree of freedom — hard-won from the church during the religious reforms — that the university would now lose as a result of the state's involvement. The Protestant theologian and philosopher of hermeneutics Friedrich Schleiermacher advocated for a close relationship with the state as a way to achieve the larger goal of scholarly independence. In what Friedrich Paulsen called the "intellectual charter" of the German university, Schleiermacher argued that scholars must rely on the state to offer certain guarantees, like freedom from censorship, that were required for the pursuit of knowledge.[19] Schleiermacher shared Fichte's emphasis on philosophy and the Romantic devotion to the "inner unity" of science.[20] And though his statement expressed the requisite patriotism of the day, Schleiermacher also supported a closer relationship between states to advance knowledge and warned against a "scholarly embargo" that would prevent "citizens from taking part as they wish in the scholarly pursuits of neighboring states."[21] Potentially warring states must nevertheless engage with each other if science was to advance, according to Schleiermacher. In his corresponding blueprint for the organization of the theological faculty, Schleiermacher drew on the institutional antecedents of Halle and Göttingen to show how cross-disciplinary research housed in the newly conceived university might work.[22]

The cosmopolitan cultural world that Schleiermacher promoted was a poor consolation to many aspiring statesmen, who would have preferred political and military might. A skeptical public had to be persuaded of science's utility and scientists' loyalty, for the latter took (and gave away) ideas wherever they could, and operated in a "Union of Men of Letters and Students," as Goethe and Schiller referred to Jena, without concern for territorial borders.[23] Reflecting those fears of rootless cosmopolitanism, the Berlin public was unsure of what a descent of scholars on their city would mean. In the war-torn capital of the largest German state, many asserted the university's patriotic responsibility to serve. "The university is not being founded as a mere feast for the scientific *gourmands* of Europe," the founding publisher of Berlin's main newspaper argued, "[but] the immediate purpose of all higher education is the preparation [*Bildung*] of civil servants."[24]

These various strands of aspirations and anxiety came together in Wilhelm von Humboldt, a linguist by training, who applied his love of languages to patriotic purposes, serving as ambassador for the Prussian state. Born into a wealthy aristocratic family, Wilhelm Humboldt and his younger brother Alexander, who would go on to become one of the most celebrated scientists of all time, were lavished by their widowed mother with education if not affection.[25] Humboldt the elder spent time studying law and classical philology at universities in Frankfurt on the Oder and Göttingen before settling in Jena, where he befriended Goethe and Schiller. Over the course of his distinguished career Humboldt alternated between basking in the private search for *Bildung* among his classical heroes, and periods of civil service in which he worked to make the state a conduit for culture.

Humboldt's early quest for *Bildung* was realized in his relationship with his future wife, Caroline Dacheröden, a young woman from an upper-class Huguenot family whom he met through his companions in the Tugendbund (League of Virtue), the secret society he cofounded. In the subculture of the Jewish *salonnière* Henriette Herz, Christians and Jews mingled, members used the familiar *Du*, and dedicated themselves to collective moral improvement.[26] Schiller, who married Caroline's childhood friend, found Humboldt's fiancée to be a "lovely genius." "Bill and Li," as they were known, married as the French Revolution was beginning and became staples of the eighteenth-century literary salons. In the egalitarian spirit of the time, they chose to live as (mostly) equals in a *Seelenliebe* (higher friendship), as reflected in their voluminous correspondence.[27] For Humboldt, as for his contemporary Romantics, *Bildung* was primarily expressed in private life, including one's marriage and child-rearing, art collecting, and letters (of which his brother Alexander wrote around fifty thousand).[28]

And so when Humboldt learned in 1808, while stationed in Rome as ambassador to the Holy See, that he had been chosen for the very public task of remaking the Prussian education system, his first reaction was hesitation. "On the few occasions when people still approach me, I only give in when . . . I can be sure that I will make a genuine contribution," he wrote to his wife.[29] For such an ambitious project would certainly ruin his *Ruhe*, or "peace," which would be "horrific to have tasted . . . once and then lost . . . forever."[30] And besides, he said, "how much can you really accomplish in Prussia today with such limited resources? Managing a crowd of scholars," he complained to Li, was not much better than "running a traveling circus."[31] His sigh of resignation is almost audible two hundred years later.

Humboldt's early writings offer few indications that he would become one of the most significant education reformers of all time. In his first work, *The Limits of State Action*, drafted in the year the Prussians fought their first battle against the French (but not published until after his death), he wrote: "National education—or that organized or enforced by the State—is at least in many respects very questionable."[32] If Humboldt, a man who had never been to school and barely went to university, became known as a *Bildungsdiktator*, he was a reluctant one, who preferred to write himself out of the script.[33] Humboldt assumed his duty the following year as the director of the newly created Department for Religion and Public Instruction (Ministerium für den Kultus und öffentlichen Unterricht), which reported to the Ministry of Interior. His charge was to modernize the Prussian education system. While he was not the originator of the main ideas that would be embodied in the University of Berlin, any more than he was the originator of his main scholarly ideas in the budding field of linguistic anthropology, many of which he translated from the French and British milieu, Humboldt expertly synthesized these into a coherent (and marketable) whole.

Humboldt himself remained a liminal figure in the academic revolution that he enabled, as he and his younger brother continued to conduct much of their learned work outside the university. Nonetheless, Humboldt ultimately ushered *Bildung* from an aesthetic private project of self-formation to its fulfillment in state-run public institutions.[34] The true ends of life that Humboldt exalted were the "cultivation to the full of the talents with which we have been endowed," a belief that would become the cornerstone of higher education's aspiration for excellence. "The signs are favorable, and new institutions are being established for the future," Humboldt wrote confidently shortly after the Kaiser signed the document that brought the university into being; "under a benevolent government, this great new institution is destined to make history in Germany" (fig. 1).[35]

Humboldt's "great new institution" reflected the balance between cultural cosmopolitanism and growing German nationalism that would shape the German education system. In contrast to Alexander, who enjoyed the company of his colleagues in Paris while their estate was ransacked by French soldiers, Wilhelm always put his duty to the state above all.[36] While subsequent scholars and students of the university lamented the failure of the institution to live up to the ideal of self-cultivation, Humboldt conveyed a pragmatism that would become characteristic of the academic innovators of that century and beyond. Crucially, with respect to autonomy

Figure 1. The tension between education and politics is evident in the statue of ur-academic innovator Wilhelm von Humboldt in front of the partially destroyed Humboldt-Universität (opened in 1810) on the Unter den Linden boulevard in 1946. (Photo by Friedrich Seidenstuecker © bpk Bildagentur/Art Resource, NY.)

and responsibility, Humboldt advised balancing the two interests. "The state must always remain conscious of the fact that it never has and in principle never can, by its own action, bring about the fruitfulness of intellectual activity," wrote Humboldt, making clear the nation's reliance on the university for useful knowledge. But in exchange for generating that useful knowledge, Humboldt maintained, the university was entitled to an unprecedented amount of autonomy for the unbounded pursuit of knowledge, since "effective intellectual accomplishment is to be sought in ceaseless effort."[37] The academies of the previous generation were "sanctuaries" from the state, but "the university always stands in a close relationship to practical life and the affair of training the younger generation."[38]

Humboldt's writings eloquently affirmed the condition that was the sine qua non for the emergence of the modern research university—the nation's interest in useful knowledge. In a proposal to the King in July of 1809 Humboldt made the case for establishing a seat of learning in the Prussian capital.[39] Administrators of the absolutist states of the previous era had already begun to see the advantage of better-trained bookkeepers and tax collectors. The necessity of useful knowledge and men trained in its applications was accentuated by the defeat in war, which created an urgency for Prussia's leaders and an opening for its hungry scientists and scholars. Insofar as it both trained students for civil service and focused on self-cultivation, then, the ur-university that opened to students in October 1810 in a former royal palace on the magnificent Unter den Linden boulevard was more transactional than usually assumed.[40]

To be sure, beginning in February 1810 Humboldt offered a "call" to many of the most famous scholars of his day including Fichte (philosophy), Friedrich Karl von Savigny (law), August Boeckh (classical philology), and Christoph Wilhelm Hufeland (medicine).[41] No doubt these scholars were attracted by Humboldt's support of "solitude and freedom" (*Einsamkeit und Freiheit*) and what subsequent academics and scholars later distilled as the four elements of the "university ideal": the freedom of teaching and learning (*Lehr- und Lernfreiheit*); the unity of teaching and research (*Einheit von Lehre und Forschung*); the devotion to "pure" research as connected to character formation (*Bildung durch Wissenschaft*); and the unity of the natural sciences and the humanities (*Einheit der Wissenschaft*). But he made crucial compromises in the implementation of that ideal, a transaction that constituted the first modern academic social contract.[42]

Viewed from a contractual perspective the university was permitted to stand apart from national, political, and economic concerns in teaching the subjects it chose and, to a certain degree, in hiring the faculty it wished. But these privileges came with responsibilities. Research could be unified with teaching only as long as scholars provided instruction that prepared students for state exams. *Bildung* could remain the core of higher learning only as long as that learning produced an educated workforce for the modern civil service and army. The unity of natural sciences and humanities prevailed only as long as the broader notion of *Wissenschaft* under which they were contained served those professional goals. And, perhaps the most long-lasting contradiction, solitude and freedom was justified by the eventual application of knowledge. In sum, the academic social contract Humboldt negotiated endowed the university with an autonomous and privileged position in society in exchange for providing a set of services to society.

The demands of the contract became clear almost immediately. Ultimately frustrated by the constraints on his freedom, Humboldt decamped for Vienna, where he took up the Prussian ambassadorship. He was replaced by a professional civil servant and Prussian authoritarian who put the interests of the state ahead of those of pure science. Embattled in a dispute over disciplining students, Fichte, too, resigned, months after his triumphal address as rector. The university that students and professors attended following the eventual defeat of Napoleon was already very different from the one the Romantics envisioned. Medicine was incorporated in 1817 into the so-called ministry of the mind (the new title was the Ministry of Ecclesiastical, Educational, and Medicinal Affairs, hereafter, Education Ministry), signaling the beginning of more money being funneled into the sciences, displacing the humanities. And the "bread" students and courses made a comeback. On the other hand, after this slow start, the synergy between the new university and Berlin's original assets, including the Academy of Science and the Charité hospital, and an expanded university library and public lecture series, turned Berlin into a hub of intellectual activity that continued largely unabated until the Second World War. Despite the deep conservatism that swept Prussia from 1810 to 1861, Berlin flourished. When a less progressive ruler came to power in the Kingdom of Hanover in 1837 and threatened to alter the constitution, seven Göttingen professors resigned in protest (the so-called Göttingen Seven); three of them went to Berlin, strengthening Berlin's call to be the prototype for the modern university.[43] Neither the theological experiments at Halle nor the enthusiasm for the seminars at Göttingen extended far beyond academic circles. But with the support of the state the university in Berlin became a model the world over. "The two together," as Humboldt observed, university and the state, "are a fruitful combination."[44]

The university's position in Berlin was also shaped by its relationship to other German cities. Other centers of knowledge surfaced, as in Giessen and Leipzig, and proved to be vital incubators for knowledge, but a hierarchy—albeit a dynamic one—materialized, with Berlin at the top. Berlin received almost as much money as all the other universities combined: 43 percent of total state university funding in 1878–1880.[45] Vibrant universities on the periphery, however, were also supported and proved formidable competitors, particularly in the disciplines in which they had historic strengths—chemistry in Giessen, mathematics in Göttingen, and psychology and cultural history in Leipzig. The unique combination of the German lands' federal structure and the emergence of reformers eager to capitalize on what the historian R. Steven Turner called the new "research imperative" solidified these dynamics.[46]

Other countries tried to emulate Germany's success but weren't able to achieve the robust cultural and scholarly competition that flourished in Germany. In France, the reasons were manifold. For much of the eighteenth and nineteenth centuries, during which it was the envy of scientists and literati throughout the world, France did not actually have a system of universities that thoroughly combined research and teaching. The French National Convention in 1793 abolished existing institutions and replaced them with a centralized educational system that included lycées and, later, the *université impériale* and academies divided by regions.[47] Victor Cousin's 1832 laudatory report on Prussian education, and France's primary school law passed a year later, emphasized centralization in teacher training and rigorous measures, but was more focused on staving off revolution than on advancing instruction.[48] Upstaged at the International Exhibition in 1867 in Paris by Germany's advances in research, French education minister Victor Duruy sent envoys again to Prussia and elsewhere to investigate the competition.[49] At a conference organized a year later by Napoleon III at the Tuileries, scientists and sometime collaborators Louis Pasteur and Claude Bernard attempted to persuade the emperor of the need to direct more resources to the provinces. Minister Duruy supported the scientists: "I venture to request the Emperor to read this description of the physico-chemical laboratory which the Prussians are building at Bonn. It is heart-rending for your minister of education, and menacing for French science."[50] Only larger salaries and better-equipped laboratories would create a healthier scientific landscape, they argued. But other than the École Pratique des Hautes Études (EPHE), founded that year, little else was done.[51]

French reformers uniformly saw the French defeat by the Prussians in 1870 as a symbol of cultural decadence and scholarly stagnation, and, under Louis Liard, the director of higher education in the Ministry of Public Instruction from 1884 to 1902, they sought to modernize the French university system.[52] Liard's comprehensive plan for six universities in strategic locations around the country was diluted, however, resulting in seventeen underfunded regional institutions. And his autonomous financial structure that encouraged regional fundraising did not in the end produce enough resources in the provinces to make a difference.[53] Such scholars as the historian Jules Flammermont advocated for a decentralized system like the

German one, in which provinces competed more effectively for resources, but the clutches of Paris remained too powerful, the German system too controversial, and the regional purses too thin to complete the transformation.[54] Of course, there were countervailing success stories. Some resourceful French scientists and administrators in Nancy, Grenoble, Lyon, Toulouse, and Bordeaux raised money from regional industrialists—efforts that produced significant research, especially in chemistry, electrical physics, and engineering.[55] Under the leadership of Mayor Éduoard Herriot (later prime minister) from 1905 and the famous architect Tony Garnier, Lyon became a "pioneer in French town planning" and part of an international network of reformers.[56] And the joint Nobel Prize in Chemistry to Victor Grignard and Paul Sabatier in 1912 (products of Lyon and Toulouse, respectively) would become a symbol of provincial achievements in science. These moments remained anomalies, however, and as Paris continued to dominate internally, French scholars worried about lagging behind Germany.[57]

Great Britain, too, struggled to match German success. As the first major country to be influenced by German innovations in higher education, Great Britain underwent attempts to "Prussianize" its educational system.[58] The philosopher Matthew Arnold, whose day job was school inspector, greatly admired Humboldt, whom he called "one of the most beautiful and perfect souls that have ever existed," and envied Germany's success with his model.[59] In his *Higher Schools and Universities in Germany*, originally published in 1868, Arnold praised Humboldt for impressing upon statesmen like Bismarck the need to reform the universities so they could raise the culture of the nation even higher, and suggested that the German schools "offer an abundance of . . . lessons."[60]

Arnold met considerable resistance, however. At Cambridge and Oxford, the individual colleges still enjoyed autonomy and remained devoted to the training of clergy within religious orthodoxy.[61] According to the sociologist Joseph Ben-David, the British system also labored under structural challenges separate from translation or ideology—namely, it never developed a productive cultural relationship of center to periphery, even if it is held out as a model for political federalism. With two traditions of education—one for the aristocratic elite and one for the utilitarian and vocational training of the middle classes—it showed early signs of developing the "pioneering diversity" that could become the basis for competition-driven innovation, especially in such Enlightenment-era Scottish institutions as the University of Edinburgh.[62] In 1852, Cardinal Newman became rector of a newly founded Catholic University in Dublin and proposed the idea of a university based on "knowledge for its own sake." But this midcentury Irish example remained an anomaly, a "golden age" invoked as inspiration and out of step with the global turn to applied research.[63]

The British system of higher learning, like its wider culture, never became competitive, and its components, "like so much else in that society, arranged themselves in a relatively neat hierarchy." In this rigid and inert system research and talent flowed to the "two leading universities." In this duopoly, as Ben-David once observed, there was "no incentive for academic innovations: the two leading universities did not need it, and the rest had limited chances of competing with them."[64] To be sure, Cambridge would later become a leader in the natural sciences, and such institutional innovations as the London School of Economics, as we will see in chapter 8, would certainly be influential, but the lack of internal competition held Britain back. Indeed, it was in many ways the counterexample for the simultaneous embrace of meritocracy and stratification based on inherited privilege that, as we will see in chapter 5, proved a winning combination for America.[65]

For reasons political as much as intellectual, Humboldt's model was particularly suited for the United States. Though it would be overly teleological to assume that unification was on the horizon for Germany, it is equally important to recognize that academic leaders increasingly aspired to cultural nationalism to mitigate political fragmentation.[66] Americans must have seen that political diversity went hand in hand with cultural unity, and wondered how they might achieve both. The German university model accordingly took shape across the Atlantic in the form of the land-grant colleges authorized by the Morrill Act of 1862. Though usually considered to be quintessential American institutions of higher learning, their implementation reflecting a distinctively American federalism, the land grants were conceived in transatlantic dialogue.[67] Even as the land-grant movement and the Morrill Act laid the groundwork for "national" coordination, the system in fact remained diffuse and devolved. Devolution was a hallmark of both the German and the American systems, though the peculiarities of the two produced divergent results.

PRUSSIA, MY MICHIGAN

The American founders aimed to spread knowledge, but just how to create a distinctly American system of higher learning that did not rely too much on their European past was another story altogether. In 1779 Thomas Jefferson introduced "A Bill for the More General Diffusion of Knowledge," which called for public support for common schools. In the same year he also reorganized the College of William and Mary; by eliminating chairs for theology and supplementing the faculty with new positions in the arts and sciences, he hoped to turn his alma mater into the pinnacle of a new statewide system.[68] After the Revolution, however, American leaders began to worry whether the American Republic would ever produce artistic and literary luminaries and scientific geniuses.[69] Many American intellectuals and academic leaders emerged who pursued cultural nationalism to strengthen the international face of the new nation.

Despite the good intentions of many reformers, a disparate flotilla of colleges anchored in Reformed Protestantism launched in antebellum America, exacerbating incoherence for half a century. The Second Great Awakening, the religious revival that created major sectarian divisions, produced many colleges, all under religious sponsorship and, although lay governed, effectively under religious control. Judged even by their own standards, these religious colleges were places of little intellectual freedom, limited professional training among instructors, and marginal scientific contributions.[70] Moreover, unlike their European counterparts, they did not emerge in cities that they anointed as centers of learning; rather, as Richard Hofstadter once observed, "They were small and scattered . . . [and] in the nineteenth century . . . this tendency got completely out of hand."[71] Anyone with a charter could start a college in their own religious community, and many did just that. Over four hundred were attempted in just sixteen states in the Republic. While in 1780 there were a mere nine institutions that called themselves colleges, that number amounted to no less than 182 by the eve of the Civil War.[72]

The absence of a superior center of knowledge worried George Washington and his colleague Benjamin Rush, lesser-known founding father, physician, and school reformer, who would go on to improve schools in his native Philadelphia and found Dickinson College. Inspired by Washington, Rush initiated in 1787 the first formal proposal for a "federal university under the patronage of Congress." For Rush, who wanted to employ European-style researchers to collect scientific data from different states, the dangers of not following this plan were clear: America would have an uneducated populace and risk mob rule.[73] The benefits, on the other hand, could be enormous: "Should this plan of a federal university or one like it be adopted, then will begin the golden age of the United States."[74]

A debate ensued about the cultural contours of federalism—did the promotion of science and literature lie within the domain of Congress's responsibility? The American Philosophical Society, a cosmopolitan literary and scientific society founded by Benjamin Franklin in 1743, began to view itself as a vehicle for creating national consciousness, and in 1795 offered a prize for an essay on "the best system of liberal Education and literary instruction, adapted to the genius of the Government of the United States; comprehending also a plan for instituting and conducting public schools in this country, on principles of the most extensive utility."[75] The following year, Washington and John Adams supported the establishment of a national university, and James Madison assured naysayers that such a national university would expand "features of national character," even if it first meant drawing on European expertise. (So desperate were Adams and Jefferson for a national university of their own that they considered taking up the Swiss on their offer to transplant the University of Geneva to the United States.)[76] But there was deep and widespread antipathy toward a centralized national university—James Monroe warned that a constitutional amendment would be required—and the first movement for a national university petered out.[77]

With separate professional schools in medicine, theology, and law, the American colleges were dominated by an educational position typified by the famous Yale Report of 1828. In response to the suggestion that they should forgo the "dead languages" of Latin and Greek for "other studies," the Yale faculty announced the university's commitment to general education rather than research, and expressed self-satisfaction in its independence from the European model: "We hope at least, that this college may be spared the mortification of a ludicrous attempt to imitate . . . [the German universities]."[78] Nevertheless, Americans soon began to crave access to the intellectual stars of the world and as cosmopolitan-minded students and professors started going abroad they discovered the reality: their American colleges barely stood up to a German gymnasium or French lycée (all the more distressing since colleges were postsecondary institutions).[79] When the young George Ticknor arrived in Göttingen from Harvard in 1816 and toured its magnificent library he was shocked: while at Harvard there were twenty professors and fewer than twenty thousand volumes, the German university had forty professors and more than two hundred thousand volumes. Jefferson requested that he buy him German versions of classical texts to furnish a major American library.[80]

Exuberant following his *Wanderjahr*, Ticknor became lecturer in modern literature at Harvard and attempted to reform its curriculum by dividing the college into specialized departments in which related studies would be grouped, a move that met resistance among his colleagues and was unsuccessful. Meanwhile, Jefferson abandoned his aspirations for William and Mary for the students were too juvenile and the curriculum irreparable. He also gave up on a true national university (he tried again as president and got a military academy at West Point instead). Following his presidency Jefferson trained his sights on creating a centrally located state university in Virginia that would be the "last great act of his life and the crowning achievement of nearly a half century of thought and activity for the benefit of education."[81]

Established in 1819, the University of Virginia was Jefferson's attempt to educate a new southern leadership class. Like future supporters of a national university Jefferson worried that without a countervailing force the New England colleges would control the production of the American elite. Jefferson wanted at Charlottesville what was no longer possible at his alma mater: a secular university steeped in republican values and classical education.[82] If he borrowed models of freedom of teaching and learning and democratic faculty governance from German universities these adaptations were only identified as such in hindsight.[83] He was most focused on hiring serious instructors and, in 1824, dispatched his friend and lawyer Francis Walker Gilmer to Europe to recruit German-trained English professors—a mission for which Jefferson was mocked and resented in the northern press.[84] When the university opened to students in 1825, it quickly became clear that the university would contribute to, rather than overcome, the intensifying American sectional politics. Indeed it is difficult to see how a national education system would develop in a climate in which Jefferson worried about native Virginians going to Princeton and Harvard, where they might be indoctrinated by northern ideology on the Missouri question.[85] Even if such reformers as Ticknor yearned for a Göttingen in America, the most natural place for a distinguished university would be hotly debated. Where was the intellectual center of the early American Republic?

Ticknor was only the most well-known of the American sojourners who began to travel regularly to German universities; others included George Calvert, who was one of the first Americans to study in Göttingen and went on to become a popularizer of German literature; Theodore Dwight Woolsey, who parlayed his studies in Leipzig, Bonn, and Berlin to become president of Yale College; and Barnas Sears, who learned biblical theology and ancient languages in Germany and led Brown University after the Civil War.[86] Although many of these "academic missionaries," including Ticknor, were too early to implement structural change, they did not hold back spreading the new gospel back at home.[87] One of the most fervent of these apostles was Karl (later Charles) Follen, a native of Brandenburg and revolutionary exile. He once aspired to found a German university in America but settled for becoming the first professor of German literature at Harvard University, where he instructed the next generation of travelers.[88] Ticknor's traveling partner Edward Everett encouraged his pupil George Bancroft to read German literature, philosophy, and theology, and, supplying him with letters of introduction, sent him off to Germany.[89] Bancroft traveled to Jena and

Weimar and received his doctoral degree two years later. He was welcomed by Goethe and studied in Berlin with Hegel, among others, and wrote letters to the Harvard president about his impressions of the capital city and its enthralling university.[90] Upon his return, the gap between the American college and the German university now felt uncomfortably wider.[91]

Antebellum New England witnessed a "German craze," including music tutors, the Kindergarten, and the common schools movement.[92] What was different about the new generation of American scholars and higher education reformers who emerged in the 1850s was that they mastered the argument Humboldt once made: science is useful for the state. Young people needed to be prepared to become the scientists, farmers, and engineers who could help the United States industrialize. As these priorities came to the fore, education took a utilitarian turn. In 1844, no less than two decades after the Yale Report promoted intellectual protectionism, an enthusiastic orator at Yale told undergraduates that the "age of *philosophy* has passed. . . . That of utility has commenced."[93]

Scientists took the lead in asserting the usefulness of their disciplines. Modeling themselves on the German chemist Justus von Liebig, American scientists joined an emerging international effort to make the case that research improvements in chemical agriculture supported states' interests. Wildly influential all over Europe and America in the 1830s and 1840s, Liebig became the center of an "international laboratory movement" at the University of Giessen, where he regularly received visiting scientists from around Germany, including Alexander von Humboldt, Wilhelm's younger brother, as well as others from at least a dozen nations. Liebig, who made regular speaking tours, was the "established darling of English agriculturalists," and even published a popular cookbook. He represents the first of many scientists who sought, rather than fended off, market interest—a prototype for today's academic celebrity.[94] By 1862 there were fifteen experiment stations in German states based on Liebig's research, and acolytes in America believed they were critical both to Germany's industrial success and as a model for a permanent institutional home for science in America.[95] Among the strategies that American adherents of Liebig's experimental method supported were the adaptation of a chemical approach to the choice of seeds and fertilizers, and the scientific breeding of animals. Liebig's main innovation—the laboratory—solidified the turn from the system building of the late Enlightenment and Romantic reformers to the age of experimentation.[96]

One American reformer who brought together strands of German idealism, the new experimentation, and cultural nationalism was Henry P. Tappan, who merged the French philosopher Victor Cousin's analysis of the Prussian education system with the new laboratory-based science. One historian has called him the "John the Baptist" of the modern research university for the fervor with which he spread this university gospel back home.[97] Tappan's pulpit would become the University of Michigan, whose Board of Regents made him its first president in 1850.[98] In his 1851 work *University Education*, Tappan borrowed heavily from Germany in his efforts to identify the appropriate model, the relevant stakeholders, and the funding for a new American education. For Tappan, the German lands were the source of *echt* professors and invaluable books and equipment.[99] In his report to the Board of Regents of 1853, Tappan extolled the virtues of the University of Berlin, whose ideals did not adhere to "mere commercial utility." At the same time, he insisted that his institution would produce men who could promote economic productivity. "The man, when he is truly educated as a man, is best fitted for all the future of a man, and for all the employments of human life," Tappan intoned. "The result is seen in the substantial and elegant character of [the Prussians'] public works, in the perfection of their manufactures and all the products of the mechanical arts, and in that wonderful agriculture which extorts plenty from a barren soil."[100]

In Tappan's vision the city of Ann Arbor, to which the school had moved in 1837, would breathe "the very air" of "freedom" like his inspiration in Berlin. If the University of Berlin was possible under a "despotic government with an expensive court, a large standing army, and the consequent imposition of burdensome taxes," it must be possible, Tappan reasoned, for America to have an intellectual "life of national prosperity." The sale of lands in Michigan would add income and permit the hiring of professors and purchasing of equipment, but Tappan knew that the university would have to appeal to the state for financial support: "As the University of Michigan it must be worthy of its name. We say to the State, it is yours, we are but the servants whom you commission to do this great work. Give us the means that we may carry out your design, and make good your hopes."[101]

Tappan did not accomplish these lofty aspirations. As a "broadminded evangelical," he assumed the university would be Christian, and this entailed support for voluntary religious organizations and a requirement that all students attend a Sunday service.[102] But he also pursued a proactive campaign against what he called "sectarianism" and abolished the various "chairs" in different denominations. Tappan was never able to manage all the interests required: the scientists did not like his focus on religion; the religious leaders did not like his support of science; and the Regents took issue with his authoritarian personality. (He insisted on being

called Chancellor, which his critics linked to his "empire-building pretensions.")[103] In 1863, the board dismissed him, and Tappan moved his family
to "self-imposed exile" in Berlin, but not without announcing that "the pen
of history . . . [which is] held by the hand of Almighty Justice" was on his
side.[104] Notwithstanding his religious rhetoric, Tappan's legacy established
the framework for the modern secular relationship between the research
university and the American state, and created a new role for the university as an institution of both economic and cultural regeneration.[105]

Tappan's early attempts at the adaptation of the German model were set
against the background of congressional debates about federalism. In issues ranging from law enforcement to the staffing of the executive branch,
railroad regulations and labor management, lawmakers debated whether
locality or the nation was the proper locus of power. Inspired by state initiatives to allocate the proceeds of land sales for the founding of local universities, Congressman Justin Smith Morrill of Vermont introduced legislation in 1856 to create a national program in which Congress would "endow
a system of industrial universities."[106] To a certain extent, the lawmakers'
debates about these "land-grant universities" followed the same ambivalent pattern as those about the proper locus of authority in such other fields
as interstate commerce and agriculture, and Morrill's first two attempts
to pass his bill failed.[107] Once the rebellious Southern states seceded and
the land was expropriated from indigenous people, however, the ensuing
economic and military crisis created for Morrill and his legislation — in his
telling — "a more favorable auspices."[108]

Though strictly speaking an internal crisis, the Civil War was also, as
historians have increasingly shown, a "global" war, with soldiers arriving from Europe to take sides in an economic and an ideological battle.[109]
Northerners were compelled to come to terms with the inadequacy of their
military and their agriculture. As Morrill admonished, had his legislation
been implemented a half quarter century earlier "the young men might
have had more fitness for their sphere of duties, whether on the farm, in
the workshop, or in the battle field."[110] The message was clear: to become
a serious nation-state in an industrializing world Americans must determine what changes they would make. The notion that the United States
would take its place among nations not merely by applying the inventions
of others, but in becoming a source of those inventions, would preoccupy
Americans well into the twentieth century. The Morrill Act was the first
legislative expression of that desire.

American lawmakers nonetheless entered tentatively into what political
scientists call the "second state" of national administration. Congressman
Morrill was not an advocate of what we might call "big government." A

states' rights fiscal conservative, he cautioned against spending and financial dependency.[111] Indeed it was his emphasis on local governance that motivated the bill. But as this was the first time since the Northwest Ordinance of 1787 that the national government would sponsor a national education agenda, many of his colleagues were fearful of its implications. According to one historian, Morrill succeeded in 1862 because he "created a measure that could be interpreted in both a nationalist and a local orientation."[112]

There was another reason for Morrill's success: as the author of the Tariff Act of 1861 and chairman of the House Ways and Means Committee, Morrill championed American industry. With no formal education he had built a successful dry goods business and promoted policies that would protect the American economy.[113] Morrill's economic protectionism motivated his support of a federally coordinated system of higher education for working people with whom he identified. Skeptics were thus willing to overlook the competition among states vying for resources that would arise from the law's implementation. At a moment of tremendous division, when national coherence was in question, Morrill used the ambivalence of federalism to his advantage and brought into his tent both those whose priority was maintaining a loose federation of states and those who wished for a country that was internationally competitive.

The Prussian model proved significant in reconciling the centralizing and localizing interests and was a constant presence in the debates about the Morrill Act. One Union Party member who had served as an American ambassador to Prussia warned his colleagues in Congress that "without scientific investigations into our nation's resources . . . we shall gradually sink into a mere dependency of Europe." The discussion of agriculture and the common schools movement followed similar lines, reflecting an influence and impetus from Prussia, while lawmakers aimed to disguise the Prussian origins of their ideas to ward off associations with executive power.[114]

With respect to pedagogy and purpose, Morrill's thinking was coherent and timely. Drawing on regret about his own lack of education, Morrill was keen that "at least one college in every state" be "accessible to all, but especially to the sons of toil." The land-grant movement has often been hailed as the university "of the people"; however, the lofty goal of inclusion would not have succeeded had Morrill not underscored the centrality of agriculture for "the foundation of all present and future prosperity" and its potential for "elevating it to that higher level where it may fearlessly invoke comparison with the most advanced standards of the world."[115] In his speech before Congress, which was later reprinted in the publication of the New York State Agricultural Society in June 1862, Morrill sounded alarms concerning America's international competitiveness. "Should no effort be made to arrest the deterioration and spoliation of the soil in America, while all Europe is wisely striving to teach her agriculturalists the best means of hoarding up capital in the lands on that side of the Atlantic, it is easy to see that we are doomed to be dwarfed in national importance, and not many years can pass away before our ships will be laden with grain not on their outward but homeward voyage."[116] Morrill's message is especially evident in section 4 of the bill that President Lincoln signed into law on July 2, 1862, in which what is described is the creation of opportunity for those in the "industrial classes" to receive training in the "practical avocations of life." The institutions of higher learning established under its aegis would teach the "practical arts" alongside "other scientific and classical studies" and encourage "economic development through research."[117]

Defining who the students were and how to meet their needs created opportunities and divisions. In contrast to the realms of law and economics, where the creation of bureaus brought order and systemization, the implementation of the land-grant legislation was patchwork, albeit effective.[118] Some grants were awarded to existing state universities such as Wisconsin, while in other states new ones, such as Cornell University (itself a hybrid of private and public monies) and the University of California, were created. Some states chose to bypass their public universities altogether and established separate A&M institutions; and four colleges for African Americans were given land-grant designations by Southern states, though they would remain systematically underfunded.[119]

In Michigan in the decades following the passing of the legislation, both the advantages and disadvantages of the emerging state system became evident. If Tappan struggled with just what the German model meant for the American higher education landscape, James B. Angell, the longest-serving president of the University of Michigan, identified the feature that would be essential in its American implementation—the devolution of authority to the states. In Angell's conception of the academic social contract this entailed, the university aspired to a system of education that served the state and expected its support in return. While not a land grant itself, the University of Michigan under Angell's presidency drew impetus from the land-grant movement and the German advancements in science to develop an alternative model that focused more on research than on application in his midwestern empire—underscoring the lack of consensus over whom the state-sponsored institution would serve.

Angell was as exuberant about German ideas as Tappan had been, recounting for his midwestern audience at his presidential inauguration in 1871: "It was with no exaggerated estimate of the functions and power of a university that Stein and William von Humboldt and Niebuhr and

Schleiermacher and Savigny and their coadjutors laid the foundations of that splendid school at Berlin as the mightiest instrumentality in lifting Prussia from her deep abasement to that height of power from which she could look down in defiance upon her conqueror from beyond the Rhine." For Angell the implementation was as important as the philosophy of German idealism. Echoing Germany's dual commitments to the military and to science, Angell argued that the university was an expression of the state's political — and military — might.[120]

Angell was neither the first nor the last American university president to be influenced by Germany's nation-building project. The proper scale for implementing the German university model in the United States, however, was the American state, not the nation, as was implicit in the Morrill Act. Angell made this explicit in an address given at the dedication of the new building in 1885 at the University of Missouri, which had been awarded land-grant status in 1870 on the condition that it open two more schools of agriculture and the mechanical arts. Angell identified each American state as analogous to a nation that required its own university. "Each of these states has the territory and the resources of a European kingdom: There should be in each at least one vigorous university. Germany has one for each two million inhabitants. Most of these states will at no distant day each have more inhabitants than that number. Some of them have more already. Can any one who measures the strength the State universities have already attained cherish a doubt that the one great university in each one of these States, if there is to be one great university in each, will be the State university? Then the State in its legislation and the university in shaping its development should lay their plans in view of this fact."[121]

The University of Michigan has been hailed as a success story of international knowledge exchange. According to two historians, "The transmogrification of German practice was the really substantial American contribution to the research university. The Germans invented the research ideal. The Americans invented an institution to house and perpetuate it."[122] When the New York journalist Edwin E. Slosson visited Ann Arbor in 1910 he would remark that there were more undergraduates at Michigan than anywhere in the country.[123] And Angell campaigned to bring the standards of incoming students up to par with their European counterparts. More significant than his singular institutional achievement, however, was his insight into a feature of the system — that it should remain true to its federalist origins. State university presidents in the coming years would rely heavily on the language of federalism and federations.[124]

Yet not every state university could become an Ann Arbor, and even within Michigan tensions emerged between those who viewed the "Michigan Plan" as a critique of the impact of industrialization on agriculture and those who aimed to help farmers address the changing times. At the University of Missouri, where Angell detailed his research-driven vision for the university, this approach prevailed only after several years of political struggles.[125] The University of Minnesota, chartered in 1851, faced similar challenges and could not open for collegiate instruction until 1869. And the Illinois Industrial University opened in 1868 amid a debate about structure and location and an overbearing body of Regents.[126] These struggles recalled Tappan's advice from 1853: "It is better to have one strong and well-endowed institution than a multitude of feeble ones."[127] And indeed that is precisely what later reformers would aim to calibrate—the redundancy, unevenness, and disorder created by the Morrill Act. The path of diversity and pluralism, of course, would be difficult to reverse; it would also prove to be the source of considerable advantages.

THE FEDERALIST ADVANTAGE

The potential and limits of federalism for science were borne out in the last quarter of the nineteenth century as American innovators transformed the German university model into a state system of higher education, creating what Clark Kerr later dubbed a unique "American mixture."[128] The state system was also shaped by a transatlantic debate about the utility of education and state-sponsored research. These debates occurred in all industrializing countries at the time, including France and Great Britain, where the perceived decline of both science and universities was the source of much anxiety. As educational leaders in budding nations in a globalizing world, German and American administrators found that their respective "special paths" collided in debates concerning how to create a system of higher learning that housed scientific research and in turn served the needs of the state.[129] In both contexts, federalist questions about the centripetal and centrifugal forces of politics paralleled questions about the best way to organize and fund the pursuit and dissemination of knowledge. In America, in contrast with the German case, war did not create a national university, nor did it facilitate a synecdochic relationship between the nation's capital and science. As Christopher Jencks and David Riesman observed in 1968 at the height of unrest in American universities, because of the "preference of local spokesmen for local institutions," "America got a Balkanized pattern that made even the decentralized and polycentric German approach look orderly and monolithic."[130]

The continued maligning of America's decentralized system, as reflected in Jencks and Riesman's observation, has obscured its wisdom.

Whereas decentralization posed challenges for infrastructure and political unity, it simultaneously fostered conditions under which higher learning thrived.[131] Later American reformers would view decentralization as a disadvantage, and extoll the virtues of standardization and centralization, but in America, at moments of institutional change, the voices of "localizers" were often louder.[132]

At the same time, nations with more centralized systems, such as France, learned about the disadvantages of their approach. Despite efforts to buttress provincial universities with private funding, France failed to develop an alternative to the cultural center of Paris.[133] From one perspective the French and German institutional approaches were not all that different. They both pursued teaching and research; they both integrated technical skills into education; and they both envisioned elite roles for a university-trained professional class. To be sure, Germans would play up the rejection of the French, but their similarities suggest that the federalist political context is as important as any "internal" logic in explaining what by the twentieth century would be called the French "decline."[134]

Matthew Arnold shrewdly observed, "The French university had no liberty, and the English universities have no science; the German universities have both."[135] Many an observant American marveled at the freedom in Göttingen and Berlin despite the autocratic political context. And while, as we will see in chapter 7, these Americans had an inflated sense of what they anointed as "academic freedom" back at home, the disconnect between the university and the political worlds in which it existed remained a puzzle: How could Americans account for the fact that a monarchy seemed to be surpassing a democracy in higher education? And how could they overcome the political challenges of democracy to get the same benefits?

Tappan was not the only university president to reservedly admire the German university as "a glorious achievement of an enlightened and energetic despotism." Francis Wayland, "Whig university leader" of Brown University, shared Tappan's ambition to emulate the success of Europe's institutions of cultural nationalism—without the political ramifications of an anarchic revolution or a repressive monarchy.[136] What good was higher learning if it came at the cost of freedom? Tappan asked. We must prove that a "republic, too, can create and foster the noblest institutions of learning, can patronize the arts and artists, and learning and learned men."[137] One could say that Tappan and the Americans hoped to avoid the sacrifice that Humboldt had made to exchange democratic politics for educational excellence.[138]

The wisdom of the federalist system reflected in the land-grant movement was its apparent evasion of national partisan politics to the end of supporting these "learned men." The Morrill Act achieved the centralization and funding for which Jefferson had labored—but in a distinct formulation that provided federal funding for state-based implementation. Since the grants would be awarded on the basis of the state's ability to provide matching funds, and states had autonomy to promote (and exclude) those schools they desired, the domestic landscape would remain uneven. Skeptics were willing to go along with the plan because Morrill persuaded them of the necessity of keeping up with the Prussians. When the land-grant universities are viewed from a transatlantic perspective, domestic competition and inequality emerge as the price Morrill and his colleagues were willing to pay for international competitiveness.[139]

By reconsidering the relationship of the center to the periphery, the Morrill Act rewrote the terms of Humboldt's contract. Now all the states would have universities—Michigan, Wisconsin, and Iowa too!—in exchange for producing educated farmers, scientists, and engineers who would ensure the competitiveness of their states and the United States. As Morrill assured, "With such a system as that here offered—nurseries in every State—an efficient force would at all times be ready to support the cause of the nation and secure that wholesome respect which belongs to a people whose power is always equal to its pretensions."[140] As was already visible in the first decade of the land-grant universities' founding, however, states became miniature empires themselves—as Angell had predicted—replete with the problems of European nation-states.

Daniel Coit Gilman, then a professor at Yale's Sheffield Scientific School, itself a recipient of a land grant, noted the parallel: state universities encompassed "a vast domain, surpassing the area of many of the kingdoms and duchies of Europe."[141] In 1871, as Germany became a nation, the US secretary of the interior asked Gilman to survey science education in America. In his report he contrasted "useful education" with his own research-based notion of "national schools of science," a vision that he later tried in vain to implement as president of the University of California.[142] After learning the hard way about the challenges that these mini-empires wrought, Gilman returned to the East Coast to launch an entrepreneurial venture that reflected a different formulation of the university ideal, one that embraced pure research—rather than utilitarianism—as its ethos. Supported by local and regional philanthropists, Gilman had the opportunity to redraft the terms of the contract yet again. He would reach back to the German university model as the inspiration for a new institution. The result of his efforts showed the competitive advantage of an institution with global ambitions embedded in, and closely identified with, a city.

CHAPTER TWO

GÖTTINGEN AT BALTIMORE

THE STAKES OF KNOWLEDGE EXCHANGE

Certainly Gottingen is the best place to gather genuine learning; but I hardly think, a man would learn there how to use it properly.
GEORGE BANCROFT, 1820

In February 1876, Daniel Coit Gilman presided over the opening of the Johns Hopkins University in Baltimore. In his memorable oration, Gilman presented the new university as the culmination of a history that began in 1676 with the founding of a grammar school in New Haven, continued to the founding of the American Republic in 1776, and was now, one hundred years hence, "distinguishe[d by] a university foundation."[1] A few months later, at the International Exhibition of Arts, Manufactures and Products of the Soil and Mine, delegates from around the world gathered in Philadelphia's Fairmount Park to celebrate the 100th anniversary of the signing of the Declaration of Independence. On the three thousand acres of the grounds of this "world's fair," America displayed its marvels of technology alongside those of other nations, including its traditional rivals, Great Britain and France, and the new nation of Germany.[2]

The sophistication of the US-made machines elicited worries among Europeans. Friedrich Engels dubbed the Philadelphia World's Fair Germany's "Industrial Jena," recalling Prussia's defeat at the hands of Napoleon seventy years earlier to suggest that Germans should feel a similar degree of humiliation in their industrial performance.[3] Engels's metaphor was apt, because nations were now competing as much for economic dynamism as they were for military might. He would have been even more concerned had he known that the opening of Hopkins only months before heralded America's rapid advance in science, which undergirded economic growth and military power. In the increasingly competitive and interconnected world of the late 1800s, the transatlantic exchange of knowledge, scholars, and ideas for organizing education would take on greater significance, with ironic consequences for the nature of educational competition and its effects on innovation.

SERVING A NEW MASTER

Uniquely in American higher education Daniel Coit Gilman understood the need to acquire knowledge from elsewhere "in order to know what to avoid and abandon, what to test and adopt."[4] Abraham Flexner, America's educational trailblazer of the next generation, would make Gilman his model and declare, "No other American of his day had a comparable equipment in knowledge of coming educational change or in experience with innovation."[5] Born in 1831 in Norwich, Connecticut, to founders of that city, Gilman began his career in New England cataloging the library of George Washington. Reverence for the library as central to an institution of higher learning would remain a cornerstone of his beliefs throughout his career.[6] After graduating from Yale in 1848 he spent a few months studying at Harvard College, where he experienced the "lure" of the German university. When the opportunity arose in 1854 to travel as an attaché of an American delegation to St. Petersburg with his classmate Andrew Dickson White, Gilman seized it. At a serendipitous meeting in Europe with Noah Porter, a Yale professor who would become that college's next president, Gilman confided, "When I go home to America, I must have some definite notions. I long for an opportunity to influence New England minds."[7] Gilman subsequently toured throughout Europe and studied in Berlin. A self-described "close observer" of the "three typical institutions," the residential college, the technical school, and the research university, Gilman was poised to define the purpose of higher learning in post–Civil War America.[8]

Upon his return to the United States, Gilman took a job with Yale's library and became involved in Yale's emerging Scientific School, which had been reorganized while he was in Europe to include courses in chemistry and engineering. Gilman showed fundraising savvy and institutional farsightedness in his "Proposed Plan for a Complete Organization of the School of Science Connected with Yale College," which he published in 1856 in New Haven:

> For a long time past, every European government . . . has made provision for the thorough training of men who wished to study science for its own sake, or who desired to fit themselves for such practical occupations as Engineering, Architecture, Agriculture, Mining, and Manufacturing. The observations of intelligent travelers, the testimony of manufacturers, agriculture and commerce, and the recent "Universal exhibitions of industry and art," unite in showing that the welfare of any nation is immediately affected by the maintenance of such scholars. Such training has been almost wholly neglected in the

United States. We are consequently far behind European nations in many important branches of industry.[9]

American investments in science were behind, and the country's agricultural and mechanical output was suffering the consequences. Gilman referred his readers to an appendix, "Notes on Schools of Science in Europe," in which he enumerated the schools and faculties in France and Germany, along with their courses and requirements, that might serve as models.[10] Largely as a result of his leadership, Gilman secured in 1860 both a building and benefaction for Yale's Scientific School in the amount of $100,000 and bestowed the honor of the school's name on its primary donor, Joseph E. Sheffield. Gilman's influence is evident in the reorganization of the school, especially in the new admissions requirements implemented that year based on those he had admired in Germany.[11] The newly minted Sheffield School received the crucial right to grant the German-style PhD, which it began to do the following year (the first awarded in America).[12] With a land grant, also negotiated by Gilman, the Sheffield Scientific School's future was secure. Gilman was named a professor of physical geography in 1863, but his passion lay not with instruction but with administration, in which he was inspired by what he had seen abroad, and he continued to push for more financial support and the elevation of standards.[13]

In a public report that he published in 1867, Gilman praised the benefactor of the Sheffield Scientific School for recognizing the double duty of "National Schools of Science," since he "had clearly seen the value of training in mathematical, physical, and natural science as a preparation for life, as well as the importance of scientific researches in promoting the development of our natural resources."[14] Other philanthropists, including Stephen Van Rensselaer, James Smithson, and Abbott Lawrence, the latter of whom gave Harvard $50,000 to begin a scientific institute, agreed, and, following the Civil War, institutions dedicated to the practical arts were added to Columbia University (1864), Lafayette College (1866), Dartmouth College (1871), the University of Pennsylvania (1872), and Princeton University (1873).[15] For Gilman these nascent institutions required guidance: "We regard it as highly important that the scientific schools of Europe should be understood in this country. . . . Their influence, in the first place, on the advancement of science and its application to human industry, on invention and discovery, deserves to be unfolded; and in the second place, their influence on the training of manufacturers, agriculturists, miners, engineers, architects, for the various positions of the industrial world."[16] America was still a pupil of Europe.

The German model could help Americans achieve their scientific aspirations and industry's demands for technical expertise. Technical schools in Europe, Gilman wrote, "are adapted to the wants of different classes of students, to those who are competent to pursue the highest scientific investigations, and to those who seek only a technical preparation for active life. We need very much at the present moment an examination of the influence of foreign scientific institutions in promoting the efficiency of industrial undertakings."[17] This duality inspired Gilman's lifelong balancing of what he later called "Hand-craft and Rede-craft," or mechanical and logical skills. "They are brothers, partners, consorts, who should work together as right hand and left hand," Gilman espoused, "as science and art, as theory and practice."[18]

Though Gilman continued to respect the mechanical arts, he believed that what we would call today basic research was foundational to society's advancement. Often it seemed that research for its own sake was the favored son. As he reflected on the Sheffield Scientific School, "Everyone knows that the country depends for agriculture on crops, but not everybody remembers, when he sees the heavily laden trains, the well-filled elevators, and the wharves burdened with wheat, cotton, and tobacco, that the national supplies are largely results of advances made by science."[19] In other words, Gilman wanted to bring the pure science that made the marvels of the Philadelphia World's Fair possible to the fore. At the same time, by praising research on the basis of its eventual application he approached a utilitarian defense of *Wissenschaft* to which Humboldt, too, had subscribed.

Ultimately unable to adapt Yale's college model any further, Gilman looked for a new institutional opportunity within which to realize the union of pure and applied research. Offered the presidency of another land-grant institution, the University of California, twice, Gilman finally accepted and threw himself into becoming a "native Californian."[20] To a certain degree, he was successful. He lectured on geography, conferred with the Regents, negotiated with legislators, and tried in earnest to create an institution that reflected the needs of its constituents. Gilman's sensitivity to the university's community is evident in his inaugural address as president: "[The University of California] is not the university of Berlin or of New Haven which we are to copy . . . but is the University of this State. It must be adapted to this people, to their public and private schools, to their geographical position, to the requirements of their new society and their undeveloped resources. It is not the foundation of an ecclesiastical body, nor of private individuals. It is 'of the people and for the people'—not in any low or unworthy sense, but in the highest and noblest relations to their intellectual and moral well-being."[21]

Following "one year of glory," however, Gilman found the breaches between the ecclesiastical and the secular, the scientific and the applied, to be irreparable. Viewing Gilman as elitist, Henry George, a San Francisco newspaper editor who supported the Grangers, California's populist movement for the mechanical and agricultural arts, claimed "the Regents . . . have perverted the University from its original design into a college of classics and polite learning." Moreover, a new political code passed at the beginning of Gilman's presidency tied the University of California's Regents more closely to the state legislature, narrowing his executive latitude. Gilman complained of his limited authority to his former travel companion White, who was now himself president of Cornell University: "The University of California is . . . nominally administered by the Regents; it is virtually administered by the legislature" and "liable 'to be sponged out' in a single hour of partisan clamor."[22] Since Cornell was part public land grant and part private, White would find his own hands tied similarly by government regulations.[23]

Charles Eliot, who had recently been named the twenty-first president of Harvard College and with whom Gilman maintained a "strong sense of colleagueship," not surprisingly saw the problem differently, beginning with the "utterly unrepublican and un-American" notion that the state should be the benefactor of education at all.[24] "The whole country—including most of our public men—is inoculated with the idea of government benefice. . . . If the people are suffering the inevitable ills of an irredeemable currency, the President and the Secretary of the Treasury are the kind gods who must set all things right," Eliot wrote disparagingly in 1873 to a beleaguered Gilman.[25] Eliot had another idea of who the new gods ought to be: a rising class of university presidents. Gilman's California predicament symbolized a larger national debate about whether education would best be addressed by the government or through voluntary institutions and will. The academic social contract required a new model of higher education, one that evaded both the English college's sectarianism and the overreaching power of the state.

A "princely gift" of $7 million from a railroad magnate afforded Gilman with the opportunity to realize that model in a new institution. One of the "foremost of the moneyed men of Baltimore," Johns Hopkins was known to "gather around the table the brightest and most intellectual people of the community" of Baltimore, a growing hub of culture due to the generosity of the philanthropist George Peabody. The principal owner of the Baltimore and Ohio (B&O) Railroad, young Johns, it had long been thought, had been forced to abandon his education at a young age when his abolitionist father freed their slaves. Though we now know this story to be apocryphal, there remain unanswered questions about the motivations of this childless philanthropist.[26] What is certain is that the model of private philanthropy for higher education, with its distinctly personal advantages and disadvantages, would have a long-term influence.

At the age of seventy-three, he incorporated the Johns Hopkins University under the laws of the state of Maryland and appointed a group of trustees to be its guardians.[27] Following his death in 1873, the distinguished group met to make arrangements for the future of the institution.[28] Gilman later lauded the dutiful trustees as "large-minded men" who comprised the city's finest businessmen and merchants—praise that stemmed from their shared approach to education.[29] One trustee, George Washington Dobbin, was a jurist and amateur scientist who kept a lab at his summer home and regularly attended scientific lectures. Another was George William Brown, the former mayor and then judge of the Supreme Bench of Baltimore, who had professed the centrality of research in a lecture at St. John's College in 1869. For Brown, instructors "should be teachers in the largest sense, that is, should have the ability and the leisure too, to add something by their writings and discoveries to the world's stock of literature and science."[30] Gilman couldn't have agreed more.

The next summer, after assembling a library on higher education, the trustees invited to Baltimore several university presidents, including Angell, Eliot, and White, to share their wisdom. White suggested a focus on "men over buildings," and Angell urged the board to emphasize "the practical applications to science and arts," given Baltimore's identity as a mechanical and industrial city. Eliot was doubtful about a de novo institution accomplishing anything in the range of graduate education: "It is impossible that [the organization of such an institution] should spring full-armed from anybody's brain."[31] About one point the presidents were in utter agreement—the "one man" for the job. Angell confided in his friend Gilman the "remarkable" fact that "without the least conference between us there, we all wrote letters, telling them that the one man was Daniel C. Gilman of California."[32] Gilman would perform the remarkable trick—he would pull the university "full-armed from [his] brain."

The letter from the Hopkins board members that Gilman received in October of 1874 altered his destiny: they offered him the opportunity to lead this new university with a fund of $3.5 million (the other half of Hopkins's gift was reserved for a hospital) "with no shackles of state or political influence, and with no restriction but the wisdom and sound judgment of the Board of Trustees." The president of the board (as the title was then) emphasized that the institution would be "not denominational" and "entirely plastic in the hands of those to whom its founder has entrusted its organization and development." The American pragmatist philosopher Charles S. Peirce, who would later lecture at the university, praised the philanthropist's will as being "happily free from all definite ideas."[33] Gilman could not conceal his excitement: "When I think of the immense fund at your control; and when I think of the relations of Baltimore to the other great cities of the East, and especially of the relations which this University should have to the recovering states of the South, I am almost ready to say that my services are at your disposal."[34]

If the university was to be neither a college for ministerial preparation nor a "National School of Science" that promoted the agricultural and mechanical arts for the benefit of the state's economy, then whom would this new institution serve? Gilman's answer to that question established an institutional model that outlived him. Judge Brown had reportedly deemed America's educational system "a temple without a dome, a column without a capital, a spire without a pinnacle."[35] Gilman shared Brown's aspiration to create that peak and implored the other trustees to aim for "something more than a local institution" and "to bring to Baltimore, as teachers and as students, the ablest minds that we could attract."[36] The first step was distinguishing what the university was not. According to Gilman, "To certain persons, the university simply means the best place of instruction that the locality can secure." In contrast, he advanced his notion of making Hopkins a "means of promoting scholarship of the first order," a project that would require "leaving the kind of work now done by undergraduates to be done elsewhere."[37] Calling an institution that was little more than an advanced high school a "university" degraded the idealistic as well as practical ends to which Gilman aspired.[38]

To achieve that higher goal, Europe and Germany would be both model and competition, as Gilman made clear at his first appearance before the board at the end of 1874. Compared with Europe, he said, "our intellectual progress bears no sort of proportion to our progress in the accumulation of wealth and in the mechanical arts. . . . To the higher thought of the world we contribute shamefully little. The books that rouse and stimulate men in the various great fields of speculation to-day are almost invariably European."[39]

Unfortunately for Gilman, not all Baltimoreans—even on the board of trustees—shared his ambitions for a world-class university. The railroad magnate John Garrett broke with the board when they rejected his advice to become an institution with local goals.[40] As Angell had advised, a great city of the steam engine could use an institution devoted to "the practical application of chemistry, for instance, to the useful arts—such as working in the metals, dyes, etc.," not a research university at the expense of local needs.[41] Unbeknownst to Gilman, an editor at the *Nation* got hold of Gilman's private remarks and published them, replete with their condescending asides about college students—unleashing a torrent of criticism.[42] A local editorial listed the pros and cons of the proposed institution, and the author noted that because there already existed ample opportunities for higher learning in America, "this part of the country" could not possibly justify a "school of philosophy."[43] A relentless stream of articles followed in Baltimore's *American* that castigated Gilman as out of touch with the needs of Baltimoreans.[44] The Baltimore writer Edwin Spencer defended the university against critics who thought the benefaction would better have been "applied to augment the already large resources of Harvard or Yale," but also counseled Gilman privately on the city's "clannish and provincial" attitude and predicted that the "commercial spirit, the idea that the horizon of education and the practical are identical, will be apt to give you a trouble like that which you have had from the 'Grangers' in California."[45]

If Gilman were to be successful, then, he would need to persuade Baltimore's citizens—his new contractual partners—of the connection between their city's needs and his institution's lofty ambitions. To this end, the chair of the board of trustees advised Gilman to consider the "double aspect" of higher education; that is, to offer not only the German PhD but also the American BA.[46] In his formal acceptance letter of January 1875, Gilman identified a solution: to establish "not a scientific school, nor a classical college, nor both combined; but a faculty of medicine, and a faculty of philosophy."[47] A hybrid of the best of earlier institutions—German and American—began to emerge.

Although Hopkins's bequest was the largest single gift to an institution of higher learning at the time (in contrast, the Harvard University's endowment in 1873 was $2.5 million) the $3.5 million allocated for the university was swiftly accounted for.[48] Since the charter restricted the university's yearly income to $200,000, and Gilman believed it crucial to reserve $45,000 for the library, equipment, and administration, that left $155,000 for instruction. Gilman calculated he could secure four senior professors at $6,000 each. The remaining instructors would receive an average of $4,500 or less (in contrast, a Harvard professor made on average $4,000 a year).[49] Out of necessity Gilman turned to recruiting "young men of genius, learning, and talent," since, as one confidant warned him, "old men who are great; these you can rarely move." Young people would be willing to move and take a risk on a new institution, and would be more open to change. As Gilman remarked, "There were none to say, 'This is not our way'; none to fasten on our ankles the fetters of academic usage. Duty, youth, hope, ambition, and the love of work were on our side."[50]

In the year before Hopkins opened its doors Gilman traveled far and wide seeking "ideas and scholars," in particular, men who exhibited not only an aptitude for research and a "gift for sharing knowledge," but also an organizational interest in the new university. As he explained to the trustees, in Germany "scholars of distinguished reputation readily consent to be transferred from one place to another," but in America they would have to persuade their recruits of their new institution's advantages or find those with reason to move.[51] He conferred with a number of leading American thinkers, including the "local Hegelians" in St. Louis, and traveled to Washington, DC, and West Point, recruiting his first faculty member, Henry A. Rowland, a promising young physicist at Rensselaer Polytechnic Institute. The quintessential undiscovered talent, Rowland signed on to Gilman's initiative just as he was being scouted by MIT. Gilman's further domestic tour led to appointments for Basil Gildersleeve in classics and Ira Remsen in chemistry. Rowland accompanied Gilman to Europe that summer for further recruiting and fact-finding. The trip took Gilman and Rowland to Britain, France, Germany, Switzerland, and Austria in search of "men of promise rather than of fame." A visit to the International Geographic Congress in Geneva reinforced Gilman's commitment to training specialists in surveying and engineering. Gilman successfully recruited Charles Morris as an assistant professor of classics, Henry Newell Martin in biology, and the mathematician James Sylvester—all from Britain. In Germany they received advice if not personnel.[52]

Gilman's American version of the German university followed some elements of the original and adapted others. The most significant German ingredient was Gilman's emphasis on independence. As Gilman insisted, the "head of a great department . . . shall be as far as possible free from the interference of other heads of departments, and shall determine what scholars he will receive, and how he will teach them." The organization of faculties was also borrowed directly, but the American university departed significantly from the German model in the design of departments. The German *Lehrstuhl*, or "professor's chair," was organized around one individual's expertise; the American academic department was organized around a discipline and included several chairs. The German *Lehrstuhl* enjoyed his own infrastructure, including a library and laboratory, that was not afforded the American version at Hopkins.[53] In America, by tying tuition to the department, faculty were forced to work together more than their European counterparts.[54] Despite attempts to integrate German teaching formats, certain elements were out of the control of even as adept an entrepreneur as Gilman. The German graduate seminar was centered on a single charismatic master, which the American version attempted to emulate. But as historian Laurence Veysey once speculated, "Magnetism was too rare to flourish wholesale," and most instructors would never achieve the level of charisma that the system required.[55]

With respect to architecture Gilman heeded the European model to emphasize "men not buildings." When he visited Baltimore in 1876 at the opening of the university, the British scientist Thomas Huxley is reported to have advised, "Get an honest bricklayer, and make him build you just such rooms as you really want, leaving ample space for expansion."[56] Despite initial interest among members of the board to use the donor Hopkins's remote Clifton estate as the site of the university, Gilman secured two modest buildings downtown as the base. The decision was more than merely sound financially; it had the added benefit of physically linking the university and the city. Unlike the cloistered campus of an English college, as Jefferson had sought with his "academical village" in Virginia, Hopkins envisioned the "university as city" (fig. 2).[57]

Of course a university always risked being viewed as a city unto itself, and so Gilman intentionally made no distinguishing features separating the university buildings from those of the surrounding neighborhood—a strategy he saw successfully employed in Göttingen. Indeed German universities were known for being so integrated with their towns that many a traveling American joked that when one arrived in Göttingen looking for the university he would find himself, without any "tangible evidences of its existence, its reality," confused about just where it was. In the guide that

Figure 2. Focused on "men not buildings," Johns Hopkins University's main campus was designed on the German model of integrating the university into the city. (Image #04261, University Archives, Sheridan Libraries, Johns Hopkins University.)

he prepared for students visiting German universities, James Morgan Hart observed that the English college "was all body, all bricks and mortar; the [German university], no body and all soul."[58] Gilman aimed to bring that soul to Baltimore and he expected Baltimore to reciprocate.

In his inaugural address, Gilman made explicit his expectations for this new contractual relationship. Despite Hopkins's record-breaking endowment, Gilman immediately expressed the need for more funds. For "till the original benefaction is supplemented by other gifts, or the growth of Baltimore increases the value of our present investments, we must be contented with good work in a limited field." This rhetoric reflected a financial model that required constant fundraising and whose success depended on the capital markets.[59] To win over the university's patrons Gilman balanced international aspirations with local practicality: "At the present moment Americans are engaged in promoting institutions of higher education in Tokio [sic], Peking, and Beirut, in Egypt and the Hawaiian Island the oldest and the remotest nations are looking here for light." What motivated this exchange and this pursuit was "a reaching out for a better state of society than now exists."[60] Gilman hoped Baltimoreans would help Hopkins step into this leading role by financially supporting the institution.

For those for whom a "better state of society" was too abstract, Gilman promised the useful application of the university's research. Chemistry is a "child of the nineteenth century," Gilman announced, noting Hopkins's indebtedness to Liebig and his laboratory in Giessen, which, as we saw, spurred the Morrill Act.[61] Gilman understood that the university must offer benefit to society: "It renders services to the community which no demon of statistics can ever estimate, no mathematical process ever compute. These functions may be stated as the acquisition, conservation, refinement, and distribution of knowledge." Just as much as the world likes outcomes, however, Gilman reminded his audience that these results came "not of industrial fabrics, not of mercantile corporations, not even of private enterprises, and that the motive which inspired their founders and directors was not the acquisition of wealth, but the ascertainment of fundamental law."[62] Gilman appealed to establish an American institution that balanced knowledge for its own sake and the benefits of applied science. And in the tradition of Humboldt, it was never entirely clear which was his priority. Did Gilman promote application to win donors but in fact believed in pure research in his heart? Or was he really captured by industry and using the language of pure inquiry to appease the faculty? That one was never sure was the mark of his strategic genius.

Yet even Gilman's impressive chameleon-like quality could not hide Johns Hopkins's peculiar and unprecedented decision that the university be nondenominational. In fact, despite accusations of secularism, the philanthropist as well as three of his board members were Quaker, and Gilman, a "moderately liberal Congregationalist," was described by one contemporary as having a "Christian calling" to the "academic ministry."[63] This was of little consolation to the orthodox religious groups, however, who decried the decision not to build a chapel or to have a theology department. Indeed, just how secular the institution would be was made dangerously clear when Thomas Huxley was invited to speak at an opening ceremony in September 1876. Huxley, a biologist, was associated with the agnosticism that was most offensive to religious leaders. By declining to have an opening prayer the trustees fed Gilman to the wolves. News of the "storm-signal" traveled far and wide: one Presbyterian minister of New York wrote to his colleague in Baltimore, "It was bad enough to invite Huxley, It were better to have asked God to be present."[64]

It probably did not help Gilman deflect accusations of running a "godless institution" that he used the freedom of nondenominationalism to hire a Jew, the British mathematician James Joseph Sylvester, as the first chair of the Department of Mathematics. Sylvester's appointment was less a product of religious pluralism than of Gilman's strategy to tap underutilized talent, and he shared reservations about the eccentric Sylvester's ability to cooperate with others. Having placed second in Cambridge University's prestigious Tripos examinations in 1837, Sylvester was considered one of the best mathematicians of his generation. He was unable to receive a degree from Cambridge, however, because he was—as he said snidely—born into "the faith in which the founder of Christianity was educated" and would not sign an oath of allegiance to the church. Earlier in his career Sylvester was run out of the University of Virginia following violent opposition by the Richmond newspapers and an altercation with an antisemitic student in Charlottesville.[65] In Baltimore, the Jewish community welcomed Gilman's support.[66] Gilman's views on female and African American education were more complicated—as we will see, he condoned and contributed to the hierarchical thinking of the time. Nonetheless, the connection he made between talented outsiders and academic innovation gave Hopkins an early advantage, identifying a strategy that subsequent entrepreneurs would adopt.[67]

Gilman would be compelled to further compromise on undergraduate education. The undergraduate program became a local college, a "feeder" to higher work, and "a most valuable adjunct to this work itself."[68] Gilman would not have had the success he did had he not determined that this was a way to gain local support. The undergraduate college eventually drew the resources and attention of the university; however, the compromise that made the undergraduate-graduate hybrid work would prove to be the university's weakness.

To complement this awkward merger, Gilman innovated one final structural component—the fellowship system, which offered graduate students an annual stipend of about $500 to pursue their studies at Hopkins.[69] It was a system that hybridized the English and German models of student support for the new American context; and yet, like most of these adaptations, this system, according to one former fellow, the American philosopher Josiah Royce, was perceived to be a pure German import. It was perhaps to assuage skepticism that Hopkins was merely imitative that Gilman reminded audiences that "in following the example of Germany, as we are prone to do in educational matters, we must beware lest we adopt what is there cast off; lest we introduce faults as well as virtues."[70] Nonetheless Royce reported in 1877 hearing professors at Hopkins, nearly all of whom had studied in Germany and many of whom had received doctorates there, speaking of Germany, rather than England, as the "mother country."[71]

Hopkins had a solid foundation as an undergraduate school with a graduate program led by promising faculty. If Hopkins was to compete internationally in the scientific realm, however, the university would need the validation of peers. Gilman identified academic publishing as one route to that status and made the establishment of academic journals a near requirement of his faculty. Hopkins thus became the site for several foundational publications, including the *American Journal of Mathematics*, the *American Chemical Journal*, and the *American Journal of Philology*. Despite his skepticism, Sylvester, who, as he recalled, "again and again . . . threw all the cold water I could on the scheme," nonetheless solicited foreign contributions—the only way to garner respect for the enterprise.[72] In the six volumes that appeared under his editorship foreigners comprised 25 percent of contributors. Nearly 45 percent of each volume, however, came from scholars with some connection to Hopkins itself—a fact that suggested the limits of this strategy.[73]

Gilman rightly intuited that raising the status of English-language scholarly publications relative to German was crucial to gaining prestige in the academic world, but in the 1870s the fulfillment of this bold move was still far off.[74] Gilman had wisely focused his attention on youth and undiscovered talent in order to recruit his improbably excellent faculty. This strategy proved advantageous to such undervalued professors as Sylvester, who, at the age of sixty-nine, returned to England in 1883 to accept a position as the Savilian Professor of Geometry at Oxford. (With the effects of the University Test Act of 1871 finally felt, both Cambridge and Oxford were now, like Hopkins, nonsectarian.)[75] In the next round of recruiting, however, Gilman strained to promote Baltimore's advantages. Despite the city's "attractive . . . climate, proximity to Washington, abundance of good society, and a moderate scale of domestic expenditure," the German-trained Harvard chemist Oliver Wolcott Gibbs was unmoved to leave Cambridge.[76] Moreover, while Hopkins's faculty was nearly all German-trained, Gilman had not succeeded in attracting any *echt* Germans to his cause—a move that would be necessary if Hopkins was to extend its reputation beyond America. To fill the chair Sylvester vacated, Gilman identified the German mathematician Felix Klein, a uniquely versatile thinker who was looking for a home for a school of his own.

THE GERMAN PLAY FOR THE APPLIED SCIENCES

While Gilman launched "Göttingen at Baltimore," the peak of America's scientific landscape, Germans were consumed by another American event of 1876—the Centennial Exhibition in Philadelphia. Just as Göttingen inspired Gilman to accelerate American scientific progress, the display of American technology in Philadelphia convinced Germans that their efforts in this area lagged. One German delegate to the exhibition was Franz Reuleaux, head of the Royal Industrial Academy (Gewerbe Akademie), who had trained under Ferdinand Redtenbacher, the pioneering Austrian scientist of mechanical engineering. Redtenbacher's belief in the potential of technology found common purpose with the Centennial Exhibition, which, organized around the idea of human progress, took visitors from exhibits of raw material inputs to the machines and methods of the diffusion of knowledge. "This ability to direct, dominate and control the forces of nature," Redtenbacher observed, "thus making them work for us, has, especially in our epoch, assumed great importance."[77]

In the main exhibition hall of the Philadelphia fairgrounds, Reuleaux would have seen ample evidence of America's domination of the forces of nature, including refrigeration, the telephone, and the Westinghouse Air Brake, an important system for trains invented by George Westinghouse. One American visitor, Walt Whitman, was compelled to stop at the Corliss engine, the crown jewel in Machinery Hall, and stare, "contemplating the ponderous motions of the greatest machinery man has built."[78] Of course the Centennial Exhibition was more than a celebration of human progress. The event's main organizer, Joseph Hawley, revealed the patriotic motivation in his opening speech: "Comparison is vital to the success of any exposition. . . . You can never discover your success or your failure without comparison."[79] An "installation by the races" showed England, France, and Germany prominently displayed alongside America, with other nations cordoned off in less desirable areas.[80] The Germans did not need any more motivation than that. The German industrial products were, as Reuleaux put it bluntly in the first of ten letters he published on the event that summer in Berlin's liberal *National-Zeitung*, "cheap and shoddy," and the jingoistic ornamentation of Krupp's giant guns and "the Bismarcks, Moltkes, Roons, in porcelain, as biscuits, in bronze . . . painted, embroidered, knitted, printed, lithographed, closing in from all sides," an embarrassing sign of "chauvinism and sycophancy."[81]

By exposing Germany's inferior industrial products, Reuleaux showed how international competition played a role in national industrialization. In Reuleaux's assessment, "our efforts in many areas remained contrived and convulsive, aimed merely at short-term profits and deals, and blind to a more dignified, long term vision. . . . Talk of [Germany's] destiny and fate is so pervasive, and the song of its glory has been performed so often, that it has lost sight of the forces required in international competition. It is a simple fact that our defeat is obvious."[82] Though some Germans called Reuleaux a traitor, German engineers largely concurred with him.[83] Against the backdrop of the economic depression that had begun in 1873 on both sides of the Atlantic, German engineers, who had previously defined themselves in terms of the technical institutes' "school culture" with little regard to practical application, began to emulate the American "shop culture" and reoriented their training toward application.[84] The German Royal Industrial Academy was soon merged with the architecture-based Bau Akademie in 1879 to become the Royal Technical University in Charlottenburg, and Reuleaux assumed a new chair in the design of machines and tools. The Technical University quickly became the world's largest of its kind, with more than three thousand students and three hundred professors. The German American Association of Technical Engineers, which Reuleaux founded five years later, would permit Germans and Americans to institutionalize the value of simultaneous comparison and competition—or competitive emulation—to stay on top of the field.[85]

The history of Germany's technical institutes and research universities collided in the life and work of the German mathematician Felix Klein, who would draw on an American visit to remake the relationship between the two. Born in 1849 in Düsseldorf, a center of German industry that had been a battleground in the revolution a year before his birth, Klein benefited from the increase in Prussia's power and influence, and his career tracked the rise and fall of his beloved German Empire. Having received his doctorate in Bonn at only nineteen, Klein became a sensation in the field of mathematics for his groundbreaking research in geometry. An appointment as an *Ordinarius* professor at Erlangen in 1872 made him, at twenty-three, one of the youngest professors in the field.[86] There he delivered his famous inaugural address on the "Comparative View of Recent Researches in Geometry," later known simply as the "Erlangen program," which is still fundamental to this field.[87]

Since Erlangen was too small for a significant mathematics program, Klein left for the Technische Hochschule in Munich where he began to develop a laboratory for mathematical research and worked on issues at the intersection of group theory, algebraic equations, and function theory. By the time he was thirty he had published seventy papers, a few of them landmarks, and was the indisputable "rising star" of the field. When the University of Leipzig created a chair of geometry the opportunity was his. Seemingly in search of the right place to establish his expansive school, Klein assumed the position in 1880 and announced his intention "for a comprehensive and unified approach to mathematics unencumbered by narrow specialization and free from the insularity of one-sided schools."[88]

Klein's career was unique for three reasons: he moved in and out of the applied world of the technical universities and the pure world of the research universities; he was a professor who would advocate for taking secondary education seriously; and he was an unconverted Jew with an *Ordinarius* position and all the privileges that this civil service position entailed. In fact, as a result of these overlapping suspicious identities, Klein would be periodically accused of being "superficial and sometimes a charlatan"—slander that was, in part, antisemitically motivated. A fierce competition with the French mathematician and author of automatic functions theory Henri Poincaré worsened his physical (he suffered asthma) and mental health, and in 1882 he suffered a nervous breakdown. Though it was not entirely unusual for a mathematician to be most productive in his early years, Klein's mathematical career was basically over by 1883.[89] It was at the end of that year that Gilman, in need of German scientific blood to nurture the nascent Johns Hopkins University, reached out to Klein.

Given his ambitions for Hopkins, what likely caught Gilman's eye was less Klein's mathematical abilities than his institutional leadership prowess.[90] At his farewell reception, Sylvester professed his faith in his chosen successor: "I may venture to say that I have done, to the best of my power, a good turn to this University in suggesting the name of one who can do all that I can do, and a great deal more besides."[91] Already at Munich and Leipzig, Klein had proved himself to be a scholar of breadth and interdisciplinarity, an ambassador for the union of the pure and applied sciences, and a canny organizer. Klein, however, was exhausted by the resistance he faced to institutionalizing his style of mathematics. The combination of administrative duties, ill health, and cutthroat competition had worn him down. So when Gilman offered Klein a position as Hopkins's senior mathematics professor he was intrigued. Might Baltimore provide the place and opportunity for his long-desired school?

The thirty-four-year-old Klein responded in December of 1883 in German to Gilman's query: "I am inclined to accept the position. I am attracted by the novelty of the task and the grandeur of the perspective that it offers; I am even young enough to find something enticing about the change itself."[92] Klein saw the possibility for Baltimore as the site for his would-be school and a way out of oppressive rivalries.[93] Klein's enthusiasm was tempered, however, by the specifics of the offer. Klein remained frustrated with the knowledge that Sylvester had made $1,000 more than the $5,000 Gilman offered him. Moreover, as Germany was increasingly guaranteeing financial support for widows and orphans in the event of a professor's death, Hopkins and America would not provide a similar guarantee until the early twentieth century, exposing a liability in the new private university model and its ability to recruit talent abroad.[94] Though he was tempted that he "would have an influential journal at [his] disposal and lastly not so many hassles with faculty meetings and exam work as in Germany," Klein ultimately declined the offer.[95]

The correspondence between Klein and his confidants revealed that his decision rested on Hopkins's perceived viability. While Paul Haupt, who had left Göttingen to take a chair in Semitic languages at Hopkins, insisted to Klein that Hopkins was "fully capable of competing with the German universities," the mathematician William Storey, who studied in Berlin and Leipzig and was now a tutor at Hopkins, worried Klein when he suggested that where teaching was concerned, the American university was already unmoored from the German model.[96] For Haupt the lack of coherence in a "specific system" for the seminars was a benefit: "There is the overarching opinion here that our university is still too young for firm rules to be beneficial." What was clear was that Klein would have "total freedom, a point Sylvester himself echoed."[97] Arthur Cayley, a British mathematician who had lectured at Hopkins and acted as a go-between for Gilman, insisted, "Most certainly there is no ground whatever for the imputation of a 'humbug'—the university is a solidly established, very wealthy institution, conducted in a liberal manner, and with a brilliant future before it."[98] But Klein was not so sure. The disadvantage was that even if later Hopkins would be lauded for its contribution to graduate education in America, at the time it seemed possible that this educational "start-up" could fail.

Fortunately for Klein, around the same time, "Göttingen [was] beginning to make noises," and the education director Friedrich Althoff soon reached out to him to fill a position at the Enlightenment-reformed university.[99]

And though Klein had not been the first choice (one of the other candidates declined, and the other died), Klein and Althoff soon found that they shared the ambition of "reviving the justifiable pride of the University of Göttingen in its magnificent tradition of mathematics dating back to the times of the great mathematician and astronomer Carl Friedrich Gauss."[100] Klein's letter of appointment highlighted his "versatility" with respect to science and his organizational ability—precisely the qualities Gilman would have admired.[101] What happened next proves that Gilman was not wrong to see in Klein a partner in innovation. He did turn a town into a world center of applied mathematics, but to Gilman's chagrin, it was Göttingen, not Baltimore. Ironically, Gilman's offer marked the beginning of Klein's interest in America and undoubtedly shaped his innovation in Germany.[102]

Crucial to Klein's success was his navigation of the German academic sea that Weber later called the "Althoff system."[103] To say that Althoff served as director of higher education in the Prussian Education Ministry doesn't do justice to his influence. Contemporaries called him the "almighty departmental director," and following his death one newspaper remarked that Althoff was the "Bismarck of the university system" over which he reigned for twenty-seven years. With his commanding personality, he maintained strict control over the university's policies and the budget.[104] One historian identified Althoff as a proto–scholarly manager, but according to Ulrich von Wilamowitz-Moellendorff, the classicist and rector of the University of Göttingen during Klein's ascent, "The bureaucracy *per se* was as inconvenient to him as to the Imperial Chancellor." Indeed, Althoff's gift was in the way he bridged the civil service, the scholars, and the emperor, who called him a "man of genius" and with whom he had the unusual privilege of unmediated and direct address.[105] Wilamowitz-Moellendorff was among the many German professors who later recalled Althoff's ability to manipulate faculty and intra-university politics to achieve his desired end—often keeping professors stewing in his foyer just to intimidate them.[106] Althoff for his part was said to have boasted, "I can buy professors and prostitutes on every street corner." Weber enjoyed quoting this line, though not without adding his own boast that he and other sociologists couldn't be bought.[107]

A more compliant professor, however, could in exchange for supporting Althoff's hiring and policy choices count on financial subsidies and even an institute with a budget, equipment, and assistants. Althoff was effective at raising money from the finance minister and, during his tenure, succeeded in establishing no fewer than eighty-six medical institutes, laboratories, and clinics, nine seminars in law, four in theology, and twenty-seven institutes and seminars in the philosophical faculties among the nine Prussian universities.[108] Klein was among those referred to as Althoff's "spies and lackies," who included, as we will see, Rudolf Virchow and Adolf von Harnack, in addition to Wilamowitz-Moellendorff, who capitalized on Althoff's support and, occasionally, circumvented him.[109] As early as 1893 Klein shared with Althoff his desire to improve collaboration between the mathematical sciences and technology and his belief that the admission of female students would alleviate the shortage of secondary school teachers. On both issues, Klein was in the vanguard, and Althoff, while supportive—"I fully agree with what you write about the admission of women"—made it clear that he "reserve[d] the right to come back to the matter verbally on occasion."[110]

Soon thereafter, Klein traveled with Althoff's support to America for the latest Congress of Arts and Science held in conjunction with the Chicago World's Fair in 1893.[111] There America dazzled foreign visitors, as it had in Philadelphia seventeen years previously, with a spectacle of industrial progress, including GE's seventy-foot tower of light bulbs and an enormous Ferris wheel.[112] In America, Klein identified a strategy, involving private money, technical training, and coeducation, to accomplish his ambitious program in the applied sciences. Wilamowitz-Moellendorff called Klein a "born organizer," but Klein was more than that. He counted among the most impactful cultural brokers of his time.[113]

Notwithstanding Klein's decline of Gilman's job offer, the German mathematician's reputation was as strong as ever in America. As early as 1892, William Rainey Harper, the founding president of the University of Chicago, informed Klein that his "coming would furnish [inspiration] to scores of young men interested in this great department."[114] A series of lectures was arranged for Klein, solidifying his position as a representative of the Prussian Education Ministry at the Chicago Congress. Even before his departure Klein had his doubts about how Germany would fare. He shared confidentially with his colleague Oscar Bolza, who had emigrated from Germany to America, his concern that the German university exhibit was sorely underfunded and disorganized and "will only come together very imperfectly: the whole thing was taken up too late and lacks the right personalities to lead it."[115]

In his correspondence with Althoff, Klein was, in contrast, diplomatic when he expressed measured praise for the Americans and a mentor role for the Germans. Of the "University Exhibit," Klein later reported, "It was very rich, and I myself became acquainted for the first time with a large number of models and apparatus that had not yet come on the market." As a university professor (rather than an instructor at a technical school), Klein's voice mattered more than Reuleaux's had, and Klein used his privileged position to argue for better integration of technical instruction into universities. Althoff, for his part, supported Klein and other traveling scholars

to represent and bring back ideas to German science. In Klein's official report he presented America's role for Germany as an extension of Althoff's
international cultural policy: "We may take satisfaction that everywhere
where representatives of German science were present [the congresses]
were successful. . . . You will be aware that mathematics in America is still
in its early stages of development, much unlike her sister sciences, physics
and astronomy, which are in their full flowering. I am very hopeful that
the exhibition, congress, and colloquium will together remain a source of
inspiration for the development of American mathematics."[116]

Klein suggested to Althoff privately, however, that the tide might be
turning: "There is no doubt that indeed now and for the near future America represents for us the greatest and most advantageous object of scholarly colonization. Americans have already studied in the last years in great
numbers at German universities. But that has happened until now without
any special initiative on our part. My trip evidently signifies a change in
this system [of exchange]."[117] American higher education had evolved more
than Klein or Althoff predicted. Klein's report showed that he returned,
as two historians of mathematics put it, "singing a different tune."[118] The
colonial undertones gave way to marveling at such American advances as
engineering education, the movement toward coeducation, and the private
financing of scholarship. Klein later reflected, "I returned in the firm belief
that our teaching institutions are most urgently called to establish a direct
relationship with the prevailing forces of practical life, notably to the world
of engineering, but then also with the most pressing questions of education
as such."[119]

Klein's American colleagues would have liked to engage Klein more—
E. H. Moore wanted to elect Klein "honorary president" of the American
Mathematical Society—but Klein remained focused on Göttingen and returned ready to implement the vision for a collaboration among technology, science, and industry that he had proposed to Althoff the previous
year. He didn't wait for a state appropriation; rather, he began to raise
money on his own.[120] Klein found ample support in his hometown of Düsseldorf, a stronghold of the steel and chemical industries. In spring of 1894,
Klein reported his success to Althoff: "Convinced that industry itself must
have very considerable interest in this matter, I contacted outstanding specialists and I have managed to organize a committee whose purpose is
to support us materially."[121] Klein's advisory committee boasted several
prominent names in German industry, including Emil Schröter, the director of the German Steel Association, Fritz Asthöwer, the technical director
of Krupp, and Henry Theodore von Böttinger, the director of Elberfelder
Dye Works and a member of the Prussian parliament. When it was formally

founded in 1899, Böttinger became chair of the Göttingen Association for the Promotion of Applied Physics (which would expand the following year to include mathematics).

The results of Klein's organizing were felt immediately. Composed of forty-two professors and fifty members of industry, the association funded the infrastructure—the buildings, equipment, and professorships—for Klein to turn Göttingen into a center of applied mathematics. To appeal to the industrialists Klein emphasized the practical importance of the scientific discoveries, and utilized Böttinger's connection to the government to arrange matching grants for the private contributions. Klein's achievement rested on finding a point of common interest between industrial progress through scientific advancement. Klein tapped what in America had seemed "especially impressive to me . . . the self-sacrifice of private individuals and groups whose unwaning energy is spent supporting and advancing American universities."[122] Insofar as the triad included the private sector the partnership that emerged was more American than German.

Given Klein's successes, Althoff was more than happy to support subsequent trips to America, especially to keep German scholars abreast of American developments in engineering and natural sciences. On a second trip to America in 1896, Klein was accompanied by the German engineer Alois Riedler, ostensibly to attend a mathematical conference on the East Coast. The two made the most of their journey, crossing the United States from the Massachusetts Institute of Technology (then known as Boston Tech) to the California Institute of Technology (then known as Throop Polytechnic Institute) in Pasadena, California.[123]

As technical institutions that were themselves hybrids of the European technical institute and the American research university, MIT and CalTech must have held a particular fascination for Klein and Riedler, who aimed to elevate technical training to the level of the university.[124] The continuing impact of American institutional innovations and the cross-fertilization of ideas is evident in Klein's administrative achievements of the 1890s, in which he implemented American applied science, American private philanthropy, and American actuarial science, and succeeded in adding to his institutional empire a Royal Department of Actuary Science with a Division of Actuarial Theory.[125] As a result of Klein's administrative and lobbying efforts the German technical institutes received the right in 1899 to award the coveted doctoral degree.[126] This privilege effectively created a parallel system of universities in Germany, and it arose through transatlantic adaptation.

Klein didn't only borrow academic innovation from America; he also accumulated students. Approached by American students at his lectures,

Klein encouraged them to visit him in Göttingen, and many did the subsequent year. At a time when German universities experienced a decline in enrollments because of a lack of jobs, Klein, who was in need of graduate assistants, received aspiring American mathematicians warmly—even the women. It is ironic that soon after Klein declined the call to Hopkins, America came to play an even more central role in his life. Though he would never become an instructor at an American university, Klein would train a generation of American mathematicians. From across the ocean the German mathematician sparked a "Kleinian era" in American mathematics.[127]

THE GÖTTINGEN EFFECT, OR THE
IRONY OF SHARING IDEAS

The founding of Hopkins and Klein's American-style revitalization of Göttingen showed that domestic as well as international competition fueled the development of research institutions. Aspiring American academics had ample reason to be motivated by the German university, including its devotion to pure inquiry, its spirit of academic freedom, and its high level of scholarship across multiple fields, all of which fed the competitive emulation between America and Germany in the 1850s and 1860s. Among American academic leaders, however, already in the 1870s the central rivalry in higher education had shifted: competition among American universities superseded that with German universities.

If Germany was a symbol of excellence, the knowledge race among domestic institutions would soon amount to creating the best version of the German university in America. Domestic competition created pressure to innovate; Gilman's innovations at Yale, for example, spurred Harvard president Charles Eliot to take action. Of the German university model the Harvard president was initially known to have said that it would "suit the 150 young men who enter Freshman [at Harvard] every year, about as well as a barn-yard would suit a whale."[128] But when Eliot saw the success of German-style graduate schools in America, first at Yale and then at Hopkins, he changed his mind. Nine years after Gilman's first efforts at Yale, Eliot instituted a "University Course of Instruction," and gradually expanded eligibility to study for the AM degree, in 1872 consolidating these offerings into a graduate school. With a false naïveté, Gilman later observed, "It is a striking coincidence that Harvard and Yale caught the laboratory quickstep at almost the same time."[129]

Later, thunderstruck by Gilman's ambitions and success at Hopkins, Eliot became fully caught up in a competitive fervor. According to the sociologist Everett Rogers's classic diffusion of innovation theory, for an idea to catch on, a clear motivation must spur "early adopters" who then compel a "significant majority" to take it up. Eliot now had a motivation: to beat Johns Hopkins.[130] The competitive emulation fueled by such aspiration would help the modern research university eclipse the undergraduate college and become a constitutive feature of American higher education.

That competition was motivated by the presumed advantages of becoming a knowledge center as much as acquiring any specific institutional model. Eventually Gilman was credited for making Johns Hopkins "not only the pride of Baltimore but of America as well, and [it] commands for us the respect and admiration of the world." Baltimoreans, in turn, saw the benefits of a "Göttingen at Baltimore," which included weekly public lectures attended by over two hundred people, public praise, and an influx of students into their mid-Atlantic city from over a dozen states.[131]

Mayors, civic leaders, and academic innovators, therefore, soon wanted "a Göttingen" in their own cities. At a speech delivered in 1882 at the opening of Western Reserve College in Cleveland, titled "The Dawn of a University," Gilman posed the question that was on everyone's mind—how did a university become a Göttingen? "It is worth while for the citizens of Cleveland, engaged in founding a university, to ask what has given Göttingen its power."[132] Gilman believed Göttingen provided "models of instruction to Cleveland and Baltimore. [The education minister's] wise methods secured great teachers; great teachers drew able scholars; those able scholars carried to distant lands the lessons they had learned."[133] A stopover in Göttingen became a rite of passage for any up-and-coming scholar, and what was once a "dull little town" now dispatched students and ideas the world over.[134] If Cleveland followed Gilman's blueprint for "Göttingen at Baltimore," it, too, could become a knowledge center.

Yet success was far from assured. Without a mutually beneficial contract, as Gilman achieved with the Baltimore public, many more experiments faltered. Such was the fate of Clark University, established as the first all-graduate institution in the United States in 1887. Clark's first president, the psychologist G. Stanley Hall, persuaded many of Klein's former students, nearly the entire mathematics department at Hopkins, to join his endeavor. He also established a strong psychology department.[135] But because of a lack of funds and poor management, Clark's development was thwarted. Bolza, who joined the Department of Mathematics department in 1889, complained in 1892 of the financial starvation and reported the "lack of confidence" vote that the faculty had recently given Hall.[136] Harper, the aggressive new president of the University of Chicago, eagerly poached Bolza and others for his venture that year.[137] Freud, who received an honorary degree from Clark in 1909, praised the university as the most

Figure 3. Though Freud (*front row, left*) called Clark University the "most European in the world," his visit in 1909 did not help its flagging reputation. (RGB Ventures/Superstock/Alamy Stock Photo.)

European institution in the world, but that proved problematic (fig. 3).[138] Without the undergraduate "compromise" that Gilman made, Clark struggled to maintain a connection to the surrounding community, and new universities in Chicago and Palo Alto, both claiming in different ways to represent better American versions of the German university, would rise to take its place. Even when university presidents did not follow the German model, as with Woodrow Wilson at Princeton University, it was a conscious decision to defy the trend.[139]

Gilman and Klein were part of a complex system in which academic leaders and their institutions competed with counterparts across the Atlantic and at home for leadership in educational innovation and scientific progress. Soon the reality (and irony) of knowledge exchange became clear. Exchanges now shaped innovation. That innovation, in turn, raised the stakes of the exchange. Insofar as partners in exchange drew on innovations to seek prominence, status, and prestige for their own institutions, cities, and nations, they became competitors. But competitors are also those from whom one has the most to learn.

Germany was the leader in 1902, when Ira Remsen assumed the presidency of Hopkins, whether measured by publication output or by linguistic dominance.[140] By the end of the decade, however, America had the upper hand. When the German political historian Friedrich Wilhelm Keutgen visited Hopkins in 1905 he could speak confidently of that institution's formative role in "a new era in American university history."[141] The German American scholar Albert Bernhardt Faust announced in 1909 that Germans treated Johns Hopkins now as a "sinister institution."[142] Even if Faust projected a bit, the power dynamics were clearly shifting, as Klein saw in America's mathematical encyclopedia that charted the Americans' impressive achievements.[143] Klein understood the paradoxical logic responsible for the American ascent. As Klein explained to Althoff, "Whatever supremacy we may have enjoyed earlier will be lost through our own doing, and we will have to regain it through efforts of our own as well."[144] Klein would know—he trained many of the Americans.

At the same time, the academic playing fields looked different from domestic and international vantage points. Hopkins's status abroad as flagship of the American system contrasted with its growing pains at home, where it now faced a crowded market of "fast followers" and competitors.[145] Already in the 1890s the university had its first major financial crisis, and by 1910 the journalist Edwin E. Slosson observed there was "a great deal of talk—in other universities—about the decline of Hopkins." In a sense, Hopkins had become a victim of its own success. "It is lost in the crowd of its imitators," Slosson observed.[146]

Competitive emulation contained another irony. Germans like Klein were self-assured about their place in pure science but argued that Germany must emulate America in applying that science for Germany's advancement. Americans like Gilman, in contrast, thought what America needed was a pure research institution, and only grudgingly accepted some measure of application. Desperate to succeed, these parallel innovators sought their competitor's secret ingredient.

Success arose from hybrids responsive to academic social contracts, the results of which became visible—even to the founders—only over time.[147] In this iterative process, new formulations recombining the productive tension between pure and applied research, or other models in productive tension with one another, would continue to emerge.[148] Sometimes, as in the case of Hopkins, the new combination was richer than anything Gilman could have imagined. Education innovators hailed Gilman's success to justify a variety of ventures. And while the multiplication of rivals eclipsed Hopkins's preeminence at home, it gave rise to a system of higher education that made America a challenger with which Germany would have to contend.

CHAPTER THREE

MEET ME IN ST. LOUIS

DILEMMAS OF THE KNOWLEDGE ECONOMY

Le savant a une patrie, la science n'en a pas.
The scientist has a homeland, science does not.

LOUIS PASTEUR, 1888

At the opening of the Congress of Arts and Science, held in conjunction with the Louisiana Purchase Exposition in St. Louis in 1904, the director, Howard J. Rogers, announced the congress's lofty purpose: "Under national patronage and under the spur of international competition the best products and the latest inventions of man in science, in literature, and in art are grouped together in orderly classification. Whether the motive underlying the exhibits be the promotion of commerce and trade, or whether it be individual ambition, or whether it be national pride and loyalty, the resultant is the same. The productive genius of every governed people contends in peaceful rivalry for world recognition and the exposition becomes an international clearing-house for practical ideas."[1]

As a component of America's third World's Fair, the congress at St. Louis presented not only an "international clearing-house for practical ideas," but signaled the amplification of "cultural diplomacy," in which science became more intertwined than ever with the politics of nation-states.[2] At St. Louis the stakes of the German-American two-way cultural diffusion represented by Gilman and Klein were evident: industrializing nations were competing not just for status and influence but also for economic, political, and military power—and the work of the university was proving to be essential to that global race.

With the success of Hopkins, America had "come of age" in the academic world and was now applying its scientific acumen and industrial might amid a new imperialism to overtake Britain and France and become a world power on par with Germany.[3] In an earlier period, as those older empires expanded their influence around the globe for economic, cultural, and religious reasons, their universities trained civil servants, developed new technologies for building wealth and power, and spread their "imagined communities." Although many intellectuals in the colonial world looked to Britain and France for inspiration, the relationships among settler and core universities remained asymmetrical.[4] Now, around

1900, the modern research university came to serve the new German and American empires in ways that were unique to their late, parallel, and intertwined periods of "liberal imperialism," an ideology that attempted to reconcile racially charged colonial expansion with their liberal societies.[5] German and American universities facilitated exchanges in the social sciences—in fields such as naval science, foreign policy, anthropology, and psychology—that would justify their respective systems. But the universities did not only "divide the world"; they also provided new opportunities for scholars to act as cultural mediators.[6] Those who stepped into those roles were forced to make decisions on what terms they would participate in exchanges that were subject to new and increasingly contradictory pressures.

TO STAY OR GO? THE POLITICS OF TWO-WAY TRAFFIC

The terms of the rivalry between the Germans and Americans began to change around 1900 when rumors circulated in the Prussian Education Ministry that the number of American students enrolled in German universities was declining. This was concerning for two reasons. First, American students made up the largest contingent of foreign students in Germany before 1914. Between 5 and 10 percent of all foreign students in Germany came from the United States, though the number could be as high as 20 percent in German universities with American "colonies," like Heidelberg and Göttingen.[7] These numbers peaked in the middle of the 1890s and then began to tail off. The German concern was not economic—foreign students' registration and lecture fees to professors were not substantial. Rather, their fear stemmed from the intangible though no less powerful understanding of Germany's status in international science, and perhaps—as disturbing as it was for the Germans to consider—America's newfound scientific self-confidence.

America's scientific rise did not catch all Germans by surprise. In a speech delivered to his colleagues at the Academy of Sciences of Berlin back in 1882, Emil Du Bois-Reymond had identified the challenge posed by America and warned against accepting "cynical" characterizations of "Americanization" as mere utilitarianism. "The names of American historians, philosophers, and linguists," he said, "are mentioned among the best, and are cherished as worthy by this Academy." In other words, Americans were good for more than the mere application of science; they were producing original scholarship as well. As noted in the introduction, Du Bois-Reymond had predicted that "with time, the scholarly center of gravity will . . . move more decisively towards the west."[8] As extensions of nation-states, universities were, even in 1882, embroiled in a race variously measured by publications, foreign student enrollments, and (after 1901) Nobel Prizes—all of which contributed to determining the "center of gravity." Du Bois-Reymond warned his colleagues that if they didn't treat America seriously then that position just might get away from them.

Du Bois-Reymond possessed exceptional foresight. Within three decades, German scholars and scientists had caught on to the changes occurring in the academic ecosystem. Dispatched on a three-month tour of America in 1902, the German chemist Fritz Haber announced that Germans had "long underestimated the advancements of the United States. Now the mood has turned around."[9] Key to that "change of mood" in the Prussian Education Ministry was, as we saw, Felix Klein, who had traveled twice to America at Althoff's behest and emphasized the necessity of the international free exchange of ideas despite the evident increase in American contributions to scholarly life. "And, in fairness, this is not a bad thing," Klein intoned, "but something we should embrace, since academia is sustained and thrives only when there is competition. Further, the effect is not one-sided, and every new research effort is a gift to us as well."[10]

Yet not all Germans saw the benefits of exchanging ideas with the Americans so clearly. Commenting on a decree under consideration in 1898 to exclude foreigners from engineering programs in Berlin, a German official rationalized, "There is no question that the German technological schools and industrial and scientific institutions will soon be forced to adopt a less liberal policy with foreigners. The tricks of trade we have been teaching them so long are now being used against us to the great injury of our industry."[11] Germans wished for Americans to visit German universities to provide sought-after validation. They just wished they weren't such good students. In fact, two separate approaches emerged in response to what Haber deemed "the American danger."[12] The first, in accordance with Klein's view, grew out of the notion of the university as apart from the politics and economics of nation-states. This position promoted an openness to outsiders, sharing of research, and a free trade of ideas that we might call internationalist. The second position emphasized the role of the university in furthering the interests of the nation-state and promoting intellectual self-sufficiency. Coalescing in the critical and condescending reactions to the idea of an American congress itself and the professor exchange that grew out of it, this defensive position amounted to intellectual protectionism.

That the once obligatory German educational experience for up-and-coming American scholars and civil servants seemed to be becoming obsolete was worrying for those who held either position. Internationalists saw a loss in exchange of ideas, and protectionists saw it as a signal of Germany's declining influence. Germany's place as the scholarly "center of gravity" was in jeopardy. To regain Germany's grip on cultural dominance, the Prussian Education Ministry launched a series of international initiatives to formalize a response influenced by both these approaches. In the same year that Haber toured American universities and industry, Althoff created the central organizing administration (*Hochstift*) to oversee these visits and begin collecting reports and bibliographies on universities. He also established the Office of Ministerial Academic Information (Amtliche Akademische Auskunftsstelle) at the University of Berlin in 1904, on the model of the Sorbonne's Bureau de reinseignments scientifiques, to monitor developments in research and higher education abroad "so that it may be possible to see where other countries are ahead of us, and where we have the upper hand."[13]

Althoff began to see the urgency of sending German scholars to America, to keep abreast of American innovations in higher education and to promote German scholars and scholarship. Althoff's "favorite" professor, the eminent church historian Adolf von Harnack, concurred. After learning of the founding of the American Society of Church History he remarked, "America has put us in Europe to shame," and advocated for strategies to ensure the "international recognition of German scholarship."[14] While he was writing some of his most enduring multivolume works on the expansion and missionaries of Christianity, Harnack was strategizing how the German university as a site of scientific research would maintain its cultural grip on the world.[15] Althoff's support for such scholars as Weber, Troeltsch, and Lamprecht to attend the congress in St. Louis was as much an effort to keep tabs on the competition as it was to spread the German gospel of science. When, in 1907, the Austrian-German philologist Alois Brandl observed that "the American research university is the best conquest that we have made in the world since Goethe," he also suggested that this occurred somewhat accidentally: "It happened, admittedly, without our doing anything directly, and it took a long time before we even noticed it."[16] But exchanging ideas was a delicate courtship. As the German professor from Breslau Eugen Kühnemann was dispatched to America, Althoff apparently advised him, "Let people woo you like a virgin, but don't offer yourself like sour beer."[17] Althoff would have preferred to be the courted, but, in fact, he was destined to be the suitor.

While Althoff worried that American students were no longer coming to German universities, German professors weighed the opportunities and costs of leaving the fatherland to go to America, the upstart. Klein, as we saw, declined job offers at Hopkins, Clark, and Yale—American universities were destinations for creative inspiration, perhaps, but not for employment. Of course differences existed across fields; one would expect a historian of America, for example, to show more interest in that country. While he advised Gilman, Hermann von Holst, the preeminent German historian of America in his day, also declined a job offer at Hopkins. The situation appeared to have changed fifteen years later. When Harper offered a job to Holst at the newly founded University of Chicago he accepted—paving the path for others. According to a young German instructor in the new field of applied psychology, Hugo Münsterberg, "If a former rector [at Freiburg] found it worthwhile, the youngest instructor might risk it."[18] The stream of scholars began to flow in the opposite direction.

The emigration of scholars out of Germany depended as much on German professors' desire to cross the Atlantic as on America's need to draw them over. These German recruits to American universities would ensure America did not fall into the trap of permanent "followership" experienced by other modernizing empires. When Japan revised the Meiji Constitution, for example, its leaders looked to Germany for inspiration and a supply of civil servants to model their new legal, political, and educational world. The Japanese diplomatic voyage known as the Iwakura Mission was highly influenced by its four-week academic reconnaissance trip to Germany in spring of 1873—producing ten chapters about Germany in their three volumes of final recommendations. The Berlin newspapers, for their part, reported on the visit of the Japanese education commissioners, "Japan is learning, buying, copying. . . . Some day we will have to learn from Japan."[19] But Japan never made the shift from an asymmetrical to a two-way scholarly relationship, for the Japanese were never able to recruit foreigners to work in their universities in a role other than mentor, and by the late Meiji period this relationship had declined.[20] The American challenge was rather to use their latecomer status, as the historian Daniel Rodgers has written, "to leapfrog over their competitors by cashing in on the advantages of delay."[21]

Given the lack of homegrown intellectual culture, America, like Japan, had enormous use for German professors in the late nineteenth century, but there were many Americans who wished for this to change. Looking back on the German-American relationship as it existed before World War I, the American Charles Thwing reflected on "the value which highly educated foreigners bring to America." "The value may not be measured in terms of dollars," wrote Thwing. "It is to be measured in terms far mightier than gold. America has not been able to produce of itself a proper number of scholars, literary, philosophic, scientific. It has drawn upon older, and scholastically richer, lands."[22] The conditional need for European culture, science, and personnel to seed America's own culture, as Thwing observed, was as old as British America. The goal had always been pragmatic—that is, America would eventually outgrow the crutches of European scholars and scholarship and walk on its own feet, firmly grounded on a national culture and institutions of science. The "rise and fall" of the German American psychologist Münsterberg, who organized the St. Louis congress and was known as a cultural mediator, illustrates precisely this shift in the cultural and scientific relationship between Germany and America.[23]

As a German from Danzig descended from Breslau Jews, Münsterberg had to consider his prospects for employment in his fatherland when he charted his career plans. After Münsterberg's father died, he and two of his brothers converted—the "ticket of admission" to German society, as the German-Jewish poet Heinrich Heine once remarked. Heine had added that conversion was one of the places in which water was ineffective, and despite his conversion Münsterberg found his options constricted by cultural convention and antisemitism. He selected medicine, as was common for Jews, and after attending lectures by Wilhelm Wundt at Leipzig, soon expanded into the new field of psychology. (G. Stanley Hall and James McKeen Cattell, with whom Münsterberg would later become colleagues in America, also studied with Wundt.) Wundt aimed to devise a scientific field for assessing mental states by connecting the laboratory methods of physics with the metaphysical inquiry into the mind. After he received his degree in physiological psychology from Leipzig in 1885, Münsterberg went to Freiburg, where he pursued this research further. Though he drew criticism from conservative psychologists for his attempt to investigate the problem of will, his experimentalism earned him intense interest in the Anglo-American world, where William James hailed his dissertation as "a little masterpiece."[24]

Not even Münsterberg's emphatic nationalism, however, could guarantee that a Jew intent on forging a new discipline would ever achieve a senior *Ordinarius* position with the full rights and status of the German professoriate.[25] More likely was that Müsnterberg would have remained among the ranks of the subordinate *Extraordinarien* and *Privatdozenten*, the latter of which the art historian Erwin Panofsky designated the realm of academic Jewish purgatory—a fitting moniker since Jews would notoriously remain overrepresented in these adjunct positions.[26]

So when James offered Münsterberg an opportunity to improve Harvard's Psychology and Philosophy Departments and laid on the flattery— "We need a man of genius if possible"—America provided a way out. James, for his part, remarked that hiring Münsterberg was the "best stroke I ever did for our University." Since he truly hoped to be an applied psychologist, Münsterberg rationalized, "I would see and hear much that is new; I would get out of the muggy atmosphere of the German universities and into the free air of grand affairs and would be able to serve practical ends."[27] The European prejudice against American "applied" science resonated with Münsterberg as it had with Klein. He would "take a leave of absence for six semesters and . . . use it for a kind of scientific expedition to the New World, with a chance to build up a model laboratory in a distant land."[28]

To a certain degree Münsterberg's move in 1892 showed how quickly loyalty could be transferred. America's regionalism permitted him to take pride in a particular aspect of American culture without giving up his German nationalism. A converted New England patriot, Münsterberg wrote that "all the best aesthetic and moral and intellectual impulses originate in New England," and after attending the World's Fair in Chicago and touring Niagara Falls, the midwestern colleges, Berkeley, and Palo Alto, Münsterberg urged his fellow Germans to do the same. They would see that Americans were "at work with a restless energy."[29] At heart a self-promoter, Münsterberg became more invested in America as it became associated with him.

Despite his public protestations, however, he was clearly not persuaded of America's equal scholarly worth, and he likely would have left for good had he been offered a senior position in Germany. When he returned to his impermanent position in Freiburg in 1893, he found to his dismay that antisemitism blocked an appointment for an *Ordinarius* position for which he had been recommended in Zurich.[30] Nonetheless, he made sure that Charles Eliot knew that he would be doing Harvard a favor if he returned, and now expressed his desire to become a cultural mediator: "I came to Harvard not *in spite* of the fact that I am foreigner, but *because* I am foreigner. I take it that in your opinion it is good for the organism of the Harvard Faculty that a transfusion of some drops of German university blood may be made, just at the critical time when the College is so splendidly growing into a university." In other words, Harvard needed *echt* Germans, and Münsterberg was for Eliot a valuable commodity. Privately Wundt assured Münsterberg that he was not in exile, after all: "America is not the end of the world." Indeed, some, like Gilman, would say America was now the center. When Münsterberg made the move definite in 1897—"burning his ship" as Eliot requested—he contributed to moving the scholarly "center of gravity" westward.[31]

Once settled at Harvard, Münsterberg's stock rose. He was elected the president of the American Psychology Association (APA), and his talents were appreciated by his new American colleagues, like James Cattell, who relied on his German American friend to facilitate a scholarly dialogue among psychologists across the Atlantic.[32] Münsterberg also embraced the position as spokesman for what one German historian has called the "Wilhelmian scholar's National Liberalism."[33] He helped to organize a memorial at Harvard for the German physicist Hermann von Helmholtz, who had died shortly after returning from the Chicago Exhibition.[34] As Münsterberg later reflected, it was a good time to be a German academic in America.[35]

Already by the turn of the century, however, there were signs that Münsterberg's fortune—and that of German American academics more broadly—was too good to last. A series of missteps, including an excessive reception he organized in honor of the Kaiser's brother, led to Münsterberg's falling out with his Boston Brahmin colleagues.[36] Cattell tried to take advantage of Münsterberg's decline in Cambridge and win him for Columbia University to buttress its rival psychology department. After all, as he told Columbia's president, Nicholas Murray Butler, Münsterberg is "a true man of genius," even if he is "vain to excess, but in a childlike way that is not displeasing. He is not altogether liked by his colleagues at Harvard. It is not improbable that he would come to Columbia University, but he would probably return to Germany, should he receive a call to a German University."[37]

Cattell's instinct was, in part, correct—had Münsterberg received a position at the University of Berlin he would most certainly have taken it. But the only call that came from Germany was at the University of Königsberg and, while that city and university carried prestige as Kant's home, the port city on the Baltic was no Berlin. After initially accepting "in the name of German science," he quickly retracted. Münsterberg may have claimed later that in America he "was needed for more than the mere professional work."[38] And it was equally true that at Harvard he was still at the center of America's scholarly life, which was better than being on the periphery in Germany. Münsterberg presented his decision as out of duty for cultural mediation, but the truth was that it was also his best option.[39] The common good was also in his self-interest.

As a cultural mediator Münsterberg walked a thin line. Though he was certainly no spy, as one viscous rumor suggested, his self-presentation undoubtedly changed depending on his audience. On one hand, Münsterberg advocated for mutual understanding between his fatherland and his adopted home.[40] On the other, he insisted to the Prussian elite his priority was the "increased prestige of *Kultur*." Above all, Münsterberg became, according to his biographer, "the most aggressive publicist in a fast professionalizing discipline" and his real opportunity to shine arose with the World's Fair in St. Louis in 1904.[41]

THE FACE-OFF

Münsterberg was not the only one looking for the spotlight. The announcement of a World's Fair in St. Louis presented the opportunity for comparison, as had the previous events in Philadelphia and Chicago, but the competition would now be among institutions as much as nations. In America, where competition among cities and states was woven into the federalist fabric of the nation, the rivalry between St. Louis and Chicago over the World's Fair extended to Olympic-esque competition among its universities.[42] It is likely that President Harper of the University of Chicago promoted a scholarly congress tied to the fair because of his own ambitions to feature his young institution at the event. As we saw, Harper had engaged Klein to deliver a series of speeches at the Chicago Congress in 1893, and, with more lead time, he worked together with Walter Wever, the German consul in Chicago from 1900 to 1908, and conspired to use the 1904 World's Fair to gain attention and funds for the university. The University of Chicago would offer honorary degrees to such distinguished scientists and scholars as the professor of medicine Paul Ehrlich, the professor of ancient history in Berlin, Eduard Meyer, and the professor of Sanskrit in Jena, Berthold Delbrück, as much to distinguish the university by associating it with so prestigious a foreign name as to give the receiver the imprimatur of the new university.[43]

In the context of these various local, institutional, and national (not to mention scholarly) interests, an advisory board coalesced in the fall of 1902 that included, in addition to Harper and Butler, the German-born American diplomat Frederick Holls, who served as a delegate to the Hague Peace Conference of 1899. Münsterberg counted Holls among his diplomatic friends and dedicated his study *American Traits* to him; Holls repaid the favor and included Münsterberg in the planning. Given Harper's ambitions for the University of Chicago it was natural that one of the rising stars of his faculty, the emerging sociologist Albion Small, be included. Eager for this congress to outdo its predecessors, the board gave Münsterberg and Small the charge to propose plans.

An aspiring world power required a comprehensive system of social science to explain the world. But what that would look like was the subject of disagreement. Both Small and Münsterberg sought to put their imprint on a vision for the organization of the disciplines. Having studied under Adolf Wagner and Gustav Schmoller, Small was steeped in the German Historical School—in fact, while abroad as a student in 1881 he married the daughter of a Prussian general, Valeria von Massow. In 1892, Small founded the Department of Sociology at Chicago and, within a few years, published the first journal in English in the field, the *American Journal of Sociology*. Distressed by excessive specialization, Small, like Münsterberg, aimed to connect disparate strands from multiple fields, but their proposals for the congress were radically different, and their clash rippled throughout the academy. Small assumed "that human interests not logical categories make the world," and proposed organizational categories like the promotion of health, the production of wealth, and the harmonization of human relations that concerned society's problems. Münsterberg, in contrast, grounded his proposal in the abstract Fichtean categories of normative, historical, physical, and mental realms, with sections for each. As he wrote to the congress planners, "Instead of a hundred congresses, let us have one congress . . . and let us give to this one congress the definite purpose of working toward the unity of human knowledge."[44]

The American pragmatist John Dewey was among those irritated by Münsterberg's plans for a priori logical categories as the basis for organizing the event, and a battle among idealists and pragmatists ensued.[45] The disagreement was also culturally and politically motivated. Münsterberg wanted to promote American scholarship to Europeans, but he also wanted to prove to the Europeans that the Americans had become sufficiently sophisticated. After all, just two years prior, Münsterberg had had difficulty getting German psychologists to travel to America for a professional conference.[46] Small resented Münsterberg's self-presentation as the cultural mediator. "Some of my most respected teachers have been, and still are, German scholars; yet I am sure that I understand my countrymen well enough to interpret their feeling with reference to Old World opinion," Small wrote to Münsterberg. "We are far enough advanced so that we are no longer jealous of estimates passed upon us from the Old World standpoint."[47] Münsterberg played to the Americans' insecurities, however, and insisted that only his plan would get the Germans on board. Münsterberg's proposal was subsequently adopted by the congress officials, and he was named one of two vice presidents of the congress and one of the three members of the planning committee responsible for the speaker invitations.

Münsterberg and Small divided up Central Europe and the disciplines to seek attendees (the astronomer Simon Newcomb took France), and they received 117 affirmative replies from 150 invitees. Münsterberg's daughter Margaret reported that he had the "earnest support" of Althoff and his assistant Friedrich Schmidt-Ott.[48] Münsterberg proved to be an effective mediator and spoke differently—condescendingly even—about America when writing to his fellow Germans. In a confidential memo sent to German participants, Münsterberg lectured that the *university* in America "should not be taken as synonymous with the German word *Universität*." Rather, he explained, it is "a collective name for about 600 institutions of vastly different standards . . . the highest of which might well be on par with a German *Universität* while the lowest are merely equivalent to the *Sekunda* [the sixth grade of a German high school]."[49]

The largely positive American assessments of the congress bordered on self-congratulation—some of which was justified. The volume of speeches delivered suggested an impressive breadth of scholarly inquiry. Lectures on the college from the presidents of Bryn Mawr (Martha Carey Thomas) and Swarthmore (Frank Aydelotte) conveyed a picture of an American system that was distinct from the European in its preservation of the English residential college and its elevation of single-sex education.[50] However, fractures emerged barely beneath the surface of the conference, and absences haunted it—as we will see in the next chapter. Münsterberg, for his part, remained frustrated by the lack of interest among Americans in engaging with the foreigners, whose lectures had conspicuously meager attendance.[51]

Germans who traveled to America for the congress returned largely self-assured of their superiority. While the Germans were disproportionately represented across various fields, the French had objected to the small number of invitations they had received, and threatened to withdraw, causing what one organizer called "the French bombshell."[52] While Weber was captivated by America's "fortified castles of capitalism" and collected data for an essay on churches and sects in North America, his own early enthusiasm gave way to criticism. Even if Ernst Troeltsch, who traveled with Weber, became interested in William James's modern psychology of religion, he was unwilling to attribute James's scholarship to anything distinctly American.[53] "That the execution had true scientific value and brought seed often to the best American soil is essentially your achievement," Troeltsch wrote in praise of Münsterberg. "But otherwise you must grant a strongly individualist European scholar—as far as the congress is concerned—a great measure of humor, which at least for me is connected with this scholarly exhibition."[54] The German philosopher Max Dessoir concurred—the German American organizer was impressive even if the conference itself was inferior.[55] The Leipzig-based chemist Wilhelm Ostwald had a similar reaction; he returned from St. Louis gloating about Clark University's apparent setback. In his telling, not only were the American students undeterred, but they exhibited an unbridled (and inexplicable) ambition. Uncertain of how seriously to take the Americans, Ostwald later recalled the American chemist Arthur Amos Noyes "with rosy cheeks and a beaming smile," posturing, "We are hoping in due time to shift the scholarly center of gravity of all mankind across the entire Atlantic Ocean to us."[56]

Despite their assuredness, Germans, by simply attending, had already confirmed that America was not at the edge of the world, as Wundt had consoled the young Münsterberg, but was fast moving to the center. The most decisive effect of the congress internationally was to show that the exchange between German and American scholars and scientists was a necessary condition of the global academic world. Harnack justified his new position based on his own experience: "My trip afforded me powerful, inspiring impressions of a kind not available in Europe. I had a magnificent time, untroubled by any awkwardness or unpleasant encounter. In America, Germany and especially its universities are still able to capitalize on a tremendous amount of respect, love, veneration, and admiration! May they always justify this trust and remain worthy of it."[57]

Following the congress, Harnack, together with Karl Lamprecht and Friedrich Schmidt-Ott, traveled to Harvard to meet with Eliot and discuss the implementation of an official German-American professor exchange, an idea that Francke had raised years earlier and now seemed more compelling than the "little German university" in the New World for which Althoff once pined.[58] Together with the German-Jewish industrialist Leopold Koppel, Althoff founded the Koppel Foundation for the Promotion of Intellectual Relations Between Germany and Foreign Countries especially "the United States of America and Also with Other Culturally Important Countries, Particularly France."[59] The following fall Althoff sent Eliot a proposal outlining that every year the University of Berlin and Harvard would send one to two professors to teach at the other school. The visiting professors would receive stipends for travel and accommodations in addition to their home institution salaries.[60] Münsterberg offered assistance to work out the remaining details, including offering credit for American students to attend the German scholars' lectures, and assigning assistants to the German visitors.[61] That Münsterberg's own esteem would rise with the success of the program no doubt motivated him to facilitate the negotiation.[62]

Beginning in the academic year of 1905–1906, the interchanges that German and American scholars had been enjoying for decades were formalized by the scholars' respective countries and anointed with imperial pomp. When the Kaiser announced the program in the presence of the American ambassador, Charlemagne Tower, in January 1905 at his New Year's reception, he expressed his ambition to expand beyond Harvard and Berlin. In the subsequent years, until the outbreak of World War I, professors from Harvard and Columbia visited Berlin on yearlong Theodore

Roosevelt Professorships, while the Prussian Education Ministry, aided by the imperial Ministry of the Interior, sent German scholars as Kaiser Wilhelm Professors to Cambridge and New York. As a result of this exchange, American students at Harvard heard lectures on the "Atlantic" qualities of the Kaiser's leadership, and Germans were introduced to "multicolored charts and diagrams to illustrate industrial statistics" of the nineteenth-century American economy.[63] Schmitt-Ott later referred to the exchange as one of the most successful examples of international cultural cooperation. The professor exchange was followed by other exchanges of university presidents, teachers, and students, and the creation of German Houses on American university campuses.[64]

The German-American professor exchange may have signaled a new phase of imperial cultural politics, but in this overseas knowledge exchange localities and regions became players as important as nation-states and empires. In fact, much as it had with the world's fairs, the success of the German-American professor exchange rested on its ability to straddle intranational and international competition. Thus Columbia was added to the exchange, as a result of the lobbying of its president Nicholas Murray Butler and prominent political scientist John William Burgess, and the program's mission altered to encompass cultural as much as scholarly exchange.[65] Harper sought "his" direct scholarly exchange for the University of Chicago with German universities and scholars. Designed to promote American scholars in Germany and German scholars in America, the exchanges also brought renown to the participating institutions. Ironically, this only accentuated local competition.[66] In fact, so proprietary did Münsterberg feel about the exchange that he went to great lengths to sabotage its expansion, which he must have seen as diminishing his own influence.[67]

The career of Saxon-born historian Karl Lamprecht similarly highlights how savvy, resourceful, and ambitious academic managers could take advantage of the multiple levels of identification in an empire to benefit their cities and institutions.[68] A visionary iconoclast who found his place on the edge of the traditional academy, Lamprecht was the director of the Institute for Cultural and Universal History and later rector of the University of Leipzig from 1910 to 1911. Despite his reservations about America, he used his 1904 *Amerikareise* (American sojourn), in particular the ideas of the private financing of scholarship and the American campus, to revive Leipzig as a regional cultural center.[69] Though not wholly successful in his attempts, Lamprecht seized an opening that Butler created when he tacked Columbia onto the German-American professor exchange, and, in 1912, Lamprecht negotiated a similar exchange for Leipzig.[70] Of one fact Lam-

Figure 4. One of Lamprecht's many photographs taken on his 1904 *Amerikareise*, this photo of Yale University reflected his interest in the American campus, which he would unsuccessfully try to adapt to Leipzig. (ULB Bonn, Nachlass Lamprecht, NL Lamprecht: 47.)

precht was sure—participation in global knowledge exchange could give a regional city like Leipzig the basis on which to compete with Berlin (fig. 4).

This domestic intramural competition notwithstanding, the symbolism of American parity with Germany was not received well in Berlin. The notion that American professors were equals with their former German teachers, as the formalization of German-American academic exchange implied, was unacceptable for many. Ignoring indications of the Americans' ascent and declaring it all bravado, the philosopher and historian of education Friedrich Paulsen urged the University of Berlin's philosophy faculty not to participate.[71] If Paulsen decried the second-class status of American thinkers, other Germans worried that a formal exchange would make Germans vulnerable to Americans' stealing trade secrets.[72] The British also raised concerns about the budding German-American partnership, which they dubbed a "cartel," and did not like the idea that they would find themselves on the outside of whatever economic and scientific benefits it might bring.[73] The French, too, must have been concerned. Refusing to draw on the German model, they found little success recovering from their 1870 defeat by the Prussians. Seeing an opening, some Frenchmen now wedged themselves into a transatlantic partnership to attract American students and establish their own American professor exchange.[74] Münster-berg complained of the difficulty of finding an appropriate American candidate for the German exchange because Harvard professors, including his colleague William James, preferred Paris.[75] Both international competition and national backlash threatened to sink the Theodore Roosevelt and Kaiser Wilhelm Professorships before they even set sail.

To head off further controversy, Harnack was enlisted to defend the program from the skeptical German nationalist professors.[76] In a timely essay that we might translate as "On the Big Business of Academia" ("Vom Großbetrieb der Wissenschaft"), Harnack distinguished the international character of research and the national character of teaching.[77] "The ways, degrees and means by which findings are disseminated are all rooted in the character and experiences of a people. They cannot simply be exported to another country or devised according to an abstract formula." This situation was admittedly different from the Middle Ages, when nations were not yet developed and a student encountered "the same science wherever they [went]." But in the modern university, as Harnack explained, "the links between research and teaching are subtle and intimate. Teaching (i.e. dissemination) cannot be stripped off from research (that is, science) like a robe." Thus, both must be brought in line to meet the new international demands of industry. Just as Liebig and Humboldt required the exchange of ideas not only through books, but also with foreigners, so too did students wish to learn from professors all over the world. But unlike in the Middle Ages, scholarship was not uniform. Rather, "there are disciplines which are pursued with greater interest in one nation than in another, certain methods are more sophisticated here than there, and certain tools more advanced or useful."[78] Whatever risks were involved in opening the nation's academic borders must be overcome, therefore, for scientific advancement and for the chance to extend international influence. Harnack not only saved the German-American professor exchange; he also paved the way for a new internationally aware and motivated scientific strategy befitting two emerging world powers.

GLOBAL CONTRACTS

Althoff found a lot to admire in Harnack's defense of the German-American professor exchange. It was neither the first nor the last time Harnack made a pragmatic argument for a strategic national scientific policy.[79] In conversation with his assistant Schmidt-Ott, however, Althoff noted that Harnack's emphasis on the "big business" of academic knowledge missed

another part of the equation—what we might call today the "global knowledge economy" (*Weltbetrieb der Wissenschaft*), in which higher learning and research were embedded.[80] It was in the latter context that the
German-American professor exchange program found its purpose. If the
"big business" of academia addressed the conditions for research in one's
own country, the global knowledge economy addressed the new role of the
university in an increasingly interconnected world. As we have seen, universities became building blocks for the nation-state and brought competitive advantage to their cities. Insofar as the political goal of Germany and
America by the 1890s was to become a world powers, these new empires
now required knowledge institutions that were similarly global.

But what made a university fit for an empire? And how did the geopolitics of empires interact with universities' unique border-crossing ecosystem? For one, empires required comprehensive knowledge systems to
scientize, rationalize, and justify their politics. The fight over who would
dominate at the congress in St. Louis was charged, in part, because it
seemed to dictate who would have those rights. Empires also needed universities to project power into the world, a particular kind of power that
was often hidden and opaque, and depended on the tacit participation of
others. In this way, universities emerged as early manifestations of what
political scientists have called "soft power," the use of "nontraditional
forces such as cultural and commercial goods" to achieve national aims.[81]
Though they never developed any universities in Togoland, Cameroon, Na-
mibia, or other German colonies, German scholars, scientists, and museum
directors, in partnership with the Education Ministry, harnessed institutions of science and culture to promote colonial interests—from lending
authority to a German-funded railway project to increasing cultural prestige by adorning the New World with art objects donated by the Kaiser.

University expressions of American soft power were manifest as early
as 1900, when, in the midst of the Philippine-American War, Harvard
president Eliot and Secretary of the Navy John Davis Long addressed the
thirty-fourth annual dinner of the Harvard Club of New York. After sharing
memories of his time at Harvard, Secretary Long identified the significance
of the moment: "There is . . . a tide in the affairs of countries as well as of
men. We can no more hold a college or a country to the old limitations than
we can hold the wind. The expansion going on in college life is such that
the expansion going on in the territory of the United States is insignificant
compared with it." For Long, who had overseen the Spanish-American War,
the university seemed a natural extension of America's emergence as an
imperial power. "There is no doubt that in a few years, in some pillared
hall in far off Manila," Long mused, "the dusky native-born Filipino will

lead the cheering for his college and his country and thank God that he lives under the Stars and Stripes." America was then embroiled in a bloody battle with the Filipinos to control their country, and Long hoped that the creation of an American university in Manila would be part of the American footprint in that region—a desire that expanded from holding territory to a broader cultural imperialism of the "Greater United States."[82]

The awkward but necessary transatlantic conversation between Germany and America as simultaneous allies and rivals in "liberal imperialism" meant that cultural mediators like Münsterberg could purport to represent both Germany in America and America to visiting Germans. As ambassadors of empire, German and American scholars traded ideas about how to cultivate world power. Germans looked to the American continent for a colonial model, seeding an interest in American empire, the Monroe Doctrine, and various iterations of realist foreign policy that would continue into the National Socialist period.[83] In the meantime, the American naval scientist Alfred Mahan was sympathetic to Germany, and his work *The Interest of America in Sea Power, Present and Future* was "devoured" by the Kaiser.[84] Germans' and Americans' scholarly codependence persisted despite—and because of—their political rivalry.

For the time being. When President Theodore Roosevelt forced Germany to back down in the Venezuela naval blockade of 1902, Germans learned that their shared commitment to science did not mean that the Americans would necessarily take their side in an international confrontation. Either out of misunderstanding the emerging American imperial interests in Latin America or in an attempt to magnify his connection to political power, Münsterberg had erroneously assured the German emperor that the Monroe Doctrine meant that the United States would not get involved if a crisis occurred.[85] The German flexing of economic and military muscles in South America unnerved leadership in Washington, DC, and offered a prelude to the colonial skirmishes that would lead to World War I. But politics didn't curtail the exchange of ideas. As Lamprecht and Klein, as well as Butler, Eliot, and Münsterberg, understood, there was no way out of that exchange, and potentially much to be gained, for the advancement of knowledge and their institutions. For this reason, German and American academics depended on one another in an even more fundamental way—to validate each other's institutions.

Over the last quarter of the nineteenth century, academics and their universities increasingly competed over science and vied to prove that their institutions were at the center of the scientific world. That competition could involve comparing numbers of publications, students, and prizes. It often wasn't clear what the main source of competition was. These accolades had meaning because universities required external validation. Foreign visits were valuable because they were connected to the most intangible, and most precious, fruit of validation—status. This led to a contradiction for universities and their faculties: the same foreigners who conferred status were the ones who represented the greatest threat. Such contradictions were inescapable. They were part of what the modern research university was creating: a new currency—a universally accepted framework for exchange and comparison—that mediated the relationships among foreign scholars and their countries. This currency, enabled by nation-states and their interconnected economies, operated on a complex value system of trust, exchange, and openness—and it was required for universities to thrive and knowledge to advance.

When Althoff died in 1908, the German American scholar Eugen Kühnemann was among the many who noted the education director's idealistic commitment to international exchange.[86] Burgess of Columbia recalled Althoff claiming that "an exchange of scholars . . . once more represents progress over trade in the direction of the intellectual unity of the human race."[87] Though he didn't speak English and never visited America himself, Althoff was of the late imperial belief that internationalism emanated from the nation-state.[88] On one side of the Atlantic, Althoff was the fourth German to receive an honorary degree from Harvard, and on the other, he won over the emperor and earned the title of Excellency. It is not a coincidence that German-Jewish industrialist Koppel provided the funding for the German-American exchange, as well as such evolving projects as the German medical school in Shanghai and the publication of the *Internationale Wochenschrift*, which ran from 1907 to 1921 and provided a significant vehicle for scholarly collaboration across borders. Koppel understood and believed in the need for international partnerships.[89] As with Humboldt before him, Althoff's internationalism and nationalism were woven together, so where one saw "mutual understanding of two kindred nations," another intuited a strategic partnership with a country with many susceptible German American immigrants.[90]

Harnack for his part developed his double-sided reality into modern *Realpolitik*. Following the traumatic break of the First World War many American scholars exaggerated their own prewar cosmopolitanism or pointed fingers at the Germans for their nationalism.[91] But Americans were being disingenuous if they didn't recognize the ambition and self-interest that motivated their participation in exchange. Harnack best described not only the German, but also the American, policy when he observed that sharing scientific secrets with the world represented more than fulfilling an ideal of universal knowledge, as prevailed in the Middle Ages; it was in fact also in the nation's self-interest. According to Harnack, "The exchange of students in the university is one of the rare enterprises in which the givers and the receivers both in an equal way win, if one makes the right use of it."[92] In admitting the transactional nature of this relationship, Harnack's defense of the German-American exchange program was, then, not all that different from Paulsen's critique of the credential-seeking Americans who aimed to use their experience in Germany to raise their professional status at home. The difference was that Harnack felt the risks were outweighed by the opportunity to influence those American students and scholars and, thereby, increase the prestige of German scholarship in the world.

Harnack's defense reflected a keen insight into the relational quality of scholarly validation. Engagement in the world economy of scholarship required balances of openness and protection. One need not be a cosmopolitan to see the benefits of academic exchange. The elaborate machinations that Münsterberg undertook to remain at the center of the "global economy" of knowledge reflected this self-interested strategy. He was right to link the success of the German-American professor exchange to the international political context when he later recounted, "It is appropriate for the two fittest, strongest, and most promising nations of the world to have, through their most worthwhile cultural institutions, universities, vibrant contact and permanent harmony."[93] As long as Germany and America were secure in their respective spheres of influence and power, Münsterberg's career benefited from this wider context; but by 1905 the stakes were changing.

That fall, at a lavish ceremony in the presence of the German emperor, the Harvard theology professor Francis Greenwood Peabody delivered the inaugural address as the first visiting Theodore Roosevelt Professor in Berlin. One prominent journalist, Maximilian Harden, reflected the frustration of many in Berlin when he noted the irony of a middling American preacher drawing the Kaiser to the university. "The lectures of Ranke, Helmholtz, Treitschke, Mommsen, Virchow, Schmidt, and all the other world-famous German docents," Harden scoffed, "were met with less appreciation than the idle talk of Mr. Peabody."[94] The new rituals of cultural diplomacy reflected the changed reality that the Germans and Americans were now equal partners, as Du Bois-Reymond predicted (and feared) they would become. In this changing "balance of payments," America, too, was transitioning from openness to protectionism. When asked to report to Althoff on where Germans stood with respect to American universities, the German embryologist Alfred Schaper confirmed Münsterberg's experience that "the Americans are beginning amongst themselves to cultivate capable academic instructors and scholars; even today, they hardly see

Figure 5. Imperial pomp, including the attendance of Kaiser Wilhelm II and Empress Augusta Victoria, at the inauguration of the Roosevelt Professorships in Berlin, showed that when scholarly exchange was concerned, America and Germany were now on equal footing. (Photo © bpk Bildagentur/Art Resource, NY.)

the need, and certainly don't have the wish, to hire any more foreigners to their faculty" (fig. 5).[95]

In 1908, Münsterberg circulated in the Prussian Education Ministry an alarmist report in which he assessed where the Germans stood with respect to science.[96] The outlook was not good. That year the protectionists sought to end unlimited admission of foreigners to German technical colleges. A professor of the technical college at Charlottenburg told a journalist, "Don't you ever admit a Yankee to your plant. For an American needs only see a machine to go home and make a better one."[97] But neither openness nor protectionism seemed to have succeeded in helping the Germans keep up. To be sure, Münsterberg always had his career interests in mind, and his 1908 report led to his stint as a Roosevelt Professor in 1910 and his founding directorship of the America Institute in Berlin. Münsterberg never ceased to raise those alarms: "the influence of German intellectual work upon the American universities" always seemed to be in "frightening decline." Scare tactics were good for the business of a cultural arbitrageur.[98] But that doesn't mean he was wrong. As the organizer of the congress, Münsterberg played all sides, lauding the Americans in the presence of the Germans while assuring the latter of their continuing preeminence, all the while promoting his own career. Even though he would eventually fall from his glory, Münsterberg remained a proponent of open scholarly borders, rooted in both the pragmatic need for international validation and the idealistic pursuit of universal knowledge.

Around 1910, it was clear that the Germans could not prevent the westward movement of the scholarly center of gravity. It is unlikely that any strategy would have thwarted this shift. In fact, it would be ideology — not pragmatic self-interest — that would ultimately envelop the German university in the nation-state and lead to its irreversible decline. Althoff and Harnack, like their contemporary Americans, were simply doing what their universities demanded of them. Universities forged in the nineteenth century by the Germans as the undisputed centers of higher learning now entered the twentieth century with the Americans prepared to make full use of their models at Germany's expense.

CHAPTER FOUR

RELUCTANT INNOVATORS

CHANGE FROM THE MARGINS

I do so want *girls to have the opportunity for culture without having to exile themselves for years to obtain it.*
MARTHA CAREY THOMAS, 1882

During the late nineteenth century and into the early twentieth, most of the Americans who went to Germany to study were white, male, wealthy, and Protestant. For many young white men of privilege, going to a German university was a recognized pathway to success in business, science, government, or administration. Some would return to have significant leadership roles in the development of higher education in America. But a small minority of Americans taking classes, and sometimes degrees, in German universities were not white or male or privileged, or some combination of these. The stories of those exceptional individuals and their impacts on American higher education—or lack thereof—shed light on how Americans used the German model to create a higher education system that served mostly the elite but also gained the appearance, at least, of offering equality of access.

As we have seen, European Jewish scholars like Sylvester and Münsterberg mitigated the limited professional options at home with prospects they saw abroad. Each capitalized on transatlantic travel to revolutionize whole fields. Similar international "open door" polices afforded opportunities for American women and blacks, who pursued study in Europe in the hopes of earning a degree that might help them break into America's academic establishment. For these individuals, further from the American centers of power, the German university provided cultural capital, ideas, and inspiration. The white men at the helm, they reasoned, would have to take a German doctorate seriously and let them into their institutions.

When they returned to the United States after immersing in the tradition devoted to the twin German educational ideals of *Bildung* and *Wissenschaft* (and, if they were fortunate, degrees), these outsiders sought professional advancement for themselves and for the interest groups they represented, within a system that had been strongly influenced by German models. They found their paths constrained, however, not only by institutionalized sexism and racism, but also, paradoxically, by the very ideals they had absorbed in German universities. Their pioneering efforts to alter an emerging system that had not yet hardened into formal structures led to robust debate about whom higher education should serve, but also prompted stricter gatekeeping. Ultimately, their greatest impact was to shape the way that the top strata of American colleges and universities managed to remain the preserve of the elite throughout the twentieth century, despite the growth of a middle class and a discourse—if not an actual policy—focused on equality of opportunity and the promise of social mobility.

THE GERMAN UNIVERSITY AS OUTPOST FOR AMERICAN WOMEN

For an ambitious American female student Germany offered a potential way out and way up. The education available to women in mid-nineteenth-century America was fragmentary and largely vocational. The arguments in support of educating women generally revolved around improving their contributions to society as mothers and teachers of young boys. Activists founded women's academies in the first quarter of the century, the most enduring of which was Mount Holyoke, which began in 1837 to train women to be teachers. Religious schools were often at the vanguard of women's education (as well as racially integrated education). Catherine Brewer Benson became the first "female college graduate in the South and in the nation" in 1840 when she graduated from the Methodist Wesleyan College in Macon, Georgia (then the Georgia Female College). Founded as "God's college," Oberlin admitted white and black men and women; awarded BAs to a group of three white women—Mary Hosford, Elizabeth Smith Prall, and Caroline Rudd—in 1841; and was the first, in 1862, to award a BA to an African American woman, Mary Jane Patterson.[1] Boston University admitted women to every department in congruence with the "religious and feminist ideals of its Methodist founders."[2] Despite these isolated examples, women had few opportunities to gain a college education until after the Civil War.

The expansion of university education precipitated by the land grants provided new opportunities for women in employment and education, but the idea of coeducation continued to meet a strong current of opposition throughout the country. Not all the states that accepted women into their land-grant schools between 1867 and 1870—Wisconsin, Kansas, Indiana, Minnesota, Missouri, Michigan, and California—did so willingly. Only after Michigan women raised $100,000 for the institution did University of Michigan president Angell see beyond his successor Tappan's shortsightedness to make his university "one of the most desirable academic places for women to study." Privately, he told Gilman that "the system was forced on the Institution by public opinion." Andrew Dickson White, the president of Cornell University, which had been the recipient of a land grant, was caught off guard by the demands of a persistent young woman named Jenny Spencer and eventually acquiesced, though he assured the trustees that "boarding school misses" would never be welcome there.[3]

Individual land-grant university presidents may have been reluctant to accept women, but even greater structural challenges to female education persisted throughout the country. Women activists relied on what has been called "coercive philanthropy," or money with strings attached, as a strategy to pressure institutions to admit women.[4] But cash wasn't always an antidote to sexism. Eliot failed to keep his promise of coeducation, even after proactive women had raised money for Harvard, changing the amount required at least twice, and he advised Gilman to keep women out of Hopkins. He justified this exclusion with pseudoscience: "The world knows next to nothing about the natural mental capacities of the female sex." In the Southeast, cultural mores remained opposed to coeducation, and, as late as 1912, only seven universities admitted women.[5]

A secondary path for women emerged with the founding of a host of new single-sex schools, including Vassar (1865), Wellesley (1875), and Smith (1875), which educated women in a classical curriculum. Ambitious women, such as Margaret E. Maltby, Ida Hyde, and Martha Carey Thomas, remained skeptical of the value of such schools and kept their focus on something higher—complete equality through coeducation. These women sought not only secondary and collegiate training, but also the new PhD that was now being awarded to their male counterparts. With the latter goal they had only limited success. Sixteen years after the first PhD was awarded by Yale to a white male American, in 1877, Boston University awarded one to Helen Magill, an alumna of Swarthmore and the daughter of its second president. (Magill went on to marry Cornell president White.) In 1880, Cornell, Syracuse, and the University of Pennsylvania also awarded PhDs to women.[6]

At Johns Hopkins, which presided as the pinnacle of graduate education from its opening in 1876 through the close of the century, the experience of women was mixed. When Sylvester wanted to accept Christine Ladd-Franklin, a teacher and graduate of Vassar, to study with him in 1878, Gilman complied.[7] Moreover, Gilman showed some interest in pursuing the concept of a women's college like Girton College at the University of Cambridge, which he admired, but was ultimately cowed by the trustees "on this important matter . . . [who] prefer to declare their own views by the expression of which I am ready to be governed."[8] Ladd-Franklin (the wife of another student of Gilman's) was denied a PhD in psychology despite having completed the work for her degree (she was awarded one retroactively in 1926).[9] Martha Carey Thomas was a student at Cornell when Hopkins opened, and was disappointed that she was accepted for "only" an MA degree. Barred from attending classes, she was forced to rely on notes from her male colleagues and to meet with professors privately. Florence Bascom received a PhD in geology at Hopkins, but only as an "exception."[10] Given persistent gender discrimination, many women looked for an alternate route.

Graduate training in the German lands provided precisely that route, and beginning in the 1870s, American women with adequate resources went to study in Germany to bypass the barriers in America and to acquire the education and degrees they believed would help them advance professionally. The standards for women's education in Germany, determined on a state-by-state basis, were as fragmented as those in America. Though women did not gain the right to earn degrees at German universities until 1900 (the state of Baden was first), they could acquire status as *Gasthörer* to audit lectures with the professor's permission, and on a private basis in a welcoming university, could receive some of the benefits of a world-class education.[11]

Germany wasn't without barriers of its own. The height of public debate on women's education in Germany coincided with the birth of the German Empire and the perceived crisis of the university.[12] Many states began to use the matriculation requirement of the *Abitur* (secondary school exam) to keep women out, and the women's movement accordingly focused on improving secondary education, which the activist Helene Lang believed as late as 1928 was still too focused on producing educated housewives "so that they don't bore men."[13] With respect to women's chances, Prussia, which held out enrolling women until 1908, was the worst, as perhaps was to be expected from a place where the leading university boasted such traditionalists as Heinrich von Treitschke and Friedrich Paulsen, the latter of whom echoed Eliot in his belief that "real creative activity has, in general, been bestowed by nature in a larger measure upon the male than upon the female." The centrality of the fraternities, where dueling and drinking were the main activities, further cemented the male-centered notion of academic citizenship.[14]

Cornell president White, appointed US ambassador to Germany in 1879, wrote to an inquiring young Martha Carey Thomas that "it is hardly likely that a lady would be admitted to the University of Berlin," but with "some little fortitude," one could achieve a German education, especially if one was willing to move around.[15] Aspiring and resourceful American female scholars sought German professors who were known to be inclined to women's education. Anonymous letters published in the *Nation* from such seasoned travelers as Thomas offered advice for this "back-door method," including where to go (Leipzig and Göttingen), what to study (art history would be easier than theology), and what to say at the German professor's office hours, or *Sprechstunde* (some phrase like "I crossed the sea for the sole purpose of hearing him" was probably in order). Then one might hope for the noncommittal yet meaningful reply: "If you choose to attend my lectures, no one will interfere with you."[16] As a result of these extraordinary individual efforts and networks, clusters of American women gathered around willing German professors, including the art historian Ernst Curtius and the psychologist Wilhelm Wundt at the University of Leipzig, where the unofficial acceptance of women was the best kept secret in the German Empire.[17] Since women still could not earn their degrees, however, even from Leipzig, they often finished their studies in Zurich, home to the most permissible of European institutions where coeducation was concerned. According to one female American visitor, the experience abroad was such that eventually "all women are shoved to Zurich."[18]

Upon their return to the United States, many of these pioneering female scholars were not content to merely enjoy their singular triumphs. Using the tactic of shaming American educational leaders, these women, or a subset of them, drew on their experience to fight for coeducation in America for all women. Ladd-Franklin rightly pegged Hopkins and Harvard as "susceptible targets" for peer pressure and wrote William James that she was "optimistic" about her prospects in Göttingen. The extent to which Ladd-Franklin understood her audience is evident when James replied, "Of course we are going to have women in Harvard soon. Göttingen mustn't be allowed to get ahead of us."[19] Another female budding scholar, Ida Hyde, had similar success playing institutions off one another. With opportunities in America sparse, Hyde accepted an offer to work in an embryology lab in Strasbourg. Despite its reputation for openness, however, she found the administration there as disinclined to award her a degree as in America and she moved on to Heidelberg where her petition for a degree was accepted. In a laboratory in Bern where Hyde found postdoctoral work she met the physiologist Henry P. Bowditch of Harvard Medical School, who declared, "If Heidelberg and Bern opened their doors to women, there was no reason why Harvard Medical School should not admit them also."[20] Peer pressure worked to a limited degree: Though Bowditch arranged for her to conduct research at Harvard she would not be employed there. She did, however, go on to a professorial position at the University of Kansas, and in 1902 became the first woman elected to the American Physiological Society.[21]

Using one's German education to pressure an American institution could be a successful strategy, but expanding that option would require funds. To facilitate sending women to Europe, Ladd-Franklin organized the Association of Collegiate Alumnae (ACA). The newspaper heiress Phoebe Apperson Hearst was persuaded to support the ACA's new "missionary work" in the "prejudiced land" of Germany. In 1890, the year that the ACA began distributing fellowships, Hyde was among the first recipients. When a woman was declined a fellowship, as in the case of the promising young mathematician Mary Winston, sometimes Ladd-Franklin picked up the tab herself.[22] Without this organization, and both formal and informal networks, like the General Federation of Women's Clubs, which provided cultural and financial capital, these pioneering women academics would never have been so successful.[23]

The movement to advance women's educational opportunities was also supported by mutually beneficial relationships. The arrival of Felix Klein in America in 1893 coincided with the activities of the ACA and led to his accepting American female students in Germany. The confidence Klein developed in women's abilities then fueled his academic innovation, in which he saw the admission of women in his own country as a way to restock the depleted pool of secondary teachers. Beyond these utilitarian needs, Klein may also have been inclined to feminism. Klein noted that his own marriage to Anne Hegel, the beautiful and impressive granddaughter of the great philosopher, represented the "beginning of an ordered existence" in his own life, and the mathematician and his wife made the women students feel welcome.[24] Among them were Margaret E. Maltby and Mary Winston, who approached Klein in Chicago when he visited on the occasion of the World's Fair, and then traveled to Göttingen supported by the ACA and Ladd-Franklin the following year. The women would have to be ready to fight, as Klein warned. According to a high-level university official, women were "worse than social democracy, which only seeks to abolish the difference in possessions," because Klein wanted "to abolish the difference between the sexes."[25] But Klein was willing to support smart and persistent women by petitioning their cases one by one, and the next year, in winter 1894–1895, he had nine men and four women working with him.[26]

Word got out fast. By 1900, women "were applying by the dozens for special permission to matriculate at Göttingen."[27] Maltby and Winston were the first American women to receive PhDs in physics and mathematics, in 1895 and 1896, respectively, at a Prussian university (their roommate Grace Chrisholm, an Englishwoman, passed her doctoral exam shortly before them).[28] Klein, for his part, drew on the influx of American women academics to supply his program with a steady stream of assistants, and no doubt to pressure his own government to permit the same privileges to German women.

Not all women could share in the success enjoyed by white women from elite backgrounds. Racial, ethnic, class, and religious barriers still loomed large. Hyde was one of the exceptions. Despite being Jewish and working class, Hyde found support in the new philanthropic network of the ACA for her career aspirations. African American women would have to wait even longer; the first three African American women to receive PhDs all did so in 1921.[29] African American women did begin making their way to Europe, too, though largely after World War I.[30] Racial and class discrimination stacked the deck even more against African American female aspiring scholars. It is revealing that once German universities began admitting German women in 1900 the openness to foreign women waned.[31] Aristocratic Russian women, who had sought educational opportunities in Germany as avidly as their American counterparts, soon found the doors closed especially to them, as, for instance, when Prussian universities added particular hurdles for Russian women entering German universities.

Anticompetitiveness motivated some of the arguments against foreign female students, as it had against their male counterparts, but antisemitism seemed equally if not more significant, given the large percentage of Jewish women in the Russian contingent. Between 1880 and 1914 the share of Jews among female Russian students was as high as 80 percent.[32] Nationalists pointed to the large presence of Jewish, foreign, and female scholars around Klein in Göttingen, for example, as a sign of the Judaizing of Aryan science. In this context, Klein's support of female students is all the more remarkable.[33] To be sure, the fiercest opposition was reserved for Russian Jewish female scholars, but all foreign female students and foreigners suffered from the erosion of openness that had characterized the world's fairs of Chicago and St. Louis. Even if the presence of American women in German universities precipitated the admission of German women, that development led to the exclusion of American and other foreign women. By the time the gates began to close in Germany, however, the American female reformers were taking on new challenges back home.

MARTHA CAREY THOMAS—A UNIVERSITY BUILDER FOR WOMEN

In the 1890s, before Maltby and Winston made their marks, and when American female attendance in German universities was ascending, the transatlantic experience of one ambitious student—Martha Carey Thomas—had transformative consequences. Steeped in the East Coast world of Orthodox

Friends, Thomas took advantage of the Quakers' growing interest in educating women and seized every opportunity. Fortunately for Thomas, her mother's family was wealthy enough to support a town house, servants, and a country estate, as well as participation in Quaker charities. Privileged and ambitious, Thomas was described by friends, family, and colleagues as charismatic, persistent, and shrewd. Beautiful and persuasive, she allowed herself to be courted by male suitors while she played female lovers off one another. Thomas wasn't afraid to use her special relationship with her mother to advance and finance her cause, sometimes defined as women's educational advancement and always involving her own.[34]

Like Hyde and Maltby, Thomas found a favorably inclined professor in Leipzig where she went to study for two years, and was among the first to report on the experience to women back home.[35] Yet unlike the others, Thomas found the Prussian universities closed to her. When Leipzig denied her a degree, she moved on Zurich in 1882 to complete her work and in that same year graduated with a PhD summa cum laude. When she reported her achievement to her ever-supportive mother, her false modesty revealed her ambition: "I never dreamed of taking the highest possible degree—a degree which no woman has ever taken in Philol. before and which is hardly ever given." Before she closed the letter (and lest her mother lose sight of her achievement's significance) she added, "Be sure and tell Uncle James."[36]

Thomas's request was strategic, since Uncle James, as well as her father and other relatives, had recently been appointed trustees of a college in Philadelphia whose founding was imminent. Funded by the Quaker Joseph Taylor, this college would be the "women's Haverford," the Quaker liberal arts college just outside Philadelphia, and it was in need of a founding president. The calculating Thomas had seen the possibility coming and selected her discipline (philology) and dissertation topic (a medieval English text) to make herself attractive to the board. As Thomas wrote her mother two years earlier, "I shall certainly be better qualified than any other woman in the Society and it may sound conceited, but I have not the slightest fear of my being able to teach girls of that age. I am sure I have this power and these lectures in Germany have given me the method."[37] Other letters Thomas sent from Leipzig detail her potential male competition and her plotting to garner other relatives' support.[38]

Never without confidence, the twenty-seven-year-old Thomas wrote to the board, proposing herself for the job. Among her qualifications she listed her "American Univ. education to begin with, two and a half years at Leipzig, one of the Universities of Germany, six months at Zürich and the highest honor the University could award my scholarship." The German scholars had helped shape her understanding of "what a college might become," and she believed she "could make it the very best women's college there is, so that English and German women would come and study there." And besides, "it is best for the president of a woman's college to be a woman."[39] Her ambitious plan was only temporarily thwarted by a compromise mediated by her aunt in which she was initially made professor and dean. Soon, however, because of the failing health of her competitor, Thomas became founding president "in all but name."[40] She hired faculty, established entrance requirements, and wrote the founding documents. When she warned that "the best undergraduate training can never be given by a college which is not able to guide advanced students," Thomas sounded like the female version of Daniel Coit Gilman. That imitation was not coincidental. She used Hopkins to mediate between the German university and the American educational experiences for women. She changed the direction of the new institution—Bryn Mawr—so it would no longer be the female equivalent of Haverford that Taylor originally envisioned, but instead a Johns Hopkins University for women.[41]

Thomas was so successful in her de facto presidential role that she was made the official president in 1894 when the male executive director succumbed to ill health. Known in later years as P.T. (for "President Thomas"), she continued to adhere to the German research university model for her nearly three-decade tenure at Bryn Mawr. P.T. insisted from the beginning that Bryn Mawr award the PhD; as she explained, "A College without graduate students never occurred to us."[42] She "boldly claimed descent from the male collegiate tradition" and recruited a "young, largely male faculty, newly trained in the German universities." In the early years she emphasized academic standards over gender, much to the chagrin of her critics; the faculty was made up largely of unmarried young men.[43]

Thomas ruthlessly pursued her strategy of "coercive philanthropy" to promote the inclusion of women and herself. No doubt it helped her case for Bryn Mawr that Mary Garrett, the unmarried B&O Railroad heiress and Thomas's sometime lover, offered to pay $10,000 (or 10 percent) annually of Bryn Mawr's budget if her beloved was named the next president. Touched by Garrett's generosity and savvy, Thomas called it a "sweet and clever attempt to use Mammon for righteousness."[44] Together with four Baltimore women, she founded and raised an endowment for the Bryn Mawr School of Baltimore, to provide a secondary education for young women to better prepare them for university, and, drawing on her large network, formed a Women's Medical Fund Committee to lobby for the acceptance of women to Johns Hopkins Medical School. Knowing that Gilman was struggling to open the promised new medical school because of a decline in the university's investment income, Thomas urged Garrett to offer the seed money on the condition that the new medical school admit women on equal terms. The offer was initially $100,000, but Gilman and the trustees, much to the consternation of Thomas and Garrett, held them hostage for another $500,000. After substantial (understandable) complaining on the part of Thomas—"[Gilman] would much much rather *never* have the medical school than have it with women"—they struck a deal. As one grateful alumna recalled, "Their conditions were accepted along with their cash," which appeared to convert even the skeptical trustees into believers in coeducation.[45]

P.T. was a trailblazer for women's education, which took off in the 1870s and rose for the following thirty years. Both Stanford and the University of Chicago began as coeducational institutions when they opened in 1891 and 1892, respectively. Between 1870 and 1900 the number of women enrolled in higher education in the United States multiplied almost eightfold, from 11,000 to 85,000. The share of women among all students rose from 21 percent to at least 35 percent in the same period.[46] In 1899 at the inauguration of Wheeler as president of the University of California, even the ambivalent Gilman observed that the "admission of women to the advantage of higher education" was one "of the remarkable changes of recent years."[47] Thomas concurred. In 1900, she published *Education of Women*, a monograph series edited by Nicholas Murray Butler that made her the leading national voice for educating women. Like Gilman, Eliot, and Butler, Thomas insisted on high standards on par with the German universities and that those standards be applied equally regardless of sex—a mission that she pursued with vigor at Bryn Mawr.

In her continuing communications with German scholars, however, P.T. defended coeducation even as she presided over a single-sex college. In 1904, when she was invited to address a largely German audience at the International Women's Congress in Berlin, Thomas used the opportunity to pursue the argument in favor of coeducation. Following an address by Marianne Weber, whom Thomas would later have the opportunity to host in America on the occasion of the St. Louis World's Fair, the Bryn Mawr president expressed that like "many American professors I owe to Germany a debt of gratitude that I can never pay." She also offered a surprising recommendation: "As I happen to be the President of one of the four largest and best endowed separate colleges for women in the United States, you will not think me unduly biased, if I say that, as women, we should throw all our influence in favor of unrestricted co-education of the sexes from the Kindergarten through the university."[48] Anticipating the debate as to whether equity and excellence are best achieved for women in separate or coeducational institutions, it is significant that the foremost president of one of the leading women's colleges recommended coeducation—at least when out of American earshot—as the wisest strategy.

P.T.'s insistence on coeducation is revealing on another level as well. Women's education had been trending toward coeducation from at least the 1880s, a fact that P.T. felt supported her claim to the board of trustees that Bryn Mawr would have to be exceptional to compete.[49] At the University of Chicago's opening in 1892, women were a minority in the Junior College by a ratio of two to three. In just ten years, the enrollment of women outstripped that of men and, in 1902, women received 56.3 percent of Phi Beta Kappa awards.[50] But a victim of this success, the egalitarian spirit of the western universities gave way to reactionary policies. In December of 1901, attuned to this development, President Harper of Chicago undermined women students when he announced that coeducation should "cultivat[e] the life which is peculiarly woman's." Attempts at Chicago, and at Stanford and Wisconsin—which experienced similar demographic shifts—to implement entrance quotas to limit the acceptance of women and to segregate classes based on sex tempered any sense of success.[51] By the time Thomas represented America in Germany in 1904 coeducation had rebounded somewhat, but the future of women in elite universities was insecure. Why then did Thomas offer a full-throated endorsement of coeducation abroad? Back in the United States at the Congress of Arts and Science in St. Louis later that year, P.T. expressed in her public talk that she was "struck by the similarity" in the electives taken by men and women, a fact that disproved the suggestion that women opted for vocational over theoretical fields. Any changes that would be made in the curriculum, she insisted, would have to be made for men and women's education equally.[52]

In front of American audiences, P.T. remained a passionate advocate for high standards for women's education, but shied away from supporting anything other than single-sex education. She continued to draw on her German education and German networks to insist on her inclusion and that of her German-inspired institution in the solidifying American elite system. At home P.T. worked to change from within the bounds of what was possible. Bryn Mawr reflected the possibilities of transatlantic exchange for altering—if not fully upending—the all-male tradition in America.

W.E.B. DU BOIS—A BLACK BISMARCK

For African Americans the German PhD was even further out of grasp than it was for white American women. That only increased the determination of the young and ambitious W. E. Burghardt Du Bois to acquire one. Born in 1868 to a poor home with a mother who worked as a housekeeper in

Great Barrington, Massachusetts, Du Bois attended an integrated school where he received a classical education, and by the time he was fifteen, he was covering local black issues for the *New York Globe*.[53] Du Bois's lifelong preoccupation with German culture was sparked at Fisk University, where German had been taught since 1869 and where Du Bois entered as a sophomore in 1885.[54] One of the first black institutions of higher learning, Fisk remained devoted to classical education in a growing sea of technical schools. The university taught Romance languages, hosted a Mozart Club, and in 1872 sent its Jubilee Chorus to a warm reception in Europe.[55] When he graduated in 1888 as valedictorian, Du Bois chose to deliver his public oration on Bismarck. While previous winners had selected as their topics "Anglo-Saxon influence," "women in public life," and "feudalism," Du Bois explained his decision as political: "This choice in itself showed the abyss between my education and the truth in the world. Bismarck was my hero. He had made a nation out of a mass of bickering peoples. He had dominated the whole development with his strength until he crowned an emperor at Versailles."[56] The contemporary philosopher Kwame Anthony Appiah imagines that Fiskites who listened to his address might very well have seen that Du Bois "had a vision of himself as a black Bismarck."[57] Perhaps the black Humboldt might have been even more fitting considering Du Bois's lifelong efforts to build a people's identity through educational excellence.

Through a combination of exceptional talent, unusual tenacity, and a growing network of supportive professors and preachers, Du Bois found himself the recipient of a Price Greenleaf Fellowship at Harvard in 1888. Though he never truly felt "of" Harvard, Du Bois received his degree in 1890 cum laude, was named one of the commencement speakers, and subsequently entered Harvard Graduate School to study social science, for which he received a Bromfield Rogers Memorial Fellowship. Harvard was significant for Du Bois for another reason—it provided another gateway to the German tradition through William James, whom Du Bois described as his "friend and guide to clear thinking," the inaugural Roosevelt exchange professor Francis Peabody, and Albert Bushnell Hart, from whom he learned German.[58] At Harvard Du Bois wrote two seminar papers devoted to Germany, already showing signs of how he might develop his interest in the "color line" on the German model.[59] After hearing that John F. Slater had set up a fund to support African American education abroad and that its chairman, Rutherford B. Hayes, formerly the nineteenth president of the United States, was seeking "young colored men in the south" to send to Europe for further educational training, Du Bois saw his opening. He quickly dashed off a letter to Hayes making his case.[60] As Du Bois later reflected, "I wanted then to study in Germany. I was determined that any failure on my part to become a recognized American scholar must not be based on lack of modern training."[61]

The John F. Slater Fund joined a number of new foundations in the 1890s, including the Daniel Hand Fund, the Southern Education Board (SEB), and the Anna T. Jeanes Fund, that distributed thousands of dollars a year to help schools train African American teachers. Motivated by a combination of Christian noblesse oblige and modernizing ideology, the philanthropists who established these funds saw African American education as a means to improve the Reconstruction-era South.[62] In this context, vocational education had begun to emerge as a component of fulfilling the commitment to educating all Americans, albeit at different levels. As we saw, Gilman as president of Hopkins had supported education in Hand-craft (manual training) to complement the elevation of Rede-craft (classical studies in logic). It is not a coincidence that Gilman joined the Slater Fund as a trustee. Du Bois's application to the Slater Fund was reviewed as a group of philanthropists and academic leaders convened the Mohonk Conferences to discuss the "Negro Question," and this all-white male panel determined that the vocational model, as epitomized by Booker T. Washington's industrial education, would provide a solution.[63]

Despite his obvious qualifications for the fellowship and the support of his Harvard professor Albert Bushnell Hart, Du Bois's application had been declined. As his biographer David Levering Lewis commented, "Most assuredly a Du Bois fellowship was not the appropriate symbol for a policy of training of 'heart and hand.'"[64] This was not the first or the last time that Du Bois would not take no for an answer. He took it upon himself to try again with a "manifesto" of a letter, which Du Bois later "described as nothing less than impudent," and Lewis identified as "the most significant for his race."[65] Calling out the foundation's offer as an empty one, Du Bois declared, "As to my case I personally care little. I am perfectly capable of fighting alone for an education if the trustees do not see fit to help me. On the other hand the injury you have . . . done the race I represent . . . is almost irreparable. . . . When now finally you receive three or four applications for the fulfillment of that offer, the offer is suddenly withdrawn. . . . I think you owe an apology to the Negro people."[66] Not unlike those of the German-educated American women, his shaming tactics worked and they won him an ally in Gilman. The second time around Du Bois toned down the ambition of his request for the white committee, assuring them that travel to Germany was "merely for personal interest."[67] Du Bois met with Gilman in spring 1892 in New York City and left "walking on air." Self-assuredly, he bought a dress shirt for $3—four times as much as he'd ever paid—and exuberantly prepared to sail for Europe.[68]

Du Bois settled into the small town of Wartburg, where he planned to improve his German before the semester began. With his Baedeker in hand he explored Cologne's massive cathedral and mastered the libretto of *Tannhäuser*, and he was pleasantly surprised to find himself the object of romantic attention from the innkeeper's daughter—the first of his many German dalliances. In Germany he became attuned to the universalism of humanity beyond the particular distinctions that divided people: "Slowly [the Germans] became, not white folks, but folks. The unity beneath all life clutched me. I was not less fanatically a Negro, but 'Negro' meant a greater, broader sense of humanity and world fellowship. I felt myself standing, not against the world, but simply against American narrowness and color prejudice, with the greater, finer world at my back."[69]

Du Bois was determined to use the German tradition to buttress his own ascent and that of the African American people. In a letter to the *Fisk Herald* he encouraged his classmates to do the same and master Goethe to raise themselves and the race.[70] He soaked up Hegel's notoriously difficult work "Lordship and Bondage," which traced the dialectic between master and slave, and Herder's notion of *Volk*, a concept that gave structure and meaning to his emerging racial philosophy.[71] His embrace of the German tradition was tempered by one hesitation: did he aim to capitalize on his mastery of the highest scholarly tradition to enter white society or to emulate it in his reformulation of the black one? Du Bois jotted down in his notebook: "These are my plans: to make a name in [social?] science, to make a name in literature and thus to raise my race. Or perhaps to raise a visible empire in Africa thro' England, France or Germany."[72] He was conflicted.

Even as he relished the shared humanity he discovered in Germany, Du Bois worried about his loyalty, a concern that would persist:[73] "[How] far can love for my oppressed race accord with love for the oppressing country? And when these loyalties diverge, where shall my soul find refuge?"[74] Moreover, imperial Germany could hardly be described as a "land of the free"—its genteel constitutional monarchy was predicated on a racial and class war that politicians—some of whom were his new beloved teachers—waged against Catholics, Socialists, Poles, and Jews. Though this played out before his eyes, some of it remained opaque to him. Du Bois's private writings bear the imprint of the antisemitism that was standard fare for the National Liberal professors with whom he studied.[75] He may even himself have been the object of racism from the fiery professor Heinrich von Treitschke, who once called out in a class in which he was present "Die Mulattin [en] sind niedrig! Sie fühlen sich niedrig." (Mulattoes are inferior! They feel themselves to be inferior.) Intent on capturing the "positive" aspects of nationalism and evading those racial hierarchies of the nation-state, Du Bois ignored this and likely other racist comments.[76] A classmate urged him to visit Krakow to see a real "race problem"—that between the Germans and the Poles—an experience that instilled a new sense of empathy.[77]

In his intimidation by the German bureaucracy and its seemingly endless hallways, documents, stamps, and queues, Du Bois echoed Mark Twain's jovial travelogue. But despite his claims to the contrary, Du Bois's pursuits were of course more than merely "personal." Du Bois faced a version of a problem common to all visiting American students—that Germany would not accept work completed at Harvard toward his graduate degree and required at least six semesters in a German university to sit for the PhD. The administrative hurdles were compounded by the expense of living in Berlin. Du Bois understood that his case was different than that of other visiting American students, and when he asked the Slater Fund to renew his fellowship in the spring of 1893 he admitted to Gilman that "even more than to the white, is the contact with European culture of inestimable value in giving him a broad view of men and affairs."[78]

Intellectually Du Bois had already proven himself worthy, attending lectures from the most challenging and awe-inspiring professors of the German Historical School, including Adolf Wagner and Gustav Schmoller, under whose guidance he worked on his thesis concerning the nineteenth-century agricultural system in the southern United States.[79] In other courses he assimilated the use of statistics for the social sciences and heard lectures from Lenz on the Reformation and from Weber, who fortuitously was in Berlin at the time, on political economy. He became a member of the Verein für Sozialpolitik, which included the *Kathedersozialisten* (social-ists of the lectern) who opposed the laissez-faire school of economics and advocated for an interaction between social science and policy, and even took on the local political cause of social democracy.[80]

Du Bois's German supporters were willing to waive two of the semester requirements, but he would still need to remain for a fourth semester in order to get his PhD, which would mean obtaining one more renewal of his grant from Slater Fund. His fate rested with the white philanthropists. It was Gilman's job to share the bad news that his fellowship renewal was not accepted. In the "recent meeting" to which Gilman referred in his letter he underscored that the trustees "express, with great earnestness, the hope that . . . you will devote your talent and learning to the good of the colored race."[81] Lewis interprets the elusive meeting: "How useful to the education of a people one generation removed from slavery could a University of Berlin-minted teacher be, after all? . . . Black Ph.D.s from Germany were not a priority in Booker T. Washington's America." Lewis identifies the so-cial significance of the status marker of which the sociologist Du Bois was

Figure 6. Denied the funding he needed to complete his PhD in Germany in 1892, W.E.B. Du Bois would receive an honorary degree from Humboldt University in Berlin (then in East Germany) in 1958. (W.E.B. Du Bois Papers, Special Collections and University Archives, University of Massachusetts Amherst Libraries.)

no doubt aware: "To return to the United States with a coveted Heidelberg or Berlin doctorate would be the ultimate seal of professional standing, a personal triumph and a racial marker."[82] But the white gatekeepers would not permit him to earn it (fig. 6).[83]

Du Bois's inclusion—and then exclusion—from the German-American encounter was symptomatic of the structures that were emerging in American higher education at the time. One aspect of the solidifying system was that American philanthropists and academic leaders could use money and decision-making power to maintain a hierarchy and determine who would get which opportunities.[84] While Thomas had access to her family's resources—and had no trouble draining those—as well as the substantial capital of her wide network of heiresses, artists, literary figures, and publishers, Du Bois did not possess the same kin, connections, or capital.[85] Access to philanthropy required that proximity, and even then, as we saw in the varying experience of American women, inclusion was not guaranteed.

Though he did not in the end receive the German PhD, Du Bois did become the first African American to earn a PhD at Harvard (and one of the first to earn a PhD in America at all). Although this marks an important milestone, the meaning of the Harvard PhD in 1894 has been lost in the thicket of history. For as Lewis points out and Gilman would have conceded, "Harvard's degree, after all, was regarded in about the same light by the leading German universities as his Fisk bachelor's had been by Harvard."[86]

Du Bois remained a faithful advocate of the German research university. With his Harvard PhD as consolation prize, he arrived at the first African American college, Wilberforce, in 1894 to teach Latin, Greek, and German as the chair in classics. His work reflected the "rapid growth of interest in the field of modern foreign languages in the Negro Colleges" and a stronghold against Booker T. Washington's utilitarian educational program for African Americans.[87] Du Bois's education at the University of Berlin fed new concepts, including the "Talented Tenth," and new organizations, like the American Negro Academy in Washington, DC.[88] In fact, Du Bois's counterpoint to Washington's vocational education rang like an endorsement for the German notion of *Bildung*: "The object of all true education is not to make men carpenters, it is to make carpenters men."[89] He applied the lessons of Gustav Schmoller's social policy to the study of race, and culled huge amounts of quantitative data for his groundbreaking sociological study *The Philadelphia Negro*. He emulated the empirical approach of the Berlin School with the school of sociology that he established when he arrived in Atlanta from Wilberforce in 1897.[90] Through unwavering devotion to *Bildung* and his interdisciplinary approach to the social sciences, Du Bois reformed black colleges and institutions on the German model even as American academic leaders overlooked him. But his adherence to the German tradition had a contradictory legacy. Du Bois carried into his own system a German sense of superiority and a "marrow-deep elitism" that were the source of both pride and, for some, culpability.[91]

MERITOCRACY—*BILDUNG*, AMERICAN STYLE

Against the backdrop of German influence, the encounters between academic leaders and marginalized individuals like Thomas and Du Bois reveal how the murmurings of a new ideology of meritocracy became a salve for the American adaptation of the German educational ideal. Among the lectures delivered at the congress in St. Louis was a contribution from the newly appointed Yale president Arthur Twining Hadley concerning the social implications of the developments in America education over the preceding century. "When careers were thrown open to ability instead of being determined by birth," Hadley expounded, "each man was anxious to have the ability of his children developed instead of remaining content with those traditional studies which had once seemed a birthright."[92] Hadley's account traced the meritocratic logic of American education to

Jacksonian egalitarianism, linking an individual's ability to opportunity. Though he held conservative views on property rights and was suspicious of government power, Hadley also—like most of his contemporary university presidents—believed education to be an essential public good.[93] But what kind of education, and for whom?

Gilman was typical of such American academic leaders in his support of expanding educational opportunity while preserving a hierarchy that favored the elite. Gilman was protective of the "university" name itself. It belonged only to institutions that measured up, and only some communities would get to have one. "Just after the war the enthusiastic sympathy of the North for the enfranchised blacks led to the bestowal of the highest term in educational nomenclature upon the institutes where the freedmen were to be taught," Gilman observed. "Fortunately, Hampton and Tuskegee escaped this christening, but Fisk, Atlanta, and Howard foundations were thus named."[94] That is, institutions for black students did not qualify for the elevated status of universities.

Through his apparent support of educational hierarchy, then, Gilman was a perfect spokesperson for the Slater Fund, which ostensibly funded educational expansion for African Americans but on a highly tiered system that focused on technical institutions that provided primarily manual training. When a donor funded a building at the Hampton Normal and Agricultural Institute, named, in part, for John H. Slater, Gilman spoke in 1896 at the opening about the "three great benefits—political freedom, the Christian religion, and the opportunity to acquire knowledge," which black men were now receiving. Gilman equivocated on what that knowledge might comprise and suggested—citing Booker T. Washington—that "right here comes the value of industrial education combined with first-class literary training." Nonetheless, the goal was to "make each race as good as it can be made." Education for all, but each in his place.[95] Du Bois had found out firsthand how confining those places could be.

Gilman remained conflicted, and his ambivalent support of Du Bois was itself a sign that the boundaries were not as defined as he hoped. Even by 1904, America boasted a variety of institutions, including schools, colleges, and universities, and often the lines between these were not clear. Working with one's "mind and hand," for example, as in the motto of MIT, could lead one to become either a mechanic or a manager. Even within the category of the college, as Bowdoin's seventh president, William DeWitt Hyde, observed, there were both "school-colleges" and "university-colleges," each of which tended in a different direction on the spectrum.[96] In Germany the boundaries between the technical institutions and research universities, as well as between the lower and higher secondary schools, were much stricter.[97] The porosity of borders between institutional categories in America, however, meant that resourceful and industrious individuals could find openings, however narrow, to wedge themselves into higher education and move up.[98]

In offering opportunities for the upwardly mobile, meritocracy unleashed anxiety among those whose privilege was granted by birth. P.T.'s oft-reported (though perhaps unreliable) statistic that at least half of Bryn Mawr graduates married and had children had less to do with managing fears concerning the birthrate than those related to the "feminization" of the academy.[99] As the women's rights activist Helen R. Olin wrote when the University of Wisconsin was considering a rollback of coeducation, "So long as men predominate in state universities, no problem is presented to these educators. As soon as the number of women begins to equal or exceed that of the men serious questions arise."[100] President Charles Van Hise of Wisconsin stoked these fears with hyperbole: there were so many women, he insisted, "that some of the colleges of liberal arts in the state universities, not the universities as a whole, may in large measure cease to be coeducational by becoming essentially women's colleges."[101]

Assuaging the fear of being replaced by those on lower rungs of the status ladder was becoming a feature of American meritocracy, and when it came to personifying the threat, Jews followed quickly on the heels of women. At Columbia University status anxiety sparked an antisemitic backlash, as evidenced by a campus ditty heard in Morningside Heights around 1910:

> Oh, Harvard's run by millionaires,
> And Yale is run by booze,
> Cornell is run by farmer's sons,
> Columbia's run by Jews.
> So give a cheer for Baxter Street,
> Another one for Pell,
> And when the little sheenies die,
> Their souls will go to hell.[102]

Much like the women of the ACA, Jewish philanthropists used "coercive philanthropy" to counter their exclusion and fund opportunities for Jewish scholars. The German-Jewish philanthropist Leopold Koppel and James Speyer, an American banker of German-Jewish origin and donor to Columbia, had provided the funds for the German-American exchange program and Münsterberg's America Institute. Butler, for his part, was content to take their money until there were too many Jews or the Jews became too demanding.

So when Speyer asked Butler to commit to regularly naming Jews to the Theodore Roosevelt Professorship in Berlin, Butler was incensed. In consultation with Althoff, and Professors Burgess and Paulsen, Butler evidently decided it was better to stick to "native-born American stock." Even more egregiously, when somehow Felix Adler, the Jewish political and educational radical, squeezed through, Butler exploited him to provide cover for his bigotry. How could a Jewish donor say we were antisemitic if we had a Jewish professor?—so his logic went.[103] At the same time, to alter the perception of the college, Butler began an aggressive campaign to limit the number of Jewish students at Columbia, instituting a quota system intended to halve the Jewish population of the university. Many years later, when Butler was on the verge of hiring Lionel Trilling, the first Jewish English professor at an elite American university, Butler rewrote the story of the German-American professor exchange and his unequivocal support of Adler. In his revisionist account, he assured Diana Trilling that he had told his German colleagues, "At Columbia, sir, we recognize merit, not race."[104] Merit was indeed a useful criterion of selection when it aligned with institutional goals.

The muckraking journalist Upton Sinclair spoke for many leftists when he expressed little faith in the American higher education system to provide access for all. In fact, by World War I, he would attribute the American university's continuing role as the bastion of privilege to the insidious German influence and identified its roots in the late nineteenth-century transatlantic partnership: "Our educational system is not a public service, but an instrument of special privilege; its purpose is not to further the welfare of mankind, but merely to keep America capitalist." Columbia, which Sinclair dubbed the "University of the House of Morgan," was the worst offender, but none of the American university presidents were exempt from the "Goose-step under the Kaiser." Sinclair's populism was precisely the scourge Hadley and Gilman feared. Sinclair fumed that while American academic leaders were keen to draw on the German university model to reinforce American aristocracy, they "ignored that Kaiser Wilhelm had established old-age pensions and unemployment insurance in Germany."[105] On one matter Sinclair was correct: the ideology of merit came to justify exclusion on a broader scale and to perpetuate a higher education system on the German model that would remain largely the preserve of the elite.

Thomas's and Du Bois's lives and careers bear this out but also show that they each held a certain responsibility for their own fate. Since those on the edges of the academy wanted desperately to be insiders, they often shared and performed the elitism of the establishment: women and African Americans imbibed antisemitism; male African Americans embraced sexism; and those who assimilated *Bildung* viewed themselves as part of a select class who participated in this cultural and scientific tradition.[106] Thomas, for her part, believed that she was destined for greatness and that most women (and men for that matter) were "socially beneath her," a feeling that likely intensified with her marginalization.[107] She viewed selective limitation of the student body as vital to the institution's success and compiled ancestry statistics of her students as proof of their ascribed status.[108] That classism extended to antisemitism and racism, and Thomas expressed both freely. Upon dining with Booker T. Washington, she noted she found him "disappointing" and "like a Negro in the way his mind works." And this racism extended to the strategy for her nascent school.[109] Though early in her presidency she hired the German-Jewish physiologist Jacques Loeb and insisted on an official tolerance policy, she kept other Jews out of the faculty and blocked their promotions. When in 1901 an African American student, Jessie Redmon Fauset, won a scholarship designated for Bryn Mawr, Thomas donated her own money to send her to Cornell instead.[110] So desperately did she want to be part of the new aristocracy that Thomas feared being associated with anyone who wasn't already in it.[111]

The results of Thomas's and Du Bois's efforts were mixed at best, as evidenced by the transatlantic networks in which they continued to associate. For Thomas this meant that coeducation—complete inclusion—remained the higher goal. In the short term, she expressed pride that Bryn Mawr conferred a large proportion of the PhDs awarded to women as late as the first decade of the twentieth century.[112] Yet after the 1870s the majority of undergraduate women enrolled in coeducational institutions, and, by 1900, there were more than twice as many women in these as in women's colleges. P.T. did not lament this development. As she said to her German colleagues while abroad, "Let me beg of you, ladies . . . to oppose the founding of separate universities for women. Such separate foundations will tend to close to women your world renowned universities for men. Be content with nothing less than unrestricted co-education. It will profoundly influence for good not only your girls but your boys."[113] Visibility and achievement for women at the highest ranks of the establishment would mean the disappearance of her own single-sex world.

Being on the institutional periphery, as were P.T. and Bryn Mawr, created a certain set of challenges, which, though difficult, could be overcome.[114] Du Bois's marginalization based on race presented greater obstacles embedded in the history of slavery and the politics of Reconstruction. Though he was unable to challenge racial hierarchy, Du Bois, like Thomas, capitalized on the openings he found. He modified his rhetoric when speaking to the board of white philanthropists—emphasizing his multiracial background and his humble mission.[115] Given the choice, Du Bois, like Thomas, would rather have been accepted by mainstream academia; his exclusion, in Thorstein Veblen's formulation, was a condition "by force of circumstances over which he ha[d] no control."[116] And the separation ignited an ambition to be—in Pierre Bourdieu's words—"visible."[117] Though he was already an established scholar with a published study in sociology, Du Bois was not invited by Albion Small, a fellow student of the Berlin School, to present at the St. Louis Congress. He would become an institutional founder, but he was never hired in a nonblack institution.

Like Thomas, Du Bois maintained relationships in Germany, and Weber, in particular, arranged to meet him on the sidelines of the St. Louis Congress.[118] Weber was as interested in Du Bois as American sociologists were aloof. When a group of Schmoller's former American students organized a Festschrift to honor their former professor, Du Bois was again excluded. Except for a female social scientist (equally marginalized) no one recognized the African American sociologist's contribution to transatlantic social reform.[119] The Chicago School of Sociology eventually came to embrace ideas of racial constructs similar to Du Bois's, but arguably the assimilation of his ideas was belated and superficial.[120] Du Bois would have the last word, his absence haunting the American university for decades to come.[121]

Even when it helped educate, and thus raise the status of, Americans outside the white, male, Protestant elite, the German university system ended up reinforcing the role of American higher education as a mechanism for the preservation of elite dominance and inherited privilege. German *Bildung*, self-cultivation, was always elitist; the elitism traveled with it to the United States—among other ways via Thomas and Du Bois. Given their immersion in German philosophy, and facing entrenched racism and sexism, all that Thomas and Du Bois could do was establish separate systems of higher education that mirrored the elitist principles of the top universities while remaining inferior to them, leaving untouched the ideological and institutional foundations of elite dominance. Their institutional innovations were impressive and admirable, classic examples of "hybridization" as a strategy of institutional emergence, but they were a consequence of their marginalization that left the core of the system intact.[122]

The German model required a particular high school education and the mastery of Latin and Greek, all of which was expensive and onerous to acquire. These requirements threw up additional barriers even as exceptional individuals tried to break them down, much as others would attempt in

Germany. American education leaders used the weight and inaccessibility of the German philosophical tradition and the expense of equipment and books to create a system that reinforced the determinants of status within the emerging stratification. To be sure, not all the shortcomings of American meritocracy can be blamed on German influence. But reading the debates about access and standards against the background of the "lure" of the German university model illuminates the fault lines.

The American equivalent of the German *Bürgertum* was based on intersecting gendered, racial, ethnic, and class hierarchies. The difference was that at the same time an ideology of meritocracy was emerging in America that seemed to hold out the promise for movement within those structures. Though the gates would be less open at different points in America's history, as in the early 1920s at the height of elite schools' discriminatory admissions, a glimmer of hope remained, and for those who made it through, the logic of the system dictated that once they did, they close the door tightly behind them. The ensuing clash among pioneering individuals, academic leaders, and emerging interest groups created the conditions under which higher education could remain the preserve of the elite—a hallmark of America's "credential society"—while paying lip service to the ideals of equal access and meritocracy.

CHAPTER FIVE

AN "ARISTOCRACY OF EXCELLENCE"

THE RISE OF THE PROFESSIONS

In the absence of a system of hereditary ranks and titles, without a tradition of honors conferred by a monarch, and with no well-known status ladder even of high-class regiments to confer various degrees of cachet, Americans have had to depend for their mechanism of snobbery far more than other peoples on their college and university hierarchy. In this country, just about all that's finally available as a fount of honor is the institution of the higher learning.

PAUL FUSSELL, 1982

At his inauguration as the twenty-first president of Harvard in 1869, Charles Eliot announced that the reform of professional education would be his administration's top priority. "A university is not closely concerned with the applications of knowledge," he maintained, "until its general education branches into professional."[1] Over the next several decades, capitalizing on the Progressive-Era political demand for specialists for the new administrative state, Eliot and his colleagues pushed through higher admissions standards and introduced new requirements for the BA and the medical and law schools.[2] By the turn of the century, pre-professionalism in American higher education was ascendant, prompting William James to complain, in the *Harvard Monthly* of March 1903, that a "Ph.D. octopus" was taking over the American university. Believing, as many Harvard men of his day did, that the pursuit of knowledge was justified only for its own sake, James balked at the German obsession with titles—even the doctorate—that seemed to be ensnaring young men and eager administrators with its vocational tentacles.[3]

The professionalization of the university was not merely a response to the outside forces of industrialization and business needs. It was as much a result of academic leaders like Eliot, as well as such reformers as Henry Pritchett and Abraham Flexner, engaging with the economic, political, and social concerns of their communities and seeking to raise the status of their fields and institutions.[4]

The professionalism that arose in the United States had domestic influences to be sure, but Americans aimed explicitly to use the German model of professionalization to advance beyond what Germany had achieved. As in other areas of transatlantic competitive emulation, the Americans never adopted wholesale the German model but hybridized Prussian-inspired changes with their evolving ecosystem. While Americans were impressed by German professionalism and inspired by features of German professional education—in particular in medicine—ultimately American innovators developed very different career paths for their students. The result was a hybrid that separated the BA from the professional degree (albeit only for the most elite students), confirmed privilege, and provided a mechanism for social mobility. But there was friction in adopting a system based on a rigid class structure for a democracy that idealized merit and egalitarianism. That system proved pliable in certain ways, but it ushered in new inequalities, particularly for those in the lower social strata for whom middle-class life was now further out of reach.

GERMANY AND THE NEW SCIENTIFIC WORKERS

Professionalization has roots in the guild and court traditions of early Europe, which controlled who could enter such fields as law, medicine, and the skilled trades.[5] The origins of American professionalization, in particular, can be located in the cultures of science and medicine of the early nineteenth-century German university. Over the course of one generation of physicists—between those born around 1770 and those born around 1800—the character of the field changed. While the former had no specialized training and often worked other jobs and dabbled in multiple fields, the latter all attended universities, where they earned the now requisite PhD and then worked in full-time university positions.[6] The second dissertation, or *Habilitation*, which granted the right to teach, became obligatory in 1816 for all *Privatdozenten* at the University of Berlin, and other universities soon followed. By the 1830s, advanced courses in science appeared in university catalogs, and a series of periodicals emerged in which professors were expected to publish their findings. The beloved Society of German Natural Scientists and Medical Doctors, a haven for generalists like Alexander von Humboldt, was split up in the following decade into various groups for subspecialties. The new leader of the Physical Society, Hermann von Helmholtz, who later rose to become pro-rector of the University of Heidelberg, lauded the disciplinary expertise required for this new era in the natural sciences, which "also taught us best to harness the powers in our immediate natural environment, and to put them in the service of our will."[7]

It was not lost on Helmholtz, who once called the new "scientific workers" "an organised army, labouring on behalf of the whole nation, and generally under its direction and at its expense," that the culture of science would be indebted to the state.[8] This new regime of empirical science was best conducted in laboratories with large teams, and that required more resources. Just as Liebig secured support for agricultural chemistry in the 1820s and 1830s because of fears about agricultural depression, Helmholtz and his colleagues argued for the utilitarian benefits of "big" science, from physics and physiology. In this climate Robert Bunsen's chemistry lab in Heidelberg and Carl Ludwig's physiology lab in Leipzig were just two of the many built in the 1860s that earned ample funding and widespread fame over the next decade.[9] Sought out by scientists and encouraged by state "top-down" reform, these new laboratories made discoveries that had tangible benefits for public health and such industries as dyestuffs.[10]

One of the original pillars of the university's four faculties, medicine was an early beneficiary of the new institute system that rewarded top researchers with laboratory space, assistance, and resources to pursue their specialized fields. The pioneering Rudolf Virchow, a contemporary of Helmholtz's, set many of these developments in motion. A political idealist and key member of the generation of 1848, Virchow often used political metaphors to describe his new cell biology, uniting medicine and social policy.[11] His pupil Robert Koch emerged as one of the leading experts in public health. In Koch's laboratory devoted to infectious diseases, Emil von Behring and Paul Ehrlich competed to make discoveries in bacteriology—leading to Nobel Prizes for both in physiology or medicine. The Koch Institute (1891) became a symbol of the potential for scientific advancement through public support and prestige. One need only compare medicine with dentistry to see how professionalization brought gains that other fields coveted. The Central Union of German Dentists (CVDZ), founded in 1859, also aimed to "raise the profession" by establishing a university curriculum and clinic in dentistry, yet it took much longer to develop regulations and, therefore, receive similar recognition. That lag had an impact on the progress of the field. The benefits of professionalization were evident—higher pay, greater status, and more government support.[12]

Yet the new academic social contract had its drawbacks, particularly when the balance of pure research and the applied benefits was upset. The university's philosophical faculties trained most *Gymnasiallehrer* (secondary school instructors), who were required as of 1810 to pass a competitive state qualifying exam to become civil servants. That exam thus effectively controlled the curriculum. As it was, only between 10 and 25 percent of students continued for the PhD, and further reforms in 1893 threatened to make the doctorate "superfluous" for medicine, since it would no longer be a condition for taking the exam, which alone conferred the right to practice.[13] At the same time, those scientists who did wish to pursue a faculty career now needed to follow a specific path, from *Privatdozent* to professor, by publishing, since, as the physicist Paul Erman put it, "The gentlemen in the Ministry . . . love tangible literary merit. . . . It wouldn't hurt if the work were at the same time good, too."[14] While on the surface the state's investment in science benefited all knowledge workers and universities, this new regime led to an unprecedented split in *Wissenschaft* between the natural sciences (*Naturwissenschaften*) and the humanities (*Geisteswissenschaften*).[15] Chemistry and not philology, laboratory experiments and not Greek and Latin, would be the gateway to society's progress.[16]

The state also used licensure exams as a form of social engineering—that is, to control the number and variety of students in increasingly crowded professions.[17] Adding a tenth required semester of study in 1901 as well as a practical year effectively reduced entrants into the profession. The costs of pursuing a degree of medicine already exceeded those of other fields, and those in Berlin were higher still, approaching those of the private Harvard Medical School. Hikes in fees—both of the *Gymnasium* and of the medical courses—were utilized to slow the attendance of students from working-class backgrounds.[18] The university professoriate thus remained the domain of mostly educated and propertied middle-class men.[19] Similarly, professional associations adopted discriminatory policies to keep out unwanted ethnic groups—namely, Jews—who flocked to specific specialties and often went into private practice to avoid discrimination.[20] German humanists worried about the threat of *Berechtigungswesen* (credentialism) to the ideals of learning, but their retreat to pure inquiry in a system that was conditioned to preserve social hierarchy also limited opportunities for individual advancement. In America, where the education system aspired to the meritocratic ideals of democracy, the unliberal aspects of the liberal self-regulating profession would be more contested.

STANDARDIZING ADMISSIONS

Before it could develop the standards, regulations, and incentives needed to produce graduates qualified to practice in the professions of law, engineering, business, and medicine, American higher education first had to implement a coherent system with uniform goals. As the urban middle class swelled in the closing decades of the 1800s and meritocratic ideals gained steam, it could no longer be assumed that a college education was reserved for male members of the privileged classes. With many other kinds of people clamoring for the mobility-enhancing benefits of postsecondary education, it became necessary to regulate entry to higher education and for university administrators to assume the role of gatekeepers. What developed was a system of certificates that was an early precursor to selective admissions policies and related associations governing accreditation.

When American higher education consisted mostly of small colleges that comprised no more than a few hundred students each, and very few people attended college, the notion of selective admissions was purely hypothetical.[21] After the Civil War and the passing of the Morrill Act a debate emerged concerning who should be admitted to college, but the focus was on increasing the enrollment of students deemed most fit, not on exclusion. As African Americans, women, and immigrants pressed for the right to receive a college education, institutions responded in an ad hoc manner, and public discourse fragmented. There was confusion concerning just who had access to this kind of institution and who was the arbiter who made the selection.

In search of a method to standardize admissions, University of Michigan president Henry S. Frieze, who served between Haven and Angell in 1870–1871, identified a German model as a solution. In Germany, the secondary education system that was standardized in the 1830s had three tiers, the *Gymnasium*, the *Realschule*, and the *Volkschule*. While the first provided a classical course of education for students from the upper class, the latter two had what was considered a more modern curriculum for students from the working class.[22] What impressed Frieze seems to have been the *Abitur*, the diploma that permitted entrance to German universities, earned by *Gymnasium* students who successfully completed an exam. Implemented in 1834, the *Abitur* helped reduce the excess of educated men in the labor market by making the *Gymnasium* the sole route to the university.[23] Following travel in Germany, Frieze sought to create an American diploma system that would accomplish a similar filtering.[24] As elaborated by Frieze's successor Angell, Michigan succeeded in establishing what he called an articulation agreement between the university and the secondary schools, "carrying out, in some respects," as he explained to the interested Trustees of Johns Hopkins, "the plan of the German Gymnasium."[25]

Yet in the American version there was a crucial difference. Whereas in Germany the state controlled the *Abitur* through its selection of inspectors and oversight of the curriculum, in the United States that power was decentralized, so authority over admission was shared by states and universities. The university presidents did not control the levers of admission as the German state did. As Angell explained, the process occurred on a state-by-state and, in some cases, a school-by-school basis: "Any School may invite a committee of the [University of Michigan] Faculty to come down and visit you. If the Committee find that the School has, in our opinion, well-prepared students for all our courses, organized upon a plan large enough to do that, and is doing its work satisfactorily, in our opinion, then we will leave to you the responsibility of saying when the student is prepared to come to the University."[26] A uniquely American system of checks and balances emerged through which university presidents tried to influence high schools' curricula in exchange for accepting the diplomas awarded by those high schools as a basis for admission. In the German case a student who did not attend the *Gymnasium* could not take the *Abitur*—making the state the gatekeeper.[27] In the United States, in contrast, the door opened wider, at least to varying interpretations in different states.

Seeking tighter control of the admissions pipeline, university leaders committed to raising standards sought influence through a second avenue: the National Education Association (NEA). With roots in the early nineteenth century, the NEA consolidated a number of professional teacher organizations in 1870 and emerged at the end of the nineteenth century as a vocal exponent of professional identity. Under the guidance of his mentor, Columbia president Frederick A. P. Barnard, Butler began to use various teachers' organizations, including the Industrial Education Association, as a "stalking horse" for their collective cause of professionalization.[28] Among other leadership positions, Butler was elected to the sixty-person NEA board and convened its first conference on secondary education. From this conference the Committee of Ten arose, to which he named his trusted friend Eliot as chair.[29] Hailed as "the most important educational document ever issued in the United States," the report of the Committee of Ten addressed the core question of how to create a secondary curriculum that catered to the needs of both college-bound and terminal students. The committee laid out four different curricula for high schools, thereby providing alternatives to the earlier Greek and Latin requirements.[30] But ultimately the NEA had no regulatory force, and Eliot failed to persuade secondary schools to adopt the committee's recommendations.[31]

Devolved authority and the absence of accountability to shared commitments remained a persistent challenge to professionalization in America. Decentralization permitted each university to balance the maintenance of general standards and local values. University of Michigan presidents Frieze and Angell raised standards while increasing and widening enrollment. Butler, who became acting president of Columbia in 1901, and formal president in 1902, shows the lengths to which a university leader could go to make institutions more exclusive. In 1887, he founded the New York College for the Training of Teachers (later Columbia Teachers College). In 1901, as executive secretary of the College Entrance Examination Board, he advocated for standardized entrance exams and created a modified diploma system in New York to curtail lower-class students from using the Regents exam as a stepping-stone to Columbia. Eager to feed a new "aristocracy of intellect and service" and to control an influx of undesirable students, Butler would pursue one of the most stringent selective admissions strategies.[32]

Professionalism conferred status and controlled social mobility. The incomplete efforts of the state-based early articulation agreement and the NEA's Committee of Ten focused on the inputs—who would get to attend—while the other side of reform focused on the outputs—what professions the degrees permitted a graduate to pursue. Medicine was the field where these concerns came together most visibly and with the most long-standing consequences for the professionalization of the academy at large.

THE AMERICAN AGE OF THE SPECIALIST

Eliot made a comprehensive reorganization of Harvard's professional schools the "leading item on his agenda" when he assumed the presidency in 1869, and he made good on his promise. That goal would persist throughout what turned out to be a forty-two-year tenure. By his own estimation, selecting Christopher Columbus Langdell as dean of Harvard Law School was one of the "three best" accomplishments of his presidency, in part because of the professionalization Langdell brought to the school.[33] Under Langdell's leadership, even as Harvard Law School became a center for legal scholarship, it also advanced legal training through the case study method. Langdell cultivated the notion that one could make a career not only in the practice of law, but also in teaching and writing about it. And he encouraged uniform written examinations rather than the more relaxed oral examinations—developments that led to the first bar associations. Harvard Business School, which Eliot began to develop in 1900, would be shaped in part on the law school's model.[34] In his book *College Administration*, which he dedicated to "the great president" Charles Eliot, the historian Charles Thwing declared, "The age of the specialist has come."[35]

Because it was impossible to create nationwide standards in the field of law, given the states' insistence on separate bar examinations, Eliot's impact on the profession had its limits. Before 1869 no one would have guessed that medicine would lead the march toward professionalization. "The ignorance and general incompetency of the average graduate of American Medical Schools, at the time when he receives the degree which turns him loose upon the community, is something horrible to contemplate," Eliot observed at the outset of his presidency. Harvard Medical School, which had only a "faint connection to the university," fared not much better. "The whole system of medical education in this country needs thorough reformation," said Eliot.[36] Gilman, too, singled out medical education, which, as we saw, was notable for its hybridization of the German and American models and critical to the university's success.[37] In fact, Johns Hopkins was the first to require a BA degree for admission to its new medical school, and Eliot announced that Harvard Medical School would do the same for the incoming class five years hence. Speaking before the Medical Society of the State of New York in 1896 in a lecture titled "Medical Education of the Future," Eliot reminded his audience of the benefits of professionalization: "The physician needs thorough education, that he may hold his own in public estimation with other professional men who undergo a prolonged and vigorous preparatory training. Social power and standing come with recognized cultivation."[38]

Eliot's and Gilman's efforts to promote professionalization received crucial support from what might seem an unlikely source: an extra-university organization called the Carnegie Foundation for the Advancement of Teaching (CFAT), which was founded in 1905. CFAT would come to play a large role in raising educational standards in the early twentieth century. For this achievement the director of CFAT and former president of MIT, Henry Pritchett, was responsible. The quintessential academic innovator, Pritchett harbored ambitions beyond running any single institution, and was an organizer more than a scholar. The offspring of a father who founded a small college in Missouri, Pritchett quickly rose through the ranks of astronomy. He traveled to Munich in 1894 to obtain the "coveted doctorate," which he completed in eight months, and upon his return he landed a position as superintendent of the US Coast and Geodetic Survey.[39] Abraham Flexner later attributed the alacrity of Pritchett's ascent to his skill and the support of a German astronomer who was willing to "cut through no end of red tape so as to make it possible to Pritchett to become a candidate for his degree within a year." Pritchett was also the recipient of the accolade summa cum laude, which foreigners, as he boasted to his father in 1895, were seldom awarded, let alone for one semester's work. No wonder his associates at Washington University in St. Louis, where he worked upon his return, "could scarcely believe it."[40]

Pritchett reflected the opportunities and anxieties surrounding Americans' studying abroad. On one hand, his time in Munich "enabled him to understand the great strength of the German universities because of the freedom which they gave to the advanced student and their emphasis upon original research." The German university, according to Flexner, "made upon him a deep impression, which was never effaced." Yet he was an easy target for those concerned about the careerist motives of such sojourns and the superficiality of their scholarship. Of Pritchett's "quick rise," one German scientist said it was "Echt amerikanisch."[41] Pritchett's dubious credentials—it is not clear whether he even earned a BA—coupled with his rapid-fire ascent in academic administration contributed to a paradoxical situation: that is, he himself may have manipulated a system that he sought to reform.

Unlike the Boston Brahmin Eliot, Pritchett hailed from the cultural periphery, but he shared with Eliot the vision of elevating the professions. Speaking at the inauguration of C. S. Howe as president of the Case School of Applied Science in 1904, Pritchett had asked, "Shall engineering belong to the liberal professions?" For Pritchett, as for Eliot, that answer was clear: "We endow the older professions of the law, of medicine, of theology with the possession of a certain altruistic attitude toward mankind. Is there any reason why the Engineer should not have a similar ideal?"[42] Such views informed a far-fetched plan to merge MIT and Harvard—to unite the best technical engineering institute with the best liberal arts program—and create an exceptional institution in the true mold of the German research university. The merger failed, however, and Pritchett was pushed out of MIT. The *Boston Transcript* surmised that the whole thing had been "one of Mr. Carnegie's schemes."[43] This was not the case, yet insofar as Andrew Carnegie would give Pritchett the chance to pursue reforms stymied at MIT, that editorial was not entirely off base. Carnegie offered him a "broader sphere of influence" and promised that he would come "into touch with the world at large."[44] CFAT provided him with precisely that opportunity.

Pritchett and Carnegie combined forces to use CFAT to standardize American professions under the pretext of providing pensions for universities. As Pritchett announced, he wanted CFAT to be "one of the Great Agencies . . . in standardizing American education."[45] One of the organization's first achievements under Pritchett's leadership was to initiate a private pension system adapted from the pioneering public German model—yet another example of the way that the efforts to resolve social questions were part of transatlantic competitive emulation.[46] At universities that met certain criteria, professors could participate in a pension program that Carnegie endowed. This program, though already unprecedented in its scope and ambition, was never Pritchett's singular goal. Rather, he "saw that, before pensions could be widely or intelligently bestowed, fundamental distinctions must be made." As Flexner himself admitted, "I am not sure I appreciated the distinction, which had been perfectly clear to Pritchett when he first conceived the Carnegie Foundation for the Advancement of Teaching."[47] Pritchett, for his part, sought a revised charter in 1906 that allowed CFAT to expand work to other fields, and he published bulletins on athletics, vocational training, retirement, and state educational systems. (Once it became clear in 1917 that the pension system vastly exceeded even Carnegie's wealth, Pritchett created the Teachers Insurance and Annuity Association of America, or TIAA, as a nonprofit stock association.)[48]

CFAT became a supra-institutional entity that exerted considerable influence on higher education in the United States as a "centralizing and standardizing influence" extending far beyond the purpose and scope of the fund.[49] But too often scholars have attributed to Carnegie and his foundation a humanitarian agenda. As Ethan Ris persuasively argues, however, the impetus behind pensions was less likely humanitarian than ideological: "Carnegie was not interested in professors, but he was interested in reform. The pension fund came with strict terms, requiring participating institutions to modernize and align with his vision of efficiency." Among those terms were a minimum endowment, separation from any religious affiliation, and the admission only of students who had completed the requisite number of so-called Carnegie Units, which counted the credit hours students needed for graduation.[50] To receive the benefits Carnegie offered, universities were required to adopt these standards, to secularize and modernize.[51] Given all of these burdens, it makes sense that the standardization was the end goal rather than the means, for schools would have to get in line if they wanted to participate.[52] And get in line was precisely what Pritchett wanted institutions and professions to do.

Germany provided Pritchett with a model, impetus, and mirror—for it was only possible for these American academic leaders to comprehend the challenge before them by viewing themselves through the eyes of their chief interlocutor. To further the transatlantic exercise, the foundation authorized a study entitled "The Financial Status of the Professor in America and Germany," which compiled statistics on the professional status of educators in the two countries. The study revealed that the German university professor could expect "far greater financial and social reward than comes to his American colleague. He has, furthermore, a place of far greater security and with full protection for old age and for his wife and children." German senior faculty—namely, the *Ordinariat*—had it better than their US counterparts. Pritchett also noted the unevenness of the German system, which "is particularly in contrast with that in the United States by reason of the fact that it includes a scale of remuneration which can fit a wide scale of merit. The struggling privat-docent has a bare living, but the better known teacher may hope to get a financial return comparable with that of a well-established lawyer or physician." Not everyone had it better, but that did not seem to bother Pritchett. Rather, to achieve excellence, Americans required standardized education and uniform credentials—conditions that would necessarily produce a distinct class that would command higher status and higher pay. As Pritchett observed in his summary of the study, "[The professor] lives . . . in the only recognized aristocracy in America."[53]

Admiration for Germany's centralized hierarchy reflected the growing interest among Pritchett and his colleagues in regulated competition. Competitive emulation with Germany seemed to fit that mold. At the same time, however, Pritchett lambasted the unfruitful competition between Harvard and MIT, which he and Eliot tried to end through the merger. Monopolies were justified in education as in business, as Pritchett made clear with the apt metaphor of the railroad.[54]

To parse these distinctions, it is helpful to remember that social Darwinism was essential to American Progressivism: it was an ideology that applied the scientific theory of natural selection to rationalizing social competition in which only the best traits survived. An admirer of Herbert Spencer, who popularized the "survival of the fittest" for its social application, Andrew Carnegie governed in philanthropy as he did in business— with a "visible hand" aiding the natural dynamics of the market.[55] With Carnegie's support, Pritchett set out to create a method that would place institutions and individuals into a hierarchy of fitness in which the "weaker men are weeded out."[56] As in social Darwinism this process of evaluation would yield winners and losers.

THE BOMBSHELL REPORT

The debased condition of American medical schools at the turn of the century presented the perfect opportunity for Pritchett to test his ideas about centralization, efficiency, and standardization. Market competition had not produced high-quality medicine, nor, without regulation or incentives, had it weeded out the subpar physicians and institutions. Quite the contrary: the redundancy of institutions and lack of standards had created "confused lawlessness."[57] In the commercial world of nineteenth-century American medical education, medical schools competed for students to enroll in what was no more than two or three years of ungraded curriculum.[58] Ambitious doctors went abroad, while efforts at educational improvements occurred at home in fits and spurts. The American Medical Association was incorporated in 1897 to reform the schools, and its main achievement by 1900 was that 96 percent of medical schools required three or more years of study.[59] Pritchett saw that unregulated competition, along with lack of consequences for the worst-performing schools, was the source of the problems. He was aware that the University of Pennsylvania, home to one of the oldest medical schools in the country, attempted in 1847 to lengthen the course of study but abandoned it when competing schools refused to "fall in line."[60] Incentives for others to follow the leader would be required to achieve the sweeping transformation that the system demanded.

To effect this change Pritchett found an ally in Abraham Flexner. Like Pritchett, Flexner was a midwesterner—born in Louisville, Kentucky. Flexner was the son of German-Jewish immigrants, and his life was transformed by his undergraduate experience at Johns Hopkins and his European travels. His first study, *The American College: A Criticism*, appeared in 1908; a testy critique crafted while he was studying in Heidelberg, it presaged a grouchiness that would become characteristic of Flexner's intellect. In this case, he took to task Eliot's elective curriculum and university lectures—features that many American educators praised as contributing to America's ascent.[61] By Flexner's admission, the book "fell quite flat."[62]

When Pritchett approached Flexner in 1908 about authoring a report on medical education, Flexner assumed that Pritchett was confusing him with his brother Simon. A physician, scientist, and, since 1901, the director of the Rockefeller Institute for Medical Research, Simon Flexner would have been the more likely pick. Pritchett assured him, however, that he was not mistaken. He was drawn to Flexner's ruthlessness in *The American College* and viewed the author's lack of medical credentials as an advantage. "What I have in mind is not a medical study, but an educational one," Pritchett clarified. "Medical schools are schools and must be judged as such. . . . Henceforth, these institutions must be viewed from the standpoint of education. Are they so equipped and conducted as to be able to train students to be efficient physicians, surgeons, and so on?"[63] For Pritchett the transformation of medicine had less to do with practice than with education and required someone with a system-wide view.

Between the time when he was hired in the fall of 1908 and when he set out to conduct his research in January 1909, Flexner pored over the literature in the field, consulted with his brother Simon and the Hopkins anatomist Franklin Mall, and maintained contact with Pritchett. His visits to schools were admittedly short—he arrived and made inquiries, he compared the school's claims with the credentials of students, he scrutinized the school's source of income, and strolled through laboratories, sometimes in less than an hour. What Flexner found was shocking and occasionally humorous: small and filthy quarters with no equipment to speak of, bolted laboratory doors, and deceptive deans. In Des Moines, Flexner feigned his departure and then paid a janitor to let him through locked doors marked with different specialties—Anatomy, Physiology, and Pathology—and was horrified to discover they were each identical with only "a desk, a small blackboard, and chairs." On another occasion, when he appealed to the dean in Salem, Washington, to direct him to the physiological laboratories, the dean disappeared upstairs and returned a few moments later with an instrument in a small case that measured a pulse.[64]

Following his visits to 155 schools in the United States and Canada — since Canada provided a number of doctors for American communities — Flexner returned to New York to write his report. When the work was complete in 1910, Pritchett authorized the printing of an unprecedented fifteen thousand copies. The report was widely distributed, and Flexner was invited to speak at a number of professional meetings.[65]

Pritchett believed that what came to be known simply as "The Flexner Report" signaled the demise of for-profit medical education and unregulated competition among medical schools. In his heavy-handed introduction to the report, Pritchett announced that the task before CFAT was to determine the "safeguards as will limit the number of those who enter [the professions] to some reasonable estimate of the number who are actually needed . . . and will safeguard the right of society to the service of trained men in the great callings which touch so closely our physical and political life."[66] In his analysis, Flexner, for his part, emphasized standardization as an antidote to the uneven quality and excess quantity of medical schools. He marshaled statistical and demographic data about America and Germany: "Our forty-nine states and territories have now eighty-two different boards of medical examiners. . . . It cannot allow one set of practitioners to exist on easier and lower terms than another. . . . A single board should subject all candidates, of whatever school, to the same tests at every point."[67] While America possessed on average one doctor for every 568 people, an astronomical number of doctors that was for Flexner a sign of the failure of quality control, Germany, in contrast, maintained one doctor per 2,000 people, a ratio that the historian Friedrich Paulsen noted represented many more doctors than in the past. Of course the number of doctors was suppressed in Germany, as Flexner accounted, because there "the road to a professorship involves a period of training and of self-denial far longer and more exacting than that to which the American professor submits."[68] What America needed was fewer, better doctors, Flexner insisted; his report included maps to illustrate where the 155 schools were and how they might be reorganized and reduced.[69]

Flexner's report-cum-exposé was meant to kick-start that rationalization. And he did not hold back: Flexner found the "combination of business, religion, and pseudo-science" at Michigan's Missionary Medical College in Battle Creek "very revolting"; Bowdoin College Medical School in Portland was a "disgraceful affair"; Birmingham Medical College amounted to no more than a "joint stock company, paying annual dividends of 6%"; and the California Medical College whose "outfit in anatomy consists of a small box of bones and the dried-up filthy fragments of a single cadaver" was a "disgrace to the state whose law permits its existence."[70]

The only "bright spot" in Flexner's survey was Johns Hopkins University Medical School.[71] (Incidentally, visiting Germans, in their formal reports to Althoff, agreed with Flexner.)[72] Hopkins had, after all, under Gilman made the most "radical departure" when it founded a medical school in 1893 and modeled the new medical school, like its university, on the German example.[73] John Shaw Billings, who was Gilman's "chief advisor," designed the curriculum following a trip to Germany as librarian of the US surgeon general's office. Hopkins's curriculum distinguished itself with the "important peculiarity" of German medical education, in particular, laboratories, research, and clinical training.[74] Billings recommended entrance requirements, a four-year graded curriculum, and small classes that integrated preclinical training.[75] Billings also developed departments in pediatrics, psychiatry, public hygiene, and medical history and handpicked William H. Welch for pathology and William Osler as physician in chief, both of whom had "imbibed in Germany a zeal for research and for the freedom which this implied."[76]

While Pritchett's introduction to Flexner's report acknowledged the exceptional nature of Johns Hopkins—"It is not expected that a Johns Hopkins Medical School can be erected immediately in cities where public support of education has hitherto been meager"—he insisted on "a certain minimum of equipment and a minimum of educational requirement without which no attempt ought to be made to teach medicine."[77] Not all universities could be Johns Hopkins, but Pritchett and Flexner were unapologetic that Hopkins was the standard by which others were judged. If the inferiority of medical education amounted to a structural problem the solution would involve emulating the German centralization with the German-rooted Johns Hopkins Medical School at the core.[78]

University presidents did not enjoy Flexner's scrutiny. Flexner's report yielded complaints about the criteria for assessment from medical school deans embarrassed about how their schools had fared. In June of 1910 Pritchett and Flexner were sued for libel by the St. Louis College of Physicians and Surgeons for $100,000. In Chicago, where Flexner had recently declared that twelve of its fifteen medical schools should be shut down, he was told that if he showed up for an upcoming talk he would be shot.[79] However, Pritchett assured Flexner it was "pure bluff. The medical report is bringing us both a shower of stones and a number of good opinions."[80] Pritchett drew on his "moral authority" as a former university president to come to Flexner's defense.[81]

Once the groaning ebbed, change came swiftly. A number of medical school deans who had criticized the report publicly then went to Pritchett quietly, as he boasted to Flexner, "to consult as to what they can really do."[82] Many aspects of medicine we now take for granted date to the collective response to Flexner's report, including the high standards of admission for medical school, uniform prerequisites for medical training, and the strength of state regulation of medical licensure.[83] The core recommendation—a four-year graded curriculum with two years of basic medical sciences and two years of clinical work—was also adopted. The American Medical Association's Council on Medical Education endorsed the report and became the de facto accrediting agency through its rating system that judged schools on their ability to meet these goals. From a numerical standpoint the Flexner Report was transformative. By 1915 the number of for-profit schools had dropped to 95 from 131 five years earlier.[84] And this consolidation symbolized a wider reform in which the control of medical training was wrested from the private business of practicing medicine and placed under the governance of an academic system—a shift that ensured that training of physicians was linked to the vanguard of scientific research. These successful changes also cemented Flexner's relationship with the General Education Board (GEB), where he would spend the next thirteen years shaping the wider research landscape in America.[85]

DEMOCRACY AND ITS DISCONTENTS

Germany remained Flexner's guiding star, as it was for Pritchett, throughout his career in higher education. Flexner later recalled his first visit to Germany in 1906 with his wife, Anne, and their daughter Jean, when "with throbbing hearts" they made their way to Berlin. The theme that surfaced there and persisted was German excellence. Upon visiting a *Gymnasium* Flexner reflected, "Education must, of course, be provided for the mediocre, but not at the expense of the able." As he later reflected, the "danger of democracy" was that it "will fail to appreciate excellence, for in very truth an *aristocracy of excellence* must judge the children of the well-to-do by precisely the same standards as are applied to the children of the poor."[86] The simultaneous pursuit of excellence and commitment to the democratic values of meritocracy—in his words, achieving an "aristocracy of excellence"—would be Flexner's life's mission.

The first challenge was how to work within a democracy to compel its citizens to raise educational standards. In 1910, following the completion of his report, Flexner returned to Europe to research European medical education for a complementary survey. With one major study under his belt and two children in tow, the experience was, he recalled, "one of the richest episodes of my life." Since he was not interested in reforming the German schools, he was free to "find out the principles upon which . . . medical education had been organized, in order that I might so describe them, not that they would be imitated in America, but that, as the founders of the Johns Hopkins had done, significant features, in so far as possible, might be adapted to American conditions."[87] Pritchett assisted with introductions to ambassadors in Vienna, Paris, London, and Berlin.[88] Together with Franklin Mall, who was in Munich with his family, Flexner visited laboratories and attended lectures in Strasbourg, Munich, and elsewhere and received numerous responses to his survey concerning the ratios of clinical students and patients, the makeup of the student body, and the structure of courses.[89]

As much as institutional inspiration, what he found in Germany was an enviable political culture that revealed much about the roots of American professionalization. Once again he praised the *Gymnasium* but also noted the wise choice to maintain a separate secondary educational track in the more practically oriented *Realschule*, since "Latin and Greek make but a faint appeal to many able youths." In the German monarchy it was possible to impose requirements and tracks, yet "can our boys and girls be disciplined to work without the use of force or compulsion?" Flexner asked. He yearned for the power to make top-down change: "Organization comes relatively easy to monarchical, aristocratic, or other kinds of paternal government. They can go a long way without asking permission; they possess a good deal of initiative; within fairly large limits, they make up their minds as to what is good for the people in the interest of the governing class and 'jam it through.'"[90] As Flexner was reminded shortly after he published his survey, reform was nearly impossible to "jam through" in a democracy. That America needed education for "salvation" made it no easier to reform it. Nonetheless, Flexner insisted that the "democratic venture [would] pay."[91]

The Europeans watched intently. More than forty thousand copies of the two reports were eventually distributed across America, Britain, and the European continent, and a wave of editorials appeared—135 in response to the European report alone. Hundreds of letters addressed to Flexner arrived at the Carnegie Foundation office while he was abroad. Most read Flexner's 1910 report as praising the German system above all, but Flexner insisted that was not the case.[92] In fact, although Flexner found that in "Germany medical education was sound precisely where . . . American medical education [was] deficient," the classes there were too large, the provision of equipment too inadequate, and access to hospital beds too restricted. The Germans reluctantly began to agree, and the flow of knowledge became more bidirectional.[93]

If the impacts of German psychiatry, pathology, physiology, and bacteriology were decisive, there was one specialty in America "whose debt to Germany was always somewhat ambiguous": surgery. In this area of medicine, "Americans never needed to make apology for their skill and achievements."[94] The Civil War had given an unfortunate boost to American military surgery. Just ten years after the war, a physician from a prominent family toured European hospitals and attested to American advancements in surgery.[95] The American surgeon Richard Dewey, who volunteered for the German army in the Franco-Prussian War, favorably assessed the Americans' technique if not their tools: "The Germans are pre-eminent in deep investigation and thorough information; but in candor, one may say an American is not led to think less highly of the surgeons and surgery of his own country [i.e., America]. One who has seen and studied practical surgery in any of the chief American Hospitals will scarcely see here [i.e., in Germany] order, skillful manipulation, rapidity and brilliance in as great a degree as he is accustomed to see at home."[96] By the time Flexner's report appeared, Europeans and foreign students were traveling to New York and Chicago to witness with their own eyes the "order, skillful manipulation, rapidity and brilliance" of American surgeons.[97]

The main medical journal in Germany, the *Deutsche Medizinische Wochenschrift*, ran a regular common *Amerikanische Briefe* with dispatches from traveling doctors that reflected growing interest in—and fear about—American medical advancements. When German doctors visited America in the 1890s they already noted features of the American system that they admired, including the privately funded hospitals with their impressive equipment, records, and routines, and compulsory attendance for students.[98] Upon returning from a visit to America, Julius Hirschberg, a German-Jewish eye surgeon, wrote of his "conviction" that "we can learn much from the Americans—just as they can from us."[99] Needless to say, when such luminaries in German medicine as Ehrlich and Koch arrived, they received a "hero's welcome" in Baltimore and New York. They also repaid the favor. Thanking Carnegie for a gift to his institute, Koch was said to have remarked, regarding sanitation and public hygiene in New York, "You must admit that most of the scientific discoveries in this area were made in Germany. But I must admit that you here in America, especially in New York, are far ahead of us in their practical application."[100]

In 1910, the Munich surgeon Fritz Lange was so impressed by the more than three hundred beds in the Boston hospital available for orthopedic cases, compared with the fewer than fifty at home, that he raised doubts about the superiority of German medicine.[101] For Lange, Americans were a young people for whom "lack of tradition" was a disadvantage and an advantage. "Intellectual, social, and political problems are solved so much faster there than here. This is why traveling to America is such a fascinating experience," wrote Lange. "The more Germans visit America, the better for us. We can learn so much from the Americans!"[102] Of surgery Flexner's biographer observed, "It was once more a case of American dependence on Europe for the theoretical foundations of a science, while excelling in the practical application of new knowledge to concrete situations. . . . Truly, the medical exchange between America and Germany was no longer a one-way proposition!"[103]

American and German doctors—like engineers and scientists—increasingly valued a higher level of professionalism. Just as Pritchett's elevation of engineering from the mechanical arts to a profession gave Klein the impetus to lobby for the PhD for the technical schools, a similar condition made American dentistry the envy of German dentists. In fact, so many German dental students came to America to study before 1914 and subsequently adapted what they learned to Germany that the Berlin dental clinic of American expatriate Willoughby Dayton Miller became a center for modern German dentistry.[104] When in 1884 the University of Berlin opened a dental institute, the director observed, "Many of these students would have gone to America to study at the place where modern dentistry has been raised to such great significance, if they had not found opportunity in the Institute to learn scientific and practical dentistry."[105] While in America dentistry was elevated to the level of medicine, in Germany it was considered one of the mechanical arts, a categorization that doomed it to less support and lower status. Even if Flexner could not see this comparative advantage and called for a "fearless investigation of the dental schools," American dentistry in fact was the world leader.[106] As a counterpoint to medicine, dentistry underscores how the professionalization of a specialty—rather than anything deterministic in one country—could be the source of superiority.

Research and travel in Germany helped Flexner clarify his thoughts on knowledge transfer. "The importance to us of German methods is quite independent of their and our relative greatness," he mused in an article in the *Atlantic* in 1913.[107] In other words, Germany no longer represented the standard so much as standardization. As Flexner explained, "[A] wise and powerful government had drawn a sharp line below which no medical school can live."[108] Implementing that kind of standardization and accountability in the United States became Flexner's and Pritchett's shared strategy.

The Flexner Report had a ripple effect across the professions. Other fields would soon (willingly or not) be subjected to similar training reforms. Even though law schools had begun their reform ten years earlier, the dean of Harvard Law School was so impressed by the results of Flexner's report that in 1913 he wrote to Carnegie and inquired if they would fund a similar investigation for law. Aspiring lawyers and law professors like future US Supreme Court justice Felix Frankfurter admired Flexner and advocated for the law to be professionalized as had medicine.[109] The result eight years later was a report that called for a reduction in the number of law schools and standardization of training—a more difficult feat in a more fragmented field.[110] Business schools soon followed and subsequently urged the introduction of "scientific management" in organization.[111]

But professionalization was not good for everyone. Humanists on both sides of the Atlantic bemoaned the degradation of the humanities implicit in the new definitions of science that were linked to practical application. Previously combined in the meaning of the German term *Wissenschaft*, the natural sciences and humanities now seemed to be parting ways. By separating the BA from the professional schools, Eliot for his part may have made a "devil's bargain": as he saved the liberal arts he redefined them as merely pre-professional. To be sure, Eliot did not disallow classics, art history, or literature, but his elevation of the administrative sciences would have the long-term consequence of making the humanistic fields preparatory and subservient to the graduate professional training that followed.[112]

The elevation of standards for professors degraded those for secondary school teachers and hurt those—notably African Americans and women— for whom teaching in high school was the only professional option as educators. And since academic leaders viewed the entrance of women into a profession as evidence of its lower status, this motivated sexist and discriminatory policies.[113] In fact, the ambiguities of professionalization are revealed in Flexner's observations about African Americans and women in the report. Since women's choices were now "free and varied," Flexner concluded in his 1910 report, separate education for women was not necessary. Society opened a professional door for women; it had no obligation to open all of them, such as a career path for female doctors. It was a position that placed tacit confidence in merit and overlooked the obstacles women faced to gain access to the newly elevated institutions.[114]

Flexner's attitude toward "negro education" similarly reflected the paternalism that became the primary feature of northern philanthropies that vied to control the education of African Americans and the historically black colleges and universities (HBCUs). Despite any original good intentions, these foundations, including Rockefeller's GEB, the Carnegie Corporation, and the Rosenwald Fund, would all be cowed by southern interests in maintaining segregation.[115] Since African Americans were more likely to be "taken in" by deceptive and inadequate schools, Flexner reasoned, and only two of the seven medical schools devoted to African American education—Howard and Meharry—were worth saving, "nothing will be gained by way of satisfying the need or of rising to the opportunity through the survival of feeble, ill equipped institutions quite regardless of the spirit which animates the promoters."[116]

The Flexner Report was only the first in a series of reports ostensibly focused on standards that would adversely impact HBCUs. Since most of the black medical colleges were unable to fund the changes Flexner demanded, they were in effect regulated out of existence.[117] To force the "undeserving" institutions to close was certainly the desire of another report, authored by William Buttrick of the Rockefeller-funded GEB, begun in 1907 and published ten years later. In paying lip service to African American education, a report like Buttrick's placed Du Bois in a bind. As a German-trained sociologist and proponent of Greek and Latin instruction and rigorous standards, Du Bois tried to persuade philanthropists like Rockefeller to fund not only industrial, but also liberal arts education for African Americans. While he hoped to gain support for the best black colleges, however, the cost of working with a foundation with more aggressive social Darwinist intentions would be the obsolescence of some black-serving institutions, which, like the mediocre medical schools, didn't make the cut.[118]

In the widespread efforts toward professionalization, the "losers" were schools on the geographic and institutional periphery that were forced to close. Advocates of the medical schools with lower standards emphasized the need they fulfilled—in particular, providing physicians for rural America.[119] One could have said the same of the "subpar" black colleges. Critics of the Flexner Report expressed legitimate concern that if schools like Chattanooga Medical College were eliminated, there would be no doctors to serve the communities surrounding them. Flexner always responded that the poor medical school did not serve the poor man but only itself.[120] But demographically speaking, advocates for Chattanooga and similar schools had a point. And sometimes a school with a "lower standard" like that in Louisville produced a Simon Flexner, as one editorialist pointed out—a single accomplishment that "justified its existence."[121]

Flexner was attuned to the accusations of the antidemocratic strand in his reforms and insisted that a "spontaneous dispersion" would spread graduates of top medical schools around the country. As it turned out, however, doctors gravitated to wealthier areas, and a 1920 study showed that the distribution of physicians was correlated with per capita income.

Disparities between urban and rural medicine only widened over time.[122] Despite these realities, the Flexner Report established a pattern that Pritchett pursued ruthlessly as president of CFAT: he aimed to elevate the best universities and institutes devoted to research at the expense of those on the edges.

The much-lauded German model of professionalization cast a shadow on a system that was simultaneously beginning to embrace meritocracy.[123] Education reform was certainly easier to implement in a monarchy than in a democracy, where voluntary associations were required for change. But the educational systems in Germany and America also did vastly different work for their respective political cultures. As Flexner admitted, "Education has therefore in a democracy a positive function in reference to an ideal hoped for, as against a negative function in reference to a status already established."[124]

With an increasing awareness of the elitist implications of professionalization, academic leaders shifted their rhetoric to emphasize the public service that these professions performed. "The medical profession has before it an entrancing prospect of usefulness and honor," Eliot announced to the Medical Society of the State of New York. "It offers to young men the largest opportunities for disinterested, devoted, and heroic service. The times are past when men had to go to war to give evidence of endurance, or courage, or capacity to think quickly and well under pressure of responsibility and danger. The fields open to the physician and surgeon now give ample scope for these lofty qualities."[125] "Service" to society was a rhetorical strategy that accompanied professionalization and solidified institutional and social hierarchies.[126]

The Flexner Report and its aftermath made clear that the decentralized, free-market system that Weber had observed on his 1904 visit to America continued to present opportunities for innovation while also being the source of new anxieties. In the field of medicine the free market, left to its own devices, did not mitigate the shortcomings of meritocracy and the role of higher education in reinforcing the power of the elite; if anything, it exacerbated them. Concerned that the free market did not necessarily promote excellence, such American education reformers as Flexner and Pritchett would advocate, beyond medical schools, for external measures to ensure that American universities would become the paragons of quality that German institutions represented.

To reach this goal Pritchett and Flexner emphasized the pursuit of excellence over any systematic attention to the democratization of the German model for its use in America. In so doing, they fulfilled Weber's prediction about how technical expertise would replace inherited privilege: "The role played in former days by the 'proof of ancestry' as a prerequisite for equality of birth . . . is nowadays taken by the patent of education. The elaboration of diplomas from universities, business and engineering colleges and the universal clamor for the creation of further educational certificates in all fields serve the formation of the privileged stratum in bureaus and in offices."[127] Insofar as universities now decided whom to admit, certified graduates, and defined competence through their curricula, these institutions became the new gatekeepers.

They would become responsible for maintaining what the sociologist Randall Collins, inspired by Weber, termed in 1979 our "credential society"—a society "stratified around an educational credential system with a stranglehold on occupational opportunities and a technocratic ideology that cannot stand close examination."[128] The conservative core of the system the elite university presidents and educational reformers admired was not shed in its American garb. To the extent that American higher education retained much of the German elitism, the preservation of privilege countered any new opportunities the market provided. This proved a winning combination for American higher education as a system if not for all of its individuals and institutions.

CHAPTER SIX

CARNEGIE, CAPITAL, AND THE KAISER

All history testifies to the gradual up-building of universities by individual benefactions. . . . Private philanthropy will do all it can, but public interest demands that the State should do its part.

HERBERT BAXTER ADAMS, 1889

Scholarship has reached the point in its expansion and in its workings in which the state can no longer be responsible for its needs. Developing forms of cooperation between the state and wealthy, academically inclined members of the community should now be on the agenda.

ADOLF VON HARNACK, 1909

"Research in the natural sciences always secures the base for technical progress," wrote the scientist-entrepreneur and philanthropist Werner von Siemens in 1883. "Never will a national industry arrive at an internationally leading position, if the same country does not lead in the sciences."[1] Increasingly sharing Siemens's assessment of the scientific "competition" among nations, academic and industry leaders alike became so enthusiastic about the economic potential of science that by the first decade of the twentieth century, research began to find an institutional home outside the confines of the university, in Germany and the United States.[2] With new specialties and applications requiring bigger teams, larger spaces, and more money, science was outgrowing the ability of universities to support it.[3]

In rethinking the funding and sites of advanced research in the first decade of the twentieth century, the United States played the role of transatlantic innovator. Americans were becoming leaders in applying research to spur economic development and project international power. Philanthropy funded much of these efforts. In 1901, Andrew Carnegie began devoting his fortune to institutions of science and scholarship, drawing attention on both sides of the Atlantic.[4] "The readiness of the American to give," declared the Harvard psychologist Münsterberg, "is in every case the secret of American success."[5]

Motivated as ever by one-upmanship in the decades leading up to World War I, Germany now looked to America for iterations of the model it had invented a century earlier in Berlin. They saw private philanthropic support of science as the innovation most worthy of emulation. Not to be out-done, Althoff planned a group of research institutes modeled on Carnegie's example, and these, seeded in 1911 by the emperor, became the Kaiser Wilhelm (later, Max Planck) Institutes.[6] Ironically, the different ways these developments unfolded in the two countries meant that the German-born modern university model would be best preserved in the United States, providing the foundation for the Americans to solidify their lead in the global knowledge economy.

A DOME FOR THE TEMPLE

Although at the end of the nineteenth century a smaller number of Americans were going to Germany to earn higher degrees, the flow was nevertheless substantial. Thus when German education administrators expressed frustration with the varying levels of preparation of American students seeking entry into German universities, US academic administrators listened. Having studied in Germany, the president of the University of California, Benjamin Ide Wheeler, described to President Seth Low of Columbia the obstacles to the exchange of students with Germans: "At present no adequate uniformity exists in the requirements for admission to the various schools of our own country, nor in the standard of graduate work which lead to the higher degrees."[7] Wheeler believed that establishing standards would, in turn, promote American students' acceptance abroad. In this respect, international pressure forced a domestic reckoning with the questions of hierarchy and systematization, the same inspiration that moved Pritchett, Eliot, and Flexner, with his Carnegie-backed landmark report.

The need for standardization spurred the creation of a new professional organization: the Association of American Universities (AAU). In the letter of invitation to this new initiative, sent in 1900 by Eliot, Gilman, Harper, Low, and Wheeler to nine colleagues at the nation's leading institutions, one hears the impatience: "The time has arrived when the leading American Universities may properly consider the means of representing to foreign Universities the importance of revising their regulations governing the admission of American students to the examinations for the higher degrees." The signatories sought "credit as legitimately due" American students, and "to protect the dignity of our Doctor's degrees."[8] In other words, they wanted Americans to be treated on equal scholarly terms—and they wanted a seat at the international table of learning.

While the academic leaders might have begun their conversations about the AAU focused on the rather mundane issues of standards in admissions and graduation, they quickly saw an opportunity to realize a greater ambition— *high* standards. And in the pursuit of academic excellence, not all of America's universities were quite up to snuff. Wheeler hoped that the association they were proposing would elevate the weaker institutions and exclude those that didn't measure up from "counting" among these elites. Given the American respect for the diversity of institutions, not everyone was initially supportive. But ultimately Wheeler persuaded them of the benefits of the "greater uniformity of the conditions." Following their efforts, the Germans recognized the American bachelor's degree as the equivalent of the *Abitur* (provided that it came from an AAU member institution). It represented a turning point in German-American scholarly exchange and it made the AAU into an accrediting agency.[9]

The founders of the AAU set a high bar for institutional qualification in their elite organization. Their standards left them open, though, to charges of exclusivity. The question arose as to whose responsibility and privilege it was to make judgments about those credentials. Could the association be broad enough to justify its representative status but remain narrow enough to maintain high standards associated with the research universities? And if there were to be standards for membership, who would determine them and what would they be? In fact the organization's selectiveness so dismayed some that when the 1903 AAU meeting was held in New York and scholars from New York University were invited to attend, they adamantly declined and accused the group of elitism.[10]

In the American academic leaders' preoccupation with standardization they had arrived at a conflict that would come to define the higher education landscape in the early twentieth century and beyond: how to balance the desire for quality and excellence with concern about access. In the debate about standardization, the elite institutions of the AAU were pitted against those that served a wider constituency. This occurred against the backdrop of regional battles between the eastern and western schools and new issues provoked by increased ethnic diversity due to immigration. To respond to the growing power of the elite schools, presidents of other institutions of higher learning had already begun to organize along professional and regional lines by founding the Association of American Agricultural Colleges and Experimental Stations (1887) and the National Association of State Universities (1895).[11] Building coalitions at the regional level was one way to oppose centers of power.

Out of the movement to counter the influence of the AAU came a drive to establish a national university. Its proponents argued that such a university could better standardize American higher education without the elite universities being in control. The main supporters were the presidents of nonelite schools, including the governor of Wyoming and president of its first university, John Wesley Hoyt. In the last quarter of the nineteenth century Hoyt became the spokesman for a university in a "federal city" and found a compatriot in Henry Pritchett, the director of CFAT.

The national university as envisioned by Hoyt and Pritchett would accomplish what many had hoped for Hopkins—a "dome" for the American temple of learning and a center of American culture and science. Flexner and Pritchett worried that Hopkins would remain an exception. Moreover, while Hopkins had received substantial domestic admiration, it never became America's national university in the way that the universities of Berlin and Paris did. One of the unresolved issues for the American system of higher education remained, as Gilman announced in 1893 at the Columbian Exposition in Chicago, "the establishment of a university in the Federal City," which would serve as the scholarly center of America.[12] A new national university was needed as an exemplar.

When he stepped down from the presidency in 1902, Gilman conceded the lack of an undisputed American academic center.[13] As the director of a new organization established and lavishly funded by Andrew Carnegie, Gilman would get another chance to make the case for such an institution. As we have seen, Carnegie nurtured aspirations to further research excellence. Though the AAU represented wealthy research universities, the organization possessed limited funds and had minimal regulatory impact. Carnegie had the potential, in contrast, to use his resources to effect major change in the American system. Carnegie's new institution would become the touchstone for debates about federalism, research organization, and international competition.

MONEY, MONEY, MONEY

America looms large in the history of philanthropy. Writing in 1888, the British academic James Bryce, who would later serve as ambassador to the United States, observed, "Not only are the sums collected for all sorts of philanthropic purposes larger relatively to the wealth of America than in any European country, but the amount of personal effort devoted to them seems to a European visitor to exceed what he knows at home."[14] In the two decades between 1878 and 1898 private donation to higher education totaled at least $140 million.[15] Much of the money donated in this period was given to local causes.[16] Enterprising German academic entrepreneurs like Felix Klein and university presidents like Karl Lamprecht saw this fundraising firsthand and aimed to recreate it in their own communities. Already a savvy fundraiser, Lamprecht found financial support outside Saxony to fund his own institute at the University of Leipzig in 1907 and establish the new field of cultural history. When he became rector of the university in 1910, he applied these skills at a larger scale. His outgoing address, in which he enumerated the donors he had cultivated, reads like a contemporary report to an American university board of trustees.[17]

Private philanthropy demonstrates how the scholarly exchanges of the pre-First World War period went beyond merely sharing ideas. When Pierpont Morgan announced in 1912 a gift of $50,000 to the University of Göttingen, where he had fond memories of being a student, the philanthropic model itself traversed the Atlantic. Europeans must have worried that the "Morganeering" of their art, which wealthy Americans like Morgan were buying in bulk, was now encroaching on their other store of cultural capital—higher education.[18] In an earlier period, the rich had devoted money to founding universities like Hopkins, Stanford, and Chicago; in the early twentieth century, philanthropic gifts went to existing universities or independent agencies. For this development Carnegie himself was largely responsible.

Carnegie had begun to chart his philanthropic path in the last decade of the nineteenth century. A writer from youth, he outlined his ideas about the best uses of private money for the public good in a series of articles, beginning in 1889. The most famous of these became known as "The Gospel of Wealth." He wrote: "The best means of benefiting the community is to place within its reach the ladders upon which the aspiring can rise . . . [and] in this manner returning their surplus wealth to the mass of their fellows in the forms best calculated to do them lasting good."[19] Late in 1900, Carnegie wrote the mayor of Pittsburgh encouraging him to establish technical schools and offering supplemental support: "For many years I have nursed the pleasing thought that I might be the fortunate giver of a Technical Institute to our City fashioned upon the best models, for I know of no institution which Pittsburg, as an industrial center, so much needs."[20] For those models Carnegie looked to Great Britain and Germany, in particular Charlottenburg in Berlin, home to the Technical University: "Nothing in Pittsburgh will be one of Greater usefulness."[21] For Carnegie international exchange was meant to promote local and regional hubs rather than centralize resources nationally. Moreover, trade in ideas and not just goods, Carnegie believed, would eventually lead to not only a more prosperous world but also a more peaceful one.

In 1901, Carnegie's charitable horizon expanded, and he announced his intention to endow an institution, the Carnegie Institution of Washington, with $10 million (to which he would add another $12 million by 1911).[22] An influx of this kind of money presented opportunities to American scientific leaders. Although charitable gifts in the year of 1902 amounted to more than $17 million, funds specifically marked for scientific research amounted to less than $3 million.[23] With resources at the scale of Carnegie's directed specifically to science, it would be possible to make America the international center of scientific research, a role Germany had held in the previous century.

But how would the goal of strengthening research in the United States be best accomplished? Would it be in a university or in some separate organization? Spread geographically or lavished on an exceptional institution in a knowledge capital? For those who supported a national university in America as an answer to its "inferior position" in the scientific world, Carnegie's philanthropic ambition seemed to present an opportunity, and they began to lobby Carnegie for their cause.[24] Carnegie for his part was initially moved "to fulfill one of Washington's dearest wishes—to establish a university in Washington."[25] But he proved impressionable to both sides of the argument. The institution that arose as a solution to the quandary reveals cultural differences between America and Germany concerning the relationship between the center and periphery and differing assumptions about economic and scientific competition.

The national university camp was promoted by those who believed that the only way to compete internationally was to build a research institution that would rival the great centers in Europe. Leading advocates included Hoyt as well as the American historian and first president of Cornell University Andrew Dickson White, who also sought a graduate institution in Washington, DC.[26] Then there were the skeptics—including Charles D. Walcott, director of the US Geological Survey; John Shaw Billings, the physician who modernized the library of the US surgeon general and developed the New York Public Library; and Robert Woodward, a civil engineer who succeeded Gilman as president of the Carnegie Institution in Washington—who doubted that universities were "the home of science." Unpersuaded that the German scientific system was right for them, they looked to other foreign models—namely, the Royal Institution of Great Britain, whose laboratories were home to such great scientists as Humphry Davy and Michael Faraday.[27]

Hoyt's argument was predicated on a critique of American federalism that excessively protected regional centers. While political centralization was "fatal if carried to a certain limit," Hoyt believed educational centralization "a prerequisite to that diffusion of knowledge which insures health and security to every part of the body politic."[28] Indeed by putting a representative from each state on its governing board, a national university would provide a safeguard *against* the unequal distribution of knowledge, and in particular the marginalization of nonelite institutions and newer cities.[29] Committed to laissez-faire principles, however, Harvard's president Charles Eliot shuddered at the un-American idea of the national government being involved in controlling an American institution of higher education, especially if it were meant to promote republican principles.

Known for the "Massachusetts method," or private donor method, Eliot believed that control over the character and financing of education should be the domain of private citizens.[30] Mocking as "childish" the inferiority complex that motivated the national university's supporters, Eliot assured, "As American life grows more various and richer in sentiment, passion, thought, and accumulated experience, American literature will become rich and more abounding; and, in that better day, let us hope that there will be found several universities in America, though by no means one in each state, as free, liberal, rich, national, and glorious as the warmest advocate of a single, crowning university at the national capital could imagine his desired institution to become."[31] Columbia University president Nicholas Murray Butler echoed Eliot's argument with his characteristically acerbic rhetoric—a national university would be "an educational blunder of the first magnitude."[32]

No doubt Eliot's trepidation, like Butler's, was motivated in no small part by fear of the competition that such a generously endowed institution would bring for their own institutions. The divide that emerged in these debates was largely (though not exclusively) that between the private elite university presidents and those, like Hoyt and Edmund James, who were or would become presidents of state universities. These presidents of institutions on the periphery knew that a national university, with the symbolic advantage of the nation's capital as its home, could be a good check on the elite universities' power and could potentially redistribute cultural influence more evenly across the country. Pressed by Eliot about his disparaging remarks concerning the current conditions of the American university, Hoyt argued that Eliot was disingenuous, given how much of Harvard's success rested on the shoulders (and subsidies) of Boston, Massachusetts, and the nation.[33] Hoyt was, however, perhaps overly optimistic or else naïve when he suggested that "opposition based on local ambitions will also disappear when a just view is taken of the relation that is normally sustained by a central and national post-graduate university to all other institutions."[34] Butler and Eliot were not interested, and their "local ambition" did not disappear.[35]

Carnegie shared Eliot's and Butler's antipathy to greater competition. As an industrialist and monopolist in business, Carnegie clearly identified the advantages of centralization as a corporate strategy. But how did that apply to higher education? Was a national university an appropriate counterbalance to the unequal distribution of cultural capital across the states? Or was it a statist move to deny private citizens the right to shape their own institutions of learning? We have already seen how Carnegie likely supported Pritchett in his attempt to merge Harvard and MIT, so it is consistent that he suggested a compromise that would incorporate Hopkins into a new institution in Washington, thereby eliminating some redundancy. In written correspondence, White tried in vain to assure Carnegie that competition on a state level, such as that between Berkeley and Stanford, was not unproductive.[36] After meeting with Carnegie, Hoyt expressed his bitter disappointment that despite Carnegie's interest in the national university idea, he had "library on the brain." Hoyt must have seen the writing on the wall— that without a national university, a natural monopoly would arise among elite private institutions of higher learning that would hurt regional public universities like his. Unfortunately for Hoyt, Carnegie had been "made to think that . . . [a national university] would injure existing institutions."[37]

Carnegie was also increasingly influenced by his European counterparts. Thanking him for his $10 million endowment for Scottish universities in the summer of 1901, Arthur James Balfour, who was soon to be prime minister, wrote to Carnegie, "We ought to regard our Universities not merely as places where the best kind of knowledge already attained is imparted, but as places where the stock of the world's knowledge may be augmented. One discovery . . . may do far more for mankind than the most excellent teaching of what is already known, absolutely necessary to national welfare as this latter is."[38] Carnegie's elevation of research over teaching was evident to leading American educational reformers who that June established the Washington Memorial Institution, a supra-institutional research organization that they hoped Carnegie would fund.[39] Following a meeting with Gilman and Billings that November, Carnegie produced the first draft plan for an institution devoted to research. So much confusion persisted over the institution's purpose, however, that newspapers erroneously reported the development with the headline: "Carnegie founds new university."[40]

As the excitement mounted in the summer and fall of 1901 around Carnegie's largest benefaction to date, the question of how the institution would be configured—as a national university or as a center of research support—came to the fore. The mistake in the newspaper opened the door to continual suggestions and counter-suggestions; Hoyt even thanked Carnegie, believing he had prevailed. The first meeting of the institution's board—consisting of twenty-seven men selected by Carnegie—convened in Washington in January 1902 with Gilman now acting as the institution's president.[41] Carnegie finally announced his highly anticipated decision: "Because one of the objections—the most serious one, which I could not overcome . . . was this: That it might tend to weaken existing institutions, while my desire was to cooperate with all kindred institutions, and to establish what would be a source of strength to all of them and not of weakness, . . . therefore I abandoned the idea of a Washington University of anything of a memorial character."[42] The university presidents Eliot and Butler seemed to have gotten their way.

On January 4, 1902, the Carnegie Institution was incorporated as an independent funding agency "to conduct, endow, and assist investigation in any department of science, literature, or art, and to this end to cooperate with governments, universities, colleges, technical schools, learned societies, and individuals." Among the goals enumerated were to "promote original research," "to discover the exceptional man," and "to increase the efficiency of the Universities."[43] Between the November draft plan and the Deed of Trust, however, the statement supporting universities went from first to fourth place, while the charge "to promote original research" moved to the first position. Moreover, what was initially meant to be the "Carnegie National Institution for Research" morphed into the "Carnegie Institution" and then the "Carnegie Institution of Washington," reflecting the debate over whom it served—nations, states, or localities. In the end, the establishment of the Carnegie Institution weakened, if it did not completely halt, the national university movement, and therefore played a role in countering centralization, and ensuring the diversity that has become a hallmark of the American higher education system.[44]

In the debate that emerged in the eight-month fact-finding period that Carnegie initiated upon founding the institution Germany loomed large as the model to emulate and as the nation with which to compete. The report of chemist Theodore W. Richards (the first American to receive a Nobel Prize in Chemistry) about America's appalling research conditions provoked frustration among the scholarly reformers, who felt it did not accurately represent their institutions. Ira Remsen, who succeeded Gilman as the president of Johns Hopkins, further argued that the status of German research was exaggerated by the report's focus on Berlin, which was not representative of Germany's universities on the periphery. Moreover, at Hopkins anyway, Remsen assured, professors were free from routine teaching and administrative work. "I am gradually getting the impression that the only truly overworked men in America are the Harvard men," Remsen commented sarcastically.[45]

Notwithstanding Remsen's condescension, his observation touched on an important recognition. The conditions for scholarly productivity were not only to be measured internally at one institution or another, but also across institutions. The collective research output was the determining factor for the system's success. As Münsterberg noted, the most meaningful difference in his adopted home was the "supporting activity in the periphery of the national circle as over against the German governmental support. In Germany the aid came in centrifugal paths, in America in centripetal ones." For this German-born and trained scholar, too much "external" money would discourage alumni from giving to their universities; that is, it would weaken the local base, which "not only sums up in the long run to a much greater result than any single central aid, but it is also more wholesome, more educative, more adjustable, more American."[46] It is ironic that in this era of consolidation of wealth and industry, Weber would concede, after visiting America in 1904, that America's advantage was its healthy domestic competition among localities. Viewing the decentralized design of American higher education through Weber's eyes underscores how higher education was not reducible to mere corporate capitalism. Whether it was accidental or not, healthy local competition encouraged innovation and offered benefits that went far beyond the material.[47]

Münsterberg's observations further raised a set of questions that were as much about comparison as exchange. In the last quarter of the nineteenth century Americans' confidence was growing. As the American sociologist Lester M. Ward already boasted in 1885, "It [cannot] be considered un-American for the government to encourage and actively prosecute scientific researches. . . . In this respect we are becoming the envy of European nations, and they are just now beginning to learn from us that it is sound national policy."[48] The creation of the Carnegie Institution exemplified that self-assuredness. The physicist, former president of MIT, and current president of CFAT Henry Pritchett put it bluntly in 1903: "Germans need fear in the industrial world neither the Englishman nor the Frenchman, only the American."[49] The distinction between Ward and Pritchett is significant, however, for the two drew different conclusions from the investment in the new social scientists. Ward was part of a group of transatlantic-oriented reform-minded sociologists who sought to mitigate the inequalities that resulted from such crude social Darwinist thinking as practiced by Pritchett and Carnegie. It is not a coincidence that he was married to one of the few female sociologists, Elizabeth "Lizzie" Vought, and the two fought for solutions to social problems (including women's rights) through what he called "sociocracy." Ward's social-reform version of Progressive-Era social science did not win out.[50]

Carnegie and other Americans remained more concerned about the consequences of scholarly competition in the international realm. In his 1902 address at St. Andrews in Scotland, Carnegie presented to the British the ascent of the Germans, who held a special place in his intellectual and his geopolitical views: "It is in [the German] workmen that the Continent has one of its chief advantages over Britain, and America over the Continent."[51] Reflecting in 1913 on his decade-long friendship with the Kaiser, Carnegie recalled their meeting at the Kiel Regatta in 1907 at which they bonded over the Scottish tradition.[52] To be sure, Carnegie had his reasons in 1913 for praising the "peace-preserving German Emperor" and "born leader of men," and his exaggerated descriptions of the emperor's lifelong service to the "Federation of Europe" read like wishful thinking at a moment when repeated crises threatened to plunge the world into war.[53] Carnegie also had much to admire in the German emperor's support for the agricultural sciences and social services.[54] This transatlantic *Wissenstransfer* reveals that America and Germany shared both the Progressive Era's response to social questions and the bellicose ambitions of late imperial rivals.

GERMANY RESPONDS

Carnegie's ideas had already had a considerable impact in Europe before news of his institution reached its shores. Carnegie's first essays, "The Gospel of Wealth" and "The Best Fields of Philanthropy," had sparked such a robust debate in England concerning the proper response to the "social question" that even the prime minister was moved to respond.[55] These essays were translated into German in 1894, just five years after they first appeared.[56] A German translation of Carnegie's *The Empire of Business*, published in English in 1902, followed in 1903 as the *Kaufmanns Herrschergewalt*, while an English version for German students appeared in 1911 alongside only William Shakespeare and Herbert Spencer.[57] The significance of Carnegie's gospel was manifest, but just where the Germans fit, with their very different relationship between state and society and role for the university, which for Carnegie "[stood] apart by itself" as a "field for philanthropy," was less certain.[58]

Wilhelm II, the powerful and unpredictable king of Prussia and German emperor from 1888 to 1918, loved to surround himself with wealth. As the historian Lamar Cecil observed in his multivolume biography, "There was more than a trace of jealousy in the Kaiser, who resented the ability of American magnates to buy anything they wanted, from British steamship lines to European art and divas for New York's Metropolitan Opera." Wilhelm II entertained these new wealthy American, including J.P. Morgan, Vanderbilt, Drexel and others with Scandinavian cruises, regattas, and hunting expeditions and even adorned Morgan with a high decorations in exchange for a gift of a letter by Martin Luther to a Reformation museum in Wittenberg. Morgan for his part offered no more than a reticent endorsement: "[The Kaiser] pleases me," he reportedly said.[59]

Farsighted German reformers saw an opportunity in American-style techniques of private financing, and welcomed Carnegie's gospel as a source of guidance.[60] In early 1902, a report appeared in the *Hochschulnachrichten*, the main German higher education publication, about the imminent founding of the Carnegie Institution.[61] The following year, the theologian and scholarly reformer Harnack, published "Carnegies Schrift über die Pflicht der Reichen" in the *Allgemeine Zeitung* in Munich, in which he praised the American philanthropist's energy and zeal. But he also cautioned that Carnegie's philanthropic model would face challenges taking root in Germany because of "what stands in the way of the realization of these 'duties of wealth,' both generally and in our country, and where the commitment of people falls short and which statutory provisions could enable donations of any amount." He refrained, however, from "weakening the enthusiasm" of readers, since it "would be petty to do so, and contain a lesson that the author [i.e., Carnegie] does not require."[62]

The "almighty" Prussian education director Althoff, together with his circle of advisers, worried about what American education philanthropy and Carnegie's Gospel of Wealth meant for the international standing of German science. He sent Harnack's article to leading Prussian bureaucrats as well as the Kaiser, with whom he had developed a relationship. Though the Kaiser had conservative taste in art, was deeply antisemitic, and self-absorbed and insecure, Wilhelm II also considered himself a "modern man" who understood the significance of applied science for Germany's future as a leading military and industrial nation. He was increasingly receptive to Althoff's arguments for funding science and reportedly declared to him in 1902, "The new century will be ruled by science, including technology and not by philosophy as was its predecessor."[63] The Prince of Eulenburg, the Kaiser's close friend who became notorious when he was outed as homosexual, accused Wilhelm II of being drawn to inventors only for their wealth. But the historian Cecil reminds us that the emperor's two favorites, the aircraft pioneer Count Ferdinand von Zeppelin and the inventor of the X-ray Wilhelm Röntgen, made no money on their inventions. Nonetheless, when Röntgen discovered the X-ray in 1906, the Kaiser sent him a personal telegram with the message, "I praise God for granting our German fatherland this new triumph of science." As historian Fritz Stern wrote, there was "the whole legitimating dogma in one sentence."[64]

In 1907 the Office of Ministerial Academic Information, which Althoff had founded when he launched the German-American exchange professorship, had troubling news that would ultimately spur the Kaiser to more than mere rhetorical support.[65] The office had been tracking developments in research and higher education abroad. That year the office published a report listing nineteen privately funded research institutions that the Education Ministry should take note of, including the Pasteur Institute in Paris, the Norwegian Nobel Institute, the Rockefeller Institute for Medical Research in New York, and the Carnegie Institution in Washington.[66] Though he retired because of ill health in 1907, Althoff was, at the time of his premature death the following year, strategizing Berlin's answer to Pasteur and Rockefeller.

After a visit from Klein, Althoff's collaborator in uniting science and industry in Göttingen, Althoff developed plans for turning Dahlem, the southwest inner suburb of Berlin, into a protoresearch park devoted to science.[67] Intrigued by this idea and eager to win support from a discontented middle class, the Kaiser charged Friedrich Schmidt-Ott and the chief of his Civil Cabinet, Rudolf von Valentini, with synthesizing the late Althoff's plans.[68] According to Schmidt-Ott, Althoff had apparently discussed with the director of the Zoologische Museum, August Brauer, the possibility of using the Museum of Natural History as a classroom for the people, and dedicating the Ethnology Museum, the Institute for Oriental Science, and other spaces exclusively to research. The plans presumed that professors who held a university chair could not bear the double assignment of research and teaching.[69]

Harnack was uniquely attuned to German industrialists' growing interest in the academic world. Harnack's meteoric rise as an evangelical theologian and leader reflected the ascent of critical historical study of the Bible—and his strategic acumen. In 1890, he was offered membership in the Prussian Academy of Science, and his lectures in 1899 on the essence of Christianity attracted more than six hundred students. He also served as director of the Prussian National Library from 1905 to 1921. His outsized salary reflected that he was both a highly valued scholar and an effective negotiator.[70] In 1914 Harnack would be ennobled by Wilhelm II, and in America, where he retained a significant presence following his visit of 1904, he would be posthumously elected to the Society of Biblical Literature and Exegesis. The New York press eulogized him as "much more than a great scholar and critic, he is a great man."[71]

Harnack's professional and public position was complemented by a carefully cultivated private world that exemplified progressive Protestant intellectualism. He married Amalie Thiersch, a Catholic from Munich who was raised Protestant and was the granddaughter of the celebrity scientist Justus von Liebig. "Much more than his reader," Amalie, together with

Adolf, hosted a weekly coffee *klatsch* that included Amalie's sister Lina and brother-in-law Hans Delbrück, Germany's leading military historian and former tutor to the royal family, and Karl Bonhoeffer, psychiatrist and father to Dietrich Bonhoeffer, who would become Harnack's pupil. Though a monarchist close to the Kaiser, Harnack was an independent thinker often at odds with the Lutheran clergy and a progressive on women's education (two of his three daughters received PhDs).[72]

Harnack and Althoff were soon joined by a number of German professors eager to take advantage of the financial support of the sciences from business, and thereby improve their own professional standing. The paleontologist Otto Jaekel proposed to Althoff as early as 1904 an institute that would free scientists from the burden of teaching. In a memorandum of 1909, Jaekel used a nationalist argument to support an institute for biology but argued that the fundraising model would be American.[73] Another scientist, Emil Fischer, whom Althoff had lured to Berlin, shared his ideas with Harnack on a new form of science organization to keep up with American institutional developments.[74] And Hugo Andres Krüß, who was appointed to the Prussian Education Ministry in 1907 and later became the director, also suggested a "Kaiser Wilhelm Foundation for Scientific Research," a title that itself betrayed its American institutional influences.[75]

The American model appealed especially to reformers in German cities, such as Frankfurt on the Main and Hamburg, that enjoyed looser institutional structures and a civically active upper middle class. Indeed, Harnack reminded his readers of precisely this distinctive urban history in his coverage of Carnegie in 1903.[76] As early as 1904, industrialist and philanthropist Wilhelm Merton wrote to a colleague who was headed to the St. Louis exhibition, asking if he could collect information about American advances in the "private character" in social welfare. Merton planned to use the material to develop his Institute for the Common Good in Frankfurt.[77] A similar spirit, as we will see, motivated the founding of the privately funded university in that city during the Weimar Republic.

Just as the Americans had discovered, the rapid advancement of the natural sciences meant the work could not be done by a single professor and required funding beyond what the state could provide. Rather, this work required a consolidation of researchers in costly labs. The problem in Germany, as in the United States, was how to finance these operations and where to house them. Even before Carnegie wrote his first essay, a fluid but delicate cooperation between industrialists and scientists had emerged. In 1887, Siemens was crucial in founding the Imperial Institute of Physics and Technology, which became a model for a privately funded research institute.[78] Unlike in America, where philanthropy was spearheaded by donors, in Germany a growing group of forward-thinking and resourceful chemists, including Emil Fischer, Wilhelm Ostwald, and Fritz Friedland Nernst, saw an opportunity and lobbied for a similar institute devoted to chemistry.[79] While unsuccessful, their lobbying set a precedent for fundraising in the German domain. The "Kaiser's chemists" failed to achieve their institute without the cooperation of the Prussian bureaucracy. But they piqued the Kaiser's interest. Once he proved willing to exchange aristocratic titles for money (in particular, among upwardly mobile German-Jewish industrialists), he unleashed the potential for raising large sums among those interested in acquiring such privileges.[80]

In the fall of 1909, the German education reformers got the boost they needed. Sufficiently persuaded by the American example—and threat—the Kaiser supported the scholars' plans with the establishment of the Kaiser Wilhelm Society. In fact, Fischer did not believe in Germany's inferiority but willingly exploited the anxiety of others to raise funds for their cause.[81] Harnack, for his part, had an instinctive appreciation for the productive tension between nationalism and internationalism in the scholarly realm. He knew when to emphasize the international aspects of sharing knowledge and when the national research imperative should take precedence.[82] Years later, after the world war, when Harnack was president of the society and trying to reintegrate Germany into the international scientific community, he would try to reconcile the two: "Education is national, but scholarship is international. What does this imply? Two things: first, that we are in a constant competition with other civilized peoples; second, that we must exchange our scholarship with theirs."[83] It was in that spirit that he had, together with Althoff, promoted the multiyear German-American professor exchange over objections that visiting Americans might "steal German trade secrets."[84]

Harnack walked a delicate line between embracing openness to outside ideas and foreign scholars and the economic and cultural nationalism befitting a Prussian academic leader. In his defense of the German-American exchange professorship, Harnack echoed Carnegie's endorsement of a "bigger system [that] grows bigger men"; Harnack saw science as "big business" (Großbetrieb).[85] He found support in strange corners. The humanist Theodor Mommsen had introduced Harnack to the Berlin Academy nearly fifteen years earlier with what one scholar calls "prophetic words," when he observed that "like big government and big industry, so has big scholarship [or big science]—performed by many but led by one—become a necessary element of our developing civilization. . . . Big science, like big industry, needs operating capital."[86]

In an ambitious 1909 memorandum to the Kaiser, Harnack expressed his belief that to stay competitive Germany would have to found extra-university institutes to support the basic research they were no longer able to accommodate entirely on their own. Humboldt's famous writings on the university, which represented the ur-academic innovator's contribution to the founding of the University of Berlin, had been discovered only in the last decade of the nineteenth century and recently published. Harnack drew on his predecessor to lend authority and gravitas to his argument that new research institutions would not be an aberration but would be based on Humboldt's vision.[87] Moreover, Harnack's formulation would address the university's long-standing limitations: the incompatibility of research and teaching. These twin tasks would remain together, but the protection of this model required supplemental institutions. After all, Humboldt himself had called these *Hilfsinstitute*, and through careful coordination they would assure the university a continued existence.[88]

Of the motivations Harnack identified for founding these extra-university institutions, among the most significant were the time required for research, the needs of industry for scientific support, and the benefits of an interdisciplinary space for intellectual advancement. But the most pressing, he insisted, was that competition demanded them.[89] German scientists were running the risk of being overtaken by the Americans, whose own universities were on the ascent. Science was no longer concerned only with the universal pursuit of truth; rather, "this state of affairs is already very damaging in terms of the politics of the nation and will gradually become ever more damaging in economic terms too. It is damaging to the nation in that now, in these times of heightened nationalism, and unlike in the past, a national label is attached to every scientific result."[90] For Harnack, scientific leadership was not a lofty ideal but a practical need. If Germany failed to act fast, it would risk falling behind not only in science, but also in military strength and economic advancement.

According to Valentini, the Kaiser read Harnack's memorandum in December 1909 "word for word."[91] In the following academic year, the Prussian Culture Ministry deemed twelve American public and private universities formidable competitors to the twenty-one of the German system. More worrisome, it found that American expenditures per university had quadrupled since the mid-1890s, at twice the growth rate in Germany.[92] (The German historian Charles McClelland confirms the alarming drop after 1908 in German spending on science; funds were diverted to defense, which increased to 2.3 billion M or over half the budget in 1913.)[93] Given what they perceived as the dire state of the German sciences, the Prussian bureaucrats welcomed Harnack's memo and in November published it, along with reactions from the wider public, in the illustrated *Die Woche*.[94] The Kaiser drew on his words for his remarks at the celebrations in honor of the one-hundred-year anniversary of the University of Berlin, where he announced that 10 million M had been raised for the new Kaiser Wilhelm Society. Never had so much money been devoted to research.

Yet criticism had already been mounting from the left about the take-over of "big scholarship," like "big business," and the top-down organiza-tion of the Kaiser Wilhelm Society—piquing even Harnack's own latent reservations about the mixing of "clique and capital."[95] Some of these criti-cisms, expressed in terms of unwanted Americanization, no doubt assumed additional meaning amid a strike and police crackdown the following year. Such critics as Weber noted that science was also becoming increasingly politicized. In the so-called Era of Althoff, Harnack and others coined new terms to describe the process through which culture, ideas, and science became weapons in the political crossfire, including *Bildungspolitik* and *Schulpolitik* (1896), *internationale Kulturpolitik* (1910), and *auswärtige Kul-turpolitik* (1908/12), in which Weber and others invoked fierce critiques of the establishment.[96] Finally, the founding of the Kaiser Wilhelm Society precipitated palpable anxiety on the part of the University of Berlin's rec-tor, Max Lenz, who struggled to claim that the university was both nation-alist and cosmopolitan: "Scholarship is shared between everyone in the civilized world. . . . And yet . . . may the University of Berlin be mindful at all times that it is a German university." The university itself was at the center of intellectual life and yet now fueled domestic competition from new research institutions. The university's centennial celebrations celebrated the "unity of knowledge" even as it witnessed the creation of a rival institution that would challenge its future. "May this day mark not only the anniversary of the founding of Berlin's University but the next step in the development of German intellectual life," the rector declared.[97]

As the architect of the Kaiser Wilhelm Society, Harnack mediated among interest groups to create the society's strategy, dubbed the "Harnack Prin-ciple," in which institutes replete with assistants, funds, and equipment were awarded to "the personalit[ies] of the leading scholars," who, in turn, unburdened by teaching, were free to pursue their research.[98] But he did not get his way on every detail. Harnack wanted the new institution to be funded equally from private donations and state contributions, but the minister of finance refused. In the end, the Prussian government agreed only to provide land for the society's buildings and to pay the salaries of directors. The society, in turn, was expected to fundraise for the construc-tion of the buildings and their ongoing operations.[99] The society met its initial 10-million-M fundraising goal easily and, according to one historian, received more donations that it could spend on operations. By 1914, the society was largely independent of government subsidies.[100]

The second major issue was how the society would be organized. One camp, led by the industrialist Walter Rathenau, envisioned a broad-based membership with a low entrance fee that he believed would help the German people connect with the society's scientific mission.[101] The cultural diplomat Friedrich Schmidt-Ott, who rose from a position as Althoff's assistant to become head of the Emergency Association of German Science (the predecessor of the German Research Foundation), fought for a more hierarchical structure of senators, founders, and members, with the highest-level paying a 20,000-M entrance fee and another 1,500 M in annual dues. That approach would ensure the organization would become an elite club of millionaires.[102]

Schmidt-Ott's plan for Althoff and Harnack's vision won out: the Kaiser Wilhelm Society became a hierarchical organization that avoided corporatization by diversifying its funding among private and public sources. The various tiers of individual contributors were enticed to support the cause alongside the patron Kaiser, who acknowledged their gifts with membership medals, handwritten notes, and senatorial robes.[103] At the first meeting of the membership in January 1911 the eighty-three voting members represented the most prominent names in industry, including Krupp, Siemens, and Böttinger. With Harnack as its first president, the society served as an umbrella organization for new institutions devoted to basic research, the first of which were constructed in 1912, to Chemistry with Ernst Beckman as its director, and Physical Chemistry and Electrochemistry with Fritz Haber as its director. The institutional strategy would remain tied to the so-called Harnack Principle of seeking out talent before scientific fields. According to Fredrick Glum, the secretary general of the society from 1922 to 1937, "The Kaiser Wilhelm-Gesellschaft should not build institutes and then search for the proper man for them, but rather first find the man and then build an institute around him."[104]

At the first of many institute inaugurations in Dahlem surrounded by the roofs in the style of Kaiser's "helmet façade" and scientists, scholars, and society members donning top hats and uniforms, the two pillars of German society that Harnack proclaimed in his 1909 memo coalesced. "Military might and scholarship are the two strong factors underpinning Germany's greatness and the Prussian state derives from its glorious traditions the responsibility for upholding both," Harnack announced (fig. 7).[105] Harnack straddled religious, economic, and military influences for the advancement and diffusion of German science, and his agility lent itself to

Figure 7. Harnack (*right*), in formal dress, accompanies Kaiser Wilhelm II (*left*) on the occasion of the inauguration of a new Kaiser Wilhelm Institute. Harnack believed that scholarship and the military were the two pillars of German society. (Photo © bpk Bildagentur/Art Resource, NY.)

the modern university's interstitial character, a feature that contributed to its ascendancy.[106]

Yet it was not without consequence. For all his skill at creating new opportunities, Harnack gave his blessing to an industrial science that would pray to a new god. He was not naïve about this trade-off, which he noted only a few months after the society's founding, but he had faith in his own organization to mitigate the downsides: "Science today requires for the pursuit of everything it does considerable resources; by and large, these are only made available in return for other benefits. If the state does not provide them, the daily workings of science will become dependent on the views of those who give money—see America, Rockefeller, Carnegie! Just as in the Middle Ages scholarship was entirely bound up with the church, since the church gave money and bestowed honors on individuals and institutions; there is a danger now that we shall have a science which is party-political and subordinate to high finance or industry. The creation of our very own Kaiser-Wilhelm-Gesellschaft is a powerful antidote; the state and academia are thereby channeling capital into an 'untained' bed."[107] In response to the increasing costs and industrial needs, Harnack helped craft a new institutional iteration of the "Humboldtian contract," in which scholars reclaimed some autonomy in exchange for new services to society. Hybridizing pure and applied science, and universities and research institutions, Harnack ingeniously staved off a reductive corporatism that accepted utility as the only metric for research and protected the relevance and competitiveness of German research.[108]

PARTING WAYS

To reformulate Virginia Woolf's memorable observation, "on or about December, 1910," the transatlantic character of the university changed.[109] The contemporaneous foundings of the Carnegie Institution and the Kaiser Wilhelm Society arose from similar growth in interest among industrialists in the economic benefits of science and increasing needs for financial support of the sciences. The philanthropists on both sides of the Atlantic who funded these extra-university research entities were motivated as much by international competition as by humanitarian goals.[110] Carnegie represented an activist managerial capitalism that supported exceptional men at the expense of others.[111] The Kaiser Wilhelm Society shared this preoccupation with excellence and promoted the "great personalities" of individual "scientific genius" in its founding mission.[112] But despite the commonalities, there were differences in the design and implementation of these organizations, and those differences set America and Germany on divergent paths of knowledge organization. That divergence had epistemological and wider social significance for the two countries.

Gilman's hybrid university model was already considered "indigenous" in America by 1906, when the question of research versus teaching arose at a presidential meeting of the Association of American Universities. For the president of Stanford University, David Starr Jordan, "the American university [was] emphatically a teaching university." Quoting one of the many professors he surveyed, Jordan relayed, however, "It seems to me so hopeless to look for the career of research in many departments of learning outside of the universities, and its presence in the university is so helpful, that the wiser solution seems to me frankly to include the research program within the larger cultural and practical ends for which universities exist." His "final answer to the question . . . is this: The university should recognize the necessity of research to university men, and in a much greater degree than is now the case in any American university. It should provide for this by furnishing all needed appliances, material books, clerical help, artists, assistants, leisure, and freedom."[113] Others, like Yale president Arthur T. Hadley, agreed that teaching and research should remain in one institution but expressed concern that, if not carefully integrated, two classes of professors would emerge—"some whom it values for their ability in teaching old truth, and others whom it values for their ability in bringing out new truth."[114] While both Jordan and Hadley had their reservations, the Americans felt invested enough to improve on the university rather than abandon it.

Pritchett was fighting an uphill battle, then, when he made a last-ditch effort to generate interest in a national university, a dome for America's uneven temples of higher education. In January 1908, while on a fact-finding mission in Iowa and Illinois, Pritchett received a letter from Carnegie that read like an innovator's dream: "Dear Friend: If you have any spare time at your command, will you kindly give me an answer to this question: If you had say five or ten millions of dollars to put to the best use possible, what would you do with it? Prize given for the best answer. Always very truly yours, Andrew Carnegie."[115] Seeing an opening, Pritchett dashed off an argument that presented a national university as an antidote to what he decried as the low standards of the state universities, which were designed for the masses, the "average member of society." Rather, a national university would "breed great men in philosophy, in Science and in Literature. A Pasteur, a Hemholtz or a Tennyson in a half century, would be abundant justification for its existence. Over and above this, it will hold up the ideals of true learning and true freedom to all other Colleges and Universities. Ten Million Dollars would compass it."[116] Pritchett staged a congressional hearing for the plan in 1914, but the elite university presidents mounted a formidable opposition, and the bill failed one final time. With respect to the organization of research, both in its abandonment of the European-style European university and in its reinforcement of the bond between research and teaching, American higher education parted ways with Germany.

While American university presidents like Jordan and Hadley were re-
stating their commitment to a modern research university that encompassed
both research and teaching, the founding of the Kaiser Wilhelm Society
dealt an unquestionable blow to the research university ideal in Germany.
Despite attempts by University of Berlin rector Max Lenz to defend the university as the authority for the advancement of knowledge, the announcement of the Kaiser Wilhelm Institutes at the celebration of the hundred-year
anniversary of the University of Berlin only exposed the widening fissures.
Speakers at the centennial celebrations as well as in the published volume
on the history of the university all seemed to protest too much.[117]

If the Kaiser Wilhelm Society did not precipitate a complete "exodus of
research" from the university, it certainly created conditions, with more
funding, plentiful staff assistance, and lack of teaching, that made the institutes more attractive to scientists.[118] The institutes the society spawned in
effect created the tiered system that Hadley had feared for America. The majority of the Nobel Prizes given to Germans in chemistry, physics, and medicine between 1901 and 1930 would go to institute affiliates, and, even more
remarkably, its scholars won over one in six of all prizes in the sciences—
constituting what an observer called a "particular breed of elite science."[119]

The extra-university research institute was more open and flexible than
the university system in either Germany or America. To be sure, its adoption of a hierarchical rather than egalitarian membership structure war-
ranted charges of elitism similar to those that had been directed at the AAU
in America. (Indeed, it would be difficult to suggest that the institutes of
the Kaiser Wilhelm Society, which awarded "life tenure" to directors with
commanding "personalities" but no one else, was democratic.)[120] And the
financial inaccessibility of membership in the society was matched by the
geographical unevenness; though the society aimed to represent the empire at large, half of the senators came from the Berlin region.[121] What was
crucial, however, was that directors were not limited in their hiring, as
were universities, by traditions of discrimination.

For philanthropists who cared about career prospects for Jews this
opening gave a reason to support the institutes. The baroness and patron
Mathilda von Rothschild complained to the district president of Wiesbaden
in 1910 that the "imperial state government continuously avoids making
Jews *Ordinariat* professors at the university," and then went on to name the
scientist Jacques Loeb as an example of what had happened as a result—he
emigrated to the United States.[122] Jewish donors wishing for structural
change in Germany used their money to support new institutions. Indeed,
25 percent of the society's senators were Jewish, and as of 1914 their contributions made up 39 percent of the donations.[123]

Such Jewish donors as Leopold Koppel, Franz von Mendelssohn, and Paul von Schwabach aimed to reduce the impact of institutional antisemitism.[124] With their contributions—Koppel would give 1 million M in 1912 for the construction of a Kaiser Wilhelm Institute for Physical and Electrical Chemistry—these donors created extra-university spaces that would be open to Jews. (Koppel even insisted that the Jewish scientist Fritz Haber be made director, and created an independent appointment system for his institute to achieve this.)[125] German-Jewish philanthropists borrowed the "coercive philanthropy" from American women of means, in which donations secured concessions for their interest groups. Even without such agreements, a number of open-minded directors welcomed women and Jews, and even made their institutes "refuge[s] for female scientists" who could not find employment in the traditional university, the most famous of whom were the chemist Lise Meitner, the physicist Isolde Hausser, and aeronautical engineer Melitta Schiller (fig. 8).[126] In light of the fact that American elite research universities were beginning as early as 1910 to restrict the numbers of Jewish faculty and students, the progressive policies of privately funded institutions in Germany are all the more remarkable. The institutes' openness to talent would accelerate German science in the period before World War I.[127]

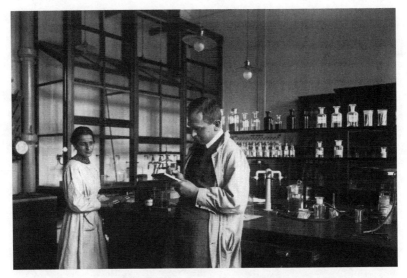

Figure 8. Otto Hahn with Lise Meitner, a Jewish physicist, who was the second woman to receive a PhD at the University of Vienna, and among those who received a permanent position at a Kaiser Wilhelm Institute in 1913. (Photo © bpk Bildagentur/Art Resource, NY.)

At the same time, while in both countries the boundaries between the scientific and industrial worlds were disappearing, German scientists were unable to take advantage of the new, privately funded model as fully as did the Americans. This resulted less from cultural reasons than is often assumed. When the culture minister August von Trott zu Solz appealed to Prussians to give as "rich Americans do," one reporter commented, "What comes most natural to Americans would be quite abnormal in Germany, in light of its different social and political conditions. If Germany wanted to see similar results to America in terms of charitable commitments, it would have to create the same framework conditions as in America first. . . . How different is Germany, then, where no Rockefeller was needed to set up a 'University of Chicago' on entirely new premises and turn it, with money, money, money, into the leading and most productive academic institution in the land, if not the entire world, within a very short space of time."[128]

Nonetheless, as early as the scholarly congress in St. Louis in 1904, Germans had been aware of the American ascendancy and sought private financing of scholarship to improve. Despite criticisms of what we might call the American corporatization of science, the Kaiser Wilhelm Society was initially funded largely by individual private donations that drew on willing donors in local communities with active philanthropic cultures like the Berlin suburbs, much as the Göttingen Association for the Promotion of Applied Physics and Mathematics had been supported ten years prior by steel industrialists in Düsseldorf. Whatever will did exist, however, was limited by regulatory constraints, including, in particular, a 5 percent tax on donations instituted in 1906 that undoubtedly handicapped any philanthropic momentum built up in the last quarter of the nineteenth century.[129] A further requirement that endowments be invested in state bonds and the government's subsequent decision to devalue the currency during the inflation thwarted the scant munificence that remained.[130] By the end of the Weimar Republic more than half of the funding for the Kaiser Wilhelm Society would come from the state rather than from private sources, effectively undermining whatever independence it had achieved.

These early roots of philanthropy would take some time to diffuse throughout Europe and the wider world.[131] But one pattern persisted: when the university was threatened by external stressors, including economic or political pressures, some academic leaders invoked an ideal separate and apart from the market and the nation.[132] With the advent of war, as universities faced more constraints, these leaders would reach back to the nostalgic myth of the autonomous university as a source of authority and a basis for a renegotiated academic social contract.

CHAPTER SEVEN

WORLD WAR I AND THE INVENTION OF ACADEMIC FREEDOM

A university must be indigenous; it must be rich; and above all, it must be free.

CHARLES ELIOT, 1869

The "freedom of science" exists in Germany within the limits of political and ecclesiastical acceptability. Outside these limits, there is none.

MAX WEBER, 1908

In 1915 at least eleven American professors were summarily dismissed from their positions. One had spoken favorably of the Roman Catholic Church at the University of Utah, where Mormon influence was profound; another at Wesleyan had drafted the Workmen's Compensation Act in Middletown, Connecticut; and a law professor at the University of Colorado had represented striking coal miners in a US congressional investigation.[1] It was nothing new for professors to be fired for saying and doing things that rubbed administrators and their communities the wrong way. What we call academic freedom and take for granted as a feature of American university life did not yet exist.[2] In fact the convention that prevailed before 1915 in America dictated that American faculty possessed no formal rights, legal guarantees, or economic security with respect to their employment.[3]

The beginning of World War I in Europe was the catalyst that would eventually alter these circumstances, providing American professors the opening to legitimize academic freedom—ushering in the professionalization of the American professoriate. The war between the United States and Germany complicated the process. The vaunted (but often mischaracterized) freedom of teaching, or *Lehrfreiheit* of German universities inspired American professors seeking protection from politically motivated dismissal.[4] At the same time, Germany was now using poison gas and engaging in the U-boat warfare that would sink the *Lusitania*, tainting the earlier idealization of Germany and bringing to a head conflicts over freedom of expression versus presumed loyalty to the nation. The war further gave the state the prerogative to limit precisely those freedoms that academics sought.

Although academic freedom would not be fully institutionalized and codified in law for several more decades, American professors' efforts in 1915 produced its "philosophical birth cry" in the United States.[5] Meanwhile, in Germany, the war and its aftermath would have the near-opposite effect. On both sides of the Atlantic, the new arrangement portended changes in the relationship between the nation-state and the university. The formalization of academic freedom occurred, despite, or perhaps because of, the state's demands that most threatened it. This phenomenon, and the gaps between freedom on campus and in broader society, would later blunt professors' long-term ability to engage in public debate and guard against pseudoscience.

HOW FREE WERE GERMAN SCHOLARS REALLY?

In 1902, the German historian Friedrich Paulsen observed, "In general, there are no limits imposed on teaching at German universities, and this freedom enjoyed by instructors is a codified and undisputed right."[6] But there is no doubt that many, including foreign visitors, greatly overstated this freedom. Either unaware or willfully ignorant of its limitations, G. Stanley Hall, the psychologist who founded Clark University, expressed an academic canard when he announced in 1908, "The German University is today the freest spot on earth."[7] The gap between the American perception of German academic freedom and the German reality matters, not only because it points to how Americans may have exaggerated it for their own professional aggrandizement, but also because that gap exposes the different political cultures in which academic freedom emerged. If freedom worked only in a nationalist monarchy, and required faculty to prepare students for state-administered exams, was this any freedom at all? And in America, an, in theory, even more free country, shouldn't academics expect still more freedom?

Though German professors had enjoyed some freedom since medieval times, the reformed universities of Göttingen and Halle and the new university in Berlin were only beacons of freedom when compared with the darker seventeenth and eighteenth centuries.[8] Before German unification, free thinkers were often punished. The myth of Jewish iconoclast Baruch Spinoza's declined invitation to join the University of Heidelberg in 1673 is the exception that proves the rule. Religious tests and oaths were common; the University of Marburg barred Cartesian philosophy; at Jena unanimous consent was required to challenge Aristotelian principles. Even the fates of such prominent thinkers as Christian Wolff and Immanuel Kant were subject to the whims of the intermittently enlightened Frederick the Great. The Enlightenment happened despite, not because of, these constraints.[9]

Having experienced the free thought that prevailed in the first quarter of the nineteenth century at the University of Göttingen, Humboldt viewed it as central to that university's success and worked to secure the principle of *Freiheit von Forschung und Lehre*, the freedom of research and teaching, through the abolition of censorship in the University of Berlin. But his victories were short-lived. The Carlsbad Decrees a decade later, which imposed strict censorship and a tight administrative grip on the universities, represented a major setback, as did the dismissal in the nearby kingdom of Hanover (not yet part of Prussia) of the Göttingen Seven—the professors who refused to swear allegiance to a new and less liberal constitution in 1837. Even though a certain autonomy for higher education was inscribed in the 1850 Prussian Constitution, which stated that "scholarly research and teaching shall be free" and academic freedom would be awarded to scholars who proved "to official powers that they have the moral, intellectual, and technical capability," the policies as enforced proved otherwise.[10] By 1870 Du Bois-Reymond, who, as we saw, also vigilantly tracked the rise of the American applied sciences, referred to his colleagues at Berlin as "the intellectual bodyguards of the Hohenzollerns, billeted right across from the royal palace," earning him the approval of Wilhelm II.[11] A quid pro quo between the German state and its academics offered the faculty a measure of autonomy.

Crucially, the freedom guaranteed by the state applied only to German scholars at the top of the academic pyramid—the *Ordinarius* professors who were civil servants and comprised the self-governing body of the university. They constituted less than half of the professoriate.[12] A debate brewed in Germany in the last third of the nineteenth century and beginning of the twentieth century about the standing of those in the *Extraordinarius* and *Privatdozent* categories, who demanded more rights and better pay. In response to the demands of these adjunct instructors, German *Ordinarius* professors were, understandably, protective of their status. (In America, where academic freedom would be, after 1915, linked to tenured faculty, tenured professors were similarly protective, demonstrating again how the privilege of autonomy was tied to the stratified hierarchy of the university system.)[13]

Notwithstanding the expansion of freedom of inquiry at the reformed universities, the professorship at the University of Berlin was defined religiously. Protestantism was considered a prerequisite for scientific objectivity, though a few Catholics managed to squeeze through.[14] Similarly, in the British system, a religious test barred Catholics, Jews, and nonconformists from earning a degree or a position at either Cambridge or Oxford—a restriction only abolished in fits and starts. Just as a Jew could get neither out of Cambridge nor into Oxford, as the joke went, so, too, could he become a *Privatdozent* even if he had virtually no chance of ever becoming an *Ordinarius*.[15] Weber famously observed that the Jewish academic should "abandon all hope" (or, as Münsterberg might have added, move to America).[16]

Socialists were even more suspect, as was uncomfortably revealed when the Prussian authorities removed a *Privatdozent* in physics, Leo Arons, from the University of Berlin for delivering lectures defending the Social Democratic Party.[17] The faculty defended Arons against the Prussian state not out of any great love for socialism but because they resented the government infringing on the institution's ideological independence—that is, they wanted the right to reprimand him themselves.[18] The "Arons affair" demonstrates that academic freedom was connected more to desires for institutional autonomy than to a generalized value of freedom of thought.

Even taking these restraints into account it would be difficult to argue (though admiring Americans nonetheless did) that German faculty had the autonomy in the last quarter of the nineteenth century to make professorial appointments, which the historian Charles E. McClelland called the most "significant litmus test of academic freedom." Instead, what existed was closer to a compromise in which the faculties produced a list of often three final candidates, and the Education Ministry—usually, but not always—selected from this list.[19] Despite an occasional obvious political appointment based on the wishes of the emperor, this allocation of powers between the university and the state was generally a guarantee of the German university's autonomy.[20] As Walter Metzger observed, "The German universities were state institutions, but the combination of governmental restraint, limited professorial co-option, elected administrators and cultural isolation gave them the appearance, and a good deal of the reality, of self-governing academic bodies."[21] While the state drew up budgets, created chairs, appointed professors, and framed the instruction, the power to elect academic officials, appoint lecturers or *Privatdozenten* (at least until the Arons case), and nominate professors lay with the faculty.

It is a reflection of the reality of constrained autonomy that when such German scholars as Fichte and Helmholtz spoke in the early nineteenth century of "academic freedom" (*akademische Freiheit*), they usually meant *Lernfreiheit*—the absence of administrative constraints on the conditions of learning; that is, the freedom for students to roam and sample the academic wares of various professors rather than being bound by a particular institution or curriculum.[22] When Germans referred to freedom of teaching—closer to what Americans would adopt in 1915 as *academic freedom*—they used the term *Lehrfreiheit* or *akademischer Lehrfreiheit*.[23] It is this latter freedom—the freedom to examine bodies of evidence and to report their findings in lecture or print—to which the *Ordinarius* professors would cling to preserve their status vis-à-vis those outside their rank.

This arrangement had its advantages. In the pre-Althoff era, the faculty succumbed to bickering and squabbles. In the so-called family university, it was not uncommon for a theology student to be expected to marry his professor's daughter to get his mentor's job.[24] Nepotism was curtailed by Althoff, who played interest groups off one another and cultivated certain professors. Under his benevolent rule, neutrality and objectivity thrived. When the Kaiser reportedly insisted to Althoff in 1897, "I will tolerate no socialist among my officials," Althoff insisted that freedom of expression was a constitutive feature of academic excellence.[25] When the "academic Kulturkampf" led to opposition against Catholics and Jewish fraternities, Althoff, who boasted of never engaging in any "rabble-rousing propaganda, not against Catholics and not against Jews," resolved the manner with his characteristic charm in a principled speech to the State House of Representatives, saying "that the universities guaranteed the same freedom to every student, including the Catholics, the Jews, and foreigners."[26]

Yet there is no doubt that Althoff pulled the strings—"Er liess die Puppen tanzen, ohne dass man ihn sah" (He pulled the puppet strings without one seeing him do so) —a situation that many, including Weber, resented.[27] To complicate matters further, the faculty occasionally cried "academic freedom" when the state imposed a professor—even if the imposition was in the name of progress and Enlightenment, as in the controversy that erupted over the appointment of the Catholic Martin Spahn to the all Protestant history department at the University of Strasbourg.[28] As McClelland observed, "When it worked well the division of labor between the ministry and faculty circumvented both despotism by the former and the sway of sectarian schools and coteries, which opened a disastrous leeway for personal interests and intrigue."[29] Althoff's priority was German scientific superiority, and, like Gilman on the other side of the Atlantic, he was willing to tap outsider talent to achieve it. But a less pragmatic director of higher education would lead to very different results.

The kind of enlightened despotism that the Althoff system reflected had deep roots in Prussia—indeed it was what had enabled Enlightenment thinking to flourish under Frederick the Great. The power of the state and the royal government was never in question. And the duality of Kant's classic formula "Argue as much as you will, but obey!" provided a philosophical rationale. This duality persisted in the next century in the university fraternities, where students purportedly sang a folk song dating to the sixteenth century, "Thoughts are Free" (*Die Gedanken sind Frei*).[30] Kant's academic *Streitkultur*, which in a previous era thrived out outside the university, ensured that the university would thereafter remain a locus of robust debate.[31] As Metzger observed, however, "A sharp distinction between freedom *within* and freedom *outside* the university was implicit in the German conception."[32]

At the second annual conference of German faculty in 1908 in Jena, academic freedom was on the agenda. Academics gathered to discuss the protection of religious or political views of adjunct faculty. Weber complained that the state's meddling in hiring appointments and promotion was leading to the appointment of scholars deemed "unexceptionable," and political conformism.[33] He believed the same criteria should apply to those seeking a new position and professors who already held a chair, and was angered that his colleagues expressed an alternative view at the conference. "Only when this perfectly obvious point has been acknowledged can one begin to discuss the question as to which kinds of actions—public or private—may be regarded as incompatible with the role of a university teacher."[34]

Given the controversy concerning hiring and firing for religious and political reasons, the University of Berlin rector's claim, in 1910, that the faculty had "the right of corporative self-replenishment" was implausible.[35] But such freedom may not have even been desirable. Schleiermacher and Humboldt had warned against the medieval and early modern "self-replenishment" model and favored more enlightened direction: if the government "imposed" certain theologians on the faculty, it was in support of the critical historical school—that is, it usually represented scientific advancement. Once Althoff retired, the competing flaws of "professorial capitalism" and academic interest groups and their patronage powers reminded many of the benefits of benevolent despotism. Even if he complained about Althoff's nefarious influence, Weber's own value-free scholarship was, at least in part, culpable for professors' acceptance of political nationalism in exchange for academic freedom.[36] One had to ask if freedom of thought in exchange for political conformism was any freedom at all.

The outbreak of World War I, when the German professoriate overwhelmingly defended German wartime actions, showed how German universities were precariously held together by the expectation of patriotism.[37] Though America would not enter the war until 1917, many US faculty would be accused of leading America into battle to enhance their professional status. Now that the detached, relatively unimportant group of schools that had existed in early nineteenth-century America had been transformed into a centralized and professionalized system, it was necessary to retranslate the German influence into a uniquely American Progressive-Era trope: scientific service to the state.

THE BIRTH OF THE SERVICE UNIVERSITY

The *idea* of freedom of thought had long been held dear among American academics. Since Ticknor's visit to Göttingen in 1815, the American "return-ees" had noted the centrality of freedom to the German university's success.[38] Say what you will about German politics, but the "German literary world is a perfect democracy," George Bancroft noted.[39] Gilman had identified freedom as the essential ingredient in the modern research university and organized Hopkins's departments with that independence in mind: "The institution we are about to organize would not be worthy the name of a University, if it were to be devoted to any other purpose than the discovery and promulgation of the truth; and it would be ignoble in the extreme if the resources which have been given by the Founder without restrictions should be limited to the maintenance of ecclesiastical difference or perverted to the promotion of political strife."[40] Harper concurred: "When for any reason . . . the administration of the institution or the instruction in any one of its departments is changed by an influence from without, when an effort is made to dislodge an officer or a professor because the political sentiment or the religious sentiment of the majority has undergone a change, at that moment the institution has ceased to be a university."[41]

As the German-trained economist and president of the American Economic Association (AEA) Richard Ely observed, what "impressed in the German university . . . [was] a certain largeness and freedom of thought."[42] But what was meant by "freedom" was debated. Though Ely was unique in having a nuanced understanding of the German version of academic freedom, many German-trained Americans often confused *Lehrfreiheit* with *Lernfreiheit*.[43] Before the 1890s such American education entrepreneurs as Eliot focused on the freedom of students to take elective courses, and drew on this principle to reshape the curriculum.[44] This focus changed by 1900.[45] Eliot's increased attention to both freedom of instruction and freedom of learning made clear why the translation of the notion of academic freedom to America would be so complicated. The American professor was neither a civil servant as in Germany nor a director of a self-governing corporation as in England, but rather an employee of a lay board. Americans became preoccupied with the conflicting identities of a professor as an employee and a scholar. Arguably the lack of professional status for faculty limited their role in governance, and the emergence of academic freedom was tied up with improving both.[46]

In contrast to the German model of pseudo-self-governance, American universities had, during the nineteenth century, developed a balance of power among trustees, administration, and faculty. At their best, these "checks and balances" created what one contemporary sociologist calls "complex autonomy," a distinctive feature of the American system.[47] But under this arrangement, individuals held varying levels of power. In particular, the president, part of both the governing board and the faculty, was essentially a permanent member of the university, whereas an individual professor was employed only at the will of the board.[48] This lack of parity created the circumstances under which the presidents threatened to become "monarchs" in Clark Kerr's later description. One hoped that they would lead benevolently, but there were no guarantees. If in their capacity as scholars they put forward ideas at odds with employers, faculty were not protected from dismissal.

One question that defined the American fault lines around 1900 was knowledge for its own sake versus the advancement of a greater social vision like democratic citizenship or, at minimum, the democratic governance of the university. Arthur Lovejoy, the renowned Johns Hopkins intellectual historian, advocated for the "professionalization of the professoriate" based on the idea of a "self-governing republic of scholars." Lovejoy envisioned a university that was more egalitarian in its governance, with professors assuming more control over the university's affairs.[49] His friend the psychologist James McKeen Cattell, who would later become the center of a defining controversy at Columbia University, shared this view. In a series of essays titled "University Control," Cattell drew on the long history of universities from Bologna and Paris to Berlin to argue that freedom was essential to their success. In a faculty survey Cattell found that 58 percent supported a "complete change which would make the administration responsible to the faculties. This is surely a condition which foretells reform or bankruptcy." Only one favored the current system, and he was an executive.[50]

This debate took shape in a series of cases that began in the 1890s in the social sciences, the "new body of studies," as John Dewey called them. When Ely's socialist activities were scrutinized by officials at the University of Wisconsin the controversy raised the question of the separation between fact and value.[51] In a university that was increasingly linked to industry—one study found that while 48 percent of board members were businessmen, bankers, and lawyers in 1860, that proportion had risen to

64 percent in 1900—social scientists found themselves embattled against their employers over such hot-button topics as labor unions and corporate monopolies.[52] Professional associations were formed, including the AEA (1885), the American Political Science Association (1903), and the American Sociological Society (1905), largely to provide support to aggrieved social scientists.

The most visible academic freedom fight involved Edward Alsworth Ross, a Hopkins-trained economist, who taught at Stanford until he was dismissed in 1901.[53] As the new institution had only one trustee, Jane Stanford, the widow of founder and railroad magnate Leland Stanford, Stanford was an exception in the university structure described above. When Ross opposed the railroad's importation of Chinese labor and criticized its labor practices, Jane Stanford demanded that the president, David Starr Jordan, ask for Ross's resignation. Columbia economist E. R. A. Seligman, then president of the AEA, led a successful campaign on behalf of Ross. Then a young professor at Stanford, Lovejoy was one of the first faculty members at Stanford to resign in protest. Facing mounting bad publicity and a newly confident professoriate, Jordan relented and rehired Ross, who soon departed for Wisconsin.[54]

The Ross case, as it was known, was a win for academic freedom and institutional due process. The case also brought legitimacy to social scientists and accelerated their inclusion in the associations and institutions of academia. In an essay published after Ross resumed his position, Dewey, however, cautioned that American scholars should be wary of the costs of professionalization. Once "specialized," a discipline enjoyed the acceptance of its conclusions as scientific truth, but there were drawbacks: "Specialization, in its measure and degree, means withdrawal."[55] Dewey feared that, in exchange for protection from meddling, disciplines disengaged from world affairs and lost their ability to impact society. The desire for acceptance and academic status for social science would shape the context and scope of the formalization of academic freedom for the entire academy.[56]

For a group of academics led by Lovejoy and Seligman, a series of professorial dismissals in the first decade of the twentieth century provided a wedge to challenge the power of the Carnegie Foundation for the Advancement of Teaching (CFAT), which they thought was in thrall to industry. As we saw in chapters 5 and 6, Carnegie, his administrators, and program officers played an outsized role in the promotion of academic standards and, indeed, the direction of scholarship. CFAT was effective at creating incentives for professors to participate in expansive programs that were intended to standardize the higher education system. Pritchett, Flexner, and

Carnegie believed that an increase in faculty control would reduce their prized efficiency, so they often clashed with this new academic-freedom-minded coterie.[57] Lovejoy and Seligman aimed, in contrast, to wrest power from the presidents and return it to the faculty in a more egalitarian form of governance. Indeed, Carnegie and his allies could have been said to pursue precisely the meddling that Lovejoy and Seligman aimed to end. The struggle resulted in the founding of the American Association of University Professors (AAUP—not to be confused with the earlier AAU).

Though Dewey would become the organization's first president, the meeting was organized by Lovejoy, who served as the association's first secretary in 1915, and its de facto investigative agent. Tipped off by regional newspaper headlines, Lovejoy traveled the country that spring—with Dewey sometimes footing the bill—and amassed reams of dossiers about the infractions being committed by less-than-benevolent university monarchs.[58] Led by the experienced and judicious Seligman and Lovejoy as well as esteemed "midwives" Ely, Henry Farnam, and Roscoe Pound, Committee A of the AAUP birthed the 1915 Declaration of Principles of Academic Freedom and Academic Tenure. (There would ultimately be sixteen committees on pressing issues, each designated with a letter of the alphabet.) Divided into sections of proposals and principles, the 1915 Declaration translated academic freedom from something akin to common law into a written constitution. "Academic freedom in this sense comprises three elements," the authors wrote, "freedom of inquiry and research; freedom of teaching within the university or college; and freedom of extra-mural utterance and action."[59]

The Declaration attempted to clarify the fraught relationship between trustees and faculty, the source of so much recent grief, and to establish the status of professors and due process for dismissals. The Declaration left many unsatisfied and much ambiguous. It permitted trustees to make ultimate decisions about dismissals—albeit after faculty consultation—an ongoing source of frustration for Lovejoy, who sought more radical change and found the focus on individual cases a distraction.[60] The authors announced, moreover, their interest in freedom for the instructor, not the student. In the American version of academic freedom, therefore, *Lernfreiheit* would be disassociated from *Lehrfreiheit*. Nor were the AAUP professors concerned with the university's *institutional* freedom, a category of academic freedom that would be enshrined in US constitutional law in 1957 and be the primary focus of the Supreme Court's subsequent jurisdiction over these issues.[61] President Van Hise of Wisconsin for his part objected that the Declaration was written only from the perspective of professors and did not consider the rights of students or the public.[62]

Van Hise identified a main flaw of the document: it left the scope and purpose of academic freedom undefined. While the primary justification for academic freedom in the Declaration of Principles rested on what Charles Eliot had called the "social function" of the professional scholar, the authors never made clear what that would mean in practice. University faculty, who were not employees "in the proper sense," had a responsibility to the public, much like judges. The public good was crucial to making the association and its Declaration palatable to a public that had misgivings about unionism. Dewey openly worried about the university professor becoming a "hired hand," and expressed concern about the narrowing of scientific scholarship, but he played a critical role nonetheless in crafting "science as service," an ideology that shaped a new age for academia.[63]

Despite Dewey's attempts at reconciliation, however, a paradox remained at the heart of his logic and that of the AAUP's principles. For Dewey the demand for experts was the rationale for concurrent industrialization and professionalization. "With the decay of external and merely governmental forms of authority," he had written as early as 1902 about the Ross case, "the demand grows for the authority of wisdom and intelligence. This force is bound to overcome those influences which tend to withdraw and pen the scholar within his own closet."[64] Progressives likewise saw the potential for science to mitigate the negative effects of government. Viewed from one perspective, scholars received academic freedom in exchange for not meddling in the public debate.[65] But professors' willingness to serve government was emblematic of a new academic social contract between the university and the nation-state into which such scholars as Dewey willingly entered. The war would make clear just how exacting the terms of that contract could be. In a letter to the editor, Lovejoy expressed hope that the AAUP may in the long run "do a good deal to keep up on our guard against our own potential sources of corruption in the profession."[66] His hopes were soon dashed.

RETRACTIONS

Understanding the AAUP's Declaration of Principles against the backdrop of the war illuminates the contradictions of academic freedom. It was probably overdetermined that the AAUP would find itself at the center of controversy. Not only had its members justified their new freedoms in terms of service to society, which would become more taxing during wartime, but the association had at its helm prominent American academics trained in Germany, with which the United States was now at war. Lovejoy, who studied in France, was an exception; more than half of the signatories of the AAUP's founding Declaration had studied and or received degrees in Germany.[67] Even as World War I unleashed nativist attacks against German Americans and anti-German American nationalism, the AAUP statement opened with an acknowledgment of German influence.[68] As Metzger observed, it is "not too fanciful to see also in their remarkable showing a pattern of withdrawal-and-return wherein American scholars, temporarily abandoning their world and drawing courage from alien springs, returned to dispense their inspiration."[69]

The growing anti-German sentiment in America strained the already competitive relationships between academics in Germany and in America and put pressure on knowledge brokers, many of whom were German Americans. Lovejoy called the German professors' endorsement of their nation's war effort the most "scandalous episode in the history of the scholar's profession." But many American scholars also saw affinity rather than distance in the German scientific community's nationalist response and worried about what it meant for America.[70] Given the cultural currency that German degrees and pedigree held, German Americans had always been privileged despite the rise of American nativism. But in this new phase of wartime jingoism, German Americans—at 2.5 million, one of the largest ethnic groups in America—found themselves vulnerable to personal and professional attacks.[71]

Many German American academics felt conflicted about their identities and allegiances. Among them was Kuno Francke, the cultural historian who had negotiated the donation of the German Museum to Harvard and was an early supporter of the German-American professor exchange. Francke had lived in Cambridge, Massachusetts, since 1875, became an American citizen in 1891, and now had an American wife and two American-born children. Moved by a calling as a mediator as much as a scholar, Francke felt close to Germany. Despite the war, he was invited to lecture at Cornell in 1915. There he shared his hope with his friend, President White, that the war would come to a peaceful end. White was far from sympathetic. "If the Germans only had been content to take the ordinary route to Paris," he evidently snickered. Following the entrance of the United States into the war, Francke could not help but feel hurt as he saw Harvard students in uniform from his Cambridge window.[72]

The friendship between Francke and White was not the only one damaged by the war.[73] Very few Americans could embrace "the friendly feeling of American Universities" promoted by the German University League, founded in 1914.[74] Burgess, who had served as a Theodore Roosevelt Professor in Berlin and retired in 1912, published a charitable analysis of Germany in 1915 and came closest.[75] When the German American anthropologist Franz Boas was asked by the *New York Times* about his thoughts on Germany his answer reflected the strained position of many German Americans at that moment. As an American citizen Boas said he remained most concerned about American affairs and our "readiness to plunge into a war which I consider unjustified on account of the vigor with which the militaristic agitation is being carried on; on account of the attempts to restrict freedom of expression, of which private and public administrators have been guilty, and on account of the attempts to coerce those who do not join in the clamor of the day."[76] Then there were those like Yale's president Arthur Hadley, who sought to reconcile the "Two Germanies" and mined the works of the arch-nationalist Heinrich von Treitschke for glimmers of Germany's cosmopolitan *Kultur*. Even Hadley must have known this was a stretch, since he then donated the proceeds from his article to the Belgian relief fund, apparently out of guilt.[77]

American campuses mostly became pro-Allies, out of American interest and a shared view of Germany as aggressor. Because of the large presence of German Americans in Wisconsin, President Van Hise at first aimed for neutrality; however, his silence was misinterpreted, and he was ultimately shunned.[78] Instigated by Georg Simmel, who complained that the world was believing lies about Germany, Albion Small, who remained proud of his German pedigree and wife, laid out the counterargument for Germany's culpability for World War I. Jordan of Stanford evolved from pacifist intervention to supporting American involvement in the Allies' war effort. Even German nationals living in America imbibed the anti-German sentiment.[79]

The tendency toward intellectual conformism was troubling to some. And the constraints fed a long-brewing resistance to administrative autocracy in a public controversy at Columbia University at the center of which was President Nicholas Murray Butler. The consummate education entrepreneur, who successfully turned scholarship into a form of international diplomacy, Butler had, in the 1910s, aspired to a political career with an internationalist platform. Together with Carnegie he had delivered speeches abroad about a peaceful Europe. Butler's institutional success at home rested on his strategic relationships with government officials around the world, including the Kaiser and those in the cultural ministries of Germany and their equivalents in Great Britain and France. It is, therefore, all the more alarming that Butler shifted so radically from advocate for international peace to bellicose American nationalist. Well before America entered the war, Butler paved the way for a new path of influence with lectures around New York boosting an image of the university as a service institution for the state.[80]

When in June 1916 Congress approved the creation of the Reserve Officers' Training Corps (ROTC) to train officers at universities, Butler signaled that Columbia was ready to mobilize. Butler's eagerness to become an agent of the government was not shared by his faculty. Seligman, the political economist who had been tasked by the AEA to investigate the Ross case and became part of the AAUP's Committee A, advocated for a more autonomous role for the university. In his 1916 address, "The Real University," Seligman professed, "The function of the state is to supplement the individual; the function of the church is to moralize the individual; the function of the university is to emancipate the individual. The state stands for order; the university for freedom. The church seeks for spiritual truth; the university for intellectual truth. The state stands for power; the church stands for unity; the university stands for independence."[81] While Seligman was a reformer who supported the progressive income tax, he opposed socialism and often mediated between leftism and the establishment. His message of the university ideal was pitched in that tone.

Seligman's colleague Cattell was less diplomatic. A student of Wilhelm Wundt in Leipzig, Cattell joined Columbia in 1891 as a professor of experimental psychology and rose to become one of the most prominent scholars in that discipline and a leader in the profession. A founder and president of the American Psychological Association and of the American Association for the Advancement of Science, Cattell was also elected to the National Academy of Sciences. As founding editor of the *Psychological Review* and editor of the magazine *Popular Science*, his imprint on the publishing world was no less impressive. According to the historian of psychology Dorothy Ross, Cattell was "second only to William James, in the esteem of his colleagues."[82] Cattell was also a "difficult and fiercely independent man," possibly "the most prominent academic gadfly of his time."[83]

The gadfly in Cattell surfaced at least a decade prior to the incident in 1916. Philosophically, Cattell was no more radical than Lovejoy, but he proposed institutional reform measures, including the right for departments to nominate candidates for appointments, that threatened the executive authority of the president. Whereas Lovejoy framed his vision of university governance in terms of republican ideals, Cattell was deliberately provocative and belligerent. In one of his essays for the series "University Control," Cattell wrote, "The more incompetent the faculties become, the greater is the need for executive autocracy, and the greater the autocracy of the president, the more incompetent do the faculties become. Under these conditions it appears that the university must be completely reorganized on a representative basis."[84] Cattell almost always presented his recommendations and positions as attacks against Butler, and even when he didn't, Butler saw them as personal.

On April 6, 1917, America entered the war, and the professors and administration at Columbia geared up to fight—each other. Neither Butler nor Cattell wasted any time. Speaking at commencement on June 6, Butler declared his readiness to serve: "The responsibility for action and for service cannot be devolved upon someone else, least of all can it be devolved upon government officials and government agencies . . . but [it must be taken up] by men and women who are the support of all these and whose convictions and stern action are the foundation upon which government and armies and navies rest."[85] Universities must play their part, and that role involved self-sacrifice and the constriction of free speech. Most startlingly Butler announced in a statement that was republished in newspapers across the United States, "This is the university's last and only word of warning to any among us, if such there be, who are not with whole head and mind and strength committed to fight with us to make the world safe for democracy."[86]

Cattell, for his part, seems to have been begging to be fired since his commentaries on the "autocratic" university system were published in 1913. By the summer of 1917, when Butler announced the new university policy on academic freedom, Cattell had just recently dodged one bullet from Butler after he suggested in a "confidential memorandum" that was leaked to the press that the faculty club be moved to Butler's grand and spacious home. Seligman pressured Cattell to apologize and managed to defuse the situation at first, but Cattell's second infraction would be more difficult to reconcile. Just two months later, Cattell sent a petition on Columbia letterhead to three congressmen urging them not to approve a bill that would have permitted the use of American conscripts on European battlefields.[87] This time, given Butler's professed commitment to the university's "special obligations" in wartime and Cattell's unwillingness to cooperate, Seligman and Dewey were at a loss, and Butler seized the opportunity to fire Cattell.

The incident, which led to a decades-long libel and pension lawsuit, left ill will all around. Dewey, who disapproved of Cattell's manner and urged him to apologize, was nonetheless disturbed enough to resign from the committee responsible for investigating his colleague's case. After a second professor, Henry Wadsworth Dana, was dismissed for similar opposition to the war effort, the historian Charles Beard resigned from the university completely, issuing a statement to the *New Republic* and the *New York Times* about the embarrassing state of affairs, in which faculty were being subjected to "humiliating doctrinal inquisitions by the trustees."[88]

The press was less than sympathetic. In an editorial in the *New Republic*, World War I was dubbed a "thinking man's war," and professors were accused of leading America into it. They may have had in mind not only Butler's "asylum," as Cattell later dubbed it, but also his inmates.[89] Dewey's *German Philosophy and Politics*, which appeared at the end of 1915, seemed to justify the American involvement in the war by analyzing what was problematic about German idealism. Dewey's evolving position, which appeared in a series of essays, including notably "In a Time of National Hesitation," revealed, as his student Randolph Bourne contended, the "poverty of pragmatism."[90] Written before the declaration of war and published thereafter, the essay opposed Americans' unwillingness to fight for a cause not their own. He argued for a transition from American isolationism to a new principled internationalism.[91] On reflection Dewey insisted that it was "idle to appeal to reason [since] [f]or the time being the conservative upholders of the Constitution are on the side of moral mob rule and psychological lynch law. In such an atmosphere a sober effort to locate the real abode of folly and wrongheadedness would itself appear treasonable."[92] In short, Dewey ultimately came around to endorse American involvement—on the terms that winning the war would mean a more enduring peace. For Bourne this set a dangerous precedent for professors complying with the states' demands.[93]

The "poverty" of Dewey's philosophical pragmatism was further exposed by a report from the AAUP's Committee on Academic Freedom in Wartime at the end of December 1917 that revised the Declaration of 1915. Rarely included in the celebratory histories of the AAUP, this document shows just how difficult it would be to protect academic freedom. An effort to strike a balance between suppression and irresponsibility—"It is a paradox of a war waged by a people in defense of law or freedom that the state of war may itself weaken within the respect for law or justice or freedom"—the document suffers under disclaimers as the authors weakly dial back freedom. Indeed, part of their claim is that they have played a role in preparing the American people for war even as they insist on the space for their work to continue.[94]

Aggravating the disappointment concerning the 1917 addendum was the fact that universities were now being mobilized for the war effort. In the fall of 1917 institutions of higher learning became centers for military training. And on October 1, at simultaneous assemblies of 516 colleges and universities around the country, 140,000 male students were inducted into the US Army and became student soldiers in the Student Army Training Corps (SATC). According to the US War Department Committee on Education and Special Training, universities were "like railroads, essentially government institutions."[95] The AAUP's retreat and the mobilization of students elicited little criticism, outside circles at the *Nation* and the *New Republic*, lone voices of opposition to the war.[96] And the new AAUP guidelines provided little protection for Cattell, even if he hadn't worn out the patience of his sole supporters at Columbia, Dewey and Seligman.

When the dust settled there were few heroes left standing. While French, British, and American academics expressed disdain in one breath at the German embrace of war, many seized the opportunity to expand their roles in their own societies, an uncomfortable fact that justifies the moniker of World War I as the "professor's war."[97] Francke entertained fantasies that had he lived until the war, William James would not have fallen prey to the "mad rush of American scholars against Germany" but would have joined the few independent scholars, including the British philosopher Bertrand Russell and the French poet Romain Rolland, who spoke out against nationalism. Perhaps. But even so, the list of scholars who retained their independence was short. Even Dewey, who protested the firing of Cattell, left the committee but not the university that was complicit in this act. And his split from his former student Bourne is a good indication of the disappointment many felt in the failure of intellectual leadership. To be sure, other professions, such as journalists and clergy, also used the war to raise their status, but the academic social contract was unique in that it entitled faculty negotiated autonomy that lasted through the end of the twentieth century.[98]

Beard's resignation is an example of one noble alternative path of a scholar who chose not to comply with the new terms of such a contract. In a dramatic letter that was later published in *Columbia Alumni News*, Beard announced that since he no longer had faith in a university run by a "few obscure and willful trustees who now dominate the University and terrorize the young instructors," he would leave the university in which he had served for over a decade but not the "great republic of Columbia students, alumni, and professors."[99] The historian Thomas Bender points out the irony that Beard, who had been tasked to head the Civics Division within Butler's new framework for the "Organization of Columbia University for National Service . . . would indeed give Columbia a lesson in civics, but certainly not the one Butler intended or wanted."[100] And he made good on his promise. Though the university had been able to withstand religious and economic orthodoxy, at least where the early academic freedom cases were concerned, it was impotent in the face of nationalism.[101]

Notwithstanding the promises of the AAUP, aggrieved scholars like Cattell, whose positions fell outside the societal demands put upon them, were unable to defend themselves. The possibilities for expressing discontent and remaining within the system were limited. The American professional professoriate was born of World War I and defined national service as constitutive of professional integrity. The German professoriate fared no better, because—as Weber, Ben-David, and subsequent sociologists surmised—there was no independent corporation and no corporate identity independent of the scholars' obligations to the state. Even if the German university was truly populated by conservative professors who believed that the state was above reproach this would be impossible to verify because of the pressure to conform. Pacifists were silenced or exiled. It was the first of many moments to come in which a professor would have to face the dilemma of what the sociologist Albert O. Hirschman later called "exit, voice, and loyalty." For Beard the best possibility of preserving the university ideal (and the only choice of integrity) was to exit, whereas other scholars continued to express—and to benefit from—their loyalty.[102]

EXIT, VOICE, LOYALTY

Given the academic social contracts on both sides of the Atlantic, it was unavoidable that universities would in some degree serve their states during World War I.[103] In Germany, this service was formalized, as described in chapter 1, following war with Napoleon: universities received some degree of autonomy in exchange for the expertise that assured Germany would never again suffer such a humiliating defeat. These "bodyguards of the Hohenzollerns" were expected, when the time came, to step up and certainly not to stand in the nation's way. In America, the Civil War was the conflict that crystallized university service, albeit in regional terms. Education entrepreneurs, whether at private or public universities, enacted the "will of the community," and trustees acted as "public servants." When World War I created the conditions for American universities to be viewed as potential resources for the nation, university leaders would be compelled to alter their rhetoric. The German American scientist Jacques Loeb shared the frustrations of many when he observed in 1914, "The whole trouble comes from their identifying themselves with their governments and their diplomats." When one considers the original contract, however, it was unreasonable to feign surprise. Mobilization was part of the deal.[104]

With respect to the "philosophical birth" of academic freedom, the faculty could have aimed higher. In Germany, the *Ordinariat* class clung to their freedom of inquiry partially as a proxy for social and economic status, and they resented technical school instructors and *Privatdozenten* for encroaching on their privileged position. Anxiety about professional status and privilege proved to be an equally important motivation in America, where many academics came from the lower middle class. One consequence was that academic freedom in America became attached to tenure, and adjunct instructors were left with little to no job protection.[105]

Academic freedom had its beginnings in the defensive demands of scholars acting in response to suppression. Even if they had loftier ideals, academic freedom was from its inception a freedom *from* rather than a freedom *to*, making it more akin to what the philosopher Isaiah Berlin called a negative freedom rather than a positive one. This is all the more surprising, since one of its framers, Dewey, for his part came to be celebrated for his commitment to shaping democratic character through positive claims.[106] But the founding Declaration was far from a positive claim; it was the quintessential negative procedural document. This permitted the authors of the AAUP's Declaration of Principles to skirt the issue of the purpose of academic freedom. The current courts' lack of agreement concerning the scope of academic freedom has its origins in the muddled philosophical legacy and the lack of clear boundaries and ends delineated at the very beginning.[107] As a practical matter, the failure of the Declaration's authors to determine what constitutes legitimate academic speech (both intramural and extramural) weakened the ability to defend not only against further infringements on the faculty, but also against faculty members promoting, for example, racist ideology under the guise of science.

Weber's support of value-free scholarship as the university's true purpose hardly did any better. "Universities do not have it as their task to teach any outlook or standpoint which is either 'hostile to the state' or 'friendly to the state,'" Weber insisted in his defense of Germany's vanishing academic freedom. "They are not institutions for the inculcation of absolute or ultimate moral values. They analyse facts, their conditions, laws and interrelations; they analyse concepts, their logical presuppositions and content." Even Weber understood the limitations of this neutrality as the last defense against political and religious fanaticism penetrating the university.[108]

The irony is that while the balance worked best when the university was kept at arm's length from society, the precious freedom enjoyed by the *Ordinariat* in Germany was connected to their role as civil servants, and the demands of war activated the expected loyalty that came with this role, making them inevitably less free. The post–World War I culture minister Carl H. Becker declared in 1919 that the power of the *Ordinariat* was "near absolute."[109] But so was their obligation to the state. At those moments of friction, the fragility of the arrangement became evident. Ben-David reminds us of the anomalous status of universities in Germany, which "started thriving as a hot-house flower mainly on the whimsical support of a few members of the ruling class, and desperately attempted to establish wider roots in society. . . . It was, therefore, a precarious status based on a compromise."[110]

That compromise constrained intellectuals during dark times, as we will see, but it also meant that the environment of the garden was important for the flower's growth. Given the greater political freedom in the United States, many American (and British) academics who had visited Germany in the preceding decade noted what one scholar calls the "paradoxical inversion" of the relationship between freedom in the university and freedom in society. That is, the German university was more permissive than its surrounding political culture, while in America, the political culture was freer than the university.[111] At the same time, American visitors to Germany absorbed unrealistic expectations about the German ideal. Academic freedom would later become unhinged from its historical context and elided with American civil liberties, which were in fact more expansive than even those the Germans imagined for the professoriate.[112]

If the war was the fertilizer for the "planting" of academic freedom in America, a new relationship between the university and society emerged from the distinctive American context. In the process, the relationships and loyalties between professors and their institutions, and between their institutions and the state, were redrawn, and an "indigenous" American system was born. As the authors of the AAUP founding document observed, freedom of inquiry was blurred by the diversity of higher education, with public and private, as well as religious, institutions whose explicit objective was to evangelize. "But it is manifestly important that they should not be permitted to sail under false colors," the committee intoned. "Genuine boldness and thoroughness of inquiry, and freedom of speech, are scarcely reconcilable with the prescribed inculcation of a particular opinion upon a controverted question."[113] At stake were the terms under which an institution was entitled to call itself a university. When it came to public goods, the authors of these principles believed that both state and private universities had a contractual agreement to provide them, and it was on the basis of their value that freedom of inquiry was earned.[114]

Some American professors welcomed the expansion of their role; they wanted to be advisers to the political elite.[115] Not anticipating the anti-intellectualism that awaited them at the end of the war, many professors embraced their new elevated social status.[116] Others, disillusioned by "Clio's debauch in the arms of Uncle Sam," were dismayed that faculty were so easily swayed by the proximity to power.[117] For them the war was a crisis of the university's purpose, which birthed not only academic freedom, but also other institutional reform. In Frankfurt on the Main, German scholars would seize the moment of revolutionary change following World War I to create a new university and a new research institution, both of which were more autonomous than their forebears. In New York, the aggrieved Beard gathered like-minded colleagues and moved downtown with the lofty goal to reform the research university itself—heralding the greatest changes to higher education yet.

CHAPTER EIGHT

THE "HOUR FOR EXPERIMENT" IN NEW YORK AND FRANKFURT

It is our American habit if we find the foundations of our educational structure unsatisfactory to add another story or a wing. We find it easier to add a new study or course or kind of school than to reorganize conditions so as to meet the need.

JOHN DEWEY, 1916

No university is complete today without its research institute.

HAROLD LASKI, 1928

In 1918, the American chemist Willis R. Whitney, who founded the General Electric laboratory, wrote to Robert A. Millikan, vice chairman of the National Research Council, requesting that more funding be provided for scientific research. What was notable about Whitney's letter was not the appeal—as we've seen, this was becoming the order of the day—but its urbanist rationale: "We who know geography even now recall many European cities largely through the research laboratories or scientists they contained. Take Leipzig, Berlin, Heidelberg, Bonn, for example. Who would know of Göttingen, Freiburg, or Jena but through the researches done there? . . . Why should we fail to produce in many of the cities of our country just such Meccas of learning and research as Leipzig or Jena?"[1]

Whitney's rhetoric reflected the growing importance of urban centers relative to nation-states that resulted from the war's toppling of the political order. It was consistent with a new climate of competition and innovation that followed the parallel disruption of the international scientific order. Because World War I ended Germany's hundred-year reign as the global center of knowledge, for the first time since the founding of the University of Berlin there was no single leading authority in higher learning. This vacuum proved to be motivation for the competitive development of universities inside and outside Germany. Academic entrepreneurs hardly waited for the armistice to be negotiated before pushing their institutions to the top of the new pyramid. Amid the widespread suffering, the war and its aftermath precipitated a great deal of innovation—as usual a mixture of idealistic and self-serving—that marks the interwar period as what one group of academic reformers in New York called the "hour for experiment."[2]

America's European allies, France and Great Britain, rushed to take Germany's place by isolating it with harsh restrictions and an official boycott, cultivating new "interallied" partnerships, and courting credential-seeking students abroad.[3] Americans could barely conceal their schadenfreude at Germany's fall from scientific grace. The American astrophysicist George Ellery Hale, who was initially prepared to forgive the Germans, clearly perceived the opening the war represented, calling it "the great opportunity of the United States."[4] Even nations that adapted the German university model, like China, Japan, and now Palestine, strove to capitalize on the decline of German hegemony.[5]

With the international realignment of scientific organization came opportunities for cities unhindered and untainted by nationalism to become bigger players in the world order. A new crop of academic leaders welcomed the return of the local as an organizing principle for intellectual and scholarly life. In the revitalized federalism of the Weimar Republic in interwar Germany, cities with histories of milder nationalism (as well as with deeper pockets and independent infrastructures) were ready to compete internationally.[6] Unencumbered by the tradition and hierarchy of Germany's centuries-old universities, these "Weimar-era" institutions, including those founded in Frankfurt on the Main (1914), Hamburg (1919), and Cologne (1919), had an affinity for America in their financial models and became home to intellectual schools that were eminently exportable.[7]

One condition of the decline of German science and the rise of regional centers was the emergence of a new institution: the privately funded social science research institute. Citing the strained relationship between research and teaching, and the damaged ideal of autonomy, German and American education entrepreneurs established institutions of higher learning outside the traditional structure of the research university. These new extra-university institutions, the "Forschungsinstitute," were often supported by private funding and valued autonomy above all.[8] Part of a wider embrace of the "un-university" that included experiments in adult education and the revival of the liberal arts college, the research institute, which often still incorporated some element of teaching, emerged as both a supplement and a challenge to the modern university.[9]

NEW YORK—A FREE SCHOOL FOR SOCIAL THOUGHT

As the bloody war drew to its conclusion, the social scientists Charles Beard and James Harvey Robinson, and the publisher Herbert Croly, formulated

an institutional experiment in New York City that aimed to radically rede-
fine the university's purpose and relationship to the world. Drawing on the
history of New York as a "laboratory" for the social sciences and a city with
a strong literary base, these innovators challenged Columbia, the city's major university, with one of the most consequential "un-university" projects
of the twentieth century: the New School for Social Research.[10]

Beard was emblematic of the social scientists who moved between the
municipal and university worlds, and his fluidity supported the close relationship between theory and practice that he espoused. In his first text-
book, published in 1910, Beard formulated his activist historical position by
revising the German tradition in which he was trained: "Man is not made
for the state . . . but the state for man."[11] Believing in scholarship's engagement with the public discourse, Beard helped to found a number of metropolitan organizations, including the Bureau of Municipal Research, a city
fact-finding agency that played a central role in the professionalization of
public administration. Based at the bureau three afternoons a week, Beard
crafted his controversial work, *An Economic Interpretation of the Constitution*, which aimed to apply activist economics to an understanding of
American politics. He subsequently assumed responsibilities at the Training School for Public Service; in 1915, the year he published *The Economic
Origins of Jeffersonian Democracy*, Beard became director of that school.[12]
Together with the historian Robinson, Beard set out to develop a school of
"New History" that drew equally on German anti-laissez-faire economic
thought and American pragmatist philosophy to produce a more engaged
form of scholarship.

Robinson shared Beard's German economic historical training and a
belief in the ability of science to improve the world. Beginning his graduate work with William James at Harvard, Robinson completed his dissertation, "The Original and Derived Features of the Constitution of the
United States," at Freiburg in 1890 under the direction of Hermann Edward von Holtz, whose own departure for Chicago signaled the strength of
this transatlantic partnership in the social sciences. Hired by Columbia in
1895 as a professor of European history, Robinson developed friendships
with Dewey and Thorstein Veblen (the latter of whom became, as we saw,
a keen observer of the relationship between exclusion and innovation).[13]
Together, Veblen, Beard, and Robinson constructed a formidable critique
of the embeddedness of the university in a class system and became advocates for the newly formalized academic freedom. Through these activities
Beard and Robinson developed a commitment to grounding training for
public service in social science.

As early as 1916 Beard and Robinson had corresponded with Croly, the publisher of the nascent magazine the *New Republic*, about starting an independent institute to offer lecture courses and research opportunities to adult students. Croly lent his offices at West Twenty-First Street to the disaffected Columbia professors for weekly planning sessions.[14] The magazine became a platform in which Croly laid out one form the school could take. Given the emerging hierarchy of international science, it is not entirely surprising that he referenced France rather than Germany as its foreign model, but it is revealing that the institution Croly cited was not the Sorbonne (the main research university of Paris and France) but the École Libre des Sciences Politiques (ELSP), an independent institute. The French innovation that should most interest Americans, according to Croly, was that which emerged from private citizens' desire to train students for public administration and to apply scientific methods to the problems of politics. Sharing "a faith in the creative power of ideas which is no less implicit in the American than in the French national tradition," Croly yearned for "an enlargement, adapted to American conditions, of the idea underlying the École Libre des Sciences Politiques."[15]

There was a paradox at the heart of Croly's conception of the New School. To allow the school to "pursue its work without a fear of interference from those class and official interests whose social behavior it would necessarily investigate," he sought "independence" from business and the state. But insofar as he aimed to improve public administration with highly trained experts, Croly presented the school's raison de être as serving the state. The founders aimed to rewrite the academic social contract, which they felt had foundered at Columbia with an opportunist like Butler at the helm. Under their guidance, the university would be independent but not remote, Croly wrote, "so the American school hopes to make social research of immediate assistance to a bewildered and groping American democracy." For Croly, as for most American Progressive intellectuals, science was a valuable tool: "The war has helped us to realize at once what enormous resources science has placed at the disposal of the human will."[16] It needed only to be wielded for good rather than ill.

In the pages of the *Columbia University Quarterly*, where he was still on the faculty, Beard expressed a similar desire for autonomy and was weighing the extent to which this union of research and praxis fit into the research university. "This fortunate combination of research and teaching, so peculiarly American, makes the lot of the university instructor in politics a happy one," Beard wrote, "and it will in time have a wholesome effect upon our learning." Though Beard made his first institutional home at Columbia, he also set his gaze on a future when social science training would be more in tune with government needs: "The number of government positions requiring special training is multiplying, and they are especially attractive to university men. . . . The day is not far off when some great university will work a happy union of physics and politics . . . and thus help to give to public service a greater efficiency, and the real dignity which it deserves."[17]

Beard, like Croly, believed that scholarly integrity and the application of social science research to social problems depended on professors coming from all class backgrounds. But how was that to be accomplished? At the very least, he knew in 1917 it was no longer possible under Butler at Columbia, a realization that was not easy. He had devoted over a decade to strengthening political science at Columbia and in so doing had contributed in no small part to the premier status that Columbia held at the turn of the twentieth century. In agreement with Croly that "the truth about social processes and relations will never set us free if it is sought only or chiefly by contemplation," Beard departed Columbia in 1917.[18]

Beard, Croly, and Robinson continued to hash out the details of their plan on the pages of the new "Journal of Opinion," as Robinson dubbed the *New Republic* in 1915.[19] His description of the magazine's founders applied to their educational innovation, a "growing class of thoughtful men who have no undue reverence for established habits of thought, and who feel that our final extrication from the present muddle must come in part at least through unhampered scientific criticism, not only of existing moral, social and political institutions, but of the very ideas and standards that have been underlying them."[20] And Robinson's position had the least "reverence for established habits of thought" as expressed in the university's educational model. As Robinson observed, "Teaching and learning are assumed to go hand in hand. But no one who is not professionally pledged to this assumption can fail to see that teaching commonly fails to produce learning, and that most we have learned has come without teaching, or in spite of it."[21] In his desire for real learning he shifted his attention to a different audience—adults—"who after some experience of life are eager to extend, elaborate and elucidate their personal experience by studying matters which have aroused their curiosity, shown up their ignorance or puzzled them."[22]

These discussions brought together diverging strands of reform—the distrust of elite universities; the self-improvement movement that sought, in the words of Robinson, to "humanize" knowledge; and the politically driven workers education and labor colleges that coalesced in the 1920s.[23] So it is not a surprise that two competing visions for the school emerged—an independent social policy institute versus a provider of extended adult education. The debate reflects broader unresolved tensions concerning the relationship between research and teaching and the purpose of each. Into the mix stepped John Dewey, whose ideas of democratic education were used in the school's promotional materials, as well as Thorstein Veblen, whose anticapitalist work was becoming increasingly influential. Dewey would never actually resign his position at Columbia to join the New School—a decision that was revelatory of the gap between vision and reality and the problematic structure of the school. Veblen, for his part, was now revising what would become his classic, *The Higher Learning in America,* and his interactions with the Croly circle provided occasion to consider how the war damaged the American university and created an opening for a new, more independent institution.[24]

In a passage that would become famous, Veblen criticized the corporatization of the university: "In this view the university is conceived as a business house dealing in merchantable knowledge, placed under the governing hand of a captain of erudition, whose office it is to turn the means in hand to account in the largest feasible output." Even if the "captain" Veblen had in mind was Harper of Chicago or Jordan of Stanford, the characterization applied equally to Butler and his "business house" of knowledge. For Veblen as for Robinson, teaching and research in their current formulation were incompatible. What Veblen sought was a new establishment where "teachers and students of all nationalities, including Americans . . . , may pursue their chosen work as guests of the American academic community."[25] His observations set the stage for Beard, Robinson, and Croly's plans, and he eagerly signed on to the New School as a lecturer.

The distinct proposals for a social policy institute and an adult education school might never have united had the philanthropist Dorothy Straight not seen the latter as a way to train progressive leaders. Without consulting her husband, she pledged $10,000 a year for ten years and became the first and main patron of the New School.[26] In combining the two visions for the school, the institution also isolated the most radical strand.[27] Beard himself had been involved in the Rand School of Social Science, which had ties to the labor union movement and communism.[28] But he was tempered by Robinson, whose student, Emily James Putnam, argued with her mentor that he was not "revolutionary" enough and often signed her letters "Yours for Anarchy." In certain matters Putnam's persistence succeeded; it was her idea to do away with tenure and limit faculty appointments to contracts, and these became signature features of the first version of the school.

In the December 28, 1918, issue of the *New Republic,* the New School ran an advertisement listing its course offerings and inviting "intelligent men and women" to enroll.[29] The New School was from the beginning coed and egalitarian, a combination that, as we have seen, was far from a given. In their "Proposal for an Independent School of Social Sciences for Men and

Women," the founders committed to educating individuals to make sense of the world's complexity and to producing the "new type of leadership" demanded by the war. Since the "legal control of all our institutions is placed in the hands of bodies of trustees, composed for the most part of men whose views of political, social, religious and moral questions are in no way in advance of those of the average respectable citizen," a new institution with a different organization was needed to encourage more than "established thought," one that was "free from ancient embarrassments, where well qualified investigators and thinkers can enjoy the advantage of one another's thought and discoveries."[30] Openness to a new system, new ideas, and new kinds of scholars and students went hand in hand.

In February 1919, the New School welcomed students in its first home — six brownstones on West Twenty-Third Street in the Chelsea neighborhood of New York City. The offices of the *New Republic* were right around corner on Twenty-First Street, and a new literary world was emerging in Greenwich Village to the south. The offer of adult education drew more students than anticipated. In its first year the school enrolled 348 students, but registrations more than doubled over the next four years to 800. From the beginning, two-thirds of those students were women (in comparison to 40 percent of college students nationwide and 35 percent in New York state). Nearly 30 percent seem to have been Jewish.[31] The New School faculty also contained a number of prominent women and Jews, as well as socialists. The overlap among these groups explains the endorsement the New School received from the International Ladies' Garment Workers' Union. The school's identification with "respectable radicalism" may have appealed to women in social-reform movements, many of whom were Jewish.[32] In the previous decade, when prejudice barred them from jobs as professors, women PhD social scientists were often pushed into social work.[33] It is equally important, therefore, that the opening of a new "ununiversity" provided an unprecedented academic route for a host of female social scientists.

One remarkable such woman was Clara Mayer, who belonged to all these categories. Mayer was amenable to Robinson and Beard's adult education plan and became a champion for the idea that "learning has no age limit."[34] She was, according to one biographer, "a student in search of a teacher," and she followed Robinson from Columbia to the New School. Beginning as a student, she became the school's most significant administrator.[35] She also established a close relationship with Alvin Johnson, the Nebraska-born, Columbia-trained editor of the *New Republic*, whom Mayer would later approach to lift the New School out of its financial troubles.

Johnson was exuberant in his recollection of the school's founding. As he later wrote, "The New School opened, with éclat, for the spring term of 1919. Every liberal in the city was excited by the novel venture of an institution headed by two such dynamic figures as Robinson and Beard, self-disfrocked from the conventional academic life."[36] Johnson's recollection echoed the 1919 proposal in which the founders announced of the school's novelty, "Nothing like it has ever been attempted; this is the hour for experiment; and New York is the place, because it is the greatest social science laboratory in the world and of its own forces attracts scholars and leaders in educational work."[37]

Not everyone in New York shared his enthusiasm. Almost immediately the New School came under attack for being "pro-Hun" and "Teutonic" (despite its claims of Gallic inspiration). The conservative T. Everett Harré argued that the New School proved how "Germanism had invaded American universities and schools during a quarter of a century, the extent to which the minds of American professors had been tainted by the Teutonic virus." Of course Harré acknowledged that the new German influence was no longer transparent and urged vigilance against its new domestic form as "the propaganda of social discontent, revolution and civil strife, which seeks to deviate and destroy the nations through a cunning, deceptive and destructive internationalism."[38] In reality, a number of diverse foreign sources influenced the New School's founding, including the ELSP, the London School of Economics (LSE), Ruskin Hall (later College) in Oxford, and the German *Volkshochschule* adult education movement.[39]

In America the New School was not alone in its attempt to emancipate the social sciences from the clutches of the university, which was corrupted by its association with the dominant classes. Two groups of institutions emerged in America to pursue this goal. One group provided instruction and training grounded in a new vision of service. Manifestations of this movement included the Rand School of Social Sciences (1906, New York City) and Brookwood Labor College (1921, Katonah, New York).[40] A second group devoted to research included the Brookings Institution (1916, Washington, DC), the National Bureau of Economic Research (1920, New York City), and the Council on Foreign Relations (1921, New York City).[41] The New School, then, was part of a wider American institutional response to a transatlantic movement, which addressed the perceived shortcomings of the modern research university, be they in teaching or research. This eclectic list of institutions illustrates a duality: if the Columbia émigrés worried about the university's association with the upper class and wished to create a space free of capitalist and nationalist influence, others wished to enhance the influence of the social sciences to get closer to the seats of political power.

These frictions persisted among the New School founders themselves, appearing in the divide between those who favored a program of labor-oriented adult education and those who wanted a social policy institute. This tension carried over into the semipublic lectures that provided the substance of the curriculum. Students paid for these à la carte and could select from the leading social scientists of the day. When it worked as intended, the instructors brought what Johnson and Mayer called a "pioneer's persuasiveness" to their lectures, using the authenticity of the platform to explore cutting-edge lines of inquiry in their fields or establish new ones. This was the case for psychoanalysis, which was not represented in the university and which Mayer would persuade Johnson to support by inviting Sándor Ferenczi, the psychoanalytic theorist and close associate of Freud, from Budapest to teach a course. Not all star social science researchers turned out to be good instructors. Veblen mumbled and refused to speak clearly—by some accounts he did not want to be heard—which led to numerous student complaints and his ultimate firing.[42]

The founders of the New School opposed what they saw as the corrosive influences of excessive bureaucracy, institutionalization, and external influence. Alvin Johnson envied how free British political theorist Harold Laski was at the LSE during the war while in America faculty became accustomed to the newspaper headline "Another Professor Goes Pop." Johnson pined for a school that "was not handicapped by mobs of beef-devouring alumni, passionate about football and contemptuous of scholarship."[43] Beard believed that the endowment was the rot of an institution, and promoted a "hand-to-mouth plan" because "every endowment tempts pirate educators to clamber over the gunwales, dirk in teeth."[44] And so they eschewed an endowment altogether. The administration, they believed, only served to cripple the university—so they did away with administration; there would be no one in charge until Robinson took the reins. And like modernist artists they peeled off successive layers of artifice and pretense, tradition and expectations, until there was nothing but a pure white canvas remaining. Was it still a university?

Perhaps as an ideal, but that proved only so useful when just three years after its founding the New School found itself on the verge of bankruptcy. Had it not been for Mayer, who with a group of students appealed to Alvin Johnson for his administrative leadership and financial support, the school would have closed. Johnson agreed to both requests and, in turn, appointed Mayer to the board of trustees to "interpret the school to the other trustees." Mayer soon became its secretary and then principal officer. By 1930 she was assistant director and then codirector.[45] Together, Mayer and Johnson came up with a new financial strategy.

Johnson, who had always been—along with Mayer—less opposed to the traditional formalities of the university, began an endowment campaign. The tortured language of the promotional materials reveals how complicated it was to backtrack on one of the founders' most cherished principles.[46] In its second founding (there would come a third as well) an opportunity arose to clarify the vision.[47] Here again competing ideas were promoted, and though the battle between the social scientists and the adult education advocates was not entirely resolved, the need to generate revenue outweighed philosophical opposition to vocationalism. Student fees represented 22 percent of income in 1919; over the next ten years that percentage doubled.[48] Tellingly, one tactic that Johnson pursued was to embrace the arts wholeheartedly. Welcoming modernist artists like John Cage and Roscoe Pound and giving them a platform saved the school in terms of enrollment and income, yet this "popularizing" era threatened to change the complexion of the school's intellectual mission entirely. As Peter Rutkoff and William B. Scott observe in their history of the school, "Until 1933, its contribution to the arts notwithstanding, the New School maintained its commitment to social research in its name alone."[49]

Given how unrealistic they were, it is perhaps not surprising (though no less disappointing) that the New School failed to live up to the hopes of its founders. Already in July 1921 Charles Beard expressed disillusionment. Responding to an editorial titled "The Vanishing University," Beard tried to resurrect the original ideal while expressing frustration with the failure of the current project: "Having just returned from stricken Europe, to which so many of our educated classes turn for enlightenment, I must say, however, that if the present state of that continent is the fruit of high culture, we may profitably be spared some of the bitter harvest." Beard cautioned against nostalgia for the European medieval universities, which "were free in the sense that they were not managed by boards of weary business men; but trustees were not the only limitations on the human spirit."[50] In a moment of idealism Beard took one last stab at describing his ideal school:

It would be a group of teachers, freely associated in the pursuit of wisdom and knowledge (two very different things), and surrounded by a band of able and zealous students. It would have no buildings, no alumni associations, no academic red tape. Each teacher would be free to pick his own students from among the applicants and to dismiss wasters and mediocrities on five minutes notice. Freedom of thought would be encouraged; that would of itself impose moral responsibilities upon teachers. They would not turn their chafing at the restraints of trustees into a wild and foolish chafing at the restraints of life. Such an institution would necessarily be conservative because responsible thinking, baffled by the world's complexities, never produces half-baked radicalism.[51]

Beard did not mention the New School by name, but the conspicuous absence of it was damning enough. The New School was for Beard as for Robinson a "personal disappointment . . . [a] failure . . . to measure up."[52]

ACADEMIC EXPERIMENTS ON THE MAIN

Germany's Weimar Republic is now a synonym for desperation and precipitous political decline and, as a historical period, seems to offer an awkward parallel to the America of 1919.[53] Strapped with mounting inflation, burdened by a parliamentary stalemate, and cursed by a lack of legitimacy, the Weimar Republic was "a gamble which stood virtually no chance of success."[54] But in its encouragement of new ideas and seemingly boundless idealism, Germany's first democratic Republic shared with postwar America a similar gasp of "hope." The intellectual historian Peter Gay once observed that "Weimar was an idea seeking to become a reality."[55] For however much Weimar's fragile institutions teetered on the verge of collapse, Germany's first experiment with democracy also held cultural and scholarly possibilities. Elements of society previously excluded were more welcome. And Weimar encouraged the implementation of ideals of truth and beauty and new communities of higher learning. Their legacies would last well beyond the Republic and would extend to America.

In the Weimar cultural world, as Gay noted, traditional outsiders had the opportunity to become insiders.[56] Gay's claim of the potential for inclusion may have overstated the case, but in scholarship new institutions of higher learning were indeed more welcoming alternatives than the established academic world. To be sure, the German professors in the traditional "mandarin" mold of the empire only reluctantly accepted the Weimar Republic. They disdained the Treaty of Versailles and the hateful terms the Allies imposed on the German nation.[57] But a different potential emerged in cities outside the political center that boasted cultural traditions that dated to the Roman period and were protected in their status as "free imperial cities." Much like New York, these cities stood to gain from the federalist revival of localities over nations.[58]

One of the capitals of this "other" Weimar was Frankfurt on the Main, a city of about a half a million people that was shaped by finance and trade. Frankfurt lacked a university until 1914. As in Hamburg, for much of the nineteenth century, Frankfurt's sibling free city to the north, the merchants sent their sons abroad to train in affiliate family businesses and believed that a university was unnecessary. Those who did attend university could easily travel to nearby Heidelberg or Giessen. This was not to say that Frankfurt's merchant class was uninterested in art and culture. Since Frankfurt had no state-sponsored institutions, the merchants drove the creation of its cultural world, which, in turn, reflected the city's cosmopolitan identity. In the prewar period, Frankfurt was home to many of Germany's largest foundations, which operated as an ersatz university and conducted the scholarly, cultural, and aesthetic work of the city.[59] Though they had been outsiders of the German Empire, Frankfurt's Jews, who after World War I numbered thirty thousand, or 6 percent of the city's population, played a large role in sponsoring and cultivating the cultural world of the city and were involved in approximately one-third of its foundations.[60] The Senckenberg Nature Research Society, the Institute for the Common Good, and the city opera, constructed in 1880, were all products, at least in part, of Jewish munificence.

Franz Adickes's arrival as the Lord Mayor of Frankfurt in 1891 led to a shift in the relationship between donors and the municipality.[61] In particular, Adickes capitalized on the public institutions that had been founded through the benevolence of its citizens and incorporated them into a municipal governance.[62] He galvanized local support and attracted talent to the city. In an early win, Adickes persuaded the renowned physiologist Paul Ehrlich in 1899 to move his Royal Institute for Experimental Therapy from Berlin to Frankfurt. Crucial to Adickes's ambitious plans for the city was a university, and he soon found a partner in Wilhelm Merton, a British-German industrialist who ran one of Frankfurt's largest metal conglomerates. A baptized Jew with transatlantic connections who gave generously to Frankfurt's scientific and public causes, Merton was, as we saw, an "early adopter" of American-style philanthropy through both his Institute for the Common Good and its associated Academy of Commercial and Social Sciences.[63] Joining forces, Adickes and Merton received further financial support from the Frankfurt Jewish Speyer family, whose foundation endowed chairs and funded a growing number of medical institutes. The incremental merger of these disparate beginnings would provide the infrastructure for the biggest project of all.[64]

The duo drew on this foundation and Frankfurt's spirit of initiative and private generosity to raise funds for an endowed university (*Stiftungsuniversität*)—the first of its kind in Germany. Since the university would not be created by a monarch, prince, or duke, it would require the support of the local community. Gilman had found this to be a challenge in Baltimore, even with America's philanthropic tradition to draw on. Merton's success rested on his ability to persuade those in his personal network to support this unprecedented project. Accordingly, the Georg and Franziska Speyer Foundation funded an institute for Romance language, the Ludwig Braunfels Foundation paid for a library for languages, and Wilhelm Bonn donated the law library. Due in part to Merton's fundraising, at least a dozen Jewish foundations and philanthropists gave money for professorships and funded various medical clinics and institutes. Jewish benefactors provided three-quarters of the university's endowment.[65]

While Merton continued to solicit donations, Adickes persuaded the skeptical Prussian state, of which Frankfurt had been an ambivalent member since 1866, to permit the new enterprise. He would have to prove first that Germany—replete in universities—actually needed another one. Adickes proved a consummate negotiator and offered as consolation to the Prussian Education Ministry an arrangement in which a representative from the ministry would attend the university senate's meetings (but not vote). One correspondent in the *Kreuz-Zeitung* worried in 1912 that a university outside national control would only hire professors who shared the beliefs of the dominant local paper, the *Frankfurter Zeitung*. "Can the state renounce its vigilance over appointments to professorships?" he asked.[66]

In fact, that is precisely what the Jewish donors wanted. Despite the war and the revolution, the number of Jewish *Ordinarius* professors at Prussian universities was still remarkably small and had been declining steadily since the gains made at the end of the nineteenth century. (By 1917, there would be thirteen Jewish *Ordinarius* professors at German universities compared to twenty-five in 1909 and twenty-two in 1889.) Given the continued exclusion of Jews from the Prussian universities, the Rothschilds insisted that the new university abide by a condition of nondenominationalism in appointments at the new university, as they had urged Harnack to do with the Kaiser Wilhelm Society.[67] Drafted by Ludwig Heilbrunn, who would also write the history of the nascent university, the university's constitution included the stipulation that "religious or confessional status shall not in any instance be grounds for exclusion in filling a Chair."[68] And the founders made good on this promise. When the University of Frankfurt opened on October 16, 1914, four Jews were appointed for chairs: Berthold Freudenthal to the Chair of Public Law, Ludwig Edinger to the Chair of Neurology, Josef Horowitz to the Chair of Oriental Philology, and Paul Ehrlich (finally, at the end of his life) to the Chair in Experimental Therapy. As the historian of Germany Peter Pulzer observed, "It was a victory for the spirit and letter of the constitution achieved on a narrow front and in uniquely favorable circumstances."[69]

The University of Frankfurt declared structural and pedagogical independence from the traditional model. First, a council composed of representatives of the university, donors, and the city decided appointments of faculty, who in turn were not civil servants, but employees of the municipal institution. This autonomy was only possible in a city like Frankfurt that had both municipal and private wealth (the city contributed half of the 30 million M required for the endowment). When the mark lost value to inflation private sources of funding (those with access to foreign currency in particular) became even more important. Unlike the traditional university, faculties were established in five subject areas—philosophy, law, economics and social sciences, medicine, and natural sciences. By integrating practical education into these fields, the university accommodated the city's economic priorities. In a more unusual move, the university eschewed a theological faculty altogether (it established an institute for Semitic philology instead), and even added a chair for Jewish religion and ethics in the philosophy department that was first held in 1924 by the esteemed German-Jewish philosopher Martin Buber.[70]

When the Institute for Social Research was founded in 1923 as an independent entity affiliated with the university, it would become the "second anomaly" in this anomalous German city.[71] As with the university itself, loyal and visionary patrons were the sine qua non. The Weil family was first among them. Styled after the fashion of American robber barons, the Weils stuck out in Germany.[72] Hermann Weil was a prosperous German-Argentine businessman who in 1910 was the biggest transatlantic grain trader with three thousand employees in locations all over the world. He used his international connections and currency to remain successful after the First World War. An impactful philanthropist, he donated 120 million M during his life.[73] His son Felix Weil, raised in Argentina until he was eight, otherwise followed the tried-and-true path of the socialist-cum-son of a banker: he studied in Tübingen with Robert Wildebrandt, one of the few openly socialist German university professors, was arrested for revolutionary activities in October 1919, and then, expelled from Tübingen, returned to Frankfurt with a radical vision for a new institution of higher learning devoted to the study of Marxism as a legitimate social science.[74]

Scholars evidently teased Weil junior for being a "salon Bolshevik," but this moniker diminishes the significance of his contribution as "the only man in the field of socialist activity . . . who possessed the resources to actually realize such a Marxist research institution." Motivated by this calling, the resourceful son persuaded his generous father to finance an institute to study the international trade union movement, antisemitism, and the relationship of mass politics to poverty.[75] Felix Weil then successfully recruited Kurt Albert Gerlach, a left-wing Social Democrat and the youngest and most radical adviser to the Verein für Sozialpolitik, to join his venture. Weil intended the new institute in Frankfurt to emulate the Kiel Institute of World Economy and Marine Transport (of which Gerlach had been part) and the Cologne Institute, both of which had successfully negotiated semi-independent status. Both institutions, however, remained financially dependent on the university and city, respectively, so neither was in a position to stray too far.

Weil had a different institutional arrangement in mind to ensure the autonomy of his budding institute: to delineate an intellectual space between the Culture Ministry and the university, an institute that would have the support of both, but the input of neither. Weil showed as much aplomb as Adickes in tailoring his message to different audiences. As early as 1922 he began negotiations with the registrar of the university and with the Culture Ministry concerning his proposed institute. Weil contacted the ministry first and was open about his intended subject matter—Marxism—which he later recalled "had not counted as 'worthy of the university' until then." In his letter to the university trustees, Weil's explanation for his institute emphasized the organizational independence needed for the new social science, which might take on a variety of questions, of which Marxism was but one: "It is only possible through large-scale organizations, and in any case the complexity of social interrelations demands intellectual co-operation and collaboration. The creation of an Institute for Social Research specifically dedicated to these tasks is therefore an urgent necessity, and would help to fill a continuing gap in the ranks of established institutions."[76] As far as the university was concerned, Weil insisted that the Institute for Social Research complemented, and did not challenge, the institutional and intellectual norms.

In his intellectual interests Weil found supporters in Konrad Haenisch, the first Social Democratic minister of culture in Prussia, and his successor Carl H. Becker, who, from his installation in 1921, approved of Weil's and Gerlach's plan to support sociology, a field that Becker felt suitable for extra-university settings because of its contentious relationship to politics.[77] Weil's nuanced messaging was as revealing of the university's anti-Marxism as it was of Weil's own entrepreneurial savvy. The Weils' generosity in the meantime gave the institute leverage to affiliate with but remain independent from the university. Per their agreement, the Weils financed the building and equipment; agreed to provide an annual grant of 120,000 M; offered a lower floor in the building to the university's faculty of economics and social science; and funded the professorial chair that the institute's director held in that faculty.[78] Housed in a building designed in the cold, hard style of "new objectivity," the institute also declared its independence aesthetically, with what the Frankfurt journalist and intellectual Siegfried Kracauer later noted was an "almost fortress-like character" distinct from the surrounding *bürgerlich* environs.[79] Weil wanted the institute to have access to private money but not be mired in its influence, and to be close enough to the university to benefit from its legitimacy but not lose its autonomy.[80]

Not everyone was happy with the institute's arrangement. When Gerlach died prematurely in 1922, and Weil reached out to the Berlin historian Gustav Meyer to take his place, Meyer demurred, criticizing Weil as an *Edelkommunist* who exhibited dictatorial tendencies.[81] Weil's second choice as Gerlach's successor was Carl Grünberg, who ran the *Archive for the History of Socialism and the Labor Movement*, a journal founded in Vienna in 1910. Grünberg jumped at the opportunity to lead an institute dedicated to the history of the labor movement and the scientific study of Marxism. Grünberg shared Gerlach's desire to part ways with the traditional university. In his inaugural address, Grünberg expressed concern about the durability and integrity of the modern university. Historically devoted to research, these universities, Grünberg claimed, "have assumed the character of professional schools, or more precisely, of an aggregate of professional schools." In fact, given the training they provided to students for the learned professions, he argued, the universities had become no more than institutes for the training of mandarins (*Mandarinen-Ausbildungs-anstalten*).[82]

Like his American social scientist counterparts, Grünberg worried about the ill effects of teaching. More could be achieved in the social sciences in German and Austrian universities if "at least from a particular period in their life onwards, [scholars] could withdraw from the paralyzing effects of excessive teaching loads and administrative work brought on by contemporary university life; that they could achieve far more if they could live freely for research instead of always conducting the same introductory courses or mass seminars."[83] Like the founders of the New School for Social Research, Grünberg and his colleagues reimagined the student-professor relationship as a form of apprenticeship.

An institute devoted to Marxist studies was incongruous in post–World War I Germany for a number of reasons, not the least because it was funded by a billionaire in a capitalist university and housed in a building designed by a future Nazi.[84] The Bolshevik Revolution had changed the terms for leftist intellectuals everywhere, especially for Germans, who had to decide whether to give up their revolutionary roots and join the liberal Weimar Republic or join the Communist Party and undermine it. As Martin Jay observed in his account of the Frankfurt School and its members' "dialectical imagination," the group assembled at the institute would investigate the foundation of Marxism "with the dual hope of explaining past errors and preparing for future action."[85] The institute was the first serious attempt to study Marxism at the university level and welcomed communists to its professorial ranks. Under Grünberg the institute coordinated scholarly work with the Marx and Engels Institute in Moscow. The library contributed to the *Collected Works* of Marx and Engels, published a wide range of scholars in the *Archive*, accumulated forty thousand volumes, and subscribed to four hundred journals and newspapers. Drawing on this vast collection, one of its affiliates, the economist Henryk Grossman, produced his famous theory of Marxian crisis, in *The Law of Accumulation and Collapse of the Capitalist System*, which he would publish in 1929 just months before the stock market crash.[86]

Like New York, Frankfurt had a flourishing institutional environment ripe for innovation, and the founders of the Institute for Social Research were not the only ones to take advantage of the confluence of private wealth, a new university, and a politically conscious and supportive municipality. The Frankfurt School of Fine and Applied Arts, the product of a merger between the fine arts–focused Städelschule and the municipal academy of applied arts in 1923, taught an approach similar to that of the famous Bauhaus school founded by architects Walter Gropius and Ludwig Mies van der Rohe in 1919 in Weimar. Drawing on the same robust Jewish community that supported the university, a group led by the philosopher Franz Rosenzweig in the 1920s opened the Freies Jüdisches Lehrhaus. Organized like an adult education institute—there were lectures and no examinations—the Lehrhaus held classes in different spaces, including other Jewish institutes throughout Frankfurt, and contributed to Frankfurt's international reputation as the interwar center of Jewish higher learning.[87] Finally, as the seat of the independent *Frankfurter Zeitung* and at the forefront of radio culture, Frankfurt was home to a sophisticated media culture with an eclectic and rich extra-university intellectual life.[88]

Like Gerlach, Grünberg suffered a premature death following a stroke in 1928, and the fraught search for a replacement gave way to the very different and arguably more famous chapter in which it joined the pantheon of twentieth-century "schools" of thought. This began with the "charismatic intellectual personality" of Max Horkheimer at the helm. In his inaugural speech of January 1931, "The Present Situation of Social Philosophy and the Tasks of an Institute for Social Research," Horkheimer laid out the goals of the institution and the need to reintegrate German idealism and Hegelian *Geist* into the analysis of class. Alluding to Grünberg's description of the institute's autonomy as operating under the "dictatorship of the director," Horkheimer announced his intention to direct toward a new phase of "philosophically oriented social research," a union that would define critical theory and become the Frankfurt School's manifesto.[89] That year the Frankfurt Psychoanalytical Institute of the South-West German Psychoanalytical Association (another extra-university privately funded institution) opened in the same building as the Institute for Social Research, and the Freudian Erich Fromm, who had been teaching at the Jüdisches Lehrhaus, joined the institute as a researcher and a member of the teaching staff.

Horkheimer's call for philosophical and sociological unity would have a lasting impact on multiple fields. Through his reintegration of Marxist analysis with philosophy, Horkheimer turned away from the labor movement to more abstract philosophical concerns. He halted publication of the Marxist *Archive* and began a new publication with the politically anodyne title *Journal of Social Research*.[90] His main collaborator, Theodor Adorno, who assumed a primary role at the institute, had "little interest in politics." In contrast to their predecessors, neither Horkheimer nor Adorno was a member of any party—obscuring the earlier period of institutional innovation that grappled more actively with the relationship between scholarship, teaching, and the purpose of the university.[91] With their ideals and limitations, the founders of the city's eponymous school linked the conditions of possibility for the nonconformist institution and for their socially controversial scholarship with their urban surroundings.[92] Largely because of the synergy between the city, the university, and the institute, Frankfurt was considered a stronghold of Jews and Marxists, even if Horkheimer tried his best to keep the institute out of politics.

MISSED OPPORTUNITIES

There are similarities in the foundings of the New School for Social Research and the Institute for Social Research. In both cases influences crossed the Atlantic. The New School possessed clear disciplinary ties to German social science even if its founders presented the institution as sui generis and with French, if any, antecedents. And the success of one of Germany's only privately funded urban "prestige" universities, to which the institute would be attached, would not have been possible without Frankfurt's American-style philanthropy. Both cities boasted long-standing publishing, literary, and philanthropic infrastructures. Both institutions, though differently constituted, comprised social scientists who valued their independence above all. And both founding circles tried to evade the class divisions of the traditional university and cultivated strong but complicated relationships with the political Left.

Finally, both gave voice to at least some of the university's historical outsiders. The founding members of the Frankfurt School were mostly Jews and leftists—which led some students of critical theory to conclude that "in their own ways, Jews must have had a sense of the alienatedness and inauthenticity of life in bourgeois-capitalist society no less acute than that of the working class."[93] Horkheimer's own assessment of his worldview revealed this connection. "The only thing which is serious is the competitive struggle within classes and the struggle between classes," he wrote in 1935 in *Materials for the Reformulation of Basic Principles*. "Every friendly act is offered not to a person but to his place in society—this fact is shown in all its brutality when the same person loses his position as a result of minor or major changes in the conditions of the struggle (stock exchange, persecution of Jews) . . . solidarity forever with the victims."[94] The Frankfurt School was notoriously less kind to women. Women in the institute's circle, including the sometime chemist Gretel Adorno, were marginalized and consigned to the menial labor of typing up their husbands' manuscripts—including the erotic dreams of their lovers—their own careers pushed aside.[95]

The New School for Social Research had an equally ambivalent legacy. On one hand, celebratory histories of the New School valorize Dewey—who never actually gave up his day job at Columbia—over Clara Mayer, the unrecognized administrative backbone of the operation. On the other hand, Alvin Johnson became a tireless advocate for the underrepresented, and in the second half of the 1920s the student body became more educationally diverse and remained 65 percent female and 30 percent Jewish.[96] As other American universities in this period became more elitist and stratified as part of the broader "culture of aspiration," the New School's gates remained open.[97] The demographic shifts resulting from selective (and discriminatory) admissions in the elite universities—Columbia, for example, halved its Jewish population by 1921—made the experiment of places like the New School even more radical.[98] In fact, the New School's openness would later extend to German-Jewish and socialist refugees from this German milieu, as we will see, bringing the paths of these two storied institutions together.

Like the pre–World War I Kaiser Wilhelm Institutes in Germany and the Carnegie Institution in Washington, DC, the Weimar-era institutions in Frankfurt and New York arose as responses to the perceived inadequacies of the modern research university. In the 1919 proposal, the New School founders betrayed their ambition that "they could in a short time build up a new school as powerful in modern life as some of the great universities were in the Middle Ages. They sought to dominate political and social sciences, just as the Johns Hopkins University dominated the American university world for twenty-five years."[99] Alvin Johnson later confirmed that the New School was to be an alternative, more perfect, university.

"Where were our views different from the professed views of any ordinary university?" Johnson asked rhetorically. "At no point, except that we were trying to work out an educational plan under which professions of academic liberty could be taken seriously."[100]

The Institute for Social Research, on the other hand, especially once it assumed its gestalt as the home of the Frankfurt School, demonstrated no interest in the research university. Given the robust intellectual life and research productivity the institute made possible outside the university, Paul Tillich, the theologian and Frankfurt colleague of Horkheimer, posed in 1931 the rhetorical question "Is there even still a university?" The obvious and damaging answer was no. Arguing that the curriculum was threatened by professionalization and commercialization, Tillich encouraged his colleagues to admit the failure of the humanistic university and to establish yet another new institution.[101] In that same year the sociologist Hans Freyer and the legal theorist Carl Schmitt debated the "crisis of *Bildung*" at a conference in Davos. Caught between factions in an increasingly polarized political environment, the traditional university was the object of disdain among both the leftists of the Frankfurt School and the right-leaning Freyer and Schmitt. Like the Weimar Republic, the research university seemed hollowed out and devoid of substance, besieged from all sides for its inauthenticity.

To be sure, some Germans, including the Prussian culture minister Becker, the sociologist Georg von Below, and the historian Eduard Spranger, drew on Humboldt and *Bildung* to tie the German university to the Anglo-French tradition and buttress the Weimar Republic. But most within the universities concluded that the Weimar Republic was the "shameful result of a lost war," and following its failure in 1933, the future of the modern research university in Germany did not look good.[102] In fact, the founders of both the New School and Institute for Social Research believed that true learning would no longer be found in the university. Their institutions identified as "un-universities" that encompassed learning without the ossifying effects of bureaucracy, capitalism, and political conformism. Adorno and his later colleague Walter Benjamin wore the rejection of their dissertations by the university as badges of honor. For this *un-wissenschaftliche* group of scholars, such rejection was proof of their intellectual autonomy. The exodus of learning from the university made the university itself increasingly vulnerable. For one of the dilemmas of Hirschman's options of "exit, voice, and loyalty" was that if the best exited, who would be left standing to defend the principles of the institution? For its part as an extra-university institute devoted to increasingly abstract theory, the Institute for Social Research could boast of autonomy and untainted cultural criticism, but would no longer be in a position to exercise institutional resistance—be it through petition, boycott, or professorial pressure—to thwart the takeover of the university by the National Socialists.[103]

From a pedagogical perspective, the New School came to resemble an outpost of the German *Volkshochschule* adult education movement more than a social sciences think tank. The administration, such as it was, struggled to define the curricular choices and the population it should serve. Despite its attention to adult education, however, most of the founders believed teaching was secondary to research.[104] Its abolition of tenure in favor of hiring temporary instructors from other schools was similar to today's system of adjunct labor, which can hardly be called emancipatory. Despite the antiadministrative vision from which it arose, this choice had the practical benefit of freeing resources to recruit more distinguished faculty. By the late 1920s the New School became trapped within the contradictions of its own rebellion.

Isolated in their parallel journeys, the New School and the Institute for Social Research reflect a different kind of missed opportunity: that of transatlantic exchange in the nineteenth-century tradition. That absence became clearer in the 1920s as Americans realized they needed Europeans—and, in particular, Germans—to achieve their ambitions for the interdisciplinary social sciences.

Other research organizations, with more ambitious goals of uniting multiple fields, universities, and countries, joined the extra-university ecosystem during the 1920s. These included the American Council of Learned Societies (ACLS) and the Social Science Research Council (SSRC), the latter founded in 1923 in New York with the help of Beard's Columbia colleague economist Wesley Clair Mitchell. One of the SSRC's goals was to publish edited volumes on new methodological perspectives and thus codify an emerging field. It was in this context that the SSRC appointed Johnson in 1927 as associate editor of the Encyclopedia of Social Sciences and sent him to Europe to engage German scholars as contributors. On a series of visits Johnson connected with, among others, Emil Lederer of Berlin's Deutsche Hochschule für Politik. (Like the New School, the Hochschule was concerned with adult education and had invited as Carnegie Guest Professors James T. Shotwell, Charles Beard, and Nicholas Murray Butler.)[105] The ACLS and SSRC were designed more to project what would now be called "soft power" than to foster genuine exchange, more concerned with self-sufficiency than with open borders—signaling a departure from the earlier period and foreshadowing Cold War cultural diplomacy.

With funding from the Culture Ministry, Becker and his colleagues also initiated a series of additional German organizations to reignite transatlantic exchange, including the Academic Exchange Service (1923; later the German Academic Exchange Service) and the Alexander von Humboldt Foundation (1925), which awarded twenty-one American fellowships for graduate study in Germany between 1925 and 1930. These investments do not appear, however, to have nurtured rich transatlantic partnerships among Germans and Americans in the social sciences before the Second World War.[106] Johnson, at least in retrospect, claimed to have seen the American need for Europeans as early as 1930 and worried about the violence and antisemitism that he saw overtaking Germany.[107] Horkheimer, for his part, remained uninterested in America and was only beginning in the 1930s, as the Weimar Republic was crumbling, to conduct comparative work on Europe.

It is difficult to account for why something did not happen historically, but in this case, the decline of intellectual exchange between Germany and America seems to have been a result of the war. The war damaged the ability of scientists and scholars from the two countries to collaborate in its aftermath. The archives are littered with imagined and half-begun joint projects that show what might have been. They include a liberal arts college in a former castle of Prince Albrecht in Dresden that would have combined elements of the American, German, and English systems, and the International Commission for Intellectual Cooperation (a predecessor to UNESCO), which was supported by Einstein and the French philosopher Henri Bergson. Both remained unfulfilled because of a lack of funds, political will, and the fear of another world war.[108]

By the early 1930s the research university found itself once again in a paradox. The ideal of higher learning was preserved in Germany *outside* the institution, which itself was declared empty of both research and teaching. In America, in contrast, the university as an institution was robust, but criticized by many as devoid of ideals. The New Schoolers joined a cadre of reformers who expressed fatigue with the German research university and sought inspiration in alternative models, including the Socratic method (Deep Springs College, 1917), the Oxbridge tutorial system (Sarah Lawrence, 1926), and euthenics, the parallel improvement of one's living conditions and one's self (Bennington, 1932).[109] But the "un-university," the New School, was not realized as its founders Beard and Johnson had hoped. The New School traded one model of academic social contract for another and fell into many of the same traps as had the modern research university.

Not all moments are conducive to exchange, and in this period despite their similarities, New York and Frankfurt remained sequestered in their respective social science experiments. That we think of this moment as the height of transatlanticism has to do more with what came next. Its isolationism notwithstanding, this period created the preconditions for a historic merger between the American higher education system and German-Jewish refugees fleeing the persecution that accompanied the rise of Hitler. The double-edged sword of the academic social contract was never more visible than when Hitler funneled unprecedented sums into research at the same time that he undermined the university ideal and sacrificed objectivity and scientific excellence for his racial state. In this unwelcome climate, Thorstein Veblen's hope that Europeans would come to America for scholarly opportunities as "guests of the American academic community" would soon come true. And whereas some Americans would be wary of concentrating too many Jews in one institution, the refugee scholars' Jewishness and Social Democrat status would not make them "uncongenial" at the New School.[110] Indeed they would fit right in.

CHAPTER NINE

1933

ANNUS HORRIBILIS

At the base of the modern social order stands not the executioner but the professor. . . . The monopoly of legitimate education is now more important, more central than is the monopoly of legitimate violence.

ERNEST GELLNER, 1983

On April 7, 1933, just three months after his appointment as chancellor, Adolf Hitler passed the Law for the Restoration of the Professional Civil Service (Gesetz zur Wiederherstellung des Berufsbeamtentums). Described by one historian as a "legalistic fig leaf for the purge of the German universities," the law excluded Jews and political opponents of Nazism from civil service positions.[1] Though it initially exempted, among others, those who had held their positions since 1914 and who were veterans of World War I, the law's impact was vast. The *Manchester Guardian Weekly* ran a cover story less than a month later titled "Nazi 'Purge' of the Universities" with a long "list of dismissals" of well over one hundred names.[2] Within a year, an estimated twelve hundred individuals had been fired. The purge did not affect all universities (or all fields) equally. Three universities accounted for 40 percent of those dismissed (including Frankfurt, which vindicated the fears of those in the 1920s who said it was too Jewish). Whereas academia lost on average 39 percent of its faculty, some disciplines suffered greater losses. Among economists and social scientists the loss was nearly 47 percent (and even higher at centers like Heidelberg, where 63 percent of economists were let go).[3] By 1936 more than two thousand Jewish scholars and scientists had been dismissed or forced into retirement—about one-fifth of the German professoriate.[4] When the director of the Kaiser Wilhelm Society, Max Planck, went to meet with Hitler to make the case for retaining Jews at his institute, Hitler was said to have told him, "Our national policies will not be revoked or modified, even for scientists. If the dismissal of Jewish scientists means the annihilation of contemporary German science, then we shall do without science for a few years!"[5]

Although Hitler preferred fidelity to his racist policies to scientific advancement, his rejoinder to Planck greatly overstated the extent to which he was willing to turn his back on both science and the university. Even in 1933, Hitler knew very well that the Nazi regime was dependent on what scientists, scholars, and educators could deliver. The purge of the universities and institutes was just one facet of a broader effort to co-opt German higher education and make it serve Nazism and the state. Hitler's "coordination" of the university showed that a state could force the university to serve its interests so directly as to make the university one of its constitutive features.[6] At the same time, scholars' willingness to go along with this co-option showed how nationalism had also become a constitutive feature of the university.

Hitler's nationalist mobilization of the university and his openness to adapting models from the outside suggest surprising and disturbing continuities with the emergence and evolution of the modern research university. His politicization of the university showed the extent to which mobilization extended into the higher education system. No doubt Hitler exploited the university and scientific research to serve his regime, but that co-option also exposed a vulnerability that was—and is—inherent in the university model.

HITLER'S *AMERIKABILD*

The British philosopher of education George Frederick Kneller was right to identify Hitler as "intensely anxious . . . to root [National Socialist] principles in the hearts and minds of the German people." But Kneller and other early Anglo-American commentators took Nazi educators' claims at face value when they said that their educational philosophy was an "original creation—without a prototype."[7] In fact, Hitler was utterly unoriginal in his mobilization of science and the educational system, and, in his search for international validation, he drew on the long history of transatlantic knowledge exchange.

In 1934, Alfred Rosenberg, who led the most ideological of the Nazis' education projects, declared that the "so-called internationality of culture and science" was a fiction that had never existed.[8] In addition to being historically inaccurate, this assertion was contradicted by Hitler, who made ample use of the international routes of exchange established in the previous century. In fact, Hitler's life and career provide evidence that interest in foreign models and international exchange does not necessarily align with liberal values but can be employed for nefarious purposes. Though he showed only contempt for the diversity of cosmopolitan life in fin-de-siècle Vienna, Hitler would draw freely on American manufacturing techniques and engineering prowess, exploiting over a half century of competitive emulation that began at the 1876 World's Fair in Philadelphia.

Following his failed political coup in Bavaria, Hitler exhibited early signs of becoming a student of *Wissenstransfer* during a nine-month stay in Landsberg prison. There in the cell that he called his "university on the state's dime," Hitler crafted *Mein Kampf*, his political coming-of-age story that would be used to present him to the world.[9] In the pages of his notorious memoir, he not only makes his case against Jews and Marxists—claiming they stabbed Germany in the back and allowed the Allies to steal victory in World War I—but also tellingly cites America as a key inspiration for his new political vision. Hitler would come to admire—envy even—three features of America that came to be part of his *Amerikabild*: manifest destiny, industrialization, and anti-immigration policies.

Hitler was not the first German to rhapsodize about America's resources and landscape, as we saw, nor the first to acknowledge the darker side of its conquest. As early as 1884, when Germany acquired its first colonies, Germans found in American expansion an exemplar for "imperial liberalism," the reconciliation of nineteenth-century liberalism and imperialist conquest. The ethnographer Friedrich Ratzel, a former 1848 revolutionary, in his support of Germany's version of manifest destiny, cited the American historian Frederick Jackson Turner's "frontier thesis," which identified the "colonization of the Great West" as essential to American history.[10] In the year he became the secretary of state for colonial affairs, the banker-cum-politician Bernhard Dernburg lauded American colonization and its "complete extermination of its native people" as a model for the burgeoning German colonial project in German Southwest Africa.[11] Like most Germans, Hitler was reared on Karl May's adventure novels of the American West, fanciful descriptions of cowboys and Indians that mimicked James Fenimore Cooper.[12] Though May himself was a pacifist, Hitler drew on his stories as evidence of the "Native problem." By the time he was planning his political comeback in the Bavarian mountains, Hitler praised Americans for having "gunned down the millions of Redskins to a few hundred thousand." Over a decade later, in World War II, when he embarked on his own expansionist policy, Hitler justified it by referring to Poland and Ukraine as his Wild West.[13]

If America modeled successful colonialist expansion, it also demonstrated the potential of rapid industrialization. Hitler was only the latest in a long line of German leaders who saw in the United States the kind of technological economic growth that would be necessary if Germany were to project power in the world. The German engineer Reuleaux's visit to Philadelphia in 1876 for the World's Fair prompted German industry to try to catch up. In 1900, another impressive showing of American machines and appliances at the American Mechanical and Civil Engineers Association in Berlin, together with the American fairs in Chicago and St. Louis, propelled a "second discovery of America."[14] Fredrick Taylor's publications on improving industrial efficiency, including his 1911 *The Principles of Scientific Management*, which was translated into German within two years, provided a blueprint that Germans were eager to follow.[15] Fifty or so books in which the idea of America played a central role in the new youth-centered and consumer-oriented culture flooded the Weimar Republic book market. What one historian calls the "shock" of America in Europe was inescapable: "Everywhere there emerged the centrality of America—whether loved or loathed—as the crucial term of comparison."[16]

Hitler was drawn into the American vortex of planes, trains, and automobiles. Less than two weeks after he took office and before he expelled Jews from the universities, Hitler appeared at the Berlin Automobile Show to proclaim his vision for the Volkswagen. Especially taken by Henry Ford's personal biography and transformation of the automobile industry, Hitler aimed to use this most American of all exports to fuel his new German nation. He affectionately called his private train *Amerika* in reference to this strategy. When Goebbels launched the Volkswagen in 1938 it was this adoration for the automobile that gave Nazi propaganda the "steely romanticism" for which the Nazis became known.[17] It remained a source of delight to Hitler that Charles Lindbergh, the aviation hero of the 1920s, expressed anti-Roosevelt and pro-Nazi views; Hitler returned the favor by awarding him the highest honor given to a foreigner—the Service Cross of the German Eagle. On one memorable evening at Hitler's *Tischgespräche* the Führer asked his guests to share stories from America and one confidant showed him a picture of the Golden Gate Bridge. Hitler vowed to build one bigger and better than the American version.[18]

The most successful and chilling Nazi adoption of American techniques was in the social sciences. By the early 1930s the social scientists who applied the quantitative methods of classification, statistics, and surveys to analyses of social problems were no longer tentative newcomers. The social sciences were making inroads in a range of real-world applications, from improving business efficiency to guiding government policy. The same methods that permitted scholars to quantify, calculate, and sort for the progressive ends of aiding labor movements and challenging monopolies also enabled the expansion of a modern American bureaucracy and the administrative state. Exemplifying the technology of state administration was the sorting system developed by the surgeon and librarian John Shaw Billings for library catalogs and then adapted by the US Census Bureau. Though not initially viewed as invasive—many saw "being known" as an avenue to rights and protection—this technology would become a double-edged sword.[19]

The Nazis showed a keen interest in American bureaucratic technologies of efficiency, from office management to factory lines, and they applied them to make German society and research more efficient. They reorganized the government- and industry-funded collaborative projects at the Kaiser Wilhelm Institutes, sometimes to deadly effect.[20] At the Research Institute for Eugenics and Population Biology, for example, scientists began in 1936 compiling certificates of descent to assess racial origins and classified more than twenty-three thousand Roma as varying degrees of "gypsies"—a designation that after 1941 meant certain deportation and death. Most nefariously, in its adaptation by the Deutsche Hollerith Maschinen Gesellschaft, a subsidiary of IBM, the electronic punch card technology that emerged from the matrix of the American social sciences expedited the counting, identification, and murder of six million Jews by the Nazis.[21]

While American social sciences provided compelling methodologies, America's notorious interwar anti-immigration policy offered legal rationale for Germany's racial laws. The Nazi Program of 1920 had already laid out a notion of citizenship grounded in "German blood," but by the time Hitler began to craft *Mein Kampf* in Landsberg Prison he had a new "source of authority" available—America's 1921 and 1924 anti-immigration statutes. The significance of American discriminatory policy in shaping Hitler's own racial state becomes clear in a laudatory passage in the second volume of his memoir:

> There is currently one state in which one can observe at least weak beginnings of a better conception [of race law]. This is of course not our exemplary German Republic, but the American Union, in which an effort is being made to consider the dictates of reason to at least some extent. The American Union categorically refuses the immigration of certain races. In these respects America already pays obeisance, at least in tentative first steps, to the characteristic *völkisch* conception of the state.[22]

Hitler continued to speak admiringly about America in 1928, and in his "Second Book," which he drafted that year (and which was discovered posthumously), he commented on the goal of racial purity that he felt Americans shared with Germans: "That the American Union feels itself to be a Nordic-German state and by no means an international *Völker*-porridge is also revealed by the apportionment of immigration quotas among the European *Völker*."[23] Hitler especially admired the American Southeast, where Jim Crow laws prevented marriage between people of different races. Hitler's legal advisers, including Herbert Kier, surveyed the antimiscegenation laws of these states for legal models that would allow Germany to escape the fate of becoming a "*Völker*-porridge." The 1935 Nuremberg Laws, which codified racial hierarchy, criminalized intermarriage, and deprived Jews of their citizenship, drew liberally on the same arguments used in America to deprive African Americans and Chinese of voting rights.[24]

Though it was once considered uncouth to point out the resemblances between New Dealers and the corporatist fascists of central Europe, scholars have in recent years noted their unnerving similarities in the period between 1933 and 1935, when support for wide-ranging government expansion increased in both places. In America the administrative state swelled, taking part in everything from social engineering projects to corporatist capitalism. Justified by the Great Depression, policies sought control over previously independent corporate entities and obscured the line between the private and public realms.[25] As an institution with apparent if not always clearly defined obligations to the state, the modern research university was poised to be swept up in this tide of state expansion.

THE PURGE—A NEW RELATIONSHIP BETWEEN THE UNIVERSITY AND THE STATE?

Despite his anti-intellectualism and mistrust of experts, Hitler depended on science to provide rationale and policy for his ethno-nationalist racial empire. As the German-Jewish Hannah Arendt observed in 1946, "This 'scientificality' is indeed the common feature of all the totalitarian regimes of our time. But it means nothing more than that purely man-made power—mainly destructive—is dressed in the clothes of some superior, superhuman sanction from which it derives its absolute, not-to-be-questioned force."[26] Speaking of racist ideology, Arendt noted that science had two roles. It both provided an authoritative voice that served as ideological justification for Hitler's discriminatory, and ultimately, genocidal policies, and served the educative—or propagandistic—function of inculcating these ideas into pupils and the public. In his early assessment of the educational philosophy of National Socialism, the British philosopher Kneller concurred. National Socialism was "in itself a gigantic education enterprise." Germany, Kneller wrote, was "saturated with the word Schulung [schooling]."[27]

As the First World War had made clear, research and scientific knowledge were directly related to the development of military and industrial technology. The nations that had the best science would have the most productive agriculture, the most efficient factories, and the most destructive and deadly weapons. This is another reason to suspect that Hitler's retort to

Planck in 1933 was a mere rhetorical flourish: Hitler knew that scientific research undergirded national power, and he wanted to reap the full benefits for the Third Reich. Since universities not only served the propagandistic function of education but also provided the institutional home for much scientific research, it was natural that they should become the objects of Hitler's attention, together with the rest of the educational system.

In the same Nazi Program of 1920 in which the National Socialists announced their racial goals, the party also laid out its plans to expand and control the educational system to meet the state's needs. Teaching was to be aligned with the practical needs of life and was to be based on meritocratic principles: "Education, at the expense of the state [should support] exceptionally gifted children of poor parents without regard to their social position or occupation."[28] National Socialism scorned pure and aloof science. The German philosopher and Nazi ideologue Ernst Krieck announced, "We perceive and acknowledge no truth for the sake of truth, no science for the sake of science." The *Allgemeine Deutsche Lehrerzeitung* (General German Teacher's Journal) circulated a pamphlet that announced that objective history was "only one of the numerous fallacies of liberalism."[29] And Bernhard Rust, the unemployed Hanover teacher who was named the Nazi minister of science, education, and national culture, replaced science lessons with Reich youth days and spiritual training.[30]

Following the passing of the Civil Service Law, the universities were tightly "coordinated" under Nazi control. Krieck's "election" in the spring of 1933 as the rector of the University of Frankfurt (he was the only candidate) sealed the connection between the *Führer* of the university and that of the state.[31] That spring and fall, many recently appointed rectors delivered speeches declaring their willingness to contribute to the Nazi state.[32] Newly appointed University of Hamburg rector Adolf Rein declared, "The German people will only survive in the world and seize the objectives to which they have been called if they become political, in the true and essential meaning of the word."[33] The philosophers Hans Heyse and Alfred Baeumler were appointed rectors at the universities of Königsberg and Berlin, respectively. Baeumler became active in Rosenberg's ideology office of the Nazi Party. To ensure that a vigorous National Socialist spirit infused the university, additional political training and proof of Aryan ancestry were now required after one submitted the *Habilitation*, and professors were pressured to join the National Socialist Party.[34] In 1933, hundreds of university instructors joined the party, and by 1938 nearly two-thirds belonged to it (fig. 9).[35]

Hitler's suspension of academic freedom and the politicization of the university went well beyond previous efforts to press scientific institutions

Figure 9. *Gleichschaltung,* or the total "coordination" of the German university, was a crucial part of Hitler's malign strategy. (Photo © bpk Bildagentur/Art Resource, NY.)

into state service. The Civil Service Law of 1933 could be applied to any institution that received more than 50 percent of its funds from the state — and because hyperinflation had made them more dependent on public funding, this included the Kaiser Wilhelm Institutes. Nearly one-third of the Kaiser Wilhelm Society's staff was dismissed, along with ten of its thirty-five institute directors.[36] As with the universities, however, the law affected the institutes differentially. At Fritz Haber's Institute for Physical Chemistry and Electrochemistry, one-quarter of the personnel were Jewish. Funded primarily through the private (and Jewish) Koppel Foundation, the institute was still vulnerable, since Haber's own position was tied to the Prussian government budget, and his salary was paid through the state. Despite various machinations on the part of the institute, including moving annuities to a non-Jewish-owned bank, the Nazis eventually were able to seize these and other Jewish assets.[37] In Göttingen, where three out of the four institute directors were Jewish, the new Civil Service Law decimated the global center of applied mathematics for which Felix Klein had so labored. The responses of the ousted directors, James Franck, Max Born, and Richard Courant, which ranged from public protest to silent emigration to legal opposition, showed the limited options for those not designated as Aryan under the new regime.[38]

In this climate, the veto and oversight powers of the state, rarely used previously, became levers of control. As a semiautonomous government entity with the influential Max Planck at its helm, the Kaiser Wilhelm Institutes preserved a degree of autonomy until 1937, when the Nazis implemented a Four-Year Plan that included a more coordinated *Wissenschaftspolitik* to support self-sufficiency and military dominance. At that point some scientists who remained tried to connect their work to population or race studies, but only those whose research related to military production were viewed as valuable. Planck—for whom the postwar society would be renamed—sold himself to Hitler in exchange for the promise of protection for the society. Even if he is credited for advocating for "valuable" Jews like Haber and Otto Warburg, his institute became a pawn of the state.[39] Recalling how Planck reluctantly invoked "Heil Hitler" at the opening of the Kaiser Wilhelm Institute of Metals in Stuttgart in 1934, the physicist P. P. Ewald offered, "It was the only thing you could do if you didn't want to jeopardize the whole Kaiser Wilhelm Gesellschaft."[40]

Perhaps, but it would be misleading to speak of the Kaiser Wilhelm Society as an institution that suffered in this period. The society's administrators actively sought an arrangement with the National Socialist state that resembled more what one scholar has called a "Faustian pact" than a "gilded cage." The result of their lobbying led to more generous funding than the institutes had seen in any previous period and more than any other contemporaneous German research organization received. The budget for the natural sciences increased from 5.1 million RM in 1932 to 14.5 million RM in 1942. From a certain perspective of science—if not all scientists—the Kaiser Wilhelm Society under the Nazi regime was a "success story."[41]

The Nazis commandeered other institutions as well, including the Deutsche Hochschule für Politik in Berlin and the German Academy for the Scientific Investigation and Cultivation of Germandom in Munich, and founded dozens more to support their own research interests (and out of fear of insubordination among existing institutions). Some of these were explicitly propagandistic. Others, including the Academy of German Law and the Reich Institute for the History of the New Germany, were established to provide scientific and legal bases for the regime.[42]

As the Nazi state expanded so did its system of higher learning and science. Between 1938 and 1944 the Nazis established thirty-eight institutes, including several devoted to aviation science—a field that had a virtually unlimited budget and nearly ten thousand people working on related research. In 1938, to facilitate Germanization of annexed territory, Hitler incorporated the universities and technical schools in Prague, Gdansk, and Brno into the Nazi system and founded "new Reich universities" in Strasbourg (1940) and Poznan (1941). Culture provided a foundation for the military empire.[43]

The Nazis' enthusiastic support of applied science tells a different story than one that focuses on the purge, for it highlights the beneficiaries of the new regime. To begin with, doctoral students who faced low odds of becoming full professors, further reduced by the Depression of 1932, stood to benefit immediately from the firing of their superiors. It is no surprise, then, that the younger generation of assistant professors and students, overcome by feelings of "hopelessness," were among the strongest supporters of the Nazis and eagerly helped oust professors and burn books.[44] Early on, Planck evidently identified the challenge that opportunism posed to any unified protest in such an environment. "If today 30 professors stand up and criticize the government for its actions," he disclosed to a confidant, "tomorrow 150 persons will declare their loyalty to Hitler because they want the positions."[45] In describing his own stance, Planck later used the metaphor of withstanding an enormous storm like a "tree in the wind": under such conditions some degree of accommodation was unavoidable, but the goal was to "stand back upright."[46] Even if Planck sought minimal accommodation, many teachers and scholars actively moved in the direction the wind was blowing.

As with other professionals in the Nazi period, in their stance on National Socialism academics encompassed the spectrum from diehards to minimalists.[47] Nonetheless, given the willingness of scholars and scientists to adjust their work to receive the benefits of Nazi support, the mobilization of science might best be understood as a form of "self-mobilization" in which scientists aimed to show how their work contributed to "Nazi sciences." Indeed, as in other revolutionary moments, including 1914 before it and 1945 and 1989 afterward, some professors saw the new political demands as an opportunity to gain influence.[48] For apolitical Germans, be they humanists or natural scientists, the generally accepted position was disinterested nationalism. Many were happy to interject praise of the Führer in scholarly works.[49] And why not? As the German historian Helmuth Plessner, who went into exile in the Netherlands in 1934, wrote derisively of his colleagues who remained, the Nazis offered professors, in particular humanists, the opportunity to be "redeemed" from potential obscurity.[50]

Some of the continuity of scholarship from the Weimar Republic to the Nazi period is explained by the fluidity among post–World War I anti-Republican views, invalidating the understanding of this period as a complete caesura.[51] The zealous Nazi sounded like many a Weimar-era social scientist when he claimed that National Socialism would achieve scientific totality where there was previously fragmentation. Leftist scholars in the Weimar era, as we saw, criticized the university's erosion of true learning, or *Bildung*, by scientization and bureaucracy. In their effort to connect *Bildung* and *Wissenschaft*, right-wing Nazi scholars often resembled their leftist predecessors.

This was the route the philosopher Martin Heidegger took to become rector of the University of Freiburg. In his notorious rectorial address, "The Self-Assertion of the German University," Heidegger rejected the traditional definition of academic freedom as negative freedom and advocated "self-assertion" of the university's service in the pursuit of knowledge. Nazi officials complained that Heidegger's philosophical politics promoted "a kind of 'private national socialism' that circumvent[ed] the perspectives of the [Nazi] party program," and removed him.[52] Heidegger's brief rectorship is revealing not only of his moral shortcomings, but also underscores how the Nazis were interested in complete subservience, not just any expressions of nationalism. Despite his demotion, Heidegger did enough damage in lending scientific credence to a racist worldview.[53]

Heidegger was one of the more famous examples of scholars' political opportunism, but he was hardly an exception. When the Nazis appointed the Kiel University rector and law professor Paul Ritterbusch to organize the "wartime mobilization of the humanities" to support the regime's eastern expansion, over five hundred humanists volunteered to contribute. The communal work of "Aktion Ritterbusch" preoccupied scholars from 1940 until the invasion of the Soviet Union on June 22, 1941, and offered historical support for the annexation of the eastern regions as rightfully part of German *Lebensraum* and a new European order under German rule. That so many participated is itself alarming.[54] The work clearly opened the door to more fanatical visions as well; in a statement that echoed Heidegger's seminars, the historian Werner Conze called for the removal of Jews from Polish cities and the Germanizing of Poland. Two German scholars have accused these humanists of being the "architects of annihilation."[55]

Even if this verdict may go too far, the role of professors and universities in the Nazi period was hardly abstract. Many of those in the *Einsatzgruppen*, which led the genocidal mission on the ground alongside Hitler's military invasion of the Soviet Union, were educated. Of the four *Einsatzgruppen* commanders, three held a total of four doctorates; of the seventeen *Vorkommando* chiefs a further seven possessed doctorates.[56] Most rose through the ranks of Reinhard Heydrich's Sicherheitsdienst (SD); all shared a similar outlook toward Jews, Slavs, and Bolsheviks and believed that Germany's rightful imperial expansion should be promoted and coordinated by its scientific institutions. Even acknowledging his bias, it is difficult to argue with Jewish refugee Max Weinreich's contention that "German scholarship provided the ideas and techniques which led to and justified this unparalleled slaughter."[57] Nevertheless, not all Americans were as clear as Weinreich about the debasement of the modern research university that occurred as the Nazis appropriated it for their ends.

INTERNATIONAL EXCHANGE—TO FIGHT RACISM OR EXTEND IT?

Only three years before Hitler's rise to power in 1933, international cultural exchange seemed to have recovered from the setback of World War I. Culture Minister Carl Becker had long praised American *Kulturpolitik* as the "conscious employment of spiritual values in the service of the people and of the state" and once observed admiringly: "What have the Americans not done to hammer the idea of America into the variegated mishmash of their immigrants! They have created a new people with a victorious idea."[58] In 1930, Becker went on a tour of the United States organized by the director of the nascent Institute for International Education (IIE), Stephen Duggan. After receptions from Flexner and the new president of the University of Chicago, Robert Maynard Hutchins, among others, he delivered a final lecture at Columbia University's Teachers College.[59] Apologizing for his English, he offered, "I know that I can count on your indulgence toward me as a stranger, and also because I firmly believe that the problems of secondary education and the training of teachers are matters of international interest, despite the strictly national demands which these two functions of our educational systems have to fulfill."[60]

Organizations and institutions founded under the banner of "internationalism" in the 1920s—including the IIE and its German counterpart, the newly established German Academic Exchange Service—seemed finally to have found their footing after the isolationist period earlier that decade. A new understanding of "national self-consciousness rather than national self-assertiveness," as Becker recommended, appeared to have set in.[61] Becker was aware of the long history of transatlantic exchange in which he now participated. Aided by university presidents like Butler and a new generation of culture brokers in America that included Becker, Hermann Oncken, Eugen Rosenstock, Alfred Weber, and Alice Salomon, a regular flow of student exchange resumed, and the IIE alone brought more than 2,500 foreign students to American universities and sent over 2,000 American students abroad in the period between 1920 and the outbreak of World War II.[62]

These extra-university philanthropic organizations also promoted and funded international centers and houses on American campuses, while the Kaiser Wilhelm Society's unveiling of the Harnack House in 1928 embodied the spirit of foreign cultural exchange of its eponymous dedicatee: "Education is national, research is international."[63] University donations kept flowing, in particular, from former exchange students. In 1931, the University of Heidelberg refurbished its classroom building with funds, in part, from its American alumni, a campaign organized by the US ambassador to Germany and Heidelberg graduate Jacob Gould Schurman.[64] (Schurman, for his part, received a Heidelberg honorary degree for his transatlantic fundraising efforts alongside foreign minister Gustav Stresseman, architect of Germany's reconciliation with the West.)[65] This renewed internationalism—represented in a flow of both dollars and visitors—was essential to Germany's recovering its role as a force in scientific research. By 1930 Germany had won substantially more Nobel Prizes in science than any other country—more than Britain and America combined. As British historian Peter Watson observed, on reflecting on this fact alone, "Germany's way of organizing herself intellectually was a great success."[66]

Two very different streams flowed through the conduits of international exchange. The first circulated the values of international peace and the universal pursuit of science, as embodied by the IIE and its companion organizations. The second fomented racist, nativist, and eugenicist ideas and politics. In the first category the greatest example was Albert Einstein, who advocated for international peace and cooperation. His efforts were constrained, however, by pressure from both sides. Einstein was warned by Fritz Haber, with justification, that he would be viewed as a traitor in Germany for his politics and stands against antisemitism.[67] At the same time, organizations that sought to rescue German science from the dire economic conditions during hyperinflation, such as the Emergency Association of German Science (Notgemeinschaft der Deutschen Wissenschaft), were compelled to consider the concerns of American Jewish donors about rising German antisemitism.[68]

The second group of scientists hardly experienced any lull in international exchange despite, or because of, their racism—the eugenicists. Drawing on the growing understanding of genetics and social Darwinist thinking, eugenicists sought to improve mankind—a goal shared by adherents across the political spectrum. The American sociologist Edward A. Ross, whose dismissal from Stanford had spurred the academic freedom case that launched the AAUP, was one example of the overlap between American Progressivism and eugenics that seems strange to us today. In the same year that colleagues defended his right to pursue scholarship that undermined the railway lobby, Ross coined the term "racial suicide" to describe the danger of not intervening in the quality control of the population. Ross's formulation captured the imagination of President Theodore Roosevelt as well as that of Margaret Sanger, the feminist who campaigned for birth control, both of whom shared the fear that inferior segments of the population were outbreeding others.[69]

American eugenicists found willing partners on the other side of the Atlantic. Among these was the German eugenicist Alfred Ploetz, who nurtured international ambitions for the German Society for Racial Hygiene. Two years after he founded the society in 1905 (but before he would debate Max Weber about W.E.B. Du Bois and the virtues of African Americans), Ploetz reoriented his organization as the International Society for Racial Hygiene. Together with Fritz Lenz and Eugen Fischer in Munich, Ploetz cultivated contacts in America, Great Britain, Sweden, and elsewhere and routinely brought together eugenicists from Europe and the United States in conferences with several hundred participants. At the same time that Münsterberg and Kuhneman bemoaned the rift of World War I, the Society for Racial Hygiene in Berlin admired the "dedication with which Americans sponsor research in the field of racial hygiene and with which they translate theoretical knowledge into practice."[70] Though the international congresses of eugenicists were postponed until 1919 for what the congress organizer Charles B. Davenport called "international complications," Davenport reintegrated German racial scientists into the movement, and by 1924, well before the wider international community of scientists had reconciled, the German and American racial scientists had resumed their communication.

Not only were American eugenicists active in promoting German racial science, but American dollars sustained it. Before 1933 the Rockefeller Foundation had distributed a half a million dollars through the Emergency Association of German Science—about 5 percent of the government's contribution and more than the contribution from German industry.[71] Private money—especially donated in foreign currency—was a crucial feature of both Germany's state-based Weimar-era system and the National Socialist regime. The Rockefeller Foundation, furthermore, financed the research of German racial hygienist Agnes Bluhm on heredity and alcoholism in 1920 and, six years later, helped to establish both the Kaiser Wilhelm Institute for Psychiatry and the Kaiser Wilhelm Institute for Anthropology, Eugenics, and Human Heredity. When Emil Kraepelin founded the Institute for Psychiatry in Munich, the foundation donated $325,000 for the new building—substantial support that ensured that Germany and America would surpass Great Britain as the leading centers of eugenic research and advocacy.[72]

In the Nazi period many of these same institutions, including the Institute for Psychiatry, the Institute for Anthropology, and the Institute for Brain Research all were beneficiaries of American philanthropy, much of it from the Rockefeller Foundation. (The Carnegie Foundation was also complicit; its support of eugenics continued stateside in the Carnegie Institute of Washington's Station for Experimental Evolution, the Eugenics Record Office, and Charles Davenport's Biological Laboratory, all in Cold Spring Harbor.) In April 1930, the Rockefeller Foundation gave $650,000 for the Kaiser Wilhelm Institute of Cell Physiology and pledged more, a promise it would keep. The foundation's contributions came to over 3 million M by 1934, and though much of its funding tapered off around 1936, some continued through 1939.[73]

The transatlantic flow of money and ideas spread race science. By the second half of the 1920s, the center of gravity in eugenics had shifted to America largely as a result of the legislative achievements of advocates of forced sterilization in a number of states. Marveling at the tenfold increase in sterilization in America over the course of the decade, German racial scientists commented how strange it was that sterilization seemed easier to implement in the "country of freedom." To help the Germans catch up, Harry H. Laughlin, the assistant director of the Carnegie-funded Cold Spring Harbor laboratories, shared information with German readers about the legislative successes in over twenty states and the 1927 Supreme Court decision that deemed compulsory sterilization constitutional. When in 1932 there was an opening to propose sterilization legislation before the Prussian Health Council, German racial scientists drew on this law and its apparent benefits. Hitler kept up with progress in the field with the help of the Munich book publisher Lehmann, which published racist literature, and occasionally had assistants acquire materials from the American Eugenics Society directly. He was particularly enamored of Madison Grant's 1916 work *The Passing of the Great Race*, which argued that the Nordic gene pool was being undermined by inferior blood. Grant boasted that Hitler reported the book to be "his bible."[74]

Enabled by this infrastructure, Hitler used the university to give his racial science the imprimatur of the international scientific community. As the Americans had done in 1904 on the occasion of the St. Louis World's Fair, Hitler planned a series of anniversary events at universities to honor foreign scientists, and in so doing confirm the esteem in which the world held the German university. In 1934, on the twentieth anniversary of the University of Frankfurt, Hitler showed just how far that child of the Weimar Republic, had strayed from its liberal origins when he bestowed an honorary degree on Henry Fairfield Osborn, the founder of the American Eugenics Society (and president of the Museum of Natural History). The event went off without much resistance.

The international community began to turn against Hitler in June of 1934 following the violent purge that came to be known as the "Night of Long Knives," in which he orchestrated the murders of dozens of political rivals. In the following year, flush from a recovering economy and employment, Hitler began to plan his expansionist foreign policy and his war against the Jews. After the passing of the first Nuremberg race laws in September 1935, Hitler committed to a year of events to promote the new "national Socialist university" and carve out a more visible and purposeful role for scholars and institutions of higher learning in the Nazi regime. The main event would be the upcoming 550th anniversary of the University of Heidelberg, one of Germany's oldest and most distinguished institutions.[75] While planning began for the jubilee in the "new spirit" at the end of 1935, the university ended the year with a dedication of the new Philipp-Lenard Institute, an event that made clear to the international community just what that spirit would bring.

The Philipp-Lenard Institute was the stronghold for what Minister of Education Bernhard Rust celebrated as "Aryan Physics," and the paragon for scholarly support of the Nazi regime. Johannes Stark, who also served as president of the Physical Society, was its zealous director. Stark led the campaign to rid German physics of Jewish "thinking," a loose designation attached to such subfields as relativity theory and nuclear physics. So adamant was Stark about snuffing out Jewish influence that he would even accuse the non-Jewish father of quantum mechanics Werner Heisenberg of thinking like a "white Jew."[76] Judging from his pronouncement at the dedication the Education Minister Rust wholeheartedly agreed: "The problems of science do not present themselves in the same way to all men. The Negro or the Jew will view the same world in a different way from the German investigator." Stark, for his part, was "particularly zealous against the followers of Einstein and attacked with the greatest frankness the scientific methods of Prof. Planck." According to a disapproving report of the journal *Nature*, the ceremony concluded with a Sieg Heil.[77]

The purpose of these celebratory events in June 1936 extended beyond the borders of the academy and even Germany. In the long tradition of interinstitutional university relations, Hitler sought the respect, and thus validation, of the University of Heidelberg's peers. But the three-day celebration earned the wrong kind of attention.[78] *Nature* called out the participants' "narrow views" and condemned the upcoming anniversary as a propaganda event and an affront to the international science community. As its correspondent reported, "The official [German] spirit cannot at present make any claim to be working for the international co-operation which most scientific workers desire to promote." German universities evidently "no longer believe in the internationalism of science—or, at any rate, think it inexpedient to give public utterance to this principle."[79] Another correspondent in *Nature* recalled the memory of Spinoza, the heretic Jewish philosopher who was once invited to teach at the University of Heidelberg, as evidence that the Germans had lost their way.[80]

In the buildup to the Heidelberg jubilee the moral neutrality of international exchange and the university model itself came under the microscope. The British were the first to decline. In a letter to the *Times* of London the Bishop of Durham Herbert Dunelm explained England's refusal to participate and urged other countries to do the same: "It cannot be right that the Universities of Great Britain, which we treasure as the very citadels of sound learning, because they are the vigilant guards of intellectual freedom, should openly fraternize with the avowed shameless enemies of both."[81] The bishop's letter unleashed a torrent of replies—both for and against. Declines from the University of Birmingham and Oxford followed, and soon after, the Nazis withdrew invitations to try to save face.

Dismayed by the absence of a similar discussion in the American forum, a group of British scholars republished the bishop's letter along with the responses in a pamphlet. The collection is a helpful indication of the impact of the Nazi regime on the integrity of the university model worldwide. The vice-chancellor of the University of Birmingham disclosed that the University of Heidelberg had dismissed forty-four people since 1933. If an individual scholar chose to visit a German university that was one matter, but the "presence of British delegates will be proclaimed throughout Germany as a considered gesture of British approval of Nazi policy in the universities." The senate of the University of Birmingham resolved not to attend.[82] The commentators reminded readers of the ideals of higher education: "The essential solidarity of academic purpose, the broadly human interest of science, the supreme and universal claim of truth, the indispensableness of liberty in this pursuit—these are the policies that govern the practice of civilized universities, and apart from their honest acceptance, no genuine academic fellowship can exist."[83] And they urged Americans to ask themselves whether the university in question still actually embodied those ideals. Could a distinction be made between the university's policy and the state's? Once the values of the state and the university diverged, how could higher learning survive?

While Hitler was occupying the Rhineland in March 1936, Americans debated whether its universities should send delegates to Heidelberg for the celebration. Several American alumni of the University of Heidelberg expressed outrage at the prospect of American participation. Comparing the university jubilee to the 1936 Olympics, one commentator cautioned, "The Hitler regime is not so indifferent to the moral opinion of the outside world as it professes. . . . The learned visitors who come to Heidelberg University for the June 30 festival will become in the hands of the Nazi propagandists a foreign endorsement of something far different from the Heidelberg idea or the university idea."[84] Despite all that Hitler was doing to co-opt the university and repudiate its ideals, American university presidents Butler and the newly appointed James Conant of Harvard were all too eager to maintain relationships with Nazi Germany. In May Hitler invited the two Americans to receive honorary degrees. They accepted and joined what could not be said to be good company: the psychiatrist and euthanasia advocate Foster Kennedy, who supported killing the mentally handicapped, and Laughlin, for his lifelong work in eugenics.[85] Ignoring ever louder protest from Columbia students, Butler sailed back and forth to Europe between 1933 and 1935 on German liners under the swastika flag. Butler welcomed the Nazi ambassador to Columbia, while Conant permitted him to lay a wreath on campus. Both sent delegates to the Heidelberg celebration in 1936.[86]

Butler's disingenuous response to criticism was that "academic relationships have no political implications."[87] As usual, Butler's opportunism knew no limits—he was ready to pivot to whatever political system reigned, even a regime that by the summer of 1934 had taken a violent turn. That he and other leading American university presidents were willfully indifferent to the victims of Nazi regime should make us question the integrity of the fabric that held the system together. It is heartening, however, that a number of students at Columbia were vocal in their opposition to the Nazi regime and to Butler's accommodation of it.

The three-day Heidelberg celebration included the usual Nazi pomp replete with swastikas, flags, and parades. Goebbels delivered a speech in a castle to invited guests, and a telegram from Hitler was read. At Heidelberg the erosion of the most fundamental value—pure scientific inquiry—would soon be complete.[88] In his speech that was published in German and English, Krieck declared that the age of "pure reason" and "objectivity and neutrality" was now over. "Every worthwhile achievement in the sphere of the natural sciences, no less than in the sciences of culture," he declared, "has been intimately bound up with the fundamental racial characteristics of the people concerned."[89] The jubilee accelerated the careers of the most visible Nazi education theorists and leaders, including Krieck, who replaced Wilhelm Groh as rector of the University of Heidelberg. Groh went on to a position with the Reich Education Ministry in Berlin. Six months later the Nazis completed their purge of the academy by extending dismissals to professors with Jewish wives.[90]

The 200th anniversary of the University of Göttingen in 1937 marked the end of the esteem in which the international community held German universities. An editorial in the London *Spectator* declared, "To celebrate the humiliation of Göttingen on such a day would be, for delegates from England, a betrayal of everything for which our universities are supposed to stand, a disavowal of the ideals which have made the German universities great in the past, and will one day make them great again."[91] The historian Kneller claimed in 1941 that American universities "generally shared" this disapproving attitude.[92] In March the editors of the *Columbia Daily Spectator* argued that Columbia should abstain, and the Jewish anthropologist Franz Boas wrote to Butler that Niels Bohr had just arrived in the United States and confirmed "that practically all the mathematicians in Göttingen have been ousted." Finally persuaded, Butler opened the academic year of 1937 by condemning "the three military dictatorships of Japan, Italy, and Germany."[93]

Butler's career, which oscillated between advocacy for international peace and the abetting of the transatlantic circulation of nativist theories of racial hierarchy, underscores that exchange itself is not necessarily positive. Exchange relies on systems that can be used or abused. The European-born American scientist Jacques Loeb, who in 1918 worried about the jingoism of Europeans during World War I, held the German-inspired American professors accountable for diffusing racist ideology in America: "It happened that a number of American exchange professors and presidents, as for instance President Butler of Columbia University, President Wheeler of the University of California, and others, became the agents of the Emperor and the Junkers in spreading this race propaganda in America; of course, in a quiet way."[94] If transatlantic scholars failed to be guardians against intolerance, "international science" was furthermore not inherently liberal. The Hitler of the 1930s was arguably a cosmopolitan man eager to borrow foreign models.[95] To advance right-wing science and ideology Hitler capitalized on the exchange infrastructure built in the nineteenth century. Conferences, publications, and academic networks all enabled the movement and flourishing of eugenics and their corresponding legal expressions.

Historians often use the term "pseudoscience" to describe the eugenicists, a rhetorical decision that smears individuals but protects institutions. The fact was that the racial scientists and Nazi jurists used the methods, techniques, and infrastructures of science, including the most central institution of all, the university, to promote their malign cause. And the university proved susceptible to the takeover. Perhaps full-scale resistance is unthinkable, but even so, far too few German scholars took advantage of "voice"—either through petition against their Jewish colleagues' dismissal or boycott. Most succumbed to the government's pressures and the easy route of loyalty.[96] Academia had no Dietrich Bonhoeffer, the admirable German pastor who was executed for his participation in the plot against Hitler. By claiming to assent to the Nazis' "coordination" of the university in order to forestall even worse measures, many scholars, from Planck to Heidegger, claimed the university's autonomy when it suited their purpose, and resigned themselves when passivity was more convenient.

The web of complicity extends abroad as well, for if this moment revealed one feature of the university that remained unchanged in the Nazi period it was its porosity. Even under Hitler, the university required foreign validation. The universities in Heidelberg and Göttingen had long and distinguished histories of academic freedom and international exchange and, as we saw, had hosted the most active "colonies" of American students. Many commentators noted the additional injury that the Nazis did to this past. One American Heidelberg alumnus dubbed the event the "Heidelberg Funeral"; another lamented, "In three years the work of centuries has been undone. Academic slavery is the order of the day."[97] But too few American academic leaders drew on the university's global ties to counter insidious nationalism, especially when compared with the courageous British. As the *New York Times* editorialist who likened the university's jubilee to the Olympics wrote, "Indeed, precisely because Governments and statesmen are silent, it would be the duty of unofficial opinion to raise its voice against de facto oppression in any land."[98] Franz Boas provided a model for possible resistance when he promoted a petition in 1938 to oppose Nazi science as an "attack on democracy itself."[99] When the Americans returned to Heidelberg in 1945 they would replace the Athena that the Nazis had removed in 1935 and contribute to rebuilding that and other universities, but their leadership in the intervening years was embarrassingly absent.[100]

The Heidelberg jubilee has been overlooked by scholars or dismissed as a propagandistic event unworthy of scholarly attention.[101] Yet it also sheds light on the nature of interuniversity relationships and what makes universities unique: that they require—crave, even—the validation of peers. Despite the nationalist tone of the event's coverage, the local press recorded foreigners' memories of the university and one commentator even insisted on "making clear the face of the New Germany to his foreign comrade." The leading pro-Nazi Heidelberg professors were similarly sensitive to foreign opinion, and Krieck, in particular, believed the anniversary would be a "great demonstration of the German will to science" that would nullify foreign vilification.[102] Had more academics—both German and foreign—used Germany's reliance on America as a scholarly partner to put pressure on Hitler and his regime, different outcomes might have been possible. Instead Hitler found willing partners, Americans among them, who legitimized his worldview.

Hitler's admiration for America did not wane until he understood that Roosevelt would not support his expansionist policies. Hitler's "split image" of America reflected the two Americas that had existed side by side since at least the 1770s, when Jefferson simultaneously grounded the American Republic in natural law and condoned the institution of slavery.[103] Hitler endorsed the latter philosophical strand even if he chastised everything associated with the liberal tradition.

RETREAT TO AN IDEAL

While Heidegger prepared his lectures entitled "History, Nature, and the State" in the winter of 1933, Max Horkheimer, the Jewish philosopher and director of the Institute for Social Research in Frankfurt, redirected his research to focus on freedom. Since his house had been occupied by storm troopers, Horkheimer spent the rest of the semester commuting from Switzerland to teach. In the preface to *Dawn and Decline*, which he completed in February (and which would be published the following year in Switzerland) Horkheimer wrote, "This book is obsolete. The thoughts it contains are occasional jottings made in Germany between 1926 and 1931. . . . Again and again, they refer critically to concepts 'metaphysics', 'character', 'morality', 'personality', and 'human value' . . . they refer to a period before the final victory of Nazism . . . which is today already out of date."[104] Horkheimer would soon find asylum for his institute and his colleagues at Columbia University—Butler's conservatism notwithstanding—and begin a new chapter in a country in which he previously showed little interest.[105]

After 1933, there were admittedly few avenues for "voice" open to German scholars who wanted to preserve the university ideal. In opposition to Heidegger's 1933 rectorial lecture, his former student Karl Jaspers reworked an earlier publication on the "idea of the university" in which he showed how even those with good intentions were locked in the contradictory logic of the university-as-contract. Equally influenced by Weber, Jaspers wrote that the conditions of the university dictated that "the state's role with regard to this independent entity is, then, one of ubiquitous oversight. The university, in turn, acknowledges this function, neither secretly rejecting the underwriter of its independence as a necessary evil nor obediently bowing to every whim of the State. It confidently accepts state supervision so long as this does not conflict with the cause of truth. Rejecting it would be perilous."[106]

As Jaspers's construction suggests, much depends on the precise nature of the state's role as the "overseer," and the contrast between the autonomous university and the state as the "underwriter of its independence." Jaspers himself would be dismissed from his position in 1937 and prohibited from publishing, but he remained faithful to the university ideal. That Jaspers first drafted his thoughts on the university in the 1920s, rewrote then in 1933, and then revised them again in the postwar period, all while the university's independence was historically contingent, suggests the persistence of the academic social contract model.[107]

It is indicative of the insufficiency of universities' resistance to an oppressive regime that many in Germany sought "exit," or refuge, outside the traditional academy. The women who were never fully included were, ironically, poised to act as guardians of academic ideals in the home. Chief among them was Marianne Weber, whose fame had grown in the decade since the death of her husband, Max, in 1920. At some point in the mid-1920s Marianne decided to revive the tradition of Sunday afternoon salon in their home that she and her husband had initiated during the war. Marianne envisioned her salons as an "intellectual tea," and they were soon visited by such well-respected scholars as the archaeologist Ludwig Curtius and the social scientist Emil Lederer. With a certain self-contained quality, these salons possessed the "lasting power of attraction which a certain academic circle regarded as belonging to itself."[108]

Following enactment of the Civil Service Law of 1933, informal gatherings like Frau Weber's took on decidedly more importance as colleagues were evicted from universities and free exchange was no longer possible inside institutional venues. Marianne never understood the "unresisting compliance" of those who condoned the university's takeover. As she wrote, "The world outside Germany wondered about this and we women, despite the ingenious justifications which certain friends gave us, will never understand this kind of conduct."[109] Marianne's husband, Max, had once seen charisma as an antidote to the excessive bureaucratization of the modern university—a solution available only to individuals who possessed that masculine-defined characteristic. In her unassuming way—she was but a "guide"—Marianne proposed instead "academic conviviality" as the intellectuals' saving grace. Even if not traditional resistance, Marianne's salon university should be considered a passionate defense of the ideal in domestic exile.

In a similar vein, women who had embraced the new internationalism of the 1920s were well positioned to help refugees. Agnes von Harnack, the daughter of the education reformer, embodied one heroic example of resistance. As the first president of the German Women Academics' Association (DAB), which drew inspiration from the Anglo-American "female academic tradition," she participated in the International Federation of University Women (IFUW). At great risk to herself, Harnack harbored opponents of the Nazi regime in her home. She utilized the network of female academics she and others built in the 1920s to offer funding, support, and ultimately escape routes for women.[110] Other academic leaders joined these efforts and navigated between isolationism and internationalism, humanitarianism and opportunism. Their efforts changed the landscape of higher education.

Hitler's politicization of the university—compelling science to serve the state—was far from an aberration. It reveals the uncomfortable fact that the Nazis' "coordination" could be included within the bounds of university service as defined by the academic social contract. Rather than a rupture, the Nazification of the German universities highlights the malleability of the preexisting relationship. If anything, Hitler's regime exposed how vulnerable the university was to deployment in the service of goals most academics today find repugnant. The ease with which higher education fell to Hitler should have raised questions earlier about the viability of the German university ideal itself.[111] But soon that ideal, vulnerable as it was, would become even more entrenched in America—a result, in part, of the university's subjugation in Germany.

CHAPTER TEN

1933

ANNUS MIRABILIS

If I only had a name for the idea! The "New School Faculty of Political Science" wouldn't do. There was no barb in that hook. A "Faculty of Exiled Scholars" wouldn't do. That would be a hook with a broken point. . . . A "University in Exile"—that sounded good. For it was the university itself that was being exiled from Germany.

ALVIN JOHNSON, 1952

Hitler's academic purge brought forth the largest exile of scholars in modern history. The dismissal of non-Aryans from German universities thinned the ranks of the German professoriate, further dimming Germany's scientific star. But the diffusion of German-Jewish scholars across the globe also nourished the German research university model abroad and precipitated new institutional hybrids, especially in America. As Hitler brought universities under his control, academic reformers around the world tapped the efflux of Jewish faculty to establish new institutions. Walter Cook, whose Institute of Fine Arts at New York University, reconstituted in 1937, benefited from this "excess labor," famously joked, "Hitler is my best friend, he shakes the tree and I collect the apples."[1] The new institutions founded in the wake of the expulsion included the aptly named University in Exile, launched in 1933 as an appendage to the New School for Social Research, Black Mountain College in North Carolina (1933), the Warburg Institute in London (1933), Istanbul University (reorganized in 1933), and the Institute for Advanced Study in Princeton, which opened in October 1933. If 1933 was the German annus horribilis, it was annus mirabilis for academic innovators elsewhere.[2] Representing the final chapter in the "long nineteenth century" of scholarly exchanges, these foundings also marked the beginning of an era, fully realized after World War II, in which the American version of the German university would spread worldwide. In the United States itself, these new ventures both transformed and reinforced the system of higher education that had emerged in the 1920s.

Refugees from Hitler's Germany redirected the intellectual currents of the Anglo-American world. Shortly after the war, in early accounts of this period, humanitarians and historians identified its only historical precedent as the mythologized 1453 exile of Byzantine Greek scholars from Constantinople after its capture by the Ottomans. Just as their move to Western Europe heralded an early renaissance based on a rediscovery of Greek texts, exiles from totalitarianism ignited an intellectual and scientific renaissance in America in economics, physics, mathematics, and the humanities.[3] Moreover, much like the Byzantine exodus in the fifteenth century, the emigration of German and European scholars altered the geopolitical organization of science writ large. It also left certain areas untouched.

Even as this transformation clinched American post–World War II cultural and intellectual hegemony, it preserved ethnic and racial hierarchies. On a personal level German-Jewish refugees became the paradoxical bearers of a tradition that excluded them and indeed had deemed them unfit to pass on. But pass it on they did. Such luminaries as Erwin Panofsky and Erich Auerbach became the "founding fathers" of the fields of art history and comparative literature. Others, including Hannah Arendt, Franz Neumann, Theodor Adorno, and Max Horkheimer, affected by their own upheaval, devoted their studies to understanding the rise of totalitarianism and the authoritarian personality, producing works that remain definitive in their fields. The influx of émigrés also shaped the American higher education system—underscoring certain patterns, such as the relationship of outsiders to innovation, while undermining others, such as the benefits of exchange at all. As a whole, this international shift—the rise of Nazism, the reception of refugees, and then the experience of World War II—highlighted the complex relationship of the university with the state, and demanded a reconsideration of just what universities owed their communities, nations, and the world.

AMERICA THE BEAUTIFUL

Americans took some pleasure in the Nazis' self-defeating strategy of ridding German academia of Jews and socialists. In an anonymous poem that circulated in the 1930s titled "Nazi [pronounced Nasty] Dilemma," the author sneered:

How sad that Nazis still must use
The Mental wares made by the Jews,
And that they cannot confiscate
The minds as well as real-estate
Of all those bad, ignoble men,
Who toil with microscope and pen.[4]

Any schadenfreude that Americans felt, however, should have been tempered by the knowledge that their own policies signaled to Hitler the world's condonation of persecution. After all, the American university, as we have seen, was not a beacon of tolerance. As Karl Shapiro, who attended the University of Virginia, home of the Nazi-sympathizing Institute of Public Affairs, wrote in a 1940 poem, "To hurt the Negro and Avoid the Jew / Is the curriculum."[5] As a result of discriminatory selection criteria initiated by Harvard, Yale, and Princeton beginning in 1920, the number of Jews at the leading universities fell precipitously—an outcome that university presidents Conant (and his predecessor Abbot Lowell) and Butler congratulated. President Jack Hibben, who led Princeton in this era, robustly denied ever resorting to a quota, though his feisty wife, Jennie, remembered otherwise when he was queried by the University of Chicago's Robert Maynard Hutchins: "Jack Hibben, I don't see how you can sit there and lie to this young man. You know very well that you and Dean Eisenhart get together every year and fix the quota." In fact Princeton's celebration of the school's social exclusiveness aimed to discourage Jews from applying at all. This double-pronged strategy seems to have had the intended effect. Princeton's class of 1933 contained thirteen Jews.[6]

It was therefore far from a fait accompli that refugee German-Jewish scholars would be welcome in American higher education. The diversity of the academy that we now take for granted was largely the result of tense negotiations and conservative acquiescence enabled by undeniable opportunity.[7] How did this cultural and institutional transformation occur? With the Americanization of European refugee scholars as their top priority, the architects and leaders of the American higher education system, some of whom became accidental humanitarians, carefully managed resettlement efforts to leave intact the perception of Anglo-Saxon Protestant whiteness.

In a scathing critique published in 1922 as *The Goose-Step*, the muckraking journalist Upton Sinclair exposed the racism of elite universities' admissions—he called this an "academic pogrom"—against those who were "trying to break into 'society.'" He offered a proposal to the excluded: "If I were a cultured Jew in America . . . I should make it my task to persuade wealthy Jews to establish an endowment and gather a faculty of Jewish scientists and scholars—there are enough of them to make the most wonderful faculty in the world. And then I should open the doors of this university to seekers of knowledge of all races—save that I should bar students who had anti-Semitic prejudice!"[8] Though his language might seem in poor taste from the post-Holocaust perspective, it is helpful for thinking about strategic responses to exclusion in higher education.

Historic outsiders to the university, as we have seen, often drew on private philanthropy to support new positions or entirely new institutions that would be more open and inclusive. What we might call the Sinclair model, reminiscent of Thomas and Garrett's "coercive philanthropy," was practiced in American cities, in the American-esque German cities of Hamburg and Frankfurt, and in the American-inspired and significantly Jewish-funded Kaiser Wilhelm Society. In the last quarter of the nineteenth century, Jews had funded positions in Semitic languages and, in the 1920s, supported the creation of innovative institutions like the New School for Social Research.[9] The institution that would aid German-Jewish refugee scholars grew out of this tradition. The New York Foundation was incorporated in 1909 with a gift from Alfred Heinsheimer of the investment firm of Kuhn, Loeb & Co. Its trustees included Jacob Schiff, Herbert Lehman, Felix and Paul Warburg, and other Jewish bankers with German family backgrounds.

Philanthropy certainly wasn't limited to women or Jews. As we have seen, it was a strategic tool wielded by insiders like Carnegie to shape higher education. It could be used to disrupt or to reinforce social hierarchy. In the 1930s, the needs of Jewish outsiders and the desire for "soft power" came together in the Rockefeller Foundation, which played a significant role in responding to the plight of refugee scholars. The foundation had since the early 1920s supported science and research abroad and was deeply invested in the German-speaking world. It supported European research centers and academic travel. Even with the rise of the National Socialist regime the foundation continued to fund ongoing projects in Germany. Given Rockefeller's presence in America and Europe, it was natural for displaced scholars to appeal to the it for help; some even began to show up at the European office in Paris. The grant officers, however, were hardly free of antisemitic prejudice.[10] Before he set out on a trip to Germany in 1933, John Van Sickle, assistant director of the Paris office, cautioned against any "large aid" to Frankfurt, since it was perceived as "international and Jewish."[11]

The moral shortcomings of their colleagues notwithstanding, a different set of voices emerged from the foundation in favor of aid to refugee scholars. Two program officers who worked in the division for medical sciences, Robert Lambert in Paris and Alan Gregg in New York, came up with a plan. When Lambert wrote the New York office in April 1933 to express his concern for the treatment of German-Jewish scientists he included a letter that detailed the hardship of an exceptional young scholar in Freiburg. Lambert suggested to Gregg that a "considerable number of these first-class unemployed might find opportunities [in America]." They jointly developed a cost-sharing system to place refugees with universities.[12] In June 1933 the foundation circulated "A Report Concerning the Present Situation at German Universities In So Far as Mathematics and Theoretical Physics Are Concerned," the first of many ominous statements on the "much more profound effect" the "revolution" seemed to having "on the spirit of the universities."[13] After hearing from prominent scientists and scholars, including Niels Bohr and Joseph Schumpeter, Rockefeller approved Lambert's and Gregg's plan. As one historian argues, "A certain moral pressure for action was inescapable."[14]

American Jews in New York City established another organization—the Emergency Committee in Aid of Displaced German Scholars (later "Foreign Scholars")—to "represent the cultural interests of the country," and it would be led by Stephen Duggan, the director of the IIE. (The deputy role of assistant secretary was held by Edward R. Murrow, from 1933 until 1935, when he left to become a broadcaster.)[15] Based on a principled opposition to prejudice and antisemitism, Duggan and the Emergency Committee began a concerted program to "exert pressure gently" on universities to receive exiled Jews.[16] The New York Foundation provided the seed money, and the American Joint Distribution Committee supported administrative expenses. The Rockefeller Foundation agreed to pay part of each refugee's salary for three years. But it became clear that Jewish philanthropists were expected to shoulder much of the financial burden.[17] What was crucial was that the hiring initiative come from the university, which was required to provide matching funds and, therefore, commit financially to the scholar's future.[18]

This constellation of organizations proceeded cautiously, with overriding concern not to encourage American antisemitic backlash. In correspondence with Lambert, Gregg cautioned, "If too many Jews are introduced into American universities, we shall run a surprisingly good chance of creating an uncontrollable amount of precisely the same sort of illiberal attitude here. The men I talked to on this committee would prefer anything to fanning the flames of anti-Semitism on this side of the water."[19] Moreover, the Emergency Committee estimated that more than two thousand (or almost 10 percent of) American university instructors had lost their jobs since the beginning of the Great Depression, and the program officers wanted to assuage fears that German scholars might edge Americans out of the limited opportunities.[20] Duggan therefore wrote to the university presidents to assure them of the temporary nature of the program.[21]

The different levels of anxiety exhibited by the Emergency Committee and the Rockefeller Foundation were reflected in the distinct ways these entities presented their work. While the Emergency Committee avoided news coverage, Johnson, who aimed to recruit refugees for the New School, courted it. Worried as it was about "fanning the flames of anti-Semitism," the Emergency Committee did not even wish to present its work as a protest against Hitler and declined an invitation from the American Jewish Congress to sponsor a 1934 demonstration against Nazi dictatorship. Johnson, for his part, hired a publicity agent and published articles headlined "Thank you Hitler," clearly linking his institution to the intellectual world that the dictator exiled.[22] To be sure, Johnson as a gentile had more latitude in showcasing his humanitarian gestures. The Jewish bankers who gave their support financially did not have that luxury.

The Emergency Committee was justified in its worry that antisemitism was like a smoldering ember that could be fanned into flames. In 1938, a poll by Opinion Research Corporation found that 82 percent of American adults were opposed to large-scale immigration of German Jews. The violent pogrom known as Kristallnacht, in November 1938, was a turning point for many who previously gave the National Socialists the benefit of the doubt. Notwithstanding this change of heart, the situation did not improve for refugees, and antisemitic sentiments actually climbed.[23] Raymond Fosdick, the lawyer and public administrator who served as president of the Rockefeller Foundation for twelve years, expressed concern in December 1938 that with respect to Jewish immigration "we have reached the saturation point."[24] University presidents appeared to agree. Betty Drury, executive secretary of the committee from 1937 to 1944, reported that St. Lawrence University made a request for a displaced economist-sociologist, but since "the Jewish problem . . . exists in that particular community . . . it would be better if the candidate were not Jewish."[25] Congressional bills in 1939 and 1940 to bring twenty thousand Jewish children to the United States from Austria and Germany failed spectacularly.

Ultimately it was utilitarian and not humanitarian arguments that swayed those concerned about an influx of German-Jewish refugees. As one commentator wrote in a forum titled "Are Refugees a Liability?" "The madness of Brown Bolshevism [i.e., fascism] has presented us with the opportunity of admitting to our country educated, well-trained, skilled individuals who not only can fit readily into our economic and social life but also can furnish us with talents and industries we did not heretofore possess." "America Needs Them!" he announced emphatically.[26] Behind the scenes the Rockefeller Foundation developed a system for rating scholars, which consisted of three tiers: List A included "outstanding scientists of world wide [*sic*] reputation; in most instances they are men in or past middle age," for example, Richard Courant or Otto Stern. List B included "similar men whose reputations, are, perhaps, not quite so outstanding." While List C included "younger men who are nevertheless of first rate scientific importance." But all seemed to agree that they must focus on "world-class men," particularly if they were Jews. The hierarchy of scholarly worth had life and death consequences.[27]

Continuing concerns influenced the divergent strategies that the Rockefeller Foundation and Johnson pursued. While the foundation favored the strategy of spreading Jews across the country to assimilate them into the national system, Johnson aimed to concentrate them in a new institution, the University in Exile, which would preserve their distinct European identity and that of the social sciences. As we saw, Johnson harbored ambitions to turn the New School into a center for the social sciences, but for all his fundraising, recruiting, and curricular innovation, he was unable to accomplish that feat. In 1927, when the newly founded Social Science Research Council appointed Johnson as associate editor of the Encyclopedia of Social Sciences he had jumped at the opportunity to travel to Europe and interview social scientists for the project. Now in 1933 he had contacts he made on this trip—Emil Lederer in Berlin, for example—to very quickly assemble a willing and interested body of emigrants. Historians of the New School Rutkoff and Scott identified the absence of an "established group opposed to their recruitment" as a contributor to the absorption of the refugees, since they were not "under any compulsion to blend in or to become Americanized."[28] In fact, not only did they *not* "blend in," but the New School developed a new entity that was neither European nor American but a hybrid of the two. Faculty were encouraged to lecture in whatever language they preferred and were said to have developed their own language—a mixture of German and English, sometimes referred to as "Newschoolese," that mirrored the intellectual hybridization.[29]

Given the resistance of university leaders and the thinly veiled antisemitism, it is remarkable that the work of these foundations (by 1938 more than a dozen) achieved so much. By 1940 nearly two thousand scientists and scholars had emigrated from Germany and Austria, about seven hundred of whom made their way to America—far from an émigré's first choice.[30] The Emergency Committee placed over three hundred of these, and the Rockefeller Foundation another two hundred. (The New School itself hired about 180 refugees.) There is no doubt that America was a great beneficiary as well, both quantitatively, in terms of the influx of educated immigrants, and qualitatively, with respect to the numbers of Nobel Prize winners and significant contributors in the Who's Who of science.[31] By 1946, the proportion of tenured faculty among the Rockefeller recipients was 82 percent—a measure of its success.[32] The absorption of refugees, therefore, should be viewed in light of other academic contracts; this global one was similarly transactional.

INSTITUTE FOR ADVANCED STUDY—A
PARADISE TOO GOOD TO BE TRUE?

Abraham Flexner's desire to establish a research institution coincided fortuitously with Hitler's expulsion of the Jews. The Institute for Advanced
Study, which Flexner announced in 1930 and opened in the spring of
1933, embodies the tensions between humanitarianism and opportunism that higher education reformers navigated in that decade. Privately
funded, Flexner's institute resembled the "Sinclair model," in which philanthropy carved out a place for institutional innovation. Its early history
highlights the possibilities and limitations of academic entrepreneurship
and the changing relationship of higher education to nationalism and
internationalism.

Flexner's plan to found an institution originated in the early 1920s, when
he was working for the Rockefeller Foundation's General Education Board.
Unsatisfied with the direction that the American university had taken, and
claiming that Chicago and Hopkins had "yielded to the pressures of undergraduate education to an extent which stultified the graduate school,"
Flexner argued that Hopkins should divest itself of its undergraduate college and become a graduate school focused exclusively on research. Although his plan attracted the support of Johns Hopkins president Frank J.
Goodnow, and he wrote excitedly about the new "experiment" in the *Atlantic*, not everyone at Hopkins looked upon it favorably and, short on money
and faculty approval, Flexner's plan collapsed.[33]

As he considered retirement at age sixty-two, an invitation to deliver
the Rhodes Trust Memorial Lectures gave Flexner new direction. He and
his wife left in the spring of 1928 for Oxford, with its "great scholars and
great educational opportunities."[34] From the autumn of 1928 through the
summer of 1929 Flexner visited universities in Great Britain and Germany
for the purpose of obtaining a "fresh view of their situation, problems, and
efforts."[35] When he returned to America, his brother Simon, director of the
Rockefeller Institute, gave him an office to write. Expanding his critique
that the university had become an "educational department-store contain-
ing a kindergarten at one end and Nobel Prize winners . . . at the other,"
Flexner could not have known that a literal department store would be his
savior.[36] Louis Bamberger and his sister Caroline Bamberger Fuld had just
sold their department store to Macy & Co. two weeks before the crash for
some $25 million. Seeking to identify "the most beneficial use to which
their fortunes could be put" and inspired by their father's interest in medicine, they sent their representatives, Samuel Leidesdorf and Herbert Maas,
to seek advice from Flexner. The pair left with copies of Flexner's writings

and shared them with the Bambergers, who were taken by the idea that "progress might be greatly assisted by the outright creation of a school or institute of higher learning, a university in the post-graduate sense of the word . . . a free society of scholars."[37]

Flexner persuaded the Bambergers to adapt their initial vision of a medical school—one without quotas or restrictions against Jews—into an institute of higher learning, but he had difficulty shaking their exclusive focus on Newark. Indeed the subject of location remained a source of friction between them and Flexner, for Flexner was certain that Newark did not have the required infrastructure.[38] The certificate of incorporation for the "Institute for Advanced Study—Louis Bamberger and Mrs. Felix Fuld Foundation," which was filed on May 20, 1930, reflects a growing compromise—to establish "*at or in the vicinity* of Newark, New Jersey . . . an institute for advanced study."[39] That summer Flexner set off again to Europe to seek counsel on his book and his institute. The Bambergers agreed with the newly appointed trustees on a number of principles, including that the institute would be in the State of New Jersey (the "vicinity of Newark" now abandoned), that personnel decisions should be made in "the spirit characteristic of America . . . with no regard whatever to accidents of race, creed, or sex" (so as to preserve the family's initial desire to create a space of higher learning for Jews), that the endowment should not be spent on buildings (following Gilman's dictum of "men not buildings"), and that the institute would never accept money from donors who did not agree with these principles.[40] Flexner made an ex libris seal with the institute's name to celebrate, and the new fund was announced in the *New York Times*. When he saw the announcement, the Princeton professor Oswald Veblen wrote to his friend Flexner immediately and offered Princeton "so that you could use some of the facilities of the University and we could have the benefit of your presence."[41]

In the fall of 1930 Flexner began to flesh out his experiment. He confided to a colleague, "There is really nothing yet to be said about the new Institute except what you find on this letterhead. . . . I want to spend the next year listening."[42] Flexner was still drawn to the idea of research institutes, yet the example of Germany suggested that he should proceed carefully. Although Althoff had "made it a point to relate research institutes to universities," and the relationship had "proved to be a fruitful one for both parties concerned," Flexner knew that the development of the Kaiser Wilhelm Institutes had drained talent from the universities, suggesting that research institutes could be a mistake: "The term 'university' [had] lost its meaning."[43] He believed America was at a crossroads, and the next move would determine whether it would take its place as the leader. "The country cannot, of course, dispense with Europe," Flexner wrote, "but in the realm of higher education America has become in certain fields a country with which Europe cannot any longer dispense, either."[44]

Given his respect for his European colleagues, Flexner felt justified in hearing from them that "universities have everywhere undergone changes that have impaired their fundamental and essential character," and, therefore, an institute was the only solution.[45] Yet he held onto the notion that that institute could combine the best of both, as it would be "neither a current university, struggling with diverse tasks and many students, nor a research institute, devoted solely to the solution of problems. It may be pictured as a wedge inserted between the two—a small university, in which a limited amount of teaching and a liberal amount of research are both to be found."[46]

As for which discipline with which to begin, Flexner was inclined to mathematics despite active lobbying by his friends and colleagues for their own fields, including an impassioned letter on the humanities from the Oxford-based British historian E. L. Woodward.[47] Flexner believed mathematics represented "the severest of all disciplines, antecedent, on the one hand, to science; on the other, to philosophy and economics and thus to other social disciplines." There existed no strong university department that had already monopolized the field; and finally, mathematics was cheap—"It requires little—a few men, a few students, a few rooms, books, blackboards, chalk, paper and pencils."[48] To build his department, Flexner would need to appeal to foreigners, including those in the center of applied mathematics in Göttingen. In spring 1932 Flexner traveled to California to meet Einstein, who was visiting the California Institute of Technology, and reported that he was now ready to "take the first step looking towards the selection of men and a site."[49] Flexner's early recruiting efforts were mixed. David Birkhoff, the most important American mathematician of his day, accepted Flexner's offer and then rescinded eight days later;[50] in Göttingen, Hermann Weyl expressed interest but agonized about leaving his home.[51]

Hitler would help make Weyl's decision easier. In May of 1933 Veblen spoke with Simon Flexner about "what can be done to help the Jews and Liberals who are driven out of their positions in Germany."[52] One month before the Civil Service Law was implemented in Germany, Flexner indicated ambivalence about staffing his institute with German-Jewish refugees. In a letter to Veblen, he wrote, "whatever we may do for foreigners, we must try to develop American culture and civilization. . . . We can only do this is if in the main we seek out Americans and give them every opportunity. Meanwhile, I think we should lose no opportunity to supplement what Americans can do by drawing sometimes temporarily, sometimes permanently, upon the best that other nations have produced."[53] Flexner clearly agonized about the conflict between his nationalist aspirations for the institute to become America's "seat of higher learning" and the empathy he felt for refugees. His donors' intention to form an institute that would benefit their own provided a serendipitous pretext to alter his plans. Desperately wanting to make a "fresh start" like Gilman and Harper (who once raided Clark's failing mathematics department), Flexner now swooped in to take much of Göttingen back to America.[54] Reluctantly assuming the humanitarian role, Flexner helped extract Weyl—and his wife and children—from Germany.[55] In the end, eleven refugee scholars, in part funded by the Emergency Committee, joined the Institute for Advanced Study.

Among them was Albert Einstein. Einstein's arrival created the largest challenge, for he was not only the most renowned of the German refugee scientists but also the most outspoken about his Jewish identity and his opposition to the Nazi regime—both of which were taboo for the circumspect American Jewish philanthropists. Flexner complained to the German-Jewish American banker Felix Warburg, who was a founding member of the Emergency Committee, about Einstein's "everlasting publicity." In fact, Flexner shared with Warburg that a Jewish colleague had pleaded with him to "shut Einstein up," since Einstein was "doing the Jewish cause in Germany nothing but harm and that he is also seriously damaging his own reputation as a scientist and doing the Jewish situation in America no good."[56]

Flexner was so determined to deflect attention that he intercepted a White House invitation for the Einsteins. This angered Mrs. Einstein immensely, though Flexner assured her his intentions were pure, and he did not "wish to limit your husband's freedom." Albert Einstein assured Eleanor Roosevelt that the invitation never reached him. He continued to spar with Flexner, who tried to prevent him from aiding a benefit concert for refugees in New York at the end of that year (fig. 10).[57]

Flexner's "paradise for scholars" was not without friction or shortcomings.[58] First, the striking absence of women faculty, though not unusual compared to America's elite universities, including the one next door, came under extra scrutiny, as accomplished female mathematicians were among the refugees who fled Germany. Among them was the algebraist Emmy Noether, one of the "most talented and creative female mathematicians" in the twentieth century and "maybe even of all times," who was given a temporary position at the institute as a "visitor." Noether is sometimes hailed as representative of the institute's egalitarian spirit, and her obituary by Einstein recalls her happy time at the institute, yet the memory was likely

Figure 10. Albert Einstein, Abraham Flexner, C. Lavinia Bamberger (the sister of the benefactors), and others attend the ceremony in honor of building Fuld Hall, at the Institute for Advanced Study, 1939. (Photographer unknown. From the Shelby White and Leon Levy Archives Center, Institute for Advanced Study, Princeton, NJ, USA.)

exaggerated; Flexner would never afford her a "permanent commitment."[59] In fact, the contingency of her situation is reflective of the second-class status of the institute's women scholars: the archaeologist Hetty Goldman's father paid her salary, and the topologist Anna Stafford, then a postdoctoral student, supported herself by teaching secondary school.[60] The situation took a toll on Noether. Though Flexner helped secure a permanent position for her at Bryn Mawr, from which she would commute to the institute to lecture, she referred to Princeton as "a men's university, where nothing female is admitted."[61] Her outspoken nature was unwelcome, and her premature death after routine surgery symbolized the tragedy of her unfulfilled promise. Most refugee scholar wives were as highly trained as they were ignored and, since German-Jewish women of the upper middle class often learned English, found themselves in a subordinate position as their husbands' translators.[62]

Flexner favored the governance of a board of trustees, an unpopular idea among many professors. For Flexner this organization was fundamentally egalitarian, since the director was (like a rector) on par with the faculty, as in Europe.[63] Flexner insisted that a board was in the faculty's interest, as "complete faculty rule would mean . . . mathematicians would do what I am doing, namely, devoting their entire time to things that do not bear upon mathematics," and besides it "exists nowhere on earth."[64] That the institute itself would be governed by a board and not the faculty, however, angered Oswald and Felix Frankfurter, who, like Cattell two decades earlier, promoted "self-governance" as the only authentic model for a university.

Flexner also differed with Frankfurter on compensation. Flexner favored generous pay for faculty (the institute would later be nicknamed by Princeton's graduate students the "Institute for Advanced Salaries") and felt strongly that the low "financial status of the American professor" accounted for the lack of research output in the country. He insisted early on to his brother Simon, "Unless the University Professor can be placed upon a sound economic basis, talent will be thrown into business and professional life even more strongly than to-day."[65] In 1934 when Flexner added additional schools he introduced salary differences, however, and that controversial decision once again angered Frankfurter.[66]

Yet it was Flexner's conservatism—nostalgia even—that most irked his colleagues in his "educational Utopia."[67] The Nazi suppression of academic freedom in general and the Jews in particular made Flexner's interlocutors weary of his enthusiasm for the "German model." Writing to Flexner in 1934, Frankfurter said, "I don't want to hear anything more about the German Universities for a good long while anyhow." For Frankfurter "a university is something more than a means for contributing to knowledge. . . . In successive moral crises not only have the universities of Germany failed to reveal the accumulated wisdom that we call civilization, but to a large extent they have been the centres of decivilization."[68]

Flexner's experiment, which would have a huge impact on American science, had an ambivalent relationship with the system at large. As the concrete manifestation of an alternative vision for American higher education, it was not as well received as Flexner's 1910 report on the inadequacies of medical schools. His jibes in his 1930 publication on the poor state of American universities, which left none untouched, rested less easily with presidents who now had more students and bigger endowments—in short, more to lose and more power with which to fight back.[69] Flexner later insisted that he purposely did not poach talent from the universities, because he wanted to leave them intact as he built the institute.[70] He understood that the exceptional nature of the institute meant it would not alter the system as a whole.

FROM BAUHAUS TO BLACK MOUNTAIN

If the Institute for Advanced Study succeeded as an institution but failed as a replicable model, another start-up of the same era, Black Mountain College, was the opposite: an enterprise that failed as an institution but succeeded as a model—the experimental liberal arts college—still widely emulated and admired. The founders of Black Mountain College in the mountains of western North Carolina eagerly collected Hitler's "apples," and the result was entirely different from Flexner's. The circumstances that gave rise to the founding of the college echoed those of the 1919 "hour for experiment" in which the New School for Social Research originated: increasing tension between an institution and faculty, a public series of dismissals, and a wave of resignations in protest.

In this case the college with which the Black Mountain founders split was less illustrious and well endowed than the "House of Morgan" in Manhattan's Morningside Heights. Founded in 1885 by the Congregational Church, Rollins College was the first institution of higher learning in Florida and one of the more extreme examples of the rejection of the German research university. As the historian Frederick Rudolf once wrote, "The basis of the Rollins idea was the concept of leisure, the tendency to aristocratic emphases, which led President Hamilton Holt to declare that Rollins was on the road back to Socrates, to that relaxed atmosphere which recognized leisure as fundamental to the full discovery and development of self."[71] Even for this eccentric college, the classics professor John A. Rice was still too eccentric, and, following a tense fight over curricular reform, Holt dismissed him.[72] Arthur Lovejoy of the AAUP was dispatched to Florida to investigate, and at a hearing the college president presented a litany of complaints about the former professor including that Rice spoke too loudly in chapel, posted "obscene" pictures to discuss the nature of art, and wore a jockstrap on the beach.[73] Rice did not deny most of these charges (though he said the beach costume amounted to running shorts), and Lovejoy, somewhat at a loss, concluded that "the committee finds in the case nothing seriously reflecting upon either the private character or the scholarship of Mr. Rice, or upon his ability as a teacher."[74] The initial AAUP report put Rollins on notice, but instead of relenting, the college doubled down. In June two tenured professors of political science, historian Ralph Reed Lounsbury, and chemist Frederick Raymond Georgia, who supported Rice by sitting with him during the AAUP hearings, were dismissed.[75]

Rice didn't wait for his name to be cleared.[76] Instead he did what any academic innovator would do—he conspired with three colleagues to resign and establish a new college instead. The motley crew included Lounsbury and Georgia, assistant professor of physics Ted Dreier, and drama coach Bob Wunsch. Having roomed at the University of North Carolina at Chapel Hill with the novelist and Asheville native Thomas Wolfe, Wunsch suggested the Blue Ridge Mountains as a site for their venture. Academic rebels with a vision, they were also well-connected white Protestant men. Benefiting from advice from, and connections with, some of the leading philanthropists, including the Guggenheim Memorial Foundation, which let them use their New York City offices that summer, and the Forbes family, who were close friends of Dreier, they raised $14,500 in the summer of 1933.[77] And with that minimum underwriting (but no endowment), no trustees, and a bare-bones administration, the would-be founders set off for North Carolina.

The Black Mountaineers (much like the early New Schoolers) dreamed of a truly democratic educational institution. This applied equally to the classroom and the administration, which was entirely in the hands of the faculty and was influenced by Quaker meetings. Rice, who would serve as rector (not president) from 1934 until 1938, came from a line of Methodist church planters. As an academic entrepreneur, he sought to avoid the problems of institutional hypocrisy he had seen in the religious institutions he attended, and gravitated to the Socratic dialogue and the Oxbridge tutorial as purer models.[78] John Dewey, on whose educative ideals of "mutual consultation and voluntary agreement" the college was based, called it "a living example of democracy in action."[79] In a later interview, the architect Buckminster Fuller, who spent time teaching at the college, attested that the founders "felt there was no demonstration anywhere of a college where the trustees were the professors themselves, and they thought it would be very worthwhile to have such an experiment."[80] It would emphasize intellectual and aesthetic freedom, to an extent unparalleled in American higher education. The college became an embodiment of opposition, not just to Rollins College or the Nazi regime, but also to mainstream American academia.

Rice knew art would be central to the curriculum but had neither the resources nor the expertise among his founding faculty, so he must have been elated to learn from the architect Philip Johnson that Anni and Josef Albers were looking for work. As Johnson wrote to Josef Albers in August 1933, "My description of your work has caused a great deal of interest here. . . . Since [Black Mountain College] is new, I do not exactly know what you will be called upon to do, but you would presumably head the Department of Creative Art which they consider of vital importance rather than, as in most American schools, a subject of secondary importance."[81] Both Alberses had been instructors at the Bauhaus, founded by Walter Gropius in 1919 as an innovative challenge to the traditional academy that integrated aesthetic and industrial design. Associated with leftist and communist politics, the Bauhaus was run out of Weimar—the Republic's eponymous city—following a change in local leadership in 1925. The architects, painters, and designers set up shop in Dessau before being shut down again by the Nazis in the summer of 1933.

Seeing the opportunity, the German-speaking Ted Dreier wrote to Josef Albers inviting him to join the college and appealing to Edward Warburg to help secure the Alberses visas to the United States.[82] "Our venture (*Unternehmen*) has the character of a pioneering venture and represents an adventure," Dreier told Albers. Albers responded in German that though he was nervous about his English, he was excited "by the young organization and its institutions and its lively purpose."[83] The Alberses arrived in New York on the SS *Europa* during Thanksgiving week and shared their first American Thanksgiving with the Dreier family in Brooklyn. One of the Dreier women evidently notified the press, prompting the *Brooklyn Daily* to run a story—"Art Professor, Fleeing Nazis, Here to Teach." Following a visit to the Museum of Modern Art (MoMA) and a meeting with avant-garde artist Marcel Duchamp, the couple traveled south on a train and arrived in the small mountain town of Asheville, where the local paper, the *Asheville Citizen Times*, announced—though hardly celebrated—their arrival with the headline "Germans to Teach Art Near Here" and a large photograph of the couple. Warburg declared, "Professor Albers may exert an influence in this country that will fundamentally change present methods of approach to art education."[84] His upper-class English-speaking Jewish wife, Anni, translated for reporters, "He says that in this country at last he will find a free atmosphere. . . . He says that art must have freedom in which to grow, and that is no longer possible in Germany. There a professor must teach only the art that the government thinks is forwarding the German ideal of government."[85] With Anni adorned in a mink and fur hat, Weimar had arrived in America (fig. 11).

After surviving his first weeks with the help of Anni as his translator, Josef learned English from his students, beginning with an old copy of *Alice in Wonderland* and advancing to the *New Yorker*. As Albers immersed himself in his new milieu, his "Prussianism"—for which he was both adored and feared—remained just beneath the surface. At one faculty meeting, Josef spoke of the need for education to achieve the proper balance between self-cultivation and the acquisition of facts: "When I came to this country,

Figure 11. Donning a mink and a fascinator, Anni Albers, along with her husband, Josef, seemed to announce that Weimar had arrived in Black Mountain, North Carolina, in 1933. (© AP Photo.)

I found that you had one general term [for education] which included the instruction part of teaching and the purely educational part, which means the development of the will. We have two words: one for the real giving of methods of facts (information), and another for the development of character. I do not know whether the English language has words for these two things."[86] The German tradition encompassed *Erziehung* and *Bildung*. The former, as we have seen, has more to do with character, and the latter with knowledge; it was a distinction that was reconciled, albeit tenuously, in the German research university ideal. Albers wanted to recombine them in his new home.

At the Bauhaus Josef Albers rose from relative obscurity to teaching painting and color theory in the *Meister* class, while Anni, excluded from the "masculine" arts of metalwork and painting, devoted herself to the weaving section, which she would ultimately head. (Johnson had tried but failed to secure her a "better position in a woman's college" in America.)[87] United at the Bauhaus by their shared outsider status—Josef was working class, and Anni was a Jew—these marginal figures came into their own, ideologically and aesthetically, in America.[88] At Black Mountain, Josef expanded from sandblasted glass painting (for which the college lacked facilities) to abstract painting and instructed students in his first-year Bauhaus-style *Werkstatt*. Albers, who never mastered English, was said to have announced that his goal for his students was "to make open the eyes." Since there was no loom immediately available, Anni also changed course, initially working with other materials and later advocating weaving to support industrial production. While her husband built a school devoted to his performative techniques, her elaborate creations pushed the boundary of a previously neglected art form.

At the early Bauhaus Albers had developed a preliminary course and taught the applied arts of wallpaper design and typography. At Black Mountain, also a "new beginning," Albers developed an art course designed to break the bad habits of overly instructed students. Influenced by the Pre-Columbian art of Central America, Mexico, and the Southwest, where he and Anni traveled in the summers, Albers assigned students to make their own paintbrushes from chewed sticks to reconnect with the fundamentals of art as experience.[89] According to former student and Black Mountain historian Emma Harris, "Albers guided Black Mountain students in the re-creation of Bauhaus studies."[90] But there was also a crucial difference. While at the Bauhaus the Alberses trained artists, at Black Mountain College they shaped individuals with art at the center of a general education.[91] And before the Bauhaus ideas found a foothold in Cambridge, Chicago, or elsewhere, the Alberses helped translate this storied institution into a liberal arts college in western North Carolina.

When Yugoslavian-born writer Louis Adamic visited in 1936 he reported on the self-conscious desire of the college to provide a space for American culture unmoored from the European ship. Rice reportedly told Adamic, "In great part I blame Hitlerism on German education, which always concerned itself only with intellect, with stuffing the head full of facts, and thus prepared for Hitler a nation of emotional infants ready to succumb to his demagoguery. Essentially the same danger exists here, now that our national life is lurching into a general crisis, and for the same reason; our education has been powerfully influenced by Germany."[92]

The job of a college, Rice insisted, was to bring young people to intellectual and emotional maturity:

> If we do think as we want to think, it looks as if we ought to begin to consider education as a thing concerned at least in part with how people feel. If we do not, somebody else will, and all our structure of thought will disappear as quickly as it has in Nazi Germany. There was a country where the universities were concerned with pure thought, where the keenest thinking of the modern world was being done. And yet not a word was heard from the seats of learning when the house-painter appeared and roused the Germans of feeling. While intellection was being sharpened and polished, savagery was going its way, waiting for a chance. If we think this cannot happen here we are fools.[93]

The irony is that, despite Rice's noble desire to break with the German tradition, the school wedged between the Blue Ridge and Craggy Mountains became a refuge for German-Jewish émigrés who were some of the best exemplars of German educational ideals. Drawing on the abundance of German refugees allowed Black Mountain to become an unlikely and unexpectedly influential site of midcentury learning. Beginning with friends of the Alberses, other refugees began to turn up. The psychoanalyst Fritz Moellenhoff arrived with his wife, Anna (also a psychiatrist); in 1936, Alexander (Xanti) Schawinsky, an artist, dramatist, and fellow Bauhausler made his way to the college following an escape through Italy with his wife, Irene. Erwin Straus, another psychiatrist and former editor of the journal *Nervenartz*, took refuge there with his wife, Gertrud Lukaschik Straus, in 1938.

Resources were short, and some would have to be turned away. In May 1939 Albers initially told Heinrich Jalowetz, the former director of the Cologne Opera, that there was no open position. After a letter of recommendation arrived from his former teacher Arthur Schoenberg, now in Los Angeles, a space was found for Jalowetz (and for his wife, who was employed as a bookbinder and singing teacher).[94] By 1940, Black Mountain College had hired twenty-eight refugees; in 1943 ten more were added when Albers initiated a "money-raising campaign" to help them.[95]

By the end of the 1940s the college would become a chrysalis for the American avant-garde, nurturing such artists as Willem de Kooning, John

Cage, Merce Cunningham, and Robert Rauschenberg, who would transform American art, music, and dance. Not everyone was impressed. Clement Greenberg later quipped, "Not much art came out of Black Mountain
(only some famous names)."[96] Greenberg had an antipathy for Albers,
whom he believed represented the geometric abstraction that was being
imported from Europe.[97] There is no doubt that Black Mountain had a central role in making German culture the foundation for American modernism. At the heart of that translation were the Alberses, who numbered
among the few émigré intellectuals and artists who had successful careers
on both sides of the Atlantic.

By the time Walter Gropius arrived in America in 1937, Albers had already instructed several cohorts at Black Mountain in his Bauhaus-based
three-pronged preliminary course, or *Vorkurs*, in drawing, color, and design. During the war, this course would be further Americanized, and
renamed the Design Course, with exercises that recreated imagery from
Coca-Cola cans and cigarette boxes.[98] In the year of Gropius's arrival, Black
Mountain College purchased property at Lake Eden, a few miles across the
valley, and Albers enlisted Gropius and Marcel Breuer to design a complex
of buildings, though owing to lack of funds and organization their designs
were never implemented. Gropius, nonetheless, showed great interest
in the college's experiment, touted its "teamwork" ethic as an aesthetic
and pedagogical innovation, and joined the college's advisory council.
He encouraged his Harvard students to travel to North Carolina to take
Albers's architectural course and invited Albers to Cambridge for temporary stays.[99] John Dewey visited the campus twice in the academic year of
1934–1935, one time bringing his friend Albert Barnes, who implemented
Dewey's philosophy in his art collection. Dewey became a member of the
advisory council of the college in 1936.[100] Albers may not have read the
German translation of Dewey's work before arriving in North Carolina, but
like Gropius, he soon found a pedagogical ally. The American Black Mountaineers Gropius and Albers were links to a nearly lost European culture.

Other aspects of the Bauhaus culture that traveled with the Alberses to
North Carolina were less attractive—namely, its notorious gender politics.
Despite the egalitarian spirit of the Bauhaus, the director Gropius became
concerned in the institute's early years that certain workshops were "over-
flowing with women," and recommended in a closed-door meeting early
in 1920 that "gradually the female element be reduced to one-third of all
available spaces." A letter six months later made this quota de facto Bauhaus policy. Not only was the number of women students reduced, but
also, following Gropius's guidance, women were directed into a "women's
section" to work in the "heavy craft areas" of textiles, bookbinding, and

pottery.[101] It is perhaps no surprise, then, that Black Mountain College was even further behind with respect to women's opportunities. In the college's promotion of community and a work ethic, women were, as art historian Eva Díaz calls them, "stowaways," often tirelessly compiling and toiling in the background as their husbands took credit.[102] Anni earned a salary of $200 to her husband's $1,500.[103] As in the German case of the Bauhaus, unfazed women kept applying to the college, and Anni Albers went on to an exceptional career despite being sidelined at Black Mountain.

The summer of 1948 brought tensions between Europeans and Americans to the fore. The college had become a destination for up-and-coming artists thanks to its summer institutes, which attracted illustrious guests. That year John Cage, Buckminster Fuller, Willem de Kooning, Robert Rauschenberg, and poet and critic Charles Olson all attended. For many of these artists the time was productive. Fuller, one of the most influential figures in twentieth-century industrial design, entertained students with his experiments on the geodesic dome. De Kooning produced a single painting filled with shapes and lines painted from what the artist said was "a glimpse of something, encountered like a flash," considered a masterpiece of his oeuvre.[104]

That summer the participants debated whether to reorganize the college as an arts school or to situate the arts in a broader curriculum. Albers, who became rector in September of 1948, advocated the former position, and the lack of support for his position led to his stepping down. Abutting the curricular dispute was a growing divergence between those who advocated for the more "traditional" experimentation of the Bauhaus and those who subscribed to a more aleatory aesthetics based on chance and spontaneity.[105] Although this did not divide strictly along national lines, there is no doubt that younger American artists like Cage and Rauschenberg reflected the latter trend. Exhausted and ready to move on, the Alberses departed the following spring, first for Harvard and then for Yale, where they recreated their studios.

In the vacuum left by their departure, new leaders emerged, and the summer institute continued to attract promising artists to present experimental work. During a storied summer evening in 1952, Cage held what is largely considered to be the first "happening." Later dubbed *Theatre Piece No. 1*, the happening was a multilayered, multimedia performance in which Cage persuaded Cunningham and Rauschenberg, along with Charles Olson, pianist and composer David Tudor, dancer Nicholas Cernovich, and potter and poet M. C. Richards, to take part. With memories of the evening often contradicting, this first happening has acquired mythic status: in one version, Cunningham was chased by barking dog; in another Olson distributed a poem while Cunningham danced; in a third Cage spoke about Buddhism while Rauschenberg's *White Painting* was projected on the ceiling. With Albers gone, a distinctly American art form emerged.

The features that made Black Mountain distinctive, however, also contributed to its downfall: the anti-institutionalism held dear by teachers and students alike was not sustainable. It didn't help that the college directed money to studios rather than dormitories, counted on the "idealism" of its faculty to forgo salaries, and depended on the manual labor of its community to erect its buildings.[106] Between 1948 and 1952 the college petered out to fifteen students, called the "subsistence dwellers." In place of a course catalog in these years, Charles Olson, together with Robert Creeley, published the *Black Mountain Review*, one of the most influential small-press journals of the period. In the early 1950s the writing was on the wall: individuals and their art would survive, but the college would not. As the poet and former student of Creeley's Michael Rumaker reflected wistfully, "Perhaps, too, and the most likely, it was that the hour had finally come, unaware to us, that the varied and multiple shapes and ideas and perceptions spawned at Black Mountain over its last years were ready to be scattered out into the world, after a long-protracted and overdue birth."[107]

Plagued with financial troubles since at least 1936, and mired in debt to local merchants and faculty members, the college made a last-ditch effort in the spring of 1956 to lease the lower campus for use as a camp for Christian boys. In March 1957, the debt unresolved, the college was unceremoniously forced to suspend classes for the few students who remained. Nonetheless, despite its apparent decline during the 1950s, and until its closure, the college produced an impressive array of partnerships whose legacies long outlasted the institution itself. And the college's faculty and alumni—including Rauschenberg, Susan Weil, Kenneth Noland, Esteban Vincente, V. V. Rankine, and Ray Johnson—were eager to differentiate themselves.[108] In this respect, Black Mountain replicated the history of the Bauhaus with a burst of creative exports and communities founded in the wake of the school's disintegration: the beatniks in San Francisco, Gate Hill in Stony Point, New York, and the Bauhaus itself in New York and Chicago. With European refugee artists and intellectuals as the handmaidens, American modernism was born.

RACISM, REFUGEES, AND THE JIM CROW SOUTH

In one less glorious way Black Mountain College adhered to the conventions of higher education on both sides of the Atlantic.[109] The issue of integration apparently emerged in Black Mountain's first year, when the Board of Fellows unanimously decided against admitting an African American, and eleven students signed a petition in protest. Just over a decade later, with the war underway and the civil rights movement a glimmer on the horizon, the small and scrappy college in western North Carolina quietly entered the fray. That spring Black Mountain's lawyer researched whether North Carolina's segregation laws applied to the unaccredited college. In the intense debate that ensued, two camps emerged: those in favor of immediate integration and those opposed to "precipitous action." The vote split the faculty. Among those opposed to integration were prominent refugees, including the Alberses.[110]

In April of 1944, the faculty convened to discuss the "problems and possible risks involved in taking Negro students in the summer institutes or in regular sessions of the College during other quarters."[111] A lawyer was consulted, and his report was discussed at a special meeting. The lawyer, who was also an adviser to the college, warned them that though "there was no actual legal restriction in the way of taking such students . . . there were dangerous consequences possible from taking such a step, *because of public opinion in the state*."[112] After a group of faculty traveled to Fisk University to research black colleges, they returned to negotiate a "compromise." Though a number of the refugee faculty members favored integration in principle, for "practical reasons" the college decided to admit just one "qualified" African American—Alma Stone Williams—for the college's first summer music institute.[113]

The summer institutes became the main mechanism for racial integration. The prominent African American singers Roland Hayes and Carol Brice and the Harlem Renaissance artist Jacob Lawrence visited in this context.[114] According to one recollection, Hayes and Brice both expressed interest in participating because of Black Mountain's reputation for tolerance: "It is perhaps the only place in the south where [they] would be accepted completely as a member of the College community without any discrimination."[115] Alma Williams made a similar observation: "Black Mountain College was ready for me; the rest of the white South, not yet."[116]

The "compromise" of welcoming African Americans to the summer institutes but not the regular program can be seen as either an endorsement of integration ten years before *Brown v. Board of Education* or a reflection of the pervasive racism of the time, even among progressives.[117] The European refugees had a unique perspective on exclusion, yet not all of them favored enrolling African Americans.[118] The attitude of these refugees toward the prospective African American students was no doubt connected to their self-consciousness as faculty of a peripheral institution and ambivalence about their Jewishness, which Anni famously dismissed as only "in the

Hitler sense."[119] (Anni nevertheless made Torah ark covers for prominent Reform temples suggesting a more complicated identity and a longing to belong.) Josef, who was not Jewish, did not so much reject integration as articulate a broader concept of race that included "members of the yellow or other races." In his correspondence with foundations, including the Rosenwald Fund (which later cut the college's funding because of insufficient numbers of African American students), Josef anticipated the identity politics of the post–civil rights era.[120]

The institutional racism of colleges and universities was reinforced by the foundations. Indeed, the racism that governed the Emergency Committee's staffing decisions is cast in higher relief by the Rockefeller Foundation's initial exclusion of black colleges in their resettlement of refugee scholars. Part of this omission stemmed from the marginalization of the South in the organizations that governed higher education that extended back to Flexner's days at the General Education Board, and it was reflected in the inclusion of only one southern institution on the Emergency Committee—Vanderbilt University.[121] Given this asymmetry of organization and funding, it follows that the black colleges would not reap the same benefits of the scholarly migration as other schools.

It would have made perfect sense for the deans and presidents of black colleges to capitalize on the excess of academics, especially considering that they were short of qualified African American instructors in every desired field and northern whites were disinclined to teach at these institutions. Yet it seems that neither the Rockefeller Foundation nor the Emergency Committee reached out to any of the more than one hundred black colleges until 1941, and even then the effort was lackluster. In a field survey of southern universities in which concern was expressed about institutional matching, no mention was made of black colleges.[122] When resourceful academic leaders at black colleges, including E. P. Davis, dean of the College of Liberal Arts at Howard University, contacted the Emergency Committee and the Rockefeller Foundation, their inquiries were either overlooked or the HBCUs were unable to provide the matching funds.[123]

The triangular relationship among African Americans, German-Jewish refugees, and native whites in the American Southeast in this period, as reflected in the integration debate at Black Mountain, may account for the advice that the American Friends Service Committee apparently gave President Thomas Jones of Fisk University in 1944: "In general, we do not recommend the placement of refugees in these institutions because of the double handicap it places them under." This systematic exclusion did not mean that no refugee scholars ever made their way to universities or historically black colleges in the South. Between 1934 and the end of the war, at least fifty refugees found jobs at these institutions.[124] Some German-Jewish refugees, including the historian George Iggers, were politicized by their experience in the Southeast and devoted their lives to the civil rights cause.[125] Yet many more were like the philosopher Ernst Moritz Manasse, who arrived at North Carolina College for Negroes (now North Carolina Central University, NCCU) in 1939 and felt alienated by both the white and the black worlds.

The experience of Manasse, who with his wife, Marianne, taught German, Latin, and philosophy in Durham from 1939 to 1973, shows how German Jews threatened not only the anti-Jewish quota system of the elite northern universities but also the racial hierarchy of the South. Born in Dramberg, a small town northeast of Berlin, where his father was a respected agricultural trader and president of the Jewish community, Manasse earned a PhD in classical studies from the University of Heidelberg in 1933.[126] But things quickly took a turn for the worse when his father's non-Jewish customers were pressured by the Nazis to boycott the business. Manasse's depressed father died that May. Following the announcement of the Nuremberg Laws in 1935 that stripped Jews of citizenship, Manasse left Germany by way of Italy, where he temporarily found work at a school for Jewish refugees in Florence. Arriving in the United States on a visitor's visa, Manasse became an instructor at NCCU. He would eventually rise to full professor and department chair.[127]

Manasse later described his circumstances when he began teaching in North Carolina: "I came from a situation of forceful segregation where we were the victims and now suddenly I was on the other side; I belonged not to the oppressed but to the oppressor."[128] It may have been the case symbolically that he was on the side of the oppressor, but he was not entirely welcome in either community. As the first full-time white professor at Central, Manasse's second-class status was reflected in his salary—he received $1,750 per year whereas a number of professors received closer to $3,000.[129] An outspoken advocate of his students in the community, he found meaning in what he called the "encounter between two diverse groups of people, both victims of extreme manifestations of racist oppression and persecution."[130] Manasse encountered resistance to his progressive ideals of racial harmony, notably when he sought to host black students at his Durham home in violation of the norms of segregation, or when his recommendation of a black colleague for membership in the Southern Society for the Philosophy of Religion was rejected (he resigned in protest).[131] The segregated American Southeast was a difficult place for a German-Jewish idealist.

Manasse's own discomfort recalls the ugly mirror that the Jim Crow

South held up to Nazi Germany—a parallel the African American press was quick to note. One commentator in the *Philadelphia Tribune* in 1938 echoed countless others when he announced, "Hitler Learns Jim Crow Art from America." Even as they often pointed to the mistreatment of Jews in Germany, these countless editorials often did so to underscore the American hypocrisy on race issues (and some even displayed antisemitism in the process). In this way one editorial pointed to the Nazi persecution of Jews as paling in comparison to Jim Crow—"We rejoice that our newspapers condemn German Nazi atrocities. It's a good sign that they may yet discover the Nazism which is outside their own doors." Such statements may have been accurate, but they could not have helped German-Jewish refugees feel at home.[132]

W.E.B. Du Bois's predicament as a German-trained sociologist reflected a similar bind. As we saw in chapter 3, Du Bois was in awe of Bismarck and the German Historical School, both of which united a disparate people into a compelling cultural force. Thirty years later he must have felt both the limitations of that project and the exclusion by his white colleagues, the latter a betrayal that could only have strengthened his belief in Germany's cultural superiority. That conviction does not appear to have been diminished by Hitler's Jim Crow–inspired antisemitic racial policies. In 1936, Du Bois traveled to Germany on a grant from the Oberlaender Foundation, much to the consternation of his Jewish friend Franz Boas.[133] Du Bois claimed that his interest was scholarly, and eventually he came around to speak out against the Nazi regime. Du Bois's ambivalence was shared by other African American intellectuals who looked to European politics—and fascism—in the 1930s for inspiration for an emerging Pan-Africanism. African American children in the South were known to sing a parody of "America the Beautiful"—"My country's tired of me / I'm going to Germany / Where I belong"—underscoring an alienation that was internalized by African American academics during the German-Jewish refugee crisis.[134]

The hierarchy of knowledge as reflected in the treatment of HBCUs persisted in the later scholarship. The German American sociologist Lewis Coser once hailed the German-Jewish scholars who joined the faculty of black colleges as the "unsung heroes" of the refugee story, though he excluded them from his own research because they were instructors first and scholars second—if at all. Had they been the latter they would have been called to the elite schools in his estimation. For Coser, teachers were mere "retailers of knowledge."[135]

The fact that Coser could plausibly label any professor so disparagingly was symptomatic of a system that had lost its way, in the eyes of Abraham

Flexner. Flexner's final attempt to reform American higher education reveals how far he felt universities had fallen since 1876. Even the elite universities were troubled. The refugee scholars presented an opportunity for redemption, but also exposed the conservatism of academic leaders who resisted any vision of the university as a mechanism for social mobility. The refugees' absorption—and any future academic innovation—would have to be handled with great care.

HOW TO CHANGE A UNIVERSITY

What Ludwig Mies van der Rohe had said about the Bauhaus applied to the modern research university: "The Bauhaus was not an institution with a clear program—it was an idea, and Gropius formulated this idea with great precision. . . . The fact that it was an idea, I think, is the cause of this enormous influence the Bauhaus had on every progressive school around the globe. You cannot do that with organization, you cannot do that with propaganda. Only an idea spreads so far."[136]

The idea of the modern research university had already diffused from Germany in the late 1800s. The oppressive political conditions of 1933 ensured its exile. At the same time, the American university builders of the late nineteenth century had been so successful at rooting the idea of the German university in their institutions that by 1933, hardly more than fifty years after the founding of the first German-style research university in America, Americans already considered the modern research university to be indigenous and unmalleable.

By the 1930s research had taken priority over teaching in America, as it already had in Germany. For the Institute for Advanced Study this meant eschewing undergraduate education altogether in favor of what Flexner called in 1939 the "usefulness of useless knowledge," a philosophy that became a paradigm for the postwar funding of the basic sciences.[137] The feature that made the institute exceptional—its remoteness from the rest of the system of higher education—made it nearly impossible to replicate. If all the faculty left universities for such a research "paradise" no instructors would remain to carry on the teaching. To mitigate this fear and avoid the fate of the German universities that were overshadowed by the towering Kaiser Wilhelm Institutes, Flexner left the university model intact and made the institute fellowship attainable only as a laurel for established researchers. But there was a built-in contradiction in his vision, which he hoped to be both an exemplar and an exception, for he continued to insist that the institute would one day impact the entire higher education system, as Gilman's Hopkins had.[138] He embraced the research institute as a supplement to—rather than a substitute for—the university. Flexner's design highlighted the ongoing challenge of delivering high-quality teaching and research under one roof.

If Flexner was concerned with the university's research inadequacies, the idealists of Black Mountain College were concerned with the failure of the university to offer authentic learning and meaningful education for citizenship. But they refused to succumb to the deleterious effects of institutionalism and suffered ephemerality as a result. At the same time, their principles often fell short for women, Jews, gays, and blacks. The anti-institutionalism and impecuniosity of Black Mountain College lent it a magical quality during the Depression, an aura that was as attractive as it was unsustainable. Unwilling to compromise, successive leaders of Black Mountain accepted that its legacy was destined to be perpetuated in the work products of its faculty. An institution designed to be an exception, by definition, could not spread. And what was fully integrated into the mainstream of higher education could be only so innovative.

From the perspective of cultural transfer, Flexner and Rice faced a dilemma familiar to American innovators before them—how much of the ideas of another culture to adopt and how much of their own to preserve. Unlike the Founding Fathers, who were dependent on the Europeans for their intellectual culture, the Americans of the 1930s and beyond could afford to absorb outsiders and their intellectual gifts while maintaining native hierarchies. Those hierarchies were based on two sets of related values. One assigned the university's twin purposes—namely, who would do research and who would teach. The second defined the ethnic, racial, and social expectations of scholars and students, which were inherited from the Germans but had their hierarchical origins obscured by the ideology of meritocracy. What was made visible by the foundations' tacit exclusion of the black colleges in the resettlement of refugee scholars—as much as by the phenomenon of white "mere" instructors being sent to black colleges as a last resort—was that academic leaders aimed to keep the hierarchy of knowledge production in line with the hierarchy of race.

The absorption of German-Jewish refugees was less a victory for cosmopolitanism than the imposition of American higher education hierarchies on outsiders. Though he was one of the most outspoken supporters of absorbing refugees, even Johnson wrote: "Much as I wish to alleviate the lot of scholars thrust out of their institutions by bigotry and tyranny, I could not wish to bring them to American institutions if I did not believe, as I do, that the cross-fertilization of American and European scholarship will raise the American intellectual life to a higher level."[139] The obfuscation of Jewish identity through this "cross-fertilization" had consequences for scholarship. Jews played a significant role in the parallel and intertwined transatlantic histories of academic innovation in which tolerance was tied to matter-of-fact utilitarianism.[140] In fact, the debate between humanitarianism and opportunism was resolved once skeptics were persuaded that open borders for ideas and scholars was, in fact, in America's self-interest.[141] The Manhattan Project would continue this approach to refugee scientists, including Hans Bethe, Felix Bloch, and Niels Bohr, who directed their expertise to American defense.[142]

Notwithstanding the individual experiments in Princeton and at Black Mountain, the modern research university would remain predominant in the postwar period, aided by a new Cold War military-industrial-academic complex.[143] Indeed, Flexner's and Rice's attempts foreshadowed just how challenging it would become to alter higher education at the systemic level in America. Once an open frontier for German traveling scholars, the American education landscape was now settled by incumbents with a vested interest in maintaining the status quo.

OLD DILEMMAS, NEW CONTRACTS

The university has become a prime instrument of national purpose. This is new. This is the essence of the transformation now engulfing our universities.

CLARK KERR, 1963

In June 1949 the president of the University of California announced that all university employees were required to take a loyalty oath in which they pledged allegiance to the state constitution and denied involvement in subversive organizations. The measure reflected the paranoia that would come to be associated with the McCarthy era. At a packed meeting of the academic senate, the German-Jewish émigré and University of California, Berkeley, professor Ernst Kantorowicz inveighed against this dangerous precedent: "There are three professions which are entitled to wear a gown: the judge, the priest, the scholar," Kantorowicz intoned in his foreign sing-song accent. "This garment stands for its bearer's maturity of mind, his independence of judgment, and his direct responsibility to his conscience and to his God. It signifies the *inner sovereignty* of those three interrelated professions: they should be the very last to allow themselves to act under duress and yield to pressure."[1] Kantorowicz was a proven anti-Communist—he was known to joke, "Right of me is only the wall"—yet he refused to take the oath and was fired.[2]

Kantorowicz's argument against the notorious oath was that the university was outside politics—a status that bestowed it with *inner sovereignty*. As a medievalist, he knew that this claim to extrapolitical authority was somewhat ahistorical. The celebrated open medieval university, the *studium generale,* resulted from a compact with religious and princely authorities that put limits on scholars' freedoms. Kantorowicz's claim of inner sovereignty to defend the university's autonomy was inflected with myth.

The battle in which Kantorowicz was engaged should by now seem familiar. The academic social contract provides a framework for understanding the relationship between the university and society. As the university evolved, the levers of change were the different contracts negotiated by academic innovators with political and social partners. The varying terms of these contracts yielded iterations of the university design. In the parallel histories of German and American scholars, we see the modern research university caught between the benefits conferred by the state and society, and the demands they made in return.

When Kantorowicz, a former German nationalist and émigré, rose to defend the autonomy of the faculty, it was neither the first time nor the last that the state made demands that constituted a breach of contract.[3] To be sure, different historical contracts have been more or less productive for the advancement of knowledge and learning, or more or less favorable to society or scholars. To their consternation sometimes the contracted autonomous space expanded, and sometimes it contracted. Moreover, different disciplines, including theology, applied mathematics, and the social sciences, were variously positioned to benefit, and some may have been more willing to serve the goals of professionalization or nationalization.[4] Because of the cyclical quality of this process, a linear periodization is not possible. As the sociologist Pierre Bourdieu observed, "Autonomy is not a given, but a historical conquest, endlessly having to be undertaken anew."[5] Nonetheless, there was more wrestling with the balance of autonomy and responsibility in the period from 1890 to 1910 than in the interwar period of 1919 to 1939. Even if it amounted to a "Sisyphian heroism," the nineteenth-century scholars reasserted autonomy whenever it was threatened.[6]

A pattern emerges: once a contract was exhausted, academic entrepreneurs found new partners, formulated new ideas, and established new institutions—sometimes outside the university. During World War I, on both sides of the Atlantic, the demands to mobilize for the nation threatened the integrity of the university. That repression spurred intellectual and institutional innovation, in both the formalization of academic freedom and the creation of research institutions that scholars hoped would be better protected from the whims of the state. By the time Kantorowicz opposed the loyalty oath in 1949 it was becoming clear that the Germans' academic social contract, undermined by Hitler, would be more difficult to rebuild than the economy. As postwar leaders moved to fill the void, new forces were yielding new formulations.

With these inauspicious beginnings, the Cold War brought momentous changes in which the university assumed forms and roles that would be unrecognizable to the early twentieth-century leaders. Do the lessons of this book help us understand the landscape of higher education during the Cold War period and beyond? Or are they peculiar to the period that ended with the Second World War? Clark Kerr, whose "liberal and conciliatory stance" in the loyalty oath controversy propelled him to the chancellorship of the University of California, Berkeley, from 1952 to 1957, and then the presidency of the expanding University of California system, identified the novelty of the fact that the "university has become a prime instrument of national purpose."[7] But if the conditions and terms were new, the academic contract itself was not. With the perspective of the full arc of the development of the modern research university, the lessons of this book do indeed apply to the post–World War II era.[8]

If we follow Kantorowicz around the corner to the Cold War, we see an exceptional era in which university enrollments and research funding reached unprecedented heights.[9] The expansion of higher education in the 1950s and 1960s, directed toward training teachers and meeting the needs of the rising knowledge economy, occurred both in the United States and in Europe. At the height of veteran influx in the United States, in 1947, 51 percent of college students were veterans. Within a little over a decade, the GI Bill would send over two million American veterans to colleges and universities—breaking down class, religious, and some racial barriers.[10]

Research in post–World War II American universities grew similarly. In 1947 President Truman convened a committee to rethink the role of science and education (the so-called Truman Commission); it released a six-volume report that represented "the U.S. government's first effort to set national goals for higher education." In connecting science to democratic citizenship the report was ahead of its time, but it grossly underestimated the amount of money that would actually be spent on graduate training and scientific education in the 1950s with the establishment of, among other institutions, the influential National Science Foundation (NSF).[11] Founded after a multiyear battle pitting New Deal senator Harley Kilgore, who favored a centralized federal science policy, against Vannevar Bush, who wanted a decentralized system run by scientists, the NSF assumed responsibility for distributing research grants to universities.[12] By the end of the Korean War spending for academic research topped nearly $5.5 billion a year.[13]

The compact between the state and the university was a common denominator between the Cold War university and the earlier period.[14] Vannevar Bush was the main author of the Cold War version. As the blueprint for this era of "Cold War Science," Bush's 1945 report on the "frontiers of knowledge" distilled the ambition of the previous century for intellectual self-sufficiency: "We cannot any longer depend upon Europe as a major source of this scientific capital."[15] To achieve this goal under Bush's plan, the Atomic Energy Commission and the National Institutes of Health poured money into government laboratories and preferred universities, including MIT, Cal Tech, and Michigan. The Soviets' launch of Sputnik in 1957 added urgency, and the passage of the National Defense Education Act supported graduate fellowships and research centers on the Soviet Union and other strategic areas—the new Area Studies—as well as behavioral and social science research on societal needs.[16]

With its lavish funding, the federal government found eager partners among university leaders. On the California Bay Area's peninsula, Bush's former student and Stanford provost Frederick Terman capitalized on the growing technological needs of industry to court federal grants and turn a provincial university in Palo Alto into a world center for physics and engineering, laying the groundwork for a new three-way partnership among industry, government, and the university.[17] Philadelphia, Atlanta, and other cities would seek to emulate the "city of knowledge" Palo Alto, with varying degrees of success.[18]

Elsewhere in California, Kerr carried the tradition of the university builder into the latter half of the twentieth century.[19] An author of ideas and institutions, Kerr was described by colleagues as an "in-between" figure, skilled at negotiating the interests of government, philanthropy, and the university.[20] An "American pragmatist," Kerr brokered the California Master Plan of 1960, a tiered organization of higher education accomplished through multiple campuses that struck a balance between excellence and access and made a lasting imprint on American higher education.[21]

With respect to funding, status, and professionalization—the sirens that lured the academic leaders of the previous century—this period duly earned its moniker of the Golden Era. Scientists and humanists, the latter working in fields like creative writing, music, and dance, were the beneficiaries of this new vision of the nation-state and its Cultural Cold War.[22] Nonetheless, these benefits came at a cost, and the Cold War contract was different from its predecessors in degree, not in kind. As in the previous two hot wars, scholars arguably gave up too much, including the transparency of research projects and autonomy of interests, as was noted by the Columbia University sociologist C. Wright Mills and other skeptics at the time. Alvin Weinberg, a physicist at Oak Ridge National Laboratory and originator of the term "Big Science," observed at the height of cultural discontent in 1968 that it was difficult "to tell whether the MIT is a university with many government research laboratories appended to it or a cluster of government research laboratories with a very good educational institution attached to it."[23]

In search of new vocabulary to describe the post–World War II university, critics have invented terms like "multiversity," the "corporate university," the "instrumental university," and the "neo-liberal university"— missing the longue durée history of the university's relations to external interests.[24] But the contractual framework still applies. The essence of the contract between the university and its partners remained the same—scholars received relative autonomy in exchange for services to society. What obscured the contractual nature of this relationship was that the balance point had shifted so much toward service to society and the state that the benefits scholars received in return were harder to recognize.[25]

The imbalance of the Cold War contract was equally clear to West Germans. Under the Marshall Plan the conditions for German universities were as asymmetric as those in America, with the added dimension of demands not just from the German state but from the United States as well. The Fulbright Program, founded in 1946, envisioned international exchange as part of advocacy for democratic values. In a similar spirit, the Free University of Berlin was established in 1948 with a large contribution by the Ford Foundation.[26] In the meantime, America continued its covert efforts to co-opt the best of Nazi science through the controversial "Paperclip Project," aided by the extensive transatlantic exchange of the previous age.[27] America was a prominent model when new modern universities were called for in Germany, including the University of Konstanz (1966), referred to as "Small Harvard on Lake Constance," and the new "reform" university of Bielefeld (1969).[28] Eventually, a student countermovement positioned itself against American hegemony, but the "Other Alliance" of student activists, from Rudi Dutschke to Angela Davis, which found passage on the old transatlantic routes, was equally dominated by America.[29] Even the Humboldt University of Berlin, the ur–research university that was once the object of American admiration, was as late as 2013 adorned with a banner reading "Excellence in Research and Teaching" (in English) in celebration of its inclusion in the Excellence Strategy (then called "Initiative"), Germany's new Ivy League (fig. 12). German—and European—universities have yet to emerge from postwar Americanization.[30]

With hindsight, it is clear that the transatlantic "military-industrial-academic complex" couldn't hold.[31] Based on extraordinary conditions, including the void left by the destruction of European science, massive federal funding, and the ready availability of nearly free graduate student labor, the Cold War American academic contract could never be sustainable. The demographic explosion of enrollments masked unresolved tensions between American ideals of meritocracy and the hierarchical European system based on privilege. These cracks, temporarily covered over, would slowly and painfully be exposed with the erosion of public support for higher education and the rise of tuition and student debt. With the "permanent tax revolt" that began in California in the 1980s and the turn

Figure 12. Humboldt University, on the occasion of the "Excellence Initiative,"
shows the Americanization of the German university. (Alamy Stock Photo.)

to private sources of income like tuition, the fat years of the Cold War era
ebbed. They are not likely to return.[32]

It is hard in these lean years not to envy the scholars of the previous
era, and it has become commonplace to call for its return. Some do so,
however, without acknowledging the trade-offs.[33] Where to go from here
is complicated by the fact that the contractual framework of the Cold War
still prevails. Universities are strapped by the regulations of the earlier
period but no longer enjoy its benefits.[34] At the same time universities are
faced with the need to revise financial models, address inequality, and
work with new assumptions about what it means to be educated and who
should get educated.

Clark Kerr's rebuttal to criticism of his multiversity was that "higher
education cannot escape history." The 1990s produced a set of conditions
that called for ever larger institutional conglomerates.[35] Kerr has been criticized for this historicist position, but linking the university to the "logic
of history" does not mean passively accepting an institution that hovers
above the world as a mere Hegelian expression of the material, social, and
political conditions of its time. Rather the university is both an ideal and
an institution, neither explained fully by such external forces as nationalization and globalization, nor understandable solely through philosophical
exegesis. Only a combined materialist/idealist history captures the dialectic of the university that occupies a space of negotiated autonomy.

The academic social contract governs this in-between space. And the individuals who negotiate it are, like Kerr, in-between figures, whose success as academic entrepreneurs lies in their ability to cross borders between the university and the state, between the goals of the professional world and knowledge for its own sake, and among adjacent educational and international systems. The language of academic innovators was thus deliberately vague, since they addressed different audiences with various appeals to the ideal and pragmatic realities, as in Flexner's enduring formulation of the usefulness of useless knowledge. We can't take at face value the words of academics representing their interests. Upon inspection, it is possible that Kantorowicz's argument against the oath was not a naïve invocation of an ideal of academic freedom remote from the world but in fact a savvy attempt to publicly enforce the terms of the academic contract before the press and the world.

Academic leaders are agents not objects of this history. That the university must strike a bargain with the state and society should be viewed not as a hindrance but as a principle that provides strategic guidance, through the help of history. Any new contract must value autonomy and responsibility equally. That is what it means to wear the gown.

▲ ▲

The university encompasses two intersecting domains.[36] While the contract governed the relationship between the university and society, competitive emulation motivated the relationships among academic institutions. Academic leaders had to manage these two interacting systems. Negotiated autonomy created the space for universities to engage in exchanges outside the logic of nations and markets. Academic entrepreneurs tapped the competitive international dynamics of states to stimulate investments that would allow their institutions to succeed in the interuniversity system. The prestige earned through the validation of peers reflected back on the societies that supported them, and, in turn, justified greater autonomy.[37] The best academic innovators were able to convert the currencies of these two economies—academic contracts and competitive emulation—into thriving modern research universities in global knowledge centers.

Exchanges among Germans and American academics of the kind investigated in this book helped to shape today's university, but they also exemplify a universal process of the vicissitudes of knowledge centers, the "life cycle" of knowledge. The life cycle is a dynamic process that is both institutional and geographic.[38] In Berlin today it is common to hear, with a sigh of regret, that the German university found its true home in America.[39]

But an analysis that focuses on the ascendancy of American higher education misses the point. Decades from now, historians will be analyzing the rise of institutions that won't be American.

What will hold true is that the history of higher education is shaped by innovators wrangling their communities and balancing national imperatives and professional gain with universalist ideals and the pursuit of truth. Gilman, Flexner, Harnack, and Klein, as well as those further from the seats of power, like Thomas and Du Bois, crafted contracts that shaped the knowledge institutions we now inhabit. Their anxieties and aspirations show where innovation comes from and who the innovators of the next century might be.

ACKNOWLEDGMENTS

Since this book addresses the German-American encounter it is a pleasure to thank the people and institutions on both sides of the Atlantic who have contributed to this project. A research leave supported by the Alexander von Humboldt Fellowship at the Free University of Berlin in 2012–2013 provided the initial exploratory year. I am grateful to Paul Nolte, Christiane Kuller, and Daniel Morat for hosting me at the Friedrich-Meinecke-Institut and for Christiane's and Rüdiger Hachtmann's help co-organizing a workshop on "Wissenschaftspolitik," which jump-started this project.

During that sabbatical year and beyond I have been honored to share this work in a number of inspiring institutional contexts. I thank my generous hosts and attendees for their thoughtful feedback: Mirjam Zadoff and Michael Brenner (LMU Munich); Sylvia Paletschek and Anna Lux (Uni Freiburg); Michael Kimmage, Uwe Lübken, Andrew Preston, and Britta Waldschmidt-Nelson (Center for Advanced Studies, Munich); Tony Michels and Jennifer Ratner-Rosenhagen (George Mosse Series, University of Wisconsin–Madison); JB Shank and Gary Cohen (University of Minnesota, Twin Cities); Paul Reitter and Frank Donoghue (Humanities Center, Ohio State University); Peter Miller (Bard Graduate Center); Simon Goldhill and Theodor Dunkelgrün (CRASSH, University of Cambridge); and Mordu Levy-Eichel (Macmillan Center, Yale University).

I am grateful for the opportunity to have worked at the University of North Carolina at Greensboro (UNCG), and in particular, to former History Department chair Chuck Bolton and the interlibrary loan staff, including the late Gaylor Callahan and Patrick Kelly. In the decade I spent in North Carolina I benefited from its robust network of scholars, including Thomas Pegelow Kaplan and Heather Perry (Davidson College and UNC Charlotte) and the Southeast German Studies Workshops where I was encouraged by Astrid Eckert, Brian Crim, and Brian Vick. This book owes much to the Triangle Intellectual History Seminar, my intellectual home where this project first took shape. I thank my co-coordinators James Chappel, Malachi

Hacohen, Lloyd Kramer, Tony LaVopa, Marty Miller, Noah Strote, Steven Vincent, and David Weinstein.

In the academic year 2017–2018 I had the honor of writing this book at the National Humanities Center (NHC). For their support I am indebted to the late Tony Kaye, Tania Munz, and the center's director, Robert Newman. The book is better thanks to the resourceful and efficient work of Brooke Andrade and the library staff. The feedback I received from every single member of my cohort had a tremendous impact on this book's direction. The NHC community offers an enduring model of what Marianne Weber called "academic conviviality."

A series of conversations with Mitchell Stevens and Adam Nelson that began in 2017 in Beijing at the Third Peking University–University of Wisconsin Workshop in Higher Education planted seeds throughout this book and ultimately changed the direction of my career. In Beijing I also had the chance to learn from Chen Honjie, Shen Wenqin, and Cai Leiluo, whose grandfather Cai Yuanpei reformed Peking University. That transpacific academic exchange gave me a clearer sense of the ambition the Americans must have harbored and the anxiety the Germans must have felt in the previous century. At a workshop in honor of David Labaree at Stanford's Graduate School of Education (GSE), I received further feedback from Mitchell and Adam, and from Ethan Hutt, John Etchemendy, Jens Jungblut, and my dear former advisers Paul Robinson and Jim Sheehan. It is a great honor to have rejoined them now at Stanford University's GSE. I am grateful to my new GSE colleagues for their confidence in me and to Dean Dan Schwartz and Priscilla Fiden for affording me the time to complete this book in my first year. I thank Debbie Belanger and Kathy Kerns for their logistical and library support, respectively. I look forward to many years of collegiality and productivity to come.

This project involved research in over two dozen archival collections in Germany and America. Many of these I visited in person and others I consulted remotely. Among the many archivists who fielded my queries, I thank Jenny Swadosh of the New School Archives and Special Collections; Casey Westerman and Erica Mosner of the Shelby White and Leon Levy Archives Center of the Institute for Advanced Study; Jim Stimpert of Special Collections at Johns Hopkins University; Michael Herkenhoff at the Universitäts- und Landesbibliothek Bonn; Dietlind Willer at the Niedersächsische Staats-Universitätsbibliothek Göttingen; and Michael Maaser at the Universitätsarchiv in Frankfurt. For their research assistance I thank Jake Stanley, Felix Czmok, and Janet Hammond. For his translation review I thank Christophe Fricker. For his comprehensive indexing I thank Derek Gottlieb. For his editing and exacting standards I owe much to Eric

Engels. I am especially appreciative of the thoughtful critiques of three anonymous readers, which greatly improved the book, as well as of my editors, Priya Nelson and Elizabeth Branch Dyson, and their assistants, Tristan Bates, Mollie McFee, Dylan Montanari, and Noor Shawaf, all of whom shepherded the book so smoothly to its conclusion. I am grateful to Christine Schwab and Marian Rogers for their copyediting and patience during the COVID-19 pandemic. I am indebted to my editor, the late Doug Mitchell, for his early interest in my work, his persistent support of this project, and his friendship. May his memory be for a blessing.

Many other colleagues have offered wisdom, friendship, and crucial leads, including Omar Ali, Aaron Allen, Sonja Asal, Steve Aschheim, Karen Auerbach, Dirk Bönker, Matthias Bormuth, Warren Breckman, Flora Cassen, Deborah Cohen, Mark Cruse, Chanchal Dadlani, Lorraine Daston, Asa Eger, Maude Ellison, David Engerman, Thomas Etzemüller, Sören Flachowsky, Christian Fleck, Julia Foulkes, Peter Galison, Eva Giloi, Timothy Goering, Adi Gordon, Udi Greenberg, Karen Hagemann, Nicole Hall, Stephen G. Hall, Charlie Hill, Adina Hoffman, David Hollinger, Hilde Hoogenboom, Tera Hunter, Sarah Igo, Konrad Jaraush, Laura Jockusch, Corey Johnson, Caroline Jones, Marion Kaplan, Claudia Koonz, Derek Krueger, Charlotte Lerg, Sue Marchand, John McGowan, Paul Mendes-Flohr, Thomas Meyer, Sam Moyn, David Myers, Susan Neiman, Jane Newman, Philipp Nielsen, Molly Nolan, Libby Otto, Anne Parsons, Claire Payton, Susan Pennybacker, Sally Poor, Till van Rahden, Hollis Robbins, Gene Rogers, Na'ama Rokem, Sophie Rosenfeld, Florian Schmaltz, Stefanie Schüler-Springorum, Mary Louise Seelig, Eugene Shepard, Penny Sinanoglou, Avinash Singh, Harleen Singh, Kathryn Slanski, John Smith, Matthew Specter, Daniel Steinmetz Jenkins, Claudia Stemberger, Claire Sufrin, Norma Thompson, Anna von Villiez, Kerry Wallach, Isaac Weiner, John Wilkinson, Andréa N. Williams, Caroline Winterer, Molly Worthen, and Sam Zipp.

As Dewey wrote, "Universities, like families and like nations, live only as they are continually reborn." My family has coevolved with this project. My father, Alan, continues to be a source of unflagging support and a paragon of career success and community service; I am always reenergized by visits with him, my stepmother, Alison, and her sparkling daughters, Lizzy and Laura. My brother Malcolm's drive and commitment to his work and family never cease to amaze me. My mother, Nancy, has always encouraged my own education and, now with her husband, Lewis, remains a source of morale and cosmopolitan inspiration. I am blessed with many aunts, in-laws, cousins, nieces and nephews, and an uncle, David O. Levine, whose expertise in American higher education still inspires.

The losses of Jacques Levine, Joel Rascoff, Joseph Rascoff, and Ellen

Shapiro have left holes that we will never be able to fill. My children, Jasper and Florence, born since I set out to write this book, are a constant source of meaning, joy, and perspective.

Most of all I am deeply indebted to Matthew Rascoff—my beloved husband and partner in life and ideas who brings light and energy to every project that he touches, including this one. I've been fortunate to observe the university's unique style of open innovation firsthand from Matthew, an academic administrator and advocate for higher education innovation and access. Through his work I have come to appreciate the precious space the university occupies, in which we share our best ideas with our fiercest competitors. Through my work I attest that innovation is hardly new. The history of the university is a history of academic innovation and the changemakers who bring their ideals into the world.

NOTES

INTRODUCTION

1. The oldest surviving institution of higher learning from this earlier era is Al-Azhar University, founded in Cairo in the ninth century. Edward Shils and John Roberts, "The Diffusion of European Models outside Europe," in *Universities in the Nineteenth and Early Twentieth Centuries (1800–1945)* (Cambridge: Cambridge University Press, 2004), 3:163–230, esp. 164. The relationship of Socrates to the polis has long provided scholars with a metaphor to orient a debate about the intellectual and politics. Stephen T. Leonard, "Introduction: A Genealogy of the Politicized Intellectual," in *Intellectuals and Public Life: Between Radicalism and Reform*, ed. Leon Fink, Stephen T. Leonard, and Donald M. Reid (Ithaca, NY: Cornell University Press, 1996), 1–25, here 4.

2. Gerard Delanty's concept of universities as "zones of mediation" for the project of modernity provides a helpful theoretical framework that is compatible with my own. Delanty, "The University in the Knowledge Society," *Organization* 8 (2001): 149–153, esp. 150.

3. Countless works by leading public figures examine the university from the perspective of the current plight of the humanities and the dearth of public support, among the most compelling of which are Andrew Delbanco, *College: What It Was, Is, and Should Be* (Princeton, NJ: Princeton University Press, 2012); Stefan Collini, *Speaking of Universities* (London: Verso, 2017); and Anthony T. Kronman, *Education's End: Why Our Colleges and Universities Have Given Up on the Meaning of Life* (New Haven, CT: Yale University Press, 2007).

4. Clark Kerr, *The Great Transformation in Higher Education, 1960–1980* (Albany: State University of New York Press, 1991), 5, 48–49, quotation on 48.

5. In contrast, the university is either absent from or completely absorbed into histories of nationalization and globalization. Mark Mazower's otherwise excellent global history typifies the silence of this genre. Mazower, *Governing the World* (New York: Penguin, 2012). Sebastian Conrad provides an excellent example of integrating political and cultural history, but his treatment of the university is minimal. Conrad, *Globalisation and the Nation in Imperial Germany* (Cambridge: Cambridge University Press, 2010), 47. In Jürgen Osterhammel's compendium, the university is treated as a "cultural export" without attention to its extranational and extramarket features.

Osterhammel, *The Transformation of the World*, trans. Patrick Camiller (Princeton, NJ: Princeton University Press, 2014), 798, 804.

6. Fritz Stern, *Einstein's German World* (Princeton, NJ: Princeton University Press, 1999), 4. For a more recent examination of the "competition over modernity" between Germany and America, see Christof Mauch and Kiran Klaus Patel, "Wettlauf um die Moderne: Konkurrenz und Konvergenz," in *Wettlauf um die Moderne: Die USA und Deutschland 1890 bis Heute*, ed. Christof Mauch and Kiran Klaus Patel (Munich: Pantheon, 2008), 9–26. On universities in particular, see Kathryn M. Olesko and Christoph Strupp, "Wissen: Universität und Forschung," in Mauch and Patel, *Wettlauf um die Moderne*, 393–424. For industrial and demographic statistics, see Mauch and Patel, *Wettlauf um die Moderne*, 11. Thank you to Konrad Jarausch for this recommendation.

7. Marianne Weber, *Max Weber: A Biography*, trans. Harry Zohn (New York: John Wiley & Sons, 1975), 281, 288, 304. For Joachim Radkau's revisionist account, see Radkau, *Max Weber: A Biography* (New York: Wiley, 2013), 224–229. On the translation of Weber's ideas in America, see Lawrence A. Scaff, *Max Weber in America* (Princeton, NJ: Princeton University Press, 2011), esp. 1–7; and on the limitations of their perspective, see Dirk Kaesler, "Man sieht nur, was man zu wissen glaubt: Max und Marianne Weber im Amerika der Jahrhundertwende," in *Amerika und Deutschland: ambivalente Begegnungen*, ed. Frank Kelleter and Wolfgang Knöbl (Göttingen: Wallstein, 2006), 10–29.

8. Max Weber, "Wissenschaft als Beruf (1919)," in *Gesammelte Aufsätze zur Wissenschaftslehre* (Tübingen: J.C.B. Mohr, 1988), 582–613; translation from Max Weber, *From Max Weber: Essays in Sociology*, ed. H. H. Gerth and C. Wright Mills (Oxford: Oxford University Press, 1958), 129–156, quotation on 149. In the late eighteenth century *Wissenschaft* came to mean systematic scholarly thought or academic knowledge. It encompassed both the humanities and the natural sciences. In this book I refer to *Wissenschaft* as science, scholarship, or academic knowledge, depending on the context, and to scientists and scholars, with a similar intention. For a helpful discussion of the nuances of this term, as well as its twin concept, *Bildung*, see Louis Menand, Paul Reitter, and Chad Wellmon, eds., "General Introduction," in *The Rise of the Research University: A Sourcebook*, trans. Reitter and Wellmon (Chicago: University of Chicago Press, 2017), 9.

9. Though he technically worked under three different culture ministers during his career, Althoff "pursued his educational and cultural politics on a world-wide scale" from 1882, when he became the officer responsible for higher education, until his retirement because of ill health in 1907. The German academic authority on Althoff is Bernhard vom Brocke whose voluminous essays have provided a rich resource and a number of leads for my work. For a helpful English summary of Althoff's career, see vom Brocke, "Friedrich Althoff: A Great Figure in Higher Education Policy in Germany," *Minerva* 29 (Autumn 1991): 269–292, quotation on 270. For the challenges in identifying the influence of a behind-the-scenes bureaucrat like Althoff, especially in the English-language sources, see Peter R. Senn, "Where Is Althoff? Looking for Friedrich Althoff in English-Language Sources," *Journal of Economic Studies* 20, no. 4/5 (1993): 201–261.

10. Max Weber, untitled, in *Verhandlungen des IV. Deutschen Hochschullehrertages zu Dresden am 12. Und 13. Oktober 1911 Bericht erstattet vom geschäftsführenden Ausschuss*

(Leipzig: Verlag des Literarischen Zentralblattes für Deutschland, 1912), 66–77. Translation from Max Weber, "American and German Universities," in "The Power of the State and the Dignity of the Academic Calling in Imperial Germany: The Writings of Max Weber on University Problems," ed. Edward Shils, *Minerva* 11 (1973): 593–600, quotation on 599.

11. Benedict Anderson's essays in the following volume show how Berlin can be viewed anew from the perspective of Jakarta. Anderson, *The Spectre of Comparisons: Nationalism, Southeast Asia, and the World* (London: Verso, 1998). Thank you to Matthew Specter for this suggestion.

12. My notion of competitive emulation builds on the history of "cultural transfer," which stems from the *Transfergeschichte* and *l'histoire croisée* pioneered by German and French literary historians like Johannes Paulmann, Michel Espagne, and Matthias Middell that provided a theoretical framework for the exchange—rather than the comparison—of cultures. See, for example, Michel Espagne, "Au-delà du comparatisme: La méthode des transferts culturels," *Historiographie de l'antiquité et transferts culturels* 145 (2010): 201–221; and Johannes Paulmann, "Internationaler Vergleich und interkultureller Transfer: Zwei Forschungsansätze zur europäischen Geschichte des 18. bis 20. Jahrhunderts," *Historische Zeitschrift* 267 (1998): 649–685. For a concise survey of cultural transfer history, see David Blackbourn, "'As dependent on each other as man and wife': Cultural Contacts and Transfers, in *Wilhelmine Germany and Edwardian Britain: Essays on Cultural Affinity*, ed. Dominik Geppert and Robert Gerwarth (Oxford: Oxford University Press, 2008), 15–37. For a transatlantic history that focuses on competition and cooperation between Germany and America, see, for example, Ragnhild Fiebig-von Hase, "The United States and Germany in the World Arena, 1900–1917," in *Confrontation and Cooperation: Germany and the United States in the Era of World War I, 1900–1924*, ed. Hans-Jürgen Schröder (Providence: Berg, 1993), 33–68. On the challenges of integrating diplomatic and political history with a history of "cultural transfer," see Jan Rüger, "Revisiting the Anglo-German Antagonism," *Journal of Modern History* 83 (2011): 579–617, esp. 584–585.

13. Christopher P. Loss's work is notable as one of the first to analyze the university's role in American political development. Loss, *Between Citizens and the State: The Politics of American Higher Education in the 20th Century* (Princeton, NJ: Princeton University Press, 2012), 2. Many more works focus on the "corporatization" of the university, including, for example, Derek Bok, *Universities in the Marketplace: The Commercialization of Higher Education* (Princeton, NJ: Princeton University Press, 2003); and Christopher Newfield, *Ivy and Industry: Business and the Making of the American University, 1880–1980* (Durham, NC: Duke University Press, 2004).

14. According to Michael N. Forster, Herder was initially offered a position in 1775 at the University of Göttingen but departed after he refused to address questions about his religious beliefs. See Forster, *Herder's Philosophy* (Oxford: Oxford University Press, 2018), 3. Randall Collins called this transformation in Germany the "academic revolution" and described how it spread through every modern country. Collins, *The Sociology of Philosophies: A Global Theory of Intellectual Change* (Cambridge, MA: Harvard University Press, 1998), 644–645. For Shils's account, see Shils, "The Order of

Learning in the United States: The Ascendancy of the University," in *The Organization of Knowledge in Modern America, 1860–1920*, ed. Alexandra Oleson and John Coas (Baltimore: Johns Hopkins University Press, 1976), 19–47, esp. 20–22. The trend of extra-university life persisted longer in Great Britain, where the Royal Institution of London housed such scientists as Humphry Davy and Michael Farady. See Hermann Helmholtz, "On Academic Freedom in German Universities," in *Hermann von Helmholtz: Science and Culture: Popular and Philosophical Essays*, ed. and trans. David Cahan (Chicago: University of Chicago Press, 1995), 328–341, here 338–339.

15. Eighteenth-century German exceptions were Göttingen and Halle, whose cases are discussed in chapter 1. As Adam Nelson shows, links between science and the college were established earlier, but nationalism provided the essential component for their advancement. Nelson, "HES Presidential Address: Citizens or Cosmopolitans? Constructing Scientific Identity in the Early American College," *History of Education Quarterly* 57 (2017): 159–184, esp. 166.

16. Despite the "shrinking" of "embarrassing" nineteenth-century Europe due to its association with sinister ideologies, it remains at the center of the history of knowledge production. Susan Marchand, "Embarrassed by the Nineteenth Century," in *Consortium on Revolutionary Europe, 1750–1850: Selected Papers*, ed. Bernard Cook, Susan V. Nicassio, Michael F. Pavkovic, and Karl A. Roider Jr. (Tallahassee: Florida State University, 2002), 1–16, quotations on 1, 4.

17. Although the founding documents are from 1809, the date commonly given for the establishment of the University of Berlin is 1810. See Heinz-Elmar Tenorth, "Geschichte der Universität zu Berlin, 1810–2010: Zur Einleitung," in *Gründung und Blütezeit der Universität zu Berlin 1810–1918*, ed. Rüdiger vom Bruch and Heinz-Elmar Tenorth, vol. 1 (Berlin: Akademie Verlag, 2012), xv.

18. Shils and Roberts, "The Diffusion of European Models outside Europe," 163–230, here 164.

19. Richard Evans, *The Pursuit of Power: Europe 1815–1914* (London: Penguin, 2016), 495. In German, a *Staat*, a sovereign political entity, is distinct from the form of state power and authority constructed in a nation-state, *Nationalstaat*. I use the former when speaking about the tradition of political theory governing the former, and the latter when speaking specifically about the emergence of nation-states.

20. At the University of Strasbourg local scholars fought Prussian reformers who aimed to use the institution in this border region as part of German political nationalization. In contrast, the University of Basel remained *unzeitgemäß* or "untimely" in reflecting the anti-national sprit of the Swiss canton. See John E. Craig, *Scholarship and Nation Building: The Universities of Strasbourg and Alsatian Society, 1870–1939* (Chicago: University of Chicago Press, 1984), 29–67, 73; and Lionel Gossman *Basel in the Age of Burckhardt: A Study in Unseasonable Ideas* (Chicago: University of Chicago Press, 2002), 8.

21. Shils and Roberts, "The Diffusion of European Models outside Europe," 164.

22. Laurence R. Veysey, *The Emergence of the American University* (Chicago: University of Chicago Press, 1965), 123.

23. Only a handful of American students enrolled in the first half of the nineteenth

century, and the numbers grew to more than 170 in 1880 and then to about 400 each year during the 1890s before tapering off after the turn of the century. Carl Diehl, *Americans and German Scholarship, 1770–1870* (New Haven, CT: Yale University Press, 1978), 1; Peter Drewek, "Die ungastliche deutsche Universität: Ausländische Studenten an deutschen Hochschulen 1890–1930," *Jahrbuch für historische Bildungsforschung* 5 (1999): 197–224. Anja Werner's work shows how these numbers varied among universities. Werner, *Transatlantic World of Higher Education* (New York: Berghahn, 2013), 45.

24. On the "returnees," see Shils, "The Order of Learning in the United States," 35.

25. According to Konrad Jarausch, at least fifteen of the 150 Americans who studied at the University of Göttingen became US university presidents. Jarausch, "American Students in Germany, 1815–1914: The Structure of German and US Matriculants at Göttingen University," in *German Influences on Education in the United States to 1917*, ed. Henry Geitz, Jürgen Heideking, and Jurgen Herbst (New York: Cambridge University Press, 1995), 195–211, here 210n6; on Leipzig, see Werner, *Transatlantic World of Higher Education*, 63.

26. Richard Hofstadter and Walter P. Metzger, *The Development of Academic Freedom in the United States* (New York: Columbia University Press, 1955), 377.

27. Daniel Coit Gilman, *University Problems in the United States* (New York: Century, 1898), 309.

28. Kuno Francke, *Deutsche Arbeit in Amerika: Erinnerungen von Kuno Francke* (Leipzig: Felix Meiner, 1930), 47 (my translation).

29. Alois Brandl, "Persönliche Eindrücke von amerikanischen Universitäten," *Deutsche Rundschau* 32, no. 7 (April 1907): 116–134, quotation on 121; cited by Hugo Münsterberg, *Das Studium der Amerikaner an deutschen Universitäten* [July 23, 1908], Bl. 114, VI. 474, Nachlass Friedrich Schmidt-Ott (hereafter NL Schmidt-Ott), Geheimes Staatsarchiv Preußischer Kulturbesitz (hereafter GStPK). Later published as Münsterberg, *Das Studium der Amerikaner an deutschen Hochschulen* (Berlin, 1911). As Münsterberg explained, this publication was "printed as a manuscript and confidentially circulated," 8. Citations are to the archival edition.

30. For America as "unlimited possibilities," see Max Goldberger, *Das Land der unbegrenzten Möglichkeiten: Beobachtungen über das Wirtschaftsleben der Vereinigten Staaten von Amerika* (Berlin: F. Fontane, 1903). For an early genealogy of Americanization, see Oscar Basler, "Amerikanismus: Geschichte des Schlagwortes," *Deutsche Rundschau* 214 (1930): 142–146. For a more recent overview, see Philipp Gassert, "The Spectre of Americanization: Western Europe in the American Century," in *The Oxford Handbook of Postwar European History*, ed. Dan Stone (Oxford: Oxford University Press, 2012), 182–200.

31. Emil Du Bois-Reymond, "Ansprache," *Sitzungsberichte der Königliche Akademie der Wissenschaften zu Berlin* 16 (1882): 314 (my translation); also cited in Hubert Laitko, "'Weltbetrieb der Wissenschaft': Reflexionen und Streiflichter vom Beginn des deutsch-amerikanischen Professorenaustausches 1905/6," *Dahlemer Archivgespräche* 12 (2006): 44–152, here 66. Gabriel Finkelstein surmises that Du Bois-Reymond acquired his information about America from Alexander von Humboldt. Finkelstein, *Emil du Bois-Reymond: Neuroscience, Self, and Society in Nineteenth-Century Germany* (Cambridge, MA: MIT Press, 2013), 226–227.

32. Harry W. Paul, *The Sorcerer's Apprentice: The French Scientist's Image of German Science, 1840–1919* (Gainesville: University of Florida Press, 1972), 15.

33. Daniel Rodgers shows how this transatlantic exchange had a profound impact on the birth of the social sciences, even though these origins were subsequently either ignored or exaggerated. His focus on "brokers" of these ideas has provided an invaluable model for my work. Rodgers, *Atlantic Crossings: Social Politics in a Progressive Age* (Cambridge, MA: Belknap Press of Harvard University Press, 1998), esp. 4–7, 77.

34. Chester Squire Phinney, *Francis Lieber's Influence on American Thought and Some of His Unpublished Letters* (Philadelphia: International Printing, 1918), 38.

35. Althoff scribbled the term *Weltbetrieb der Wissenschaft* on a note to his assistant Friedrich Schmidt-Ott in reaction to an essay by Harnack on the topic. Rep. 92, A I Nr. 309 I, Bl. 290, Nachlass Friedrich Althoff (hereafter NL Althoff), GStPK. For an interpretation of the German-American relationship that takes this as a starting point, see Laitko, "'Weltbetrieb der Wissenschaft,'" 44.

36. Daniel Coit Gilman, "The Johns Hopkins University in Its Beginning," in Gilman, *University Problems in the United States*, 24.

37. On the long intellectual history of "open source" as a model for intellectual life, see John Willinsky, *The Intellectual Properties of Learning: A Prehistory from Saint Jerome to John Locke* (Chicago: University of Chicago Press, 2018), xii, 3.

38. The best in the former category include Chad Wellmon, *Organizing Enlightenment: Information Overload and the Invention of the Research University* (Baltimore: Johns Hopkins University Press, 2015); and Jon Roberts and James Turner, *The Sacred and the Secular University*, with an introduction by John F. Wilson (Princeton, NJ: Princeton University Press, 2000). The authorities in the second category are Roger L. Geiger, *The History of American Higher Education: Learning and Culture from the Founding to World War II* (Princeton, NJ: Princeton University Press, 2015); and John R. Thelin, *A History of American Higher Education* (Baltimore: Johns Hopkins University Press, 2019).

39. Julie Rueben's important revision of Veysey remains within the national context. Rueben, *The Making of the Modern University: Intellectual Transformation and the Marginalization of Morality* (Chicago: University of Chicago Press, 1996). For the hugely influential classic work of comparison, see Joseph Ben-David, *The Scientist's Role in Society: A Comparative Study* (Englewood Cliffs, NJ: Prentice Hall, 1971). Elisabeth Crawford has argued that Ben-David failed to account for why a certain scientific discipline flourished in one setting and not in another. Crawford, *Nationalism and Internationalism in Science, 1880–1939: Four Studies of the Nobel Population* (Cambridge: Cambridge University Press, 1992), 15, 17.

40. Shils and Roberts, "The Diffusion of European Models outside Europe," 228; Hastings Rashdall, *The Universities of Europe in the Middle Ages* (Oxford: Clarendon Press, 1936), 15. On the mistaken assumption that ideas undergo "autoglobalization" like commodities, see Samuel Moyn, "On the Nonglobalization of Ideas," in *Global Intellectual History*, ed. Samuel Moyn and Andrew Sartori (New York: Columbia University Press, 2013), 187–204, esp. 197. On the challenge of separating intellectual from material exchange in the nineteenth century, see David Blackbourn, "Germany

and the Birth of the Modern World," *German Historical Institute Bulletin* 51 (Autumn 2012): 9–21, esp. 12.

41. Of the best recent histories of American higher education, all speak exclusively of the German influence on the American system and are thus preoccupied with questions of how much the American university resembles the German one—a question that I argue is less significant than the role played by exchange in the university's historical evolution. See, for example, Paul H. Mattingly, *American Academic Cultures: A History of Higher Education* (Chicago: University of Chicago Press, 2017), 255–257; and James Axtell, *Wisdom's Workshop: The Rise of the Modern University* (Princeton, NJ: Princeton University Press, 2016), 223–235. While Gabriele Lingelbach argues that the American university went in its own direction, she too takes influence as the primary object of analysis. See Lingelbach, "Cultural Borrowing or Autonomous Development: American and German Universities in the Late Nineteenth Century," in *Traveling between Worlds: German-American Encounters*, ed. Thomas Adam and Ruth V. Gross (College Station: Texas A&M University Press, 2006), 100–123. On the university as "export," see Rainer Christoph Schwinges, ed. *Humboldt International: Der Export des deutschen Universitätsmodells im 19. und 20. Jahrhundert* (Basel: Schwabe, 2001). The older work by Jurgen Herbst is an exception and provides a thorough account of how this cross-pollination worked in the historical discipline. Herbst, *The German Historical School in American Scholarship: A Study in the Transfer of Culture* (Ithaca, NY: Cornell University Press, 1965), 1; and Herbst, *And Sadly Teach: Teacher Education and Professionalization in American Culture* (Madison: University of Wisconsin Press 1991), 4.

42. The classic theory of diffusion was articulated by Everett Rogers, who described the spread of ideas as a cost-benefit analysis by the individual as to whether it makes sense to adopt the innovation at hand. Rogers, *Diffusion of Innovations*, 5th ed. (New York: Free Press, 2003), xvii. For an analysis of status as a mechanism for interinstitutional market dynamics, see Joel M. Podolny, *Status Signals: A Sociological Study of Market Competition* (Princeton, NJ: Princeton University Press, 2005). For an argument for institutional emergence as hybridization, see John Frederick Padgett and Walter W. Powell, introduction to *The Emergence of Organizations and Markets*, ed. John Frederick Padgett and Walter W. Powell (Princeton, NJ: Princeton University Press, 2012), 1–29.

43. Elisabeth Clemens, *The People's Lobby: Organizational Innovation and the Rise of Interest Group Politics in the United States, 1890–1925* (Chicago: University of Chicago Press, 1997), 47. For a recent excellent example of the incorporation of political history in the sociological analysis of higher education, see Mitchell Stevens and Alexander Kindel, "Engineering Credentials: Educational Entrepreneurship as Statecraft in the Cold-War United States," SocArXiv, May 30, 2018, https://doi.org/10.31235/osf.io/pd8c4.

44. Pascale Casanova, *The World Republic of Letters*, trans. Malcolm DeBevoise (Cambridge, MA: Harvard University Press, 2007), 23.

45. In this sense, my analysis of universities mirrors that of Roger Finke and Rodney Stark's of religion in *The Churching of America, 1776–2005: Winners and Losers in Our Religious Economy* (New Brunswick, NJ: Rutgers University Press, 2005), 1, 72, 282. Thank you to Daniel Steinmetz-Jenkins and Isaac Weiner for sharing thoughts on this text and the history of religion.

46. For an example of this method, see Thomas Bender, *A Nation among Nations: America's Place in World History* (New York: Hill and Wang, 2006); and Rodgers, *Atlantic Crossings*, 69, 112–155. I'm also influenced by Michael Mitterauer's notion of "spatial geography" as a significant factor in the emergence of the first European universities, including Bologna and Solerno. Mitterauer, "Die Anfänge der Universität im Mittelalter: Räume und Zentren der Wissenschaftsentwicklung," in *Phänomenologie des europäischen Wissenschaftssystems*, ed. Wolfgang Mantl (Baden-Baden: Nomos, 2010): 45–88, esp. 48.

47. It has become common to root around in the past to inspire current reform. But without an account of change over time it is difficult to know what lessons to take. See, for example, Mattingly, *American Academic Cultures*, 2 and 8. Cathy Davidson points to Charles Eliot's 1869 essay "The New Education" as an inspiration for our own era. Davidson, *The New Education: How to Revolutionize the University to Prepare Students for a World In Flux* (New York: Basic Books, 2017), 7–9, 17–44.

48. Randall Collins, *The Credential Society: An Historical Sociology of Education and Stratification* (New York: Academic Press, 1979), 120.

49. Without such a historical theory of change, all we have are phenotypes of different models, distinct moments, or case studies disconnected from historical evolution, as is the case for Axtell's "genealogical tale" and Mattingly's "cultures"; see Axtell, *Wisdom's Workshop*, xv; and Mattingly, *American Academic Cultures*, 2–3. In this way I disagree with the notion that American private and public universities remain too different to understand together (or for that matter, American private and German public institutions). As Thelin argues, the success of private universities always rested on the state. Thelin, *A History of American Higher Education*, 358.

50. Newfield has called this vision "mass *Bildung*," but Paul Reitter and Chad Wellmon express doubt about reconciling these traditions, the elite and democratic, in their current form. See, for example, Paul Reitter, "The Business of Learning," *New York Review of Books*, February 22, 2018; and Paul Reitter and Chad Wellmon, "The Field of Dreams: Public Higher Education in the United States," *LA Review of Books*, December 13, 2016.

51. Even the best of the recent works on higher education tend to offer 1970s neoliberalism as an explanation for today's crises. See, for example, Frank Donoghue, *The Last Professors: The Corporate University and the Fate of the Humanities* (New York: Fordham University Press, 2008); and Christopher Newfield, *Unmaking the Public University: The Forty-Year Assault on the Middle Class* (Cambridge, MA: Harvard University Press, 2011).

CHAPTER ONE

1. The quotation that serves as the epigraph for this chapter appears in Carl Schurz's memoirs published in English. Carl Schurz, Frederic Bancroft, and William Archibald Dunning, *The Reminiscences of Carl Schurz* (London: J. Murray, 1909), 3:277–278. See also the helpful opening discussion by Williamjames Hull Hoffer, who uses this observation as starting point for his analysis of US congressional debates of this period. Hoffer, *To Enlarge the Machinery of Government: Congressional Debates and the Growth*

of the American State, 1858–1891 (Baltimore: Johns Hopkins University Press, 2007), vii. Paul, *Sorcerer's Apprentice*, 5.

2. Cited in Peter Burke, *A Social History of Knowledge: From the Encyclopedia to Wikipedia* (Cambridge: Polity Press, 2012), 190.

3. Subsequent sociologists, including notably Joseph Ben-David, confirmed Weber's hypotheses about the connection between competition and scientific advancement. Ben-David, review of *Max Weber on Universities*, ed. Shils, *American Journal of Sociology* 80 (1975): 1463–1468, here 1465. See also Ben-David, *The Scientist's Role*, 19, 122–123, and 171–172; and Shils, "Center and Periphery," in *The Logic of Personal Knowledge: Essays Presented to Michael Polyani on His Seventieth Birthday, March 11, 1961* (London: Routledge, 1961), 117–130, esp. 117–123.

4. Prussia supported the North in the Civil War, while American Northerners compared the Civil War to the Prussian wars. See Herbst, *The German Historical School in American Scholarship*, 10.

5. This framework is influenced by recent scholarship on federalism and German history. See, for example, Maiken Umbach, ed., *German Federalism: Past, Present, Future*, New Perspectives in German Studies (Houndmills, UK: Palgrave, 2002); Thomas Nipperdey, "Der Föderalismus in der deutschen Geschichte," *Nachdenken über die deutsche Geschichte: Essays* (Munich: C.H. Beck, 1986), 60–109; and Günther Ammon, ed., *Föderalismus und Zentralismus: Europas Zukunft zwischen dem deutschen und dem französischen Modell* (Baden-Baden: Nomos, 1996). On cultural federalism, see Abigail Green, "The Federal Alternative? A New View of Modern German History," *The Historical Journal* 46 (2003): 187–202, here 193.

6. Cited in Green, "The Federal Alternative?," 200.

7. A number of scholars have observed Berlin's slow rise to knowledge center. Walter Rüegg describes eighteenth-century Berlin as "a wasteland, scientifically speaking." Rüegg, "Themes," in *A History of the University in Europe*, vol. 3, *Universities in the Nineteenth and Early Twentieth Century*, ed. Rüegg (Cambridge: Cambridge University Press, 2004), 3–31, quotation on 16. Charles McClelland says Berlin was still a "parvenu not an arrivé" among cities, its subsequent ascent connected to the university's success. McClelland, *Berlin, the Mother of All Research Universities: 1860–1918* (Lanham, MD: Lexington Books, 2017), 6.

8. Max Lenz, *Geschichte der Königlichen Friedrich-Wilhelms–Universität zu Berlin* (Halle: Verlag der Buchhandlung des Waisenhauses, 1910), 1:78 (my translation).

9. R. D. Anderson argues that many of the developments we associate with beginning in 1810 in fact can be attributed to the earlier Enlightenment period. Anderson, "Before and after Humboldt: European Universities between the Eighteenth and the Nineteenth Centuries," *History of Higher Education Annual* 20 (2000): 5–14, esp. 5.

10. R. D. Anderson, *European Universities from the Enlightenment to 1914* (Oxford: Oxford University Press, 2004), esp. 23–25; Zachary Purvis, *Theology and the University in Nineteenth-Century Germany* (Oxford: Oxford University Press, 2016), 91, 116–117; and Thomas Albert Howard, *Protestant Theology and the Making of the Modern German University* (Oxford: Oxford University Press, 2006), 92–98.

11. Günther Meinhardt, *Die Universität Göttingen: Ihre Entwicklung und Geschichte*

von 1734–1974 (Göttingen: Musterschmidt, 1977), 17–18, 35, 132–133; William Clark, *Academic Charisma and the Origins of the Research University* (Chicago: University of Chicago Press, 2006), 274.

12. Hilde de Ridder-Symoens and Walter Rüegg, eds., *A History of the University in Europe*, vol. 2, *Universities in Early Modern Europe* (Cambridge: Cambridge University Press, 1996), 227; Paul Gerhard Buchloh and Walter T. Rix, *American Colony of Göttingen: Historical and Other Data Collected between the Years 1855 and 1888* (Göttingen: Vandenhoeck & Ruprecht, 1976), 22; Maximiliaan van Woudenberg, *Coleridge and Cosmopolitan Intellectualism, 1794–1804* (London: Routledge, 2018), 90–103. The classic negative view of eighteenth-century universities represented by such historians as Thomas Nipperdey has largely been revised. Less exceptions than models, the universities of Halle and Göttingen are now generally viewed as the bud of the modern university's emergence. On this scholarly transformation, see Peter Josephson, Thomas Karlsohn, and Johan Östling, "Introduction: The Humboldtian Tradition and Its Transformation," in *The Humboldtian Tradition: Origins and Legacies*, ed. Josephson, Karlsohn, and Östling (Leiden: Brill, 2014), 4–5. A wealth of new literature on the academic innovations at the University of Göttingen exists. See, in particular, Martin Gierl, "Compilation and the Production of Knowledge in the Early German Enlightenment," in *Wissenschaft als kulturelle Praxis, 1750–1900*, ed. Hans Eric Bödeker, Peter Hanns Reill, and Jürgen Schlumbohm (Göttingen: Vandenhoeck & Ruprecht, 1999), 69–103.

13. The twin traditions of Enlightenment-era religious reform and Romanticism assumed in Germany a path different from that in England and France. Collins, *The Sociology of Philosophies*, 646; Anderson, *European Universities from the Enlightenment to 1914*, 64.

14. Friedrich Schiller, "Was heißt und zu welchem Ende studiert man Universalgeschichte?," in *Friedrich Schiller Historische Schriften und Erzählungen I*, ed. Otto Dann, vol. 6 of *Friedrich Schiller Werke und Briefe* (Frankfurt am Main: Deutscher Klassiker Verlag, 2000), 415. On the *Brotstudent* as a flashpoint for this transition from the *Gelehrtenstand* of the Enlightenment to the *Bildungsbürgertum* of the nineteenth century, see Tony La Vopa, *Grace, Talent, and Merit: Poor Students, Clerical Careers, and Professional Ideology in Eighteenth-Century Germany* (Cambridge: Cambridge University Press, 1988), esp. 5–6. For an excellent introduction to the concept of *Bildung*, see David Sorkin, "Wilhelm von Humboldt: The Theory and Practice of Self-Formation (*Bildung*), 1791–1810," *Journal of the History of Ideas* 44, no. 1 (1983): 55–73.

15. Theodore Ziolkowski argues that Berlin was the "institutionalization of the Jena ideal." Ziolkowski, *German Romanticism and Its Institutions* (Princeton, NJ: Princeton University Press, 1990), 286.

16. Johann Gottlieb Fichte, *Addresses to the German Nation*, trans. Isaac Nakhimovsky, Béla Kapossy, and Keith Tribe (Indianapolis: Hackett, 2013), 9.

17. Johann Gottlieb Fichte, "Deduzierter Plan einer in Berlin zu errichtenden höheren Lehranstalt," in *Die Idee der deutschen Universität*, ed. Ernst Anrich (Darmstadt: Hermann Gentner, 1956), 125–217. Translation here from Fichte, "A Plan, Deduced from First Principles, for an Institution," in Menand, Reitter, and Wellmon, *The Rise of the Research University*, 73.

18. Henrik Steffens, "Vorlesungen über die Idee der Universitäten," in Anrich, *Die Idee der deutschen Universität*, 347, 352. For additional contributions to the debate over the university's founding, see Wilhelm Weischedel, ed., *Idee und Wirklichkeit einer Universität: Dokumente zur Geschichte der Friedrich-Wilhelms-Universität zu Berlin* (Berlin: W. de Gruyter, 1960). On Halle's dire state following Napoleon's invasion, see Wilhelm Schrader, *Geschichte der Friedrichs-Universität zu Halle* (Berlin: Dümmlers, 1894), esp. 5–7; and Sam A. Mustafa, *Napoleon's Paper Kingdom: The Life and Death of Westphalia, 1807–1813* (Lanham, MD: Rowman & Littlefield, 2017), 176–181.

19. Friedrich Paulsen, *The German Universities and University Study*, trans. Frank Thilly and William W. Elwang (New York: Charles Scribners Sons, 1906), 50.

20. Friedrich Schleiermacher, "Gelegentliche Gedanken über Universitäten im deutschen Sinn," in Anrich, *Die Idee der deutschen Universität*, 223.

21. Friedrich Schleiermacher, "Occasional Thoughts on German Universities," in Menand, Reitter, and Wellmon, *The Rise of the Research University*, 53–54.

22. According to Daniel Fallon, Schleiermacher's model has served as the "basic organizational pattern for all German universities up to the present time." Fallon, *The German University: A Heroic Ideal in Conflict with the Modern World* (Boulder, CO: Colorado Associated University Press, 1980), 36. See also Herbert Richardson, *Schleiermacher and the Founding of the University of Berlin: The Study of Religion as a Scientific Discipline* (Lewiston, NY: Mellen, 1991); and Elinor S. Shaffer, "Romantic Philosophy and the Organization of the Disciplines: The Founding of the University of Berlin," in *Romanticism and the Sciences*, ed. Andrew Cunningham and Nicholas Jardine (Cambridge: Cambridge University Press, 1990), 38–54.

23. Ziolkowski, *German Romanticism*, 235.

24. Quotation from Adam Müller, *Berliner Abendblatter* (1810); cited in Ziolkowski, *German Romanticism*, 300.

25. For an authoritative biography of Humboldt, see Paul R. Sweet, *Wilhelm von Humboldt: A Biography*, 2 vols. (Columbus: Ohio State University Press, 1980). For a new biography on Alexander, see Andrea Wulf, *The Invention of Nature: Alexander von Humboldt's New World* (New York: Knopf, 2015).

26. Sorkin, "Wilhelm von Humboldt," 57; and Sweet, *Wilhelm von Humboldt*, 1:38. Though they often kissed on the lips, theirs was, as James J. Sheehan explains, a "sentimental intimacy but physical chastity." Sheehan, *German History, 1770–1866*, Oxford History of Modern Europe (Oxford: Clarendon Press, 1989), 362.

27. For the relationship between Wilhelm and Caroline, see Sweet, *Wilhelm Von Humboldt*, 1:63–71; and Gustav Sichelschmidt, *Caroline von Humboldt: Ein Frauenbild aus der Goethezeit* (Düsseldorf: Droste, 1989), esp 8–9. For the correspondence of Wilhelm and Caroline, see Anna von Sydow, *Wilhelm und Caroline von Humboldt in ihren Briefen* (Berlin: Ernst Siegfried Mittler und Sohn, 1909), vol. 3; also online at http://m-tag.de/wvh03_093.htm.

28. On the gendering of spaces during the Enlightenment, see Ian McNeely, with Lisa Wolverton, who also offer an excellent survey of different paradigms of knowledge institutions. McNeely, with Wolverton, *Reinventing Knowledge: From Alexandria to the Internet* (New York: Norton, 2008), 154. For a more cynical view of how Hum-

boldt co-opted feminine traits and spaces and masculinized them, see Claudia Lindén, "It Takes a Real Man to Show True Femininity: Gender Transgression in Goethe's and Humboldt's Concept of Bildung," in Josephson, Karlsohn, and Östling, *The Humboldtian Tradition: Origins and Legacies*, 58–79. On Alexander's letter writing, see Wulf, *The Invention of Nature*, 3.

29. Wilhelm to Caroline, November 7, 1808, in Sydow, *Wilhelm und Caroline*, 3:10–11 (my translation).

30. Wilhelm to Caroline, November 22, 1808, in Sydow, *Wilhelm und Caroline*, 3:25 (my translation).

31. The German word Humboldt used is *Komödiantentruppe*. Wilhelm to Caroline, November 16, 1808, in Sydow, *Wilhelm und Caroline*, 18–19 (my translation).

32. The original German title was *Ideen zu einem Versuch die Grenzen der Wirksamkeit des Staats zu bestimmen*, though the English title obscures the focus on the state's borders. Wilhelm von Humboldt, *The Sphere and Duties of Government*, trans. Joseph Coulthard (London: John Chapman, 1854), quotation on 65. On Humboldt's emerging beliefs concerning the ends of the state and his popularity among Atlantic revolutionary thinkers like Mill and Jefferson, see Sweet, *Wilhelm von Humboldt*, 1:38.

33. According to Sweet, it is possible that Humboldt got the idea of what a university should *not* be. Sweet, *Wilhelm von Humboldt*, 1:32–38. The moniker *Bildungsdiktator* is from Anthony Grafton's engaging review of Sweet's biography in *American Scholar* 50 (1981): 371–381, here 378.

34. Wilhelm von Humboldt, "Theorie der Bildung des Menschen: Bruchstück," in *Werke in fünf Bänden* (Darmstadt: Wissenschaftliche Buchgesellschaft, 2010), 1:234–240. See also Sorkin on the reconciliation of the personal and social versions of *Bildung* and Humboldt's transformation to accept the state; "Wilhelm von Humboldt," esp. 56, 60, and 69; Sheehan, *German History*, 365; and Ian F. McNeely on Humboldt's "ultimate marginalization" in "The Last Project of the Republic of Letters: Wilhelm von Humboldt's Global Linguistics," *Journal of Modern History* 92 (June 2020): 241–273, quotation on 273.

35. First quotation from Humboldt cited in Sweet, *Wilhelm von Humboldt* 1:51. Second quotation, my translation, from Wilhelm to Caroline, August 18, 1809, in Sydow, *Wilhelm und Caroline*, 223.

36. Alexander also irked the Kaiser with his unabating love of all things French. Wulf, *The Invention of Nature*, 137, 139, 141.

37. Wilhelm von Humboldt, "Über die innere und äussere Organisation der höheren wissenschaftlichen Anstalten in Berlin," in *Wilhelm von Humboldts Gesammelte Schriften*, ed. Bruno Gebhardt (Berlin: B. Behr, 1930), 1:250–260. Humboldt's essay, likely penned sometime between September 1809 and Summer 1810, was not discovered until 1896 and only published shortly thereafter. On the protracted history of Humboldt's work, see Sylvia Paletschek, "The Invention of Humboldt and the Impact of National Socialism: The German University Idea in the First Half of the Twentieth Century," in *Science in the Third Reich*, ed. Margit Szöllösi-Janze (New York: Berg, 2001), 37–58. Translation here from Edward Shils, in Wilhelm von Humboldt, "On the Spirit and the Organisational Framework of Intellectual Institutions in Berlin,"

Minerva 8 (1970): 244. According to Björn Wittrock, this document is "perhaps the most discussed document in the modern history of universities." Björn Wittrock, "The Modern University: Three Transformations," in *The European and American University since 1800*, ed. Sheldon Rothblatt and Björn Wittrock (Cambridge: Cambridge University Press, 1993), 303–362, quotation on 317.

38. Translation by Shils, in Humboldt, "On the Spirit and the Organisational Framework of Intellectual Institutions in Berlin," 248–249. See also Shils's note (249) on the significance of Humboldt's use of *Freistätte* (sanctuary) rather than *Zufluchtsort* (refuge) to describe the Academy, in contradistinction to the university, which was to have a more intimate relationship with society.

39. Wilhelm von Humboldt, "Antrag auf Errichtung der Universität Berlin, 24. Juli 1809," in Gebhardt, *Wilhelm von Humboldts Gesammelte Schriften*, 1:150.

40. The University of Berlin would be rechristened the Friedrich-Wilhelms-Universität in 1828 in gratitude for the royal family's munificence. The University of Berlin retained this official royal name even after the end of the Hohenzollern monarchy in 1918. When the onset of the Cold War resulted in the creation of the Free University in West Berlin, and the exodus of many scholars, the "rump institution" that remained in Berlin-Mitte was renamed for the Humboldt brothers. See McClelland, *The Mother of All Research Universities*, xii.

41. On the call of the first professors at the University of Berlin, see, for example, Humboldt, "Antrag auf Berufung Savignys, 1 March 1810," in Gebhardt, *Wilhelm von Humboldts Gesammelte Schriften*, 1:228; and Tenorth, "Geschichte der Universität zu Berlin," xxxii. Not all scholars felt called to duty. Apparently the philologist F. A. Wolf only accepted once he negotiated never having to attend a faculty meeting. Fallon, *The German University*, 21; and Lenz, *Geschichte Universität Berlin*, 157–159 and 161–276.

42. On subsequent iterations of the Humboldt ideal, see Mitchell G. Ash, "Bachelor of What, Master of Whom? The Humboldt Myth and Historical Transformations of Higher Education in German-Speaking Europe and the US," *European Journal of Education* 41 (2006): 245–267, here 245. The medieval universities also enjoyed a quasi-social contract with society and enjoyed independence by carving out free space between the papacy and the sovereign, refuge that was underwritten by both. Rashdall, *The Universities of Europe in the Middle Ages*, 401–402, 429, 431; and Walter P. Metzger, "Academic Tenure in America: A Historical Essay," in *Faculty Tenure: A Report and Recommendations*, ed. William R. Keast and John W. Macy (San Francisco: Jossey-Bass Publishers, 1973), 93–159, here 98–99.

43. McClelland, *The Mother of All Research Universities*, 3, 5; Anderson, *European Universities from the Enlightenment to 1914*, 55.

44. Translation by Shils, in Humboldt, "On the Spirit and the Organisational Framework of Intellectual Institutions in Berlin," 244. How far Humboldt had come to view the nation as the vehicle for culture is illustrated in the fact that he even fought for a direct tax and a more centralized system than was ultimately adopted. Suzanne L. Marchand, *Down from Olympus: Archaeology and Philhellenism in Germany, 1750–1970* (Princeton, NJ: Princeton University Press, 2003), 27.

45. McClelland, *The Mother of All Research Universities*, 41.

46. Historians debate whether internalist or externalist factors led to this institutional change. According to Ben-David, despite every attempt at top-down nationalization, an "accidental innovation" emerged from the decentralization of these strong urban centers of knowledge. But this must be combined with R. Steven Turner's more activist agents of change for a full portrait of causes. Joseph Ben-David, "Science and the University System," in "The Notion of Modern Educational Sociology/Der Begriff der Modernen Erziehungssoziologie/La notion contemporaine de sociologie de l'éducation," special issue, *International Review of Education/Internationale Zeitschrift für Erziehungswissenschaft/Revue Internationale de l'Education* 18 (1972): 44–60, here 48; R. Steven Turner, "The Prussian Professoriate and the Research Imperative: 1790–1840," in *Epistemological and Social Problems of the Sciences in the Early Nineteenth Century*, ed. Hans N. Jahnke and M. Otte (Dordrecht: Reidel, 1981), 109–122.

47. Individual exceptions remained exemplary, as we will see, including the École Polytechnique, the postrevolutionary institute devoted to engineering, and the École Normale Supérieure, founded by decree in 1808, both of which combined instruction with elements of research; the key reformers of this period including Charles Maurice de Talleyrand and Marquis de Condorcet seem to have influenced Fichte's notion of the university. Anderson, *European Universities*, 63.

48. Jan Goldstein, *The Post-Revolutionary Self: Politics and Psyche in France, 1750–1850* (Cambridge, MA: Harvard University Press, 2008), 186.

49. Mary Joe Nye, *Science in the Provinces: Scientific Communities and Provincial Leadership in France, 1860–1930* (Berkeley: University of California Press, 1986), 14.

50. Ashley Miles, "Reports by Louis Pasteur and Claude Bernard on the Organization of Scientific Teaching and Research," *Notes and Records of the Royal Society of London* 37 (1982): 101, 115–117. Duruy, cited in Anderson, *European Universities*, 177–178.

51. According to Nye, the institution proved not very innovative. Nye, *Science in the Provinces*, 16.

52. Liard was the analogous figure to Althoff, not the actual minister, but the director of higher education who was the dominant voice through the reforms of 1882, 1885, and 1896. See Louis M. Greenberg, "Architects of the New Sorbonne: Liard's Purpose and Durkheim's Role," *History of Education Quarterly* 21, no. 1 (1981): 77–94, here 79–80.

53. George Weisz, "The French Universities and Education for the New Professions, 1885–1914: An Episode in French University Reform," *Minerva* 17 (1979): 98–128, esp. 100.

54. Jules Flammermont, *Les universités allemandes* (Paris: Picard, 1886), 1885; Harry W. Paul, "The Role of German Idols in the Rise of the French Science Empire," in *'Einsamkeit und Freiheit' neu besichtigt: Universitätsreformen und Disziplinenbildung in Preußen als Modell für Wissenschaftspolitik im Europa des 19 Jahrhunderts*, ed. Gert Schubrig (Stuttgart: Franz Steiner, 1991), 184–197, esp. 188–189.

55. Nye investigates these developments and, drawing on quantitative evidence, attempts to refute the center-periphery assumptions about the organization of science, but even she seems to concede their defeat. Nye, *Science in the Provinces*, 7, 38, 41, 52, 200–201, 240.

56. As the urban studies scholar Pierre Yves Saunier has argued, however, these efforts were too belated to form a real counterpart to Paris, and Lyon amounted to no more than a distant "second city." Saunier, "Changing the City: Urban International Information and the Lyon Municipality, 1900–1940," *Planning Perspectives* 14 (1999): 19–48, esp. 20.

57. Weisz, "The French Universities and Education for the New Professions," 128.

58. John R. David, "Higher Education Reform and the German Model: A Victorian Discourse," in *Anglo-German Scholarly Networks in the Long Nineteenth Century*, ed. Heather Ellis and Ulrike Kirchberger (Leiden: Brill, 2014), 39–62, here 43; Rosemary Ashton, *Little Germany: Exile and Asylum in Victorian England* (Oxford: Oxford University Press 1986), xiii. See also Peter Alter, *The Reluctant Patron: Science and the State in Britain, 1850–1920* (Oxford: Berg, 1987), 25. On the general role of the German states in British reform discussions, see John R. Davis, *The Victorians and Germany* (Bern: Peter Lang, 2007).

59. Matthew Arnold, *Culture and Anarchy*, ed. Samuel Lipman (Ann Arbor: University of Michigan Press, 1994), 85; Marc Schalenberg, "Großbritannien, oder: Was ein preußischer Gesandter an englischen Universitäten ausrichten kann," in *Humboldt International: Der Export des deutschen Universitätsmodells im 19. und 20. Jahrhundert*, ed. Rainer Schwinges (Basel: Schwabe, 2001), 231–245, here 237.

60. Matthew Arnold, *Higher Schools and Universities in Germany* (London: Macmillan, 1874), v, 49.

61. Institutional reform at Cambridge and Oxford resulted from the broad church movement and the Noetics. Ultimately the Liberal prime minister Lord John Russell set up a Royal Commission in 1850 to help foster reform. Heather Ellis, *Generational Conflict and University Reform: Oxford in the Age of Revolution* (Leiden: Brill, 2012), 21–63.

62. Ben-David and Zlockower, "Universities and Academic Systems in Modern Societies," 66. See also Nicholas Phillipson, "Commerce and Culture: Edinburgh, Edinburgh University, and the Scottish Enlightenment," in *The University and the City: From Medieval Origins to the Present*, ed. Thomas Bender (Oxford: Oxford University Press, 1991), 100–118.

63. John Henry Newman, *The Idea of a University* ed. Frank M. Turner (New Haven, CT: Yale University Press, 1996); for Newman as a "golden age," see Kerr, *The Great Transformation in Higher Education*, 50. Though they are often quoted together as Arnold-Newman, they in fact don't appear to have read one another. Anderson, *European Universities from the Enlightenment to 1914*, 112.

64. Ben-David and Zlockower, "Universities and Academic Systems in Modern Societies," 64, 66, 68.

65. Labaree makes a similar argument by invoking the German sociologist Ulrich Beck's theory of the "elevator effect." David Labaree, *A Perfect Mess: The Unlikely Ascendancy of American Higher Education* (Chicago: University of Chicago Press, 2017), 97, 99–100. See also Ulrich Beck, "Beyond Class and Nation: Reframing Social Inequalities in a Globalizing World," *British Journal of Sociology* 58, no. 4 (2007): 680–705, esp. 687.

66. The mutual interest of learned American and Germans dated back to the revolutionary eighteenth century. Horst Dippel, *Germany and the American Revolution,*

1770-1800: A Sociological Investigation of Late Eighteenth-Century Political Thinking, trans. Bernhard A. Ulendorf (Steiner: Wiesbaden, 1978), esp. xv–xx, 46.

67. Mark R. Finlay examines the role of Europe as a source of competition, but not the question of federalism as a mechanism for exchange and adaptation. Finlay, "Transnational Exchanges of Agricultural Scientific Thought from the Morrill Act through the Hatch Act," in *Science as Service: Establishing and Reformulating American Land-Grant Universities, 1865–1930,* ed. Alan I. Marcus (Tuscaloosa: University of Alabama Press, 2015), 34–60.

68. Thomas Jefferson, "79. A Bill for the More General Diffusion of Knowledge, 18 June 1779," *Founders Online,* National Archives, https://founders.archives.gov/documents/Jefferson/01-02-02-0132-0004-0079; Wayne J. Urban and Jennings L. Wagoner, *American Education: A History* (London: Routledge, 2009), 72; Alf J. Mapp Jr., *Thomas Jefferson: Passionate Pilgrim* (Lanham, MD: Rowman & Littlefield, 2009), 369.

69. Caroline Winterer. *American Enlightenments: Pursuing Happiness in the Age of Reason* (New Haven, CT: Yale University Press, 2016), 7, 10–12.

70. Scholars have argued that the early American college was more dynamic, evolving, and even research driven than originally caricatured, but the point about lack of standardization and coherence still stands. Louise L. Stevenson and Hugh Hawkins, *Scholarly Means to Evangelical Ends: The New Haven Scholars and the Transformation of Higher Learning in America, 1830–1890* (Baltimore: Johns Hopkins University Press, 1986); and Hugh Hawkins, "The Making of the Liberal Arts College Identity," *Daedalus* 128 (1999): 1–25.

71. Richard Hofstadter, *Academic Freedom in the Age of the College* (New Brunswick, NJ: Transaction Publishers, 1996), 114.

72. Hofstadter, *Academic Freedom in the Age of the College,* 211; and Frederick Rudolf, *The American College and University,* intro. John R. Thelin (1962; Athens: University of Georgia Press, 1990), 47.

73. Benjamin Rush sought a universal education program that was "simultaneously democratic and hierarchical." For example, he favored education for women but not social egalitarianism. Michael Meranze, introduction to *Essays: Literary, Moral, and Philosophical,* ed. Michael Meranze (Schenectady, NY: Union College Press, 1988), vvi, xvii.

74. Benjamin Rush, "Plan for a Federal University," *The American Museum,* 1788, 444. See also Rush, "Address to the People of the United States," *The American Museum,* 1787, 9–11.

75. One of the winners was Samuel H. Smith, whom Jefferson invited to Washington to advise him when he became president in 1800. On the contest, see Allen Hansen, *Liberalism and American Education in the Eighteenth Century* (New York: Macmillan, 1926), 110. The other winner was Samuel Knox. For Smith's essay, see Samuel H. Smith, "A System of Liberal Education" (1798), in *The Liberal Arts Tradition: A Documentary History,* ed. Bruce A. Kimball (Lanham, MD: University Press of America, 2010), 241–250. For more on Jefferson's conversations with French scholars Lafitte du Courteil and Du Pont de Nemours on the idea of a national university, see Hansen, *Liberalism and American Education,* 168–199.

76. David Madsen, *The National University: Enduring Dream of the USA* (Detroit: Wayne State University Press, 1966), 16–28, quotation on 27. See also Albert Ellery Bergh, ed., *The Writings of Thomas Jefferson* (Washington, DC: Thomas Jefferson Memorial Association, 1905), XIX, 108–112.

77. James Madison, "Second Annual Message," in *A Compilation of the Messages and Papers of the Presidents*, ed. James D. Richardson (New York: Bureau of National Literature and Art, 1897), 2:470; also cited in Brian M. Ingrassia, "From the New World to the Old, and Back Again: Whig University Leaders and Trans-Atlantic Nationalism in the Era of 1848," *Journal of the Early Republic* 32 (2012): 667–692, esp. 673. See also Edgar Bruce Wesley, *Proposed: The University of the United States* (Minneapolis: University of Minnesota Press, 1936), 4–10.

78. There were in fact three reports issued by the faculty and corporation of the Yale College in 1828, but the condensed report has generally been referred to in the literature as the so-called Yale Report. Jurgen Herbst, "The Yale Report of 1828," *International Journal of the Classical Tradition* 11, no. 2 (2004): 213–231, 214; and Geiger, *The History of American Higher Education*, 187–191. For the condensed version, see "Original Papers in Relation to a Course of Liberal Education," *American Journal of Science and Arts* 15 (1829): quotations on 306 and 315. According to Frederick Rudolph, the Report "gave to the forces of reaction . . . a gospel." Rudolph, *The American College and University: A History*, intro. John Thelin (1962; Athens: University of Georgia Press, 1990), 132. Viewed from another perspective the Yale Report also embodied the American commitment to the liberal arts college, which went dormant but did not fully disappear in the age of the university. For helpful context and a reprint, see David B. Potts, *Liberal Education for a Land of Colleges* (New York: Palgrave Macmillan, 2010), 7–12 and 85–140.

79. Henry P. Tappan, *A Discourse delivered by Henry P. Tappan, D.D. at Ann Arbor, Mich., on the occasion of his inauguration as chancellor of the University of Michigan, December 21st, 1852* (Ann Arbor: University of Michigan Library, 2005), 32.

80. Orie William Long, *Literary Pioneers: Early American Explorers of European Culture* (Cambridge, MA: Harvard University Press, 1935), 6–55, esp. 13; and J. Jefferson Looney, ed., *The Papers of Thomas Jefferson, Retirement Series, 1 September 1815 to 30 April 1816* (Princeton, NJ: Princeton University Press, 2012), 9:559–561.

81. Alf J. Mapp, *Thomas Jefferson—Passionate Pilgrim, the Presidency, the Founding of the University, and the Private Battle* (Lanham, MD: Rowman & Littlefield, 2009), 369.

82. Alan Taylor, *Jefferson's Education* (New York: Norton, 2019), esp. 3–5.

83. Herbert Baxter Adams, *Thomas Jefferson and the University of Virginia, Issues 1–3* (Washington, DC: Government Printing Office, 1888), 190–193. Virginia's nearest adaptation from Germany were the secondary schools or *Gymnasien*, which Jefferson's colleagues established as feeder schools for the new university. See also Philip Alexander Bruce, *History of the University of Virginia, 1819–1919* (New York: Macmillan, 1921), 3:236.

84. Jefferson must have known there would be backlash, as he tried to keep Gilmer's mission a secret. Richard Beale Davis, *Correspondence of Thomas Jefferson and Francis Walker Gilmer* (Columbia: University of South Carolina Press, 1946), 81–82; see also Garry Wills, *Mr. Jefferson's University* (Washington DC: National Geographic Society, 2002), 119.

85. Hofstadter, *Academic Freedom in the Age of the College*, 241.

86. Reginald H. Phelps, "The Idea of the Modern University—Göttingen and America," *German Review: Literature, Culture, Theory* 29 (1954): 175–190; George Park Fisher, "The Academic Career of Ex-President Woolsey," *Century* 24 (1882): 709–717, esp. 713. The line between Germany and an emphasis on research, however, was not straight, as Veysey showed. Under the Woolsey administration at Yale, for example, science declined and the Scottish Enlightenment prevailed. Veysey, *The Emergence of the American University*, 7–8, 44, 447.

87. David B. Tyack, *George Ticknor and the Boston Brahmins* (Cambridge, MA: Harvard University Press, 1967); cited in Diehl, *Americans and German Scholarship*, 73.

88. For Follen's aspirations to found a German university (and German republic) in America, see Edmund Spevak, *Charles Follen's Search for Nationality and Freedom in Germany and America, 1795–1840* (Cambridge, MA: Harvard University Press, 1997), 119. See also George Spindler, *The Life of Karl Follen: A Study in German-American Cultural Relations* (Chicago: University of Chicago Press, 1917), 76.

89. Charles F. Thwing, *The American and the German University: One Hundred Years of History* (New York: Macmillan, 1928), 258.

90. M. A. DeWolfe Howe, *The Life and Letters of George Bancroft* (New York: Charles Scribner's Sons, 1908), 1:67.

91. Some like Bancroft concluded that "we can do nothing at Cambridge till we contrive the means of having the boys sent to us far better fitted than they are now," and set off to reform secondary education. Thwing, *The American and the German University*, 263–64.

92. For the "German craze," see Henry A. Pochmann, *German Culture in America: Philosophical and Literary Influences 1600–1900* (Madison: University of Wisconsin Press, 1957), 114. On the interest among Americans in Friedrich Fröbel's Kindergarten, see Daniel Fallon, "German Influences on American Education," in *The German-American Encounter: Conflict and Cooperation between Two Cultures, 1800–2000*, ed. Frank Trommler and Elliott Shore (New York: Berghahn, 2001), 79–81; on the diplomatic uses of high culture and, specifically, music, see Jessica Gienow-Hecht, *Sound Diplomacy: Music and Emotions in Trans-atlantic Relations, 1850–1920* (Chicago: University of Chicago Press, 2009), esp. 30–39; on Americans' interest in the common schools movement, as understood through Cousin, see Herbst, *And Sadly Teach*, esp. 39–50. For a discussion of these exchanges in the context of globalization and the challenge of separating the "intellectual and material," see David Blackbourn, "Germany and the Birth of the Modern World," *German Historical Institute Bulletin* 51 (Autumn 2012): 9–21, esp. 12.

93. Cited in Richard Hofstadter, *Anti-intellectualism in American Life* (New York: Knopf, 1963), 239. On the Yale debate between classicists and utilitarians, see Mattingly, *American Academic Cultures*, 70–75.

94. The facsimile of the original 1894 cookbook advertises Liebig Company's Extract of Meat. Justus von Liebig, *Liebig Company's Practical Cookery Book* (East Sussex, UK: Southover Press, 1999). For the quotation, see R. Steven Turner, "Justus Liebig versus Prussian Chemistry: Reflections on Early Institute-Building in Germany," *His-*

torical Studies in the Physical Sciences 13 (1982): 129–162, quotation on 130. On Liebig's tireless promotion, see Regine Zott, "The Development of Science and Scientific Communication: Justus Liebig's Two Famous Publications of 1840," *Ambix* 40 (1993): 1–10.

95. Mark R. Finlay, "The German Agricultural Experiment Stations and the Beginning of American Agricultural Research," *Agricultural History* 62 (1988): 41–50; Frank Uekötter, "Why Care about Dirt? Transatlantic Perspectives on the History of Agriculture," *GHI Bulletin* 39 (2006): 66.

96. Sheehan, *German History*, 802.

97. Victor Roy Wilbee, "The Religious Dimensions of Three Presidencies" (PhD diss., University of Michigan, 1967), 81; also cited in George M. Marsden, *The Soul of the American University: From Protestant Establishment to Established Nonbelief* (New York: Oxford University Press, 1994), 103.

98. Though it had roots dating back to 1817, the University of Michigan entered a new phase in 1850 when the state rewrote its constitution, created a Board of Regents, and established an office of the university president of which Tappan was the first inhabitant.

99. Henry P. Tappan, *Report to the Board of Regents of the University of Michigan Made November 15th, 1853* (Ann Arbor: Cole & Gardner, 1853), 3.

100. Tappan, *Report to the Board of Regents*, 15, 17.

101. Tappan, 28.

102. Henry P. Tappan, *The University: Its Constitution and Its Relations, Political and Religious* (Ann Arbor: McCaracken, 1858), 32–33.

103. Margaret Cool Root, "Tappan, Bismarck, and the Bitter Connection: Reflections on Men and Their Dogs in the Artful Memory," *Rackham Reports*, 1986–1987, 17–46, here 37.

104. Tappan, *Report to the Board of Regents*, 20; also cited in Marsden, *The Soul of the American University*, 110.

105. Ironically, as Marsden shows, future leaders would oppose sectarianism in the name of Christianity. Marsden, *The Soul of the American University*, 113. See also Willbee, "The Religious Dimensions of Three Presidencies," 59; and Ingrassia, "From the New World to the Old," 685.

106. The Illinois legislature proposed the idea to Congress in 1853, asking that each state get $500,000 worth of public land for this purpose. Michigan and Vermont also experimented with the idea before the Morrill Act itself was passed. Allan Nevins, *The Origins of the Land-Grant Colleges and State Universities* (Washington, DC: Civil War Centennial Commission, 1962), 6–21.

107. Hoffer shows how the Civil War developments in interstate commerce, agriculture, law, and education, often heralded as the beginning of a new age, emerged only through contested debate about whether the government expansion should include sponsorship, supervision, or standardization. Hoffer, *To Enlarge the Machinery of Government*, esp. 90, 119, 197, 201.

108. Justin S. Morrill, "Speech of Hon. Justin S. Morrill, of Vermont, in the House of Representatives, June 6, 1862," in *Transactions of the New York State Agricultural Society with an Abstract of the Proceedings of the County Agricultural Societies*, 1862

(Albany: Comstock & Cassidy, 1863), 122–134, quotation on 122. Robert Lee and Tristan Ahtone have recently shown how 99 percent of that land or approximately 10.7 million acres was expropriated from indigenous peoples across twenty-four states, casting a shadow over the legitimacy of this enterprise. "Land Grab Universities," *High Country News*, March 30, 2020, online at https://www.hcn.org/issues/52.4/indigenous-affairs-education-land-grab-universities.

109. See, for example, Andrew Zimmerman, "From the Rhine to Mississippi: Property, Democracy, and Socialism in the American Civil War," *Journal of the Civil War Era* 5 (2015): 3–37.

110. Morrill, "Speech of Hon. Justin S. Morrill, of Vermont, in the House of Representatives, June 6, 1862," 123.

111. Coy F. Cross II, *Justin Smith Morrill* (East Lansing: Michigan State University Press, 1999), esp. 77–89.

112. Hoffer, *To Enlarge the Machinery of Government*, 15–17, quotation on 34.

113. Craig LaMay, "Justin Smith Morrill and the Politics and Legacy of the Land-Grant College Acts," in *A Digital Gift to the Nation: Fulfilling the Promise of the Digital and Internet Age*, ed. Lawrence K. Grossman and Newton N. Minow (New York: Century Foundation Press, 2001), 73–94, esp. 74.

114. Hoffer, *To Enlarge the Machinery of Government*, 45–47.

115. Scott Gelber, *The University and the People: Envisioning American Higher Education in an Era of Populist Protest* (Madison: University of Wisconsin Press, 2011), 13; Morrill, "Agricultural Colleges," 2.

116. Morrill, "Speech of Hon. Justin S. Morrill, of Vermont, in the House of Representatives, June 6, 1862," 131.

117. "An Act donating Public Lands to the several States and Territories which may provide Colleges for the Benefit of Agriculture and the Mechanic Arts," sec. 4, chap. 130.

118. The national common schools movement, often overlapping with the land-grant movement, followed a similar disorganized path, though its systematizers, as David Tyack has argued, were ultimately successful at bringing order to it. Tyack, *The One Best System: A History of American Urban Education* (Cambridge, MA: Harvard University Press, 1974). In contrast, however, their signature legislation, the Blair Bill, which would have provided federal common schooling, including for African Americans, permitted less autonomy locally, and repeatedly failed to pass. Daniel W. Crofts, "The Black Response to the Blair Education Bill," *Journal of Southern History* 37 (1971): 41–65, here 44. It is worth noting that those American common school reformers like Henry Barnard, who wanted a broad federal role in centralizing schools, were deeply influenced by European systems. Hoffer, *To Enlarge the Machinery of Government*, 91.

119. These African American institutions in the South included Alcorn University, established in 1871 in Mississippi; Hampton Normal and Agricultural Institute, in Virginia in 1872; Claflin College, in South Carolina in 1872; and Kentucky State Industrial School, which did not use its funds from the first Morrill Act until 1897. To address the racial disparity of the first Morrill Act, the Morrill Act of 1890 established another thirteen black colleges leading to the seventeen that were designated as land-grant

historically black colleges and universities (HBCUs) in 1965. Erskine Walther, *Some Readings on Historically Black Colleges and Universities* (Greensboro, NC: Management Information and Research, 1994), 15–17. There were many more private HBCUs founded before and after. As of the early twenty-first century there were over one hundred of them. See http://www.thehundred-seven.org/hbculist.html. The history of HBCUs is instructive, since one of the main reasons that the Blair Bill never passed was likely Southerners' desire to maintain segregation. Hilary Green, *Educational Reconstruction: African American Schools in the Urban South, 1865–1890* (New York: Fordham University Press, 2016), 185–200.

120. James Burrill Angell, "Inaugural Address," University of Michigan, June 28, 1871, in *Selected Addresses* (London: Longmans, Green, 1912), 5.

121. James Burrill Angell, "University of Missouri, June 4, 1895," in *Selected Addresses*, 124.

122. James Turner and Paul Bernard, "The German Model and the Graduate School," in *The American College in the Nineteenth Century*, ed. Roger L. Geiger (Nashville: Vanderbilt University Press, 2000), 221–241, here 241.

123. Edwin E. Slosson, *Great American Universities* (New York: Macmillan, 1910), 195.

124. James Gray, *The University of Minnesota, 1851–1951* (Minneapolis: University of Minnesota Press, 1951), 62–75.

125. Frank E. Stephens, *A History of the University of Missouri* (Columbia: University of Missouri Press, 1962), 194–216.

126. Geiger, *The History of American Higher Education*, 295.

127. Tappan, *Report to the Board of Regents*, 24.

128. Clark Kerr, "The American Mixture of Higher Education in Perspective: Four Dimensions," *Higher Education* 19 (1990): 1–19. Though Kerr did recognize elsewhere how the Morrill Act, at least in part, adapted the German university model. Kerr, *The Great Transformation in Higher Education*, 260.

129. The literature on the German *Sonderweg* (special path) and American exceptionalism, both of which emerged in the post–World War II era, is too vast to address here. For a helpful discussion on the insularity of comparisons of exceptionalist histories, see Peter Bergmann, "American Exceptionalism and German 'Sonderweg' in Tandem," *International History Review* 23 (2001): 505–534.

130. Christopher Jencks and David Riesman, *The Academic Revolution* (Garden City, NY: Doubleday, 1968), 157.

131. Zachary Callen argues that with respect to railroads this decentralization led to an "inconsistent and incomplete" system that "underscores the problem of relying on local actors to foster national capacity" and contrasted with what occurred at the same time in Great Britain and Europe. Callen, *Railroads and American Political Development: Infrastructure, Federalism, and State Building* (Lawrence: University Press of Kansas, 2016), 113.

132. Heinz-Dieter Meyer offers the helpful moniker of centralizers and localizers in his analysis of the "design" of the university. Meyer, *The Design of the University: German, American, and World Class*, Routledge Research in Higher Education (New York: Routledge, 2017), 88.

133. Terry Shinn estimates that regional entrepreneurs at the Science Faculty of Lyon raised 5 million francs in private funds from 1885 to 1900 while the Science Faculty of Toulouse received 3.5 million francs to support these goals. Shinn, "The French Science Faculty System, 1808–1914: Institutional Change and Research Potential in Mathematics and the Physical Sciences," *Historical Studies in the Physical Sciences* 10 (1979): 271–323, here 310–312. As Paul observes, competition existed in Paris between provincial universities and Paris if only to "shine brightly enough to be called to Paris." Paul, "The Issue of Decline in Nineteenth-Century French Science," *French Historical Studies* 7 (1972): 416–450, esp. 416–417, 445.

134. On centralization as a factor, see Joseph Ben-David, "The Rise and Decline of France as a Scientific Centre," *Minerva* 8 (1970): 160–179; and Ben-David and Zlockower, "Universities and Academic Systems in Modern Societies," 77. Anderson says that such features as religion and politics were as important as any in shaping these systems differently. Anderson, *European Universities from the Enlightenment to 1914*, 51, 63–64. Roger L. Geiger sees the roots of the challenge to reforming the French system in the Second Empire, when tensions between professionalism and classical humanism were never resolved. Geiger, "Prelude to Reform: The French Faculties of Letters in the 1860s," in *The Making of Frenchmen: Current Directions in the History of Education in France, 1679–1979*, ed. Donald Baker and Patrick Harrigan (Waterloo, ON: Historical Reflections Press, 1980), 337–361, esp. 360.

135. This sharper comment appears to have been omitted from the later edition of this work by Matthew Arnold: *Schools and Universities on the Continent* (London: Macmillan, 1868), 232.

136. Ingrassia, "From the New World to the Old," 671–672, 693.

137. Henry P. Tappan, *A Step from the New World to the Old and Back Again: With Thoughts on the Good and Evil in Both* (New York: D. Appleton, 1852), 2:64–65.

138. Sorkin argues that Humboldt viewed the Athenians, who sacrificed democratic politics for cultural greatness, as having made this trade-off. Humboldt himself hoped for the eventual dissolution of the state, but that was in the end unrealistic. Sorkin, "Wilhelm von Humboldt," 62, 72; see also Wilhelm to Caroline, March 4, 1809, in Sydow, *Wilhelm und Caroline*, 3:106.

139. To a certain degree the Morrill Act was the denouement of a debate of more than a century about the appropriate relationship between the exchange of goods and the exchange of ideas. See Adam Nelson's forthcoming book, *Capital of Mind: American Colleges and the Making of a Modern Knowledge Economy, 1730–1860*.

140. Morrill, "Speech of Hon. Justin S. Morrill, of Vermont, in the House of Representatives, June 6, 1862," 123.

141. Daniel Coit Gilman, "Our National Schools of Science," *North American Review* 105 (1867): 496; on the Connecticut land grant, see Geiger, *The History of American Higher Education*, 286.

142. Daniel Coit Gilman, "Report on the National Schools of Science," in *Report of the Secretary of the Interior* (Washington, DC: Government Printing Office, 1872), esp. 10–11.

CHAPTER TWO

1. Gilman, "The Johns Hopkins University in Its Beginning," 3.

2. Robert W. Rydell, *All the World's a Fair: Visions of Empire at the American International Expositions, 1876–1916* (Chicago: University of Chicago Press, 1984), 11.

3. Friedrich Engels, preface to the second German edition (1892), *Conditions of the Working Class in England*, Marx and Engels Collected Works, vol. 27 (New York: International Publishers, 1975), 308; cited in Kees Gispen, *New Profession, Old Order: Engineers and German Society, 1815–1914* (Cambridge: Cambridge University Press, 1989), 117.

4. Gilman in a speech at the opening of the State Industrial School at Middletown in June 1870; cited in Fabian Franklin, *The Life of Daniel Coit Gilman* (New York: Dodd, Mead, 1910), 89.

5. Abraham Flexner, *Daniel Coit Gilman: Creator of the American Type of University* (New York: Harcourt Brace, 1946), 52.

6. See, for example, the speech Gilman delivered on the completion of the Nassau Library building at Princeton University in 1898. Gilman, "Books and Politics," in *The Launching of a University and Other Papers* (New York: Dodd, Mead, 1906), 195–219. See also his address at the opening of Sage Library of Cornell University, Ithaca, October 7, 1891. Gilman, "University Libraries," in *University Problems*, 237–261.

7. Cited in Flexner, *Daniel Coit Gilman*, 7.

8. Gilman, *The Launching of a University*, 4.

9. Gilman, "Proposed Plan for a Complete Organization of the School of Science" (1856), Yjb51 1 856 d, 26, Yale University Library, Manuscripts and Archives.

10. Gilman, "Proposed Plan," with the attached appendix, "Notes on Schools of Science in Europe"; see also his article "The Higher Special Schools," *American Journal of Education* 2 (1856): 93–102.

11. Gilman, "Proposed Plan," 31.

12. *First Annual Report of the Yale Sheffield School of Science* (New Haven, CT: Tuttle, Morehouse & Taylor, 1866), 15.

13. On Gilman's aptitude as an organizer rather than an instructor, see Flexner, *Daniel Coit Gilman*, 15.

14. Gilman, "Our National Schools of Science," 500.

15. Geiger, *The History of American Higher Education*, 307.

16. Gilman, "Our National Schools of Science," 514.

17. Gilman, 515.

18. Gilman, "Hand-craft and Rede-craft—a Plea for the First Named," in *The Launching of a University*, 281–293, quotation on 282.

19. Gilman, "The Sheffield Scientific School of Yale University New Haven," in *University Problems*, 139.

20. Gilman declined offers from the University of Wisconsin in 1867 and the University of California in 1870 before accepting the latter in 1872. Flexner, *Daniel Coit Gilman*, 21.

21. Gilman, "The University of California in Its Infancy," in *University Problems*, 157.

22. Cited in Verne A. Stadtman, *The University of California, 1868–1968* (New York: McGraw Hill, 1970), 79. For more on the rise of California's State Grangers in the later 1860s, Henry George, and their clash with Gilman, see John Aubrey Douglass, *The California Idea and American Higher Education: 1850 to the 1960 Master Plan* (Stanford, CA: Stanford University Press, 2000), 48–55.

23. In fact, Cornell's compulsory coeducation would be precisely such a case. See Barbara Miller Solomon, *In the Company of Women: A History of Women and Higher Education in America* (New Haven, CT: Yale University Press, 1985), 52.

24. According to Hugh Hawkins, Gilman was not as close to Eliot as to White, though he respected the former's "stature" and often mediated between Eliot and his Harvard faculty opponents. Hawkins, "Charles W. Eliot, Daniel C. Gilman and the Nurture of American Scholarship," *New England Quarterly* 39 (1966): 291–308, esp. 299.

25. Eliot to Gilman, October 21, 1873; in Franklin, *The Life of Daniel Coit Gilman*, 356.

26. The philanthropist founder has become the object of reconsideration by Johns Hopkins since it was discovered that the legend of his abolitionism was unfounded. Remarkably Hopkins would stipulate that the hospital he endowed had to serve both blacks and whites (albeit in a segregated setting), a vision that Martha S. Jones suggests also requires further research. See Jones, "Johns Hopkins and Slaveholding: Preliminary Findings," December 8, 2020, 8, at http://hardhistory.jhu.edu. See also "The Racial Record of Johns Hopkins University," *Journal of Blacks in Higher Education* 25 (Autumn 1999): 42.

27. The pioneering American philanthropist George Peabody, who endowed the Peabody Institute in 1857, may have influenced Hopkins. The institute and the Johns Hopkins University would have four trustees in common. Hugh Hawkins, *Pioneer: A History of the Johns Hopkins University, 1874–1889* (Ithaca: Cornell, 1960), 4. The corporation of the university was founded in 1867 as the "Johns Hopkins University of the Promotion of Education in the State of Maryland." John Thomas Scharf, *History of Baltimore City and County, From the Earliest Period to the Present* (Philadelphia: L.H. Everts, 1881), 231. See also Gilman, *The Launching of a University*, 27.

28. Daniel Coit Gilman, "The Johns Hopkins University," *Johns Hopkins University Studies in Historical and Political Science* 9 (1891): 39–73, esp. 39–42.

29. Ira Remsen and The Johns Hopkins University, *Celebration of the Twenty-Fifth Anniversary of the Founding of the University, and Inauguration of Ira Remsen, L.L.D., as Present of the University* (Baltimore: Johns Hopkins University Press, 1902), 16.

30. John French, *History of the University Founded by Johns Hopkins* (Baltimore: Johns Hopkins University Press, 1946), 20–24; for the quotation, see Hugh Hawkins, "George William Brown and His Influence on The Johns Hopkins University," *Maryland Historical Magazine* 52 (1957): 173–186.

31. Remarks of President Angell, of the University of Michigan, before the Board of Trustees of the Johns Hopkins University, Baltimore, July 3, 1874, RG 01.001, Series 4, Box 2, p. 11, University Archives, Sheridan Libraries, Johns Hopkins University (hereafter JHU). For Andrew Dickson White and Charles Eliot's remarks, see RG 01.001, Series 4, Box 3, pp. 2 and 43, respectively.

32. Cited in Franklin, *The Life of Daniel Coit Gilman*, 184.

33. Hawkins, *Pioneer*, 3.

34. Reverdy Johnson Jr. to Gilman, October 23, 1874; Gilman to Johnson, November 10, 1874; in Franklin, *The Life of Daniel Coit Gilman*, 184 and 186. Abbot Lawrence's gift to Harvard thirty years earlier was the largest of its kind in its day and amounted to $50,000. Gilman, *University Problems*, 3–4.

35. Cited in French, *History of the University Founded by Johns Hopkins*, 6–7.

36. Gilman, *The Launching of a University*, 12.

37. Franklin, *The Life of Daniel Coit Gilman*, 195; *The Nation: A Weekly Journal Devoted to Politics, Literature, Science, and Art*, January 28, 1875, 60.

38. Gilman, *The Launching of a University*, 6.

39. Cited in Franklin, *The Life of Daniel Coit Gilman*, 188–189.

40. Hawkins, *Pioneer*, 5.

41. Remarks of President Angell, of the University of Michigan, before the Board of Trustees of the Johns Hopkins University, Baltimore, July 3, 1874, RG 01.001, Series 4, Box 2, p. 11, JHU.

42. *The Nation: A Weekly Journal Devoted to Politics, Literature, Science, and Art*, January 28, 1875, 60.

43. Cited in Franklin, *The Life of Daniel Coit Gilman*, 189.

44. See, for example, articles in the *Baltimore American*, December 29, 1874, 1; December 30, 1874, 1; February 2, 1875, 4; March 6, 1875, 2; May 3, 1875, 2; May 12, 1875, 4; May 13, 1875, 4; May 18, 1875, 4; May 20, 1875, 4; June 15, 1875, 2.

45. Edwin Spencer, "Should Universities Be Provincial?," *Southern Magazine* 16 (1875): 71–86, esp. 71–72. On the difference between his publication and his private correspondence with Gilman, see Hawkins, *Pioneer*, 23–24.

46. See Reverdy Johnson Jr. to Gilman, March 8, 1875; cited in Hawkins, *Pioneer*, 23.

47. Gilman to George Brush, January 28, 1875; cited in Franklin, *The Life of Daniel Coit Gilman*, 191. This letter appears to have been in Franklin's private papers and did not survive.

48. Hawkins, *Pioneer*, 4; "The Racial Record of Johns Hopkins University," 42.

49. Gilman to George Brush, January 30, 1875; cited in Franklin, *The Life of Daniel Coit Gilman*, 191–192. Harvard annual professor salaries were raised from $2,400 to $4,000 in 1868–1869 and held steady (albeit not without complaints) throughout the 1870s. See, for example, *Forty-Eighth Annual Report of the President of Harvard College, 1872–1873*, Reports of the President and Treasurer of Harvard College (Cambridge, MA: University Press, 1874), 17.

50. Gilman, *The Launching of a University*, 48; Flexner repeats this story in his own account of Gilman and indeed heeded this same advice. Flexner, *Daniel Coit Gilman*, 59–60.

51. Gilman's strategy in acquiring professors was laid out in his notes to the board, "On the Selection of Professors," read to the trustees, and taken down by copyist from dictation; MS 137, Box 5, Folder 17, p. 2, JHU. See also Gilman, *The Launching of a University* 12–22, 47–85. This story is recounted in a number of other places including Franklin, *The Life of Daniel Coit Gilman*, 196–218.

52. "On the Selection of Professors," 12. Even in these early recruiting attempts, Gil-

man faced challenges and often had to resign himself to accepting his second choice. See Hawkins, *Pioneer*, 39–50; on his UK trip, see Franklin, *The Life of Daniel Coit Gilman*, 202, 205.

53. Gilman to Brush, January 28, 1875. On the differences in the usage of "seminar," see Senn, "Where Is Althoff?," 248n80.

54. Christian Fleck, *A Transatlantic History of the Social Sciences: Robber Barons, the Third Reich, and the Invention of Empirical Social Research* (London: Bloomsbury, 2011), 21.

55. Veysey, *The Emergence of the American University*, 157–158.

56. Cited in Franklin, *The Life of Daniel Coit Gilman*, 224.

57. Paul Venable Turner, *Campus: An American Planning Tradition* (Cambridge, MA: MIT Press, 1984), 3–4, 163.

58. James Morgan Hart, *German Universities: A Narrative of Personal Experience* (New York: G.P. Putnam's Sons, 1874), 9–10.

59. On the speculation fueled by the railroad industry, see Hannah Catherine, *Transatlantic Speculations: Globalization and the Panics of 1873* (New York: Columbia University Press, 2018), 51. As we will see in chapter 4, Martha Carey Thomas would take advantage of the plummeting of B&O Railroad stock in the 1890s to negotiate the acceptance of women to Johns Hopkins Medical School in exchange for a large benefaction.

60. Gilman, "The Johns Hopkins University in Its Beginning," 6, 12.

61. Gilman, "The Utility of Universities: An Anniversary Discourse," Johns Hopkins University, February 22, 1885, in *University Problems in the United States*, 72–73.

62. Gilman, "The Utility of Universities," 55, 74.

63. Marsden, *The Soul of the American University*, 150. See also D. G. Hart, "Faith and Learning in the Age of the University: The Academic Ministry of Daniel Coit Gilman," in *The Secularization of the Academy*, ed. George Marsden and Bradley Longfield (New York: Oxford University Press, 1992), 107–145, esp. 114.

64. Cited in Franklin, *The Life of Daniel Coit Gilman*, 221.

65. Karen Hunger Parshall, *James Joseph Sylvester: Jewish Mathematician in a Victorian World* (Baltimore: Johns Hopkins University Press, 2006). On Sylvester's four months in Richmond in 1841, see R. C. Yates, "Sylvester at the University of Virginia," *American Mathematical Monthly* 44, no. 4 (1937): 194–201, esp. 197. See also Bruce, *History of the University of Virginia*, 3:73–77.

66. See the op-eds on Gilman and the university by the young Zionist Jewish thinker Henrietta Szold, who would later found Hadassah: "Baltimore Letter," *Jewish Messenger*, October 29, 1880, 5; "The Johns Hopkins University of Baltimore," *Education: An International Magazine Bimonthly*, 1883, 544. For a discussion of how students gathered at the home of her father, Rabbi Benjamin Szold, see Lewis Feuer "The Stages in the Social History of Jewish Professors in American Colleges and Universities," *American Jewish History* 71 (1982): 433.

67. Gilman may have been swayed by Angell and Eliot, both of whom expressed opposition to coeducation in their remarks to the board. The admission of women to Hopkins was first discussed and decided against in 1877. See the Minutes of the Board of Trustees, p. 76, JHU. For the exception that proves the rule regarding race, see the story of Kelly

Miller, son of a free man from Virginia and a slave woman who attended Hopkins for two years, as unearthed by archivist Julia Boublitz Morgan, "Son of a Slave," *Johns Hopkins Magazine* 32 (1981): 20–26. The year after Miller entered Hopkins the trustees raised the price of admission. "The Racial Record of Johns Hopkins University," 42–43.

68. Franklin, *The Life of Daniel Coit Gilman*, 225–226.

69. Americans enthusiastic about the German university ideal, like Herbert Baxter Adams, who read about the new program while studying in Heidelberg, rushed to apply and would go on to help turn Hopkins into a major site for historical research. See Adams's letter to Gilman, April 16, 1876; in *Johns Hopkins University Studies in Historical and Political Science* 56 (1938): 27. According to Hawkins, the fellowship system was the crucial ingredient that assured Hopkins's success. Hawkins, *Pioneer*, 81–82.

70. Gilman, "The Johns Hopkins University in Its Beginning," 11.

71. Josiah Royce, "Present Ideals of American University Life," *Scribner's Magazine* 10 (1891): 376–388, here 383. Almost all of Hopkins's fifty-three founding faculty professors had studied in Germany, and thirteen had been awarded PhDs, four of them from Göttingen. Thwing, *The American and the German University*, 43.

72. Franklin, *The Life of Daniel Coit Gilman*, 230.

73. Karen Hunger Parshall and David E. Rowe, *The Emergence of the American Mathematical Research Community, 1876–1900: J. J. Sylvester, Felix Klein, and E. H. Moore*, History of Mathematics 8 (Providence: American Mathematical Society, 1994), 412.

74. Gilman anticipated something like the Yuasa phenomenon, named for the Japanese scholar Mitsutomo Yuasa, who traced how a country moved to the center of scientific productivity when "the percentage of scientific achievements of a country exceed[ed] 25% of that in the entire world in the same period." Yuasa, "The Shifting Center of Scientific Activity in the West: From the 16th to the 20th Century," in *Science and Society in Modern Japan: Selected Historical Sources*, ed. Shigeru Nakayama, David L. Swain, and Yagi Eri (Tokyo: University of Tokyo Press, 1974), 81.

75. On Cambridge's protracted repeal of the Test Act, see John Forrester and Laura Cameron, *Freud in Cambridge* (Cambridge: Cambridge University Press, 2017), 4, 205, 215–217, 225. Thank you to Maud Ellmann for this reference.

76. Cited in Hawkins, *Pioneer*, 45.

77. Cited in Francis C. Moon, *The Machines of Leonardo da Vinci and Franz Reuleaux: Kinematics of Machines* (Dordrecht: Springer, 2007), 279.

78. Cited in Rydell, *All the World's a Fair*, 16.

79. United States Centennial Commission, *International Exhibition, 1876: Reports of the President, Secretary, and Executive Committee Together with the Journal of the Final Session of the Commission* (Philadelphia: J.B. Lippincott, 1879), 2:14. Also cited in Rydell, *All the World's a Fair*, 32.

80. Rydell, 21.

81. Franz Reuleaux, *Briefe aus Philadelphia* (Brunswick: Friedrich Vieweg und Sohn, 1877), 5–6 (my translation).

82. Reuleaux, vi, 4 (my translation). See also the useful discussion in Gispen, *New Profession, Old Order*, 115–116; and the helpful English excerpt in Franz Reuleaux's 1876 "Letters from Philadelphia," *Executive Intelligence Review*, 1997, 39–43.

83. Franz Reuleaux, *Franz Reuleaux und die deutsche Industrie auf der Weltaustellung in Philadelphia* (Leipzig: G. Hirth, 1876), 39–40. In particular, some said Reuleaux had given foreign governments an opportunity to advertise how bad German engineers were—an opportunity that the English gladly took. H. Heine, *Professor Reuleaux und die deutsche Industrie: Eine Skizze auf Grundlage amerikanischer sowie deutscher Beobachtungen und Erfahrungen* (Berlin: Polytechnische Buchhandlung A. Seydel, 1876), 4.

84. Gispen, *New Profession, Old Order*, 9–10. Panic and information during the depression also spread along transatlantic routes. Hannah Catherine Davies, *Transatlantic Speculations: Globalization and the Panics of 1873* (New York: Columbia University Press, 2018).

85. H. J. Braun and W. Weber, "Ingenieurwissenschaft und Gesellschaftspolitik: Das Wirken von Franz Realeaux," in *Wissenschaft und Gesellschaft: Beiträge zur Geschichte der Technischen Universität Berlin 1879-1979*, ed. Reinhard Rürup (Berlin: Springer, 1979), 1:285–300. See also Karl-Heinz Füssl, *Deutsch-amerikanischer Kulturaustausch im 20. Jahrhundert: Bildung, Wissenschaft, Politik* (Frankfurt: Campus, 2004), 56; and Hans Zopke, "Professor Franz Reuleaux," *Cassirer's Magazine*, 1896, 133–139. The transatlantic relationships facilitated by immigrant communities in America were a large part of the emergence of the specialist producers of the second industrial revolution. See Philip Scranton, *Endless Novelty: Specialty Production and American Industrialization, 1865-1925* (Princeton, NJ: Princeton University Press, 1997), 3, 22–23, 171. But according to Reuleaux, the German Americans had turned on the Germans and now believed America to be the future. Reuleaux, *Briefe aus Philadelphia*, 4.

86. Sooyoung Chang, *Academic Genealogy of Mathematicians* (Hackensack, NJ: World Scientific Publishing, 2010), 28.

87. For an overview of the significance of the Erlangen program for mathematics, see Jeremy J. Gray, "Klein and the Erlangen Programme," in *Sophie Lie and Felix Klein: The Erlangen Program and Its Impact in Mathematics and Physics*, ed. Lizhen Ji and Athanase Papadopoulos (Zurich: European Mathematical Society, 2015), 59–75.

88. Parshall and Rowe, *The Emergence of the American Mathematical Research Community*, 155, 170, 175, quotation on 176.

89. On the relationship between Klein and Poincaré, see David E. Rowe, *A Richer Picture of Mathematics: The Göttingen Tradition and Beyond* (Cham: Springer, 2018), 198; Chang, *Academic Genealogy of Mathematicians*, 28–29.

90. Regrettably in a previous publication I made the following errors that are corrected in this chapter: I stated that Klein attended the St. Louis World's Fair when in fact he attended the Chicago World's Fair; and I suggested that Klein had already made his name at Göttingen when in fact Gilman contacted him the year before Klein moved to Göttingen. I referred to Althoff as the "culture minister" when in fact he led the higher education section of the ministry, and I misspelled Seth Low's last name. Emily J. Levine, "Baltimore Teaches, Göttingen Learns," *American Historical Review* (June 2016): 780–823, here 780, 792, 796, 797, and 819. See the introduction, n. 9, for a discussion of Althoff's role in the Prussian Education Ministry.

91. Parshall and Rowe, *The Emergence of the American Mathematical Research Community*, 140–141.

92. Klein to Gilman, December 18, 1883, 22 L: 7 "Berufung nach Baltimore," Nachlass Klein (hereafter NL Klein), SUB Göttingen; cited and translated in Parshall and Rowe, *The Emergence of the American Mathematical Research Community*, 140.

93. Sophus Lie to Klein, January 1884, NL Klein.

94. Arthur Cayley to Felix Klein, January 25, 1884, Bl. 6–7; Daniel Gilman to Klein, January 12, 1884, Bl. 13–14, 22 L: 7 "Berufung nach Baltimore," NL Klein. Germany pioneered a number of social security measures in the 1870s and 1880s, including the provision of pensions for widows and orphans of university instructors. In addition to the benefits afforded to professors as civil servants by the German Civil Code of 1873, Gilman might also have been thinking of a special "widow-fund" that evidently existed at the University of Erlangen. See "Pensions of Widows and Orphans of University Professors," in *The Financial Status of the Professor in America and Germany*, Bulletin no. 2 (New York: Carnegie Foundation for the Advancement of Teaching, 1908), 91. Giving up this safety net was the concern of at least one other prominent German scholar whom Gilman tried to recruit: Karl Brugman. Gilman to Brugman, February 14, 1884, Bl. 11, 2c 1860: Gilman, Daniel Coit, Staatsbibliothek zu Berlin-Handschriftabteilung. On Althoff's involvement in bringing these benefits to universities and standardizing salaries, see vom Brocke, "Friedrich Althoff: A Great Figure," 281.

95. Paul Haupt to Felix Klein, January 4, 1884, 9/1–9/2, Bl. 17–18, NL Klein. Gilman said it was not worth it to them (i.e., economically) to extend him a shorter visit. Gilman to Felix Klein, August 1, 1884, Bl. 8, 22 L: 7 "Berufung nach Baltimore," NL Klein.

96. Paul Haupt to Felix Klein, January 4, 1884, 9/1–9/2, Bl. 17–18, 22 L:7 "Berufung nach Baltimore," NL Klein; cited in part in Parshall and Rowe, *The Emergence of the American Mathematical Research Community*, 141. The various correspondence about his decision is also discussed in Constance Reid, "The Road Not Taken: A Footnote in the History of Mathematics," *Mathematical Intelligencer* 1 (1978): 21–23.

97. Paul Haupt to Felix Klein, January 4, 1884, 9/1–9/2, Bl. 17–18; and William Edward Story to Felix Klein, January 10, 1884, Bl. 19–20, 22 L: 7 "Berufung nach Baltimore," NL Klein. For Sylvester, see Reid, "The Road Not Taken," 22.

98. Translated and cited in Reid, "The Road Not Taken," 22.

99. Quotation from the 1894 letter cited and translated in Reid, "The Road Not Taken," 23.

100. Renate Tobies, "The Development of Göttingen into the Prussian Centre of Mathematics and Exact Sciences," in *Göttingen and the Development of the Natural Sciences*, ed. N. Rupke (Göttingen: Wallstein, 2002), 116–142, here 123.

101. Tobies, "The Development of Göttingen into the Prussian Centre of Mathematics and Exact Sciences," 122.

102. According to Reid, when Klein was composing his autobiography in 1913, he noted in the margins "Great desire to go there," suggesting that he may have regretted his decision not to go to Baltimore. See Reid, "The Road Not Taken," 23.

103. On the popularization of Weber's term in English, see Senn, "Where is Althoff?,"

201. See also Bernhard vom Brocke, "Hochschul- und Wissenschaftspolitik in Preußen und im Deutschen Kaiserreich 1882–1907: Das 'System Althoff,'" in *Bildungspolitik in Preußen zur Zeit des Kaiserreichs*, ed. Peter Baumgart (Stuttgart: Klett-Cotta, 1980), esp. 37, 104, 107.

104. Quotation from the *Vossische Zeitung* (Berlin), October 19, 1918; translation and citation in vom Brocke, "Friedrich Althoff: A Great Figure," 269 and 289.

105. Althoff is among the few civil servants mentioned in Wilhelm II's memoirs. See William II, *The Kaiser's Memoirs*, trans. Thomas Russel Ybarra (New York: Harper & Brothers, 1922), 183. See also vom Brocke, "Friedrich Althoff: A Great Figure," 290. On the emperor's favoritism of Althoff, see Lamar Cecil, *Wilhelm II, Emperor and Exile, 1900–1941* (Chapel Hill: University of North Carolina Press, 1996) 2:56–60.

106. Burke, *A Social History of Knowledge*, 2:228; Ulrich von Wilamowitz-Moellendorff, *My Recollections, 1848–1914*, trans. G. C. Richards (London: Chatto & Windus, 1930), 300–303, quotation on 300.

107. According to Bernhard vom Brocke, Weber retold this story, adapted by Althoff from Ernst August, and often counted Tönnies, Simmel, and himself as professors who were outside Althoff's reach. Vom Brocke, "Preussische Hochschulpolitik im 19. und 20. Jahrhundert. Kaiserreich und Weimarer Republik," in *Die Universitäts Greifswald und die deutsche Hochschullandschaft im 19. und 20. Jahrhundert*, ed. Werner Buchholz (Stuttgart: Franz Steiner, 2004), 27–56, here 48.

108. Althoff honed his administrative skills at the University of Strasbourg, where he was dispatched in 1871 to transform this former French institution into a Prussian-style university. Vom Brocke, "Friedrich Althoff: A Great Figure," 277; Arnold Sachse, *Friedrich Althoff und sein Werk* (Berlin: E.S. Mittler, 1928), 72–75. On the tension between Althoff and the Alsatian professors, see Craig, *Scholarship and Nation Building*, 59, 9–94.

109. This was an advantageous strategy since the University of Göttingen was incorporated into the Prussian system in 1868 following the Austro-Prussian War. For the mutually beneficial and strategic relationship between Althoff and Klein, see Renate Tobies, "Zum Verhältnis von Felix Klein und Friedrich Althoff," in *Friedrich Althoff 1839–1908: Beiträge zum 58. Berliner Wissenschaftshistorischen Kolloquium 6. Juni 1989*, Kolloquium Heft 74 (East Berlin: Akademie der Wissenschaften der DDR, 1990), 35–56; vom Brocke, "Friedrich Althoff: A Great Figure" 283.

110. Althoff to Klein, December 12, 1893 1C, NL Klein; cited and translated in Tobies, "The Development of Göttingen into the Prussian Centre of Mathematics and Exact Sciences," 128.

111. Sachse, *Friedrich Althoff und sein Werk*, 77.

112. Reid Badger, *The Great American Fair: The World's Columbian Exposition & American Culture* (Chicago: Nelson Hall, 1979), 77–78.

113. Wilamowitz-Moellendorff, for his part, declined to travel to Chicago. Wilamowitz-Moellendorff, *My Recollections, 1848–1914*, 346, quotation on 284.

114. Karen Hunger Parshall and David E. Rowe, *The Emergence of the American Mathematical Research Community, 1876–1900: J. J. Sylvester, Felix Klein, and E. H. Moore* (Providence, RI: American Mathematical Society, 1994), 8:304–305, quotation on 305.

115. Klein letter to Bolza marked "confidential," draft, June 6, 1893, 8, NL Klein; cited in Parshall and Rowe, *The Emergence of the American Mathematical Research Community*, 306–307.

116. Klein, in *Weltausstellung in Chicago, 1893: Reichskommissar für die amtlicher Bericht über die Weltausstellung in Chicago 1893* (Berlin: Reichsdruckerei, 1894), ii:992–993 (my translation).

117. Klein to Althoff, October 11, 1893, *Amerikafahrt*, draft, 1C, Bl. 1–3, NL Klein; cited in part in Reinhard Siegmund-Schutze, "Felix Kleins Beziehungen zu den Vereinigten Staaten, Die Anfänge deutsche auswärtiger Wissenschaftspolitik und die Reform um 1900," *Sudhoffs Archiv* 81 (1997): 21–38, here 27.

118. Parshall and Rowe, *The Emergence of the American Mathematical Research Community*, 358.

119. Felix Klein, "Entwicklungsgang meiner Vorlesungen und Arbeiten" (1913), Bl. 4, 22 L: 3, NL Klein (my translation).

120. Tobies, "The Development of Göttingen into the Prussian Centre of Mathematics and Exact Sciences," 128.

121. Cited in Tobies, 129.

122. Felix Klein, "Göttinger Professoren: Lebensbilder aus eigener Hand. 4. Felix Klein (Autobiographie)," *Mitteilungen Universitätsbund Göttingen* 5:1 (1923): 26 (my translation).

123. On this second visit, about which there exists little archival material, see Siegmund-Schutze, "Felix Kleins Beziehungen zu den Vereinigten Staaten," 37; and Bruce Seely, "Research, Engineering, and Science in American Engineering Colleges: 1900–1960," *Technology and Culture* 34 (1993): 344–386. See also S. C. Prescott, *When M.I.T. was 'Boston Tech': 1861–1916* (Cambridge, MA: Technology Press, 1954). To avoid confusion I refer to MIT and CalTech by their contemporary names.

124. A lively debate exists among historians about the precise nature of influences on MIT. One historian argues that William Barton Rodgers's preoccupation with the École Central and Edinburgh provides an alternative to the German paradigm. A. J. Angulo, *William Barton Rodgers and the Idea of MIT* (Baltimore: Johns Hopkins University Press, 2009), xii.

125. On Klein's burgeoning interest in actuarial sciences, see his letters to the New York Mutual Fund in NL Klein.

126. The emperor even overrode the universities' objections. Karl-Heinz Manegold, *Universität, Technische Hochschule und Industrie: Ein Beitrag zur Emanzipation der Technik im 19. Jahrhundert unter besonderer Berücksichtigung der Bestrebungen Felix Kleins* (Berlin: Duncker & Humblot, 1970), 85, 245, 300–305. On Klein's influence, see Sachse, *Friedrich Althoff und sein Werk*, 303–304. According to Alan Beyerchen, who draws on Manegold, Klein and Althoff understood the "logic of momentum." Beyerchen, "On the Stimulation of Excellence in Wilhelmian Science," in *Another Germany: A Reconsideration of the Imperial Era*, ed. Jack R. Dukes and Joachim Remak (Boulder, CO: Westview Press, 1988), 139–168, here 152.

127. Parshall and Rowe, *The Emergence of the American Mathematical Research Community*, 147, quotation on 189.

128. This observation appears in a letter from Eliot to his mother in October of 1864 while he was touring Europe. Excerpted in Henry James, *Charles William Eliot: President of Harvard University, 1869–1909* (New York: AMS Press, 1973), 1:136–137. Under Eliot's epochal presidency, which lasted from 1869 to 1909, Harvard introduced a Summer School (1871), and opened the Arnold Arboretum (1872) and Radcliffe College (1879), but Eliot remained skeptical of the graduate school.

129. Gilman, "The Sheffield Scientific School of Yale University," 125.

130. Rogers, *Diffusion of Innovations*, 122, 148, 188, 216.

131. Frederic C. Howe, *The Phi Gamma Delta Quarterly* 13, no. 1 (1891): quotation on 109; Allen Kerr Bond, *When the Hopkins Came to Baltimore* (Baltimore: Pegasus Press, 1927), 41. On the student makeup in 1880 and public lecture series, see John Thomas Scharf, *History of Baltimore City and County, from the Earliest Period to the Present* (Philadelphia: L.H. Everts, 1881), 231–233.

132. Gilman, "The Dawn of a University," in *The Launching of a University*, 274.

133. Gilman, 275.

134. Gilman, 276.

135. Karen Hunger Parshall and David E. Rowe, "American Mathematics Comes of Age," in *A Century of Mathematics in America*, pt. 3, ed. Peter Larkin Duren, Richard Askey, Uta C. Merzbach, and Harold M. Edwards (Providence RI: American Mathematical Society, 1989), 3–28, here, 12–22.

136. Oskar Bolza to Felix Klein, May 15, 1892, 189, Bl. 26–31, 8, NL Klein.

137. Oskar Bolza to Felix Klein, January 15, 1889, 194/1–6, Bl. 39–44, 8, NL Klein; Chang, *Academic Genealogy of Mathematicians*, 434.

138. See the un-enumerated pamphlet by William A. Koelsch, "Incredible Day-Dream: Freud and Jung at Clark, 1909" (Friends of the Goddard Library, Clark University, 1984).

139. John W. Boyer, *The University of Chicago* (Chicago: University of Chicago Press, 2015), 131. For a genealogical treatment of the German motto for the seal of Stanford University, see President Gerhard Casper's "'Die Luft der Freiheit weht—On and Off,' On the Origins and History of the Stanford Motto," October 5, 1995, online at https://web.stanford.edu/dept/pres-provost/president/speeches/951005dieluft.html. Though Wilson had attended Hopkins he believed Princeton would thrive only by being distinctive, and that the graduate school should reflect the English tradition of a gentlemanly monastery. Veysey, *The Emergence of the American University*, 247; and James Axtell, *The Making of Princeton University: From Woodrow Wilson to the Present* (Princeton, NJ: Princeton University Press, 2006), esp. 293–294, 593–596.

140. According to Michael D. Gordin, German scientific achievement peaked in 1920 and was superseded by English in about 1925. Gordin, *Scientific Babel: How Science Was Done before and after Global English* (Chicago: University of Chicago Press, 2015), 6–7. Significantly, well into the early 1890s Klein's former American students counted on their German mentor to help get their scientific work published in German journals. See Henry Burchard Fine to Felix Klein, August 31, 1886, Bl. 27, 9: 27–31; William Edward Story to Felix Klein, March 26, 1892, 11: 1203; and Mary F. Winston to Felix Klein, November 28, 1896, 363/1, Bl. 46–47, 12:363, NL Klein.

141. Cited in German in Laitko, "'Weltbetrieb der Wissenschaft'," 80.

142. Albert Bernhardt Faust, *The German Element in the United States* (Boston: Houghton Mifflin, 1909), 2:229.

143. Reinhard Siegmund-Schultze, "Ein Bericht Felix Kleins aus dem Jahre 1902 über seine mathematischen Vorträge in den Vereinigten Staaten 1893 und 1896," *N.T.M.* 5 (1997): 245–252, here 248.

144. Siegmund-Schultze, 248 (my translation).

145. Rogers, *Diffusion of Innovations*, 273, 277, 281.

146. Slosson, *Great American Universities*, 376. In this respect, Gilman was extraordinary neither for the originality nor for the monopoly of his idea, as such scholars as Franklin have debated, but for the alacrity with which it spread through America. Franklin, *The Life of Daniel Coit Gilman*, 182.

147. Johann Peter Murmann argued that research at Hopkins in its early years, in particular in chemistry, was in fact driven by practical concerns, even as onlookers continued to praise it for its pure science. See Johann Peter Murmann, Louis Galambos, and Geoffrey Jones, *Knowledge and Competitive Advantage: The Coevolution of Firms, Technology, and National Institutions* (Cambridge: Cambridge University Press, 2009), 61. Thank you to Jason Owen-Smith for this reference.

148. This contract model complements the historical debate regarding Germany's winning combination in science. Alan Beyerchen argues that Germany's success lay precisely in its combination of pure and applied science, for which Klein was largely responsible. Beyerchen, "On the Stimulation of Excellence in Wilhelmian Science," in *Another Germany: A Reconsideration of the Imperial Era*, ed. Jack R Dukes and Joachim Remak (Boulder, CO: Westview Press, 1988), 139–168, esp. 152.

CHAPTER THREE

1. The quotation that serves as the chapter epigraph was recorded as Louis Pasteur's comments at the opening of the Pasteur Institute in Paris. Pasteur's words at the inauguration of the Pasteur Institute were actually the following: "Si la science n'a pas de patrie, l'homme de science doit an avoir une, et s'est à elle qu'il doit reporter l'influence que ses travaux peuvent avoir dans le monde." Louis Pasteur, "Inauguration de l'Institut Pasteur," *Annales de l'Institut Pasteur* 2 (1888): 29–30. But the citation by Pasteur was memorialized by Robert Merton in English as the basis for universalist scientific ethos and has been repeatedly drawn on since. See Robert K. Merton, "The Normative Structure of Science," (1942), in *The Sociology of Science: Theoretical and Empirical Investigations*, ed. Norman W. Storer (Chicago: University of Chicago Press, 1973), 272; Howard J. Rogers, "The History of the Congress," in *Congress of Arts and Science: Universal Exposition, St. Louis 1904; History of the Congress; Scientific Plan of the Congress; Philosophy and Mathematics*, ed. Howard. J. Rogers (Boston: Houghton Mifflin, 1905), 1:1.

2. On the early history of *Kulturpolitik*, see Jürgen Kloosterhuis, "Deutsche auswärtige Kulturpolitik und ihre Trägergruppen vor dem Ersten Weltkrieg," in *Deutsche auswärtige Kulturpolitik seit 1871: Geschichte und Struktur; Referate und Diskussionen eines*

interdisziplinären Symposions, ed. Wolfgang F. Dexheimer, Kurt Düwell, and Werner Link (Cologne: Böhlau, 1981), 7–45; and Rüdiger vom Bruch, *Weltpolitik als Kulturmission: Auswärtige Kulturpolitik und Bildungsbürgertum in Deutschland am Vorabend des Ersten Weltkrieges* (Paderborn: Ferdinand Schöningh, 1982).

3. A. W. Coats, "American Scholarship Comes of Age: The Louisiana Purchase Exposition 1904," *Journal of the History of Ideas* 22 (1961): 404–417.

4. See Benedict Anderson, *Imagined Communities: Reflections on the Origin and Spread of Nationalism*, rev. ed. (1983; London: Verso, 2016). The best work on the relationship between universities and colonization is Tamson Pietsch, *Empire of Scholars: Universities, Networks, and the British Academic World, 1850–1939* (Manchester: University of Manchester Press, 2013). Notwithstanding Pietsch's argument to view the empire not in terms of core and periphery but as a network of "inter-colonial influences," the relationship that developed between Oxbridge and these "settler" universities was one of mentor-supplicant. Pietsch, *Empire of Scholars*, 103, 110. The same can be said of the older Iberian countries and the missionary universities of the early colonial period. See Shils and Roberts, "The Diffusion of European Models outside Europe," 227.

5. Matthew P. Fitzpatrick, *Liberal Imperialism in Germany: Expansionism and Nationalism, 1848–1884* (New York: Berghahn Books, 2018); Jens-Uwe Guettel, *German Expansionism, Imperial Liberalism, and the United States, 1776–1945* (Cambridge: Cambridge University Press, 2012); and Andrew Zimmerman, *Alabama in Africa: Booker T. Washington, the German Empire, and the Globalization of the New South* (Princeton, NJ: Princeton University Press, 2010). These scholars persuasively show how ideas of empire and colonialism entered liberal progressive society in Germany and America through a robust transatlantic debate about expansion and race.

6. John Willinsky shows how education today still reflects the deleterious imperial legacy of modern Europe. Willinsky, *Learning to Divide the World: Education at Empire's End* (Minneapolis: University of Minnesota Press, 1998), 17. A number of scholars take the transatlantic conversation between German and American scholars in this period as a given but do not thematize the university itself as a mechanism for this exchange or examine how this cross-pollination occurred. This chapter explores the unique competitive dynamics of that exchange against the heightened political stakes of the competition for imperial dominance.

7. For an overview, see Thomas Adam, "American Students and German Universities," in *Germany and the Americas: Culture, Politics, and History*, ed. Thomas Adam (Santa Barbara: ABC-CLIO, 2005), 70. For Heidelberg, see Thomas Weber, *Our Friend "The Enemy": Elite Education in Britain and Germany before World War I* (Stanford, CA: Stanford University Press, 2007), 214.

8. Du Bois-Reymond, "Ansprache," 314 (my translation). According to Oscar Basler, Du Bois-Reymond's lecture was the first German definition of *Amerikanismus*, though Basler missed that the appeal went beyond scare tactics. Basler, "Amerikanismus: Geschichte des Schlagwortes," *Deutsche Rundschau* 214 (1930): 142–146.

9. Cited in Dietrich Stoltzenberg, *Fritz Haber: Chemiker, Nobelpreisträger, Deutscher, Jude* (Weinheim: Wiley, 1994), 80 (my translation).

10. Cited in Siegmund-Schultze, "Ein Bericht Felix Kleins aus dem Jahre 1902," 248 (my translation).

11. "Berlin Educational Institution Exclude Foreigners," *Scientific American* 78, no. 17 (April 23, 1898): 263. Also reported in *Science* 7, no. 174 (April 29, 1898): 603; see also Sandra L. Singer, who discusses this debate with respect to Russian female students in Berlin. Singer, *Adventures Abroad: North American Women at German-speaking Universities, 1868–1915* (Westport, CT: Praeger, 2003), 20.

12. Quotation on the "amerikanische Gefahr" in Stoltzenberg, *Fritz Haber*, 83; the German American historian Alfred Vagts also wrote of "die amerikanische Gefahr." Vagts, *Deutschland und die Vereinigten Staaten in der Weltpolitik* (New York: Macmillan, 1935), 1:345–425. For a discussion of this anxiety in the context of the buildup to World War I, see Frank Trommler, "Inventing the Enemy: German-American Cultural Relations, 1900–1917," in *Confrontation and Cooperation: Germany and the United States in the Era of World War I, 1900–1924*, ed. Hans-Jürgen Schröder (Providence: Berg, 1993), 99–125.

13. One such report from 1907 brought at least nineteen privately funded research institutions from Washington, DC to Paris to the attention of the Prussian Culture Ministry. VI. HA, A I Nr. 123, Bl. 233–236, NL Althoff. Published as Wilhelm Paszkoswki, *Die Akademische Auskunftsstelle an der Königlichen Friedrich-Wilhelms-Universitiät zu Berlin* (Berlin: Univ. Buchdr. G. Schade, 1907). See also Rudolf Vierhaus and Bernhard vom Brocke, eds., *Forschung im Spannungsfeld von Politik und Gesellschaft: Geschichte und Struktur der Kaiser-Wilhelm-/Max-Planck Gesellschaft aus Anlaß 75 jährigen Bestehens* (Stuttgart: Deutsche Verlags-Anstalt, 1990), 127. For the Althoff quotation, see vom Brocke, "Friedrich Althoff: A Great Figure," 286.

14. Adolf Harnack, "Future of Church History," *New York Independent*, April 11, 1889; cited in Elizabeth Clark, *Founding the Fathers: Early Church History and Protestant Professors in Nineteenth-Century America* (Philadelphia: University of Pennsylvania Press, 2011), 46.

15. Adolf von Harnack, *Die Mission und Ausbreitung des Christentums in den ersten drei Jahrhunderten* (Leipzig: Hinrichs, 1902); English translation: Harnack, *The Mission and Expansion of Christianity in the First Three Centuries*, ed. and trans. James Moffatt (London: William and Norgate, 1908). One could say he was diffusion theorist avant la lettre. For an explicit adaptation of this theory to religious conversion, see Richard Bulliet, *Conversion to Islam in the Medieval Period: An Essay in Quantitative History* (Cambridge, MA: Harvard University Press, 1979), esp. 27–32.

16. Brandl, "Persönliche Eindrücke von amerikanischen Universitäten," 121.

17. Eugen Kühnemann, "Eulogy of Althoff at Harvard," *Harvard Graduates' Magazine* 18 (1909–1910): 77–78, quotation on 77.

18. Hugo Münsterberg, "Twenty-Five Years: The First Chapter of an Unfinished Autobiography," *Century Illustrated Magazine* 94 (1917): 37.

19. Cited in Ulrich Wattenberg, "Germany 7–24 February 1873," in *The Iwakura Mission to America and Europe: A New Assessment*, ed. Ian Nish (Richmond, UK: Japan Library; Taylor and Francis ELibrary, 1998), 71–79. Shils and Roberts speculate that

Tanaka Fujimaro could have been canvassed on his trip by Germans who desired influence in Japan, though they did not do so for the Americans. Shils and Roberts, "The Diffusion of European Models outside Europe," 228.

20. Reform in 1881 and the founding of the Tokyo University in 1877, oriented as it was to the Western sciences, brought Japan further into line with Germany. The Meiji regime then hired dozens of foreign professors (*oyatoi*) to staff new universities, where they lectured in German. Scholars have attributed the success of the German-Japanese mentor-mentee relationship to the Japanese military victory in 1895 over China. Osterhammel, *The Transformation of the World*, 803–807; Gordin, *Scientific Babel*, 192; Philip G. Altbach, *Comparative Higher Education* (London: Mansell Publishing, 1979), 28; and Sebastian Conrad, *Globalisation and the Nation in Imperial Germany* (Cambridge: Cambridge University Press, 2010), 47.

21. Rodgers, *Atlantic Crossings*, 265–266, quotation on 265.

22. Thwing, *The American and the German University*, 103–104.

23. Julia Spillmann and Lothar Spillmann, "The Rise and Fall of Hugo Münsterberg," *Journal of the History of Behavioral Sciences* 29 (1993): 322–338.

24. Cited in Matthew Hale Jr., *Human Science and Social Order: Hugo Münsterberg and the Origins of Applied Psychology* (Philadelphia: Temple University Press, 1980), 23.

25. This is a significant distinction since in the highly tiered structure of the German university, which also included more lowly regular professors and regular associate professors, the *Ordinariat* comprised the most important committees, participated in the university senates, determined appointments, and formed the pool from which the administration was selected. I thus disagree with Hale, who argues that Münsterberg could have assumed he would eventually be promoted. Hale, *Human Science and Social Order*, 25. See Michael Grüttner's overview of this organizational structure in "German Universities under the Swastika," in *Universities under Dictatorship*, ed. John Connelly and Michael Grüttner (University Park: Penn State Press, 2005), 75–111, here 77.

26. Panofsky, cited in Emily J. Levine, *Dreamland of Humanists: Warburg, Cassirer, Panofsky, and the Hamburg School* (Chicago: University of Chicago Press, 2013), 182. For the statistics, see chapter 7, n. 15.

27. Hale, *Human Science and Social Order*, 45, 48.

28. Münsterberg, "Twenty-Five Years," 36.

29. Hugo Münsterberg, "Der Amerikaner: Eine Weltausstellungsbetrachtung," *Vossische Zeitung* (Berlin), August 3, 1893, 3; also discussed in Hale, *Human Science and Social Order*, 49.

30. William D. G. Balance, "Frustrations and Joys of Archival Research," *Journal of the History of the Behavioral Science* 11 (January 1975): 37–40.

31. Cited in Hale, *Human Science and Social Order*, 54–55.

32. James McKeen Cattell to Nicholas Murray Butler, June 22 1901, Nicholas Murray Butler Papers, Rare Book & Manuscript Library, Columbia University in the City of New York (hereafter RBMLC).

33. Vagts, *Deutschland und die Vereinigten Staaten in der Weltpolitik*, 2:1920–1921.

34. Hugo Münsterberg, "The Helmholtz Memorial," *Science*, n.s. 1 (17 May 1895): 547–48.

35. Münsterberg, "Twenty-Five Years," 38.

36. See "Prince Henry's Visit," *Harvard Graduates' Magazine* 10 (June 1902): 566–73; also Hale, *Human Science and Social Order*, 90.

37. James McKeen Cattell to Nicholas Murray Butler, January 11, 1902, Butler Papers, RBMLC.

38. Münsterberg, "Twenty-Five Years," 46.

39. Hale argues that Müsnterberg's self-presentation bares the signature stamp of self-sacrifice. Hale, *Human Science and Social Order*, 97–98.

40. Hugo Münsterberg, "The Germans and the Americans," *Atlantic Monthly* 84 (September 1899): 396–409.

41. Cited in Hale, *Human Science and Social Order*, x.

42. Paul Greenhalgh, *Ephemeral Vistas: The Expositions Universelles, Great Exhibitions, and World's Fairs, 1851–1939* (Manchester: Manchester University Press, 1988), 130.

43. According to Boyer, "Although the March convocation originated as an act of reverence by local faculty for *their* locally distinguished German *Ordinariat,* Harper turned it into an opportunity to elevate his young University such that other senior German *Ordinarius* professors would not only want to visit but also from which they would gladly receive honorary degrees." *The University of Chicago,* 142–143, 520n353, quotation on 144.

44. Hugo Münsterberg, Committee on the Plan and Scope for International Congress of Science and Art (New York, January 19, 1903), Box 26, MS Acc 1501-2500, Hugo Münsterberg Collection, Boston Public Library, Archives and Manuscripts (hereafter BPL).

45. Coats, "American Scholarship Comes of Age," 404–17. See also the articles by John Dewey and Hugo Münsterberg in *Science* in 1903; published in John Dewey, *The Middle Works, 1899–1924* (Carbondale: Southern Illinois University Press, 1980), 3:145–150, 151–152.

46. James McKeen Cattell to Nicholas Murray Butler, June 22, 1901, Butler Papers, RBMLC.

47. Albion Small to Hugo Münsterberg, February 11, 1903, Newcomb Papers, Library of Congress (hereafter LOC); also cited in Hans Rollman, "'Meet Me in St. Louis': Troeltsch and Weber in America," in *Weber's Protestant Ethic: Origins, Evidence, Context,* ed. Hartmut Lehmann and Guenther Roth (Cambridge: University of Cambridge Press, 1995), 362.

48. Margaret Müsnterberg, *Hugo Münsterberg: His Life and Work* (New York: D. Appleton, 1922), 105.

49. See both the official invitation to St. Louis and the confidential letter sent from Münsterberg to the European visitors to St. Louis, March 1904, D/5/2, Archivzentrum Frankfurt, Nachlass Max Fürbringer, UBF.

50. Martha Carey Thomas, "The College," in *Congress of Arts and Science: Universal Exposition, St. Louis 1904,* ed. Howard J. Rogers (Boston: Houghton Mifflin, 1905–1906), 8:133–150.

51. Weber, *Max Weber: A Biography,* 290.

52. Of 106 foreign speakers, 41 were German, compared with 21 English, and 17 French, even after Newcomb's concession to French demands. Hale, *Human Science and Social Order*, 97.

53. Rollman, "'Meet Me in St. Louis,'" 367, 376.

54. Troeltsch to Münsterberg, October 15, 1904, Hugo Münsterberg Collection, BPL; cited and translated in Rollman, "'Meet Me in St. Louis,'" 382.

55. Max Dessoir, "Zur Erinnerung an Hugo Münsterberg," in *Grundzüge der Psychotechnik* (Leipzig: Verlag von Johann Ambrosiüs Barth, 1918), xhi.

56. Wilhelm Ostwald, *Lebenslinien: Eine Selbstbiographie* (Berlin: Klasing, 1926), 2: 399.

57. Agnes von Zahn-Harnack, *Adolf von Harnack* (Berlin: Hans Bott Verlag, 1936), 381 (my translation).

58. A number of individuals including Münsterberg and Butler later took credit for the exchange. Friedrich Schmidt-Ott, *Erlebtes und Erstrebtes 1860–1950* (Wiesbaden: F. Steiner, 1952), 107.

59. Vom Brocke, "Friedrich Althoff: A Great Figure," 287.

60. A I Nr. 309 II, Bl. 2, 92, NL Althoff.

61. Hugo Münsterberg to Friedrich Schmidt-Ott, December 2, 1904, A I Nr. 309 I, Bl. 4–9, 92, NL Althoff.

62. For a history of the German-American professor exchange as a chapter in the history of international "cultural politics," see Bernhard vom Brocke, "Der deutsch-amerikanische Professorenaustausch: Preußische Wissenschaftspolitik, internationale Wissenschaftsbeziehungen und die Anfänge einer deutschen auswärtige Kulturpolitik vor dem Ersten Weltkrieg," *Zeitschrift für Kulturaustausch* 21 (1981): 128–182.

63. Arthur Twining Hadley, "The University of Berlin: President Hadley Relates His Impressions of German Student Life," *Yale Daily News* 119 (March 2, 1908): 1

64. Schmidt-Ott, *Erlebtes und Erstrebtes*, 107. For a more recent interpretation of "academic diplomacy" in the transatlantic context, see Thomas Adam and Charlotte A. Lerg, "Diplomacy on Campus: The Political Dimensions of Academic Exchange in the North Atlantic," *Journal of Transatlantic Studies* 13 (2015): 299–310; and the corresponding essays in that special issue. A number of essays in the *Educational Review* detail these exchanges. See, for example, J. H. Canfield, "America and Germany: An Academic Interchange," *Educational Review* 32 (December 1906): 679–682. So-called *Deutsche Häuser* were established at Harvard (1903), Columbia (1911), and the University of Pennsylvania (1912) in this period. Vom Brocke, "Friedrich Althoff: A Great Figure," 288.

65. Nicholas Murray Butler, *Across the Busy Years: Recollections and Reflections* (New York: C. Schribner's Sons, 1939), 2:65–74.

66. Albion Woodbury Small also noted the intense competition between Butler and Harper. Senn, "Where Is Althoff?," 241.

67. Laitko, "'Weltbetrieb der Wissenschaft,'" 68.

68. On regions and nationalism in German history see Maiken Umbach, "Introduction," *European Review of History/Revue européene d'histoire* 15 (2008): 235–242. On

the centrality of the local in the global turn, see Jeffry M. Diefendorf, "Introduction: Transnationalism and the German City," in *Transnationalism and the German City*, ed. Jeffry M. Diefendorf and Janet Ward (New York: Palgrave Macmillan, 2014), 2.

69. Karl Lamprecht, *Americana: Reiseeindrücke, Betrachtungen, geschichtliche Gesamtansicht* (Freiburg: Verlag von Hermann Heyfelder, 1906), 32; Trommler, "Inventing the Enemy: German-American Cultural Relations, 1900–1917," 113; on questions of nationalism and internationalism in Leipzig, see Glenn Penny's reading of the museum, whose promoters he calls "World provincials." Penny, "Fashioning Local Identities in an Age of Nation-Building: Museums, Cosmopolitan Visions, and Intra-German Competition," *German History* 17:4 (1999): 489–505, esp. 491–492.

70. For more on Lamprecht's failed mission to innovate the University of Leipzig on the American model, see Levine, "Baltimore Teaches, Göttingen Learns," 807–814. A number of other universities followed suit, including Strasbourg, Wisconsin, and Cornell. Bernhard vom Brocke, "Internationale Wissenschaftsbeziehungen und die Anfänge einer deutschen auswärtigen Kulturpolitik: Der Professorenaustausch mit Nordamerika," in *Wissenschaftsgeschichte und Wissenschaftspolitik im Industriezeitalter: Das "Althoff System" in historischer Perspektive*, ed. Bernhard vom Brocke (Hildesheim: August Lax, 1991), 185–242, esp. 210–215.

71. Friedrich Paulsen, *Autobiography*, trans. and ed. Theodor Lorenz (New York: Columbia University Press, 1938), 438.

72. "Prof Hoetzsch in Harvard: Der deutsche Gelehrte spricht über Kaiser Wilhelm II," *New Yorker Staats-Zeitung*, April 23, 1907, VI. HA, A I Nr. 310, Amerika 1904–1908–419, Bl. 34, NL Althoff.

73. Kuno Francke alluded to this British concern in "Das Kartell zwischen deutschen und amerikanischen Universitäten: In amerikanischer Beleuchtung," *Der Tag: Erster Teil; Illustrierte Zeitung*, May 7, 1905, A I Nr. 310, Amerika 1904–1908–419, Bl. 190, NL Althoff.

74. "American Students Encouraged in Paris, *New York Times*, May 19, 1902, 8.

75. Laitko, "'Weltbetrieb der Wissenschaft,'" 91.

76. Bernhard vom Brocke, "Im Großbetrieb der Wissenschaft: Adolf von Harnack als Wissenschaftsorganisator und Wissenschaftspolitiker—zwischen Preußischer Akademie und Kaiser-Wilhelm-Gesellschaft," *Sitzungsberichte der Leibniz-Sozietät* 45:2 (2001): 61–144, here 82.

77. *Betrieb* is usually translated as "enterprise" or "concern," but there is no exact equivalent in English for the holistic institutional activity implied. I follow William Clark here in his colloquial translation of this now classic statement from Harnack. See Clark, *Academic Charisma*, 468. For an informed discussion of how the concept of *Betrieb* became central to Weber's analysis of the capitalist state, see Joshua Derman, *Max Weber in Politics and Social Thought: From Charisma to Canonization* (Cambridge: Cambridge University Press, 2012), 104.

78. Adolf Harnack, "Vom Großbetrieb der Wissenschaft," *Preußische Jahrbücher* 2 (1905): 193–201, quotation on 196 (my translation).

79. Harnack had shared similar themes in a 1899 lecture, "Bericht über die Abfassung der 'Geschichte der Königlich Preussischen Akademie der Wissenschaften zu

Berlin.'" He was joined by Emil Fischer, the chemist, at the opening of his Chemistry Institute in 1900. Fischer, *Eröffnungsfeierdes neuen I. Chemischen Instituts der Universität Berlin am 14 Juli 1900* (Berlin: August Hirschwald, 1900), 46.

80. Laitko, "'Weltbetrieb der Wissenschaft,'" 44.

81. In fact, universities seem to have been uniquely poised to contribute to soft power, since, according to Joseph S. Nye's definition, the latter does not belong exclusively to the government in the same way that traditional power does. Nye, *Soft Power: The Means to Success in World Politics* (New York: Public Affairs, 2004), 11, 14. For a similar argument, see Gienow-Hecht, *Sound Diplomacy*, 8, 31.

82. "The Harvard Club Greets Big Men: President Hadley of Yale Meets with Marked Applause," *New York Times*, February 22, 1900, 1. As Daniel Immerwahr reminds us in his history of American imperialism, in Manila, which America held along with the Philippines from 1899 to 1946, there are streets named for US colleges. See Immerwahr, *How to Hide an Empire: A History of the Greater United States* (New York: Farrar, Straus and Giroux, 2019), 15. On Butler and his attempts to draw on the new field of anthropology to create a scientific institute based in Puerto Rico, see Jose Amador, *Medicine and Nation Building, 1890–1940* (Nashville: Vanderbilt University Press, 2015), 133–134.

83. Carl Schmitt would provide the Nazis with an interpretation of the Monroe Doctrine. For a history of these realist transatlanticisms, see Matthew Specter's forthcoming work, *The Atlantic Realists: Empire and International Political Thought between Germany and the United States* (Stanford, CA: Stanford University Press).

84. Dirk Bönker, *Militarism in a Global Age: Naval Ambitions in Germany and the United States before World War I* (Ithaca, NY: Cornell University Press, 2012), 256.

85. On Münsterberg's failed diplomacy, see Hale, *Human Science and Social Order*, 91.

86. Kühnemann, "Eulogy of Althoff at Harvard," 77.

87. John William Burgess, "Persönliche Erinnerungen an Friedrich Althoff," *Internationale Wochenschrift für Wissenschaft, Kultur und Technik* 3 (1909): 1337–1348; cited and translated in vom Brocke, "Friedrich Althoff: A Great Figure," 288; for similar observations, see also John William Burgess, *Reminiscences of an American Scholar: The Beginnings of Columbia University* (New York: Columbia University Press, 1934), 376.

88. Sachse, *Friedrich Althoff und sein Werk*, 309. On Althoff's lack of English skills, see Butler, *Across the Busy Years*, 70.

89. As we will see, Jewish philanthropists, like Koppel himself, would contribute disproportionately to the founding of the Kaiser Wilhelm Society as well.

90. Althoff wrote a letter on receipt of his honorary degree that was translated into English and published in the *Harvard Graduates' Magazine*. "Dr. Althoff to President Eliot," *Harvard Graduates' Magazine* 5 (1906–1907): 536–537; excerpted in Senn, "Where Is Althoff?," quotation on 257. Kühnemann understood the significance of the policy for German American immigrants and believed it was key to Althoff's interest. See Senn, "Where Is Althoff?," 258.

91. See, for example, Francis Greenwood Peabody, "An Academic Interlude," *Harvard Alumni Bulletin*, April 1935, 790.

92. Harnack, "Vom Großbetrieb der Wissenschaft," 193–201, quotation on 197 (my translation).

93. Münsterberg, *Aus deutsch Amerika* (Berlin: E.S. Mittler und Sohn, 1909), 21–22 (my translation).

94. Maximilian Harden, "Notizbuch," *Die Zukunft* 14 (1905): 192 (my translation). See also Reiner Pommerin, *Der Kaiser in Amerika: Die USA in der Politik der Reichsleitung, 1890–1917* (Cologne: Böhlau-Verlag, 1986), 278n732. According to Trommler, Harden thought the one saving grace of the emperor's gesture to the Americans was that it would strengthen the position of German Americans abroad. Trommler, "Inventing the Enemy," 113.

95. Alfred Schaper, "Persönliche Eindrücke und Erfahrungen," Rep. 92, A I Nr. 309 I, Bl. 196–233, NL Althoff; cited in Laitko, "'Weltbetrieb der Wissenschaft,'" 78 (my translation).

96. Althoff authorized report after report about the United States, but soon the situation seemed to be getting away from him. Exasperated, he noted in the margins of a letter from Butler, "I receive so many reports from America that I do not know where to turn." Handwritten note on Nicholas Murray Butler, October 13, 1905, A I Nr. 309 II, Bl. 85, 92, NL Althoff; cited in Laitko, "'Weltbetrieb der Wissenschaft,'" 43 (my translation). Althoff worriedly asked the director of the Botanical Institute in Germany to give him a list of former students in the United States. Laitko, 49.

97. Cited in Singer, *Adventures Abroad*, 20.

98. Cited in Hale, *Human Science and Social Order*, 165.

CHAPTER FOUR

1. The suffragist Lucy Stone was not the first woman to receive a BA in 1847 (as Solomon and others erroneously state), though she was the most famous. Solomon, *In the Company of Women*, 48. Subsequent research has uncovered earlier individual and institutional examples. For Catherine Brewer Benson, see Christie Anne Farnham, *The Education of the Southern Belle: Higher Education and Student Socialization in the Antebellum South* (New York: New York University Press, 1994), 184. Even though Oberlin is the "most frequently cited example of coeducation," David Bronson Potts argues "the Oberlin plan was more compromise than clarion call." Potts, *Wesleyan University, 1831–1910: Collegiate Enterprise in New England* (New Haven, CT: Yale University Press, 1992), 98.

2. Solomon, *In the Company of Women*, 51. On the "rise and fall of racially integrated education," see Christi Smith, *Repatriation and Reconciliation: The Rise and Fall of Integrated Higher Education* (Chapel Hill: University of North Carolina Press, 2016), 9. Lucy Stanton Day is typically cited as the first African American woman to receive a BA, but she appears to have only graduated from a women's course, without a degree. See Stephanie Y. Evans, *Black Women in the Ivory Tower, 1850–1954: An Intellectual History* (Gainesville: University of Florida Press, 2007), 22–24, 35.

3. For Angell's remarks, see RG 01.001, Series 4, Box 2, pp. 29–30, JHU. On the land grants in general, see Solomon, *In the Company of Women*, 44, 52–53, quotation on 52.

4. The term "coercive philanthropy" appears to have been coined by historian Margaret W. Rossiter, *Women Scientists in America: Struggles and Strategies to 1940* (Baltimore: Johns Hopkins University Press, 1982), 39.

5. For Eliot's remarks to Gilman, see RG 01.00, Series 4, Box 3, p. 49, JHU. He wasn't alone. Despite the philanthropist Joseph Bennet's donation in 1883 for women's education, the University of Pennsylvania did not matriculate women for another fifty years. Quotation from Eliot in Joan Marie Johnson, *Funding Feminism: Monied Women, Philanthropy, and the Women's Movement, 1870–1967* (Chapel Hill: University of North Carolina Press, 2017), 150–151.

6. Solomon, *In the Company of Women*, 134.

7. Patricia C. Kenschaft, *Change Is Possible: Stories of Women and Minorities in Mathematics* (Providence: American Mathematical Society, 2005), 8.

8. Gilman, "The Johns Hopkins University in Its Beginning," 32. See his letter to George Dobbin in Folder 5. For the trustees' correspondence regarding admitting women, see Folder 12. For individual applications, see Folders 6–8. Box 5, MS 137, JHU.

9. Judy Green, "Christine Ladd-Franklin (1847–1930)," in *Women of Mathematics: A Bibliographic Sourcebook*, ed. Louise S. Grinstein and Paul J. Campbell (New York: Greenwood Press, 1987), 121–128.

10. Simon Newcomb wrote on Bascom's behalf to Daniel Coit Gilman, November 6, 1890, MS 137, Box 5, Folder 12, JHU. See also Solomon, *In the Company of Women*, 135; Rossiter, *Women Scientists in America*, 40.

11. Patricia M. Mazón, *Gender and the Modern Research University: The Admission of Women to German Higher Education, 1864–1914* (Stanford, CA: Stanford University Press, 2003), 10.

12. Mazón, 5.

13. Helene Lange, "Higher Schools for Girls and Their Mission: Companion Essay," in Menand, Reitter, and Wellmon, *The Rise of the Research University*, 316.

14. Quotation from Menand, Reitter, and Wellmon, "Diversity and Inclusion: Introduction," in *The Rise of the Research University*, 312; see also Mazón, *Gender and the Modern Research University*, 3, 19.

15. Andrew Dickson White to Martha Carey Thomas, July 5, 1879, in M. Carey Thomas, *The Making of a Feminist: Early Journals and Letters of M. Carey Thomas*, ed. Marjorie Housepian Dobkin (Kent, OH: Kent State University Press, 1979), 164.

16. J.B.S., letter to the editor, "Women at the German Universities," *Nation*, February 15, 1894, in Menand, Reitter, and Wellmon, *The Rise of the Research University*, 320–322, quotation on 320. See also the "Contributors' Club: Girl Graduate at Leipzig," *Atlantic Monthly* 44 (December 1879): 788–791.

17. Anja Becker, "How Daring She Was! The Female American Colony at Leipzig University, 1877–1914," in *Taking Up Space: New Approaches to American History*, ed. Anke Ortlepp and Christoph Ribbat (Trier: Wissenschaftlicher Verlag Trier, 2004), 32, 31–44.

18. Nathan H. Dole, "Biographical Sketch," in Helen Abbott Michael, *Studies in Plant and Organic Chemistry and Literary Papers* (Cambridge, MA: Riverside Press, 1907), 26–87. For another account of women in Zurich, see Flora Bridges, "Coeducation in Swiss Universities," *Popular Science Monthly* 38 (1890–1891): 524–530. On Zurich's sig-

nificance for women seeking education in the nineteenth century, see Ernst Gagliardi, Hans Nabholz, and Jean Strohl, "Neuntes Kapitel: Der Einzug neuer Ideen," in *Die Universität Zürich, 1833–1933, und ihre Vorläufer: Festschrift zur Jahrhundertfeier,* ed. Gagliardi, Nabholz, and Strohl (Zurich: Verlag der Erziehungsdirektion, 1938), 62–77.

19. On identifying "susceptible targets," see Rossiter, *Women Scientists in America,* 44. William James to Christine Ladd-Franklin, March 3, 1892, Box 1, Christine Ladd-Franklin and Fabian Franklin Papers, RBMLC. Thank you to Tara Craig for sending this material.

20. Ida Hyde, "Before Women Were Human Beings: Adventures of an American Fellow in German Universities of the '90s," *Journal of the American Association of University Women,* 1938, 235.

21. Hyde, 236.

22. Rossiter, *Women Scientists in America,* 40–41.

23. Johnson, *Funding Feminism,* 145.

24. On Anne receiving women students, see Parshall and Rowe, *The Emergence of the American Mathematical Research Community,* 246.

25. Personalia, 22 L, S. 6, NL Klein. Translation from Parshall and Rowe, *The Emergence of the American Mathematical Research Community,* 244.

26. Parshall and Rowe, *The Emergence of the American Mathematical Research Community,* 250.

27. Parshall and Rowe, 249.

28. Dorothea Schlözer took the first known exam for a doctoral degree in 1787 at the University of Göttingen, albeit before the degree was modernized. Clark, *Academic Charisma,* 102. Two Russian women received PhDs, also at Göttingen, in 1874, in an open period before the first wave of backlash: Sofya Kovalevskaya in mathematics, and Julia Lermontova in chemistry. Singer, *Adventures Abroad,* 15. On the emerging support for women's education in Russia, see also Alexander Vucinich, *Science in Russian Culture, 1861–1917* (Stanford, CA: Stanford University Press, 1970), 126.

29. The first African American women to receive PhDs were Georgina Simpson (University of Chicago), Sadie Tanner Mossell (University of Pennsylvania), and Eva B. Dykes (Radcliffe). Evans, *Black Women in the Ivory Tower,* 127–128. The African American female Madame C. J. Walker presented one exception in an otherwise white world of women philanthropists. Johnson, *Funding Feminism,* 13.

30. Mary Elisa Church Terrel, who took a two-year tour in Europe before graduating from Oberlin in 1888, was an exception. Evans, *Black Women in the Ivory Tower,* 81.

31. Werner, *The Transatlantic World of Higher Education,* 88–90.

32. Parshall and Rowe, *The Emergence of the American Mathematical Research Community,* 240; Rossiter, *Women Scientists in America,* 37. Typically perceived as the "good foreigners," American and British women were permitted entrance to Prussian universities on the basis of examinations, while Russian women must have been previously accepted to a non-Prussian university. For the share of Jews among Russian female students at German and Swiss universities, see Singer, *Adventures Abroad,* 15, 19–21.

33. David E. Rowe, "Klein, Hilbert, and the Gottingen Mathematical Tradition," *Osiris* 5 (1989): 186–213. Klein was self-conscious enough about his Jewish identity to worry about hiring two Jews, including Adolf Hurwitz and David Hilbert, at once.

Though of the next generation and of unquestionable distinction, the female Jew Emmy Noether was also permitted to lecture as Hilbert's assistant. Felix Klein to Adolf Hurwitz, February 28, 1892, in *Transcending Tradition: Jewish Mathematics in German-Speaking Academic Culture*, ed. Birgit Bergmann, Moritz Epple, and Ruti Ungar (New York: Springer, 2012), 60, 84, 204.

34. Thomas to her mother, November 30, 1882, in Thomas, *The Making of a Feminist*, 266. As a result of Thomas's ambitions, the family's resources were soon depleted, and thereafter they often teetered on the cusp of financial collapse. Lawrence Veysey, "Martha Carey Thomas," in *Notable American Women, 1607–1950: A Biographical Dictionary, P–Z*, ed. Edward T. James (Cambridge, MA: Belknap Press of Harvard University Press, 1971), 3:446–450, 446, 448.

35. Thomas, "A Letter from Leipzig," *Alumnus*, March 1880, 35–36.

36. Thomas to her mother, November 25, 1882, in Thomas, *The Making of a Feminist*, 263–264.

37. Thomas to her mother, February 7, 1880, in Thomas, *The Making of a Feminist*, 208–209.

38. Thomas to her mother, no date, 1882, in Thomas, *The Making of a Feminist*, 258.

39. Thomas to her mother, no date, in Thomas, *The Making of a Feminist*, 266; and to J. B. Rhoads, confidential letter, in Thomas, 277–278.

40. Veysey, "Martha Carey Thomas," 3:446–450, 447.

41. Thomas to her mother, January 30, 1883, in Thomas, *The Making of a Feminist*, 271; Martha Carey Thomas to J. B. Rhoads, confidential letter, August 14, 1883, in Thomas, 279–280.

42. Cited in Barbara Bradfield Taft, "More Steeply to the Heights: The Graduate School of Arts and Sciences," in *A Century Recalled: Essays in Honor of Bryn Mawr College*, ed. Patricia Hochschild Labalme (Bryn Mawr, PA: Bryn Mawr College, 1987), 135–143, quotation on 137. This is consistent with her letter to J. B. Rhoads, in Thomas, *The Making of a Feminist*, 279.

43. Helen Lefkowitz Horowitz, *Alma Mater: Design and Experience in the Women's Colleges from Their Nineteenth-Century Beginnings to the 1930s*, 2nd ed. (Amherst: University of Massachusetts Press, 1993), 6, 115.

44. Cited in Johnson, *Funding Feminism*, 149.

45. Thomas cited in Johnson, *Funding Feminism*, 146; see also 139–149; and Alison Baker, *It's Good to Be a Woman: Voices from Bryn Mawr, Class of '62* (Exeter: Publishing Works, 2007), 156.

46. Helen S. Astin and Jennifer A. Lindholm, "Academic Aspirations and Degree Attainment of Women," in *Encyclopedia of Women and Gender, Sex Similarities and Differences and the Impact of Society on Gender, L–Z*, ed. Judith Worell (San Diego, CA: Academic Press, 2002), 2:17.

47. Gilman, "The Inauguration of President Wheeler," 262. Also cited in Solomon, *In the Company of Women*, 57.

48. Martha Carey Thomas, "The University Education of Women in the United States in America, with Special Reference to Coeducation," in *Der Internationale Frauen Kon-*

gress in Berlin 1904 Bericht mit ausgewählten Referaten, ed. Marie Stritt (Berlin: Carl Habel, 1905), 124–130, quotation on 128.

49. Thomas to J. B. Rhoads, confidential letter, August 14, 1883, in Thomas, *The Making of a Feminist*, 279.

50. This ratio is for the Junior College, which was President Harper's innovation for the first two years of general education. Richard J. Storr, *Harper's University: The Beginnings* (Chicago: University of Chicago Press, 1966), 323–327; and Lynn D. Gordon, *Gender and Higher Education in the Progressive Era* (New Haven, CT: Yale University Press, 1990), 112.

51. By 1900 women equaled or outstripped men at state universities in California, Illinois, Iowa, Kansas, Michigan, Minnesota, Nebraska, Ohio, Texas, Washington, and Wisconsin. Rosalind Rosenberg, "The Feminization of Academe," *Beyond Separate Spheres: Intellectual Roots of Modern Feminism* (New Haven, CT: Yale University Press, 1982), 28–53, esp. 43; and Solomon, *In the Company of Women*, 58–59. For the Harper quotation, see "President Harper on Co-Education," *School Journal: A Weekly Journal of Education* 64, no. 3 (January 18, 1902): 68.

52. Thomas, "Present Tendencies in Women's College and University Education," *Publications of the Association of Collegiate Alumnae* 3 (1908): 51.

53. Aldon Morris, *The Scholar Denied: W.E.B. Du Bois and the Birth of Modern Sociology* (Berkeley: University of California Press, 2015), 15.

54. According to Leroy Hopkins, German American teachers may have presented African American children with the German revolutionaries as a model for liberation. Hopkins, "'Black Prussians': Germany and African American Education from James W. C. Pennington to Angela Davis," in *Crosscurrents: African Americans, Africa, and Germany in the Modern World*, ed. David McBride, Leroy Hopkins, and C. Aisha Blackshire-Belay (Columbia, SC: Camden House, 1998), 65–81, esp. 70.

55. Hopkins, "'Black Prussians,'" 71.

56. W.E.B. Du Bois, *The Autobiography of W.E.B. DuBois: A Soliloquy on Viewing My Life from the Last Decade of Its First Century* (New York: Oxford University Press, 2007), 126; see also Hopkins, "'Black Prussians,'" 71.

57. Kwame Anthony Appiah, *Lines of Descent: W.E.B. Du Bois and the Emergence of Identity* (Cambridge: MA: Harvard University Press, 2014), 10–11.

58. W.E.B. Du Bois, "A Negro Student at Harvard at the End of the 19th Century," *Massachusetts Review* 1, no. 3 (1960): 353–369, esp. 354–361, quotation on 361.

59. The seminar papers are held in W.E.B. Du Bois's archive. See "Early Germanic Institutions as Mentioned by Tacitus, October 20, 1890," and "Origin and Methods of the German Railway System, March 16, 1889," Series 10, Essays and Student Papers, W.E.B. Du Bois Papers, UMass Amherst, online at https://credo.library.umass.edu (hereafter Du Bois Papers). Kenneth Barkin, "W.E.B. Du Bois and the Kaiserreich: Introduction," *Central European History* 31 (1998): 155–170, here 159–160.

60. Du Bois to Rutherford B. Hayes, November 4, 1890, in Rutherford B. Hayes and Louis D. Rubin, *Teach the Freeman: The Correspondence of Rutherford B. Hayes and the Slater Fund for Negro Education, 1881–1887* (Baton Rouge: Louisiana State University Press, 1959), 158–159.

61. Du Bois, "A Negro Student at Harvard," 366.

62. William H. Watkins, *The White Architects of Black Education: Ideology and Power in America, 1865–1954* (New York: Teachers College Columbia University, 2001), 150.

63. On the controversial relationship between Washington and white philanthropists, see Eric Anderson and Alfred A. Moss Jr., *Dangerous Donations: Northern Philanthropy and Southern Black Education, 1902–1930* (Columbia: University of Missouri Press, 1999), x.

64. Though Washington himself was excluded from these meetings, his ideology seems to have been favored. David Levering Lewis, *W.E.B. Du Bois: Biography of a Race, 1868–1919* (New York: Henry Holt, 1993), 123, 125.

65. W.E.B. Du Bois, *Dusk of Dawn: An Essay Toward an Autobiography of a Race Concept*, ed. Henry Louis Gates and intro. Kwame Anthony Appiah (1940; Oxford: Oxford University Press, 2014), 22; Lewis, *W.E.B. Du Bois*, 125.

66. W.E.B. Du Bois, May 25, 1891, in W.E.B. Du Bois, *The Correspondence of W.E.B. Du Bois*, ed. Herbert Aptheker (Amherst: University of Massachusetts Press, 1973), 1:14.

67. W.E.B. Du Bois to Rutherford Hayes, April 3, 1892, in Hayes and Rubin, *Teach the Freeman*, 247.

68. Du Bois, *The Autobiography of W.E.B. DuBois*, 157; Lewis, *W.E.B. Du Bois*, 126; Barkin, "W.E.B. Du Bois and the Kaiserreich," 161.

69. Du Bois, *The Autobiography of W.E.B. DuBois*, 157.

70. See W.E.B. Du Bois, "Letter," *Fisk Herald*, September 1893, 5–7; discussed in Lewis, *W.E.B. Du Bois*, 139.

71. On Du Bois's and Alain Locke's use of Herder's notion of *Volk*, see Ingeborg H. Solbrig, "American Slavery in Eighteenth-Century German Literature: The Case of Herder's 'Neger-Idyllen,'" *Monatshefte* 82 (1900): 38–49. An African American female scholar Georgiana Simpson, who conducted postdoctoral work in Germany in the 1920s, also wrote her dissertation on Herder. See Evans, *Black Women in the Ivory Tower*, 131–132.

72. Cited in Lewis, *W.E.B. Du Bois*, 135.

73. Appiah has argued that this tension between particularity and universalism, and even the double-consciousness for which he would become known, is traceable to this German experience. Appiah, *Lines of Descent*, 158.

74. Du Bois, *The Autobiography of W.E.B. DuBois*, 169.

75. Du Bois wrote disparagingly about the Jews who accompanied him back to America on his ship in his private notebooks—passages that did not make it into his published *Autobiography*. As is well known, he also edited similarly disparaging early passages about Jews in later versions of *The Souls of Black Folks*. See also Lewis, *W.E.B. Du Bois*, 148.

76. Appiah calls this the nationalism of diasporic communities—catching the fire of nationalism without being burned. Appiah, *Lines of Descent*, 53.

77. Du Bois, *The Autobiography of W.E.B. DuBois*, 24, 174.

78. W.E.B. Du Bois to Trustees of the John D. Slater Fund, March 1893, in Du Bois, *The Correspondence of W.E.B. Du Bois*, 1:22.

79. "Der Gross und Klein Betrieb des Ackerbaus, in den Sudstaaten der Vereinigten

Staaten, 1840-90" (The Large and Small-Scale System of Agriculture in the Southern United States). This paper that Du Bois wrote for Wagner's course is missing from the archives but was praised by Wagner in his correspondence with Gilman and mentioned by Du Bois in his accounting of his first year in Berlin. See Adolph Wagner to Gilman, Berlin, March 28, 1894; and Du Bois to Gilman, ca. March 1893; in Du Bois, *The Correspondence of W.E.B. Du Bois*, 1:19-20, 24.

80. See the Verzeichnis der Vorlesungen, Series 16; Miscellaneous Material; and Lecture notebook, ca. 1896, with bibliographies and statistics from Schmoller and Wagner's seminar; Series 10, Essays and Student Papers, both Du Bois Papers. In 1958, when Du Bois received an honorary degree from Humboldt University, he mentioned also having heard lectures of Gneist and Lenz, and then later recounted the same to William Ingersoll. But Barkin says it is certain *only* that he heard lectures from Schmoller, Wagner, and Treitschke. The Humboldt University at Berlin on November 3, 1958, Series 2, Speeches; *Oral History Interview of W.E.B. Du Bois by William Ingersoll*, 76-77; conducted for the Columbia University Oral History Project, May 5–June 6, 1960; transcripts, both Du Bois Papers; Barkin, "W.E.B. Du Bois and the Kaiserreich," 161.

81. Daniel Coit Gilman to W.E.B. Du Bois, April 13, 1894, in Du Bois, *The Correspondence of W.E.B. Du Bois*, 1:29; also cited in Lewis, *W.E.B. Du Bois*, 146.

82. Lewis, *W.E.B. Du Bois*, 146, 127.

83. When Du Bois received an honorary degree from Humboldt University in the then German Democratic Republic in 1958, he declared, "Today by your kindness I trust not prejudiced judgment that ambition is fulfilled." The Humboldt University at Berlin, November 3, 1958, Series 2, Speeches, Du Bois Papers. See also Doctor of Economics honorary degree, November 3, 1958; Series 1, Correspondence, Du Bois Papers.

84. Du Bois's protégé Richard R. Wright Jr. (who also felt more free in Germany than in America) would find himself in a similar position two decades later: beholden to gatekeepers for entrance to the professoriate. Wright, *87 Years behind the Black Curtain* (Philadelphia: Rare Book Company, 1965), 43, 46-47. See also Werner, *The Transatlantic World of Higher Education*, 84-85.

85. On the significance of Thomas's connection to capital, see Helen Lefkowitz Horowitz, *The Power and Passion of M. Carey Thomas* (New York: Knopf, 1994), xvi.

86. Lewis, *W.E.B. Du Bois*, 127.

87. Napoleon Rivers's study found sixty-nine language teachers, six of whom had doctorates, three in Germanics. W. Napoleon Rivers Jr., "A Study of the Modern Foreign Languages in Thirty Negro Colleges," *Journal of Negro Education* 2 (1933): 487-493. Cited in Hopkins, "'Black Prussians,'" 72.

88. Hopkins, "'Black Prussians,'" 74.

89. Du Bois, "The Talented Tenth," in *The Negro Problem: A Series of Articles by Representative American Negroes of Today*, ed. Booker T. Washington (New York: James Pott and Company, 1903), 33-75, quotation on 63; see also 33-34; Appiah, *Lines of Descent*, 69. Donald Generals shows how Washington was, in fact, implementing a hybrid philosophy of education that drew on Pestalozzian ideas, although Washington's position was (and continues to be) caricatured as purely vocational. See Generals,

"Booker T. Washington and Progressive Education," *Journal of Negro Education* 69, no. 3 (Summer 2000): 215–234, esp. 224.

90. Morris, *The Scholar Denied*, xviii, 55–59.

91. Lewis, *W.E.B. Du Bois*, 149. On Du Bois's favoritism toward college-educated and business men, see Mason Stokes, "Father of the Bride: Du Bois and the Making of Black Heterosexuality," in *W.E.B. Du Bois and Race: Essays Celebrating the Centennial Publication of the Soul of Black Folk*, ed. Chester J. Fontenot, Mary A. Morgan, and Sarah Gardner (Macon, GA: Mercer University Press, 2001), 289–316, here 295, 297.

92. Arthur Twining Hadley, "Educational Methods and Principles," in *Congress of Arts and Science: Universal Exposition, St. Louis 1904*, ed. Howard J. Rogers (Boston: Houghton, Mifflin, 1905–1906), 8:23.

93. Though the term "meritocracy" dates to the postwar period one can trace elements of its early history here. On Jacksonian-inspired egalitarian and meritocratic arguments for women's education, see Solomon, *In the Company of Women*, 1–17. For a history of how meritocracy emerged as a concept in response to the absence of real social mobility, see Ansgar Allen, "Michael Young's *The Rise of the Meritocracy: A Philosophical Critique*," *British Journal of Educational Studies* 59 (2011): 367–382. See also Arthur Twining Hadley, *Economic Problems of Democracy* (New York: Macmillan, 1923), 20–21, 151.

94. Daniel Coit Gilman, "A Study in Black and White," in *The Launching of a University*, 6.

95. Gilman, *The Launching of a University*, 336–338.

96. William DeWitt Hyde, "Place of the College in the Social System," *School Review* 12 (1904): 782–797, here 782.

97. Friedrich Paulsen, *Das deutsche Bildungswesen in seiner geschichtlichen Entwicklung* (Berlin: B.G. Teubner, 1920), 126–127. The debate over privileges between the technical institutes and universities mirrored those that played out among the *Realschulen* and the *Gymnasien*. James C. Albisetti, *Secondary School Reform in Imperial Germany* (Princeton, NJ: Princeton University Press, 1983), 31.

98. Since what characterized a "college" changed between 1900 and 1910, it made it difficult to identify meritocracy's gains or losses. According to Du Bois's own Atlanta Study, the number of black college graduates decreased in this time—a fact that could be attributed to the loss in status of institutions and not individuals. Evans, *Black Women in the Ivory Tower*, 41–42.

99. Veysey, "Martha Carey Thomas," 449.

100. Helen R. Olin, *The Women of a State University: An Illustration of the Working of Coeducation in the Middle West* (New York: G.P. Putnam's Sons, 1909), 141.

101. Olin, *The Women of a State University*, 142.

102. Cited in Jerome Karabel, *The Chosen: The Hidden History of Admission and Exclusion at Harvard, Yale, and Princeton* (New York: Mariner, 2006), 87.

103. On the exchange regarding Adler, see John W. Burgess to Nicholas Murray Butler, January 8, 1907; Nicholas Murray Butler to John W. Burgess, March 1 1910, John W. Burgess Papers, RBMLC; also discussed in Harold S. Wechsler, *The Qualified*

Student: A History of Selective College Admission in America (New York: Wiley, 1977), 136–137.

104. Michael Rosenthal, *Nicholas Miraculous: The Amazing Career of the Redoubtable Dr. Nicholas Murray Butler* (New York: Farrar, Straus, and Giroux, 2006), 352. The archival record differs.

105. Upton Sinclair, *The Goose-Step: A Study of American Education* (Chicago: Economy Book Shop, 1922), 39.

106. For a critique of Du Bois's sexism against African American women in particular, see Joy James, "Profeminism and Gender Elites: W.E.B. Du Bois, Anna Julia Cooper, and Ida B. Wells-Barnett," in *Next to the Color Line: Gender, Sexuality, and W.E.B. Du Bois,* ed. Susan K. Gillman and Alys E. Weinbaum (Minneapolis: University of Minnesota Press, 2007), 69–95. Du Bois's "masculinist worldview" is evident in his relationship with Anna Julia Cooper, who received a PhD from the Sorbonne in 1930 and whose advocacy for a humanist education may have provided unacknowledged influence on Du Bois. James, "Profeminism and Gender Elites,' 70, 77–78.

107. Horowitz, *The Power and Passion of M. Carey Thomas,* 69.

108. Veysey, "Martha Carey Thomas," 446–450, 448.

109. Horowitz, *The Power and Passion of M. Carey Thomas,* 342.

110. Horowitz documents a number of these cases involving Jewish scientists. It never occurred to Thomas, on the other hand, that African Americans would be in the position—intellectually or economically—to attend Bryn Mawr. Horowitz, *The Power and Passion of M. Carey Thomas,* 341, 342.

111. Horowitz, in contrast, attributes this narrowmindedness to the time period and Thomas's upbringing. Horowitz, *The Power and Passion of M. Carey Thomas,* 341.

112. Thomas, "Present Tendencies in Women's College and University Education," 58.

113. Thomas, "The University Education of Women in the United States in America, with Special Reference to Coeducation," 130.

114. One could say the same about James Kirkland of Vanderbilt, who was on the geographical periphery. See Anja Becker, "Southern Academic Ambitions Meet German Scholarship: The Leipzig Networks of Vanderbilt University's James H. Kirkland in the Late Nineteenth Century," *Journal of Southern History* 74 (2008): 855–886.

115. Du Bois to Rutherford B. Hayes, April 19, 1891, in Hayes and Rubin, *Teach the Freeman,* 194.

116. Thorstein Veblen, "The Intellectual Pre-eminence of Jews in Modern Europe," *Political Science Quarterly* 39 (1919): 41.

117. Morris presents an interesting discussion that takes Martin Bulmer's essay and sociology of knowledge as its starting point about the incomplete portrait offered by sociology that does not include an analysis of extra-intellectual factors. See Alson Morris, "The Chicago School of Sociology: What Made It a School?," *History of Sociology* 5 (1991): 61–77; and Morris, *The Scholar Denied,* 142.

118. For a discussion of this exchange and Weber's defense of Du Bois, see "Max Weber, Dr. Alfred Ploetz, and W.E.B. Du Bois," *Social Research,* 1973, 308–312.

119. A student of Thorstein Veblen's, Katherine Bement Davis, was one exception.

Axel R. Schafer, "W. E. B. Du Bois, German Social Thought, and the Racial Divide in American Progressivism, 1892–1909," *Journal of American History* 88 (2001): 932.

120. Impacted by Du Bois's work, Weber's views on race evolved, and he integrated Du Bois's sociology into his work. In contrast, the Chicago School did not, at least not with attribution—leading to a divergence between German and American sociology along racial fault lines. Morris argues that the Chicago School would have developed a political sociology had they incorporated Weberian and Du Boisian thought earlier. Morris, *The Scholar Denied*, 148.

121. My use of the term "haunting" is inspired by Avery F. Gordon, *Ghostly Matters: Haunting and the Sociological Imagination*, foreword by Janice Radway (Minneapolis: University of Minnesota Press, 2008), vi. Thank you to Libby Otto for this reference.

122. Elizabeth Clemens, "Organizational Repertoires and Institutional Change: Women's Groups and the Transformation of U.S. Politics, 1890–1920," *American Journal of Sociology* 98 (1993): 755–798.

CHAPTER FIVE

1. For the quotation that serves as the basis for the epigraph, see Paul Fussell, "Schools for Snobbery," *New Republic*, October 4, 1982, 25; and the discussion in David O. Levine's preface drawing on Fussell's observation. Levine, *The American College and the Culture of Aspiration, 1915–1940* (Ithaca, NY: Cornell University Press, 1987), 7. Charles W. Eliot, "Inaugural Address as President of Harvard College, October 19, 1869," in *Essays and Addresses* (New York: The Century Co., 1898), 1.

2. Charles Eliot even professionalized the university's management. Eliot, *University Administration* (1908; Boston: Leopold Classic Library, 2016). On the relationship between education and the administrative state, see, for example, Ellen Condliffe Lagemann, "The Plural Worlds of Educational Research," *History of Education Quarterly* 29 (1989): 184–214.

3. William James, "The Ph.D. Octopus," *Harvard Monthly* 36 (1903): 8. That he did not have a PhD no doubt motivated, in part, his fear of the Germans and their credentials. This anxiety was exacerbated by Münsterberg, who irked his colleagues with his self-promotion and represented for William and Henry James "the sort of class of future phenomena represented by the foreigner coming in and taking possession." Cited in Rollman, "'Meet Me in St. Louis,'" 362.

4. Scholars often write of the "encroachment" of management and market interests on the university, implying a passive relationship. Newfield, *Ivy and Industry*, 62; Donoghue, *The Last Professors*, 2, 101. But as Richard Hofstadter and Walter P. Metzger wrote a half century ago, "The line between business and scholarship was not crossed from one side alone." Hofstadter and Metzger, *The Development of Academic Freedom in the United States*, 416.

5. Previous eras gave distinct meaning to the term "professionalism," transforming one by one the fields of theology, law, and medicine. Bruce A. Kimball, *The "True Professional Ideal" in America: A History* (Lanham, MD: Rowman & Littlefield,

1996), 2. Collins also surveys the early history of these fields in *The Credential Society*, 131–181.

6. Ken Caneva, "From Galvanism to Electrodynamics: The Transformation of German Physics and Its Social Context," *Historical Context in the Physical Sciences* 9 (1978): 63–159, esp. 133–159.

7. Hermann Helmholtz, "Über das Verhältnis der Naturwissenschaften zur Gesamtheit der Wissenschaft," *Akademische Festrede gehalten zu Heidelberg am 22 November 1862 bei Antritt des Prorectorats*, in *Vorträge und Reden*, 5th ed. (Braunschweig: Friedrich Vieweg und Sohn, 1896), 1:157–185, 162, quotation on 177 (my translation). For an excellent translation of this and Helmholtz's other essays, see Helmholtz, *Hermann von Helmholtz: Science and Culture*. On these developments, see the essays from Steven R. Turner, in particular, "The Growth of Professorial Research in Prussia, 1818–1848—Causes and Context," in *Historical Studies in the Physical Sciences*, ed. R. McCormack (Philadelphia: University of Pennsylvania Press, 1971), 137–182.

8. Translation from Helmholtz, "On the Relation of Natural Science to Science in General" (1862), in *Hermann von Helmholtz: Science and Culture*, 92. Also cited in Sheehan, *German History*, 806. For a formidable biography, see David Cahan, *Helmholtz: A Life in Science* (Chicago: Chicago University Press, 2018).

9. Du Bois-Reymond's budget for his physiological laboratory had increased from 750 thaler in 1860 to 40,220 M in 1877 and was housed in a building that cost another 200,000 M. Timothy Lenoir, "Science for the Clinic: Science Policy and the Formation of Carl Ludwig's Institute in Leipzig," in *The Investigative Enterprise: Experimental Physiology in Nineteenth-Century Medicine*, ed. William Coleman and Frederic L. Holmes (Berkeley: University of California Press, 1988), 139–178, esp. 139–140.

10. Timothy Lenoir, "Revolution from Above: The Role of the State in the German Research System, 1810–1910," *American Economic Review* 88 (1998): 22–27. For the dyestuff industry, see Murmann, Galambos, and Jones, *Knowledge and Competitive Advantage*, 74, 85.

11. On Virchow's use of political metaphors, see Sheehan, *German History*, 811; for a fascinating rumination on the permutations of distinct metaphors for scientific inquiry employed by the generation of 1848, see Peter Galison, "Meanings of Scientific Unity: The Law, the Orchestra, the Pyramid, the Quilt, and the Ring," in *Pursuing the Unity of Science: Ideology and Scientific Practice from the Great War to the Cold War*, ed. Harmke Kamminga and Geert Somsen (New York: Routledge, 2016), 12–29, esp. 13–15.

12. Arthur Ward Lufkin, *A History of Dentistry* (Philadelphia: Lea & Febiger, 1938), 112–117.

13. Axtell surveys a number of different sources for these statistics. See Axtell, *Wisdom's Workshop*, 234; Theodor Puschmann, *A History of Medical Education from the Most Remote to the Most Recent Times* (London: H.K. Lewis, 1891), 597.

14. Condensed from citation in Caneva, "From Galvanism to Electrodynamics," 129.

15. Helmholtz, "Über das Verhältnis der Naturwissenschaften zur Gesamtheit der Wissenschaft."

16. Arleen Marcia Tuchman shows how in Baden scientists received support because it was seen as crucial for Germany's political and economic future. Tuchman, *Science,*

Medicine, and the State in Germany: The Case of Baden, 1815–1871 (Oxford: Oxford University Press, 1993), 3, and 173.

17. On overcrowding that led to an "academic proletariat" and "overproduction" of intellectuals, see Lenore O'Boyle, "The Problem of an Excess of Educated Men in Western Europe, 1800–1850," *Journal of Modern History* 42 (December 1970): 473–478.

18. Children of middle-class families declined in number from over 50 percent of the student body at the University of Berlin to 44 percent in the philosophical faculties between 1886 and 1911. There McClelland estimates the cost of Berlin medical school to have been 3,000 M (or as high as 12,000 M with housing, meals, and books), an amount that would have required an annual income to support it. McClelland, *The Mother of All Research Universities*, 111, 122, 125.

19. Between 1800 and 1850 close to one half of all who passed the *Abitur* and studied at universities were the sons of fathers who themselves were civil servants or professionals. Albisetti, *Secondary School Reform in Imperial Germany*, 27. For an analysis of the social structure of the university as it relates to the wider society, see Christian von Ferber, *Die Entwicklung des Lehrkörpers der deutschen Universitäten und Hochschulen, 1964–1954* (Göttingen: Vandenhoeck & Rubrecht, 1956), 163.

20. Jews were disproportionately represented in medicine—causing anxiety among professional gatekeepers, who placed discriminatory job ads in newspapers. John Efron, *Medicine and the German Jews: A History* (New Haven, CT: Yale University Press, 2001), 235, 253.

21. Levine, *The American College and the Culture of Aspiration*, 16.

22. Karl Schleunes traces the origin and evolution of schools oriented to each social class, including the usually overlooked focus on Bavaria, in *Schooling and Society: The Politics of Education in Prussia and Bavaria, 1750–1900* (Oxford: Berg, 1989), 33.

23. Albisetti, *Secondary School Reform in Imperial Germany*, 23.

24. James B. Angell, "A Memorial Discourse on the Life and Services of Henry Simmons Frieze, Ph.D. Professor of the Latin Language and Literature in the University from 1854 to 1889," in Angell, *Selected Addresses* (New York, Longmanns, Green, 1912), 165–167. See also Wechsler, *The Qualified Student*, 17.

25. Angell laid out his strategy to bring the secondary school in line with the university's goals in "Remarks of President Angell," 16–18; Records of Board of Trustees, Box 2.1, JHU. Though he does not refer to the German example, Marc Vanoverbeke provides a helpful summary of Angell's achievements in this area. Vanoverbeke, *The Standardization of American Schooling: Linking Secondary and Higher Education, 1870–1910* (London: Palgrave, 2008), 1–2, 126.

26. "Remarks of President Angell," 17; Records of Board of Trustees, Box 2.1, JHU.

27. In 1870, after a protracted debate, first-class *Realschulen* were given the right to administer the *Abitur* for their students to matriculate at the university. The traditionalists relented only in order to keep those students out of the *Gymnasien* and because of teacher shortages in the *Gymnasien* themselves. Albisetti, *Secondary School Reform in Imperial Germany*, 66.

28. Richard Whittemore, "Nicholas Murray Butler and the Teaching Profession," *History of Education Quarterly* 1 (September 1961): 22-37, quotation on 23.

29. James C. Mackenzie, "The Report of the Committee of Ten," *School Review* 2 (1894): 146–155; see also Mattingly, *American Academic Cultures*, 132–134.

30. Allan C. Ornstein and Daniel U. Levine, *Foundations of Education*, 5th ed. (Boston: Houghton Mifflin, 1993), 174–175.

31. *Report of the Committee on Secondary School Studies, Appointed at the Meeting of the National Education Association, July 9, 1892, with the Reports of the Conferences* (Washington, DC: Bureau of Education, Government Printing Office, 1893), iii. On the failure of Eliot's efforts on the Committee of Ten, see Vanoverbeke, *The Standardization of American Schooling*, 124.

32. On the comparison with Butler, see Wechsler *The Qualified Student*, 69, 157.

33. Bruce A. Kimball, *The Inception of Modern Professional Education: C. C. Langdell, 1826-1906* (Chapel Hill: University of North Carolina Press, 2009), 4.

34. In 1919, Langdell's former student Abbot Lawrence Lowell (president of Harvard from 1909 to 1933) then appointed another Harvard Law School (HLS) graduate, Wallace B. Donham, the dean of the Harvard Business School, with the directive to improve it on the model of the HLS. Kimball, *The Inception of Modern Professional Education*, 3–4.

35. Charles Thwing, *College Administration* (New York: Century, 1900), 306.

36. Cited in Paul Starr, *The Social Transformation of American Medicine* (New York: Basic Books, 1982), 113.

37. Gilman, "The Johns Hopkins University in Its Beginning," 22–24.

38. Charles Eliot, "Medical Education of the Future," in *Educational Reform: Essays and Addresses* (New York: Century, 1898), 366. On Hopkins's requirements for the medical school, see William Henry Welch, "The Johns Hopkins Medical School," *Papers and Addresses by William Henry Welch* (Baltimore: Johns Hopkins University Press, 1920), 3:9-13, here 11.

39. Abraham Flexner, *Henry S. Pritchett: A Biography* (New York: Columbia University Press, 1943), 37, 51.

40. Flexner, *Henry S. Pritchett*, 46.

41. Flexner, 44–46.

42. Henry Pritchett, "Shall Engineering Belong to the Liberal Profession?," Address on Behalf of the Technical Schools at the Inauguration of Dr. Charles S Howe as President of the Case School of Applied Science (1903), in *Inauguration, May 10 and 11, 1904* (Cleveland: The Imperial Press, 1904), 27–32, quotations on 27, 29.

43. Bruce Sinclair, "Mergers and Acquisitions," in *Becoming MIT: Moments of Decision*, ed. David Kaiser (Cambridge, MA: MIT Press, 2010), 47.

44. Philip N. Alexander, "Into Touch with the World at Large," in *A Widening Sphere: Evolving Cultures at MIT* (Cambridge, MA: MIT Press, 2011), 213, 215, 235.

45. Cited in Ellen Condliffe Lagemann, *The Politics of Knowledge: The Carnegie Corporation, Philanthropy, and Public Policy* (Middletown, CT: Wesleyan University Press, 1989), 22.

46. On the transatlantic discourse about social security, see Rodgers, *Atlantic Crossings*, 66 and 209–229. To develop the pension system Pritchett sought financial input from Frank A. Vanderlip, vice president of National City Bank (now Citibank) and "admirer of all things German," who believed an excellent education system was crucial to Germany's economic and industrial success. Ellen Condliffe Lagemann, *Private Power for the Public Good: A History of the Carnegie Foundation for the Advancement of Teaching* (Middletown, CT: Wesleyan University Press, 1983), 50.

47. Flexner, *Henry S. Pritchett*, 109.

48. Lagemann, *Private Power for the Public Good*, 53.

49. Steven L. Kanter, Victoria A. Groce, and Richard B. Gunderman, "Henry Pritchett and His Introduction to the Flexner Report of 1910," *Academic Medicine: Journal of the Association of American Medical Colleges* 85 (November 2010): 1777–1783, here 1777.

50. Ethan W. Ris, "The Education of Andrew Carnegie: Strategic Philanthropy in American Higher Education, 1880–1919," *Journal of Higher Education* 88, no. 3 (2017): 401–429, esp. 413–416.

51. On the long-standing impact of the "Carnegie Unit" on schools, see D. B. Tyack and Larry Cuban, *Tinkering toward Utopia: A Century of Public School Reform* (Cambridge, MA: Harvard University Press, 1995), 91–93. Bowdoin, Wesleyan, Rochester, and Hanover, were among the well-known institutions that abandoned denominationalism to qualify. On secularization, see Edward A. Purcell, *The Crisis of Democratic Theory: Scientific Naturalism & the Problem of Value* (Lexington: University Press of Kentucky, 1973), 8.

52. For the traditional interpretation of Carnegie as a humanitarian, which is also adopted by the foundation itself, see Lagemann, *Private Power for the Public Good*, 2, 42–51. On the revised interpretation that my research supports, see Ethan W. Ris's complementary work, "The American College in the Age of Reform" (PhD diss., Stanford University, 2017), 54, 76, 80.

53. Henry Pritchett, preface to *The Financial Status of the Professor in America and Germany*, v–x, quotations on vii and ix.

54. See, for example, Henry Pritchett, "The Large Number of Institutions in the United States and Canada Bearing the Name College or University," in *Carnegie Foundation for the Advancement of Teaching; Second Annual Report of the President and Treasurer* (New York, 1907), 77. Ris points out that both Vanderbilt and Stanford universities were founded from the wealth generated by railroads. Ris, "The American College in the Age of Reform," 109.

55. Alfred D. Chandler argues that this was the model for business reform in Progressive-Era America. Chandler, *The Visible Hand: The Managerial Revolution in American Business* (Cambridge, MA: Belknap Press of Harvard University Press, 1977), 1.

56. Pritchett, preface to *Financial Status of the Professor*, vii. John White, "Andrew Carnegie and Herbert Spencer: A Special Relationship," *Journal of American Studies* 13 (1979): 57–71. Ris also develops this theme: "The American College in the Age of Reform"; Ris, "The Education of Andrew Carnegie: Strategic Philanthropy in American Higher Education, 1880–1919," *Journal of Higher Education* 88 (2017): 401–429.

57. Robert P. Hudson argues that mediocrity and rising reform coexisted during the Civil War and for two decades following the war. Hudson, "Abraham Flexner in Perspective: American Medical Education, 1865–1910," *Bulletin of the History of Medicine* 46 (1972): 545–546, quotation on 559.

58. Richard H. Shryock, "The Influence of the Johns Hopkins University on American Medical Education," *Journal of Medical Education* 31 (1956): 226–235, here 227.

59. The American Medical Association had been founded in 1847 but had little impact on the condition of medical schools. Starr, *The Social Transformation of American Medicine*, 115.

60. Hudson, "Abraham Flexner in Perspective," 551.

61. Abraham Flexner, *The American College: A Criticism* (New York: The Century Co., 1908).

62. Abraham Flexner, *I Remember: The Autobiography of Abraham Flexner* (New York: Simon and Schuster, 1940), 110.

63. Flexner, *Henry S. Pritchett*, 109. See also Flexner, *I Remember*, 111.

64. Flexner, *I Remember*, 122.

65. For a quantifiable analysis of Pritchett's contribution, see the table and accompanying analysis in Kanter, Groce, and Gunderman, "Henry Pritchett and His Introduction to the Flexner Report of 1910," 1777, 1780.

66. Pritchett, introduction to Abraham Flexner, *Medical Education in the United States and Canada: A Report to the Carnegie Foundation for the Advancement of Teaching*, Bulletin 4 (New York: The Carnegie Foundation for the Advancement of Teaching), xiv–xv.

67. Flexner included three territories here in addition to the forty-nine US states in 1908: Guam (1898), Wake Island (1899), American Samoa (1900). Flexner, *Medical Education*, 172.

68. Flexner, *Medical Education*, 45.

69. Flexner, *Medical Education*, 152–153; and Flexner, *I Remember*, 130.

70. In the archives of the Library of Congress, where Flexner's notes from his visits are still held, the voyeuristic researcher can peruse amusing accounts of laboratories with no equipment and investigate the individual files of students who were admitted without high school degrees. Flexner, *Medical Education*, 190; Flexner, *I Remember*, 127–128, 129, 168.

71. Flexner, *I Remember*, 128.

72. Alfred Schaper: Persönliche Eindrücke und Erfahrungen, 92, A I Nr. 309 I, Bl. 196–233; and Frederick W. Keutgen: Einiges über amerikanische Universitäten nach eigenen Erfahrungen und urkundlichen Quellen, Rep. 92, A I Nr. 309 I, Bl. 162–174, both NL Althoff.

73. Starr, *The Social Transformation of American Medicine*, 115.

74. John Shaw Billings, "Suggestions on Medical Education," *Bulletin of the Institute of the History of Medicine* 6 (1938): 313–359, here 340. Billings also had in mind the field of "State Medicine," based on the German system in which a field developed around addressing issues of public reform, the management of municipal hospitals,

the regulation of the sale of food, the control of hygiene, and the public response to epidemics (347–348).

75. See Billings, "Suggestions on Medical Education," 353.

76. Shryock, "The Influence of the Johns Hopkins University on American Medical Education," 229.

77. Pritchett, introduction to Flexner, *Medical Education*, xii.

78. Martin Kaufman, *American Medical Education: The Formative Years, 1765–1910* (Westport, CT: Greenwood Press, 1976), 167.

79. Flexner, *I Remember*, 130–131.

80. Pritchett to Flexner, June 13, 1910, Box 19, Abraham Flexner Papers, LOC.

81. Kanter, Groce, and Gunderman, "Henry Pritchett and His Introduction to the Flexner Report of 1910," 1781.

82. Pritchett to Flexner, October 27, 1910, Box 19, Flexner Papers, LOC.

83. Barbara M. Barzansky and Norman Gevitz, *Beyond Flexner: Medical Education in the Twentieth Century* (Westport, CT: Greenwood Press, 1992); Andrew H. Beck, "The Flexner Report and the Standardization of American Medical Education," *JAMA* 291 (2004): 2139–2140.

84. Larry Cuban, "Change without Reform: The Case of Stanford University School of Medicine, 1908–1990," *American Educational Research Journal* 34 (Spring 1997): 83–122, here 86.

85. W. B. Fye, "The Origin of the Full-Time Faculty System: Implications for Clinical Research," *JAMA* 265 (1991): 1555–1162.

86. Flexner, *I Remember*, 102, 106 (italics mine).

87. Flexner, *I Remember*, 133, 136.

88. See the letters in Box 19, Flexner Papers, LOC.

89. See, for example, (illegible) Bayern, September 26, 1910, p. 2; and Berlin, July 15, 1911, in Flexner, German School Reports, Box 10, Flexner Papers, LOC. This box contains fifteen replies to Flexner's apparent inquiry. Many of the names are either omitted or illegible.

90. Flexner, "Aristocratic and Democratic Education," *Atlantic Monthly* 108 (1911): 391–392.

91. Flexner, "Aristocratic and Democratic Education," 391.

92. Thomas Neville Bonner, *Iconoclast: Abraham Flexner and a Life in Learning* (Baltimore: Johns Hopkins University Press, 2002), 99–100.

93. Paul v. Salvisberg to Flexner, January 3, 1911, Box 20, Flexner Papers, LOC.

94. Bonner, *Iconoclast*, 96.

95. Edward Wigglesworth, "Advantages of Foreign Study to American Medical Graduates," *Boston Medical and Surgical Journal* 83 (1870): 290.

96. Ethel L. Dewey, ed., *Recollections of Richard Dewey, Pioneer in American Psychiatry: An Unfinished Autobiography*, with an introduction by Clarence B. Farrar (Chicago: University of Chicago Press, 1936), 68–69.

97. Bonner, *American Doctors and German Universities: A Chapter in International Intellectual Relations, 1870–1914* (Lincoln: University of Nebraska Press, 1963), 98.

98. A. Jacobi, "Amerikanische Briefe," *Deutsche Medizinische Wochenschrift* 25 (1899): 816–818.

99. Robert Wollenberg, *Erinnerungen eines alten Psychiaters* (Stuttgart: Ferdinand Enke, 1931), 94; cited and translated in Bonner, *American Doctors and German Universities*, 141.

100. Quotations from Bonner, *American Doctors and German Universities*, 144, 146, 152.

101. Fritz Lange, "Amerikanische Reiseerinnerungen," *Münchener Medizinische Wochenschrift* 58 (1911): 1404–1408; discussed in Bonner, *American Doctors and German Universities*, 148–149.

102. Lange, "Amerikanische Reiseerinnerungen," 1408–1409 (my translation).

103. Bonner, *American Doctors and German Universities*, 102, 144.

104. Bonner, 10.

105. *Deutsche Medizinische Wochenschrift* 11 (October 8, 1885): 704–705; cited and translated in Bonner, *American Doctors and German Universities*, 10.

106. Flexner to Pritchett, October 25, 1918, Box 19, Flexner Papers, LOC.

107. Flexner, "The German Side of Medical Education," *Atlantic Monthly* 112 (1913): 655.

108. Flexner, "The German Side of Medical Education," 655.

109. Felix Frankfurter thought that Harvard Law School innovated the method for legal training, but he admired Flexner for creating a model for professionalization and urged practitioners in social work to follow this example. See Felix Frankfurter and Harlan B. Phillips, *Felix Frankfurter Reminiscences: Recorded in Talks with Dr. Harlan B. Phillips* (New York: Reynal & Company, 1960), 26 and 81. See also Edward Allan Brawley, "The Nonprofessional and the Professional Culture: A Dilemma for Social Work," *Journal of Sociology and Social Welfare* 2 (Winter 1974): 182–197, here 184–185.

110. Alfred Z. Reed, *Training for the Public Profession of the Law: Historical Development and Principal Contemporary Problems of Legal Education in the United States with Some Account of Conditions in England and Canada* (New York: Charles Scribner's Sons, 1921).

111. Chandler, *The Visible Hand*, 466–467.

112. This critique is suggested by Louis Menand, *The Marketplace of Ideas: Reform and Resistance in the American University* (New York: Norton, 2010), 52.

113. Kimball, *The "True Professional Ideal" in America*, 278.

114. The report had a "collateral effect" on female black physicians, since Flexner was highly critical of the only two schools that admitted African American women, the Medical University for Women in Philadelphia and the New York College and Hospital for Women. Thomas J. Ward Jr., *Black Physicians in the Jim Crow South* (Fayetteville: University of Arkansas Press, 2003), 27–28.

115. Evans, *Black Women in the Ivory Tower*, 45.

116. Flexner, *Medical Education*, 181.

117. Ward Jr., *Black Physicians in the Jim Crow South*, 20–24. Reports specifically on African American education were conducted in 1916, 1917–1918, 1928, and 1942.

118. James D. Anderson, *The Education of Blacks in the South, 1860–1935* (Chapel Hill: University of North Carolina Press, 1988), 254–255; Watkins, *The White Architects of Black Education*, 114–115, 125–127.

119. Kaufman, *American Medical Education*, 171.

120. Flexner, *Medical Education*, 43.

121. For these editorials, see Flexner Papers, LOC.

122. These changes aggravated shortages in rural areas. In 1880 for every doctor in South Carolina there were 894 persons, compared with 712 persons for every doctor in Massachusetts. By 1910 the number of people had risen to 1,170 in South Carolina and fallen in Massachusetts to 497. Starr, *The Social Transformation of American Medicine*, 125. The closure of Flint Medical College meant far fewer black doctors in Louisiana. Ward Jr., *Black Physicians in the Jim Crow South*, 28.

123. Law, medicine, and business adopted "the system of academic meritocracy that Langdell designed and built between 1870 and 1895." Kimball, *The Inception of Modern Professional Education*, 4.

124. Flexner, "Aristocratic and Democratic Education," 391.

125. Eliot, "Medical Education of the Future," 370.

126. Eliot also opposed taxing universities, since taxes did not fully value the public services these institutions offered. Eliot, "The Exemption from Taxation," in *American Contributions to Civilization and Other Essays and Addresses* (New York: The Century Co., 1897).

127. Max Weber, *Economy and Society*, ed. Guenther Roth and Claus Wittich (Berkeley: University of California Press, 1968), 2:1000.

128. Collins argues that racial and ethnic tensions caused these developments. Collins, *The Credential Society*, vii, 11.

CHAPTER SIX

1. Cited and translated in Peter Lundgreen, "Education for the Science-Based Industrial State? The Case For Nineteenth-Century Germany," in *History of Education: Major Themes*, vol. 4, *Studies of Education Systems*, ed. Roy Lowe (London: Routledge, 2002), 267–278, here 272.

2. As early as the 1870s, Siemens began to write about the scientific "competition" among nations and advocate for the private philanthropic support of research. See Werner Siemens, "Denkschrift, betreffend die Notwendigkeit eines Patentgesetz für das Deutsche Reich (1876)," in *Wissenschaftliche und technische Arbeiten*, vol. 2, *Technische Arbeiten* (Berlin: Springer, 1891), 561–567, esp. 561–563.

3. For a comparison of institutional budgets, see Vierhaus and vom Brocke, *Forschung im Spannungsfeld von Politik und Gesellschaft*, 86.

4. There would ultimately be over twenty institutions in the United States and a University Trust in Scotland in the Carnegie orbit. For a history of the Carnegie Corporation, see Lagemann, *The Politics of Knowledge*.

5. Hugo Münsterberg, *Die Amerikaner* (Berlin: Ernst Siegfried Mittler, 1904), 57 (my translation).

6. By World War I there would be twenty-four Kaiser Wilhelm Institutes. Following World War II, they would be renamed the Max Planck Institutes. As of January 2020 there were eighty-six institutes and research facilities, five of which are outside of Germany. See https://www.mpg.de/facts-and-figures.

7. Cited in Mark R. Nemec, *Ivory Towers and Nationalist Minds: Universities, Leadership, and the Development of the American State* (Ann Arbor: Michigan University Press, 2006), 164.

8. "The Letter of Invitation to the Founding Conference of AAU" (1900), online at https://www.aau.edu/key-issues/letter-invitation-founding-conference. The universities included were the University of California, the University of Chicago, Clark, Columbia University, Cornell University, Harvard University, Johns Hopkins University, University of Michigan, University of Pennsylvania, Princeton University, Stanford University, University of Wisconsin, and Yale University.

9. President of Yale Arthur Hadley questioned the necessity of such an institution and declined to attend the first meeting in Chicago. Nemec, *Ivory Towers and Nationalist Minds*, 160, 165, 205. On the Germans' reliance on the AAU for an assessment of institutional and degree quality, see Münsterberg, *Das Studium der Amerikaner an deutschen Universitäten* [July 23, 1908], Bl. 130.

10. Nemec, *Ivory Towers and Nationalist Minds*, 173–174.

11. Nemec, 180. For a history of the AAU, see Hugh Hawkins, *Banding Together: The Rise of National Associations in American Higher Education, 1887–1950* (Baltimore: Johns Hopkins University Press, 1992).

12. Gilman, *University Problems*, 301.

13. Gilman, "Resignation—Farewell Address, Feb. 22, 1902," in *The Launching of a University*, 130–131.

14. Cited in Merle Curti, Judith Green, and Roderick Nash, "Anatomy of Giving: Millionaires in the Late 19th Century," *American Quarterly* 15 (1963): 416.

15. Richard Hofstadter, "The Revolution in Higher Education," in *Paths of American Thought*, ed. Arthur M. Schlesinger Jr. and Morton White (Boston: Houghton Mifflin, 1970), 269–290. See also Purcell, *The Crisis of Democratic Theory*, 6–7.

16. The findings drew on a list of some four thousand millionaires from 1892 compiled by the *New York Tribune*. Curti, Green, and Nash, "Anatomy of Giving," 424.

17. Karl Lamprecht, "Bericht über das Studienjahr 1910/1911: Rede des Abtretenden Rektors Dr. Karl Lamprecht," in *Rektoratswechsel an der Universität Leipzig am 31. Oktober 1911* (Leipzig, 1911); Nr. 66: 6, Bl. 56, Nachlass Lamprecht, Universitäts- und Landesbibliothek Bonn (hereafter ULB).

18. "Morgan Gift of $50,000 Goes to University of Goettingen, Hanover, Where He Was Once a Student," *New York Times*, February 8, 1912, 1; and "The Alarm of Foreign Connoisseurs Lest America Carry Away Their Great Treasures," *Public Opinion* 37 (1904): 787.

19. Andrew Carnegie, "Wealth," *North American Review* 391 (1889): 663; this article is commonly known as "The Gospel of Wealth." See Edward Kirkland's helpful introduction to *The Gospel of Wealth and Other Timely Essays* (Cambridge, MA: Harvard University Press, 1962), vii–xx.

20. Carnegie would name the first of the technical schools he founded in 1906 the Margaret Morrison Carnegie School for Women in honor of his mother. Andrew Carnegie to Hon. W. J. Diehl (mayor of Pittsburgh), November 15, 1900, online at http://diva .library.cmu.edu/webapp/carnegie/.

21. Andrew Carnegie to Hon. W. J. Diehl (mayor of Pittsburgh), November 15, 1900. See also Carnegie, foreword to "Memorial of the Celebration of the Carnegie Institute at Pittsburgh, PA — April 11–13, 1907," 70; for the quotation, see Andrew Carnegie to Mr. Woods, April, undated, both online at http://diva.library.cmu.edu/webapp/ carnegie/.

22. According to Ethan Ris's analysis, Carnegie underwent an evolution in his philanthropy from a youthful disdain for culture to an interest in technical schools, concluding in an embrace of the education sector at the end of his life. See Ris, "The Education of Andrew Carnegie," 152.

23. Howard S. Miller, *Dollars for Research: Science and Its Patrons in Nineteenth-Century America* (Seattle: University of Washington Press, 1970), 132.

24. Carl Snyder's article "America's Inferior Position in the Scientific World," was, according to Miller, conveniently placed in Carnegie's "favorite publication," *North American Review*, in 1902 to influence Carnegie. Miller, *Dollars for Research*, 173.

25. Minutes, Board of Trustees, Carnegie Institution of Washington. January 29, 1902, in Nathan Reingold and Ida H. Reingold, eds., *Science in America: A Documentary History, 1900–1939* (Chicago: University of Chicago Press, 1981), 14.

26. Madsen, *The National University*, 80. For their own accounts, see Andrew Dickson White, *Autobiography* (New York: Century, 1917), 2:200–201; and John Wesley Hoyt, "Autobiography," unpublished manuscript, 448–449, J box 1, folder 10, John Wesley Hoyt, Wisconsin Historical Society, Madison, Wisconsin). Thank you to Lee Grady for sending these materials.

27. Nathan Reingold, "National Science Policy in a Private Foundation: The Carnegie Institution of Washington," in *The Organization of Knowledge in Modern America, 1860–1920*, ed. Alexandra Oleson and John Voss (Baltimore: Johns Hopkins University Press, 1979), 313–340, here 317.

28. John Hoyt, *Memorial in regard to a National University* (Washington, DC: Government Princeton Office, 1892), 121.

29. Madsen, *The National University*, 79.

30. Madsen, 76.

31. Charles W. Eliot, "An American National University," *The Critic* (1898): 415–416. On Hoyt's memorial, see Madsen, *The National University*, 100. Initially written in 1873, Eliot's article was reprinted in 1898 following Hoyt's memo to coincide with several attempted bills in Congress on the subject.

32. Nicholas Murray Butler to Andrew Carnegie, December 1901, Andrew Carnegie Papers, LOC; also cited in Madsen, *The National University*, 111.

33. The president of the University of Iowa John Bowman and Charles Van Hise, president of the University of Wisconsin, were also supporters of the bill. On the allegiances among state university presidents, see Ris, "The American College in the Age of Reform," 149. For the Eliot-Hoyt debate, see Madsen, *The National University*, 79.

34. Hoyt, *Memorial in regard to a National University*, 122.

35. Madsen, *The National University*, 84–86.

36. White to Carnegie, May 13, 1901 and June 21, 1901; Butler to Carnegie, December 1901, Andrew Carnegie Papers, LOC; Gilman to White, July 28, 1901, Daniel Coit Gilman Papers, Special Collections, JHU.

37. Cited in Madsen, *The National University*, 111.

38. Cited in Burton J. Hendrick, *The Life of Andrew Carnegie* (New York: Doubleday, 1932), 2:219.

39. Butler was the leading force who combined the Washington Academy of Science and the patriotic George Washington Memorial Association to found the new institution. White called this coincidence "providential," a fact that Miller sees as such only in the ironic sense that it was completely engineered. Miller, *Dollars for Research*, 171, 174.

40. Miller, *Dollars for Research*, 173.

41. White urged Carnegie to appoint Gilman as president, but, unfortunately, he was less effective than he had been at Hopkins. David Madsen, "Daniel Coit Gilman at the Carnegie Institution of Washington," *History of Education Quarterly* 9 (Summer 1969): 154–186, esp. 158–159.

42. Minutes, Board of Trustees, Carnegie Institution of Washington, January 29, 1902, in Reingold and Reingold, *Science in America*, 15.

43. Box 58, a, John Shaw Billings Papers, New York Public Library (hereafter NYPL). Also in Minutes, Board of Trustees, Carnegie Institution of Washington, January 29, 1902, 16.

44. Madsen, *The National University*, 111–114.

45. Ira Remsen to Theodore W. Richards, August 18, 1902, in Reingold and Reingold, *Science in America*, 20–21, quotation on 21.

46. Hugo Münsterberg, "The Carnegie Institution," *Science* 16 (Oct. 3, 1902): 521–529, quotation on 524.

47. For Clyde Barrow, Carnegie (as well as Flexner) were the villains who facilitated the integration of higher education into managerial capitalism. But this debate—and its results—shows that such a reading is too simplistic. Barrow, *Universities and the Capitalist State: Corporate Liberalism and the Reconstruction of American Higher Education, 1894–1928* (Madison: University of Wisconsin Press, 1990), 76–77, 87.

48. Lester F. Ward, "A National University," *Science* 6 (December 18, 1885): 539.

49. Cited in David F. Noble, *America by Design* (New York: Knopf, 1977), 137.

50. Edward Rafferty shows that this overlooked "father of sociology" admired Herbert Spencer but not the "liberal individualism and a vulgar Social Darwinism published in the United States in the early 1880s" that was inspired by him. Though Ward did not train in Germany himself, he was influenced by the anti-laissez-faire thinking of Ely, Small, and Ross, who did. Rafferty, *Apostle of Human Progress, Lester Frank Ward, and American Political Thought, 1841–1913* (Lanham, MD: Rowman & Littlefield, 2003), 125, 177. For Ward as a model for gender sociology, see Barbara Finlay, "Ward as a Sociologist of Gender: A New Look at His Sociological Work," *Gender and Society* 13 (1999): 251–265. For the relevance of Ward today, see James J. Chriss, "The Place of

Lester Ward among the Sociological Classics," *Journal of Classical Sociology* 6 (2006): 5–21, esp. 10.

51. Andrew Carnegie, "A Rectorial Address Delivered to the Students in the University of St. Andrews, October 22, 1902," 19–20, online at http://diva.library.cmu.edu/webapp/carnegie/.

52. Andrew Carnegie, "William II, German Emperor and King of Prussia," reprinted from the *New York Times* of June 8, 1913 (Dunfermline: A. Komanes & Sons, "Press" Office, 1913), 4. Carnegie recounts his visit with his wife to the emperor's annual regatta in Kiel in 1907 in his autobiography. Andrew Carnegie, *Autobiography of Andrew Carnegie* (Boston: Houghton Mifflin, 1920), 367–369.

53. Carnegie, "William II," 4, 21. "As I read this today [1914], what a change! The world convulsed by a way as never before! Men slaying each like wild beasts!" Carnegie, *Autobiography*, 371.

54. Carnegie, "William II," 5, and 9.

55. W. E. Gladstone, "Mr. Carnegie's 'Gospel of Wealth': A Review and a Recommendation," *Nineteenth Century*, 1890, 677–693.

56. Andrew Carnegie, *Die Pflichten des Reichtums: Zwei Aufsätze; Vom Verfasser autorisirte deutsche Ausgabe* (Leipzig: Schalscha-Ehrenfeld, 1894). Another version followed in 1901, published by Hobbing et Büchle in Stuttgart.

57. Andrew Carnegie, *Kaufmanns Herrschergewalt* (Berlin: Schwetschke, 1903); Carnegie, *The Empire of Business*, selections, ed. Henry Cave Ayles Carpenter (Leipzig: Teubner, 1911).

58. Carnegie, "The Best Fields for Philanthropy," *North American Review* 149 (1889): 682–698, here 688.

59. Cecil, *Wilhelm II,* 2:13.

60. Most scholars mark the birth of philanthropy in West Germany as occurring after World War II, but Thomas Adam's work offers an exception in that he points to the earlier and more varied history of private philanthropy in nineteenth-century Germany. Adam, *Philanthropy, Civil Society, and the State in German History, 1815–1989* (Rochester, NY: Camden House, 2016), 82.

61. See *Hochschulnachrichten: Monatsübersicht über das gesamte Hochschulwesen des In- und Auslandes* (later, from 1907, *Internationalen Wochenschrift*). On the Carnegie Institution, see *Hochschulnachrichten*, 1901, 69; and 1902, 93, 116, 139.

62. Adolf von Harnack, "Carnegies Schrift über die Pflicht der Reichen," in *Aus Wissenschaft und Leben* (Giessen: Verlag von Alfred Töpelmann, 1911), 1:167.

63. Cited in Cecil, *Wilhelm II,* 2:58–60, quotation on 59.

64. Cecil, *Wilhelm II,* 2:59. Quotation cited in Stern's *Einstein's German World,* 38.

65. The report was widely discussed among Prussian bureaucrats and German professors. See, for example, the German-language articles about Carnegie's recent donations in A II 75 Carnegie 600, Bl. 11, 12, 31, and 32, NL Althoff.

66. For the parallel story of the Rockefeller Institute, see George W. Corner, *A History of the Rockefeller Institute: 1901–1953, Origins and Growth* (New York: The Rockefeller Institute Press, 1964).

67. Alan Beyerchen sees Klein as a source of inspiration for Althoff. Beyerchen, "On

the Stimulation of Excellence in Wilhelminian Science," in Dukes and Remak, *Another Germany*, 156–157.

68. "Anfänge der Kaiser Wilhelm Gesellschaft," Rep. 92, Nr. 13, NL Schmidt-Ott. Partially reprinted in *Fünfzig Jahre Kaiser-Wilhelm-Gesellschaft und Max-Planck-Gesellschaft zur Förderung der Wissenschaften, 1911–1961* (Berlin: Max-Planck-Gesellschaft zur Förderung der Wissenschaft, 1961), 1:53–55; and as Appendix, "Althoffs Pläne für Dahlem: Denkschrift für Kaiser Wilhelm II" (1909), in *Idee und Wirklichkeit einer Universität: Dokumente zur Geschichte der Friedrich-Wilhelms-Universität zu Berlin*, ed. Wilhelm Weischedel (1960; Berlin: De Gruyter, 2019), 487–503. See also Jeffrey Allan Johnson, *The Kaiser's Chemists: Science and Mobilization in Imperial Germany* (Chapel Hill: University of North Carolina Press, 2010), 107–108.

69. "Anfänge der Kaiser-Wilhelm-Gesellschaft," in *Fünfzig Jahre Kaiser-Wilhelm-Gesellschaft*, 1:53–54.

70. His combined income came to 23,200 M in comparison to an average theology professor, who might be lucky to earn 7,000 M. See McClelland, *The Mother of All Research Universities*, 60–61.

71. George S. Duncan, "The Contribution of Adolf von Harnack to Theological and Biblical Learning," *Christian Education* 14 (1931): 694–698, here 694. Citation from Brysac, *Resisting Hitler*, 76.

72. For the details on Harnack's private life, see Shareen Blair Brysac, *Resisting Hitler: Mildred Harnack and the Red Orchestra* (Oxford: Oxford University Press, 2000), 79–81, quotation on 81. It is a mark of this circle's progressivism and independence of thought that both of Karl Bonhoeffer's sons, Klaus and Dietrich, as well as Harnack's niece Mildred and daughter Agnes, would oppose Hitler (three of the four would be executed for their resistance).

73. Lothar Burchardt, *Wissenschaftspolitik im Wilhelminischen Deutschland: Vorgeschichte, Gründung und Aufbau der Kaiser-Wilhelm-Gesellschaft zur Förderung der Wissenschaft* (Göttingen: Vandenhoeck und Ruprecht 1975), 19.

74. As we saw in chapter 3, Emil Fischer shared these ideas already in the first decade of the twentieth century. He reiterated this conviction in the *Internationale Wochenschrift für Wissenschaft, Kunst und Technik* 5 (1911): 129–148.

75. Harnack used the term "Royal Prussian Society for the Advancement of Science" and Theodor von Bethmann-Hollweg suggested "Kaiser's Society for the Advancement of Science" without territorial meaning in the English tradition. On the debate regarding the name, see Kristie Macrakis, *Surviving the Swastika: Scientific Research in Nazi Germany* (New York: Oxford University Press, 1993), 17.

76. Harnack, "Carnegies Schrift über die Pflicht der Reichen,"167.

77. Merton to Alfons Paquet, June 1, 1904, Nachlass Alfons Paquet (II) A 8 III, Autographen-Sammlung der Universitätsbibliothek J. C. Senckenberg, Göethe Universität, Frankfurt am Main.

78. David Cahan, "Werner Siemens and the Origin of the Physikalisch-Technische Reichsanstalt, 1872–1887," *Historical Studies in Physical Sciences* 12 (1982): 253–283. See also Frank Pfetsch's differing argument that economic and industrial concerns — not pure research — were the primary force in the Imperial Institute's founding.

Pfetsch, "Scientific Organisation and Science Policy in Imperial Germany, 1871–1914: The Foundation of the Imperial Institute of Physics and Technology," *Minerva* 8 (1970): 557–580, esp. 562.

79. See Johnson, *The Kaiser's Chemists*, esp. 48–86.

80. German Jews were especially susceptible to this exchange and were targeted somewhat mercilessly by the chemists and then the Prussian bureaucrats as potential donors for the cause. Lamar Cecil, "Wilhelm II und die Juden," in *Juden im Wilhelminischen Deutschland 1890–1914*, ed. Werner E. Mosse (Tübingen: J.C.B. Mohr, 1976), 313–347.

81. Johnson, *The Kaiser's Chemists*, 46.

82. As Macrakis points out, a nationalist phrase is omitted from the second version of this memorandum, "Gedanken über eine neue Art der Wissenschaftsförderung" (1910), Archiv zur Geschichte der Max-Planck-Gesellschaft, Berlin. Macrakis, *Surviving the Swastika*, 15.

83. Cited and translated in Johnson, *The Kaiser's Chemists*, 6.

84. Kuno Francke came to its defense with an "American perspective" in "Das Kartell zwischen deutschen und amerikanischen Universitäten: In amerikanischer Beleuchtung," *Der Tag: Erster Teil; Illustrierte Zeitung*, May 7, 1905), A I Nr. 310, Amerika 1904–1908–419, Bl. 190, NL Althoff.

85. For Carnegie's quotation, see "Popular Illusions about Trusts," *Century Magazine* 60 (1900): 143–149, here 146.

86. Cited and translated in Johnson, *The Kaiser's Chemists*, 43.

87. This complements recent German scholarship, which argues that the Humboldt ideal was in fact a response to a crisis around 1900, shortly after Humboldt's famous notes on the research university were discovered in the 1890s and published in 1903. See, for example, Paletschek, "The Invention of Humboldt and the Impact of National Socialism," 38.

88. "Denkschrift von Harnack an den Kaiser" (1909), in *Fünfzig Jahre Kaiser-Wilhelm-Gesellschaft*, 1:80, 83.

89. Rüdiger vom Bruch, "Wissenschaftspolitik, Kulturpolitik, Weltpolitik: Hochschule und Forschungsinstitute auf dem Deutschen Hochschullehretag in Dresden 1911," in *Transformation des Historismus: Wissenschaftsorganisation und Bildungspolitik vor dem Ersten Weltkrieg*, ed. Horst Walter Blanke (Waltrop: Spenner, 1994), 32–63, esp. 44–45.

90. "Denkschrift von Harnack an den Kaiser," 81 (my translation).

91. Valentini to Harnack, Berlin, December 10, 1909, in *Fünfzig Jahre Kaiser-Wilhelm-Gesellschaft*, 1:94.

92. Johnson, *The Kaiser's Chemists*, 18.

93. Military expenditure increased from 1.4 billion M in the 1910 budget, slightly less than half the entire budget, to 2.3 billion M, or 62 percent, in 1913. This is in contrast to the university budget, which went flat between 1910 and 1914. McClelland, *The Mother of All Research Universities*, 63–64. According to Adam, the Prussian state was providing 48 million M annually to fund the sciences in 1909. Adam, *Philanthropy, Civil Society, and the State*, 79–80.

94. Adolf von Harnack, "Zur Kaiserlichen Botschaft vom 11. Oktober: Begründung von Forschungsinstituten," *Die Woche* 12 (1910): 1933–1938.

95. Adolf von Harnack to Trott zu Solz, January 22, 1910, in *Fünfzig Jahre Kaiser-Wilhelm-Gesellschaft*, 1:95.

96. Vierhaus and vom Brocke, *Forschung im Spannungsfeld von Politik und Gesellschaft*, 22. For the first use of *Wissenschaftspolitik*, see Adolf von Harnack, *Geschichte der Königlich Preußischen Akademie der Wissenschaften zu Berlin* (Berlin: Reichsdruckerei, 1900), 1:4, 95. On *Schulpolitik*, see Friedrich Paulsen, *Geschichte des gelehrten Unterrichts auf den deutschen Schulen und Universitäten*, 2nd ed. (Leipzig, 1896), 1:4-5, 95. According to vom Brocke, the term *auswärtige Kulturpolitik* was first used by Lamprecht in 1908 in conversations with Althoff. Vom Brocke, "Friedrich Althoff: A Great Figure," 275.

97. Erich Schmidt, ed., *Jahrhundertfeier der Königlichen Friedrich-Wilhelms-Universität zu Berlin 10.-12. Oktober 1910* (Berlin: Friedrich-Wilhelms-Universität Berlin, 1911), 38 (my translation). For a discussion of the invocation of the "unity of knowledge," see McClelland, *The Mother of All Research Universities*, 226.

98. "Denkschrift von Harnack an den Kaiser," 88; Vierhaus and vom Brocke, *Forschung im Spannungsfeld von Politik und Gesellschaft*, 364–365.

99. Burchardt, *Wissenschaftspolitik im Wilhelminischen Deutschland*, 37, 93.

100. According to vom Brocke, these subsidies accounted for 25 percent of its budget. Vom Brocke, "Die Kaiser Wilhelm Gesellschaft in Kaiserreich Vorgeschichte, Gründung und Entwicklung," in Vierhaus and vom Brocke, *Forschung im Spannungsfeld*, 157.

101. Burchardt, *Wissenschaftspolitik im Wilhelminischen Deutschland*, 38–39, 48–49, 70.

102. Burchardt, 48–49; Adam, *Philanthropy, Civil Society, and the State in German History*, 82.

103. Burchardt, 64–65; Adam, 86.

104. Cited in Clark, *Academic Charisma*, 470.

105. "Denkschrift von Harnack an den Kaiser," 80–94, quotation on 89 (my translation). For chemist Lise Meitner's description of that day, see Patricia Rife, *Lise Meitner and the Dawn of the Nuclear Age* (Basel: Birkhäuser, 2007), 50–51.

106. Mitchell L. Stevens, Elizabeth A. Armstrong, and Richard Arum, "Sieve, Incubator, Temple, Hub: Empirical and Theoretical Advances in the Sociology of Higher Education," *Annual Review of Sociology* 34 (2008): 127–151.

107. Herbert Haevecker, "40 Jahre Kaiser Wilhelm Gesellschaft," *Jahrbuch der Max Planck Gesellschaft zur Förderung der Wissenschaft*, 1911–1951, 7–59, quotation on 15 (my translation).

108. Beyerchen, "On the Stimulation of Excellence in Wilhelmian Science," 158.

109. According to Virginia Woolf, in her essay "Mr. Bennet and Mrs. Brown" (1924), "on or about December, 1910, human character changed." The British historian Peter Stansky used this observation as a starting point to argue for a transatlantic reorientation of the cultural and aesthetic world. See Stansky, *On or about December 1910: Early Bloomsbury and Its Intimate World* (Cambridge, MA: Harvard University Press, 1997).

110. See, for example, Oliver Zunz, *Philanthropy in America: A History* (Princeton, NJ: Princeton University Press, 2012), 23–24.

111. Chandler, *The Visible Hand*, 2, 282.

112. *25 Jahre Kaiser Wilhelm-Gesellschaft zur Forderung der Wissenschaften* (Berlin: Springer, 1936); 1:25–26.

113. David Starr Jordan, "To What Extent Should the University Investigator Be Freed from Teaching?," *The Association of American Universities: Journal of Proceedings and Addresses of the Seventh Annual Conference* (Chicago: Association of American Universities, 1906), 7:23–43, quotations on 24, 29, and 32.

114. "Paper Prepared by President Arthur T. Hadley and Presented on Behalf of Yale University, by Professor Theodore S. Woolsey," in *Journal of Proceedings and Addresses of the Seventh Annual Conference Held in San Francisco, Berkeley, and Palo Alto, Cal. March 14–17, 1906* (Chicago: University of Chicago Press, 1920), 43–44.

115. Carnegie to Pritchett, January 14, 1908, Box 2, Henry S. Pritchett Papers, LOC.

116. Pritchett to Carnegie, January 21, 1908, Box 2, Pritchett Papers, LOC.

117. See the Kaiser's remarks and those of the rector, which echoed Harnack's allusion to Humboldt's original intention to found supplementary institutions. Schmidt, ed., *Jahrhundertfeier*, 36–37, 41.

118. Matthias Middell, "Auszug der Forschung aus der Universität," in *Gebrochene Wissenschaftskulturen: Universität und Politik im 20 Jahrhundert*, ed. Michael Grüttner et al. (Göttingen: Vandenhoeck & Ruprecht, 2011), 209–214.

119. Crawford, *Nationalism and Internationalism in Science*, 5, 110, and the table on 111; and Ben-David, *The Scientist's Role*, 193.

120. Clark saw the subservience to extraordinary scientific personalities as prioritizing charisma. Clark, *Academic Charisma*, 467.

121. See table 3.3 in Adam, *Philanthropy, Civil Society, and the State in German History*, 82 and 84–85.

122. District President Wilhelm von Meister from Wiesbaden to the Oberprasidenten of Hessen Nassau about Mathilden von Rothschild, cited in Michael Dorrmann, *Eduard Arnhold (1849–1925): Eine biographische Studie zu Unternehmer- und Mäzenatentum im Deutschland Kaiserreich* (Berlin: Akademie, 2002), 196 (my translation). On these rejected professors going to America, see Johnson, *The Kaiser's Chemists*, 116.

123. This number includes such converted Jews as Koppel, von Mendelssohn, and von Schwabach, who were still, for all intents and purposes, considered Jews in German society. Vom Brocke, "Die Kaiser Wilhelm Gesellschaft in Kaiserreich Vorgeschichte," 47; and Christoph Kreutzmüller, "Zum Umgang der Kaiser Wilhelm Gesellschaft mit Geld und Gut," *Ergebnisse* 27 (2005): 25.

124. I differ here from Adam's and vom Brocke's analysis of the motivations of the Jewish donors of the Kaiser Wilhelm Society, both of whom argue that Jews aimed to raise their social status or were trapped into giving but consequently do not attribute to them strategic goals. Adam, *Philanthropy, Civil Society, and the State in German History*, 83.

125. Macrakis, *Surviving the Swastika*, 13.

126. Annette Vogt shows how because of the law forbidding women who were married or had children from working at universities, those who did often found themselves at the Kaiser Wilhelm Institutes. Vogt, "Barrieren und Karrieren—am Beispiel der Wissenschaftlerinn," in *Frauen in der Wissenschaft—Frauen an der TU Dresden: Tagung aus Anlass der Zulassung von Frauen zum Studium in Dresden vor 100 Jahren* (Leipzig: Leipziger Universitätsverlag, 2010), 165–167, quotation on 171. Vogt has identified 225 women scientists with PhDs who worked at 20 different Kaiser Wilhelm Institutes between 1912 and 1945. Annette Vogt, "Women in Army Research: Ambivalent Careers in Nazi Germany," in *Crossing Boundaries, Building Bridges: Comparing the History of Women Engineers, 1870–1990s*, ed. Annie Canel, Ruth Oldenziel (London: Routledge, 2005), 186–206, here 188. Though evidently the Kaiser Wilhelm Society was not successful in attracting female donors, apart from Henriette Hertz, who bequeathed the society Palazzo Zuccari in Rome as an art history institute along with a significant library and endowment. Adam, *Philanthropy, Civil Society, and the State in German History*, 76.

127. As a result, the Kaiser Wilhelm Society became stigmatized as a "Jewish" institution by the nationalist and antisemitic physicist Philipp Lenard. Macrakis, *Surviving the Swastika*, 13. On the systematic exclusion of Jews from American elite universities beginning in the 1920s, see Karabel, *The Chosen*, 86–87, 112; and Marcia Graham Synnott, *The Half-Opened Door: Discrimination and Admissions at Harvard, Yale, and Princeton, 1900–1970* (Westport, CT: Greenwood Press, 1979), 14, 17. In contrast, by 1918 seven German Jews received Nobel Prizes, all in the natural sciences or without a university affiliation. Peter Pulzer, *Jews and the German State: The Political History of a Minority, 1848–1933* (Detroit: Wayne State University Press, 2003), 45.

128. One recent attempt to nuance this position, though it remains focused on the second half of the twentieth century, is Gregory R. Witkowski and Arnd Bauerkämper, eds., *German Philanthropy in Transatlantic Perspective: Perceptions, Exchanges, and Transfers since the Early Twentieth Century* (Cham, Switzerland: Springer, 2016). For the quotation see "One Model Does Not Fit All" [Eines Schickt sich nicht für alle], *Abendblatt der New York*, April 27, 1910, 76Vc, Sect. 1, Tit. XI, Pt. IX, No. 12, Vol. I, Fol. 72 (my translation); cited in part but with incorrect newspaper attribution in Macrakis, *Surviving the Swastika*, 16.

129. Burchardt, *Wissenschaftspolitik im Wilhelminischen Deutschland*, 85–94; and Johnson, *The Kaiser's Chemists*, 88.

130. Adam argues that the decline of philanthropy was due less to the inflation than the government's decision to forgo its responsibility to the owners of war bonds. Adam, *Philanthropy, Civil Society, and the State in German History*, 6–7.

131. The French education official Louis Liard was interested in the American model of private philanthropy, but his efforts were not matched by the state and strapped regional institutions with more applied research. See Weisz, "The French Universities and Education for the New Professions," 102–104, 109–110. The Japanese also sought an institutional model in 1913 that combined American and German influences and would ultimately take shape as the Institute of Physical and Chemical Research

(RIKEN), founded in 1917. See Bowen C. Dees, *The Allied Occupation and Japan's Economic Miracle: Building the Foundations of Japanese Science and Technology, 1945–1952* (London: Routledge, 1997), 120–121.

132. According to Peter Uwe Hohendahl, this was the case in the 1990s, when Germans conjured the myth of the Humboldt ideal to challenge the reality of the neoliberal university. Hohendahl, "Humboldt Revisited: General Education, University Reform, and the Opposition to the Neoliberal University," *New German Critique* 113 (2011): 159–196.

CHAPTER SEVEN

1. Daniel H. Pollitt and Jordan E. Kurland, "Entering the Academic Freedom Arena Running," *Academe* 84 (1998): 45–52, here 46, 48, and 49.

2. As Michael Berubé observes, "The German concept of *Lehrfreiheit*, the professor's freedom to teach, were simply added to faculty handbooks everywhere once Johns Hopkins University adopted the German research model." Berubé, foreword to Hans-Joerg Tiede, *University Reform: The Founding of the American Association of University Professors* (Baltimore: Johns Hopkins University Press, 2015), vii-viii.

3. A survey conducted of twenty-two universities (nine of which were private) on behalf of the AAU in 1910 showed that nearly all universities awarded their professors no more than one-year appointments, with anything longer granted on the basis of mere understandings. Charles R. Van Hise, "The Appointment and Tenure of University Professors," *Science* 33 (Feb. 17, 1911): 237–246, here 238. The situation at land grants was worse, where only two of forty-three institutions actually used formal written contracts, and in only five were the duties of the position enumerated specifically. E. D. Sanderson, "The Definiteness of Appointment and Tenure," *Science* 39 (1914): 890–896, esp. 891.

4. Max Weber, "Die sogenannte 'Lehrfreiheit' an den deutschen Universitäten," *Frankfurt Zeitung*, September 20, 1908; Translation from Weber, "The Alleged 'Academic Freedom' of the German Universities," in Shils, "The Power of the State," 589.

5. Walter Metzger, "Academic Tenure in America: A Historical Essay," *Faculty Tenure* 93 (1973): 148.

6. Friedrich Paulsen, *Die deutschen Universitäten und das Universitätsstudium* (Berlin: A. Asher, 1902), 291 (my translation).

7. G. Stanley Hall, "The University Idea," *Pedagogical Seminary* 15 (1908): 92–104, here 102.

8. Friedrich Paulsen's observation of academic freedom as a "recognizable and undisputed right" reflected this general common law. Paulsen, *Die deutschen Universitäten und das Universitätsstudium* (Berlin: A. Asher, 1902), 291.

9. On this earlier period, see Edward Yarnall Hartshorne, "The German Universities and the Government," *Annals of the American Academy of Political and Social Science* 200 (1938): 210–234, here 210–211; Hofstadter and Metzger, *The Development of Academic Freedom in the United States*, 384–385; and Metzger, "Academic Tenure in America," 93–95. On Gershom Scholem's debunking of the myth of Spinoza, see

David J. Wertheim, *Salvation through Spinoza: A Study of Jewish Culture in Weimar Germany* (Leiden: Brill, 2011), 46. To be sure, Frederick the Great distinguished himself from his father, who had banished Wolff in the 1720s at the request of a pietist, but nonetheless enlightened discourse was permitted only insofar as it partnered with the state. Christopher Clark, *Iron Kingdom: The Rise and Downfall of Prussia, 1600–1947* (Cambridge, MA: Harvard University Press, 2006), 252, 255.

10. Articles 20 and 22, online at http://www.documentarchiv.de/nzjh/verfpr1850.html (my translation). See also Walter Metzger, "The German Contribution to the American Theory of Academic Freedom," *Bulletin of the American Association of University Professors* 41 (1955): 214–230, esp. 218.

11. Emil Du Bois-Reymond, "Der deutsche Krieg," in *Reden von Emil Du Bois-Reymond, Erste Folge: Literatur, Philosophie, Zeitgeschichte* (Leipzig, 1886), 65–94 (my translation); also cited in McClelland, *The Mother of All Research Universities*, 18. The emperor evidently favored Du Bois-Reymond for his docility. Cecil, *Wilhelm II*, 2:59.

12. McClelland, *The Mother of All Research Universities*, 19–20.

13. The title of a 1915 report made the link between academic freedom and tenure explicit, and the third practical proposal item prioritized professional status: "to render the profession more attractive to men of high ability and strong personality by insuring the dignity, the independence, and the reasonable security of tenure, of the professorial office." E. R. A. Seligman et al., "General Report of the Committee on Academic Freedom and Academic Tenure," *Bulletin of the AAUP* 1, pt. 1 (December 1915): 20–43, quotation on 40. This document has been revised several times. In the most recent iteration—the "1940 Statement of Principles on Academic Freedom and Tenure" with "1970 Interpretive Comments," academic freedom is presented no longer as a means but an end for which tenure is justified. Online at https://www.aaup.org/report/1940-statement-principles-academic-freedom-and-tenure.

14. McClelland, *The Mother of All Research Universities*, 35. With Humboldt's backing the Catholic Sanskrit scholar Franz Bopp was promoted from *Extraordinarius* to *Ordinarius* in 1825 though it is notable that this was a new field. Ursula Wokoeck, *German Orientalism: The Study of the Middle East and Islam from 1800 to 1945* (London: Taylor & Francis, 2009), 102. As late as 1917 the Catholic scholar Max Scheler complained to Ernst Troeltsch of the difficulty getting a position at a non-Catholic university. James Chappel, "Slaying the Leviathan: Catholicism and the Rebirth of European Conservatism, 1920–1950" (PhD diss., Columbia University, 2012), 105–106.

15. David, "Higher Education Reform and the German Model," 40.

16. A respected Jewish classicist like Jakob Bernays did not receive a job at a university, but was confined to the Jewish Theological Seminar in Breslau. For the Weber quotation, see Gerth and Mills, *From Max Weber*, 134. Althoff calculated the percentage of Catholics and Jewish *Ordinarius* professors in 1880 as 15 percent and nearly 3 percent, respectively. In 1896/7 the percentage grew to 17 percent Catholic and nearly 4 percent Jewish. There was one Jewish *Ordinarius* from 1912 to 1914. McClelland, *The Mother of All Research Universities*, 37.

17. Paulsen, *The German Universities and University Study*, 105.

18. Following this case a law was passed in 1898, the so-called Lex Arons, that

prevented Social Democrats from teaching at universities. Busch, *Die Geschichte des Privatdozenten*, 114. For the American reception, see William C. Dreher, "A Letter from Germany," *Atlantic Monthly* 85 (1900): 305.

19. McClelland, *The Mother of All Research Universities*, 51–52.

20. The Kohlschutter case, the Scheimann case, and the Bernhard case were among the most notorious impositions of the will of the state over the objections of the faculty. See Senn, "Where Is Althoff?," 248.

21. Metzger, "The German Contribution to the American Theory of Academic Freedom," 217.

22. Only at the end of his inaugural lecture as rector of the University of Berlin in 1877 did Helmholtz add on to a lengthy discussion of student corporations, "The free conviction of the student can only be acquired when freedom of expression is guaranteed to the teacher's own conviction—the liberty of teaching." Helmholtz, "On Academic Freedom in German Universities," 336. In fact, the freedom of students was so central to the university experience that Fichte's attempt to constrain that freedom by, for example, requiring student uniforms or barring dueling was the source of much disagreement with Schleiermacher and caused the termination of Fichte's rectorship. See Johann Gottlieb Fichte, "Über die einzig mögliche Störung der akademische Freiheit," in *Sämtliche Werke*, ed. J. H. Fichte (Berlin: Veit, 1845), 6:449–476. See also Fallon, *The German University*, 27.

23. Paulsen, "Die akademische Lehrfreiheit und ihre Grenzen: Eine Rede *pro domo*," *Preußische Jahrbücher* 91 (1898): 515–531.

24. Ridder-Symoens and Rüegg, *A History of the University in Europe*, 2:227. Moreover, sons of university-educated officials and clergymen had privileged access to the university. La Vopa, *Grace, Talent, and Merit*, 30.

25. Cecil, *Wilhelm II*, 2:59.

26. For Althoff's attitude toward Catholics and Jews, see Friedrich Paulsen, "Friedrich Althoff," *Internationale Wochenschrift für Wissenschaft und Technik* 1 (1907): 967–978. For the quotation from Althoff's 1905 speech on the long history of academic freedom, see vom Brocke, "Friedrich Althoff: A Great Figure," 291. On the "academic *Kulturkampf*," see also Senn, "Where Is Althoff?," 248.

27. Bernhard Naunyn, German physician, cited in vom Brocke, "Hochschul- und Wissenschaftspolitik in Preußen und im Deutschen Kaiserreich," 91.

28. On the Spahn Affair, see Christian Nottmeier, *Harnack und die deutsche Politik 1890–1930: Eine biographische Studie zum Verhältnis von Protestantismus, Wissenschaft und Politik* (Tübingen: Mohr Siebeck, 2004), 162.

29. McClelland, *The Mother of All Research Universities*, 52. For a table detailing how many times professors were actually "imposed" over the suggestions of the faculty, see vom Brocke, "Hochschul- und Wissenschaftspolitik in Preußen und im Deutschen Kaiserreich," 90.

30. Charles McClelland, "Republics within the Empire," in Duke and Remak, *Another Germany*, 171.

31. See Jonathan Blake Fine, "Streitkultur: Polemic and the Problem of Public En-

lightenment in Eighteenth-Century Germany" (PhD diss., University of California, Irvine, 2013). Thank you to John Smith for this reference.

32. Hofstadter and Metzger, *The Development of Academic Freedom in the United States*, 388.

33. Max Weber, "Der Fall Bernhard," *Frankfurter Zeitung*, June 18, 1908 (unsigned); translation from Shils, "The Bernhard Affair," in Shils, "The Power of the State," 575.

34. Weber, "The Alleged 'Academic Freedom,'" 589.

35. McClelland, *The Mother of All Research Universities*, 52–53.

36. Weber, "The Alleged 'Academic Freedom,'" 21.

37. When ninety-three German scientists made their so-called Appeal to the Civilized World on October 12, 1914, it made explicit what so many American students had long ignored: freedom was granted only in exchange for loyalty to the state. The appeal was published in the American, British, and French press and within days the transatlantic intellectuals were up in arms. Manifestos and counter-manifestos proliferated across nations. See "To the Civilized World," published in English in *North American Review* 210 (1919): 284–287. For American coverage of the manifesto, see the *New York Times*, June 6, 1916, 13. On the transatlantic reaction, see Tomas Irish, *The University at War, 1914–25: Britain, France, and the United States* (London: Palgrave, 2015), 25–33.

38. Ticknor to Jefferson, October 14, 1815, on freedom of professors in Göttingen; cited in O. W. Long, *Thomas Jefferson and George Ticknor: A Chapter in American Scholarship* (Williamstown, MA: McClelland Press, 1933), 13–15.

39. Cited in Long, *Literary Pioneers*, 122.

40. Daniel Coit Gilman's Declaration on Intellectual Freedom (1875), in *American Higher Education: A Documentary History*, ed. Richard Hofstadter and Wilson Smith (Chicago: University of Chicago Press, 1961), 1:845.

41. Harper, in *The Trend in Higher Education* (Chicago: University of Chicago Press, 1905), 1–34, quotation on 7–8.

42. Richard T. Ely, *Papers and Discussions of the Twenty-Second Annual Meeting* (New York: American Economic Association, 1910), 77.

43. Samuel Eliot Morison's early history gives the false impression that freedom of teaching and not freedom of learning was what first appealed to Harvard reformers. Morison, *Three Centuries of Harvard, 1636–1936* (Cambridge, MA: Harvard University Press, 1936), 254; alluded to in Hofstadter and Metzger, *The Development of Academic Freedom in the United States*, 391, 392. The German-trained political economist Richard T. Ely represented a lone understanding of this nuance when he observed, "The freedom in German universities was the freedom given to men selecting their own professions. Public authorities minutely prescribed requirements for these examinations. In this way they controlled the university courses." Ely, *Ground under Our Feet: An Autobiography* (New York: Macmillan, 1938), 51. Ely himself was the subject of an academic freedom case at the University of Wisconsin for his socialist leanings, and his exoneration led to that university's affirmation of academic freedom as freedom of teaching. See Ely, *Ground under Our Feet*, 232.

44. See, for example, Dean Andrew F. Wester, "What Is Academic Freedom?," *North American Review* 140 (1885): 432–444.

45. In Albion W. Small's 1899 article on "academic freedom," student freedom had disappeared from the discussion. Hofstadter and Metzger, *The Development of Academic Freedom in the United States*, 397–398.

46. Larry G. Gerber, *The Rise and Decline of Faculty Governance: Professionalization and the Modern American University* (Baltimore: Johns Hopkins University Press, 2014), esp. 3–9.

47. Meyer, *The Design of the University*, xv, 209.

48. Tiede, *University Reform*, 11.

49. Arthur O. Lovejoy. "Profession of the Professorate," *Johns Hopkins Alumni Magazine* 2 (1913–1914): 186–187, 191.

50. Cattell, "University Control," *Science* 35 (May 24, 1912): 797–808, quotation on 800, survey results on 808.

51. Benjamin G. Rader in *The Influence of Richard T. Ely in American Life* (Lexington: University of Kentucky Press, 1966), 135ff. On the question as to whether Ely's socialist leanings were protected by academic freedom, see Theron Schlabach, "An Aristocrat on Trial: The Case of Richard T. Ely," *Wisconsin Magazine of History* 47 (1963): 146–159.

52. Earl McGrath, "The Control of Higher Education in America," *Educational Record* 17 (1936): 259–272, here 264–265.

53. Edward A. Ross, *Seventy Years of It* (New York: D. Appleton-Century, 1936), 64–65.

54. Tiede, *University Reform*, 36–38. One recent end to this century-long controversy over labor and Stanford University is the collaborative effort The Chinese Railroad Workers in North American Project, which aims to write the Chinese workers back into American and university history. See Gordon H. Chang on the "contradictory" legacy of Leland Stanford, who was both benefactor and exploiter. Chang, "The Chinese and the Stanfords: Nineteenth-Century America's Fraught Relationship with the China Men," in *The Chinese and the Iron Road: Building the Transcontinental Railroad*, ed. Gordon H. Chang and Shelley Fisher Fishkin (Stanford, CA: Stanford University Press, 2019), 346–364, esp. 346, 364.

55. John Dewey, "Academic Freedom," *Educational Review*, 1902, 1–14, here 12. Dewey describes the way that previous disciplines like mathematics were specialized in the face of initial opposition (3).

56. On the connection between the social sciences and professionalization, see Mary O. Furner, *Advocacy and Objectivity: A Crisis in the Professionalization of American Social Science, 1865–1905* (London: Routledge, 2017).

57. On occasion, however, Pritchett devoted resources to investigating political interference at state institutions, albeit to prove his point about their mediocre standards for scholarship. Tiede, *University Reform*, 46, 50.

58. Walter P. Metzger, "The First Investigation," *AAUP Bulletin* 47 (August 1961): 206–210.

59. Seligman et al., "General Report of the Committee on Academic Freedom and Academic Tenure," 20.

60. Tiede, *University Reform*, 113.

61. The "four essential freedoms" enumerated in Justice Frankfurter's decision in Sweezy v. New Hampshire 354 U.S. 234 (1957) crucially addressed the *institution* and not the *individual*. See Ralph S. Brown and Jordan E. Kurland, "Academic Tenure and Academic Freedom," *Faculty Scholarship Series*, Paper 2718 (1990): 334–335.

62. Tiede, *University Reform*, 129.

63. John Dewey, "Is the College Professor a 'Hired Man'?," *Literary Digest* 51 (July 10, 1915): 65. The question of whether Dewey was a handmaiden to the administrative state and corporate liberalism or an advocate of citizen participation is the matter of some controversy. For the former, see Clarence Karier, "Making the World Safe for Democracy: An Historical Critique of John Dewey's Pragmatic Liberal Philosophy in the Warfare State," *Educational Theory* 27 (1977): 12–47; and R. Jeffrey Lustig, *Corporate Liberalism: The Origins of Modern American Political Theory, 1890–1920* (Berkeley: University of California Press, 1982). For a more generous interpretation of a prudent and strategic Dewey, see Robert B. Westbrook, *John Dewey and American Democracy* (Ithaca, NY: Cornell University Press, 1991), esp. 91–92, Andrew Jewett tries to place Dewey back into his context in a long history of "scientific democrats" in *Science, Democracy, and the American University: From the Civil War to the Cold War* (Cambridge: Cambridge University Press, 2012), 7–8.

64. Dewey, "Academic Freedom," 14.

65. Jewett calls this the "disengagement thesis." Jewett, *Science, Democracy, and the American University*, 4.

66. Cited in Carol S. Gruber, *Mars and Minerva: World War I and the Uses of the Higher Learning in America* (Baton Rouge: Louisiana State University Press, 1975), 68.

67. Hofstadter and Metzger include Arthur O. Lovejoy (who was born in Berlin but did not study there) on their list. The others were E. R. A. Seligman, Henry W. Farnam, R. T. Ely, U. G. Weatherly, Charles E. Bennett, Howard Crosby Warren, and Frank A. Fetter. In addition, the leaders for professorial self-government were also German university alumni: Joseph Jastrow, James McKeen Cattell, and George T. Ladd. Hofstadter and Metzger, *The Development of Academic Freedom in the United States*, 396.

68. "General Report of the Committee on Academic Freedom and Academic Tenure," 20.

69. Hofstadter and Metzger, *The Development of Academic Freedom in the United States*, 396.

70. Arthur O. Lovejoy, "German Scholars and Truth about Germany," *The Nation* 99 (1914): 376. For American coverage of the manifesto, see the *New York Times*, June 6, 1916, 13. On this tension, see Timothy Cain, *Establishing Academic Freedom: Politics, Principles, and the Development of Core Values* (New York: Palgrave, 2012), 53–58.

71. Between 1881 and 1892, 1.7 million Germans had come to the United States. Bernd Weiler, "Thus Spoke the Scientist: Franz Boas's Critique of the Role of the United States in World War I," in *Academics as Public Intellectuals*, ed. Sven Eliaeson and Ragnvald Kalleberg (Newcastle, UK: Cambridge Scholars Publishing 2008), 70.

72. Kuno Francke, *Deutsche Arbeit in Amerika: Erinnerungen von Kuno Francke* (Leipzig: Felix Meiner, 1930), 5.

73. The correspondence between Schmitt-Ott and Eugen Kühneman is typical of the attempts to persuade one another of their cause. VI. 411, NL Schmidt-Ott.

74. See Rudolf Eucken and Ernst Haeckel's August 31, 1914 notice sent with O. J. Merkel to A. Lawrence Lowell, December 26, 1914; Peabody to Schmidt-Ott, October 20, 1914, Bl. 36, VI. 474, NL Schmidt-Ott.

75. See John William Burgess, *The European War of 1914: Its Causes, Purposes, and Probable Results* (Chicago: A.C. McClurg, 1915); Gruber, *Mars and Minerva*, 47.

76. "Considers Kaiser Sparring for Time," *New York Times*, April 9, 1917, 3. Boas's criticism of American nativism in the classroom led to protests from the Columbia alumni. See Weiler, "Thus Spoke the Scientist," 74–79. Boas later spoke out in 1919 against four anthropologists who used their cover as scientists to spy on behalf of the United States. See the reprint of his *Nation* op-ed in Franz Boas, *Anthropology Today* 21 (June 2005): 27.

77. Arthur T. Hadley, "The Political Teachings of Treitschke," *Yale Review* 4 (1915): 235–46; discussed in Gruber, *Mars and Minerva*, 74.

78. Gruber, *Mars and Minerva*, 54. For a comparison of the responses to wartime at Harvard and Columbia, see Tomás Irish, *The University at War, 1914–25: Britain, France, and the United States* (New York: Palgrave Macmillan, 2015), 69–72.

79. The American Historical Association tried to cover both points of view in 1915 and picked "a man of German extraction to represent what they expected to be the Germans' side of the question"; however, the German, Lingelbach of Pennsylvania, was more anti-German than anyone. Gruber, *Mars and Minerva*, 47.

80. See, for example, the speeches "Joseph Hodges Choate," June 7, 1917; and "Constitutional Convention," August 23, 1917, in the folder marked "Butler's Speeches," Butler Papers, RBMLC. On Butler's political ambition, see Rosenthal, *Nicholas Miraculous*, 7.

81. E. R. A. Seligman, "The Real University," *Educational Review* 52 (November 1916): 325–337, quotation on 327.

82. Dorothy Ross, "Cattell, James McKeen, 1860–1944," in *Dictionary of American Biography*, 23:148–151; cited in Thomas Bender, "E.R.A. Seligman and the Vocation of Social Science," *Intellect and Public Life: Essays on the Social History of Academic Intellectuals in the United States* (Baltimore: Johns Hopkins University Press, 1993), 49–77, quotation on 69.

83. Quotations from Bender, "E.R.A. Seligman and the Vocation of Social Science," 69; and Tiede, *University Reform*, 24.

84. James McKeen Cattell, "University Control" (1906): 476.

85. Nicholas Murray Butler, "Commencement Day Address," June 6, 1917, Box 2, Folder 31, Butler Papers, RBMLC.

86. President Lowell of Harvard issued a similar statement on academic freedom in wartime but nothing amounting to what would happen at Columbia occurred in Cambridge. A. Lawrence Lowell, "Statement on Academic Freedom in Wartime, 1917," in *American Higher Education: A Documentary History*, ed. Richard Hofstadter and Wilson Smith (Chicago: University of Chicago Press, 1961), 2:878–882.

87. Letters of Cattell to Julius Kahn of Columbia, S. Wallace Dempsey of New York, and E. R. Bathrick of Ohio, August 23, 1917, James McKeen Cattell Papers, RBMLC.

88. Charles Beard, "A Statement by Charles Beard," *New Republic*, December 29, 1917, 249–251. See also "Charles Beard Notifies Nicholas Murray Butler of His Resignation from Columbia, 1917," in Hofstadter and Smith, *American Higher Education*, 2:883–884.

89. Cited in Rosenthal, *Nicholas Miraculous*, 238. See also *New Republic* 10 (April 14, 1917): 308.

90. John Dewey, "In a Time of National Hesitation," *Seven Arts* 2 (May 1917): 3–7; and Randolph S. Bourne, "Those Columbia Trustees," *New Republic* 12 (October 20, 1917): 329.

91. Alan Cywar, "John Dewey in World War I: Patriotism and International Progressivism," *American Quarterly* 21 (Autumn 1969): 578–594, esp. 586.

92. John Dewey, "Explanation of Our Lapse," *The New Republic: A Journal of Opinion* 13 (November 3, 1917): 17–18, quotation on 17.

93. See the essays in Randolph S. Bourne, *The War and the Intellectuals: Collected Essays, 1915–1919*, ed. Carl Resek (Indianapolis: Hackett, 1999).

94. A. O. Lovejoy, Edward Capps, and A. A. Young, "Report of Committee on Academic Freedom in Wartime," *Bulletin of the American Association of University Professors (1915–1955)* 4 (Feb.–Mar., 1918): 31.

95. Gruber, *Mars and Minerva*, 213.

96. "The Professors in Battle Array," *Nation* 106 (March 7, 1918), 244. See also Arthur O. Lovejoy, letter to the editor, *Nation* (April 4, 1918): 402.

97. Francke, *Deutsche Arbeit in Amerika*, 18–19. On the mobilization of war, see Martha Hanna, *The Mobilization of Intellect: French Scholars and Writers during the Great War* (Cambridge: MA: Harvard University Press, 1996), 1; and Samuel Hynes, *A War Imagined: The First World War and English Culture* (New York: Atheneum, 1991), 10. On the "professor's war," see Stuart Wallace, *War and the Image of Germany: British Academics, 1914–1918* (Edinburgh: John Donald Publishers, 1988), 4, 39. For a more recent treatment of the differing British and French scholarly responses to the First World War, see Tomás Irish, "'The Aims of Science Are the Antithesis to Those of a War': The Debate about Academic Science in Britain and France during the First World War," in *Other Combatants, Other Fronts: Competing Histories of the First World War*, ed. James E. Kitchen, Alisa Miller, and Laura Rowe (Cambridge: Cambridge University Press, 2011), 29–54.

98. For a dated but relevant study about clergy who embraced the new professional opportunities afforded by the war, see Ray Abrams, *Preachers Present Arms* (New York: Round Table Press, 1933). There are of course similarities as Jewett notes through his comparison of scientists to "low church" Protestants. Jewett, *Science, Democracy, and the American University*, 3. On Bourne's persistent relevance for identifying resistance to compliance with the state in the period of Cold War science, see Stuart W. Leslie, *The Cold War and American Science: The Military-Industrial-Academic Complex at MIT and Stanford* (New York: Columbia University Press, 1994), 3.

99. "Charles Beard Notifies Nicholas Murray Butler of His Resignation from Columbia, 1917," 884.

100. On his "civics lesson," see Bender, "E.R.A. Seligman and the Vocation of Social Science," 68; and Bender, *New York Intellect: A History of Intellectual Life in New York City, from 1750 to the Beginnings of Our Own Time* (New York: Knopf, 1987), 301.

101. Cases like those involving Ross and Ely provide evidence against Barrow's argument of the "opportunistic historical accommodation with business interests and the state by accepting the new organizational structure of university life in exchange for limited procedural guarantees of personal security." *Universities and the Capitalist State*, 11.

102. Albert O. Hirschman, *Exit, Voice, and Loyalty: Responses to Decline in Firms, Organizations, and States* (Cambridge, MA: Harvard University Press, 1970). Jeremy Adelman describes how this book immediately shaped scholarly discourse in a way that makes one think that, had it been published earlier, it also would have influenced these early cases of academic freedom. Adelman, *Worldly Philosopher: The Odyssey of Albert O. Hirschman* (Princeton, NJ: Princeton University Press, 2013), 440–449. Thank you to John McGowan for introducing me to this framework.

103. Gruber suggests that perhaps a distinction could have been between serving society instead of the state, but I'm not certain that would have made a difference, given the global phenomenon of mobilization for World War I. Gruber, *Mars and Minerva*, 259.

104. Jacques Loeb to Svante Arrhenius, December 14, 1914; excerpted in Reingold and Reingold, *Science in America*, 231.

105. Lenore O'Boyle, "Learning for Its Own Sake: The German University as Nineteenth-Century Model," *Comparative Studies in Society and History* 25 (1983): 3–25, here 8; Brown and Kurland, "Academic Tenure and Academic Freedom," 340.

106. Westbrook, *Dewey and American Democracy*, xvi.

107. The following legal scholars provide different example and arguments for the scope of academic freedom. William W. Van Alstyne, "The Specific Theory of Academic Freedom and the General Issue of Civil Liberty," in *The Concept of Academic Freedom*, ed. Edmund L. Pincoffs (Austin: University of Texas Press, 1972), 59–85, esp. 61–63; Peter Byrne, "Academic Freedom: A 'Special Concern of the First Amendment,'" *Yale Law Journal* 99 (November 1989): 251–340; and David M. Rabban, "A Functional Analysis of 'Individual' and 'Institutional' Academic Freedom under the First Amendment," *Law and Contemporary Problems* 53 (1990): 227–301, 227, 231. See also the helpful 2002 report by AAUP counsel Donna R. Euben, "Academic Freedom of Individual Professors and Higher Education Institutions: The Current Legal Landscape," online at aaup.org.

108. In the same essay, he offers as the argument's strawman an alternative in which every religious group has the right to sponsor one university chair to counter any possible institutional bias, but here, too, the line between subjective and objective scholarship would have been no better maintained. Weber, "The Alleged 'Academic Freedom,'" 591.

109. Carl H. Becker served as culture minister in 1921 and from 1925 to 1930. See

his *Gedanken zur Hochschulreform* (Leipzig: Quelle & Meyer, 1919), 55; also cited in Michael Grüttner, "German Universities under the Swastika," in *Universities under Dictatorship*, ed. John Connelly and Michael Grüttner (University Park: Pennsylvania State University Press, 2005), 77. Becker made reform of this system a priority, though many subsequent historians judge his changes as ineffective. The philosopher Max Dessoir warned Becker to proceed cautiously regarding the "Extraordinarienfrage" or else there would be pushback from the faculty at the University of Berlin. Dessoir to Becker, February 21, 1925, 167 VI. HA, Nachlass Carl Becker (hereafter NL Becker), GStPK.

110. Ben-David and Zlockower, "Universities and Academic Systems in Modern Societies," 61.

111. See Tiede's interpretation of Metzger in *University Reform*, 23. This was potentially the case with respect to religious expression, though not with respect to socialism, which after 1890 would be legal in Germany. Incidentally Paulsen's English translator made the same observation in 1905. See Mabel Bode, *German Universities: A Review of Prof. Paulsen's Work on the German University System* (London: P.S. King & Son, 1905), 31; and Senn, "Where Is Althoff?," 203.

112. As Bender shows, one need only compare the mission of the ACLU, which was founded at the same time, to see how the goals of the AAUP were more narrow and professionally oriented; cited in Bender, "E.R.A. Seligman and the Vocation of Social Science," 62.

113. Seligman et al., "General Report of the Committee on Academic Freedom and Academic Tenure," 22. The landmark Dartmouth case in 1816 had preserved institutional autonomy for private universities with a public charter that had an express goal to serve the public, one consequence of which was also to clarify the distinction between private and public institutions of higher learning that had heretofore not been distinguished. See Rudolph, *The American College and University*, 210.

114. This is the case even today, though there is confusion between the First Amendment, which restricts the right of any public institution to suppress speech, and academic freedom, which addresses rights in educational contexts at both private and public institutions. Rachel Levinson, "Academic Freedom and the First Amendment," presentation to the AAUP Summer Institute (2007), online at https://www.aaup.org/our-work/protecting-academic-freedom/academic-freedom-and-first-amendment-2007.

115. "The Professor and the Wide, Wide World," *Scribner's* 65 (April 1919): 466.

116. Hofstadter, *Anti-intellectualism in American Life*, 211.

117. Cited in Gruber, *Mars and Minerva*, 2. Charles Angoff was also highly critical of American academics' role and contribution to the war effort. Angoff, "The Higher Learning Goes to War," *American Mercury* 11 (June 1927): 179–191.

CHAPTER EIGHT

1. Willis R. Whitney to Robert A. Millikan, February 25, 1918, dictated, February 22; excerpted in Reingold and Reingold, *Science in America*, 267–268.

2. "A Proposal for an Independent School of Social Science for Men and Women"

(circa 1918 26.16), The New School Publicity Office records, NS.03.01.05, Box 26, Folder 15, New School Archives and Special Collections (hereafter NSASC). John Louis Recchiuti connects this "hour for experiment" to the "greatest social science laboratory in the world," in Progressive-Era New York. Recchiuti, *Civic Engagement: Social Science and Progressive-Era Reform in New York City* (Philadelphia: University Pennsylvania Press, 2007), 1.

3. Brigitte Schröder-Gudehus, "The Argument for the Self-Government and Public Support of Science in Weimar Germany," *Minerva* 10 (1972): 22; Irish, *The University at War*, 5, 99, 102–105, 173. After years of resistance, in 1917, Oxford University voted to adopt the PhD (which they called the DPhil), and Cambridge followed two years later. Renate Simpson persuasively shows that the motivating factor was the new market of American aspiring graduate students. Simpson, *How the PhD Came to Britain: A Century of Struggle for Postgraduate Education* (Guilford, UK: University of Surrey, 1983), 131–140.

4. George Ellery Hale to Willian Henry Welch, June 10, 1915; excerpted in Reingold and Reingold, *Science in America*, 234

5. In Russia, scientist entrepreneurs eagerly took the place of absent British and French to forge stronger associational and publishing relationships with their German counterparts. Susan Gross Solomon, ed., *Doing Medicine Together: Germany and Russia between the Wars* (Toronto: University of Toronto Press, 2006), 8. In Beijing, in a process that began in 1912 by Cai Yuanpei, a young Chinese revolutionary thinker who studied with Karl Lamprecht in Leipzig, the Chinese revised the imperial university along the German university model. Chen Hongjie, "Die chinesische Rezeption der Humbolt'schen Universitätsidee: Am Beispiel der Universität Peking zu Anfang des 20. Jahrhunderts," in *Humboldt International. Der Export des deutschen Universitätsmodells im 19. Und 20. Jahrhundert*, ed. Rainer Christoph Schwinges (Basel: Schwabe, 2001), 323ff. And in Palestine both German models of higher learning—the technical university and the modern research university—influenced a group of German-Jewish Zionists who began to lay the groundwork for both the Technikum (now the Technion) in Haifa and the Hebrew University in Jerusalem. Steven Aschheim, "*Bildung* in Palestine," in *Beyond the Border: German-Jewish Legacy Abroad* (Princeton, NJ: Princeton University Press, 2007), 6–44.

6. On the resistance to the "centralization" of science in the Weimar Republic, see Schröder-Gudehus, "The Argument for the Self-Government and Public Support of Science in Weimar Germany," 538.

7. Both Karl Lamprecht and Hugo Münsterberg advised reformers of these new institutions to concentrate instead on the humanities and offered America as a model. Lamprecht to Rudolf Tombo Jr., undated, Nr. 22, Bl. 47, NL Lamprecht, ULB. Hugo Münsterberg, "The American College for Germany," *Science: A Weekly Journal Devoted to the Advancement of Science*, 1907, 363, 367. See also Levine, *Dreamland of Humanists*, 143–144, 205. See also Habbo Knoch, Ralph Jessen, Hans-Peter Ullmann, eds., *The New University of Cologne: Its History from 1919* (Cologne: Bohlau, 2020).

8. Ludwig Brauer, *Forschungsinstitute: Ihre Geschichte, Organisation und Ziele*, 2 vols. (1930; Tokyo: Publishers International, 1980).

9. Veysey once called these institutional experiments, which ran counter to the trend of the modern research university, "eccentricities." Veysey, *The Emergence of the American University*, 340. The very existence of these institutions in an ever-conforming milieu was evidence of the pull toward—but ability to resist—what sociologists Paul J. DiMaggio and Walter W. Powell identified as "institutional isomorphism." See DiMaggio and Powell, "The Iron Cage Revisited: Institutional Isomorphism and Collective Rationality in Organizational Fields," *American Sociological Review* 48 (1983): 147–160.

10. Rodgers, *Atlantic Crossings*, 69, 112–155; Bender, *A Nation among Nations*, 246. On the city as "laboratory" in particular for municipal reform in the decades leading up to World War I, see Recchiuti, *Civic Engagement*, 1.

11. Cited in Thomas Bender, "The Historian and Public Life: Charles A. Beard and the City," in *Intellect and Public Life: Essays on the Social History of Academic Intellectuals in the United States* (Baltimore: Johns Hopkins University Press, 1993), 93.

12. Bender, "The Historian and Public Life," 94–95.

13. Harry Elmer Barnes, "James Harvey Robinson," in *American Masters of Social Science: An Approach to the Study of the Social Sciences through a Neglected Field of Biography* (New York: Henry Holt, 1927), 327. Though Veblen, like Dewey, belonged to this first coterie of "professional academics," Veblen has long been presented as an academic outsider (much in line with his theory), a characterization that Charles Camic debunks in a revisionist biography. See Camic, *Veblen: The Making of an Economist Who Unmade Economics* (Cambridge, MA: Harvard University Press, 2020), 5–7.

14. Peter Rutkoff and William B. Scott, *New School: A History of the New School for Social Research* (New York: The Free Press, 1986), 11.

15. Croly, "A School for Social Research," *New Republic*, June 8, 1918, 167–171, quotation on 167.

16. Croly, "A School for Social Research," 167, 168.

17. Beard, "The Study and Teaching of Politics," *Columbia University Quarterly* 12 (1909–1910): 269–274, quotations on 270, 272.

18. "Charles Beard Notifies Nicholas Murray Butler of His Resignation from Columbia," 883–884; Croly, "A School for Social Research," 171.

19. Robinson, "A Journal of Opinion," *New Republic* 3 (May 8, 1915): 9–11.

20. Robinson, "A Journal of Opinion," 11.

21. Robinson, "The New School," *School and Society*, 1920, 129.

22. Robinson, "The New School," 130.

23. Joseph Kett, *The Pursuit of Knowledge under Difficulties: From Self-Improvement to Adult Education in America, 1750–1990* (Stanford, CA: Stanford University Press, 1994), 337, 340–352; and Richard Altenbaugh, *Education for Struggle: The American Labor Colleges of the 1920s and 1930s* (Philadelphia: Temple University Press, 1990), 3–4, 25.

24. David Riesman, introduction to Thorstein Veblen, *The Higher Learning in America: A Memorandum on the Conduct of Universities by Business Men* (Stanford, CA: Academic Reprints, 1918/1954), vii.

25. Veblen, *The Higher Learning in America*, 64, 54. Veblen was unique in having survived two dismissals, from Chicago and Stanford, and still remained a respectable

economist. Camic surmises that this may, in part, explain Veblen's persistent "outsider" persona. Camic, *Veblen*, 350.

26. Rutkoff and Scott, *New School*, 11.

27. Kett, *The Pursuit of Knowledge under Difficulties*, 351.

28. Altenbaugh, *Education for Struggle*, 31.

29. See *New Republic* 17 (December 28, 1918): iii.

30. "A Proposal for an Independent School of Social Science for Men and Women," 7, 9.

31. See Julia Foulkes, "The Majority Finds Its School: Women at the New School," YouTube, online at https://www.youtube.com/watch?v=Q5E6akh_DQA.

32. Rutkoff and Scott, *New School*, 26

33. Ellen F. Fitzpatrick, *Endless Crusade: Women Social Scientists and Progressive Reform* (New York: Oxford University Press, 1990).

34. Esther Rauschenbush, "Three Women: Creators of Change, Clara Mayer, Jacqueline Grennan, and Lucy Sprague Mitchell," in *The Higher education of Women: Essays in Honor of Rosemary Park*, ed. Helen S. Astin and Werner Z. Hirsch (New York: Praeger, 1978), 29–52, here 29.

35. Rauschenbush, "Three Women," 30.

36. Alvin Johnson, *Pioneer's Progress: An Autobiography* (New York: Viking Press, 1952), 278.

37. "A Proposal for an Independent School of Social Science for Men and Women," 10.

38. T. Everett Harré, "Who's Who in the New School," *National Civic Federation Review*, April 10, 1919, 4.

39. Harold Laski described how the London School of Economics presented a model. See Rauschenbush, "Three Women," 30.

40. For a full list, see William Cobb, *Radical Education in the Rural South: Commonwealth College, 1922–1940* (Detroit: Wayne State University Press, 2000), 25.

41. Bender, "E.R.A. Seligman and the Vocation of Social Science," 73, 76.

42. Rauschenbush, "Three Women," 34. Camic suggests that rumors about Veblen's "poor teaching," which coexisted with Veblen's popularity among graduate students, is yet another example of Veblen's insider-outsider status. Camic, *Veblen*, 349–350.

43. Johnson, *Pioneer's Progress*, 272–273.

44. Johnson, 276.

45. Rauschenbush, "Three Women," 32–33.

46. Promotional and fundraising printer material, 1926, The New School Publicity Office records, NS.03.01.05, Box 26, Folder 26.11, NSASC.

47. It is one of the strange facts of the New School that it is generally considered to have been founded in 1933. On these "two foundings," see Rutkoff and Scott, *New School*, xii; see also Craig Calhoun, "Academic Freedom: Public Knowledge and the Structural Transformation of the University," *Social Research* 76 (Summer 2009): 561–598, here 562.

48. Rutkoff and Scott, *New School*, 41.

49. Kett, *The Pursuit of Knowledge under Difficulties*, 344; Rutkoff and Scott, *New School*, 64.

50. Beard, "A Suggestion from Professor Beard," *Freeman* 3 (July 20, 1921): 450.

51. Beard, "A Suggestion from Professor Beard," 451.

52. Harry Elmer Barnes, "James Harvey Robinson," in *American Masters of Social Science: An Approach to the Study of the Social Sciences through a Neglected Field of Biography*, ed. Howard W. Odum (New York: Henry Holt, 1927), 343.

53. Jerry McCarter's perspective on the Americans' approach to World War I reflects a new trend to describe their participation and the end of World War I as punctuated by hope followed by despair. McCarter, *Young Radicals: In the War for American Ideals* (New York: Random House, 2017).

54. Gerald Feldman, "Weimar from Inflation to Depression: Experiment or Gamble?," in *Die Nachwirkungen der Inflation auf die deutsche Geschichte, 1924–1933*, ed. Gerald Feldman (Munich: Oldenbourg, 1985), 385.

55. Peter Gay, *Weimar: Outsider as Insider* (New York: W.W. Norton, 2001), 1.

56. Gay, *Weimar*, 3.

57. Notker Hammerstein, *Die deutsche Forschungsgemeinschaft in der Weimarer Republik und im Dritten Reich: Wissenschaftspolitik in Republik und Diktatur* (Munich: C.H. Beck, 1999).

58. Emily J. Levine, "The Other Weimar: The Warburg Circle as Hamburg School," *Journal of the History of Ideas* 74 (2013): 307–330.

59. Adam describes the shareholder companies that were an essential aspect of Frankfurt fundraising that "also contributed to the democratization of society." Adam, *Philanthropy, Civil Society, and the State in German History*, 71, quotation on 100.

60. Simone Lässig also shows that fifty-five of the 133 mostly highly taxed citizens in Frankfurt were Jews. Lässig, "Bürgerlichkeit, Patronage, and Communal Liberalism in Germany, 1871–1914," in *Philanthropy, Patronage, and Civil Society: Experiences from Germany, Great Britain, and North America*, ed. Thomas Adam (Bloomington: Indiana University Press, 2004), 198.

61. Ayako Sakurai, *Science and Societies in Frankfurt am Main* (London: Routledge, 2016), 147.

62. This model paralleled similar patterns in Leipzig, Bremen, and Hamburg. See Adam, *Philanthropy, Civil Society, and the State in German History*, 47.

63. Paul Kluke, *Die Stiftungsuniversität Frankfurt am Main 1914–1932* (Frankfurt: Kramer, 1972), 33, 91l; Hans Achinger, *Wilhelm Merton in seiner Zeit* (Frankfurt: Kramer, 1965), 112, 218; also W. E. Mosse, *Economic Elite: Jews in the German economy: The German-Jewish Economic Elite, 1820–1935* (Oxford: Oxford University Press, 1987), 81–84, 318–320.

64. To consolidate the various institutes Adickes also persuaded the Physical Society and the Senckenberg Foundation to move to the old city in exchange for a badly needed subsidy, and he began in 1905 to plan the foundation of the Academy for Practical Medicine. Sakurai, *Science and Societies in Frankfurt am Main*, 148.

65. On the Jewish philanthropic activity of Frankfurt, see Jonathan C. Friedman, *The Lion and the Star: Gentile-Jewish Relations in Three Hessian Towns, 1919–1945* (Lexington: University Press of Kentucky, 1998), 63–64. On Jewish donors to the university, see Kluke, *Die Stiftungsuniversität Frankfurt am Main*, 85.

66. Cited in Pulzer, *Jews and the German State*, 112.

67. Kluke, *Die Stiftungsuniversität Frankfurt am Main*, 130, 139.

68. Ludwig Heilbrunn, *Die Gründung der Universität Frankfurt-am-Main* (Frankfurt: J. Baer, 1915), 15 (my translation).

69. Pulzer, *Jews and the German State*, 113.

70. Kluke, *Die Stiftungsuniversität Frankfurt am Main*, 110–121; Sakurai, *Science and Societies in Frankfurt Am Main*, 149. Out of a fear of being "too" Jewish, the Jewish community of Frankfurt resisted funding such a position for several years, though it eventually supported one in 1920. Nehemia Anton Nobel died in 1922 shortly before the position was granted, and Franz Rosenzweig could not consider it because he was ill. Martin Buber assumed the position in 1924. Willy Schottroff, "Martin Buber an der Universität Frankfurt am Main," in *Martin Buber (1878–1965): Internationales Symposium zum 20. Todestag*, ed. Werner Licharz and Heinz Schmidt (Frankfurt: Haag and Herchen, 1989), 19–95.

71. Stefan Müller-Doohm, *Adorno: A Biography*, trans. Rodney Livingstone (Cambridge: Polity Press), 132. On the early history of the institute, see Ulrike Migdal, *Die Frühgeschichte des Frankfurter Instituts für Sozialforschung* (Frankfurt: Campus, 1981); and Paul Kluke, "Das Institut für Sozialforschung," *Geschichte der Soziologie: Studien zur Kognitiven, Sozialen und Historischen Identität einer Disziplin*, ed. Wolf Lepenies (Frankfurt: Suhrkamp Verlag, 1981), 2:390–429.

72. Wolfgang Schivelbusch, *Intellektuellendämmerung: Zur Lage der Frankfurter Intelligenz in den zwanziger Jahren; Die Universität, das Freie Jüdische Lehrhaus, die Frankfurter Zeitung, Radio Frankfurt, der Goethe-Preis und Sigmund Freud, das Institut für Sozialforschung* (Frankfurt: Insel Verlag, 1982), 17, 25.

73. Because of his Argentine citizenship, too, he was able to retrieve frozen assets from England. Jeanette Erazo Heufelder, *Der argentinische Krösus: Kleine Wirtschaftsgeschichte der Frankfurter Schule* (Berlin: Berenberg, 2017), 25.

74. Helmuth Robert Eisenbach, "Millionär, Agitator und Doktorand: Die Tübinger Studienzeit des Felix Weil (1919)," *Bausteine zur Tübinger Universitätsgeschichte* 3 (1987): 179–216.

75. Though he was exempt from duty in World War I as an Argentine citizen, Felix Weil nonetheless volunteered and helped clear his father's name when it became mistakenly associated with a far-right campaign. Heufelder, *Der argentinische Krösus*, 27–29, 38–40, 112, quotation on 40. See also Rolf Wiggershaus, *The Frankfurt School: Its History, Theories, and Political Significance*, trans. Michael Robertson (Cambridge, MA: MIT Press, 1995), 11–16.

76. Cited and translated in Wiggershaus, *The Frankfurt School*, 17.

77. Fleck, *A Transatlantic History of the Social Sciences*, 27.

78. Wiggershaus, *The Frankfurt School*, 19.

79. Schivelbusch, *Intellektuellendämmerung*, 10–11.

80. Schivelbusch, 19.

81. Martin Jay, *Dialectical Imagination: A History of the Frankfurt School and the Institute for Social Research, 1923–1950* (Berkeley: University of California Press, 1996), 9.

82. "Carl Grunberg's Inaugural Address, Translated and Introduced by Y. Michael Bodeman," *Insurgent Sociologist* 13, no. 3 (Spring 1986): 4–9, quotation on 6.

83. "Carl Grunberg's Inaugural Address," 9.

84. The bizarreness is the source of the dramatic intrigue of Stuart Jeffries, *Grand Hotel Abyss: The Lives of the Frankfurt School* (London: Verso, 2016), 1.

85. Jay, *Dialectical Imagination*, 3.

86. Wiggershaus, *The Frankfurt School*, 34.

87. On the Jewish life of Frankfurt, see Michael Brenner, *Renaissance of Jewish Culture in Weimar Germany* (New Haven, CT: Yale University Press, 1998).

88. Frankfurt was the third German city after Berlin and Leipzig to get the radio. Schivelbusch, *Intellektuellendämmerung*, 62.

89. Max Horkheimer, "The Present Situation of Social Philosophy and the Tasks of an Institute for Social Research," in *Between Philosophy and Social Science* (Cambridge, MA: MIT Press, 1993), 1–14, quotations on 11 and 14.

90. Ironically, as Bodeman notes, while the earlier institute was open to non-Marxist approaches, Horkheimer, despite his more apolitical stance, only welcomed leftists. "Carl Grunberg's Inaugural Address," 4.

91. "Carl Grunberg's Inaugural Address," 5.

92. Even Jay, who by his own admission was always "wary . . . of the sociology of knowledge in its more reductionist forms," commented that "what made the institution's unique achievement possible was the specific urban and academic situation in which its particular response to that decline [Fritz Ringer's 'decline of the German Mandarins'] was enacted." Jay, "Urban Flights," in Bender, *The University and the City*, 223, 231.

93. Wiggershaus, *The Frankfurt School*, 4–5.

94. Cited and translated in Wiggershaus, *The Frankfurt School*, 107.

95. See Staci von Boeckmann, "Trachodon und Teddie: Über Gretel Adorno," in *Adorno-Portraits*, ed. Stefan Müller-Doohm (Frankfurt: Suhrkamp, 2007), 335–352. Given her contribution to recording "highly abstract conversation developing at breakneck speed," it is Gretel who gave the conversation that would later be dubbed "A New Manifesto" its coherence and telos, yet her contribution is opaque in our histories of the school. See Martin Jay's 2012 review of Theodor Adorno and Max Horkheimer, *Towards a New Manifesto*, trans. Rodney Livingstone (London: Verso, 2011) in *Notre Dame Philosophical Reviews*, online at https://ndpr.nd.edu/news/towards-a-new-manifesto/.

96. Rutkoff and Scott show the demographics remained fairly eclectic throughout the first two periods of the school, from 1919 through 1924 and then from 1925 through 1930. While there was a drop in current college students, laborers, and housewives between the first and second periods, business executives and professionals made up about 15 percent in both periods. Rutkoff and Scott, *New School*, 39.

97. Levine, *The American College and the Culture of Aspiration*, esp. 19.

98. Karabel, *The Chosen*, 86–87, 112.

99. "A Proposal for an Independent School of Social Science for Men and Women," 10.

100. Johnson, *Pioneer's Progress*, 275.

101. Paul Tillich, "Gibt es noch eine Universität? Fachhochschulen und Universität," *Frankfurter Zeitung*, November 22, 1931; republished in Dieter Thomä, ed., *Gibt es noch*

eine Universität? Zwist am Abgrund—eine Debatte in der Frankfurter Zeitung, 1931–32 (Konstanz: Konstanz University Press, 2012), 16–23, esp. 18–19.

102. Wolfgang Kunkel, "Der Professor im Dritten Reich," in *Die deutsche Universität im Dritten Reich: Eine Vortragsreihe der Universität München* (Munich: Piper, 1966), 107; cited in Grüttner, "German Universities under the Swastika," 78.

103. This detached "withdraw[al] from democratic affirmations altogether in favor of a defense to the lonely voice of critical reason" is for Leon Fink the main difference between the Progressive-Era scientists and the leftist scholars of the 1930s. Fink, *Progressive Intellectuals and the Dilemmas of Democratic Commitment* (Cambridge, MA: Harvard University Press, 1997), 275.

104. Rutkoff and Scott, as well as Calhoun, make this claim of the affinity with the *Volkshochschule* movement, though this designation seems to have been attributed more post facto, as I have found no archival evidence from the 1920s in the New School Archives that supports this. Rutkoff and Scott, *New School*, 19–20; and Calhoun, "Academic Freedom: Public Knowledge and the Structural Transformation of the University," 575.

105. Max Planck Institute for Human Development and Education, *Between Elite and Mass Education: Education in the Federal Republic of Germany*, trans. Raymond Meyer and Adriane Heinrichs-Goodwin (Albany: State University of New York Press, 1983), 25. Another semiprivate research institute, the Heidelberger Institut für Sozial- und Staatswissenschaften, had under George Jellinek also planned a series of exchanges with Americans as early as 1910, but it is unclear whether they transpired. Füssl, *Deutsch-amerikanischer Kulturaustausch im 20. Jahrhundert*, 72.

106. There are, of course, exceptions: Talcott Parsons, for example, came to Heidelberg in 1928 in this period to work on a dissertation about Max Weber. Max Planck Institute, *Between Elite and Mass Education*, 22. See also Füssl, *Deutsch-amerikanischer Kulturaustausch im 20. Jahrhundert*, 73–76.

107. Johnson, *Pioneer's Progress*, 336.

108. Schivelbusch applies this analysis to post-1945 Berlin. Wolfgang Schivelbusch, *In a Cold Crater: Cultural and Intellectual Life in Berlin, 1945–1948* (Berkeley: University of California Press, 2018). According to the literature drafted in 1927, "Castle College Dresden: An American College for Undergraduates" would have been a coeducational school of two hundred American and German students that operated under a protectorate of the American and German educational authorities: "the natural link between the old seats of learning and of scientific research as represented by the German Universities and Technical Colleges, and the modern aggressive American College or University with its great resources in men and material, methods and manners and its more intimate contact between faculty and student body on the one side, and college and public on the other." R 64011, 9.1927–11.1927, Hochschul 1 Deutschland, Hochschulwesen und Studium in Deutschland, Ausländerstudium, Auswärtiges Amt, Politisches Amt, Bundesarchiv, Berlin. For an astute analysis of the shifting landscapes of science and politics in the interwar period that led to the failure of the ICIC, see Jimena Canales, "Einstein, Bergson, and the Experiment That Failed: Intellectual Cooperation at the League of Nations," *Modern Language Notes* 120 (2005): 1168–1191.

109. L. Jackson Newell, "Among the Few at Deep Springs College: Assessing a Seven-Decade Experiment in Liberal Education," *Journal of General Education* 34 (1982): 120–134; Helen Lefkowitz Horowitz, *Alma Mater*, 319–350; Helen Lefkowitz Horowitz, "In the Wake of Laurence Veysey: Re-examining the Liberal Arts College," *History of Education Quarterly* 45 (2005): 420–426; and on the revival of liberal arts as cultural criticism at Amherst, see Adam Nelson, *Education and Democracy: The Meaning of Alexander Meiklejohn, 1872–1964* (Madison: University of Wisconsin Press, 2001), 61–129.

110. Rutkoff and Scott, *New School*, 95–96.

CHAPTER NINE

1. Marjori Lamberti, "The Reception of Refugee Scholars from Nazi Germany in America: Philanthropy and Social Change in Higher Education," *Jewish Social Studies* 12 (2006): 157–192, quotation on 159.

2. "Nazi 'Purge' of the Universities," *Manchester Guardian Weekly*, May 19, 1933, 13–14.

3. Mitchell Ash, "Scientific Changes in Germany, 1933, 1945, 1990: Towards a Comparison," *Minerva* 37 (1999): 332; Edward Yarnall Hartshorne computes this slightly differently, but Frankfurt is still in the top three behind Düsseldorf Medical Academy and Berlin. Hartshorne, *The German Universities and National Socialism* (Cambridge, MA: Harvard University Press, 1937), 94. For a comparison of fields, see Claus Dieter-Krohn, *Intellectuals in Exile: Refugee Scholars and the New School for Social Research*, trans. Rita Kimber and Robert Kimber (Amherst: University of Massachusetts Press, 1993), 12–13.

4. E. Y. Hartshorne, "The German Universities and the Government," *Annals of the American Academy of Political and Social Science* 200 (1938): 210–234, here 222; and Klaus Fischer, "Die Emigration von Wissenschaftlern nach 1933," *Vierteljahreshefte für Zeitgeschichte* 39 (1991): 537. If one adds in the other professions, including doctors and lawyers, as well as writers and artists, that number climbs to about twelve thousand intellectuals who lost their jobs. Ash, "Scientific Changes in Germany," 332.

5. Cited in Alan D. Beyerchen, *Scientists under Hitler: Politics and the Physics Community in the Third Reich* (New Haven, CT: Yale University Press, 1977), 43.

6. *Gleichschaltung* or "coordination" was a Nazi euphemism for the total realignment of institutes with the state. Abraham Edelheit and Hershel Edelheit, *History of the Holocaust: A Handbook and Dictionary* (London: Routledge, 1994), 33. I use "co-option" in the English to better convey the sinister intentions of this process.

7. George Frederick Kneller, *The Educational Philosophy of National Socialism* (New Haven, CT: Yale University Press, 1942), 4.

8. Alfred Rosenberg, "Freiheit der Wissenschaft," in *Gestaltung der Idee: Reden und Aufsätze von 1933–1935* (Munich: Eher, 1936), 203 (my translation).

9. "Hochschule auf Staatskosten"; cited in Hans Frank, *Im Angesicht des Galgens: Deutung Hitlers und seiner Zeit auf Grund eigener Erlebnisse und Erkenntnisse* (Munich:

Friedrich Alfred Back Verlag, 1953), 46–47. Thank you to Stephen Comer for alerting me to this reference.

10. Bergmann, "American Exceptionalism and the German 'Sonderweg' in Tandem," 516.

11. Cited in Guettel, *German Expansionism, Imperial Liberalism, and the United States*, 1.

12. There was also a "French" James Fenimore Cooper and an "English" one. Guettel, *German Expansionism, Imperial Liberalism, and the United States*, 85–86.

13. Though historians debate the contours of the path from nineteenth-century overseas colonialism to Nazism, and Guettel complexifies this story (Guettel, *German Expansionism, Imperial Liberalism, and the United States*, 200), there is no doubt that this earlier period laid the groundwork for a Nazi imperialist strategy.

14. David W. Ellwood, *The Shock of America: Europe and the Challenge of the Century* (Oxford: Oxford University Press, 2012), 59.

15. It was also translated into French, Dutch, Swedish, Russian, Lettish, Italian, Spanish, and Japanese, and a few years later, into Chinese. Raymond Callahan, *Education and the Cult of Efficiency: A Study of the Social Forces That Have Shaped the Administration of the Public Schools* (Chicago: University of Chicago Press, 1962), 23; and Mary Nolan, *Visions of Modernity: American Business and the Modernization of Germany* (New York: Oxford University Press, 1994), 42–48.

16. Ellwood, *The Shock of America*, 73.

17. On the incompatibility of Ford with the German market, see Wolfgang König, "Adolf Hitler vs. Henry Ford: The Volkswagen, the Role of America as a Model, and the Failure of a Nazi Consumer Society," *German Studies Review* 27 (2004): 249–268. On Hitler's moniker for his train, see Klaus Fischer, *Hitler and America* (Philadelphia: University of Pennsylvania Press, 2011), 9. See also Jeffrey Herf, *Reactionary Modernism: Technology, Culture, and Politics in Weimar and the Third Reich* (Cambridge: Cambridge University Press, 2008).

18. Fischer, *Hitler and America*, 38, 35.

19. Inspired by Auden's poem of the same name, Sarah E. Igo shows how being a "known citizen" was the source of both rights and constraints. Igo, *The Known Citizen: A History of Privacy in Modern America* (Cambridge, MA: Harvard University Press, 2018), 2–3.

20. Rüdiger Hachtmann, "'Die Begründer der amerikanischen Technik sind fast lauter schwäbisch-alemannische Menschen': Nazi-Deutschland, der Blick auf die USA und die 'Amerikanisierung' der industriellen Produktionsstrukturen im 'Dritten Reich,'" in Lüdtke, Marßolek, and Saldern, *Amerikanisierung*, 37–66.

21. Edwin Black, *IBM and the Holocaust: The Strategic Alliance between Nazi Germany and America's Most Powerful Company* (New York: Random House, 2001); and Michael Zimmerman, *Rassenutopie und Genozid: Die nationalsozialistische "Lösung der Zigeunerfrage"* (Hamburg: Christians, 1996).

22. Adolf Hitler, *Mein Kampf: Eine kritische Edition,* ed. Christian Hartmann and Thomas Vordermayer (Munich: Berlin Institut für Zeitgeschichte München, 2018), 2:1115–1117; cited, translated, and discussed in James Q. Whitman, *Hitler's American*

Model: The United States and the Making of Nazi Race Law (Princeton, NJ: Princeton University Press, 2017), 45–46, quotation on 45.

23. Cited and translated in Whitman, *Hitler's American Model*, 47. For the original, see Gerhard Weinberg, *Hitlers Zweites Buch: Ein Dokument aus dem Jahr 1928* (Stuttgart: Deutsche Verlags-Anstalt, 1961), 132; see also 130.

24. Heinrich Krieger, "Das Rassenrecht in den Vereinigten Staaten," *Verwaltungsarchiv* 39 (1934): 327; for Whitman on Krieger, see *Hitler's American Model*, 65.

25. John A. Garraty was among the first to make these connections. Garraty, "The New Deal, National Socialism, and the Great Depression," *American Historical Review* 78 (1973): 907–944. For a history of this literature, see Wolfgang Schivelbusch, *Three New Deals: Reflections on Roosevelt's America, Mussolini's Italy, and Hitler's Germany, 1933–1939* (New York: Picador, 2007), 10; and James Q. Whitman, "Of Corporatism, Fascism, and the First New Deal," *American Journal of Comparative Law* 39 (1991): 747–778, esp. 747–748.

26. Hannah Arendt, "The Image of Hell," review of *The Black Book: The Nazi Crimes against the Jewish People* and Max Weinreich's *Hitler's Professors, Commentary*, September 1, 1946, 291–295.

27. Kneller, *The Educational Philosophy of National Socialism*, 1.

28. Kneller, 23.

29. Gilmer W. Blackburn, *Education in the Third Reich: A Study of Race and History in Nazi Textbooks* (1985; Albany: State University of New York Press, 2012), 37.

30. Erica Mann, *School for Barbarians*, intro. Thomas Mann (New York: Modern Age Books, 1938), 48–49.

31. Cited in Kneller, *The Educational Philosophy of National Socialism*, 219.

32. Hellmut Seier, "Der Rektor als Führer: Zur Hochschulpolitik des Reichserziehungsministeriums, 1934–1945," *Vierteljahreshefte für Zeitgeschichte* 12 (1964): 105–146; Hans Sluga, *Heidegger's Crisis: Philosophy and Politics in Nazi Germany* (Cambridge, MA: Harvard University Press, 1993), 7.

33. Adolf Rein, *Die Idee der politischen Universität* (Hamburg: Hanseatische Verlagsanstalt, 1933), 15 (my translation).

34. Macrakis, *Surviving the Swastika*, 74–75.

35. Grüttner, "German Universities under the Swastika," 82, 93. Konrad H. Jarausch and Gerhard Arminger arrive at a smaller proportion—one-quarter—by looking at instructors from university professors down to kindergarten aides. Jarausch and Arminger, "The German Teaching Profession and Nazi Party Membership: A Demographic Logit Model," *Journal of Interdisciplinary History* 20 (1989): 197–225. Membership closed after 1933—Ute Deichmann surmises, to keep out the opportunists—and when it reopened again in 1937 there was an increase in interest, in particular, among biologists. Deichmann, *Biologists under Hitler*, trans. Thomas Dunlap (Cambridge, MA: Harvard University Press, 1996), 61–62.

36. Reinhard Rürup, *Schicksale und Karrieren: Gedenkbuch für die von den Nationalsozialisten aus der Kaiser-Wilhelm-Gesellschaft vertriebenen Forscherinnen und Forscher* (Göttingen: Wallstein, 2008), 106.

37. The Kaiser Wilhelm Society mediated the transfer of Jewish-owned art and

real estate to new owners against their will (so-called *Besitztransfer*). In this way, the society benefited from the state's acquisition of Jewish-owned property, though, as Kreutzmüller shows, it is very difficult to chart precisely, since often records weren't kept or were lost in the war. Kreutzmüller, "Zum Umgang der Kaiser Wilhelm Gesellschaft mit Geld und Gut," 18.

38. Beyerchen, *Scientists under Hitler*, 16–27, 199.

39. Macrakis, *Surviving the Swastika*, 53, 84; J. L. Heilbron and Max Planck, *The Dilemmas of an Upright Man: Max Planck and the Fortunes of German Science*, with a new afterword (Cambridge, MA: Harvard University Press, 2000), 213.

40. Beyerchen, *Scientists under Hitler*, 1.

41. Rüdiger Hactmann, "A Success Story? Highlighting the History of the Kaiser Wilhelm Society's General Administration in the Third Reich," in *The Kaiser Wilhelm Society under National Socialism*, ed. Susanne Heim, Carola Sachse, and Mark Walker (Cambridge: Cambridge University Press, 2009), 20.

42. Max Weinreich, *Hitler's Professors: The Part of Scholarship in Germany's Crimes against the Jewish People* (1946; New Haven, CT: Yale University Press, 1999), 18.

43. Shelley Baranowski, Armin Nolzen, and Claus-Christian W. Szejnmann, eds., *A Companion to Nazi Germany* (Hoboken, NJ: Wiley-Blackwell, 2018), 204.

44. According to Grüttner, in 1931 there were 1,721 full professors and 2,665 *Privatdozenten* and associate professors. Grüttner, "German Universities under the Swastika," 81–82.

45. Cited and translated in Baranowski, Nolzen, and Szejnmann, *A Companion to Nazi Germany*, 205.

46. Heim, Sachse, and Walker, introduction to *The Kaiser Wilhelm Society under National Socialism*, 3.

47. Historians of science have typically assigned to scientists under the Third Reich the categories of resistance or capitulation, but most cases like that of the German Physical Society were far from clear-cut. Dieter Hoffman and Mark Walker, eds., *The German Physical Society in the Third Reich: Physicists between Autonomy and Accommodation*, trans Ann M. Hentschel (Cambridge: Cambridge University Press, 2012), 49.

48. For a review of the literature on "self-mobilization," see Jonathan Harwood, "German Science and Technology under National Socialism," *Perspectives on Science: Historical Philosophical Social* 5 (1997): 128–151.

49. Weinreich, *Hitler's Professors*, 16.

50. Wolfgang Bialas and Anson Rabinbach, introduction to *Nazi Germany and the Humanities: How German Academics Embraced Nazism* (London: Oneworld Publications, 2007), xi.

51. Paletschek, "The Invention of Humboldt and the Impact of National Socialism," 37–58.

52. Theodore Kisiel, "The Seminar of Winter Semester 1933–4 within Heidegger's Three Concepts of the Political," in Martin Heidegger, *Nature, History, State, 1933–1934*, ed. and trans. Gregory Fried and Richard Polt (London: Bloomsbury, 2009), 127–149, 131.

53. The literature on Heidegger and the political implications of his philosophy

is vast and not uncontested. For one obvious disturbing feature, see Heidegger's extended passage on the "goal of total annihilation." Cited by Slavoj Žižek, "Heidegger in the Foursome of Struggle, Historicity, Will, and Gelassenheit," in Heidegger, *Nature, History, State*, 151–170, quotation on 164.

54. Frank-Rutger Hausmann, *"Deutsche Geisteswissenschaft" im Zweiten Weltkriege: Die "Aktion Ritterbusch" 1940–1945* (Dresden: Dresden University Press, 1998).

55. Bialas and Rabinbach, *Nazi Germany and the Humanities*, xxxiv–xxxvi.

56. Christopher Browning and Jürgen Matthäus, *The Origins of the Final Solution: The Evolution of Nazi Jewish Policy, September 1939–March 1942*, Comprehensive History of the Holocaust (Lincoln: University of Nebraska Press, 2004), 225–226.

57. Weinreich, *Hitler's Professors*, 6. David Baumgart argued that Weinreich was "not . . . sufficiently objective." Baumgart, "Looking Back on a German University Career," *Leo Baeck Institute Year Book* 10 (1965): 261.

58. Carl H. Becker, *Kulturpolitische Aufgaben des Reichs* (Leipzig: Quelle & Meyer, 1919), 13; cited and translated in Max Planck Institute, *Between Elite and Mass Education*, 22.

59. Frank A. Ninkovich called the IIE a "halfway house between cultural laissez faire and governmental entrance into policymaking." Ninkovich, *Diplomacy of Ideas: U.S. Foreign Policy and Cultural Relations, 1938–1950* (New York: Cambridge University Press, 1981), 8. See also Justin Hart, *Empire of Ideas: The Origins of Public Diplomacy and the Transformation of U.S. Foreign Policy* (New York: Oxford University Press, 2013), 22–23. On Becker's trip to America, see 8315 Planung der Amerikareise, Zeitplan, Vorlesungen, Überfahrt, and 1716 Abschrift der Reiseerlebnisse in America 1930 Sept 4–1930 Nov 16, VI. HA, NL Becker. Hutchins tried to recruit Becker for his faculty, but Becker declined. See the telegram from Hutchins to Becker, February 4, 1930; and Becker to Hutchins, March 11, 1930, 2460, NL Becker.

60. Carl H. Becker, "The Present Educational Situation in Germany," *School and Society* 32 (1930): 679.

61. Carl H. Becker, "School and Society," *Educational Review* 32 (1930): 681 and 687; see also Max Planck Institute, *Between Elite and Mass Education*, 33.

62. Stephen Duggan, *A Professor at Large* (New York: Macmillan, 1943), 82–87, 175–176, numbers of students given on 86.

63. Füssl, *Deutsch-amerikanischer Kulturaustausch im 20. Jahrhundert*, 71.

64. "Heidelberg Obsequies," *New York Times*, July 2, 1936, 20. On this event and the American connection to the University of Heidelberg in this period, see Steven P. Remy, *The Heidelberg Myth: The Nazification and Denazification of a German University* (Cambridge: MA: Harvard University Press, 2002), 50. Schurman raised nearly $600,000, $200,000 of which came from John D. Rockefeller. See the overview of Schurman's personal correspondence at https://rmc.library.cornell.edu/EAD/htmldocs/RMA00006.html.

65. On the political symbolism of this moment, see Detlef Junker, "The Manichean Trap: American Perceptions of the German Empire, 1871–1945" (Occasional Paper No. 12, German Historical Institute, Washington, DC, 1995), 30.

66. Ben-David, *The Scientist's Role*, 193. For the quotation see Peter Watson, *The*

German Genius: Europe's Third Renaissance, the Second Scientific Revolution, and the Twentieth Century (New York: Harper Perennial, 2011), 35.

67. See the exchange between Albert Einstein and Fritz Haber, Archiv zur Geschichte der Max-Planck-Gesellschaft, Berlin.

68. Mandel to Friedrich Schmidt-Ott, November 23, 1923, VI. 474–478, NL Schmidt-Ott.

69. Atina Grossman, *Reforming Sex: The German Movement for Birth Control and Abortion Reform* (New York: Oxford University Press, 1995), 3–4, 82–83, 136.

70. Stefan Kühl, *The Nazi Connection: Eugenics, American Racism, and German National Socialism* (New York: Oxford University Press, 1994), 15.

71. Heilbron and Planck, *The Dilemmas of an Upright Man*, 91.

72. Kühl, *The Nazi Connection*, 20–22.

73. Fellowships also continued through 1938. Füssl, *Deutsch-amerikanischer Kulturaustausch im 20. Jahrhundert*, 63.

74. Timothy Ryback, *Hitler's Private Library: The Books That Shaped His Life* (New York: Vintage, 2010), 109; Fischer, *Hitler and America*, 291–292; and Kühl, *The Nazi Connection*, 85.

75. Remy offers an excellent discussion of this event in the context of what it meant for a university to become National Socialist in its orientation. See Remy, *The Heidelberg Myth*, esp. 50–80.

76. According to Beyerchen the official bias against "Jewish" physics might have played a role in the German government's neglect of nuclear physics and German nuclear weapons during the war. Beyerchen, *Scientists under Hitler*, 136.

77. Cited and translated in "Philipp-Lenard-Institut at Heidelberg: Ceremonial Dedication," *Nature*, January 18, 1936, 93.

78. The speeches from this event were edited by Stark's assistant August Becker and published in August Becker, ed., *Naturforschung im Aufbruch: Reden und Vorträge zur Einweihungsfeier des Philipp-Lernard-Instituts der Universität Heidelberg am 13. 14. Dezember 1935* (Munich: J.S. Lehmanns Verlag, 1936).

79. "Nationalism and International Science," *Nature*, January 18, 1936, 100.

80. From a correspondent, "Heidelberg, Spinoza, and Academic Freedom," *Nature*, February 22, 1936, 303–304.

81. Hubert Dunelm, letter to the editor, *Times*, February 4, 1936, in *Heidelberg and the Universities of America*, ed. Charles C. Burlingham, James Byrne, Samuel Seabury, and Henry L. Stimson (New York: Viking Press, 1936), 5; copy from b. 142 f. 4, Emergency Committee in Aid of Displaced Foreign Scholars Records (hereafter ECA)/NYPL.

82. Charles Grant Robertson, letter to the editor, *Times*, February 16, 1936, in Burlingham, Byrne, Seabury, Stimson, *Heidelberg and the Universities of America*, 23.

83. Hubert Dunelm, letter to the editor, *Times*, February 4, 1936, 5.

84. The *New York Times* covered both the debate around American participation at the jubilee and the protests at Columbia University with numerous articles. See, for example, "Nazis Will Push Heidelberg Fete," *New York Times*, March 2, 1936, 19; "Dr. Butler Receives Anti-Heidelberg Plea," *New York Times*, March 31, 1936, 19. Quotation from "The German Universities," *New York Times*, April 12, 1936, 71.

85. Kühl, *The Nazi Connection*, 85–86.

86. Stephen H. Norwood's work is packed with abhorrent examples of the disgraceful indifference and even complicit behavior of university presidents during the Nazi reign. Norwood, *The Third Reich in the Ivory Tower: Complicity and Conflict on American Campuses* (New York: Cambridge University Press, 2009), esp. 19, 35, 37, 82.

87. Quotation from Norwood, *The Third Reich in the Ivory Tower*, 67.

88. For details on the event, see "Programmgestaltung," B-1812/7; for the Hitler telegram see the *Heidelberger Tageblatt*, June 29, 1936, UAH B-1812/118 034; both in "550 Jahre Universität Heidelberg," Institut für Fränkisch-Pfälzische Geschichte und Landeskunde, Heidelberg University (hereafter UH). Thank you to Florian Schreiber and Ingo Runde for sharing this material. See also Remy, *The Heidelberg Myth*, 60–61.

89. Ernst Krieck, "The Objectivity of Science: A Crucial Problem," in *National Socialist Germany and the Pursuit of Learning*, ed. Bernhard Rust and Ernst Krieck (Hamburg: Reichinstitut für Geschichte des neuen Deutschlands, 1936), 17–24, quotations on 21 and 22.

90. Krieck's and Rust's addresses from the event were translated and reprinted in the German and foreign press. For the German edition, see Bernhard Rust and Ernst Krieck, *Das nationalsozialistische Deutschland und die Wissenschaft, Heidelberger Reden von Reichsminister Rust und Prof. Ernst Krieck* (Hamburg: Hanseatische Verlagsanstalt, 1936), 9–22, 23–25. For the English edition of Krieck's address, see note 89 above.

91. Kneller, *The Educational Philosophy of National Socialism*, 220.

92. Kneller, 220.

93. Cited in Norwood, *The Third Reich in the Ivory Tower*, 100–101.

94. Jacques Loeb to Maurice Caullery, February 4, 1918, in Reingold and Reingold, *Science in America*, 264.

95. The desire for validation from foreigners might even have motivated the continued publishing of "objective" scholarship. Holger Dainat, "Wir müssen ja trotzdem weiter arbeiten," *Deutsch Vierteljahrsschrift für Literaturwissenschaft und Geistesgeschichte* 68 (1994): 562–582, here 562; cited in Grüttner, "German Universities under the Swastika," 107.

96. The Nobel Prize–winning physicist Max von Laue represents one powerful example of such scientists who remained in Nazi Germany to continue opposing Nazi policies. Alan Beyerchen, "Anti-Intellectualism and the Cultural Decapitation of Germany under the Nazis," in *The Muses Flee Hitler: Cultural Transfer and Adaptation, 1930–1945*, ed. Jarrell C. Jackman and Carla M. Borden (Washington, DC: Smithsonian Institution Press, 1983), 29–44, here 30.

97. Boris Erich Nelson, "Heidelberg Funeral," *New York Times*, July 6, 1936, 14; and "The Heidelberg Obsequies," *New York Times*, July 2, 1936, 20. On the early history of the American celebrations at the colony of Göttingen, see Paul Gerhard Buchloh and Walter T. Rix, *American Colony of Göttingen: Historical and Other Data Collected between the Years 1855 and 1888* (Göttingen: Vandenhoeck & Ruprecht, 1976), 22. The percentage of Americans among foreign students at Heidelberg held steady at 17.5 percent until 1913. Weber, *Our Friend "The Enemy,"* 214.

98. "The German Universities," *New York Times*, April 12, 1936, 71.

99. "Nazi's Conception of Science Scored: 1,284 American Scientists Sign Manifesto Rallying Savants to Defend Democracy," *New York Times*, December 11, 1938, 50. For the quotation from Boas, see "Resolution Urges Scientists to War on Fascist Forces," *Harvard Crimson*, December 13, 1938, online at https://www.thecrimson.com/article/1938/12/13/resolution-urges-scientists-to-war-on/.

100. For the American role in the denazification, see Remy, *The Heidelberg Myth*, esp. 51.

101. Remy, who explains that this event took place at a "pivotal point," is an exception. Remy, *The Heidelberg Myth*, 51–60, quotation on 51. For other treatments, see Meinhold Lurz, "Die 550-Jahr-Feier der Universität Heidelberg als nationalsozialistische Selbstdarstellung von Reich und Universität," *Ruperto Carola* 28, no. 57 (1976): 35–41; Karl-Ludwig Hofmann and Christmut W. Präger, "'Volk, Rasse, Staat und deutscher Geist': Zum Universitätsjubiläum 1936 und zur Kunstgeschichte in Heidelberg im 'Dritten Reich,'" in *Auch eine Geschichte der Universität Heidelberg*, ed. Karin Buselmeier, Dietrich Harth, and Christian Jansen (Mannheim: Edition Quadrat, 1985), 337–345; and Philipp Gassert, *Amerika im Dritten Reich: Ideologie, Propaganda und Volksmeinung, 1933–1945* (Stuttgart: Franz Steiner Verlag, 1997), 194–198.

102. C. Wilhelm, "Heidelberg, von draußen gesehen," *Heidelberger Tageblatt*, Sonder-Beilage zum Heidelberger Universitäts-Jubiläum 1936, 13. Copy in B-1812/118, UH. Thank you to Florian Schreiber and Ingo Runde for sharing this material. The ministry would forbid subscriptions to *Nature* from Germany at the end of 1937, but in this earlier period, many like Krieck wanted to win over their foreign colleagues to their cause. Remy, *The Heidelberg Myth*, 55–56, quotation on 55.

103. The ambiguity of Jefferson as an author of these two Americas is inspired by Mia Bay's forthcoming work on the history of African American ideas about Thomas Jefferson. For the first chapter of this work, see Bay, "Talking Back to Thomas Jefferson," Kinder Institute on Constitutional Democracy at the University of Missouri, Fall 2020 Colloquium Series, online at https://www.youtube.com/watch?v=nGaQvkAEQpg.

104. Adapted from Wiggershaus, *The Frankfurt School*, 127.

105. The historical debate about how the Frankfurt School ended up at Columbia is recounted by Thomas Wheatland, who argues that Butler actually had very little to do with bringing the school to New York. In fact, had the choice been Butler's alone, he might have done away with sociology altogether. The negotiation fell largely to Erich Fromm and the US-born German sociologist Julian Gumperz. Wheatland, "The Frankfurt School's Invitation from Columbia University: How the Horkheimer Circle Settled on Morningside Heights," *German Politics and Society* 72, no. 3 (2004): 1–32, esp. 8, 11.

106. Karl Jaspers, *Die Idee der Universität, für die gegenwärtigen Situation entworfen von Karl Jaspers und Kurt Rossman* (Berlin: Springer, 1961), 150 (my translation). The English version collapses the two sides of this paradox into one line and omits chapter 10; see Karl Jaspers, *The Idea of the University*, trans. H. A. T. Reiche and H. F. Vanderschmidt, ed. Karl W. Deutsch (Boston: Beacon Press, 1959), 125.

107. Gregory J. Walters, introduction to *The Tasks of Truth: Essays on Karl Jasper's Idea of the University*, ed. Gregory J. Walters (Berlin: Peter Lang, 1996), 13–14.

108. Marianne Weber, "Academic Conviviality," *Minerva* 15 (1977): 214–246, quotation on 215.

109. Weber, "Academic Conviviality," quotations on 229, 231, 232.

110. Christine von Oertzen, *Science, Gender, and Internationalism: Women's Academic Networks, 1917–1955* (London: Palgrave, 2014), esp. 2, 57–58, 61–63, 78–79, 83, and on Harnack, 67.

111. Though American scientists certainly worried about the militaristic implications of science, the consequences were not at the forefront of the scientific community until 1939 when it became clear to Einstein among others that they were on the path to creating the bomb. See Einstein to Franklin D. Roosevelt, August 2, 1939, in Reingold and Reingold, *Science in America*, 469–470.

CHAPTER TEN

1. As told by Erwin Panofsky, "Three Decades of Art History in the United States: Impressions of a Transplanted European," in *Meaning in the Visual Arts* (New York: Vintage, 1955), 332.

2. While some histories refer to the "founding" of the Institute for Advanced Study as 1930, the institute's opening in October 1933 followed from discussion and planning during those first three years. For an account of this "opening day," see https://www.ias.edu/ideas/2008/batterson-opening-day. Arnold Reisman places the number of refugees from Nazism who contributed to the 1933 modernization of Turkish higher education at 188. Reisman, *Turkey's Modernization: Refugees from Nazism and Ataturk's Vision* (Washington, DC: New Academia Publishing, 2006), 474–478.

3. Stephen Duggan and Betty Drury, *The Rescue of Science and Learning: The Story of the Emergency Committee in Aid of Displaced Foreign Scholars* (New York: Macmillan, 1948), 1. See also Krohn, *Intellectuals in Exile*, 11.

4. Poem found transcribed in Folder 21 in folder marked "professional schools," Flexner Papers, LOC. Author unknown and undated. As of yet this poem remains unpublished and uncommented on.

5. Karl Shapiro, *Collected Poems, 1940–1978* (New York: Random House, 1978), 10; cited with "hate" instead of the original "hurt" in Stephen Whitfield, "Black Mountain and Brandeis: Two Experiments in Higher Education," *Southern Jewish History* 16 (2013): 138.

6. The anecdote is detailed in Robert Hutchins to Steven L. Buenning, December 17, 1970; published online at https://blogs.princeton.edu/reelmudd/2011/04/. Also cited in Axtell, *The Making of Princeton University*, 134. These policies are further discussed in context in Karabel, *The Chosen*, 17–23, 112; and Synnott, *The Half-Opened Door*, 17, 34–35, 195.

7. Lamberti, "The Reception of Refugee Scholars from Nazi Germany in America," 159.

8. Sinclair, *The Goose-Step*, 361, 363.

9. Jewish philanthropists paid for Felix Adler to teach Semitic languages at Cornell University (1874) and for Harry Austryn Wolfson to teach Hebrew literature at Har-

vard University (1915). Feuer, "The Stages in the Social History of Jewish Professors in American Colleges and Universities," 433.

10. Krohn, *Intellectuals in Exile*, 36.

11. Cited in Fleck, *A Transatlantic History of the Social Sciences*, 92.

12. Cited in Lamberti, "The Reception of Refugee Scholars from Nazi Germany in America," 162.

13. See confidential report translated from the German, June 26, 1933, b. 190 f. 7, Allan Gregg, MssCol 922, ECA/NYPL.

14. Lamberti, "The Reception of Refugee Scholars from Nazi Germany in America," 162.

15. Duggan and Drury, *The Rescue of Science and Learning*, 174.

16. Cited in Lamberti, "The Reception of Refugee Scholars from Nazi Germany in America," 164.

17. Program officers would become frustrated when "Hebrews were not generous." See, for example, E. R. Murrow to Betty Drury, July 23, 1935, b. 191 f. 4-6, Folder 5, MssCol 922, ECA/NYPL. See also Laurel Leff, *Well Worth Saving: American Universities' Life-and-Death Decisions on Refugees from Nazi Europe* (New Haven, CT: Yale University Press, 2019), 39.

18. Duggan and Drury, *The Rescue of Science and Learning*, 173–175.

19. ECA/NYPL; cited in Gabrielle Simon Edgcomb, *From Swastika to Jim Crow: Refugee Scholars at Black Colleges* (Malabar, FL: Krieger Publishing, 1993), 18.

20. Leff, *Well Worth Saving*, 36–37.

21. Duggan and Drury, *The Rescue of Science and Learning*, 173.

22. Bruce Bliven, "Thank You, Hitler," *New Republic* 93 (1937): 11–12. On Johnson courting the *New York Times* and other outlets, see Rutkoff and Scott, *New School*, 99.

23. "Sees Few Jobs for Jews, Report on Survey Finds Rise in Discrimination in U.S.," May 3, 1939, *New York Times*, Box 203, Folder 5, MssCol 922, ECA/NYPL. David S. Wyman drew on opinion polls to report this disturbing fact. Wyman, *The Abandonment of the Jews: America and the Holocaust, 1941–1945* (New York: New Press, 2007), 14–15. Discussed in Richard Breitman and Alan Kraut, *American Refugee Policy and European Jewry, 1933–1945* (Bloomington: Indiana University Press, 1987), 4, 10. While Wyman places the blame for the American failure to absorb refugees squarely on antisemitism, Breitman and Kraut identify the sluggishness of bureaucracy as equally culpable.

24. Cited in Krohn, *Intellectuals in Exile*, 24. For a helpful overview of Fosdick's life and career, see Steven C. Wheatley, introduction to Raymond B. Fosdick, *The Story of the Rockefeller Foundation* (New Brunswick, NJ: Routledge, 2017), vii–xi. The language of "saturation point" would become commonplace. See Leff, *Well Worth Saving*, 180. See also Oswald Veblen to Stephen P. Duggan, November 17, 1933, b. 143 f. 1-5, Folder 1, MssCol 922, ECA/NYPL.

25. Memo from Betty Drury, September 12, 1939, B173-5, Folder 5, ECA/NYPL.

26. Frank Ritchie, "Are Refugees a Liability? A Debate: II—America Needs Them," *The Forum*, 1939, 319–320, quotation on 319.

27. For an explanation of the rating system and lists upon lists of names, see B172-4, Folder 4, MssCol 922, ECA/NYPL. As Leff shows, the program officers were well aware

of the life-and-death consequences of these decisions. Leff, *Well Worth Saving*, 67–69, quotation on 72.

28. Rutkoff and Scott, *New School*, 86.

29. Krohn, *Intellectuals in Exile*, 97. Thank you to Sonja Asal for this reference.

30. That number includes nonuniversity scientists and younger academics. Mitchell Ash and Alfons Söllner, eds., *Forced Migration and Scientific Change: Émigré German-Speaking Scientists and Scholars after 1933* (Cambridge: Cambridge University Press, 1996), 7–8. Émigrés generally preferred to stay in Europe or to go to Great Britain or Turkey, where a German-inspired modernization program was underway. Krohn, *Intellectuals in Exile*, 16.

31. Laura Fermi tried to put a dollar figure to the cost-free gain the displaced scholars and scientists represented for higher education; with the cost of educating someone set at about $45,000, and considering seven hundred foreign-born university teachers, Fermi (and Krohn) calculated the savings as $32 million. Fermi also calculated that at least twelve refugees received the Nobel Prize before 1967, and 197 were listed in *American Men of Science*, 1944 ed. Fermi, *Illustrious Immigrants: The Intellectual Migration from Europe, 1930–1941* (Chicago: University of Chicago Press, 1968), 3, 12; and Krohn, *Intellectuals in Exile*, 17.

32. Lamberti, "The Reception of Refugee Scholars from Nazi Germany in America," 177.

33. See the discussion of the "Baltimore Plan" in Beatrice M. Stern, *A History of the Institute for Advanced Study, 1930–1950* (Princeton, NJ: Princeton University Press, 1964), 1:8–9, 28; Abraham Flexner, "A Proposal to Establish an American University," memorandum, November 1922, Flexner Papers, LOC. See also Flexner, "A Modern University," *Atlantic Monthly* 136 (July–December 1925): 530–541.

34. Flexner, *I Remember*, 347.

35. Flexner, *I Remember*, vii.

36. Flexner, "A Modern University," 530.

37. Abraham Flexner, *Universities: American, English, German* (Oxford: Oxford University Press, 1930), 217.

38. Stern, *A History of the Institute for Advanced Study*, 1:7.

39. Certificate of Incorporation, Appendix IV, in Stern, *A History of the Institute for Advanced Study*, 2:726 (italics mine).

40. Flexner to Louis Bamberger, December 1, 1932, Box 2, Folder 3202, Board of Trustees Records, Institute for Advanced Study (hereafter IAS). See also Letter addressed to Trustees, June 6, 1930, Appendix V, in Stern, *A History of the Institute for Advanced Study*, 2:729–731.

41. Cited in Armand Borel, "The School of Mathematics at the Institute for Advanced Study," in Duren et al., *A Century of Mathematics in America*, pt. 3, 119–147, quotation on 121.

42. Abraham Flexner to Paul H. Hanus, November 1, 1930, Box 11, Flexner Papers, LOC.

43. Abraham Flexner, Symposium on the Outlook for Higher Education in the United States, Address, read April 25, 1930, reprinted from *Proceedings of the American Philosophical Society*, vol. 60, no. 5, 1930, Box 33, Flexner Papers, LOC.

44. Flexner, *Universities*, 42.

45. Flexner, Confidential Memorandum to the Trustees, September 26, 1931, 1, Regular Meeting Minutes, IAS.

46. Flexner, Confidential Memorandum to the Trustees, 4.

47. E. L. Woodward to Flexner, Box 39, Director's Office Faculty Files, IAS; see also Stern, *A History of the Institute for Advanced Study*, 1:103, 106.

48. Flexner, Confidential Memorandum to the Trustees, 11, 14.

49. Extract from Abraham Flexner letter to Thomas Jones, February 11, 1932, Box 11, Flexner Papers, LOC.

50. Flexner was later enraged by David Birkhoff's antisemitism. Reinhard Siegmund-Schultze, *Mathematicians Fleeing from Nazi Germany: Individual Fates and Global Impact* (Princeton, NJ: Princeton University Press, 2009), 226.

51. Flexner, *I Remember*, 384.

52. Oswald Veblen to Simon Flexner, May 10, 1933; cited in Reingold and Reingold, *Science in America*, 447.

53. Abraham Flexner to Oswald Veblen, March 20, 1933, Box 5, Flexner Papers, LOC.

54. Abraham Flexner to Simon Flexner, March 12, 1932; cited in Reingold and Reingold, *Science in America: A Documentary History*, 441.

55. In summer 1933 Flexner received the following telegram from London. "Very urgent official invitation to German professors be expedited as they may not be allowed to leave." He then instructed Veblen to inform those involved in bringing Weyl that they not let it leak out of Germany that he intended to bring his wife and children, or he might not be permitted to leave. Abraham Flexner to Oswald Veblen, July 27, 1933, Box 5, Flexner Papers, LOC. See also Confidential Memorandum, German Scholars Appointed, Monday, July 24, 1933; and Flexner to Veblen, September 8, 1933, Box 5, Flexner Papers, LOC.

56. Flexner, September 28, 1933, to another Jew, Felix Warburg; cited in Siegmund-Schultze, *Mathematicians Fleeing from Nazi Germany*, 246.

57. Albert Einstein to Eleanor Roosevelt, November 21, 1933, in Reingold and Reingold, *Science in America*, 453.

58. Flexner, *I Remember*, 397.

59. Albert Einstein, Obituary of Emmy Noether, *New York Times*, May 4, 1935, 12; Siegmund-Schultze argues that Flexner's translation of Einstein's obituary actually exaggerates her fondness for the institute. Siegmund-Schultze, *Mathematicians Fleeing from Nazi Germany*, 212–214. On the specifics of Flexner's "free" translation and the credibility of this source, see Siegmund-Schultze, "Einsteins Nachruf auf Emmy Noether in der New York Times 1935," *Mitteilungen der Deutschen Mathematiker- Vereinigung* 15, no. 4 (2007): 221–227. Oswald Veblen attempted to persuade Flexner to offer Noether a permanent position. See Oswald Veblen to Abraham Flexner, February 28, 1939, page 48, box 32, Oswald Veblen Faculty File, Correspondence, IAS.

60. In 1936 the archaeologist Hetty Goldman was the first woman to be appointed to the institute's permanent faculty. Linda G. Arntzenius, *Institute for Advanced Study: An Introduction* (Princeton, NJ: Institute for Advanced Study, 2013), 17. Hetty's father, Julius Goldman, and Abraham Flexner worked out an agreement whereby Julius would

donate $20,000 for his daughter's excavation, and it would remain anonymous. The IAS "will bear no expense for this excavation though it will receive credit for it." See, inter alia, Flexner to Leidesdorf, January 19, 1938, box 15, Hetty Goldman Faculty File, IAS. On Stafford's tuition, see Oswald Veblen to Mary Stafford, May 9, 1933, 3; Anna Stafford Henriques collection, IAS; and Georgia Whidden, "Anna Stafford Henriques: A Member at the Institute in 1933," *Attributions* 1 (2001): 5.

61. Cited in Franz Lemmermeyer und Peter Roquette, eds., *Helmut Hasse und Emmy Noether: Die Korrespondenz 1925–1935* (Göttingen: Universitätsverlag, 2006), 204 (my translation).

62. Erica Mann was in the position of acting as her father's translator. Mann, *School for Barbarians*, 5.

63. Abraham Flexner to Simon Flexner, March 12, 1932, in Reingold and Reingold, *Science in America*, 441.

64. Abraham Flexner to Oswald Veblen, March 2, 1935, in Reingold and Reingold, *Science in America*, 458.

65. Abraham Flexner to Simon Flexner, March 17, 1931, in Reingold and Reingold, *Science in America*, 437.

66. Abraham Flexner to Felix Frankfurter, February 6, 1934, in Reingold and Reingold, *Science in America*, 454.

67. Flexner, Confidential Memorandum to the Trustees, 20.

68. Felix Frankfurter to Abraham Flexner, February 21, 1934, in Reingold and Reingold, *Science in America*, 456.

69. As one reviewer noted, Flexner took on both the "old eastern universities as well as . . . the younger institutions such as Chicago, Columbia and the University of Wisconsin." "The Universities Have Gone 'Main Street,'" *Milwaukee Journal*, February 4, 1931. That is not to say there was no discussion. Apparently Flexner was tipped off by a friend that a "list of Christmas suggestions" in 1930 was circulating with the following recommendation: "If you have a professor friend who has not already sold his shirt to get Flexner's book—send him one. It may make him mad; it may amuse him; but at any rate, it will stir him to the roots." See the reviews, including the above, and other miscellanea related to the publication in Box 35, Flexner Papers, LOC.

70. Flexner, *I Remember*, 389.

71. Rudolph, *The American College and University*, 458.

72. Emma Harris, *The Arts at Black Mountain College: A Pioneering Venture, 1933–1940* (Annandale-on Hudson: Edith C. Blum Art Institute, 1987), 2.

73. Martin Duberman, *Black Mountain: An Exploration in Community* (1972; New York: Norton, 2009), 1–5.

74. Arthur O. Lovejoy and Austin S. Edward, "Academic Freedom and Tenure: Rollins College Report," *Bulletin of the American Association of University Professors* 19 (1933): 416–439, here 439.

75. Harris, *The Arts at Black Mountain College*, 2.

76. Rice's name was eventually cleared in November by a subsequent report. Harris, *The Arts at Black Mountain College*, 2.

77. Lounsbury's participation was minimal, as he died of a stroke in October. Duberman, *Black Mountain*, 12–14, 19; Harris, *The Arts at Black Mountain College*, 4.

78. In this way, Black Mountain College resurrected the Board of Fellows model from Oxford and Cambridge in which the Fellows were elected from the faculty that was responsible for finances, hiring, and firing. Rice's brother-in-law Frank Aydelotte popularized the Quaker meeting at Swarthmore. Harris, *The Arts at Black Mountain College*, 2, 8; Katherine C. Reynolds, "Progressive Ideals and Experimental Higher Education: The Example of John Dewey and Black Mountain College," *Education and Culture* 14, no. 1 (1997): 1–9, esp. 5. See also Katherine C. Reynolds, *Visions and Vanities: John Andrew Rice of Black Mountain College* (Baton Rouge: Louisiana State University Press, 1998), 39, 100–101.

79. Apparently noted in private correspondence between Dewey and Dreier, Dewey's description of Black Mountain College was also reported in the *New York Times*. "Students to Erect Own Buildings; Black Mountain College Plans 'Living Example of Democracy in Action,'" *New York Times*, September 1, 1940, 7. For an excerpt from the letter with the reference, see Jonathan Fisher, "The Life and Work of an Institution of Progressive Higher Education: Toward a History of Black Mountain College, 1933–1949," online at http://www.blackmountainstudiesjournal.org/volume6/6-fisher-halfway-formatted-use-other-version/.

80. Interview with M. H. Buckminster Fuller, Box 30, D-Go, IV, Released Interviews, Black Mountain College Papers (hereafter BMC), North Carolina State Archives, Western Regional Archives.

81. Philip Johnson to Josef Albers, August 17, 1933, Josef Albers Papers, MS 32, Box 1, Folder 14, Manuscript and Archives, Yale University Library. Thank you to Jessica Becker for sending me this material.

82. On the discussion regarding visas, see Theodore Dreier to Josef Albers, October 16, 1933, Josef Albers Papers, MS 32, Box 1, Folder 7, Manuscripts and Archives, Yale University Library. Thank you to Jessica Becker for sending me this material. For the Dreier quotation, see Harris, *The Arts at Black Mountain College*, 9.

83. "Ueber die junge organization ihres institutes und seine lebendigen absichten." As Emma Harris noted, though he wrote in German, Albers used all lowercase, contrary to German grammatic rules in which nouns are capitalized. Albers to Dreier, October 16, 1933, BMC; cited in Harris, *The Arts at Black Mountain College*, 9.

84. "Germans to Teach Art Near Here," *Asheville Citizen Times*, December 5, 1933, 12.

85. Cited in Harris, *The Arts at Black Mountain College*, 9.

86. Cited in Duberman, *Black Mountain*, 102.

87. Handwritten in German at the bottom of Johnson's first letter to Albers. Johnson to Albers, August 17, 1933, Josef Albers Papers.

88. Charles Darwent argues that the pair were joined together by their outcast status and underscores that the Bauhaus had been no paradise for them. Darwent, *Josef Albers: Life and Work* (London: Thames & Hudson, 2019), 120–122, 149, 198.

89. Josef Albers, "Concerning Art Instruction," *Black Mountain College Bulletin*, series 1, no. 2 (June 1934): 2–7. See also Harris, *The Arts at Black Mountain College*, 10, 15–16.

90. Apparently given in an oral statement by Barbara Dreier for a BMC Reunion, 1995. Cited by Emma Mary Harris, "Black Mountain College and Its Cosmopolitan Faculty," in "They Fled Hitler's Germany and Found Refuge in North Carolina," ed. Henry A. Landsberger and Christoph E. Schweitzer, special issue, *Southern Research Report* 8 (Spring 1996): 117.

91. In an interview from the 1960s the Alberses speak of how they came to experience and be devoted to general education. Excerpted in Darwent, *Josef Albers*, 198.

92. Louis Adamic, "Education on a Mountain: The Story of Black Mountain College," *Harpers* 172 (April 1936): 516–530, quotation on 518.

93. John A. Rice, "Fundamentalism and the Higher Learning," *Harper's* 174 (May 1937): 587–596, quotation on 589–590.

94. The college also provided a student visa for Lisa Jalowetz, their daughter—a measure that no doubt saved her life. Emma Harris, *Starting at Zero: Black Mountain College, 1933–57*, with essays by Harris Christopher Benfey, Eva Díaz, Edmund de Waal, and Jed Perl (Cambridge: Kettles Yard, 2005), 13. Heinrich and Johanna Jalowetz (III.3), BMC.

95. See the document "Refugees Whom Black Mountain Has Helped to Become Established in the United States; as of December 18, 1940," II.35; Refugees at Black Mountain College, December 26, 1940, Financial Aspects; and Albers to Mattison, March 12, 1943; BMC.

96. Mary Harris, quoting an interview she conducted in 1972 with Clement Greenberg, in *The Arts at Black Mountain College*, 214. A small cottage industry has documented the impact of Black Mountain College on such fields as music, poetry, fine arts, and dance. The journal *Black Mountain College Studies* and blog are maintained at http://www.blackmountaincollegestudies.org.

97. Clement Greenberg contrasted Albers with Pollack, on whom he lavished praise. Greenberg, "Art," *Nation* 168 (February 19, 1949), 221–222.

98. Jo Ann C. Ellert, "The Bauhaus and Black Mountain College," *Journal of General Education* 24 (October 1972): 147; Harris, *The Arts at Black Mountain College*, 78.

99. See the article "Gropius Finds a College Run by Teamwork," Theodore and Barbara Dreier Collection, 1925–1988, PC 1956 49, BMC; in a telegram from April 10, 1940, Gropius accepted an invitation to join the council for three years. Folder for Walter Gropius (II.13), BMC. See also Harris, *The Arts at Black Mountain College*, 84.

100. Board of Fellows and Faculty Meetings, BMC.

101. Circular letter from the council of masters, September 2, 1920; cited in Anja Baumhoff, *The Gendered World of the Bauhaus: The Politics of Power at the Weimar Republic's Premier Art Institute, 1919–1931* (Frankfurt: Peter Lang, 2001), 58, 59.

102. Eva Díaz, "Stowaways," in *Leap before You Look*, ed. Helen Molesworth and Ruth Erickson (New Haven, CT: Yale University Press, 2015), 234–236.

103. Minutes, Board of Fellows and Faculty Meetings, September 11, 1937–April 14, 1941, BMC.

104. See http://www.phillipscollection.org/research/american_art/learning/dekooning-learning.htm.

105. Eva Díaz, *The Experimenters: Chance and Design at Black Mountain College* (Chicago: University of Chicago Press, 2015), 9–11.

106. Interview with M. H. Buckminster Fuller, Box 30, D-Go, IV, Released Interviews, BMC.

107. Michael Rumaker, "Robert Creeley on Black Mountain," *Boundary* 6/7 (1978): 168.

108. Ellert, "The Bauhaus and Black Mountain," 151.

109. A nostalgia pervades the memoirs and scholarly writings on this fleeting community in the North Carolina mountains, and more broadly, this period of German–African American encounter. Other than Stephen Whitfield's thoughtful essay, I know of no comprehensive work that critically takes up the issue. Some scholars have addressed other contradictions, including, for example, the way that this "free love" society was also homophobic. Wendy Fergusson Soltz, "Beyond the New York Intellectual: Jewish Refugees and Homosexuals at Black Mountain College, N.C., 1933–1956" (master's thesis, Brandeis University, 2007).

110. Duberman, *Black Mountain*, 179.

111. Minutes, Board of Fellows and Faculty Meetings, April 12, 1944, BMC.

112. Minutes, Board of Fellows and Faculty Meetings, April 17, 1944, BMC (italics original).

113. "Black Mountain College: A Pioneer in Southern Racial Integration," *Journal of Blacks in Higher Education* 54 (Winter 2006/2007): 46.

114. Rosenwald Fund (II.36), BMC.

115. Cited in Micah Wilkins, "Social Justice at BMC before the Civil Rights Age: Desegregation, Racial Inclusion, and Racial Equality at BMC," *Black Mountain Studies Journal* 6, online at http://www.blackmountainstudiesjournal.org/volume-6-alma -stone-williams-race-democracy-arts-and-crafts-and-writers-at-bmc-summer-2014/6 -17-micah-wilkins/.

116. Cited in "Black Mountain College," 46.

117. "Black Mountain College," 46.

118. Robert Orr and Erwin Straus dissented, while Albers, for his part, urged a more cautious approach. Minutes, Board of Fellows and Faculty Meetings, September 18, 1944, BMC.

119. Christopher Benfey, *Red Brick Black Mountain White Clay: Reflections on Art, Family, and Survival* (New York: Penguin, 2013), 123. Other Black Mountain Jews included Ben Shahn, Alfred Kazin, and Isaac Rosenfeld. For more on the connection between self-conscious Jewishness and opposition to total integration, see Whitman, "Black Mountain and Brandeis," 143.

120. Institute Refugees (II.14), BMC. See b. 135 f. 20, Mss Col 922, ECA/NYPL; Rosenwald Fund (II.36), BMC; and Albers's numerous letters to institute and foundation directors in the spring and summer of 1944, Institute Refugees (II.14), BMC.

121. Henry A. Landsberger, "America and North Carolina Respond," in Landsberger and Schweitzer, *They Fled Hitler's Germany*, 16.

122. B. 173, Folder 5, Mss Col 922, ECA/NYPL.

123. In Davis's case, he received his first refugee professor, Julius Lipps, in 1937,

but even he was an exception. See b. 142 f. 22, ECA/NYPL. See also Edgcomb, *From Swastika to Jim Crow*, 25–26.

124. Edgcomb, *From Swastika to Jim Crow*, 83.

125. Georg Iggers, "Refugee Historians from Nazi Germany: Political Attitudes towards Democracy," Monna and Otto Weinmann Lecture Series, September 14, 2005 (Printed in 2006 by United States Holocaust Memorial Museum).

126. Ernst Manasse, "The Jewish Graveyard," *Southern Review* 22 (1986): 296–307.

127. Christoph E. Schweitzer, "Ernst Moritz Manasse: A Black College Welcomes Refugee," in Landsberger and Schweitzer, *They Fled Hitler's Germany*, 43–46.

128. Edgcomb, *From Swastika to Jim Crow*, 67.

129. Folder 113, Alfonso Elder Papers, 1927–1999, Collection Number: 50002, North Carolina Central University. Thank you to Andre D. Vann for bringing this to my attention.

130. Letter from Ernst Manasse to Carla Boden, June 14, 1984; cited in Edgcomb, *From Swastika to Jim Crow*, xiv.

131. Schweitzer, "Ernst Moritz Manasse," 41–50. Whitfield mentions the second incident in "Black Mountain and Brandeis," 142; Edgcomb, *From Swastika to Jim Crow*, 68.

132. "Hitler Learns Jim-Crow Art from America," *Philadelphia Tribune*, December 29, 1938, 1. Quotation from *The Afro-American*, August 24, 1935, 6; Editorial 1, "American Nazis Quite as Bestial as Their German Brothers"; cited (along with many other similar examples) in Lunabelle Wedlock, "The Reaction of Negro Publications and Organizations to German Antisemitism" (masters thesis, Howard University, 1942), 96. See Hans Mommsen, "Hitler's Reichstag Speech of 30 January 1939," *History and Memory* 9 (1997): 147–161.

133. Boas expressed frustration that Du Bois was unwilling to join the American Committee for Anti-Nazi Literature because he was traveling to Nazi Germany. Franz Boas to W.E.B. Du Bois, April 22, 1936; W.E.B. Du Bois to Franz Boas, May 5, 1936; and Franz Boas to W.E.B. Du Bois, May 11, 1936, in *The Correspondence of W.E.B. Du Bois*, 135–136.

134. Mark Christian Thompson, *Black Fascisms: African American Literature and Culture between the Wars* (Charlottesville: University of Virginia Press, 2007). Thank you to Hollis Robbins for this reference.

135. Lewis Coser, *Refugee Scholars in America: Their Impact and Their Experiences* (New Haven, CT: Yale University Press, 1984), xiv. This passage is selectively and incorrectly cited by Edgcomb. This omission is important because it overlooks the reasons for the exclusion of these German-Jewish instructors, reasons that reveal much about the solidifying hierarchy of the American academy in the postwar period. Edgcomb, *From Swastika to Jim Crow*, xiv-xv.

136. Cited in Hans M. Wingler, *The Bauhaus: Weimar, Dessau, Berlin, Chicago* (Cambridge, MA: MIT Press, 1969), vii.

137. Though commentators and historians sometimes refer to an earlier version of Flexner's 1939 formulation of this idea, there is no archival evidence that an earlier version existed—other than the 1922 article on the modern American university

cited in note 33 above, which has a very different objective and framing. For a recent publication of this essay, see Abraham Flexner, with a companion essay by Robert Dijkgraaf, in *The Usefulness of Useless Knowledge* (Princeton, NJ: Princeton University Press, 2017). For the paradox of a utilitarian defense of knowledge for its own sake as the basis of the postwar science compact, see Donald E. Stokes, *Pasteur's Quadrant: Basic Science and Technological Innovation* (Washington, DC: Brookings Institution Press, 1997).

138. References and analogies to Gilman and Hopkins abound in Flexner's self-presentation of the institute. See, for example, Confidential Memorandum to the Trustees, 10.

139. Cited in Leff, *Well Worth Saving*, 72. For the implications of this strategy for the twenty-first century, see Harald Hagemann and William Milberg, eds., "Refugee Scholarship: The Cross-Fertilization of Culture," *Social Research* 84, no. 4 (2017).

140. Particularly helpful was that émigré Jewish scholars could situate themselves among *domestic* Jewish intellectuals in this period, notably the New York intellectuals, who similarly aimed to "nationalize" their ideas as part of a new consensus liberalism (and later neoconservatism). See, for example, Alexander Bloom, *Prodigal Sons: The New York Intellectuals and Their World* (New York: Oxford University Press, 1986), 369–373.

141. Abraham Flexner to Louis Bamberger and Mrs. Felix Fuld, July 19, 1937, Box 4, Flexner Papers, LOC.

142. Geoffrey L. Herrera, *Technology and International Transformation: The Railroad, The Atom Bomb, and the Politics of Technological Change* (Albany: State University of New York Press, 2006), 171–172, 176–177.

143. For a postwar account that centers the modern research university, see, for example, Roger L. Geiger, *Research and Relevant Knowledge: American Research Universities since World War II* (London: Routledge, 1993).

CONCLUSION

1. Ernst Kantorowicz, "The Fundamental Issue Documents and Marginal Notes on the University of California Loyalty Oath" (italics mine), online at http://www.lib .berkeley.edu/uchistory/archives_exhibits/loyaltyoath/symposium/kantorowicz .html. As Paul E. Lerner writes in his new biography of Kantorowicz, there were many nonsigners, but Kantorowicz was undoubtedly the "most militant." Lerner, *Ernst Kantorowicz: A Life* (Princeton, NJ: Princeton University Press, 2017), 317.

2. Lerner, *Ernst Kantorowicz*, 3.

3. One could argue that the Iraq War precipitated another version of this conundrum. With that escalated conflict playing out in the background, James J. Sheehan, then president of the American Historical Association and my dissertation adviser, invoked Kantorowicz as an example of the responsibility of wearing the gown. See James J. Sheehan, "A Historian's Thoughts at Commencement," May 1, 2005, in *Perspectives on History*, online at https://www.historians.org/publications-and-directories/ perspectives-on-history/may-2005/a-historians-thoughts-at-commencement.

4. On the eve of World War II the sociologist Robert Lynd worried that the social scientist always "[found] himself caught, therefore, between the rival demands for straight, incisive, and, if need be, radically divergent thinking, and the growingly insistent demand that his thinking shall not be subversive." Lynd, *Knowledge for What? The Place of Social Science in American Culture*, with new intro. by Lewis A. Coser (1939; Middletown, CT: Wesleyan University Press, 1986), 7. Subsequent scholars similarly criticized the "value neutral" sciences as destined to always justify the status quo, and see science and technology as a version of managerial capitalism or corporate liberalism. See, for example, Stanley Aronowitz, *Science as Power: Discourse as Ideology in Modern Society* (Minneapolis: University of Minnesota Press, 1988).

5. Pierre Bourdieu, *Science of Science and Reflexivity* (London: Polity Press, 2004), 47.

6. The term is Leon Fink's. Fink, *Progressive Intellectuals and the Dilemmas of Democratic Commitment*, 275.

7. Clark Kerr, *The Uses of the University* (Cambridge, MA: Harvard University Press, 2001), 66. The essays in this book were originally delivered in 1963 as the Godkin Lectures.

8. For a different version of the application of this contract model, see Emily J. Levine and Mitchell Stevens, "The Right Way to Fix Universities," *New York Times*, December 1, 2017.

9. The situation facing veterans following World War II was vastly different than following the previous war in which only 20 percent of veterans had gone beyond grade school. Mattingly, *American Academic Cultures*, 281.

10. Even this "mass" education movement, intended to democratize educational opportunity, was distributed unevenly. Since it was left to the states to administer (as had been the case with the land grants), southern states were free to perpetuate the unequal conditions of segregation. African Americans overwhelmingly used the GI Bill to attend vocational programs rather than research institutions, bringing the total number of veterans who used the bill to their educational advantage to 7.8 million. For the uneven impact of the GI Bill, see Suzanne Mettler, *Soldiers to Citizens: The GI Bill and the Making of the Greatest Generation* (Oxford: Oxford University Press, 2005), 80–82, 102–104.

11. President's Commission on Higher Education, *Higher Education for American Democracy* (Washington, DC: US Government Printing Office, 1947); Julie Reuben and Linda Perkins, "Introduction: Commemorating the 60th Anniversary of the President's Commission Report, *Higher Education for American Democracy*," *History of Education Quarterly* 47 (2007): 265–276, esp. 269–270; and Jason Owen-Smith, *Research Universities and the Public Good: Discovery for an Uncertain Future* (Stanford, CA: Stanford University Press, 2018), 40.

12. Daniel Lee Kleinman, *Politics on the Endless Frontier: Postwar Research Policy in the United States* (Durham, NC: Duke University Press, 1995), 18–21, 75–99.

13. In 1958, federal funding for education and research was $456 million by comparison. Geiger, *Research and Relevant Knowledge*, 157; Leslie, *The Cold War and American Science*, 1–2.

14. David H. Guston identifies Vannevar Bush's postwar science policy as a contract

but without its historical antecedents. Guston, "The Demise of the Social Contract for Science: Misconduct in Science and the Nonmodern World," *Centennial Review* 38 (1994): 215–248.

15. Vannevar Bush, *The Endless Frontier*, A Report to the President by Vannevar Bush, Director of the Scientific Research and Development (July 1945), online at https://www.nsf.gov/about/history/vbush1945.htm.

16. David Engerman, *Know the Enemy: The Rise and Fall of America's Soviet Experts* (New York: Oxford University Press, 20011); Nils Gilman, *Mandarins of the Future: Modernization Theory in Cold War America* (Baltimore: Johns Hopkins University Press, 2003); and Mitchell L. Stevens, Cynthia Miller-Idriss, and Seteney Shami, *Seeing the World: How US Universities Make Knowledge in a Global Era* (Princeton, NJ: Princeton University Press, 2018).

17. On the growth of physics and "Big Science" at Stanford during the Cold War, see Rebecca S. Lowen, *Creating the Cold War University: The Transformation of Stanford* (Berkeley: University of California Press, 1997); and Lowen, "Transforming the University: Administrators, Physicists, and Industrial and Federal Patronage at Stanford, 1935–49," *History of Education Quarterly* 31 (1991) 365–388; and Peter Galison, Bruce Hevly, and Rebecca Lowen, "Controlling the Monster: Stanford and the Growth of Physics Research, 1935–1962," in *Big Science: The Growth of Large-Scale Research*, ed. Peter Galison and Bruce Hevly (Stanford, CA: Stanford University Press, 1992), 46–77. For a revised portrait of Terman, see Stevens and Kindel, "Engineering Credentials."

18. Margaret O'Mara, *Cities of Knowledge: Cold War Science and the Search for the Next Silicon Valley* (Princeton, NJ: Princeton University Press, 2005).

19. Simon Marginson, *The Dream Is Over: The Crisis of Clark Kerr's California Idea of Higher Education* (Berkeley: University of California Press, 2016), online at https://doi.org/10.1525/luminos.17.

20. Sheldon Rothblatt, "Clark Kerr: Two Voices," in *Clark Kerr's World of Higher Education Reaches the 21st Century: Chapters in a Special History* (Dordrecht: Springer, 2012), 13.

21. Kerr, *The Great Transformation*, 4; cited in Rothblatt, "Clark Kerr," 1. See also Paul Mattingly, "The Unapologetic Pragmatist," *Social Science History* 36 (2012): 481–497. On Kerr's "in-betweenism" and the Master Plan, see "Clark Kerr and the California Idea," online at https://doi.org/10.1525/luminos.17. Kerr was also responsible for the founding of ten organized research units, or ORUs, which Ethan Schrum argues were essential to a new phase for the university. See Schrum, *The Instrumental University: Education in Service of the National Agenda after World War II* (Ithaca, NY: Cornell University Press, 2019), 88.

22. Eric Bennett, *Workshops of Empire: Stegner, Engle, and American Creative Writing during the Cold War* (Iowa City: University of Iowa Press, 2015).

23. Cited in Leslie, *The Cold War and American Science*, 14.

24. The first term was Kerr's, in *The Uses of the University*, v–vi. See also Schrum, *The Instrumental University*, 2; Sheila Slaughter and Gary Rhoades, "The Neo-Liberal University," *New Labor Forum* 6 (2000): 73–79; and Jennifer Washburn, *University Inc: The Corporate Corruption of Higher Education* (New York: Basic, 2005). For a

critical analysis of the historicity of these terms, see James Vernon, "The Making of the Neoliberal University in Britain," *Critical Historical Studies* 5 (2018): 267–280, esp. 280.

25. One of Kerr's colleagues, the UC Riverside professor of sociology Robert Nisbet, argued in the 1970s that the university enjoyed "a kind of social contract," in which academics were permitted "the freedom to indulge ourselves in the aristocratic pleasures of seeking knowledge for its own sake . . . [in exchange for] stay[ing] as far as possible out of the areas of society in which, not dispassionate reason and scholarly objectivity, but passionate moralism and politicization are incessantly required." In addition to explicitly putting the university's existence in terms of a contract, Nisbet crucially identified the split between research and teaching as being one of the more troublesome trends of the organizational shift of the postwar centers toward solving particular social problems financed by a combination of private philanthropy and the state. Althoff and Flexner both would have agreed. Robert Nisbet, *The Degradation of the Academic Dogma: The University in America, 1945–1970* (New York: Basic, 1971), 199–200; cited in Schrum, *The Instrumental University*, 220.

26. James Tent, *The Free University of Berlin: A Political History* (Bloomington: Indiana University Press, 1988).

27. John Gimbel, "The American Exploitation of German Technical Know-How after World War II," *Political Science Quarterly* 105 (1990): 295–309.

28. Moritz Mälzer, *Auf der Suche nach der neuen Universität: Die Entstehung der "Reformuniversitäten" Konstanz und Bielefeld in den 1960er Jahren* (Göttingen: Vandenhoeck & Ruprecht, 2016).

29. Martin Klimke, *The "Other Alliance": Global Protest and Student Unrest in West Germany and the United States, 1962–1972* (Princeton, NJ: Princeton University Press, 2010), 7, 241.

30. Stefan Paulus, "The Americanization of Europe after 1945? The Case of the German Universities," *European Review of History/Revue européenne d'histoire* 9, no. 2 (2002): 241–253, esp. 251–252. On the ebbs and flows of the "Humboldt ideal" in postwar Germany, see Johan Östling, *Humboldt and the Modern German University: An Intellectual History*, trans. Lena Olsson (Lund: Lund University Press, 2018). For similar calls for a new academic contract in Europe, see Peter Maassen, "A New Contract for Higher Education," in *Higher Education in Societies: A Multi-Scale Perspective*, ed. Gaële Goastellec and France Picard (Rotterdam: Sense Publishers, 2014), 33–50. Thank you to JB Shank for bringing to my attention the photograph that appears as figure 12.

31. This term was coined by William Fulbright. Cited in Leslie, *The Cold War and American Science*, 2.

32. Isaac W. Martin, *The Permanent Tax Revolt: How the Property Tax Transformed American Politics* (Stanford, CA: Stanford University Press, 2008). See also Mitchell Stevens and Ben Gebre-Medhin, "Association, Service, Market: Higher Education in American Political Development," *Annual Review of Sociology* 42 (2016): 121–124, here 129.

33. Owen-Smith's excellent book is a rare example of acknowledging exceptionality of period but providing ample justification of the "public goods" provided by the uni-

versity to aspire to similar levels of support again. Owen-Smith, *Research Universities and the Public Good*, 36.

34. ASU president Michael Crow, Robert Robbins, president of the University of Arizona, and Rita Cheng, president of Northern Arizona University, have expressed the desire to be permitted to run like businesses to make up the funding no longer provided by their states. https://asunow.asu.edu/20180130-arizona-impact-arizonas -universities-need-freedom-be-run-business-presidents-say. Holden Thorp and Buck Goldstein, in contrast, argue that universities should be providing more services to society. Thorp and Goldstein, *Our Higher Calling: Rebuilding the Partnership between America and Its Colleges and Universities* (Chapel Hill: University of North Carolina Press, 2018).

35. See Clark Kerr, "Higher Education Cannot Escape History: The 1990s," in *An Agenda for the New Decade*, ed. Larry W. Jones and Franz A. Nowotny (San Francisco: Jossey-Bass, 1990), 5–17. For criticism, see Schrum, *The Instrumental University*, 219.

36. Here I borrow Bourdieu's concept of "fields" as a system of relations in which autonomy is the crucial feature. Loïc J. D. Wacquant, "For a Socio-Analysis of Intellectuals; On 'Homo Academicus,'" *Berkeley Journal of Sociology* 34 (1989): 1–29, here 6.

37. Bourdieu referred to the different kinds of cultural capital that could be converted in different spheres of power as "exchange rates." See Andreas Schmitz, Daniel Witte, and Vincent Gengnagel, "Pluralizing Field Analysis: Toward a Relational Understanding of the Field of Power," *Social Science Information* 56 (2017): 49–73.

38. Ben-David and Zlockower, "Universities and Academic Systems in Modern Societies," 57.

39. Ash, "Bachelor of What, Master of Whom?," 245–267; Rüdiger vom Bruch, "A Slow Farewell To Humboldt? Stages in the History of German Universities, 1810–1945," in *German Universities Past and Future*, ed. Mitchell G. Ash (Oxford: Berghahn Books, 1997), 3–27.

ARCHIVES CONSULTED

GERMANY

Archiv zur Geschichte der Max-Planck-Gesellschaft, Berlin
Bundesarchiv, Berlin
    Auswärtiges Amt
    Politisches Amt
Dresden Hauptstaatsarchiv
Geheimes Staatsarchiv Preußischer Kulturbesitz (GStPK)
    Nachlass Friedrich Althoff (NL Althoff)
    Nachlass Carl Becker (NL Becker)
    Nachlass Adolf Harnack
    Nachlass Friedrich Schmidt-Ott (NL Schmidt-Ott)
Institute für Stadtgeschichte, Frankfurt am Main
Niedersächsische Staats-Universitätsbibliothek Göttingen (SUB Göttingen)
    Felix Klein (NL Klein)
Sächsisches Staatsarchiv—Hauptstaatsarchiv Dresden
Staatsbibliothek zu Berlin—Handschriftabteilung
    Ludwig Darmstaedter
    Adolf von Harnack
Universitäts- und Landesbibliothek Bonn (ULB)
Universitätsarchiv Frankfurt am Main
Universitätsarchiv Leipzig
Universitätsbibliothek J. C. Senckenberg, Göethe Universität, Frankfurt am
    Main (UBF)

UNITED STATES

Boston Public Library, Archives and Manuscripts (BPL)
    Hugo Münsterberg Collection
Columbia University in the City of New York, Rare Book & Manuscript Library
    (RBMLC)
    John W. Burgess Papers

Nicholas Murray Butler Papers
James McKeen Cattell Papers
Christine Ladd-Franklin and Fabian Franklin Papers
E.R.A. Seligman Papers
Duke Rare Book and Manuscript Library
R. Philip Hanes Papers, 1928–2010
Institute for Advanced Study (IAS)
Johns Hopkins University, Sheridan Libraries, Special Collections (JHU)
Daniel Coit Gilman Papers
Library of Congress (LOC)
Andrew Carnegie Papers
Abraham Flexner Papers
Simon Newcomb Papers
Henry S. Pritchett Papers
Oswald Veblen Papers
New School Archives and Special Collections (NSASC)
New York Public Library (NYPL)
John Shaw Billings Papers
Emergency Committee in Aid of Displaced Foreign Scholars Records (ECA)
North Carolina State Archives, Western Regional Archives
Black Mountain College Papers (BMC)
University of Massachusetts Amherst Libraries, Special Collections and University Archives
W.E.B. Du Bois Papers
University of Wisconsin-Madison, University Archives
Charles R. Van Hise Papers
Yale University Library, Manuscripts and Archives
Daniel Coit Gilman Papers
Arthur Twining Hadley Papers

SELECTED BIBLIOGRAPHY

This selected bibliography, organized by subject and methodology, lists secondary sources that were most influential in the shaping of this book's approach. For a full bibliography of primary and secondary sources, see http://press.uchicago.edu/sites/levine.

UNIVERSITY HISTORY

Anderson, R. D. *European Universities from the Enlightenment to 1914*. Oxford: Oxford University Press, 2004.

Axtell, James. *Wisdom's Workshop: The Rise of the Modern University*. Princeton, NJ: Princeton University Press, 2016.

Bender, Thomas, ed. *The University and the City: From Medieval Origins to the Present*. New York: Oxford University Press, 1988.

Clark, William. *Academic Charisma and the Origins of the Research University*. Chicago: University of Chicago Press, 2006.

Flexner, Abraham. *Universities: American, English, German*. New York: Oxford University Press, 1930.

Rashdall, Hastings, and F. M. Powicke, eds. *The Universities of Europe in the Middle Ages*. London: Oxford University Press, 1936.

INSTITUTIONAL HISTORY

Duberman, Martin. *Black Mountain: An Exploration in Community. 1972*. New York: Norton, 2009.

Edgcomb, Gabrielle Simon. *From Swastika to Jim Crow: Refugee Scholars at Black Colleges*. Malabar, FL: Krieger Publishing, 1993.

Kluke, Paul. *Die Stiftungsuniversität Frankfurt am 1914–1932*. Frankfurt: Kramer, 1972.

Krohn, Claus-Dieter. *Intellectuals in Exile: Refugee Scholars and the New School for Social Research*. Translated by Rita and Robert Kimber. Amherst: University of Massachusetts Press, 1993.

McClelland, Charles E. *Berlin, the Mother of All Research Universities: 1860–1918*. Lanham, MD: Lexington, 2016.

Rutkoff, Peter M., and William B. Scott. *New School: A History of the New School for Social Research*. New York: Free Press, 1986.

Stern, Beatrice M. *A History of the Institute for Advanced Study, 1930–1950*. Princeton, NJ: Princeton University Press, 1964.

vom Brocke, Bernhard, and Rudolf Vierhaus, eds. *Forschung im Spannungsfeld von Politik und Gesellschaft: Geschichte und Struktur der Kaiser-Wilhelm-/Max-Planck-Gesellschaft aus Anlass ihres 75jährigen Bestehens*. Stuttgart: Deutsche Verlags-Anstalt, 1990.

Wiggershaus, Rolf, and Michael Robertson. *The Frankfurt School: Its History, Theories, and Political Significance*. Cambridge: Polity Press, 1995.

WISSENSCHAFTSGESCHICHTE AND SOCIOLOGY OF KNOWLEDGE

Anderson, Benedict. *The Spectre of Comparisons: Nationalism, Southeast Asia, and the World*. London: Verso, 1998.

Ben-David, Joseph. "Science and the University System." In "The Notion of Modern Educational Sociology/Der Begriff der Modernen Erziehungssoziologie/La notion contemporaine de sociologie de l'éducation," special issue, *International Review of Education/Internationale Zeitschrift für Erziehungswissenschaft/Revue Internationale de l'Education* 18 (1972): 44–60.

———. *The Scientist's Role in Society: A Comparative Study*. Englewood Cliffs, NJ: Prentice Hall, 1971.Ben-David, Joseph, and Awraham Zlockower. "Universities and Academic Systems in Modern Societies." *European Journal of Sociology* 3 (1962): 45–84.

Bourdieu, Pierre. "The Conquest of Autonomy." Translated by Susan Emanuel. In *The Rules of Art: Genesis and Structure of the Literary Field*, 47–112. Stanford, CA: Stanford University Press, 1996.

———. "Forms of Capital." Translated by Richard Nice. In *Handbook of Theory of Research for the Sociology of Education*, edited by J. E. Richardson, 241–258. Westport, CT: Greenwood Press, 1986.

———. "The Genesis of the Concept of Habitus and Field." *Sociocriticism* 2 (1985): 11–24.

———. *Science of Science and Reflexivity*. Translated by Richard Nice. Cambridge: Polity Press, 2004.

Burke, Peter. *A Social History of Knowledge: From the Encyclopedia to Wikipedia*. Vol. 2. Cambridge: Polity Press, 2012.

Crawford, Elizabeth. *1880–1939: Four Studies of the Nobel Population*. Cambridge: Cambridge University Press, 1992.

Gordin, Michael D. *Scientific Babel: How Science Was Done Before and After Global English*. Chicago: University of Chicago Press, 2015.

Hirschman, Albert O. *Exit, Voice, and Loyalty: Responses to Decline in Firms, Organizations, and States*. Cambridge, MA: Harvard University Press, 1970.

Shils, Edward. "Center and Periphery." In *The Logic of Personal Knowledge: Essays*

Presented to Michael Polyani on His Seventieth Birthday, March 11, 1861, 117–130. London: Routledge, 1961.

Yuasa, Mitsutomo. "The Shifting Center of Scientific Activity in the West: From the 16th to the 20th Century." In *Science and Society in Modern Japan: Selected Historical Sources*, edited by Shigeru Nakayama, David Swain, and Eri Yagi, 81–103. Cambridge, MA: MIT Press, 1974.

ORGANIZATIONAL AND HISTORICAL SOCIOLOGY

Clemens, Elisabeth Stephanie. "Organizational Repertoires and Institutional Change: Women's Groups and the Transformation of U.S. Politics, 1890–1920." *American Journal of Sociology* 98, no. 4 (1993): 755–798.

Collins, Randall. *The Credential Society: An Historical Sociology of Education and Stratification*. New York: Academic Press, 1979.

———. *The Sociology of Philosophies: A Global Theory of Intellectual Change*. Cambridge, MA: Belknap Press of Harvard University Press, 1998.

Delanty, Gerard. "The University in the Knowledge Society." *Organization* 8 (2001): 149–153.

DiMaggio, Paul J., and Walter W. Powell. "The Iron Cage Revisited: Institutional Isomorphism and Collective Rationality in Organizational Fields." *American Sociological Review* 48 (1983): 147–160.

Owen-Smith, Jason. *Research Universities and the Public Good: Discovery for an Uncertain Future*. Stanford, CA: Stanford University Press, 2018.

Padgett, John Frederick, and Walter W. Powell, eds. *The Emergence of Organizations and Markets*. Princeton, NJ: Princeton University Press, 2012.

Podolny, Joel M. *Status Signals: A Sociological Study of Market Competition*. Princeton, NJ: Princeton University Press, 2005.

Stevens, Mitchell L., Elizabeth A. Armstrong, and Richard Arum. "Sieve, Incubator, Temple, Hub: Empirical and Theoretical Advances in the Sociology of Higher Education." *Annual Review of Sociology* 34 (2008): 127–151.

Stevens, Mitchell L., and Ben Gebre-Medhin. "Association, Service, Market: Higher Education in American Political Development." *Annual Review of Sociology* 42 (2016): 121-142.

Stevens, Mitchell L., and Alexander Kindel. "Engineering Credentials: Educational Entrepreneurship as Statecraft in the Cold-War United States." SocArXiv, May 30, 2018. https://doi.org/10.31235/osf.io/pd8c4.

HISTOIRE CROISÉE AND TRANSATLANTIC EXCHANGE

Adam, Thomas. *Philanthropy, Civil Society, and the State in German History, 1815–1989*. Rochester, NY: Camden House, 2016.

Barclay, David E., and Elisabeth Glaser-Schmidt, eds. *Transatlantic Images and Perceptions: Germany and America since 1776*. Washington, DC: German Historical Institute, 1997.

Bönker, Dirk. *Militarism in a Global Age: Naval Ambitions in Germany and the United States before World War I*. Ithaca, NY: Cornell University Press, 2012.

Bonner, Thomas Neville. *American Doctors and German Universities: A Chapter in International Intellectual Relations, 1870–1914*. Lincoln: University of Nebraska Press, 1963.

Charles, Christophe, Jürgen Schriewer, and Peter Wagner, eds. *Transnational Intellectual Networks: Forms of Academic Knowledge and the Search for Cultural Identities*. Frankfurt: Campus, 2004.

Diehl, Carl. *Americans and German Scholarship, 1770–1870*. New Haven, CT: Yale University Press, 1978.

Düwell, Kurt. "Der Einfluss des deutschen technischen Schul- und Hochschulwesens auf das Ausland (1870– 1930)." In *Interne Faktoren auswärtiger Kulturpolitik im 19. und 20. Jahrhundert*, edited by Kurt Düwell and Friedrich H. Kochwasser, 80–95. Stuttgart: Institut für Auslandsbeziehungen, 1981.

Espagne, Michel. "Au-delà du comparatisme: La méthode des transferts culturels." *Historiographie de l'antiquité et transferts culturels* 145 (2010): 201–221.

Fiebig-von Hase, Ragnhild. "The United States and Germany in the World Arena, 1900–1917." In *Confrontation and Cooperation: Germany and the United States in the Era of World War I, 1900–1924*, edited by Hans-Jürgen Schröder, 33–68. Oxford: Oxford University Press, 1993.

Fleck, Christian. *Transatlantic History of the Social Science: Robber Barons, the Third Reich, and the Invention of Empirical Social Research*. London: Bloomsbury, 2011.

Füssl, Karl-Heinz. *Deutsch-amerikanischer Kulturaustausch im 20. Jahrhundert: Bildung, Wissenschaft, Politik*. Frankfurt: Campus, 2004.

Geitz, Henry, Jürgen Heideking, and Jurgen Herbst, eds. *German Influences on Education in the United States to 1917*. New York: Cambridge University Press, 1995.

Heideking, Jürgen. *Mutual Influences on Education: Germany and the United States in the Twentieth Century*. Ghent, Belgium: Paedagogica Historica, Universiteit Gent, 1997.

Herbst, Jurgen. *The German Historical School in American Scholarship: A Study in the Transfer of Culture*. Ithaca, NY: Cornell University Press, 1965.

Jarausch, Konrad. "American Students in Germany, 1815–1914: The Structure of German and US Matriculants at Göttingen University." In *German Influence on Education in the United States to 1917*, edited by Henry Geitz, Jürgen Heideking, and Jurgen Herbst, 195–211. New York: Cambridge University Press, 1995.

Kloosterhuis, Jürgen. "Deutsche auswärtige Kulturpolitik und ihre Trägergruppen vor dem Ersten Weltkrieg." In *Deutsche auswärtige Kulturpolitik seit 1871: Geschichte und Struktur; Referate und Diskussionen eines interdisziplinären Symposions*, edited by Wolfgang F. Dexheimer, Kurt Düwell, and Werner Link, 7–45. Cologne: Böhlau, 1981.

Laitko, Hubert. "'Weltbetrieb der Wissenschaft': Reflexionen und Streiflichter vom Beginn des deutsch-amerikanischen Professorenaustausches 1905/6." *Dahlemer Archivgespräche* 12 (2006): 44–152.

Lingelbach, Gabriele. "Cultural Borrowing or Autonomous Development: American and German Universities in the Late Nineteenth Century." In *Traveling between Worlds: German-American Encounters*, edited by Thomas Adam and Ruth V. Gross, 100–123. College Station: Texas A&M University Press, 2006.

Rodgers, Daniel T. *Atlantic Crossings: Social Politics in a Progressive Age.* Cambridge, MA: Belknap Press of Harvard University Press, 2009.

Schivelbusch, Wolfgang. *Three New Deals: Reflections on Roosevelt's America, Mussolini's Italy, and Hitler's Germany, 1933–1939.* New York: Picador, 2007.

Siegmund-Schultze, Reinhard. "Felix Kleins Beziehungen zu den Vereinigten Staaten, die Anfänge deutsche auswärtiger Wissenschaftspolitik und die Reform um 1900." *Sudhoffs Archiv* 81 (1997): 21–38.

Trommler, Frank. "Inventing the Enemy: German-American Cultural Relations, 1900–1917." In *Confrontation and Cooperation: Germany and the United States in the Era of World War I, 1900–1924*, edited by Hans Jürgen Schroeder, 99–125. Oxford: Berg, 1993.

Werner, Anja. *The Transatlantic World of Higher Education: Americans at German Universities, 1776–1914.* New York: Berghahn Books, 2013.

Werner, Michaël, and Bénédicte Zimmermann. "Histoire Croisée and the Challenge of Reflexivity." *History and Theory* 45 (2006): 30–50.

Whitman, James Q. *Hitler's American Model: The United States and the Making of Nazi Race Law.* Princeton, NJ: Princeton University Press, 2017.

Zimmerman, Andrew. *Alabama in Africa: Booker T. Washington, the German Empire, and the Globalization of the New South.* Princeton, NJ: Princeton University Press, 2010.

GERMANY

Ash, Mitchell. "Bachelor of What, Master of Whom? The Humboldt Myth and Historical Transformations of Higher Education in German-Speaking Europe and the US." *European Journal of Education* 41 (2006): 245–267.

Beyerchen, Alan. *Scientists under Hitler: Politics and the Physics Community in the Third Reich.* New Haven, CT: Yale University Press, 1977.

Bialas, Wolfgang, and Anson Rabinbach, eds. *Nazi Germany and the Humanities: How German Academics Embraced Nazism.* Oxford: Oneworld Publications, 2014.

Burchardt, Lothar. *Wissenschaftspolitik im Wilhelminischen Deutschland: Vorgeschichte, Gründung und Aufbau der Kaiser-Wilhelm-Gesellschaft zur Förderung der Wissenschaft.* Göttingen: Vandenhoeck und Ruprecht, 1975.

Cahan, David. "Werner Siemens and the Origin of the Physikalisch-Technische Reichsanstalt, 1872–1887." *Historical Studies in Physical Sciences* 12 (1982): 253–283.

Dukes, Jack R., and Joachim Remak, eds. *Another Germany: A Reconsideration of the Imperial Era.* Boulder, CO: Westview Press, 1988.

Galison, Peter. "Meanings of Scientific Unity: The Law, the Orchestra, the Pyramid, the Quilt, and the Ring." In *Pursuing the Unity of Science: Ideology and Scientific Practice from the Great War to the Cold War*, edited by Harmke Kamminga and Geert Somsen, 12–29. New York: Routledge, 2016.

Gispen, Kees. *New Profession, Old Order: Engineers and German Society, 1815–1914.* Cambridge: Cambridge University Press, 1989.

Green, Abigail. "The Federal Alternative? A New View of Modern German History." *Historical Journal* 46 (2003): 187–202.

Grüttner, Michael. "German Universities under the Swastika." In *Universities under Dictatorship*, edited by John Connelly and Michael Grüttner, 75–111. University Park: Pennsylvania State University Press, 2005.

Hartshorne, Edward Yarnall. *The German Universities and National Socialism.* Cambridge, MA: Harvard University Press, 1937.

Johnson, Jeffrey Allan. *The Kaiser's Chemists: Science and Mobilization in Imperial Germany.* Chapel Hill: University of North Carolina, 2010.

Manegold, Karl-Heinz. *Universität, Technische Hochschule und Industrie: Ein Beitrag zur Emanzipation der Technik im 19. Jahrhundert unter besonderer Berücksichtigung der Bestrebungen Felix Kleins.* Berlin: Duncker & Humblot, 1970.

Oertzen, Christine von. *Science, Gender, and Internationalism: Women's Academic Networks, 1917–1955.* Translated by Kate Sturge. New York: Palgrave Macmillan, 2014.

Östling, Johan. *Humboldt and the Modern German University: An Intellectual History.* Translated by Lena Olsson. Lund: Lund University Press, 2018.

Palatschek, Sylvia. "Die Erfindung der Humboldtschen Universität: Die Konstruktion der deutschen Universitätsidee in der ersten Hälfte des 20. Jahrhunderts." *Historische Anthropologie* 10 (2002): 183–205.

Paulsen, Friedrich. *Die deutschen Universitäten und das Universitätsstudium.* Berlin: A. Asher, 1902.

Pfetsch, Frank. "Scientific Organisation and Science Policy in Imperial Germany, 1871–1914: The Foundation of the Imperial Institute of Physics and Technology." *Minerva* 8 (1970): 557–580.

Schwinges, Rainer Christoph, ed. *Humboldt International: Der Export des deutschen Universitätsmodells im 19. und 20. Jahrhundert.* Basel: Schwabe, 2001.

Turner, Steven R. "The Prussian Professoriate and the Research Imperative: 1790–1840." In *Epistemological and Social Problems of the Sciences in the Early Nineteenth Century*, edited by Hans N. Jahnke and M. Otte, 109–122. Dordrecht: Reidel 1981.

vom Brocke, Bernhard. "Hochschul- und Wissenschaftspolitik in Preußen und im Deutschen Kaiserreich 1882–1907: Das 'System Althoff.'" In *Bildungspolitik in Preußen zur Zeit des Kaiserreichs*, edited by Peter Baumgart, 9–118. Stuttgart: Klett-Cotta, 1980.

vom Bruch, Rüdiger. *Weltpolitik als Kulturmission: Auswärtige Kulturpolitik und Bildungsbürgertum in Deutschland am Vorabend des Ersten Weltkrieges.* Paderborn: Ferdinand Schöningh, 1982.

Wellmon, Chad. *Organizing Enlightenment: Information Overload and the Invention of the Research University.* Baltimore: Johns Hopkins University Press, 2015.

UNITED STATES

Barrow, Clyde. *Universities and the Capitalist State: Corporate Liberalism and the Reconstruction of American Higher Education, 1894–1928*. Madison: University of Wisconsin Press, 1990.

Bender, Thomas. *Intellect and Public Life: Essays on the Social History of Academic Intellectuals in the United States*. Baltimore: Johns Hopkins University Press, 1993.

Bledstein, Burton J. *The Culture of Professionalism: The Middle Class and the Development of Higher Education in America*. New York: Norton, 1976.

Fink, Leon, Stephen T. Leonard, and Donald M. Reid, eds. *Intellectuals and Public Life: Between Radicalism and Reform*. Ithaca, NY: Cornell University Press, 1996.

Geiger, Roger L. *To Advance Knowledge: The Growth of American Research Universities, 1900–1940*. New York: Oxford University Press, 1986.

Gerber, Larry G. *The Rise and Decline of Faculty Governance: Professionalization and the Modern American University*. Baltimore: Johns Hopkins University Press, 2014.

Gruber, Carol S. *Mars and Minerva: World War I and the Uses of the Higher Learning in America*. Baton Rouge: Louisiana State University Press, 1975.

Hoffer, William James. *To Enlarge the Machinery of Government: Congressional Debates and the Growth of the American State, 1858–1891*. Reconfiguring American Political History. Baltimore: Johns Hopkins University Press, 2007.

Hofstadter, Richard, and Walter P. Metzger. *Academic Freedom in the Age of the College*. New York: Columbia University Press, 1961.

Jewett, Andrew. *Science, Democracy, and the American University: From the Civil War to the Cold War*. Cambridge: Cambridge University Press, 2012.

Johnson, Joan Marie. *Funding Feminism: Monied Women, Philanthropy, and the Women's Movement, 1870–1967*. Chapel Hill: University of North Carolina Press, 2017.

Kerr, Clark. *The Great Transformation in Higher Education, 1960–1980*. Albany: State University of New York Press, 1991.

Marsden, George M. *The Soul of the American University: From Protestant Establishment to Established Nonbelief*. New York: Oxford University Press, 1994.

Mattingly, Paul H. *American Academic Cultures: A History of Higher Education*. Chicago: University of Chicago Press, 2017.

Nelson, Adam R. "HES Presidential Address: Citizens or Cosmopolitans? Constructing Scientific Identity in the Early American College." *History of Education Quarterly History of Education Quarterly* 57 (2017): 159–184.

O'Mara, Margaret Pugh. *Cities of Knowledge: Cold War Science and the Search for the Next Silicon Valley*. Princeton, NJ: Princeton University Press, 2015.

Parshall, Karen Hunger, and David E. Rowe. *The Emergence of the American Mathematical Research Community, 1876–1900: J. J. Sylvester, Felix Klein, and E.H. Moore*. History of Mathematics 8. Providence: American Mathematical Society, 1994.

Rossiter, Margaret W. *Women Scientists in America: Struggles and Strategies to 1940*. Baltimore: Johns Hopkins University Press, 1982.

Shils, Edward. "The Order of Learning in the United States: The Ascendancy of the University." In *The Organization of Knowledge in Modern America, 1860-1920*, edited by Alexandra Oleson and John Coas, 19–47. Baltimore: Johns Hopkins University Press, 1976.

Veysey, Lawrence R. *The Emergence of the American University*. Chicago: University of Chicago Press, 1965.

BEYOND

Ashton, Rosemary. *Little Germany: Exile and Asylum in Victorian England*. Oxford: Oxford University Press, 1986.

Dees, Bowen C. *The Allied Occupation and Japan's Economic Miracle: Building the Foundations of Japanese Science and Technology 1945-1952*. London: Routledge, 1997.

Ellis, Heather. *Generational Conflict and University Reform: Oxford in the Age of Revolution*. Leiden: Brill, 2012.

Hongjie, Chen. "Die chinesische Rezeption der Humbolt'schen Universitätsidee: Am Beispiel der Universität Peking zu Anfang des 20. Jahrhunderts." In *Humboldt International: Der Export des deutschen Universitätsmodells im 19. und 20. Jahrhundert*, edited by Rainer Christoph Schwinges, 323–334. Basel: Schwabe, 2001.

Irish, Tomás. *The University at War, 1914-25: Britain, France, and the United States*. New York: Palgrave Macmillan, 2015.

La Fargue, Thomas E. *China's First Hundred: Educational Mission Students in the United States, 1872-1881*. Pullman: Washington State University Press, 1987.

Lundgreen, Peter. "The Organization of Science and Technology in France: A German Perspective." In *The Organization of Science and Technology in France 1808-1914*, edited by Robert Fax and George Weisz, 311–332. Cambridge: Cambridge University Press, 1980.

Paul, Harry W. *The Sorcerer's Apprentice: The French Scientist's Image of German Science, 1840-1919*. Gainesville: University of Florida Press, 1972.

Pietsch, Tamson. *Empire of Scholars: Universities, Networks, and the British Academic World, 1850-1939*. Manchester: University of Manchester Press, 2013.

Shils, Edward, and John Roberts. "The Diffusion of European Models outside Europe." In *Universities in the Nineteenth and Early Twentieth Centuries (1800-1945)*, 3:163–230. Cambridge: Cambridge University Press, 2004.

Simpson, Renate. *How the PhD Came to Britain: A Century of Struggle for Postgraduate Education*. Guilford: University of Surrey, 1983.

Weber, Thomas. *Our Friend "The Enemy": Elite Education in Britain and Germany before World War I*. Stanford, CA: Stanford University Press, 2007.

Weisz, George. *The Emergence of Modern Universities in France, 1863-1914*. Princeton, NJ: Princeton University Press, 1983.

———. "The French Universities and Education for the New Professions, 1885-1914: An Episode in French University Reform." *Minerva* 17 (1979): 98–128.

INDEX

Page numbers in italics refer to figures.